FILM FACTS

FILM FACTS

by

Cobbett S. Steinberg

Facts On File Inc. #5893933
119 West 57th Street, New York, New York 10019

FILM FACTS

Copyright, 1980 Cobbett S. Steinberg

Library of Congress Cataloging in Publication Data

Steinberg, Cobbett.
   Film Facts.

   Includes index.
   1. Moving-pictures.—Dictionaries.   I. Title.
   PN1993.45.S75   791.43
   79-27427
   ISBN 0-87196-313-2

9 8 7 6 5 4 3 2 1

Printed in the United States of America

Grateful acknowledgment is made to the following for permission to reprint the following material:

American Film Now: "The Best of the Decade", Oxford University Press 1978: "The Best of the Seventies", dated July 1978 , James Monaco.

British Film Institute: Sight and Sound Surveys 1952, 1962, 1972.

Film Culture Magazine: Independent Films Awards.

Film Heritage: Film Heritage's "Women in Film Pick the Ten Best Films About Women."

Film Society of Lincoln Center: "Ten Best Editors", dated March-April 1977; "My Favorite Films/Texts/Things", dated Nov.-Dec. 1976.

Harvard Lampoon: "Movie Worsts" 1939-1976.

Los Angeles Times: "Celebrities Respond Eloquently to Vote on Film Picks", dated 1/11/70; "More Celebrities Vote for Their Film Favorites", dated 1/18/70 and "And More Celebrities Vote for Their Film Favorites" by Joyce Haber, dated 1/25/70; "The Best of the Sixties", dated January 11, 18 and 25,1970.

Motion Picture Association of America, Inc.: The Production Code; the Advertising Code; the Code of Self-Regulation; Rules and Regulations of the Classification and Rating Administration dated 8/1/77.

Newspaper Enterprise Association: chart of Motion Picture Company Profits 1952-1972, from *The Economist*, dated 7/7/72.

The New York Times: The *New York Times* Annual 10 Best Films Lists 1924-1976. Russell Baker's List of Greatest American Films, dated 11/22/77, "The Definitive List of Truly Great American Movies," dated 11/22/77.

Quigley Publications: "Stars of Tomorrow" 1941 to the present; "Top Money Making Stars" 1932 to the present.

Time, The Weekly Newsmagazine: *Time* Best Movies Lists 1945-76.

Variety Inc.: "MPAA Film Ratings, 1968-78", dated 11/1/78. Top 200 films on the All Time Box Office Champs list; Top 20 films on the annual Box Office Champs of the Year, 1947-1976; Most Popular Films on Television—top 50 films.

TABLE OF CONTENTS

Introduction

VI. THE AWARDS

VII. THE CODES AND REGULATIONS

ACKNOWLEDGEMENTS

I SHOULD LIKE to thank the Library of the Academy of Motion Picture Arts and Sciences and the Theater Arts Library of the University of California at Los Angeles. Without their facilities and the efficiency of their staffs, this book would have been difficult to compile. I should also like to extend my gratitude to Syd Silverman of *Variety* for his generosity and to the Hollywood Foreign Press Association for their friendly help. Both the Motion Picture Association of America and the *Harvard Lampoon* supplied information that would otherwise have been difficult to locate, and I thank them for their time. Albert J. LaValley of Rutgers University helped to conceive this book, Gail Winston of Random House gave numerous helpful suggestions during its gestation, and Ed Troutman provided generous help with this second edition. I should also like to thank my sister Barbara for her enthusiasm, and most of all, Larry Fields for his patience and friendship.

INTRODUCTION: "THE WHOLE EQUATION"

"You can take Hollywood for granted like I did, or you can dismiss it with the contempt we reserve for what we don't understand. It can be understood too, but only dimly and in flashes. Not half a dozen men have ever been able to keep the whole equation of pictures in their heads."
—F. Scott Fitzgerald,
  The Last Tycoon

IN THE MARCH 22, 1973, issue of *The New York Review of Books,* the well-known screenwriter and novelist Joan Didion published an essay that aroused the furor of American film critics. In her essay—prefaced by the above quotation from *The Last Tycoon*—Didion argued that film reviewers never keep "the whole equation" of pictures in their heads. Completely ignorant of the Byzantine economics of the film industry, American film critics, according to Didion, approach the truth about films only occasionally, accidentally. They refuse to acknowledge the economic reality of movies, they forget the importance of production accidents and compromises, they don't understand that a deal memo can determine a movie's success as much as the script itself, and they ignore the fact that a film can be more influenced by the clauses of its financing than by any director's "vision." Film reviewers, Didion implied, simply forget that film is first and foremost an industry, not an art.

Critics, understandably incensed by Didion's contempt, were quick to answer, claiming a reviewer should indeed work with the art *on* the screen and not with the wheeling and dealing *behind* it. After all, they argued, isn't the film itself the real magic? Regardless of the compromises, accidents and deals, movies are an art, and what is there on the screen can be "described, analyzed, and evaluated just as work in the other arts is," as one critic angrily contended with Didion.

The controversy over whether film is an art or an industry did not, of course, begin with Joan Didion. Throughout film's history, moviegoers have argued just how important or unimportant the business aspects of films really are. In one of his first columns for *The Nation,* James Agee, for example—often considered one of America's most perceptive film critics—believed it advantageous to forget the insider's preoccupation with the box office. Rather than become involved in the analysis of an industry, it was better, Agee said, simply to describe "what my eyes tell me as I watch any given screen." In the National Society's first anthology Richard Schickel, on the other hand, argued that since commerce had a way of intruding upon experiences that should ideally be free of crass consideration, responsible film criticism demanded "an alertness to factors that customarily lie beyond the purview of critics in the other arts."

There have even been swings of fashion in the controversy. During the late 1950s and throughout the 1960s, when film studies were becoming a part of American academia, it was popular to see films in terms of their directors' "artistic visions." In the 1970s, when the national economy has often been shaky and when Marxist criticism has gained popularity, it is common to stress a film's "economic profile." Paul Schrader, for example, one of Hollywood's most praised young writers, believes that most people today are interested in statistics: "You go to a film campus and eight out of ten questions will be about business."

Even as early as 1915 the controversy over whether film was merely an industry or an art form was important enough to be brought before the Supreme Court. In the famous *Mutual Film Corporation* v. *Ohio* case, the Court unanimously ruled that movies were only an item of commerce, not subject to the protection of the free-speech clauses in state constitutions. "The exhibition of moving pictures," the Court declared, "is a business pure and simple, originated and conducted for profit . . . "

In was not until 1952, in fact, that the Supreme Court reversed its position and ruled that movies were indeed a medium of public opinion subject to similar protection as books and newspapers. In this celebrated *Burstyn* v. *Wilson* decision concerning Roberto Rossellini's *The Miracle,* the Court unanimously declared that it could not be doubted that "motion pictures are a significant medium for the communication of ideas. They may affect public attitudes and behavior in a variety of ways, ranging from direct espousal of a political or social doctrine to the subtle shaping of thought which characterizes all artistic expression."

The Court's belief in the artistic expression of films, however far-reaching its consequences, hardly settled the question of film's schizy nature. People both within and outside the industry still like to give their own very definite opinions on the issue. Charlie Chaplin, for example, amused reporters after receiving an honorary Academy Award in 1972 by stating that though he appreciated the honor, he had to confess that "I went into the business for money and the art grew out of it. If people are disillusioned by that remark, I can't help it. It's the truth."

It would be easy to dismiss the controversy by saying the obvious: movies are both an art *and* an industry. But the obvious would not take into account the intricacy with which the art and the business are intertwined. If there is something like a "whole equation" of motion pictures as Fitzgerald suggested, it is certainly nothing as simple as: film = ½ art + ½ industry. Surely our familiarity with what occurs off the screen has heightened our fascination with what happens on it. The industry's fast money, big deals and rags-to-riches anecdotes are as representative of American life as the stories on the screen. The very facts of filmmaking have fed our fantasies.

Film Facts is a compendium of statistics, lists and surveys that suggests just how complicated that "whole equation" is. Some of the entries, like the Academy's technical awards, stress the practical side of filmmaking. Other entries, like the studios' incomes, emphasize the financial. Still other sections, like the New York Film Festival Programs, remind us of the personal and creative elements. And still other selections, like the annual box-office champs, record the social and popular appeal films exert. Many entries reveal how all the different elements are intertwined.

The mixture is intentional. When critics dwell on sophisticated issues like the "semiotics" of cinema, it is tonic to remember just how often the art of film has depended on such practical matters as the discovery of a new electric cable, of a spotlight or even of a new type of artifical snow. And when movie moguls go on and on about percentages, points and "bankability," it is good to be reminded just how many dazzling directors have been showcased at international film festivals. *Film Facts* is an eclectic book about an eclectic art. In collecting a wide range of information about what happens both on and off the screen, it serves a modest but, I hope, useful function: to urge us to keep "the whole equation" of pictures in our heads.

—C.S.

I. THE MARKETPLACE

1/THE TOP 200 MONEYMAKING FILMS OF ALL TIME

EACH YEAR *Variety* publishes its list of All-Time Box-Office Champion Films, one of the most interesting compilations for everyone from the movie producer to the cinema scholar to the film buff. Although *Variety's* presentation is relatively straightforward, many people don't understand exactly what the list signifies. Here are some important clarifications:

1. The figures indicate rental fees and *not* box-office grosses. The rental fee is the money the theater pays to the distributor to show the movie; the box-office gross is the money the moviegoer pays to the theater to see the film. Box-office grosses would be higher than the rental fees reported here in almost all cases.

2. The figures given here include rentals only for the United States-Canadian market and do not cover foreign-market rentals. According to the industry, the foreign-market rentals usually equal or slightly surpass domestic rentals. Thus, to determine what a film earned in world-wide rentals, simply multiply the figures given here by two.

3. Despite the fact that many old films are often reissued to considerable profit, studios tend not to report such added incomes for old films. Once a movie has passed its first success, a studio is often reluctant to revise a movie's earnings figures. As a result, many of the older films on *Variety's* list may in fact have made more money that the list would suggest.

4. For years it was said that *Birth of a Nation* made $50 million. After reportedly diligent research, the 1977 Anniversary *Variety* reported that such a figure was more legend than fact. As far as research can show, *Nation* earned $5 million in domestic rentals.

5. This list merely includes the top 200 films on *Variety's* much longer and more comprehensive compendium.

One thing quickly becomes obvious from this list: most of the big moneymaking films are recent releases. Of the top 25 Box-Office Champs, 23 have been released since 1965, 19 since 1970. Only two of the big 10 moneymakers—*Gone With the Wind* and *The Sound of Music*—were made before 1970. Inflation is obviously largely responsible for the preponderance of recent movies on this list. According to the Bureau of Labor Statistics, today's dollar would have been worth nearly $5.00 in 1939, the year *Gone With the Wind* was released.

According to industry estimates (and these *are* estimates, not exact statistics), the top moneymaking films taking inflation into account would look like this:

1. *Gone With the Wind* (1939) $382.7 million
2. *Star Wars* (1977)   187.8
3. *The Sound of Music* (1965)   173.8
4. *Jaws* (1975)   156.4

5. *The Godfather* (1972)   143.2
6. *Snow White* (1937)   128.9
7. *The Exorcist* (1973)   128.2
8. *The Sting* (1973)   123.1
9. *The 10 Commandments* (1956)   109.7
10. *Doctor Zhivago* (1965)   102.4

But other factors besides inflation may account for the large number of recent releases on this list. Ever since *The Godfather* broke the all-time box-office record established more than three decades earlier by *Gone With the Wind*, Hollywood has been hell-bent on producing the "super-grosser": a blockbuster that will soar into the "hyperspace-hyperbuck stratosphere" to use Steven (*Jaws, Close Encounters*) Speilberg's phrase. Producers no longer want to make profits; they want mega-profits, and they're determined to try to catch the largest possible audiences. So with fewer and fewer films and more and more sophisticated advertising techniques, it's not surprising that there's been a greater conformity in filmgoers' tastes in recent years.

The changes that have occurred in film exhibiting during the past decade may also be responsible for the increased revenues of recent releases. In previous decades a film would be shown on a strictly-timed three-step schedule: in first-run houses that charged the highest prices; then in neighborhood theaters where prices were lower; and finally in late-run houses that charged bargain-basement admission. But the number of theaters showing first-run films has increased considerably over the past 10 years; first-run houses have spread out from the cities into the suburbs. The result is that films are now kept at a higher level of release for longer periods of time, during which ticket prices are higher. Hence, increased revenues.

Note: Film title is followed by name of director; producer or production company; original distributor plus present distributor if different; year of release; and total rentals received to date. Whenever two or more films earned the same rental fees, the tied movies are given the same numerical rank. The film earning the next greatest rental fees is then given a numerical rank which takes into account the preceeding tie. For example, *Love Story* and *Towering Inferno* each earned 50 million dollars, giving them both 16th place. *Jaws II*, which earned 49.299 million, is then considered to occupy 18th place.

This list was compiled from the January 3, 1979 issue of *Variety* and hence does not include films released since that time.

THE TOP 200 MONEYMAKING FILMS OF ALL TIME

Rank	Title (Director; Producer; Distributor; Year)	Total Rentals
1.	*Star Wars* (Lucas; Kurtz; 20th; 1977)	$164,765,000
2.	*Jaws* (Spielberg; Zanuck/Brown; Universal; 1975)	121,254,000
3.	*The Godfather* (Coppola; Ruddy; Paramount; 1972)	86,275,000
4.	*Grease* (Kleiser; Stigwood/Carr; Paramount; 1978)	83,091,000
5.	*The Exorcist* (Friedkin; Blatty; Warners; 1973)	82,200,000
6.	*The Sound of Music* (Wise; 20th; 1965)	79,000,000
7.	*The Sting* (Hill; Bill/Phillips; Universal; 1973)	78,889,000
8.	*Close Encounters of the Third Kind* (Spielberg; Phillips; Columbia; 1977)	77,000,000
9.	*Gone With the Wind* (Fleming; Selznick; MGM/UA; 1939)	76,700,000
10.	*Saturday Night Fever* (Badham; Stigwood; Paramount; 1977)	71,463,000
11.	*One Flew Over the Cuckoo's Nest* (Forman; Zaentz/Douglas; UA; 1975)	59,000,000
12.	*Smokey and the Bandit* (Needham; Engelberg; Universal; 1977)	57,259,000

Rank	Title (Director; Producer; Distributor; Year)	Total Rentals
13.	*American Graffiti* (Lucas; Coppola; Universal; 1973)	55,886,000
14.	*Rocky* (Avildsen; Chartoff/Winkler; UA; 1976)	54,000,000
15.	*National Lampoon Animal House* (Landis; Simmons/Reitman; Universal; 1978)	52,368,000
16.	*Love Story* (Hiller; Minsky; Paramount; 1970)	50,000,000
	Towering Inferno (Guillermin; Allen; 20th; 1975)	50,000,000
18.	*Jaws II* (Szwarc; Zanuck/Brown; Universal; 1978)	49,299,000
19.	*The Graduate* (Nichols; Turman; Avemb; 1968)	49,078,000
20.	*Doctor Zhivago* (Lean; Ponti; MGM/UA; 1965)	46,550,000
21.	*Butch Cassidy and the Sundance Kid* (Hill; Foreman; 20th; 1969)	46,039,000
22.	*Airport* (Seaton; Hunter; Universal; 1970)	45,300,000
23.	*The Ten Commandments* (DeMille; Paramount; 1956)	43,000,000
24.	*Heaven Can Wait* (Beatty; Paramount; 1978)	42,517,000
25.	*Poseidon Adventure* (Neame; Allen; 20th; 1972)	42,000,000
26.	*Mary Poppins* (Stevenson; Disney; Buena Vista; 1964)	41,000,000
	Goodbye Girl (Ross; Stark; Warners; 1977)	41,000,000
28.	*Blazing Saddles* (Brooks; Hertzberg; Warners; 1974)	37,200,000
29.	*A Star Is Born* (Pierson; Peters; Warners; 1976)	37,100,000
30.	*King Kong* (Guillermin; DeLaurentiis; Paramount; 1976)	36,915,000
31.	*M*A*S*H* (Altman; Preminger; 20th; 1970)	36,720,000
32.	*Ben-Hur* (Wyler; Zimbalist; MGM/UA; 1959)	36,650,000
33.	*Earthquake* (Robson; Universal; 1974)	36,250,000
34.	*Young Frankenstein* (Brooks; Gruskoff; 20th; 1975)	34,600,000
35.	*Fiddler on the Roof* (Jewison; UA; 1971)	34,010,000
36.	*Billy Jack* (Frank; Solti; Warners; 1971)	32,500,000
37.	*Hooper* (Needham; Reynolds/Gordon; Warners; 1978)	31,500,000
38.	*The Deep* (Yates; Guber; Columbia; 1977)	31,300,000
39.	*Oh, God* (Reiner; Weintraub; Warners; 1977)	31,000,000
40.	*Godfather, Part II* (Coppola; Coppola/Fredrickson/Ross; Paramount; 1974)	30,673,000
41.	*All The President's Men* (Pakula; Coblenz; Warners; 1976)	30,000,000
42.	*Silver Streak* (Hiller; Milkis/Miller; 20th; 1976)	28,850,000
43.	*Thunderball* (Young; Eon; UA; 1965)	28,530,000
44.	*Trial of Billy Jack* (Laughlin; Carmer; TL/Warners; 1974)	28,516,000
45.	*Patton* (Schaffner; McCarthy; 20th; 1970)	28,100,000
46.	*What's Up Doc?* (Bogdanovich; Warners; 1972)	28,000,000
47.	*The Omen* (Donner; Bernhard; 20th; 1976)	27,851,000
48.	*Snow White* (animated; Disney; RKO/Buena Vista; 1937)	26,750,000
49.	*Wilderness Family* (Raffill; Dubs; PIE; 1976)	26,649,000
50.	*Funny Girl* (Wyler; Stark; Columbia; 1968)	26,325,000
51.	*The French Connection* (Friedkin; D'Antoni/Schine/Moore; 20th; 1971)	26,315,000
52.	*Cleopatra* (Mankiewicz; Wanger; 20th; 1963)	26,000,000
53.	*Airport 1975* (Smight; Frye; Universal; 1974)	25,805,000
54.	*Guess Who's Coming To Dinner?* (Kramer; Columbia; 1968)	25,500,000
55.	*Foul Play* (Higgins; Miller/Milkis; Paramount; 1978)	25,065,000
56.	*The Jungle Book* (Reitherman; Disney; Buena Vista; 1967)	25,000,000
	The Way We Were (Pollack; Stark; Columbia; 1973)	25,000,000
	Revenge of the Pink Panther (Edwards; UA; 1978)	25,000,000
59.	*The Bad News Bears* (Ritchie; Jaffe; Paramount; 1976)	24,888,000
60.	*2001: A Space Odyssey* (Kubrick; MGM/UA; 1968)	24,100,000
61.	*The Enforcer* (Fargo; Daley; Warners; 1976)	24,000,000
62.	*Around The World in 80 Days* (Anderson; Todd; UA; 1956)	23,120,000
63.	*The Longest Yard* (Aldrich; Ruddy; Paramount; 1974)	23,017,000
64.	*In Search of Noah's Ark* (Conway; Seillier; Sunn; 1977)	23,000,000

Rank	Title (Director; Producer; Distributor; Year)	Total Rentals
65.	*Goldfinger* (Hamilton; Eon; UA; 1964)	22,860,000
66.	*Bonnie and Clyde* (Penn; Beatty; Warners; 1967)	22,700,000
67.	*Papillon* (Schaffner; Dorfmann; Allied Artists; 1973)	22,500,000
	Dog Day Afternoon (Lumet; Bregman/Elfand, Warners; 1975)	22,500,000
69.	*Deliverance* (Boorman; Warners; 1972)	22,400,000
70.	*Midway* (Smight; Mirisch; Universal; 1976)	22,329,000
71.	*Shampoo* (Ashby; Beatty; Columbia; 1975)	22,000,000
	Murder By Death (Moore; Stark; Columbia; 1976)	22,000,000
	The Spy Who Loved Me (Gilbert; Broccoli; UA; 1977)	22,000,000
74.	*Jeremiah Johnson* (Pollack; Wizan; Warners; 1972)	21,600,000
75.	*Up in Smoke* (Adler; Adler/Lombardo; Paramount; 1978)	21,271,000
76.	*The Love Bug* (Stevenson; Walsh; Buena Vista; 1969)	21,000,000
	Silent Movie (Brooks; Hertzberg; 20th; 1976)	21,000,000
	A Bridge Too Far (Attenborough; Levine; UA; 1977)	21,000,000
79.	*It's A Mad, Mad, Mad, Mad World* (Kramer; UA; 1963)	20,800,000
80.	*Summer of '42* (Mulligan; Roth; Warners; 1971)	20,500,000
81.	*Midnight Cowboy* (Schlesinger; Hellman; UA; 1969)	20,325,000
82.	*The Dirty Dozen* (Aldrich; Hyman; MGM/UA; 1967)	20,300,000
83.	*Cabaret* (Fosse; Feuer; Allied Artists; 1972)	20,250,000
84.	*Magnum Force* (Post; Daley; Warners; 1973)	20,100,000
85.	*Three Days of the Condor* (Pollack; Schneider; Paramount; 1975)	20,014,000
86.	*The Valley of the Dolls* (Robson; Weisbart; 20th; 1967)	20,000,000
	The Odd Couple (Saks; Koch; Paramount; 1968)	20,000,000
	Return of the Pink Panther (Edwards; UA; 1975)	20,000,000
	The End (Reynolds; Gordon; UA; 1978)	20,000,000
90.	*Diamonds Are Forever* (Hamilton; Eon; UA; 1971)	19,620,000
91.	*Pink Panther Strikes Again* (Edwards; UA; 1976)	19,500,000
	The Cheap Detective (Moore; Stark; Columbia; 1978)	19,500,000
93.	*West Side Story* (Wise/Robbins; Mirisch/7Arts; UA; 1961)	19,450,000
94.	*You Only Live Twice* (Gilbert; Eon; UA; 1967)	19,400,000
95.	*Murder on the Orient Express* (Lumet; Brabourne/Goodwin; Paramount; 1974)	19,124,000
96.	*To Sir With Love* (Clavell; Columbia; 1967)	19,100,000
	Easy Rider (Hooper; Pando/Raybert; Columbia; 1969)	19,100,000
98.	*Swiss Family Robinson* (Annakin; Disney; Buena Vista; 1969)	19,000,000
	Bullitt (Yates; D'Antoni; Warners; 1969)	19,000,000
	Funny Lady (Ross; Stark; Columbia; 1975)	19,000,000
101.	*Bambi* (animated; Disney; RKO/Buena Vista; 1942)	18,735,000
102.	*The Other Side of the Mountain* (Peerce; Feldman; Universal; 1975)	18,647,000
103.	*The Getaway* (Peckinpah; Foster; Brower; NGP/Warners; 1972)	18,100,000
104.	*Dirty Harry* (Siegel; Warners; 1971)	17,831,000
105.	*The Longest Day* (Annakin/Marton/Wicki; Zanuck; 20th; 1962)	17,600,000
106.	*The Robe* (Roster; Ross; 20th; 1953)	17,500,000
	South Pacific (Logan; Magna/Adler; 20th; 1958)	17,500,000
	Herbie Rides Again (Stevenson; Walsh; Buena Vista; 1974)	17,500,000
	Other Side of Midnight (Jarrott; Yablans; 20th; 1977)	17,500,000
	The Gauntlet (Eastwood; Daley; Warners; 1977)	17,500,000
111.	*Romeo and Juliet* (Zeffirelli; Allen/Brabourne; Paramount; 1968)	17,473,000
112.	*Bridge on the River Kwai* (Lean; Spiegel; Columbia; 1957)	17,195,000
113.	*High Anxiety* (Brooks; 20th; 1977)	17,040,000
114.	*Walking Tall* (Karlson Briskin; CRC/AIP; 1973)	17,000,000
115.	*Tom Jones* (Richardson; UA; 1963)	16,950,000
116.	*Peter Pan* (animated; Disney; RKO/Buena Vista; 1953)	16,875,000

Rank	Title (Director; Producer; Distributor; Year)	Total Rentals
117.	*Oliver* (Reed; Woolf; Columbia; 1969)	16,800,000
118.	*Lawrence of Arabia* (Lean; Spiegel/Columbia/Lean; Columbia; 1962)	16,700,000
119.	*Marathon Man* (Schlesinger; Evans/Beckerman; Paramount; 1976)	16,575,000
120.	*Paper Moon* (Bogdanovich; Paramount; 1973)	16,559,000
121.	*Looking for Mr. Goodbar* (Brooks; Fields; Paramount; 1977)	16,542,000
122.	*Apple Dumpling Gang* (Tokar; Anderson; Buena Vista; 1975)	16,500,000
123.	*Pete's Dragon* (Chaffey; Miller/Courtland; Buena Vista; 1977)	16,100,000
124.	*Throroughly Modern Millie* (Hill; Hunter; Universal; 1967)	16,000,000
	Last Tango In Paris (Bertolucci; Grimaldi; UA; 1973)	16,000,000
	Tommy (Russell; Stigwood; Columbia; 1975)	16,000,000
127.	*Live and Let Die* (Hamilton; Eon; UA; 1973)	15,850,000
128.	*Woodstock* (Wadleigh; Maurice; Warners; 1970)	15,800,000
129.	*Hawaii* (Hill; Mirisch; UA; 1966)	15,550,000
130.	*Fantasia* (animated; Disney; RKO/Buena Vista; 1940)	15,500,000
	The Carpetbaggers (Dmytryk; Levine; Paramount; 1964)	15,500,000
132.	*This Is Cinerama* (Thomas; Cooper; CRC; 1952)	15,400,000
133.	*A Clockwork Orange* (Kurbrick; Warners; 1971)	15,400,000
134.	*Heroes* (Kagan; Foster/Turman; Universal; 1977)	15,341,000
135.	*Hello Dolly!* (Kelly; Lehman; 20th; 1970)	15,200,000
136.	*The Hindenburg* (Wise; Universal; 1975)	15,105,000
137.	*Airport 77* (Jameson; Frye; Universal; 1977)	15,074,000
138.	*Bad News Bears In Breaking Training* (Pressman; Goldberg; Paramount; 1977)	15,052,000
139.	*The Turning Point* (Ross; Ross/Laurents; 20th; 1977)	15,045,000
140.	*The Bible* (Huston; DeLaurentiis; 20th; 1966)	15,000,000
	Planet of the Apes (Schaffner; Jacobs; 20th; 1968)	15,000,000
	Rosemary's Baby (Polanski; Castle; Paramount; 1968)	15,000,000
	Little Big Man (Penn; Millar/Penn; CCF/NGP/Warners; 1970)	15,000,000
	Carrie (De Palma; Monash; UA; 1976)	15,000,000
	The Rescuers (Reitherman/Lounsberry/Stevens; Reitherman; Buena Vista; 1977)	15,000,000
146.	*House Calls* (Zieff; Winitsky/Sellers; Universal; 1978)	14,859,000
147.	*Dirty Mary, Crazy Larry* (Hough; Herman; 20th; 1974)	14,855,000
148.	*Ryan's Daughter* (Lean; Havelock-Allan; MGM/UA; 1970)	14,641,000
149.	*Spartacus* (Kubrick; Bryna/Lewis; Universal; 1960)	14,600,000
150.	*Bob and Carol and Ted and Alice* (Mazursky; Tucker; Columbia; 1969)	14,600,000
	Serpico (Lumet; Bregman; Paramount; 1974)	14,600,000
152.	*Toral Toral Toral* (Fleischer; Williams; 20th; 1970)	14,530,000
153.	*Who's Afraid of Virginia Woolf?* (Nichols; Lehman; Warners; 1966)	14,500,000
	The Vixens (Meyer; RM Films; 1969)	14,500,000
	Paint Your Wagon (Logan; Lerner; Paramount; 1969)	14,500,000
	Network (Lumet; Gottfried; MGM/UA; 1976)	14,500,000
157.	*Coma* (Crichton; Erlichman; MGM/UA; 1978)	14,400,000
158.	*True Grit* (Hathaway; Wallis; Paramount; 1969)	14,250,000
159.	*Black Sunday* (Frankenheimer; Evans; Paramount; 1977)	14,202,600
160.	*The Great Gatsby* (Clayton; Merrick; Paramount; 1974)	14,200,000
161.	*101 Dalmatians* (animated; Disney; Buena Vista; 1961)	14,100,000
162.	*The Greatest Show on Earth* (DeMille; Paramount; 1952)	14,000,000
	Giant (Stevens; Stevens/Ginsberg; Warners; 1956)	14,000,000
	Those Magnificent Young Men (Annakin; Margulies; 20th; 1965)	14,000,000
	Camelot (Logan; Warners/7Arts; 1967)	14,000,000
	Fun With Dick and Jane (Kotcheff; Bart, Palevsky; Columbia; 1977)	14,000,000
	Herbie Goes To Monte Carlo (McEveety; Miller; Buena Vista 1977)	14,000,000

Rank	Title (Director; Producer; Distributor; Year)	Total Rentals
168.	*Slap Shot* (Hill; Wunsch/Friedman; Universal; 1977)	13,957,000
169.	*Challenge to Be Free* (Farnett; Dubs; PIE; 1974)	13,914,000
170.	*Exorcist II: The Heretic* (Boorman; Boorman/Lederer; Warners; 1977)	13,900,000
171.	*The Sand Pebbles* (Wise; 20th; 1967)	13,500,000
	Freebie and the Bean (Rush; Warners; 1967)	13,500,000
173.	*Supervixens* (Meyer; RM Films; 1975)	13,450,000
174.	*Jesus Christ Superstar* (Jewison; Jewison/Stigwood; Universal; 1973)	13,291,000
175.	*The Last Picture Show* (Bogdanovich; Friedman; Columbia; 1972)	13,110,000
176.	*One-On-One* (Johnson; Hornstein; Warners; 1977)	13,100,000
177.	*Pinocchio* (animated; Disney; RKO/Buena Vista; 1940)	13,000,000
	The Guns of Navarone (Thompson; Foreman; Columbia; 1961)	13,000,000
	The Outlaw Josey Wales (Eastwood; Daley; Warners; 1976)	13,000,000
180.	*Song of the South* (animated/live; Disney; RKO/Buena Vista; 1946)	12,800,000
181.	*The Lady and the Tramp* (animated; Disney; Buena Vista; 1955)	12,750,000
	A Man For All Seasons (Zinnemann; Columbia; 1966)	12,750,000
183.	*Lucky Lady* (Donen; Gruskoff; 20th; 1975)	12,655,000
184.	*Vanishing Wilderness* (Seilmann; Dubs/Seilmann/Dubs; PIE; 1973)	12,633,000
185.	*Quo Vadis* (LeRoy; Zimbalist; MGM/UA; 1951)	12,500,000
	Seven Wonders of the World (Thomas; CRC; 1956)	12,500,000
	That Darn Cat (Stevenson; Disney; Buena Vista; 1965)	12,500,000
	Born Losers (Frank; Henderson; AIP; 1967)	12,500,000
189.	*Cinderella* (Jackson; Disney; RKO/Buena Vista; 1949)	12,450,000
190.	*Chinatown* (Polanski; Evans; Paramount; 1974)	12,400,000
191.	*Carnal Knowledge* (Nichols; Avco-Embassy; 1971)	12,351,000
192.	*The Shaggy Dog* (Barton; Disney; Buena Vista; 1959)	12,250,000
	Catch-22 (Nichols; Calley; Paramount; 1970)	12,250,000
194.	*From Here to Eternity* (Zinnemann; Columbia; 1953)	12,200,000
195.	*The One and Only* (Reiner; Gordon/Picker/ Paramount; 1978)	12,189,000
196.	*How the West Was Won* (Ford/Hathaway/Marshall; Smith-Cinerama; CRC/MGM/UA; 1962)	12,150,000
197.	*Omen II: Damien* (Taylor; Bernhard; 20th; 1978)	12,050,000
198.	*That's Entertainment* (Haley; MGM-UA; 1974)	12,020,000
199.	*White Christmas* (Curtiz; Doland/Berland; Paramount; 1954)	12,000,000
	Cinerama Holiday (DeRochemont; CRC; 1955)	12,000,000
	El Cid (Mann; Bronston; Allied Artists; 1961)	12,000,000
	My Fair Lady (Cukor; Warner; Warners; 1964)	12,000,000
	Benji (Camp; Mulberry Square; 1974)	12,000,000
	Annie Hall (Allen; Joffe; UA; 1977)	12,000,000

2/TOP TEN MONEYMAKING MUSICALS, WESTERNS, COMEDIES, HORROR FILMS, BIBLICAL EPICS, DISASTER FILMS, JAMES BOND MOVIES, WAR FILMS, ETC.

THE FOLLOWING LISTS were compiled from the "All-Time Film Rental Champs" published in *Variety* January 3, 1979 and hence do not include films issued since that time. It should be remembered that the following statistics indicate (1) rentals and not box office grosses and (2) include only rentals from the U.S./Canada market and not foreign market rentals. Again, these figures do not take into account inflation. The year of release is included for each film to remind you to consider the effects of inflation.

TOP TEN MONEYMAKING MUSICALS

1.	*Grease* (1978)	$83,091,000
2.	*The Sound of Music* (1965)	79,000,000
3.	*Mary Poppins* (1964)	41,000,000
4.	*A Star Is Born* (1976)	37,100,000
5.	*Fiddler on the Roof* (1971)	34,010,000
6.	*Funny Girl* (1968)	26,325,000
7.	*Cabaret* (1972)	20,250,000
8.	*West Side Story* (1961)	19,450,000
9.	*Funny Lady* (1975)	19,000,000
10.	*South Pacific* (1958)	17,500,000

RUNNERS-UP

1.	*Oliver I* (1969)	16,800,000
2.	*Thoroughly Modern Millie* (1967)	16,000,000
	Tommy (1975)	16,000,000
4.	*Hello Dolly* (1970)	15,200,000
5.	*Paint Your Wagon* (1969)	14,500,000
6.	*Camelot* (1967)	14,000,000
7.	*Jesus Christ Superstar* (1973)	13,291,000
8.	*White Christmas* (1954)	12,000,000
	My Fair Lady (1964)	12,000,000
10.	*Sgt. Pepper's Lonely Hearts Club Band* (1978)	11,070,000

COMMENTS: *Saturday Night Fever* and *Woodstock* are not included in this list. Some people consider them musicals; I don't. Any trends in the top musicals? Of the top ten, three star Barbra Streisand.

TOP TEN MONEYMAKING HORROR FILMS

1.	*Jaws* (1975)	$121,254,000
2.	*The Exorcist* (1973)	82,200,000
3.	*Jaws II* (1978)	49,299,000
4.	*King Kong* (1976)	36,915,000
5.	*The Omen* (1976)	27,851,000
6.	*Rosemary's Baby* (1968)	15,000,000
	Carrie (1976)	15,000,000
8.	*Coma* (1978)	14,400,000
9.	*The Exorcist II* (1977)	13,900,000
10.	*Omen II* (1978)	12,050,000

RUNNERS-UP

1.	*Psycho* (1960)	11,200,000
2.	*The Fury* (1978)	10,800,000
3.	*Orca* (1977)	9,430,000
4.	*Willard* (1971)	9,300,000
5.	*Wait Until Dark* (1967)	7,800,000

TOP TEN MONEYMAKING COMEDIES

1.	*Smokey and the Bandit* (1977)	$57,259,000
2.	*American Graffiti* (1973)	55,886,000
3.	*National Lampoon Animal House* (1978)	52,368,000
4.	*The Graduate* (1968)	49,078,000
5.	*Heaven Can Wait* (1978)	42,517,000
6.	*The Goodbye Girl* (1977)	41,000,000
7.	*Blazing Saddles* (1974)	37,200,000
8.	*M*A*S*H* (1970)	36,720,000
9.	*Young Frankenstein* (1975)	34,600,000
10.	*Hooper* (1978)	31,500,000

RUNNERS-UP

1.	*Oh, God!* (1977)	31,000,000
2.	*Silver Streak* (1976)	28,850,000
3.	*What's Up, Doc?* (1972)	28,000,000
4.	*Foul Play* (1978)	25,065,000
5.	*Revenge of the Pink Panther* (1978)	25,000,000

6.	*The Bad News Bears* (1976)	24,888,000
7.	*The Longest Yard* (1974)	23,017,000
8.	*Shampoo* (1975)	22,000,000
	Murder By Death (1976)	22,000,000
10.	*Up In Smoke* (1978)	21,271,000
11.	*Silent Movie* (1976)	21,000,000
12.	*It's a Mad, Mad, Mad, Mad World* (1963)	20,800,000
13.	*The Odd Couple* (1968)	20,000,000
	Return of the Pink Panther (1975)	20,000,000
	The End (1978)	20,000,000
16.	*Pink Panther Strikes Again* (1976)	19,500,000
	Cheap Detective (1978)	19,500,000
18.	*High Anxiety* (1977)	17,040,000
19.	*Tom Jones* (1963)	16,950,000
20.	*Paper Moon* (1973)	16,559,000

COMMENTS: Four of the top 30 comedies were written by Neil Simon; 5 of the top 30 feature Burt Reynolds; 4 of the top 30 were directed by Mel Brooks (where's Woody Allen?); and the most successful comic series represented on this list is the *Pink Panther* set of films.

TOP TEN MONEYMAKING BIBLICAL EPICS

1.	*The Ten Commandments* (1956)	$43,000,000
2.	*Ben-Hur* (1959)	36,650,000
3.	*The Robe* (1953)	17,500,000
4.	*The Bible* (1966)	15,000,000
5.	*Spartacus* (1960)	14,600,000
6.	*Quo Vadis* (1951)	12,500,000
7.	*El Cid* (1961)	12,000,000
8.	*Samson and Delilah* (1949)	11,500,000
9.	*Greatest Story Ever Told* (1965)	6,930,000
10.	*King of Kings* (1961)	6,512,000

RUNNERS-UP

1.	*Solomon and Sheba* (1959)	5,200,000
2.	*Salome* (1953)	4,750,000
	David and Bathsheba (1951)	4,750,000
4.	*Demetrius and the Gladiators* (1954)	4,250,000
5.	*Ben-Hur* (1926)	4,000,000

TOP TEN MONEYMAKING DISASTER FILMS

1.	*Towering Inferno* (1975)	$50,000,000
2.	*Airport* (1970)	45,300,000
3.	*The Poseidon Adventure* (1972)	42,000,000
4.	*Earthquake* (1974)	36,250,000
5.	*Airport 1975* (1974)	28,805,000
6.	*The Hindenburg* (1975)	15,105,000
7.	*Airport 77* (1977)	15,074,000
8.	*Black Sunday* (1977)	14,202,600
9.	*Rollercoaster* (1977)	9,974,000
10.	*Two Minute Warning* (1976)	9,110,000,

TOP TEN MONEYMAKING JAMES BOND MOVIES

1.	*Thunderball* (1965)	$28,530,000
2.	*Goldfinger* (1964)	22,860,000
3.	*The Spy Who Loved Me* (1977)	22,000,000
4.	*Diamonds Are Forever* (1971)	19,620,000
5.	*You Only Live Twice* (1967)	19,400,000
6.	*Live and Let Die* (1973)	15,850,000
7.	*Casino Royale* (1967)	10,200,000
8.	*From Russia With Love* (1964)	9,820,000
9.	*Man With the Golden Gun* (1974)	9,400,000
10.	*On Her Majesty's Secret Service* (1969)	9,100,000
11.	*Dr. No* (1962)	6,350,000

COMMENTS: The Bond series is by most estimates the most financially successful series in film history. *Moonraker* earned $33,934,074 in 1979, too late to be included in the above list.

TOP TEN MONEYMAKING WESTERNS

1.	*Butch Cassidy* (1969)	$46,039,000
2.	*Little Big Man* (1970)	15,000,000
3.	*True Grit* (1969)	14,250,000
4.	*Outlaw Josey Wales* (1976)	13,000,000
5.	*How the West Was Won* (1962)	12,150,000
6.	*Duel in the Sun* (1946)	11,300,000
7.	*Cat Ballou* (1965)	9,300,000
8.	*Shane* (1953)	9,000,000
9.	*The Professionals* (1966)	8,800,000
10.	*Life & Times of Judge Roy Bean* (1972)	8,100,000

RUNNERS-UP

1.	*Rooster Cogburn* (1975)	8,022,000
2.	*The Alamo* (1960)	7,910,000
3.	*Shenandoah* (1965)	7,750,000
4.	*High Plains Drifter* (1973)	7,694,000
5.	*Big Jake* (1971)	7,500,000
6.	*The Cowboys* (1972)	7,400,000
7.	*Missouri Breaks* (1976)	7,000,000
8.	*Hang 'em High* (1968)	6,710,000
9.	*A Man Called Horse* (1970)	6,500,000
10.	*Joe Kidd* (1972)	6,330,000
11.	*The Good, the Bad, and the Ugly* (1967)	6,030,000
12.	*Sons of Katie Elder* (1965)	6,000,000
	The War Wagon (1967)	6,000,000
	El Dorado (1967)	6,000,000
	Chisum (1970)	6,000,000
16.	*The Shootist* (1976)	5,987,000
17.	*Rio Bravo* (1959)	5,750,000
18.	*Hombre* (1967)	5,610,000
19.	*Nevada Smith* (1966)	5,500,000
	Bandolero (1968)	5,500,000

COMMENTS: *Paint Your Wagon* and *Seven Brides for Seven Brothers*, though both set in the West, are more musicals than Westerns and were not included in this list. Similarly, *Blazing Saddles* is too much of a parody (even more than *Cat Ballou*) to be considered a Western. And *Jeremiah Johnson* was also omitted here. Any trends in the top Westerns? Not surprising to notice that 9 of the top 30 moneymaking Westerns star the indomitable John Wayne, and 5 of the top 30 feature popular gunslinger Clint Eastwood.

TOP TEN MONEYMAKING WAR FILMS

1.	*Patton* (1970)	$28,100,000
2.	*Midway* (1976)	22,329,000
3.	*A Bridge Too Far* (1977)	21,100,000
4.	*The Dirty Dozen* (1967)	20,300,000
5.	*The Longest Day* (1962)	17,600,000
6.	*Bridge on the River Kwai* (1957)	17,195,000
7.	*Lawrence of Arabia* (1962)	16,700,000
8.	*Tora! Tora! Tora!* (1970)	14,530,000
9.	*The Guns of Navarone* (1961)	13,000,000
10.	*Catch 22* (1970)	12,250,000

RUNNERS-UP

1.	*From Here to Eternity* (1953)	12,200,000
2.	*The Green Berets* (1968)	9,750,000
3.	*MacArthur* (1977)	9,402,000
4.	*Battle Cry* (1955)	8,100,000
5.	*Von Ryan's Express* (1965)	7,700,000
6.	*The Blue Max* (1966)	7,275,000
7.	*Where Eagles Dare* (1969)	7,150,000
8.	*War and Peace* (1956)	6,250,000
9.	*Sergeant York* (1941)	6,100,000
10.	*Strategic Air Command* (1955)	6,000,000
	Sea Chase (1955)	6,000,000
	To Hell and Back (1955)	6,000,000

COMMENTS: *Mr. Roberts, Operation Petticoat, No Time for Sergeants,* and *M*A*S*H* are more comedies than war movies and hence are not included in this list. *Best Years of Our Lives,* though it documents the aftershocks of war, is similarly omitted from this list because it's not really a war film.

TOP TEN MONEYMAKING HITCHCOCK MOVIES

1.	*Psycho* (1960)	$11,200,000
2.	*Family Plot* (1976)	7,541,000
3.	*Torn Curtain* (1966)	6,500,000
	Frenzy (1972)	6,500,000
5.	*North by Northwest* (1959)	6,450,000
6.	*Rear Window* (1954)	5,700,000
7.	*The Birds* (1963)	5,000,000
8.	*Spellbound* (1945)	4,890,000
9.	*Notorious* (1946)	4,800,000
10.	*To Catch a Thief* (1955)	4,500,000

TOP TEN MONEYMAKING FILMS FROM THE SEVENTIES

1.	*Star Wars* (1977)	$175,849,013
2.	*Jaws* (1975)	133,429,000

3.	*Grease* (1978)	93,292,000
4.	*The Exorcist* (1973)	88,100,000
5.	*The Godfather* (1972)	86,275,000
6.	*Superman* (1978)	81,000,000
7.	*The Sting* (1973)	78,889,000
8.	*Close Encounters* (1977)	77,000,000
9.	*Saturday Night Fever* (1977)	73,522,000
10.	*National Lampoon Animal House* (1978)	68,471,000

RUNNERS-UP

1.	*Smokey and the Bandit* (1977)	61,017,000
2.	*One Flew Over the Cuckoo's Nest* (1975)	59,000,000
3.	*American Graffiti* (1973)	55,886,000
4.	*Rocky* (1976)	54,000,000
5.	*Jaws II* (1978)	50,569,000
6.	*Love Story* (1970)	50,000,000
	Towering Inferno (1975)	50,000,000
8.	*Every Which Way But Loose* (1978)	48,000,000
9.	*Heaven Can Wait* (1978)	45,300,000
10.	*Airport* (1970)	45,300,000

COMMENTS: This list was compiled from the January 9, 1980 *Variety*. All other lists in this section (as mentioned) used the earlier January 3, 1979 issue.

TOP TEN MONEYMAKING FILMS FROM THE SIXTIES

1.	*The Sound of Music* (1965)	$79,000,000
2.	*The Graduate* (1968)	49,078,000
3.	*Doctor Zhivago* (1965)	46,550,000
4.	*Butch Cassidy* (1969)	46,039,000
5.	*Mary Poppins* (1964)	41,000,000
6.	*Thunderball* (1965)	28,530,000
7.	*Funny Girl* (1968)	26,325,000
8.	*Cleopatra* (1963)	26,000,000
9.	*Guess Who's Coming to Dinner?* (1968)	25,500,000
10.	*The Jungle Book* (1967)	25,000,000

RUNNERS-UP

1.	*2001* (1968)	24,100,000
2.	*Goldfinger* (1964)	22,860,000
3.	*Bonnie and Clyde* (1967)	22,700,000
4.	*The Love Bug* (1969)	21,000,000
5.	*It's a Mad, Mad, Mad, Mad World* (1963)	20,800,000
6.	*Midnight Cowboy* (1969)	20,325,000
7.	*The Dirty Dozen* (1967)	20,300,000
8.	*The Valley of the Dolls* (1967)	20,000,000
	The Odd Couple (1968)	20,000,000
10.	*West Side Story* (1961)	19,450,000

TOP TEN MONEYMAKING FILMS FROM THE FIFTIES

1.	*The Ten Commandments* (1956)	$43,000,000
2.	*Ben-Hur* (1959)	36,650,000
3.	*Around the World in 80 Days* (1956)	23,120,000
4.	*The Robe* (1953)	17,500,000

	South Pacific (1958)	17,500,000
6.	*Bridge on the River Kwai* (1957)	17,195,000
7.	*Peter Pan* (1953)	17,195,000
8.	*This Is Cinerama* (1952)	15,400,000
9.	*Greatest Show on Earth* (1952)	14,000,000
10.	*Giant* (1956)	14,000,000

RUNNERS-UP

1.	*The Lady and the Tramp* (1955)	12,750,000
2.	*Quo Vadis* (1951)	12,500,000
	Seven Wonders of the World (1956)	12,500,000
4.	*The Shaggy Dog* (1959)	12,250,000
5.	*From Here to Eternity* (1953)	12,200,000
6.	*White Christmas* (1954)	12,000,000
	Cinerama Holiday (1955)	12,000,000
8.	*Peyton Place* (1957)	11,500,000
9.	*20,000 Leagues Under the Sea* (1954)	11,000,000
10.	*Sayonara* (1957)	10,500,000

COMMENTS: Lots of religion, lots of Disney, lots of wide screen.

TOP TEN MONEYMAKING FILMS FROM THE FORTIES

1.	*Bambi* (1942)	$18,735,000
2.	*Fantasia* (1940)	15,500,000
3.	*Pinocchio* (1940)	13,000,000
4.	*Song of the South* (1946)	12,800,000
5.	*Cinderella* (1949)	12,450,000
6.	*Samson and Delilah* (1949)	11,500,000
7.	*Duel in the Sun* (1946)	11,300,000
	Best Years of Our Lives (1946)	11,300,000
9.	*This is the Army* (1943)	8,500,000
10.	*The Bells of St. Mary's* (1945)	8,000,000

RUNNERS-UP

1.	*The Jolson Story* (1946)	7,600,000
2.	*Going My Way* (1944)	6,500,000
3.	*Sergeant York* (1941)	6,100,000
4.	*Welcome Stranger* (1947)	6,100,000
5.	*Life with Father* (1947)	6,000,000
6.	*Blue Skies* (1946)	5,700,000
7.	*Valley of Decision* (1945)	5,560,000
8.	*Mrs. Miniver* (1942)	5,500,000
	Leave Her to Heaven (1945)	5,500,000
	Egg and I (1947)	5,500,000

COMMENTS: Buena Vista (Disney) is one of the few studios that consistently revises statistics to include income from re-issues. Hence, one reason why the top five films on this list are Disney products.

TOP MONEYMAKING FILMS FROM THE THIRTIES

1.	*Gone With the Wind* (1939)	$76,700,000
2.	*Snow White* (1937)	26,750,000
3.	*King Kong* (1933)	5,000,000

4. *San Francisco* (1936) 4,000,000
   The Wizard of Oz (1939) 4,000,000

TOP MONEYMAKING FILMS FROM THE TEENS AND TWENTIES

1. *Big Parade* (1925) $5,500,000
2. *Birth of a Nation* (1915) 5,000,000
3. *Ben-Hur* (1926) 4,000,000
4. *Singing Fool* (1928) 4,000,000

3/ANNUAL TOP MONEYMAKING FILMS

HERE ARE THE top moneymaking movies for each year from 1930 to 1979. From 1930 to 1946 the films are listed alphabetically, according to the records of the *Motion Picture Herald, Motion Picture Daily* and *Film Daily*. When a film is a top moneymaker for more than one year during these years, only the first year has been listed.

From 1947 to 1979 the movies are listed according to their rental earnings as reported each year in *Variety*. These figures reflect a film's domestic (United States and Canada) and not its foreign earnings. When a picture is released late in the calendar year (October to December), its income is reported in the following year's compendium, unless the film made a particularly fast impact. *Variety*'s lists include reissues.

From 1947 to 1958, the films are listed according to their *total* domestic anticipated earnings; that is, according to the studio's educated guesses as to the film's eventual revenue in the United States and Canada. The figures were based on full market playoff as indicated by the amounts taken in at the time the list was compiled.

Beginning in 1959, however, the films are not listed according to their eventual total domestic earnings, but *only* according to their rental fees up until the end of the calendar year. Thus, the figures in the lists from 1959 are in most cases smaller than a film's eventual domestic earnings.

It is possible for a film released after 1959 to have earned considerable rental fees and yet not appear on one of these annual lists. Let's say, for example, that a film released in September 1959 had earned two million dollars by the end of the year, a sum that would not qualify for that year's Top Twenty. That movie, however, could also have earned, let's say, another two million dollars during the next year, a sum that would not qualify the film for the following year's Top Twenty either. But between those two calendar years, the film would have made four million dollars. The film would have earned an impressive sum and yet not have appeared on either the 1959 or 1960 lists of Top Twenty Moneymakers.

Whenever two or more films earned the same rental fees, the tied movies are given the same numerical rank. The film earning the next greatest rental fees is then given a numerical rank which takes into account the preceding tie. For example, in 1969 *Oliver!* and *Goodbye, Columbus* each earned $10.5 million and thus tied for eighth place that year. *Chitty Chitty Bang Bang,* which earned $7.5 million that year, is then said to occupy tenth place.

1930/31

Animal Crackers
Check and Double Check
Cimarron
City Lights
A Connecticut Yankee
Daddy Long Legs
Hell's Angels
Little Caesar
The Man Who Came Back
Min and Bill
Morocco
Politics
Reducing
Strangers May Kiss
Trader Horn

1932

Arrowsmith
Bring 'Em Back Alive
Business and Pleasure
Delicious
Dr. Jekyll and Mr. Hyde
Emma
Frankenstein
Grand Hotel
Hell Divers
The Man Who Played God
Mata Hari
One Hour with You
Shanghai Express
Shopworn
Tarzan the Ape Man

1933

Animal Kingdom
Be Mine Tonight
Cavalcade
42nd Street
Gold Diggers of 1933
I'm No Angel
The Kid from Spain
Little Women
Rasputin and the Empress
State Fair
Tugboat Annie

1934

The Barretts of Wimpole
    Street
Belle of the Nineties
Chained
It Happened One Night
Judge Priest
Kentucky Kernels
The Lost Patrol
One Night of Love
Queen Christina
Riptide
Roman Scandals
She Loves Me Not
Sons of Kong
Sons of the Desert
Wonder Bar

1935

China Seas
David Copperfield
Forsaking All Others
Goin' to Town
Les Misérables
Lives of a Bengal Lancer
A Midsummer Night's Dream
Mutiny on the Bounty
Roberta
She Married Her Boss
Steamboat 'Round the Bend
Top Hat

1935/36

Anna Karenina
The Bride Comes Home
Broadway Melody of 1936
Bullets or Ballots
Captain Blood
The Country Doctor
The Crusades
Follow the Fleet
The Great Ziegfeld
Green Pastures
In Old Kentucky
The King Steps Out
The Littlest Rebel
Magnificent Obsession
Modern Times
Mr. Deeds Goes to Town
A Night at the Opera

Rhythm on the Range
Rose Marie
San Francisco
Show Boat
The Story of Louis Pasteur
A Tale of Two Cities
Thanks a Million
These Three

1936/37

After the Thin Man
Anthony Adverse
Artists and Models
The Big Broadcast of 1937
Born to Dance
Captains Courageous
The Charge of the Light
    Brigade
College Holiday
Come and Get It
Dodsworth
The Good Earth
The Gorgeous Hussy
Green Light
I Met Him in Paris
The Last of Mrs. Cheyney
Libeled Lady
Lloyds of London
Lost Horizon
Love Is News
Maytime
Mountain Music
My Man Godfrey
One in a Million
On the Avenue
Pigskin Parade
The Plainsman
Rainbow on the River
The Road Back
Romeo and Juliet
Shall We Dance
Slave Ship
A Star Is Born
Swing High, Swing Low
Swing Time
Wake Up and Live
Wee Willie Winkie
You Can't Have Everything

1937/38

The Adventures of Robin
    Hood

The Adventures of Tom
 Sawyer
Alexander's Ragtime Band
The Buccaneer
The Firefly
The Girl of the Golden West
The Goldwyn Follies
Happy Landing
Holiday
The Hurricane
In Old Chicago
Rosalie
Snow White and the Seven
 Dwarfs
Test Pilot
Wells Fargo

1938/39

Angels with Dirty Faces
Boys Town
Dodge City
Goodbye Mr. Chips
Gunga Din
The Hardys Ride High
Jesse James
Juárez
Out West with the Hardys
Pygmalion
Stagecoach
Sweethearts
That Certain Age
Three Smart Girls Grow Up
Union Pacific
You Can't Take It With You

1939/40

All This and Heaven Too
Another Thin Man
Babes in Arms
Destry Rides Again
Drums Along the Mohawk
The Fighting 69th
Gone With the Wind
The Grapes of Wrath
Gulliver's Travels
Hollywood Cavalcade
The Hunchback of Notre
 Dame
Lillian Russell
Mr. Smith Goes to
 Washington
My Favorite Wife
Ninotchka

Northwest Passage
The Old Maid
The Rains Came
Rebecca
Road to Singapore
The Women

1940/41

Aloma of the South Seas
Blood and Sand
Boom Town
The Bride Came C.O.D.
Caught in the Draft
Charley's Aunt
Dive Bomber
The Great Dictator
Hold That Ghost
I Wanted Wings
The Lady Eve
Life Begins for Andy Hardy
Meet John Doe
North West Mounted Police
The Philadelphia Story
Road to Zanzibar
The Sea Wolf
Strawberry Blonde
That Hamilton Woman
This Thing Called Love
The Ziegfeld Girl

1941/42

Ball of Fire
Captains of the Clouds
Eagle Squadron
Holiday Inn
Honky Tonk
How Green Was My Valley
In This Our Life
Kings Row
Louisiana Purchase
The Man Who Came to
 Dinner
Mrs. Miniver
My Favorite Blond
My Gal Sal
Pride of the Yankees
Reap the Wild Wind
Sergeant York
Somewhere I'll Find You
This Above All
To the Shores of Tripoli
Woman of the Year
Yankee Doodle Dandy

1942/43

Air Force
Behind the Rising Sun
Casablanca
Claudia
Commandos Strike at Dawn
Coney Island
Dixie
Heaven Can Wait
Hello, Frisco, Hello
Hers to Hold
Hitler's Children
Immortal Sergeant
In Which We Serve
Keeper of the Flame
Lucky Jordan
The More the Merrier
Now, Voyager
Random Harvest
Road to Morocco
So Proudly We Hail
Stage Door Canteen
Star Spangled Rhythm
This Is the Army

1943/44

Arsenic and Old Lace
Cover Girl
Destination Tokyo
Dragon Seed
For Whom the Bell Tolls
The Gang's All Here
Girl Crazy
Going My Way
Guadalcanal Diary
A Guy Named Joe
Lady in the Dark
Let's Face It
Madame Curie
The Miracle of Morgan's
 Creek
Mr. Skeffington
The North Star
See Here, Private Hargrove
Since You Went Away
The Song of Bernadette
The Story of Dr. Wassell
Sweet Rosie O'Grady
Thank Your Lucky Stars
As Thousands Cheer
White Cliffs of Dover
Wilson

1944/45

The Affairs of Susan
Along Came Jones
Anchors Aweigh
And Now Tomorrow
Casanova Brown
Christmas in Connecticut
Diamond Horseshoe
Frenchman's Creek
God Is My Co-Pilot
Here Comes the Waves
Hollywood Canteen
I'll Be Seeing You
Incendiary Blonde
Irish Eyes Are Smiling
The Keys of the Kingdom
Meet Me in St. Louis
Mrs. Parkington
Music for Millions
National Velvet
Nob Hill
The Princess and the Pirate
Rhapsody in Blue
Salty O'Rourke
A Song to Remember
Thirty Seconds Over Tokyo
Thrill of Romance
Thunderhead
Son of Flicka
To Have and Have Not
A Tree Grows in Brooklyn
The Valley of Decision
Winged Victory
Without Love
Wonder Man

1945/46

Adventure
Anna and the King of Siam
Bandit of Sherwood Forest
The Bells of St. Mary's
Caesar and Cleopatra
Canyon Passage
The Dolly Sisters
Dragonwyck
Duffy's Tavern
Easy to Wed
Gilda
The Green Years
The Harvey Girls
The House on 92nd Street

Kid from Brooklyn
Kitty
Leave Her to Heaven
The Lost Weekend
Love Letters
Mildred Pierce
Miss Susie Slagle's
Monsieur Beaucaire
My Reputation
Night and Day
Notorious
Road to Utopia
San Antonio
Saratoga Trunk
The Spanish Main
Spellbound
The Stork Club
They Were Expendable
Tomorrow Is Forever
Two Sisters from Boston
Weekend at the Waldorf
Ziegfeld Follies of 1946

1946/47

The Bachelor and the
  Bobbysoxer
The Best Years of Our Lives
Blue Skies
California
Dear Ruth
Duel in the Sun
The Farmer's Daughter
The Hucksters
Humoresque
I Wonder Who's Kissing Her
  Now
It's a Wonderful Life
The Jolson Story
Life with Father
Margie
My Favorite Brunette
No Leave, No Love
Nora Prentiss
The Perils of Pauline
Possessed
The Razor's Edge
Till the Clouds Roll By
The Time, the Place and the
  Girl
Two Years Before the Mast
Variety Girl
Welcome Stranger
The Yearling

1947

1.	The Best Years of Our Lives	$11,500,000
2.	Duel in the Sun	10,750,000
3.	The Jolson Story	8,000,000
	Forever Amber	8,000,000
5.	Unconquered	7,500,000
6.	Life with Father	6,250,000
7.	Welcome Stranger	6,100,000
8.	The Egg and I	5,750,000
9.	The Yearling	5,250,000
10.	Green Dolphin Street	5,000,000
	The Razor's Edge	5,000,000
12.	The Hucksters	4,700,000
13.	The Bachelor and the Bobbysoxer	4,500,000
	Till the Clouds Roll By	4,500,000
15.	Mother Wore Tights	4,150,000
16.	California	3,900,000
17.	Dear Ruth	3,800,000
	The Perils of Pauline	3,800,000
19.	The Sea of Grass	3,650,000
	This Time for Keeps	3,650,000

1948

1.	The Road to Rio	$4,500,000
2.	Easter Parade	4,200,000
3.	Red River	4,150,000
4.	The Three Musketeers	4,100,000

Johnny Belinda
4,100,000
6. Cass Timberlane
4,050,000
7. The Emperor Waltz
4,000,000
8. Gentleman's
Agreement 3,900,000
9. Date with Judy
3,700,000
10. Captain from Castile
3,650,000
Homecoming
3,650,000
12. Sitting Pretty
3,550,000
13. Paleface 3,500,000
The State of the Union
3,500,000
15. My Wild Irish Rose
3,400,000
When My Baby Smiles
at Me 3,400,000
17. Hamlet 3,250,000
Key Largo 3,250,000
19. On an Island with You
3,150,000
20. The Fuller Brush Man
3,100,000

1949

1. Jolson Sings Again
$5,500,000
2. Pinky 4,200,000
3. I Was A Male War
Bride 4,100,000
The Snake Pit
4,100,000
Joan of Arc 4,100,000
6. The Stratton Story
3,700,000
7. Mr. Belevedere Goes to
College 3,650,000
8. Little Women
3,600,000
9. Words and Music
3,500,000
10. Neptune's Daughter
3,450,000
11. Good Old Summertime
3,400,000
Sorrowful Jones
3,400,000

13. Take Me Out to the
Ballgame 3,350,000
14. Great Lover 3,300,000
15. The Barkleys of
Broadway 3,200,000
16. Adam's Rib 3,000,000
Come to the Stable
3,000,000
Command Decision
3,000,000
Connecticut Yankee
3,000,000
20. Whispering Smith
2,850,000

1950

1. Samson and Delilah
$11,000,000
2. Battleground
4,550,400
3. King Solomon's Mines
4,400,000
4. Cheaper by the Dozen
4,325,000
5. Annie Get Your Gun
4,200,000
6. Cinderella 4,150,000
Father of the Bride
4,150,000
8. Sands of Iwo Jima
3,900,000
9. Broken Arrow
3,550,000
10. Twelve O'Clock High
3,225,000
11. All About Eve
2,900,000
The Flame and the
Arrow 2,900,000
Francis 2,900,000
On the Town
2,900,000
15. Adam's Rib 2,750,000
16. Three Little Words
2,700,000
17. Black Rose 2,650,000
18. The Great Lover
2,625,000
19. The Duchess of Idaho
2,600,000
Fancy Pants 2,600,000

1951

1. David and Bathsheba
$7,000,000
2. Showboat 5,200,000
3. An American in Paris
4,500,000
The Great Caruso
4,500,000
5. A Streetcar Named
Desire 4,250,000
6. Born Yesterday
4,150,000
7. That's My Boy
3,800,000
8. A Place In the Sun
3,500,000
9. At War with the Army
3,350,000
10. Father's Little Dividend
3,100,000
11. Detective Story
2,800,000
Kim 2,800,000
13. Across the Wide
Missouri 2,750,000
Captain Horatio
Hornblower 2,750,000
15. Halls of Montezuma
2,650,000
16. Flying Leathernecks
2,600,000
Harvey 2,600,000
Royal Wedding
2,600,000
19. Here Comes the Groom
2,550,000
20. Go For Broke
2,500,000
On Moonlight Bay
2,500,000
On the Riviera
2,500,000

1952

1. The Greatest Show on
Earth $12,000,000
2. Quo Vadis 10,500,000
3. Ivanhoe 7,000,000

4. The Snows of
   Kilimanjaro 6,500,000
5. Sailor Beware
                 4,300,000
6. The African Queen
                 4,000,000
   Jumping Jacks
                 4,000,000
8. High Noon 3,400,000
   Son of Paleface
                 3,400,000
10. Singin' in the Rain
                 3,300,000
11. With a Song In My
    Heart   3,250,000
12. The Quiet Man
                 3,200,000
13. The Bend of the River
                 3,000,000
    Plymouth Adventure
                 3,000,000
    Stars and Stripes
    Forever   3,000,000
    World in His Arms
                 3,000,000
17. I'll See You in My
    Dreams   2,900,000
    The Iron Mistress
                 2,900,000
    Just for You 2,900,000
20. Distant Drums
                 2,850,000

1953

1. The Robe
       $20–30,000,000
2. From Here to Eternity
               12,500,000
3. Shane   8,000,000
4. How to Marry a
   Millionaire 7,500,000
5. Peter Pan   7,000,000
6. Hans Christian
   Andersen
                 6,000,000
7. House of Wax
                 5,500,000
8. Mogambo 5,200,000
9. Gentlemen Prefer
   Blondes   5,100,000
10. Moulin Rouge
                 5,000,000

11. Salome   4,750,000
12. Charge at Feather River
                 3,650,000
13. Caddy   3,500,000
    Come Back, Little
    Sheba   3,500,000
    The Moon Is Blue
                 3,500,000
    Scared Stiff 3,500,000
    Stooge   3,500,000
18. Stalag 17 3,300,000
19. Little Boy Lost
                 3,000,000
    Mississippi Gambler
                 3,000,000
    The Road to Bali
                 3,000,000
    Roman Holiday
                 3,000,000

1954

1. White Christmas
       $12,000,000
2. The Caine Mutiny
                 8,700,000
3. The Glenn Miller Story
                 7,000,000
4. The Egyptian
                 6,000,000
5. Rear Window
                 5,300,000
6. The High and the
   Mighty   5,200,000
7. Magnificent Obsession
                 5,000,000
   Three Coins in the
   Fountain   5,000,000
9. Seven Brides for Seven
   Brothers   4,750,000
10. Desiree   4,500,000
11. Knights of the Round
    Table   4,400,000
12. Dragnet   4,300,000
13. Demetrius and the
    Gladiators 4,250,000
    Living It Up 4,250,000
15. On the Waterfront
                 4,200,000
16. Hondo   4,100,000
17. The Long, Long Trailer
                 4,000,000
    Sabrina   4,000,000

19. River of No Return
                 3,800,000
    Broken Lance
                 3,800,000

1955

1. Cinerama Holiday
       $10,000,000
2. Mister Roberts
                 8,500,000
3. Battle Cry 8,000,000
   20,000 Leagues Under
   the Sea   8,000,000
5. Not as a Stranger
                 7,100,000
6. The Country Girl
                 6,900,000
7. The Lady and the
   Tramp   6,500,000
   Strategic Air Command
                 6,500,000
9. To Hell and Back
                 6,000,000
   Sea Chase 6,000,000
   A Star Is Born
                 6,000,000
12. The Blackboard Jungle
                 5,200,000
13. East of Eden 5,000,000
    Pete Kelly's Blues
                 5,000,000
    The Seven-Year Itch
                 5,000,000
16. The Bridges at Toko-Ri
                 4,700,000
17. A Man Called Peter
                 4,500,000
    No Business Like Show
    Business   4,500,000
    To Catch a Thief
                 4,500,000
    Vera Cruz 4,500,000

1956

1. Guys and Dolls
       $9,000,000
2. The King and I
                 8,500,000
3. Trapeze 7,500,000

4. High Society
 6,500,000
 I'll Cry Tomorrow
 6,500,000
6. Picnic 6,300,000
7. War and Peace
 6,250,000
8. The Eddy Duchin Story
 5,300,000
9. Moby Dick 5,200,000
10. The Searchers
 4,800,000
11. Conqueror 4,500,000
 Rebel Without a Cause
 4,500,000
13. The Man with the
 Golden Arm 4,350,000
 The Man in the Grey
 Flannel Suit 4,350,000
15. Bus Stop 4,250,000
16. The Rose Tattoo
 4,200,000
17. The Bad Seed
 4,100,000
 The Man Who Knew
 Too Much 4,100,000
19. Friendly Persuasion
 4,000,000
20. The Proud and the
 Profane 3,900,000

1957

1. The Ten
 Commandments
 $18,500,000
2. Around the World in
 80 Days 16,200,000
3. Giant 12,000,000
4. Pal Joey 6,700,000
5. Seven Wonders of the
 World 6,500,000
6. The Teahouse of the
 August Moon
 5,600,000
7. The Pride and the
 Passion 5,500,000
8. Anastasia 5,000,000
 Island in the Sun
 5,000,000
10. Love Me Tender
 4,500,000

11. Written on the Wind
 4,400,000
12. Gunfight at the O.K.
 Corral 4,300,000
13. Heaven Knows, Mr.
 Allison 4,200,000
14. April Love 4,000,000
 Jailhouse Rock
 4,000,000
16. Battle Hymn 3,900,000
17. An Affair to Remember
 3,850,000
18. Bernadine 3,700,000
 Loving You 3,700,000
20. The Sun Also Rises
 3,500,000

1958

1. The Bridge on the River
 Kwai $18,000,000
2. Peyton Place
 12,000,000
3. Sayonara 10,500,000
4. No Time for Sergeants
 7,200,000
5. The Vikings 7,000,000
6. Search for Paradise
 6,500,000
7. South Pacific
 6,400,000
8. Cat on a Hot Tin Roof
 6,100,000
9. Raintree County
 6,000,000
10. Old Yeller 5,900,000
11. The Big Country
 5,000,000
 A Farewell to Arms
 5,000,000
 The Young Lions
 5,000,000
14. Don't Go Near the
 Water 4,500,000
15. Witness for the
 Prosecution 3,750,000
16. Indiscreet 3,600,000
17. God's Little Acre
 3,500,000
 Houseboat 3,500,000
 The Long Hot Summer
 3,500,000
 The Sad Sack
 3,500,000

1959

1. Auntie Mame
 $8,800,000
2. Shaggy Dog 7,800,000
3. Some Like It Hot
 7,000,000
4. Imitation of Life
 6,200,000
5. The Nun's Story
 6,000,000
6. Anatomy of a Murder
 5,250,000
 North by Northwest
 5,250,000
8. Rio Bravo 5,200,000
9. Sleeping Beauty
 4,300,000
10. Some Came Running
 4,200,000
11. Hole in the Head
 4,000,000
 Hercules 4,000,000
13. Inn of the Sixth
 Happiness 3,600,000
14. The Horse Soldiers
 3,300,000
15. Don't Give Up the Ship
 3,200,000
16. 7 Voyages of Sinbad
 3,100,000
17. The Buccaneer
 3,000,000
 The Geisha Boy
 3,000,000
 I Want to Live!
 3,000,000
20. Separate Tables
 2,700,000
 Big Circus 2,700,000

1960

1. Ben-Hur $17,300,000
2. Psycho 8,500,000
3. Operation Petticoat
 6,800,000
4. Suddenly, Last Summer
 5,500,000
5. On the Beach
 5,300,000

6. Solomon and Sheba 5,250,000
7. The Apartment 5,100,000
8. From the Terrace 5,000,000
   Please Don't Eat the Daisies 5,000,000
10. Oceans 11 4,900,000
11. Journey to the Center of the Earth 4,700,000
12. The Bellboy 3,550,000
13. Elmer Gantry 3,500,000
14. The Rat Race 3,400,000
15. Portrait In Black 3,200,000
16. Li'l Abner 3,200,000
17. Visit to a Small Planet 3,200,000
18. Home from the Hill 3,150,000
19. Who Was that Lady? 3,000,000
    Toby Tyler 3,000,000
    The Big Fisherman 3,000,000
    Can-Can 3,000,000

1961

1. The Guns of Navarone $8,600,000
2. The Absent-Minded Professor 8,200,000
3. The Parent Trap 8,000,000
4. Swiss Family Robinson 7,500,000
5. Exodus 7,350,000
6. The World of Suzie Wong 7,300,000
7. Alamo 7,250,000
8. Gone With the Wind (reissue) 6,000,000
9. 101 Dalmatians 5,800,000
10. Splendor in the Grass 5,100,000
11. Come September 4,500,000

North to Alaska 4,500,000
Fanny 4,500,000
14. Pepe 4,300,000
One-Eyed Jacks 4,300,000
16. Parrish 4,200,000
17. The Misfits 3,900,000
18. The Sundowners 3,800,000
19. Midnight Lace 3,500,000
20. Never on Sunday 3,300,000
Where the Boys Are 3,300,000
The Wackiest Ship in the Army 3,300,000

1962

1. Spartacus $13,500,000
2. West Side Story 11,000,000
3. Lover Come Back 8,500,000
That Touch of Mink 8,500,000
5. El Cid 8,000,000
The Music Man 8,000,000
7. King of Kings 7,500,000
8. Hatari 6,000,000
9. The Flower Drum Song 5,000,000
The Interns 5,000,000
11. Blue Hawaii 4,700,000
12. Lolita 4,500,000
13. Babes in Toyland 4,400,000
14. Bon Voyage 4,100,000
15. What Ever Happened to Baby Jane? 4,000,000
16. Sergeants 3 3,955,000
17. The Man Who Shot Liberty Valance 3,900,000
18. Judgment at Nuremberg 3,800,000
19. Moon Pilot 3,500,000
Splendor in the Grass 3,500,000

1963

1. Cleopatra $15,700,000
2. The Longest Day 12,750,000
3. Irma La Douce 9,250,000
4. Lawrence of Arabia 9,000,000
5. How the West Was Won 8,000,000
6. Mutiny on the Bounty 7,700,000
7. Son of Flubber 6,900,000
8. To Kill a Mockingbird 6,700,000
9. Bye Bye Birdie 5,600,000
10. Come Blow Your Horn 5,450,000
11. Gypsy 5,400,000
12. The Castaways 4,700,000
13. The Birds 4,600,000
The Great Escape 4,600,000
15. The Brothers Grimm 4,500,000
16. Diamond Head 4,300,000
17. The Thrill of It All 4,150,000
18. Spencer's Mountain 4,000,000
19. 55 Days at Peking 3,900,000
Hud 3,900,000

1964

1. The Carpetbaggers $13,000,000
2. It's a Mad, Mad, Mad, Mad World 10,000,000
3. The Unsinkable Molly Brown 7,500,000
4. Charade 6,150,000
5. The Cardinal 5,275,000
6. Move Over Darling 5,100,000

7. My Fair Lady
    5,000,000
    What a Way to Go
    5,000,000
9. Good Neighbor Sam
    4,950,000
10. The Pink Panther
    4,853,000
11. Viva Las Vegas
    4,675,000
12. Sword in the Stone
    4,500,000
13. Hard Day's Night
    4,473,000
14. Dr. Strangelove
    4,148,000
15. The Night of the Iguana
    4,000,000
    The Misadventures of
    Merlin Jones
    4,000,000
17. From Russia with Love
    3,849,000
18. Love with the Proper
    Stranger   3,500,000
19. Seven Days in May
    3,400,000
    The Prize   3,400,000

1965

1. Mary Poppins
    $28,500,000
2. The Sound of Music
    20,000,000
3. Goldfinger 19,700,000
4. My Fair Lady
    19,000,000
5. What's New Pussycat?
    7,150,000
6. Shenandoah 7,000,000
7. The Sandpiper
    6,400,000
8. Father Goose
    6,000,000
9. Von Ryan's Express
    5,600,000
10. The Yellow Rolls-Royce
    5,400,000
11. How to Murder Your
    Wife   5,380,000
12. Cat Ballou 5,150,000

13. The Sons of Katie Elder
    5,000,000
14. Help   4,140,000
15. Sex and the Single Girl
    4,000,000
16. In Harm's Way
    3,900,000
17. The Americanization of
    Emily   3,600,000
18. Monkey's Uncle
    3,500,000
19. The Train   3,450,000
20. Goodbye Charlie
    3,400,000
    Operation Crossbow
    3,400,000

1966

1. Thunderball
    $26,000,000
2. Doctor Zhivago
    15,000,000
3. Who's Afraid of
    Virginia Woolf?
    10,300,000
4. That Darn Cat
    9,200,000
5. The Russians Are
    Coming, The Russians
    Are Coming 7,750,000
6. Lt. Robin Crusoe, USN
    7,500,000
7. The Silencers
    7,000,000
    Torn Curtain 7,000,000
9. Our Man Flint
    6,500,000
10. A Patch of Blue
    6,300,000
11. The Ugly Dachshund
    6,000,000
12. Wild Angels 5,500,000
13. Harper   5,300,000
14. The Blue Max
    5,000,000
    Arabesque 5,000,000
    Nevada Smith
    5,000,000
17. The Battle of the Bulge
    4,500,000
    Fantastic Voyage
    4,500,000

Texas Across the River
    4,500,000
20. The Glass Bottom Boat
    4,320,000

1967

1. The Dirty Dozen
    $18,200,000
2. You Only Live Twice
    16,300,000
3. Casino Royale
    10,200,000
4. A Man for All Seasons
    9,250,000
5. Thoroughly Modern
    Millie   8,500,000
6. Barefoot in the Park
    8,250,000
7. Georgy Girl 7,330,000
8. To Sir With Love
    7,200,000
9. Grand Prix 7,000,000
10. Hombre   6,500,000
11. Murderer's Row
    6,240,000
12. Gone With the Wind
    (reissue) 6,200,000
13. El Dorado   5,950,000
14. Blow-up   5,900,000
15. War Wagon 5,500,000
16. Follow Me, Boys
    5,350,000
17. Divorce American Style
    5,150,000
18. In Like Flint 5,000,000
    Guide for the Married
    Man   5,000,000
    Up the Down Staircase
    5,000,000

1968

1. The Graduate
    $39,000,000
2. Guess Who's Coming
    to Dinner 25,100,000
3. Gone With the Wind
    (reissue) 23,000,000
4. The Valley of the Dolls
    20,000,000

5. *The Odd Couple*
   18,500,000
6. *Planet of the Apes*
   15,000,000
7. *Rosemary's Baby*
   12,300,000
8. *The Jungle Book*
   11,500,000
9. *Yours, Mine and Ours*
   11,000,000
10. *The Green Berets*
    8,700,000
11. *2001: A Space Odyssey* 8,500,000
12. *The Fox* 8,300,000
13. *Wait Until Dark*
    7,350,000
14. *Camelot* 6,600,000
15. *The Detective*
    6,500,000
16. *The Thomas Crown Affair* 6,000,000
17. *In Cold Blood*
    5,600,000
18. *Bandolero* 5,500,000
19. *For the Love of Ivy*
    5,075,000
20. *Hang 'Em High*
    5,000,000
    The Happiest Millionaire 5,000,000

1969

1. *The Love Bug*
   $17,000,000
2. *Funny Girl* 16,500,000
3. *Bullitt* 16,400,000
4. *Butch Cassidy and the Sundance Kid*
   15,000,000
5. *Romeo and Juliet*
   14,500,000
6. *True Grit* 11,500,000
7. *Midnight Cowboy*
   11,000,000
8. *Oliver!* 10,500,000
   Goodbye Columbus
   10,500,000
10. *Chitty Chitty Bang Bang* 7,500,000
11. *Easy Rider* 7,200,000

12. *I Am Curious (Yellow)*
    6,600,000
13. *Where Eagles Dare*
    6,560,000
14. *The Lion in Winter*
    6,400,000
    Swiss Family Robinson (reissue) 6,400,000
16. *Winning* 6,200,000
17. *The Impossible Years*
    5,800,000
18. *Three in the Attic*
    5,200,000
19. *Finian's Rainbow*
    5,100,000
20. *Support Your Local Sheriff* 5,000,000

1970

1. *Airport* $37,650,796
2. *M*A*S*H* 22,000,000
3. *Patton* 21,000,000
4. *Bob & Carol & Ted & Alice* 13,900,000
5. *Woodstock* 13,500,000
6. *Hello, Dolly!*
   13,000,000
7. *Cactus Flower*
   11,300,000
8. *Catch-22* 9,250,000
9. *On Her Majesty's Secret Service*
   9,000,000
10. *The Reivers* 8,000,000
11. *The Adventurers*
    7,750,000
12. *Beneath the Planet of the Apes* 7,250,000
    The Out-of-Towners
    7,250,000
14. *Z* 6,750,000
15. *They Shoot Horses, Don't They?* 6,500,000
16. *Anne of the 1,000 Days* 6,134,264
17. *A Boy Named Charlie Brown* 6,000,000
    101 Dalmatians (reissue) 6,000,000
    Chisum 6,000,000
    A Man Called Horse
    6,000,000

1971

1. *Love Story*
   $50,000,000
2. *Little Big Man*
   15,000,000
3. *Summer of '42*
   14,000,000
4. *Ryan's Daughter*
   13,400,000
5. *The Owl and the Pussycat* 11,500,000
6. *The Aristocats*
   10,100,000
7. *Carnal Knowledge*
   9,347,000
8. *Willard* 8,200,000
9. *The Andromeda Strain*
   7,500,000
   Big Jake 7,500,000
11. *The Stewardesses*
    6,418,170
12. *Shaft* 6,100,000
    The French Connection
    6,100,000
14. *Klute* 6,000,000
15. *Cold Turkey* 5,500,000
    Le Mans 5,500,000
    The Anderson Tapes
    5,000,000
    A New Leaf 5,000,000
19. *The $1,000,000 Duck*
    4,700,000
20. *There's a Girl in My Soup* 4,500,000

1972

1. *The Godfather*
   $81,500,000
2. *Fiddler on the Roof*
   25,100,000
3. *Diamonds are Forever*
   21,000,000
4. *What's Up, Doc?*
   17,000,000
5. *Dirty Harry* 16,000,000
6. *The Last Picture Show*
   12,750,000
7. *A Clockwork Orange*
   2,000,000

8. *Cabaret* 10,885,000
9. *The Hospital* 9,000,000
10. *Everything You Always Wanted to Know About Sex* 8,500,000
11. *Bedknobs and Broomsticks* 8,250,000
12. *The Cowboys* 7,000,000
13. *Nicholas and Alexandra* 6,750,000
14. *Frenzy* 6,300,000
15. *Skyjacked* 6,001,000
16. *Song of the South* (reissue) 5,900,000
17. *Escape from the Planet of the Apes* 5,500,000
   Butterflies Are Free 5,500,000
   The New Centurions 5,500,000
20. *2001: A Space Odyssey* (reissue) 5,395,000

1973

1. *The Poseidon Adventure* 40,000,000
2. *Deliverance* 18,000,000
3. *The Getaway* 17,500,000
4. *Live and Let Die* 15,500,000
5. *Paper Moon* 13,000,000
6. *Last Tango in Paris* 12,625,000
7. *The Sound of Music* (reissue) 11,000,000
8. *Jesus Christ Superstar* 10,800,000
9. *The World's Greatest Athlete* 10,600,000
10. *American Graffiti* 10,300,000
11. *The Way We Were* 10,000,000
12. *Lady Sings the Blues* 9,050,000

13. *Mary Poppins* (reissue) 9,000,000
   Sounder 9,000,000
15. *Pete 'n' Tillie* 8,700,000
16. *The Day of the Jackal* 8,525,000
17. *Walking Tall* 8,500,000
18. *Jeremiah Johnson* 8,350,000
19. *Billy Jack* (reissue) 8,275,000
20. *High Plains Drifter* 7,125,000

1974

1. *The Sting* $68,450,000
2. *The Exorcist* 66,300,000
3. *Papillon* 19,750,000
4. *Magnum Force* 18,300,000
5. *Herbie Rides Again* 17,500,000
6. *Blazing Saddles* 16,500,000
7. *Trial of Billy Jack* 15,000,000
8. *The Great Gatsby* 14,200,000
9. *Serpico* 14,100,600
10. *Butch Cassidy and the Sundance Kid* (reissue) 13,820,000
11. *Billy Jack* (reissue) 13,000,000
12. *Airport 1975* 12,310,000
13. *Dirty Mary and Crazy Larry* 12,068,000
14. *That's Entertainment* 10,800,000
15. *The Three Musketeers* 10,115,000
16. *The Longest Yard* 10,100,000
17. *Jeremiah Johnson* (reissue) 10,000,000
18. *Robin Hood* (reissue) 9,600,000
19. *For Pete's Sake* 9,500,000

20. *Thunderbolt and Lightfoot* 8,500,000

1975

1. *Jaws* $102,650,000
2. *The Towering Inferno* 55,000,000
3. *Benji* 30,800,000
4. *Young Frankenstein* 30,000,000
5. *The Godfather Part II* 28,900,000
6. *Shampoo* 22,000,000
7. *Funny Lady* 19,000,000
8. *Murder on the Orient Express* 17,800,000
9. *Return of the Pink Panther* 17,000,000
10. *Tommy* 16,000,000
11. *The Apple Dumpling Gang* 13,500,000
12. *Freebie and the Bean* 12,500,000
13. *Lenny* 11,100,000
14. *Island at the Top of the World* 10,000,000
15. *The Man with the Golden Arm* 9,500,000
16. *The Great Waldo Pepper* 9,400,000
17. *Three Days of the Condor* 8,950,000
18. *Mandingo* 8,600,000
19. *Escape to Witch Mountain* 8,500,000
20. *The Other Side of the Mountain* 8,200,000

1976

1. *One Flew Over the Cuckoo's Nest* $56,500,000
2. *All the President's Men* 29,000,000
3. *The Omen* 27,851,000
4. *The Bad News Bears* 22,266,517
5. *Silent Movie* 20,311,000

6. *Midway* 20,300,000
7. *Dog Day Afternoon*
   19,800,000
8. *Murder by Death*
   18,800,000
9. *Jaws* (reissue)
   16,077,000
10. *Blazing Saddles*
    (reissue) 13,850,000
11. *Lucky Lady* 12,107,000
12. *Taxi Driver* 11,600,000
13. *Outlaw Josey Wales*
    10,600,000
14. *No Deposit, No Return*
    10,500,000
15. *Ode to Billy Joe*
    10,400,000
16. *The Exorcist* (reissue)
    10,300,000
17. *Hustle*
    9,958,738
18. *Barry Lyndon*
    9,100,000
19. *Gus* 9,000,000
20. *Marathon Man*
    8,886,753

1977

1. *Star Wars*
   $127,000,000
2. *Rocky* 54,000,000
3. *Smokey and the Bandit*
   39,744,000
4. *A Star Is Born*
   37,100,000
5. *King Kong* 35,851,283
6. *The Deep* 31,000,000
7. *Silver Streak*
   27,100,000
8. *The Enforcer*
   24,000,000
9. *Close Encounters of the
   Third Kind* 23,000,000
   *In Search of Noah's
   Ark* 23,000,000

11. *The Spy Who Loved
    Me* 22,000,000
12. *Oh, God* 21,200,000
13. *A Bridge Too Far*
    21,000,000
14. *The Pink Panther
    Strikes Again*
    19,500,000
15. *The Other Side of
    Midnight* 17,000,000
    The Rescuers
    17,000,000
17. *Airport 77* 14,836,000
18. *Network* 14,500,000
19. *Slap Shot* 14,497,000
20. *Herbie Goes to Monte
    Carlo* 14,000,000

1978

1. *Grease* $83,091,000
2. *Close Encounters of the
   Third Kind* 54,000,000
3. *National Lampoon's
   Animal House*
   32,368,000
4. *Jaws 2* 49,299,000
5. *Heaven Can Wait*
   42,517,000
6. *The Goodbye Girl*
   41,000,000
7. *Star Wars* (reissue)
   38,375,000
8. *Hooper* 31,500,000
9. *Foul Play* 25,065,000
10. *Revenge of Pink
    Panther* 25,000,000
11. *Up In Smoke*
    21,271,000
12. *The End* 20,000,000
13. *Cheap Detective*
    19,500,000
14. *The Gauntlet*
    17,500,000
15. *High Anxiety*
    17,040,000

16. *Pete's Dragon*
    16,100,000
17. *Turning Point*
    15,045,000
18. *House Calls*
    14,859,000
19. *Coma* 14,400,000
20. *Omen II: Damien*
    12,050,000

1979

1. *Superman*
   $81,000,000
2. *Every Which Way But
   Loose*
   48,000,000
3. *Rocky II* 43,049,274
4. *Alien* 40,086,573
5. *The Amityville Horror*
   35,000,000
   Star Trek 35,000,000
7. *Moonraker* 33,934,074
8. *The Muppet Movie*
   32,000,000
9. *California Suite*
   29,200,000
10. *The Deer Hunter*
    26,927,000
11. *The Main Event*
    26,000,000
12. *The China Syndrome*
    25,425,000
13. *10* 25,000,000
14. *Apocalypse Now*
    22,855,657
15. *Escape From Alcatraz*
    21,014,000
16. *Meatballs* 19,674,000
17. *Love At First Bite*
    18,100,000
18. *The In-Laws*
    18,000,000
19. *Manhattan* 16,908,439
20. *Starting Over*
    15,201,000

4/MOST POPULAR MOVIES ON TELEVISION

MOVIES AND TV are natural enemies, right? Well, not exactly. Yes, it has been repeatedly argued that the birth of television almost caused the death of movies, and yes, some movie moguls in the 1950s were so anxious of TV's growing success that they actually forbade their stars to appear on the tube. But for years now, the networks have been relying on movies for blockbuster ratings, and the studios have similarly depended upon the webs for whopping profits from selling films to the tube. Movies and TV—once bitter enemies —are now willing and at times even friendly collaborators.

When did the truce begin? On September 23, 1961 when the first prime time weekly film series on television, NBC's *Saturday Night at the Movies,* made its debut with *How to Marry a Millionaire,* an ironic first presentation, perhaps, since that 1953 film —lavishly shot in Cinemascope with superstars Marilyn Monroe, Betty Grable, and Lauren Bacall—was originally made to lure viewers *away* from their TV sets and back into the movie house.

Of course there had been movies on television prior to 1961, but the films shown on TV during the late 1940s and throughout the 1950s were seldom recent releases or big hits. The major studios simply were not willing to sell their best products to the small screen, so that in its infancy TV had to depend upon independent producers and small studios like Monogram and Republic for its film fare.

In 1955 ABC had presented a package of 100 films from British filmmaker J. Arthur Rank, and in 1956 RKO sold more than 700 of its films to C & C Super Corp. which in turn leased them to the networks. But none of these aired films had been theatrically released after 1948: Hollywood still held back with its recent goods.

In 1960, however, NBC negotiated with Twentieth Century-Fox and purchased broadcast rights to 30 feature releases (vintage 1951 through 1955) for the 1961/62 season: thus *Saturday Night at the Movies* was born.

The show proved so successful* that in 1962 ABC followed with its own movie series, and in 1963 NBC even added another film series, *Monday Night at the Movies,* to its prime time schedule. CBS, the third big network, began purchasing rights to movies in December 1964, so that by the end of the 1960s as many as nine movies could be seen on national television.

Movies were so dominant during those years that a 1968 *Variety* headline nervously asked CAN TV CONQUER THE MOVIE MENACE? According to the article, the networks, in their reckless race for rating points, had turned themselves into "neighborhood theatres 7 nights a week

Saturday Night at the Movies lasted until 1978, when it was then the second longest-lived prime time series on TV: only Walt Disney had lasted longer.

. . . Are motion pictures destroying the television business? 15 years ago the question went the other way around."

Here's a chart that records the growing popularity of movies on TV during the 1960s boom:

	Saturday Night at the Movies (NBC)		Sunday Night (ABC)	
	Rating	Share	Rating	Share
1962/63	19.3	32	16.2	24
1963/64	19.2	32	18.8	31
1964/65	21.0	37	19.0	32
1965/66	21.0	36	19.0	32
1966/67	21.6	37	20.7	35
1967/68	24.3	42	19.5	33

The success of movies on televison gave birth to a new baby: the made-for-TV movie. *See How They Run* starring John Forsythe and Senta Berger was aired October 7, 1964 and hailed as the first movie made especially for television. *The Killers* with Lee Marvin and Angie Dickinson was supposed to be the first made-for-TV flic, but was deemed too violent for television and hence was theatrically released.

By 1969, movies-made-for-TV were becoming so successful that ABC had an entire weekly series, *ABC Movie of the Week*, and the popularity of movies-made-for-TV has been increasing ever since, especially during the past few years. A 1979 ABC study, for example, revealed that made-for-TV pictures had risen from 32% to 57% of the total films on TV between the 1975/76 and 1978/79 seasons. Feature films, by contrast, had decreased from 68% to 43%.

What accounts for the diminishing number of theatricals on TV? For one thing, Hollywood is making fewer and fewer films each year, so that the networks had fewer movies to fight over. Censorship concerns —most feature films are too violent and sexy by TV standards—further complicate the move from silver screen to TV tube.

Then there are the demographics: studies indicate that the largest audience for movies consists of teenage males, between 17 and 19. TV advertisers, on the other hand, want to capture the female 18-34 market, since they are the biggest consumers. So with the exception of blockbuster flics like *The Sting* and *Rocky,* many feature films aren't considered great buys by the networks.

And then, of course,there's money: theatrical movies are much more expensive than made-for-TV films. Made-for-TV flics are "so reasonably priced compared to theatricals," one top-level network executive has confessed, "you have to wonder why we're in theatricals at all."

How much *does* a studio charge a network to air a film? For its first historic season of *Saturday Night at the Movies,* NBC paid Twentieth Century-Fox $5,500,00 for 30 films, or approximately $180,00 per feature, and needless to say, prices have been skyrocketing ever since. In 1975 the average price per play of a feature film on TV was $500,000, in 1979 $1.2 million. The largest fee ever paid for a single film in the history of TV is the $35 million CBS forked over to MGM for 20 showings in 20 years of *Gone With the Wind.* ABC reportedly paid $25 million for the air rights to *Jaws I* and *Jaws II.* NBC was willing to pay some $21.5 million to air *Sound of Music* 20 times in 22 years. And CBS purchased 4 airings of *Rocky II* with an additional broadcast of *Rocky I* for $20 million.

Networks usually purchase films in packages: in 1978 CBS, for example, obtained air rights from Twentieth Century-Fox for 13 films (including titles such as *Silver Streak, Fury,* and *Lucky Lady*) for $40 million. A network will sometimes buy the TV rights to a film before it has even been made—a risky business to be sure. CBS, for example, paid $6.5 million for 3

MOST POPULAR MOVIES ON TELEVISION/31

runs of *Butch and Sundance: The Early Years* while that film was still in production. The movie was a boxoffice flop when it was released, and CBS would not have had to pay such a hefty sum if they had waited.

On the other hand, CBS—in another pre-production deal—gave only $2 million for the TV rights to *Foul Play* because the movie had no superstars. The film, however, became one of the biggest hits of 1978 and many industry experts estimate that CBS would have had to pay at least 3 times the money if they had bought the film after its release.

Movies are obviously quite good at winning ratings for the networks, but are they very profitable given their costs? Not particularly. The profit potential of an average two-hour movie aired during the 1978/79 season was $200,000 to $400,000 or $50,000 to $100,000 per half hour. By comparison, an episode of a successful show like *Three's Company* could generate a profit of $330,000 during the Fall/Winter and $430,000 during Summer re-runs.

The networks do make money from movies in another way: in recent years Hollywood has turned to TV as one of the best ways to advertise its current crop of films. Industry statistics show investments in TV time by film studios jumped more than 20% from 1975 to 1979. "Filmmakers are now utilizing their one-time archenemy, television, to sell their own product," says Arthur Trudeau Jr., an executive of the Television Bureau of Advertising. According to the Bureau, Hollywood now spends $131 million to advertise and hype their films on TV.

* * *

Local TV stations can choose from more than 20,000 feature films to show on their film series. Which pictures are the most popular? In 1977 *TV Guide* asked program directors across the nation to name the 10 most popular, most often shown movies in their markets. The results:

1. *Casablanca* (1943)
2. *King Kong* (1960)
3. *The Magnificent Seven* (1960)
4. *The Maltese Falcon* (1941)
5. *The Adventures of Robin Hood* (1938)
6. *The African Queen* (1951)
7. *The Birds* (1963)
8. *Citizen Kane* (1941)
9. *Miracle on 34th Street* (1941)
10. *Girls! Girls! Girls!* (1962)
11. *King Solomon's Mines* (1950)
12. *The Treasure of the Sierra Madre* (1948)
13. *The War of the Worlds* (1953)

The same survey revealed the most popular *series* to be the Sherlock Holmes pictures starring Basil Rathbone and Nigel Bruce.

What are the highest-rated films on TV? The following chart lists the top-rated movies on television between September 1961 and September 1979. This list is selected from *Variety*'s much longer and more comprehensive compilation that ranks every movie that has earned a national Nielsen rating of 24.0 or better.

372 individual titles make *Variety*'s list: 224 theatricals and 148 made-for-TVs. For the first seven years, the big movies on TV were all theatricals, but in recent years made-for-TVs have enjoyed enormous success.

The Wizard of Oz is cited 14 times on *Variety*'s list, a record. *The Homecoming* (the source of *The Waltons* series) with 5 appearances on the list holds a repeat record for made-for-TVs.

Postscript: Shortly after this list was compiled, *Jaws* was aired on national TV, a 39.0 rating and 57 share, earning it a 6th-place tie with *Poseidon Adventure*.

MOST POPULAR MOVIES ON TELEVISION

	TITLE	DAY	DATE	RATING	SHARE
1.	*Gone With the Wind*—Part 1.	Sun.	11/7/76	47.7	65
2.	*Gone With the Wind*—Part 2.	Mon.	11/8/76	47.4	64
3.	*Airport*	Sun.	11/11/73	42.3	63
	Love Story	Sun.	10/1/72	42.3	62
5.	*The Godfather*—Part 2	Mon.	11/18/74	39.4	57
6.	*Poseidon Adventure*	Sun.	10/27/74	39.0	62
7.	*True Grit*	Sun.	22/12/72	38.9	63
	The Birds	Sat.	1/6/68	38.9	59
9.	*Patton*	Sun.	11/19/72	38.5	65
10.	*Bridge on the River Kwai*	Sun.	9/25/66	38.3	61
* 11.	*Helter Skelter*—Part 2	Fri.	4/2/76	37.5	60
	Jeremiah Johnson	Sun.	1/18/76	37.5	56
13.	*Ben-Hur*	Sun.	2/14/71	37.1	56
	Rocky	Sun.	2/4/79	37.1	53
15.	*The Godfather*—Part 1	Sat.	11/16/74	37.0	61
* 16.	*Little Ladies of the Night*	Sun.	1/16/77	36.9	53
17.	*Wizard of Oz* (R)**	Sun.	12/13/59	36.5	58
18.	*Wizard of Oz* (R)	Sun.	1/26/64	35.9	59
19.	*Planet of the Apes*	Fri.	9/14/73	35.2	60
*	*Helter Skelter*—Part 1	Thu.	4/1/76	35.2	57
21.	*Wizard of Oz* (R)	Sun.	1/17/65	34.7	49
22.	*Born Free*	Sun.	2/22/70	34.2	53
23.	*Wizard of Oz*	Sat.	11/3/56	33.9	53
24.	*Sound of Music*	Sun.	2/29/76	33.6	49
* 25.	*The Waltons' Thanksgiving Story*	Thu.	11/15/73	33.5	51
26.	*Bonnie & Clyde*	Thu.	9/20/73	33.4	38
27.	*Ten Commandments*	Sun.	2/18/73	33.2	54
*	*Night Stalker*	Tue.	1/11/72	33.2	48
29.	*The Longest Yard*	Sun.	9/25/77	33.1	53
*	*A Case of Rape*	Wed.	2/20/74	33.1	49
31.	*Wizard of Oz* (R)	Sun.	12/9/62	33.0	55
*	*Dallas Cowboys Cheerleaders*	Sun.	1/14/79	33.0	48
* 33.	*Brian's Song*	Tue.	11/30/71	32.9	48
34.	*Wizard of Oz* (R)	Sun.	12/11/60	32.7	52
35.	*Beneath the Planet of the Apes*	Fri.	10/26/73	32.6	54
36.	*Wizard of Oz* (R)	Sun.	12/10/61	32.5	53
* 37.	*Women in Chains*	Tue.	1/24/72	32.3	48
	Cat on a Hot Tin Roof	Thu.	9/28/67	32.3	50
* 39.	*Jesus of Nazareth*—Part 1	Sun.	4/3/77	32.2	50
40.	*Sky Terror*	Sun.	9/19/76	32.0	51
	Apple Dumpling Gang	Sun.	11/14/76	32.0	47
42.	*Butch Cassidy and the Sundance Kid*	Sun.	9/26/76	31.9	51
	The Sting	Sun.	11/5/78	31.9	48
* 44.	*Heidi*	Sun.	11/17/78	31.8	47
* 45.	*My Sweet Charlie*	Tue.	1/20/70	31.7	48

* Indicates a movie made especially for television
** Indicates a repeat broadcast

	TITLE	DAY	DATE	RATING	SHARE
46.	*Airport 1975*	Mon.	9/20/76	31.6	46
•	*Feminist and the Fuzz*	Tue.	1/26/71	31.6	46
• 48.	*Something for Joey*	Wed.	4/6/77	31.5	51
•	*Dawn: Portrait of A Teenage Runaway*	Mon.	9/27/76	31.5	46
50.	*Great Escape*—Part 2	Fri.	9/15/67	31.3	55
51.	*McLintockl*	Fri.	11/3/67	31.2	54
52.	*Ballad of Josie*	Tue.	9/16/69	31.1	56
	Great Escape—Part 1	Thu.	9/14/67	31.1	51
	Wizard of Oz (R)	Sun.	1/9/66	31.1	49
	Goldfinger	Sun.	9/17/72	31.1	49
• 56.	*Amazing Howard Hughes*—Part 2	Thu.	4/14/77	31.0	53
	The Robe	Sun.	3/26/67	31.0	53
•	*Sarah T.—Portrait of a Teenage Alcoholic*	Tue.	2/11/75	31.0	44
• 59.	*Call Her Mom*	Tue.	2/15/72	30.9	46
• 60.	*A Death of Innocence*	Fri.	11/26/71	30.8	55
	Ten Commandments—Part 2 (R)	Mon.	2/18/74	30.8	48
•	*Autobiography of Miss Jane Pitman*	Thu.	1/31/74	30.8	47
• 63.	*Charlie's Angels*	Sun.	3/21/76	30.7	49
64.	*Three Days of the Condor*	Sun.	11/27/77	30.5	47
	The Graduate	Thu.	11/8/73	30.5	48
66.	*Rescue From Gilligan's Island*—Part 1	Sat.	10/14/78	30.4	52
	The Dirty Dozen	Thu.	9/24/70	30.4	53
•	*Tribes*	Tue.	11/10/70	30.4	45
•	*Yuma*	Tue.	3/2/71	30.4	44
•	*Brian's Song* (R)	Tue.	11/21/72	30.4	43
• 71.	*Mr. & Mrs. Bo-Jo Jones*	Tue.	11/16/71	30.2	45
72.	*Earthquake*—Part 2	Sun.	10/3/76	30.1	46
73.	*The War Wagon*	Sat.	10/31/70	30.0	53
	Lilies of the Field	Fri.	3/24/67	30.0	50
	Airport (R)	Sun.	2/9/75	30.0	42
• 76.	*Melvin Purvis, G-Man*	Tue.	4/9/74	29.8	49
77.	*Your Cheatin' Heart*	Fri.	4/5/68	29.7	50
78.	*Gidget Goes Hawaiian*	Thu.	3/31/66	29.6	49
• 79.	*Mrs. Sundance*	Tue.	4/9/74	29.5	43
• 80.	*The Waltons' Easter Story*	Thu.	4/19/73	29.4	48
•	*Charlie's Angels* (R)	Tue.	9/14/76	29.4	47
•	*Maybe I'll Come Home In the Spring*	Tue.	2/16/71	29.4	42
	Five Branded Women	Fri.	1/6/67	29.4	42
• 84.	*Jesus of Nazareth*—Part 2	Sun.	4/10/77	29.3	48
•	*Alias Smith and Jones*	Tue.	1/5/71	29.3	44
86.	*PT 109*	Fri.	1/13/67	29.1	50
	Escape From Planet of the Apes	Fri.	11/6/73	29.1	50
	Roustabout	Wed.	1/3/68	29.1	48
	Hombre	Sun.	1/25/70	29.1	45
90.	*Green Berets*	Sat.	11/18/72	28.9	45
	West Side Story—Part 1	Tue.	3/14/72	28.9	41
92.	*Cat Ballou*	Wed.	10/2/68	28.8	48
•	*Raid on Entebbe*	Sun.	1/9/77	28.8	41
	Gone With the Wind (R)—Part 2	Mon.	2/12/79	28.8	40

* Indicates a movie made especially for television
** Indicates a repeat

	TITLE	DAY	DATE	RATING	SHARE
95.	Valley of the Dolls	Fri.	9/22/72	28.7	50
•	The Homecoming (R)	Fri.	12/7/73	28.7	49
•	Sibyl—Part 2	Mon.	11/15/76	28.7	43
98.	Wizard of Oz (R)	Sun.	2/12/67	28.6	50
	Splendor in the Grass	Thu.	10/12/67	28.6	47
	Walking Tall (R)	Sun.	11/9/75	28.6	46
	Survive!	Sun.	2/27/77	28.6	44
	The Hospital	Sun.	11/18/73	28.6	44
•	Incredible Journey of Dr. Meg Laurel	Tue.	1/2/79	28.6	42
	In Harm's Way—Part 2	Mon.	1/25/71	28.6	42
105.	To Kill A Mockingbird	Sat.	11/9/68	28.5	49
	Mario Puzo's The Godfather—Part 4	Tue.	11/15/77	28.5	43
•	Gidget Gets Married	Tue.	1/14/72	28.5	40
• 108.	The Jericho Mile	Sun.	3/18/79	28.4	46
•	The Runaways	Tue.	4/1/75	28.4	44
•	Dr. Cook's Garden	Tue.	1/19/71	28.4	41
111.	W.W. & The Dixie Dancekings	Sun.	1/2/77	28.3	43
• 112.	Flying High	Mon.	8/28/78	28.2	46
	That Touch of Mink	Tue.	1/9/68	28.2	43
114.	Cactus Flower	Sat.	9/30/72	28.1	46
•	The Last Child	Tue.	10/15/71	28.1	44
•	Battlestar Galactica	Sun.	9/19/78	28.1	43
• 117.	SST—Death Flight	Fri.	2/25/77	28.0	47
	Buster and Billie	Mon.	3/22/76	28.0	44
	Mario Puzo's The Godfather—Part 3	Mon.	11/14/77	28.0	42
120.	Madame X	Mon.	9/16/68	27.9	47
	Oklahoma	Thu.	11/26/70	27.9	47
122.	North By Northwest	Fri.	9/29/67	27.8	50
	Tora! Tora! Tora!	Fri.	9/21/73	27.8	47
	Serpico	Sun.	9/21/75	27.8	47
•	Girl Most Likely To	Tue.	11/6/73	27.8	42
	The Cowboys	Tue.	11/13/73	27.8	42
	Earthquake—Part 1	Sun.	9/26/76	27.8	41
128.	Wizard of Oz (R)	Sun.	3/15/70	27.7	50
	Second Time Around	Tue.	10/3/67	27.7	48
	Sons of Katie Elder	Sun.	11/17/68	27.7	46
•	In Search of America	Tue.	3/23/71	27.7	42
132.	What A Way to Go!	Sat.	9/16/67	27.6	50
	The Carpetbaggers	Sun.	2/16/69	27.6	48
•	Cry Rape!	Tue.	11/27/73	27.6	43
•	Wild Women	Tue.	10/20/70	27.6	41
• 136.	Doomsday Flight	Tue.	12/13/66	27.5	48
	Billy Jack	Sat.	11/20/76	27.5	46
	What's Up Doc?	Fri.	1/23/76	27.5	44
•	Longest Hundred Miles	Sat.	1/21/67	27.5	43
•	Run, Simon, Run	Tue.	12/1/70	27.5	43
•	The Red Pony	Sun.	2/18/73	27.5	42
142.	Ten Commandments (R)	Sun.	3/25/79	27.4	48
	Send Me No Flowers	Tue.	9/19/67	27.4	47
	I Want To Live!	Thu.	2/15/68	27.4	43

* Indicates a movie made especially for television
** Indicates a repeat broadcast

	TITLE	DAY	DATE	RATING	SHARE
•	*It Happened One Christmas*	Sun.	12/11/77	27.4	42
•	*Elvis*	Sun.	2/11/79	27.4	40
•	*Second Chance*	Tue.	2/8/72	27.4	40
• 148.	*Man From Atlantis*	Fri.	3/4/77	27.3	46
•	*Smash-Up On Interstate 5*	Fri.	12/3/76	27.3	45
	Blue Hawaii	Tue.	11/29/66	27.3	45
•	*Jane Eyre*	Wed.	3/24/71	27.3	43
	That's Entertainment	Tue.	11/18/75	27.3	41
153.	*Spencer's Mountain*	Fri.	10/13/67	27.2	49
	Battle Of the Bulge—Part 2	Fri.	2/19/71	27.2	43
	Hawaii	Fri.	1/11/74	27.2	42
•	*A Taste of Evil*	Tue.	10/12/71	27.2	41
•	*Hardcase*	Tue.	12/1/72	27.2	40
•	*The Victim*	Tue.	11/14/72	27.2	40
159.	*McLintock!* (R)	Sat.	2/27/71	27.1	44
	Stepford Wives	Sun.	10/24/76	27.1	43
•	*The Loneliest Runner*	Mon.	12/20/76	27.1	42
	West Side Story—Part 2	Wed.	3/15/72	27.1	42
	Diary of a Mad Housewife	Mon.	1/24/73	27.1	42
	The Mating Game	Mon.	10/21/63	27.1	41
	In Harm's Way—Part 1	Sun.	1/24/71	27.1	41
166.	*Walking Tall*	Sat.	3/1/75	27.0	45
•	*Girl Who Came Gift-Wrapped*	Tue.	1/29/74	27.0	40
168.	*Hot Spell*	Wed.	3/17/65	26.9	44
•	*She Waits*	Fri.	1/28/72	26.9	44
	African Queen	Thu.	3/5/70	26.9	43
	Gator	Sun.	2/12/78	26.9	41
•	*Savage Bees*	Mon.	11/22/76	26.9	41
•	*Sybil*—Part 1	Sun.	11/14/76	26.9	40
•	*Crowhaven Farm*	Tue.	11/24/70	26.9	40
175.	*Diamonds Are Forever* (R)	Sun.	11/26/76	26.8	47
	I'll Take Sweden	Tue.	9/17/68	26.8	47
	Guess Who's Coming to Dinner?	Mon.	9/19/71	26.8	44
	Five Easy Pieces	Mon.	4/5/76	26.8	44
	The Last Voyage	Wed.	3/24/65	26.8	43
•	*Over-the-Hill Gang*	Tue.	10/7/69	26.8	42
	Wizard of Oz (R)	Sun.	3/14/76	26.8	42
•	*Love Hate Love*	Tue.	2/9/71	26.8	38
183.	*Thrill of It All*	Sat.	11/25/67	26.7	46
•	*Fame Is the Name of the Game*	Sat.	11/26/66	26.7	44
	Father Goose	Sat.	1/41/69	26.7	42
	The Big Country—Part 2 (R)	Tue.	3/30/71	26.7	42
• 187.	*Killer Who Wouldn't Die*	Sun.	4/4/76	26.6	45
	Tickle Me	Fri.	12/8/67	26.6	44
•	*The Homecoming* (R)	Fri.	12/8/72	26.6	43
	Life and Times of Grizzly Adams	Mon.	5/17/76	26.6	43
191.	*Wizard of Oz* (R)	Sun.	3/20/76	26.5	41
•	*Man in the Iron Mask*	Mon.	1/17/77	26.5	39
•	*If Tomorrow Comes*	Tue.	12/7/71	26.5	38

* Indicates a movie made especially for television
** Indicates a repeat broadcast

RANK	TITLE	DAY	DATE	RATING	SHARE
194.	Marnie	Sat.	11/4/67	26.4	47
•	Shadow Over Elveron	Tue.	3/5/68	26.4	43
	Wizard of Oz (R)	Sun.	4/8/73	26.4	43
•	Fantasy Island	Fri.	1/14/77	26.4	42
•	House on Greenapple Road	Sun.	1/11/70	26.4	40
•	A Cry in the Wilderness	Tue.	3/26/74	26.4	39
200.	Harlow	Sun.	10/15/67	26.3	43
•	Trapped	Wed.	11/4/73	26.3	43
	From Russia With Love	Mon.	1/14/74	26.3	42
•	Green Eyes	Mon.	1/3/77	26.3	40
•	Texas Across the River	Mon.	1/19/70	26.3	39

* Indicates a movie made especially for television
** Indicates a repeat broadcast

5/MOVIE THEATERS IN THE UNITED STATES

IN THEIR EARLIEST days, movies did not have a home of their own. The first movies were not shown on a theater screen, but were viewed by one person at a time through a medium-sized cabinet known as a kinetoscope. Kinetoscopes—which have their modern day equivalent in the peep shows of adult bookstores—could be found in such places as penny arcades and traveling tent shows, where they offered such film fare as a young woman climbing a tree, an ocean wave beating upon the shore or a railroad train speeding directly toward the viewer.

In 1895, however, the Lumiere Brothers in Paris projected film onto a screen for a commercial audience for the first time, and one year later the experiment was successfully repeated by Thomas Edison in New York. Projected films proved so popular that soon many penny arcades, storefronts and music halls were converted into movie theaters, or "nickelodeons" as they came to be called. (The name is usually attributed to John P. Harris, a showman who merged the Greek word for theater with the admission price. The name caught on, although the admission price was soon to rise.)

The interiors of nickelodeons were usually simple: the auditorium was approximately 20 feet wide and 80 feet deep, divided by a central aisle with short straight rows of wooden seats on either side. The piano was located at the front, the projection booth in the back, and the screen was often merely a square of white or silver paint.

The exteriors of nickelodeons, however, were often quite lavish. The facade almost invariably contained an elaborate arch, in the middle of which was the ticket booth. (Above the box office was a small window to provide ventilation and a possible hasty escape for the projectionist, who was handling flammable nitrate film.) The facades could be decorated in various exotic styles —Moorish, Gothic, Oriental—and were embellished with ornamentation, statutes, and above all else, with light bulbs. To attract audiences, theater managers hired barkers to announce the programs or even placed a pianist in the arched vestibule to play for passers-by.

By around 1910, film exhibitors began building theaters expressly to show movies rather than continue converting standing structures into nickelodeons. The Columbia Theater in Detroit (1911), the Regent in New York (1913) and the Coliseum in Seattle (1916) were all designed on a lavish scale that had been impossible on the pre-existing storefront sites of the nickelodeons. These new theaters held thousands of people, not hundreds, and an entire symphony replaced the solitary piano of the nickelodeon. Staffs were now uniformed, and mammoth pipe organs entertained audiences before the films. Live shows involving a great number of entertainers, dancers and singers were elaborately and professionally staged during intermissions. If one theater dressed a giant in an outlandish costume to "guard" the box office, another theater would place a midget in its foyer, or would dress its doorman as a Foreign Legionnaire to lure audiences into its splendid lobby. In short, the age of the movie palace had arrived.

Certain architects, in fact, became famous for their elaborate theaters: Thomas W. Lamb, who designed New York' Regent (1913), the Strand (1914) and the Rialto (1916), was one of the first and most prolific theater architects, having designed over three hundred movie palaces by 1921; Rapp and Rapp, whose best work included the Riviera and the Tivoli in Chicago and the famous Paramount Theater (1928) on Times Square, specialized in late-French-court architecture; and John Eberson, designer of the Majestic (1922) in Houston, was known for his "atmospheric" style that made the theater look as if it were outdoors, set in some exotic land.

Exotic styles were, in fact, quite fashionable for movie palaces, the two most famous examples being in Hollywood: Grauman's Egyptian Theater (1922) and Grauman's Chinese (1927), where on opening night Norma Talmadge pressed her hands and feet in wet cement and thereby started a tradition. Both Grauman's theaters were designed by Meyer and Holler.

The movie palace reached its apotheosis in two New York theaters: the Roxy (1927), which called itself the "cathedral of motion pictures" and proudly advertised its $10 million building costs; and Radio City Music Hall (1932), a lasting tribute to the wonders of Art Deco. Each theater seated over 6,000 people, and spared no expense in its luxurious interiors and elaborate equipment. The Roxy, designed by Walter Ahlschlager and decorated by Harold Rambusch, was named after S. L. Rothafel, the famous theater manager who had been nicknamed "Roxy" during his baseball days.

Movie-palace design is now both adamantly praised and criticized, but whether you find its architectural excesses wonderful or merely kitsch, you must admit that the movie-palace style served its function. For one thing, the fantastic décor matched the fantastic narratives of early films—as architect Thomas Lamb wrote when describing his State Theater (1929) in Syracuse, "these exotic ornaments, colors, and scenes are particularly effective in creating an atmosphere in which the mind is free to frolic and becomes receptive to entertainment." Secondly, the resplendent style paradoxically served America's "equalitarian" spirit, for despite our supposed anti-aristocratic sentiments, the American spirit has often been enamored of aristocracy and has secretly wished for everyone to be an aristocrat. The movie palaces afforded that chance: for a small admission fee, anyone could inhabit lush surroundings. As architect George Rapp noted, the movie palaces were "a shrine to democracy where there are no privileged patrons." Thirdly, the grand scale of the movie palaces served to hide the insecurity of an art form that was all too aware of its humble origins. By appropriating the style of legitimate theaters and opera houses— most movie palaces did not really pay much attention to the unique requirements of showing movies but merely imitated dramatic theaters—movies hoped to gain some of the respect conferred on legitimate drama.

But the era of the movie palace did not last very long. Both the Depression and the coming of sound brought an end to the extravagance. Physically, sound required attention to be paid to the acoustics of the theater and not merely to its decoration;

and psychologically, sound brought a certain realism to the screen that contradicted the decorative excesses of movie palaces. The Depression, of course, curtailed the extravagant spending, and by the time the country was beginning to recover, World War II had begun and it, too, curtailed theater construction.

After the war, film exhibition in this country met two problems: (1) antitrust actions that forced Hollywood studios to divorce their production/ distribution interests from their exhibition facilities, which meant that most theaters no longer had the studios' financial backing; and (2) television. During the early fifties, Hollywood found its audiences decimated by TV. The mammoth theaters, no longer able to draw large audiences, were often demolished or converted into garages, churches and bowling alleys. Hollywood tried to woo back its audiences through the technological curiosities of the wide screen— Cinerama, CinemaScope, VistaVision—but the tricks did not really work. By 1958 there were only 12,000 indoor theaters in the United States, whereas in 1948 there had been nearly 18,000.

Technology did, of course, change the shape of our theater screens. Silent films had been almost square in shape—1.33 feet in width to every 1 foot in height. Early sound films were slightly more rectangular, to accommodate the optical sound tract— their ratio was 1.66 to 1. But with the new projection techniques of the early fifties, screens were almost twice as wide as high— 18.5 to 1.

One type of theater, however, did thrive after World War II; the drive-in. In 1932 Richard M. Hollingshead, Jr., a chemical manufacturer, had set up a movie screen in front of his New Jersey garage and watched the film from his car. Hollingshead patented the idea, opened a drive-in in nearby Camden the following year and soon had located several drive-ins in other states. The patent was declared illegal and the war put a stop to drive-in construction. But after the war the idea caught on and the country found itself infatuated with drive-ins: in 1948 there were only 820 drive-ins in the United States, but by 1958 the number had increased to over 4,000.

Initially, drive-ins were small rocky lots with few accommodations. But soon they, like the movie palaces before them, turned to grandness. Some drive-ins could handle over 2,000 cars, others featured swimming pools, amusement parks, even laudromats. Complete dinners could be purchased, cars could be serviced, and of course drive-ins grew infamous for the "privacy" they afforded. In their first years, drive-ins were likely to show only B-movies, but with their growing popularity, they soon began to screen first-run films as well.

Today the number of drive-ins has decreased because of stricter zoning regulations and rising costs in land. Now the average drive-in capacity is 550 cars.

In the 1960s indoor theaters moved to the suburbs, and with that move began the rise of the multiple theater. In 1963 Stanley Durwood opened a two-unit complex in a Kansas City shopping center—two small theaters with one projection booth. The arrangement proved successful, and within a few years Durwood opened other "twin" theaters and then the first quad complex. Today, small multiple theaters—particularly in huge suburban shopping centers— are among the most lucrative of theaters. Approximately 10% of all indoor theaters in this country are now multiple units.

In recent years, much attention has been paid to the special demands of film exhibition, and several theaters have been constructed to excel in screening diverse kinds of films. The American Film Institute theater in Washington, D.C., the Pacific Film Archives theater in Berkeley, and the

American Cinematheque in New York are a few of the well-known theaters which realize that *how* we see films influences *what* we see. Although opinions differ as to what exactly constitutes ideal viewing conditions —whether each viewer should be isolated from all other viewers, whether the theater should be austere so as not to compete with the screen or decorated to enhance the magic of the movie—more and more care is now being given to film exhibition.

Film exhibition represents a considerable segment of the film industry. In 1965 the U.S. Department of Commerce estimated that 94% of the total capital invested in the motion picture industry was in theaters; and in 1974 the Department of Commerce reported that of the entire industry employment, 70% were employed by theaters.

The money a theater grosses, however, can be deceptive today. To show such popular films as *The Exorcist* or *Star Wars,* for example, a theater might have to pay a huge advance and hand over 90% of the box-office take to the distributor. Some theaters even make more money on their concession stands (popcorn, candy, ice cream) than on the ticket price.

Several years ago the Motion Picture Herald Institute of Industry Opinion reported that for every dollar spent on theater expenditures, 24.5 cents went to the House (rent, mortgages, upkeep, etc.); 26.6 cents went to the Staff; 34.4 cents went to the Show (film rentals); 9 cents went to Sales Approach (advertising, publicity); and only 3.5 cents could be counted as operating profit (before state and federal taxes).

Because Hollywood studios are making fewer and fewer pictures these days, the competition among theaters for the best new releases can be quite keen. For a while exhibitors would agree not to bid against one another in order to keep prices down, but the Justice Department has declared "product-splitting" (as this procedure is called) illegal. Because good films are so few in number, a theater will often have to bid for a film without ever having seen it ("blind bidding"), even agreeing to play the film for eight, 10 or 12 weeks regardless of the film's success or failure. "Blind-bidding," however, has been declared illegal in several states in recent years.

The following figures are only *estimates* of the number of movie theaters in America each year. Through 1966 the statistics are taken from *Film Daily Yearbook.* The Motion Picture Association of America is the source of the figures from 1967 on. Each multi-screen installation is counted as one theater in these figures. (About 80% of multiplex units have two screens; 20% range from three to seven screens per theater.) The average number of seats in indoor theaters in this country is now 500; in 1950 the average was 750. The estimated capacity of theaters at the end of 1976 was 7,320,000 seats and 1,935,000 cars.

NUMBER OF MOVIE THEATERS IN THE UNITED STATES

Year	Wired for Sound	Silent	Total
1926	—	19,489	19,489
1927	20	21,644	21,664
1928	100	22,204	22,304
1929	800	22,544	23,344
1930	8,860	14,140	23,000
1931	13,128	8,865	21,993
1932	13,880	4,835	18,715
1933	14,405	4,128	18,553
1934	14,381	2,504	16,885
1935	15,273	—	15,273
1936	15,858	—	15,858
1937	18,192	—	18,192
1938	18,182	—	18,192
1939	17,829	—	17,829
1940	19,032	—	19,042
1941	19,645	95	19,750
1942	20,281	99	20,380
1943	20,196	97	20,293

Year	Wired for Sound	Silent	Total	Year	Four-Wall Theaters	Drive-Ins	Total
1944	20,277	96	20,375	1965	10,150	4,150	14,000
1945	20,355	102	20,457	1966	9,330	4,200	14,350
1946	18,719	300	19,019	1967	9,500	3,670	13,000
1947	18,059	548	18,607	1968	9,650	3,690	13,190
1948	17,575	820	18,395	1969	9,750	3,730	13,480
1949	17,367	1,203	18,570				
1950	16,904	2,202	19,106	1970	10,000	3,750	13,750
1951	16,150	2,830	18,980	1971	10,300	3,770	14,070
1952	15,347	3,276	18,623	1972	10,580	3,790	14,370
1953	14,174	3,791	17,965	1973	10,850	3,800	14,650
1954	15,039	4,062	19,101	1974	9,645	3,519	13,164
1955	14,613	4,587	19,200	1975	9,857	3,535	13,392
1956	14,509	4,494	19,003	1976	10,044	3,536	13,580
1957	14,509	4,494	19,003				
1958	11,300	4,700	16,000				
1959	11,335	4,768	16,103				
1960	12,291	4,700	16,999				
1961	15,000	6,000	21,000				
1962	15,000	6,000	21,000				
1963	9,250	3,550	12,800				
1964	9,850	4,100	13,750				

6/THE NUMBER OF FILMS RELEASED IN AMERICA EACH YEAR

THROUGH 1968 THE following statistics are taken from the *Film Daily Yearbook.* From 1969 on, the statistics were compiled from various annual reports.

One thing quickly becomes clear from this chart: the 1950s and 1960s were not a prolific period in Hollywood. For the first time in history, foreign films outnumbered the domestic product as American studios made fewer and fewer films each year.

There has been, however, a slight surge in the 1970s, but this recent increase in the annual number of American releases is due both to the large market for porno flicks and to the increase in small, independent production. The major studios are still only making little more than a handful of films each year.

In 1978 the ten member companies of the Motion Picture Assn. distributed 111 new films in the U.S. During the 1960s the average number of new movies per year was 163; in the 1950s it was 373; and in the 1940s, 445.

The statistics printed below do not include re-issues.

DOMESTIC VERSUS FOREIGN

Year	U.S. Produced	Imported	Total	Year	U.S. Produced	Imported	Total
1917	687	—	687	1930	509	86	595
1918	841	—	841	1931	501	121	622
1919	646	—	646	1932	489	196	685
1920	796	—	796	1933	507	137	644
1921	854	—	854	1934	480	182	662
1922	748	—	748				
1923	576	—	576	1935	525	241	766
1924	579	—	579	1936	522	213	735
				1937	538	240	778
1925	579	—	579	1938	455	314	769
1926	740	—	740	1939	483	278	761
1927	678	65	743	1940	477	196	673
1928	641	193	884	1941	492	106	598
1929	562	145	707	1942	488	45	533

Year	U.S. Produced	Imported	Total	Year	U.S. Produced	Imported	Total
1943	397	30	427	1961	131	331	462
1944	401	41	442	1962	147	280	427
1945	350	27	377	1963	121	299	420
1946	378	89	467	1964	141	361	502
1947	369	118	486	1965	153	299	452
1948	366	93	459	1966	156	295	451
1949	356	123	470	1967	178	284	462
				1968	180	274	454
1950	383	239	622	1969	232	180	412
1951	391	263	654				
1952	324	139	463	1970	186	181	367
1953	344	190	534	1971	233	199	432
1954	253	174	427	1972	229	147	376
				1973	295	168	463
1955	254	138	392	1974	280	270	550
1956	272	207	479				
1957	300	233	533	1975	362	242	604
1958	241	266	507	1976	353	222	575
1959	187	252	439	1977	311	249	560
1960	154	233	387	1978	217	137	354

7/AVERAGE PRICE OF A MOVIE TICKET IN AMERICA EACH YEAR

THROUGH 1962 THE statistics printed below were compiled by *Film Daily Yearbook.* The Research Department of the Motion Picture Association of America is the source of the figures beginning in 1963.

Between 1942 and 1953, there was an amusement tax on movie tickets. In 1942 the tax was 2.7 cents; in 1953, 10 cents. The figures given below for those years include the tax.

Year	Admission Price	Year	Admission Price
1933	23¢	1957	50.5¢
1934	23¢	1958	50.5¢
1935	24¢	1959	51¢
1936	25¢		
1937	23¢	1960	69¢
1938	23¢	1961	69¢
1939	23¢	1962	70¢
		1963	84.6¢
1940	24.1¢	1964	92.5¢
1941	25.2¢		
1942	27.3¢	1965	$1.010
1943	29.4¢	1966	$1.094
1944	31.7¢	1967	$1.198
		1968	$1.310
1945	35.2¢	1969	$1.419
1946	40.3¢		
1947	40.4¢	1970	$1.552
1948	40.1¢	1971	$1.645
1949	46¢	1972	$1.695
		1973	$1.768
1950	52.8¢	1974	$1.874
1951	52.8¢		
1952	60¢	1975	$2.048
1953	60¢	1976	$2.128
1954	44.7¢	1977	$2.230
1955	49.8¢	1978	$2.340
1956	49.7¢	1979	$2.510

8/AVERAGE WEEKLY MOVIE ATTENDANCE IN AMERICA EACH YEAR

THESE FIGURES ARE only estimates of the average weekly number of American moviegoers. Industry statistics can never be exact here.

Each year the Opinion Research Corporation of Princeton conducts a study for the Motion Picture Association of America to learn more specific information concerning America's moviegoing habits. According to the 1977 survey, a whopping 74% of the moviegoers are under 30 years of age, and only 7% are 50 years or older. Although teenagers between the ages of 12 and 20 comprise only 22% of the population, they're 41% of the film audience. Here is how America's 1976 moviegoers are divided into age groups:

Age	Percent of Total Yearly Admissions	Percent of Resident Civilian Population
12-15	16	10
16-20	25	12
21-24	16	8
25-29	17	10
30-39	13	15
40-49	6	13
50-59	4	13
60 and over	3	19

The study also showed that there is a tendency toward more frequent attendance among males and that moviegoing increases as income rises. For example:

Family Income	Frequent or Occasional Attendees in Total Public
$15,000 or over	63%
$7,000 to $14,999	49
Under $7,000	35

Frequent moviegoers (those who go to films at least once a month) constitute only 27 percent of the public over 12 years of age, but they account for 87 percent of admissions. Within the age group 16-20, the majority are frequent moviegoers. Within all other age groups up to age 39, the majority are either frequent or occasional (those who go to films once in 2 to 6 months) moviegoers. From age 40 on, the majority are infrequent moviegoers.

The Princeton survey suggested that moviegoing increases with increasing education.

	Some College	High School Completed	Less Than Complete High School
Frequent	35%	22%	14%
Occasional	30	27	12
Infrequent	10	22	11
Never	25	29	63

According to industry estimates, Saturday is the best day for theater business, Friday is second, and Sunday third. Mondays through Thursdays are about equal. July is the best month, with August second and January third. May is the worst month of the year. And the worst two weeks of the year are the first two weeks in December after Thanksgiving when business drops 30-50%.

Approximately 60% of American moviegoers attend a neighborhood theater; 65% prefer single to double features; and 39% are influenced to some degree by film reviewers. Some 80% say the subject matter of a film is important in deciding what movie to see; 30% consider a film's stars. A considerable 70% like American films over foreign products, and 83% prefer color to black-and-white films.

Year	Average Weekly Attendance	Year	Average Weekly Attendance
1926	50,000,000	1953	46,000,000
1927	57,000,000		
1928	65,000,000	1954	49,000,000
1929	95,000,000	1955	46,000,000
		1956	47,000,000
1930	90,000,000	1957	45,000,000
1931	75,000,000	1958	40,000,000
1932	60,000,000	1959	42,000,000
1933	60,000,000	1960	40,000,000
1934	70,000,000	1961	42,000,000
1935	75,000,000	1962	43,000,000
1936	88,000,000	1963	44,000,000
1937	85,000,000	1964	(Not reliably reported)
1938	85,000,000		
1939	85,000,000	1965	44,000,000
		1966	38,000,000
1940	80,000,000	1967	17,800,000
1941	85,000,000	1968	18,800,000
1942	85,000,000	1969	17,500,000
1943	85,000,000		
1944	85,000,000	1970	17,700,000
		1971	15,800,000
1945	90,000,000	1972	18,000,000
1946	90,000,000	1973	16,600,000
1947	90,000,000	1974	19,400,000
1948	90,000,000		
1949	87,500,000	1975	19,900,000
		1976	18,400,000
1950	60,000,000	1977	20,400,000
1951	54,000,000	1978	21,800,000
1952	51,000,000	1979	21,6000,000

9/ANNUAL AMERICAN BOX-OFFICE RECEIPTS

THESE FIGURES CHART American box-office receipts in relation to personal consumption expenditures. The source of these statistics is the United States Department of Commerce, Social and Economic Statistics Administration, Bureau of Economic Analysis (Survey of Current Business).

According to these statistics, admissions to American film theaters decreased during the early Depression but began to pick up by 1934. The rise continued throughout the 1940s. During the 1950s and early 1960s, however, admissions dropped considerably. The past 10 years, particularly the past five, have witnessed another rise in box-office receipts.

Although Americans are now spending more money on movies than ever before, they are spending even greater amounts of money on other forms of recreation. Moviegoing no longer holds the same priority in American lives. In 1943, for example, Americans spent more than 25% of their recreation expenditures on the movies. In 1976 that figure had dropped to less than 5%.

1946 remains the industry's record breaking year: that year's $1,692 million in U.S. box office represented something like 4,067 million tickets sold at an average price of 42¢. Today's ticket dollar is not worth even 20¢ in 1946 terms. And 1978's $2,653 million box office shrinks to $562 million in 1946 dollars.

Year	U.S. Box-office Receipts (in millions $)	% of U.S. Personal Spending	% of U.S. Recreational Spending	% of U.S. Spectator Recreational Spending
1929	720	0.93	16.62	78.86
1930	732	1.05	18.35	82.06
1931	719	1.19	21.77	84.19
1932	527	1.08	21.58	83.52
1933	482	1.05	21.89	84.12
1934	518	1.01	21.22	82.88

Year	U.S. Box-office Receipts (in millions $)	% of U.S. Personal Spending	% of U.S. Recreational Spending	% of U.S. Spectator Recreational Spending
1935	566	1.00	21.14	82.74
1936	626	1.01	20.73	82.48
1937	676	1.02	19.99	82.64
1938	663	1.04	20.46	81.25
1939	659	0.99	19.09	80.27
1940	735	1.04	19.54	81.31
1941	809	1.00	19.08	81.31
1942	1,022	1.15	21.85	84.88
1943	1,275	1.28	25.70	87.63
1944	1,341	1.24	24.73	85.80
1945	1,450	1.21	23.62	84.60
1946	1,692	1.18	19.81	81.90
1947	1,594	0.99	17.23	79.58
1948	1,506	0.87	15.54	78.52
1949	1,451	0.82	14.50	77.51
1950	1,376	0.72	12.34	77.26
1951	1,310	0.63	11.33	76.34
1952	1,246	0.57	10.30	75.29
1953	1,187	0.52	9.33	73.44
1954	1,228	0.52	9.39	73.44
1955	1,326	0.52	9.42	73.63
1956	1,394	0.52	9.31	73.41
1957	1,126	0.40	7.34	68.04
1958	992	0.34	6.28	64.50
1959	958	0.31	5.51	60.98
1960	951	0.29	5.20	59.22
1961	921	0.27	4.72	56.68
1962	903	0.25	4.41	54.86
1963	904	0.24	4.07	53.43
1964	913	0.23	3.71	51.81
1965	927	0.21	3.51	51.19
1966	964	0.23	3.34	50.13
1967	989	0.22	3.20	48.79
1968	1,045	0.20	3.11	46.71
1969	1,099	0.19	2.98	48.59
1970	1,162	0.19	2.86	48.00
1971	1,170	0.18	2.74	47.74
1972	1,644	0.22	3.03	47.01

Year	U.S. Box-office Receipts (in millions $)	% of U.S. Personal Spending	% of U.S. Recreational Spending	% of U.S. Spectator Recreational Spending
1973	1,524	0.20	3.50	50.77
1974	1,909	0.28	4.10	53.99
1975	2,115	0.26	3.84	51.81
1976	2,036	0.27	4.12	53.36
1977	2,372	*	*	*
1978	2,653	*	*	*
1979	2,806	*	*	*

* figures not available

10/THE MOST EXPENSIVE MOVIES EVER MADE

ONE REASON WHY Hollywood makes fewer pictures these years is the rising cost of filmmaking. In 1949 the average feature cost $400,000 to make. By 1949 the price had risen to more than one million dollars; by 1961 to 1.5 million dollars; by 1971 to 1.75 million dollars; by 1974 to more than 2.5 million dollars; by 1976 to four million dollars. And in 1978 it jumped to five million dollars.

Of course, these are just "average" prices: many films cost more—much much more, as the following *Variety* chart shows. Remember, these figures do not take infla-tion into account: if inflation were consid-ered, *Cleopatra*'s 1963 $44,000,000 would almost approach the $100 million mark! Also remember that these are Western-financed films: the Soviet's *War and Peace,* which supposedly cost more than $100 mil-lion to make, is not included here.

According to industry estimates, the typical budget is divided as follows: the story costs 5%; production and direction 5%; sets and props 35%; cast 20%; studio overhead 20%; income taxes 5%; net profit after taxes 10%.

Film (Distibutor, Year of Release)	Budget
1. *Cleopatra* (20th Century-Fox,1963)	$44,000,000
2. *Star Trek* (Paramount, 1979)	40,000,000*
Heaven's Gate (United Artists, 1980)	40,000,000*
4. *Flash Gordon* (De Laurentiis, 1980)	35,000,000*
5. *Inchonl* (One Way Prods, 1980)	30-35,000,000*
6. *1941* (Universal/Columbia, 1979)	32,000,000
Moonraker (United Artists, 1979)	32,000,000
8. *Apocalypse Now* (United Artists, 1979)	31,500,000
9. *Waterloo* (De Laurentiis, 1970)	25,000,000+
Omar Mukhtar—Lion of the Desert (Arab Intl. Prod, 1980)	25,000,000+
11. *Toral Toral Toral* (20th Century-Fox, 1970)	25,000,000
Superman (Salkind-Warner Bros., 1978)	25,000,000
Superman II (Salkind-Warner Bros., 1980)	25,000,000
The Empire Strikes Back (20th Century-Fox)	25,000,000

15.	*Hello, Dolly!* (20th Century-Fox, 1969)	24,000,000
	The Wiz (Universal, 1978)	24,000,000
	A Bridge Too Far (Joseph E. Levine, 1977)	24,000,000
18.	*King Kong* (De Laurentiis, 1976)	23,000,000
19.	*Darling Lili* (Paramount, 1970)	22,000,000
	Hurricane (DeLaurentiis, 1979)	22,000,000
21.	*Sorcerer* (Universal/Paramount, 1977)	21,600,000
22.	*The Greatest Story Ever Told* (United Artists, 1965)	20,000,000
	Close Encounters of the Third Kind (Columbia, 1977)	20,000,000
	Jaws 2 (Universal, 1978)	20,000,000

* Approximate cost: film was still in production when *Variety* compiled list (August 29, 1979).

II. THE STARS

1/ANNUAL TOP TEN BOX OFFICE STARS

WHEN MOVIES WERE young, actors and actresses were not known by name. Although, as early as 1910, moviegoers expressed definite preferences for one actor over another and even wrote letters to the studios asking for the real names of "Little Mary" or of "The Biograph girl," producers were reluctant to release a performer's name lest the actor demand a higher salary should he grow famous.

But in 1910 Carl Laemmle (then the head of Independent Motion Pictures, which was later to become Universal) had to promise Florence Lawrence screen credit in order to make her leave Biograph to work for him. Having acquired her contract, Laemmle then performed what many people think was the first publicity stunt; after circulating rumors that Florence Lawrence had died in a streetcar accident, Laemmle took out large ads in newspapers announcing that Lawrence was in fact alive, working for him on some of the "best movies of her career," and that she would soon start to make personal appearances to dispel the rumors of her death. The stunt worked: at Lawrence's first personal appearances, a joyous mob of fans surrounded her.

Thus was the star system launched.

At first the system was employed only by the Independent companies, but stars proved so popular that soon the licensed members of the Patents Company adopted the star policy. By 1911 there was even a dog star, "Jean," and soon postcards of stars were made available in theater lobbies.

The first fan magazine, *Motion Picture Story Magazine*, was published in 1911, and although it was originally intended only for film exhibitors, it proved so popular that it had to be sold on newsstands as well. *Photoplay* followed in 1912, and *Motion Picture Stories* in 1913. Initially these magazines merely summarized movie plots, but they soon expanded to include "behind the scenes" glimpses of the stars' private lives. By 1914 *Motion Picture Story Magazine* had achieved a circulation of 270,000.

Stars, in short, became determining factors in a film's production and publicity, not to mention in its profits. Producers, wishing to safeguard their investments, soon realized that a star was the surest way to guarantee a movie's success. As a result, studios began to organize filmmaking around stars, even tailoring scripts to a particular performer's talents. (Universal even made May McLaren sign a contract with a provision that should she leave the company she was never to use her name with any other studio.)

Studios initially predicted that stars would come from the Broadway stage, but they soon learned that a successful stage actor did not necessarily make an equally successful screen actor. And so the studios started to "create" their own stars, through clever publicity campaigns, type-casting and large salaries.

By the late 1920s and early 1930s, the star system was so closely connected to the studio system that MGM, Hollywood's most successful company, wanted to be known as the studio with "more stars than there are in the heavens." The studios' rigid control of their stars' private lives—their diets, their clothes, their loves—has since become legendary. A few stars like Bette Davis and Olivia de Havilland have become well known for fighting the studios on such issues as contracts and type-casting.

But when the studio system started to collapse in the late 1940s and early 1950s, the star system also suffered. Finding their audiences decimated by television, Hollywood studios could no longer afford to pay their stars thousands of dollars a week regardless of whether they were working or not. As independent production grew more and more prevalent throughout the 1950s, it was no longer feasible or profitable for a studio to create a star. (It is often thought that Harry Cohen's grooming of Kim Novak for Columbia was the last example of a studio-created star.)

Free from the restrictions of studio contracts, stars both prospered and declined. Stars found themselves in the position to bargain for incredible salaries for a single picture: Alan Ladd got a reported $290,000 for *Boy on a Dolphin* (1957); Ava Gardner received $400,000+ for *On the Beach*; Elizabeth Taylor was paid $500,000 and 10% of the gross for *Suddenly, Last Summer*, after which time her fee was one million dollars per picture; and William Holden supposedly received a deferred salary of two million dollars for *The Bridge on the River Kwai*. Despite the advantages of such high prices, stars made fewer and fewer pictures each year, and some simply stopped making films altogether.

In recent years certain stars—Barbra Streisand, Paul Newman, Robert Redford, Steve McQueen, Clint Eastwood—can still ensure a movie's success. But many recent blockbusters, like *Jaws*, *American Graffiti*, *The Exorcist* and *Star Wars*, have been made without benefit of superstars. *Variety*, in fact, reported that 13 of the 25 top grossers between 1968 and 1972 featured performers of little or no evident box office appeal at the time of release. In comparison, only seven of the 25 biggest hits between 1963-67 achieved that success without benefit of stars, while only five of 1958-62's top grossers lacked big names.

But for those moviegoers who believe they don't make stars like they used to, it is tonic to know that as early as 1918, *Motion Picture Magazine* was lamenting: "Where Have All the Stars Gone?" And for those fans who thought a star's death could no longer arouse the mass hysteria caused by Rudoph Valentino's death in 1926, Elvis Presley's death in 1977 reminded us just how potent a star's attraction still could be.

Perhaps, as Andy Warhol once predicted, we will all be famous for 15 minutes. In any case, the very concept of fame has played an undeniably important role in the history of modern consciousness and is one of the defining characteristics of modern popular sensibility.

Each year Quigley Publications asks film exhibitors in the United States to name that year's Top Box Office Stars. Although these polls provide only approximate and not exact indexes of American tastes—a star who has had three movies released that year has an obvious advantage over an actor with only one film—the polls nevertheless afford some fascinating information. It is interesting, for example, to learn how frequently Abbott and Costello were cited during the 1940s, or how infrequently Marlon Brando has been mentioned throughout his career.

These polls suggest that during the second half of the 1930s, America must have been charmed by children: Shirley Temple was the #1 star from 1935 to 1938, followed by Mickey Rooney from 1939 to 1941. And the lists neatly trace the decline of female stars: whereas women make up 50% of the top stars of the 1930s, for example, they comprise little over 10% during the 1970s, and this 10% stems from the indomitable presence of Barbra Streisand.

John Wayne has appeared on these lists more often than any other star: between 1949 and 1974, there was only one year Wayne was not cited: 1956.

1932

Marie Dressler
Janet Gaynor
Joan Crawford
Charles Farrell
Greta Garbo
Norma Shearer
Wallace Beery
Clark Gable
Will Rogers
Joe E. Brown

1935

Shirley Temple
Will Rogers
Clark Gable
Fred Astaire/Ginger Rogers
Joan Crawford
Claudette Colbert
Dick Powell
Wallace Beery
Joe E. Brown
James Cagney

1938

Shirley Temple
Clark Gable
Sonja Henie
Mickey Rooney
Spencer Tracy
Robert Taylor
Myrna Loy
Jane Withers
Alice Faye
Tyrone Power

1933

Marie Dressler
Will Rogers
Janet Gaynor
Eddie Cantor
Wallace Beery
Jean Harlow
Clark Gable
Mae West
Norma Shearer
Joan Crawford

1936

Shirley Temple
Clark Gable
Fred Astaire/Ginger Rogers
Robert Taylor
Joe E. Brown
Dick Powell
Joan Crawford
Claudette Colbert
Jeanette MacDonald
Gary Cooper

1939

Mickey Rooney
Tyrone Power
Spencer Tracy
Clark Gable
Shirley Temple
Bette Davis
Alice Faye
Errol Flynn
James Cagney
Sonja Henie

1934

Will Rogers
Clark Gable
Janet Gaynor
Wallace Beery
Mae West
Joan Crawford
Bing Crosby
Shirley Temple
Marie Dressler
Norma Shearer

1937

Shirley Temple
Clark Gable
Robert Taylor
Bing Crosby
William Powell
Jane Withers
Fred Astaire/Ginger Rogers
Sonja Henie
Gary Cooper
Myrna Loy

1940

Mickey Rooney
Spencer Tracy
Clark Gable
Gene Autry
Tyrone Power
James Gagney
Bing Crosby
Wallace Beery
Bette Davis
Judy Garland

1941

Mickey Rooney
Clark Gable
Abbott & Costello
Bob Hope
Spencer Tracy
Gene Autry
Gary Cooper
Bette Davis
James Cagney
Judy Garland

1942

Abbott & Costello
Clark Gable
Gary Cooper
Mickey Rooney
Bob Hope
James Cagney
Gene Autry
Betty Grable
Greer Garson
Spencer Tracy

1943

Betty Grable
Bob Hope
Abbott & Costello
Bing Crosby
Gary Cooper
Greer Garson
Humphrey Bogart
James Cagney
Mickey Rooney
Clark Gable

1944

Bing Crosby
Gary Cooper
Bob Hope
Betty Grable
Spencer Tracy
Greer Garson
Humphrey Bogart
Abbott & Costello
Cary Grant

Bette Davis

1945

Bing Crosby
Van Johnson
Greer Garson
Betty Grable
Spencer Tracy
Humphrey Bogart/Gary
  Cooper
Bob Hope
Judy Garland
Margaret O'Brien
Roy Rogers

1946

Bing Crosby
Ingrid Bergman
Van Johnson
Gary Cooper
Bob Hope
Humphrey Bogart
Greer Garson
Margaret O'Brien
Betty Grable
Roy Rogers

1947

Bing Crosby
Betty Grable
Ingrid Bergman
Gary Cooper
Humphrey Bogart
Bob Hope
Clark Gable
Gregory Peck
Claudette Colbert
Alan Ladd

1948

Bing Crosby
Betty Grable
Abbott & Costello

Gary Cooper
Bob Hope
Humphrey Bogart
Clark Gable
Cary Grant
Spencer Tracy
Ingrid Bergman

1949

Bob Hope
Bing Crosby
Abbott & Costello
John Wayne
Gary Cooper
Cary Grant
Betty Grable
Esther Williams
Humphrey Bogart
Clark Gable

1950

John Wayne
Bob Hope
Bing Crosby
Betty Grable
James Stewart
Abbott & Costello
Clifton Webb
Esther Williams
Spencer Tracy
Randolph Scott

1951

John Wayne
Martin & Lewis
Betty Grable
Abbott & Costello
Bing Crosby
Bob Hope
Randolph Scott
Gary Cooper
Doris Day
Spencer Tracy

1952

Martin & Lewis
Gary Cooper
John Wayne
Bing Crosby
Bob Hope
James Stewart
Doris Day
Gregory Peck
Susan Hayward
Randolph Scott

1953

Gary Cooper
Martin & Lewis
John Wayne
Alan Ladd
Bing Crosby
Marilyn Monroe
James Stewart
Bob Hope
Susan Hayward
Randolph Scott

1954

John Wayne
Martin & Lewis
Gary Cooper
James Stewart
Marilyn Monroe
Alan Ladd
William Holden
Bing Crosby
Jane Wyman
Marlon Brando

1955

James Stewart
Grace Kelly
John Wayne
William Holden
Gary Cooper
Marlon Brando
Martin & Lewis
Humphrey Bogart

June Allyson
Clark Gable

1956

William Holden
John Wayne
James Stewart
Burt Lancaster
Glenn Ford
Martin & Lewis
Gary Cooper
Marilyn Monroe
Kim Novak
Frank Sinatra

1957

Rock Hudson
John Wayne
Pat Boone
Elvis Presley
Frank Sinatra
Gary Cooper
William Holden
James Stewart
Jerry Lewis
Yul Brynner

1958

Glenn Ford
Elizabeth Taylor
Jerry Lewis
Marlon Brando
Rock Hudson
William Holden
Brigitte Bardot
Yul Brynner
James Stewart
Frank Sinatra

1959

Rock Hudson
Cary Grant
James Stewart
Doris Day
Debbie Reynolds
Glenn Ford

Frank Sinatra
John Wayne
Jerry Lewis
Susan Hayward

1960

Doris Day
Rock Hudson
Cary Grant
Elizabeth Taylor
Debbie Reynolds
Tony Curtis
Sandra Dee
Frank Sinatra
Jack Lemmon
John Wayne

1961

Elizabeth Taylor
Rock Hudson
Doris Day
John Wayne
Cary Grant
Sandra Dee
Jerry Lewis
William Holden
Tony Curtis
Elvis Presley

1962

Doris Day
Rock Hudson
Cary Grant
John Wayne
Elvis Presley
Elizabeth Taylor
Jerry Lewis
Frank Sinatra
Sandra Dee
Burt Lancaster

1963

Doris Day
John Wayne
Rock Hudson
Jack Lemmon

Cary Grant
Elizabeth Taylor
Elvis Presley
Sandra Dee
Paul Newman
Jerry Lewis

1964

Doris Day
Jack Lemmon
Rock Hudson
John Wayne
Cary Grant
Elvis Presley
Shirley MacLaine
Ann-Margret
Paul Newman
Richard Burton

1965

Sean Connery
John Wayne
Doris Day
Julie Andrews
Jack Lemmon
Elvis Presley
Cary Grant
James Stewart
Elizabeth Taylor
Richard Burton

1966

Julie Andrews
Sean Connery
Elizabeth Taylor
Jack Lemmon
Richard Burton
Cary Grant
John Wayne
Doris Day
Paul Newman
Elvis Presley

1967

Julie Andrews

Lee Marvin
Paul Newman
Dean Martin
Sean Connery
Elizabeth Taylor
Sidney Poitier
John Wayne
Richard Burton
Steve McQueen

1968

Sidney Poitier
Paul Newman
Julie Andrews
John Wayne
Clint Eastwood
Dean Martin
Steve McQueen
Jack Lemmon
Lee Marvin
Elizabeth Taylor

1969

Paul Newman
John Wayne
Steve McQueen
Dustin Hoffman
Clint Eastwood
Sidney Poitier
Lee Marvin
Jack Lemmon
Katharine Hepburn
Barbra Streisand

1970

Paul Newman
Clint Eastwood
Steve McQueen
John Wayne
Elliott Gould
Dustin Hoffman
Lee Marvin
Jack Lemmon
Barbra Streisand
Walter Matthau

1971

John Wayne
Clint Eastwood
Paul Newman
Steve McQueen
George C. Scott
Dustin Hoffman
Walter Matthau
Ali MacGraw
Sean Connery
Lee Marvin

1972

Clint Eastwood
George C. Scott
Gene Hackman
John Wayne
Barbra Streisand
Marlon Brando
Paul Newman
Steve McQueen
Dustin Hoffman
Goldie Hawn

1973

Clint Eastwood
Ryan O'Neal
Steve McQueen
Burt Reynolds
Robert Redford
Barbra Streisand
Paul Newman
Charles Bronson
John Wayne
Marlon Brando

1974

Robert Redford
Clint Eastwood
Paul Newman
Barbra Streisand
Steve McQueen
Burt Reynolds
Charles Bronson
Jack Nicholson
Al Pacino
John Wayne

1975

Robert Redford
Barbra Streisand
Al Pacino
Charles Bronson
Paul Newman
Clint Eastwood
Burt Reynolds
Woody Allen
Steve McQueen
Gene Hackman

1977

Sylvester Stallone
Barbra Streisand
Clint Eastwood
Burt Reynolds
Robert Redford
Woody Allen
Mel Brooks
Al Pacino
Diane Keaton
Robert De Niro

1979

Burt Reynolds
Clint Eastwood
Jane Fonda
Woody Allen
Barbra Streisand
Sylvester Stallone
John Travolta
Jill Clayburgh
Roger Moore
Mel Brooks

1976

Robert Redford
Jack Nicholson
Dustin Hoffman
Clint Eastwood
Mel Brooks
Burt Reynolds
Al Pacino
Tatum O'Neal
Woody Allen
Charles Bronson

1978

Burt Reynolds
John Travolta
Richard Dreyfuss
Warren Beatty
Clint Eastwood
Woody Allen
Diane Keaton
Jane Fonda
Peter Sellers
Barbra Streisand

2/STARS OF TOMORROW

EACH YEAR SINCE 1941, Quigley Publications has also asked film exhibitors in the United States to choose from among the newer screen talent of the season the players most likely to achieve major stardom.

1941

Laraine Day
Rita Hayworth
Ruth Hussey
Robert Preston
Ronald Reagan
John Payne
Jeffrey Lynn
Ann Rutherford
Dennis Morgan
Jackie Cooper

1942

Van Heflin
Eddie Bracken
Jane Wyman
John Carroll
Alan Ladd
Lynn Bari
Nancy Kelly
Donna Reed
Betty Hutton
Teresa Wright

1943

William Bendix
Philip Dorn
Susan Peters
Donald O'Connor

Anne Baxter
Van Johnson
Gene Kelly
Diana Barrymore
Gig Young
Alexis Smith

1944

Sonny Tufts
James Craig
Gloria DeHaven
Roddy McDowall
June Allyson
Barry Fitzgerald
Marsha Hunt
Sydney Greenstreet
Turhan Bey
Helmet Dantine

1945

Dane Clark
Jeanne Crain
Keenan Wynn
Peggy Ann Garner
Cornel Wilde
Tom Drake
Lon McCallister
Diana Lynn
Marilyn Maxwell
William Eythe

1946

Joan Leslie
Butch Jenkins
Zachary Scott
Don De Fore
Mark Stevens
Eve Arden
Lizabeth Scott
Dan Duryea
Yvonne De Carlo
Robert Mitchum

1947

Evelyn Keyes
Billy De Wolfe
Peter Lawford
Janis Paige
Elizabeth Taylor
Claude Jarmon, Jr.
Janet Blair
Macdonald Carey
Gail Russell
Richard Conte

1948

Jane Powell
Cyd Charisse
Ann Blyth
Celeste Holm
Robert Ryan
Angela Lansbury
Jean Peters

Mona Freeman
Eleanor Parker
Doris Day

1949

Montgomery Clift
Kirk Douglas
Betty Garrett
Paul Douglas
Howard Duff
Pedro Armendariz
Dean Stockwell
Wanda Hendrix
Wendell Corey
Barbara Bel Geddes

1950

Dean Martin and Jerry Lewis
William Holden
Arlene Dahl
Ruth Roman
Vera-Ellen
John Lund
William Lundigan
Dean Jagger
Joanne Dru
James Whitmore

1951

Howard Keel
Thelma Ritter
Shelley Winters
Frank Lovejoy
Debra Paget
David Brian
Piper Laurie
Gene Nelson
Dale Robertson
Corinne Calvet

1952

Marilyn Monroe
Debbie Reynolds
Marge & Gower Champion
Mitzi Gaynor
Kim Hunter

Rock Hudson
Audie Murphy
David Wayne
Forrest Tucker
Danny Thomas

1953

Janet Leigh
Gloria Grahame
Tony Curtis
Terry Moore
Rosemary Clooney
Julie Adams
Robert Wagner
Scott Brady
Pier Angeli
Jack Palance

1954

Audrey Hepburn
Maggie McNamara
Grace Kelly
Richard Burton
Pat Crowley
Guy Madison
Suzan Ball
Elaine Stewart
Aldo Ray
Cameron Mitchell

1955

Jack Lemmon
Tab Hunter
Dorothy Malone
Kim Novak
Ernest Borgnine
James Dean
Anne Francis
Richard Egan
Eva Marie Saint
Russ Tamblyn

1956

Rod Steiger
Jeffrey Hunter
Natalie Wood

Dana Wynter
Tim Hovey
Yul Brynner
George Nader
Joan Collins
Sheree North
Sal Mineo

1957

Anthony Perkins
Sophia Loren
Jayne Mansfield
Don Murray
Carroll Baker
Martha Hyer
Elvis Presley
Anita Ekberg
Paul Newman
John Kerr

1958

Joanne Woodward
Red Buttons
Diane Varsi
Andy Griffith
Anthony Franciosa
Hope Lange
Brigitte Bardot
Burl Ives
Mickey Shaughnessy
Russ Tamblyn

1959

Sandra Dee
Rickey Nelson
James Garner
Curt Jurgens
Lee Remick
John Saxon
Sidney Poitier
Ernie Kovacs
Kathryn Grant
Carolyn Jones

1960

Jane Fonda

Stephen Boyd
John Gavin
Susan Kohner
Troy Donahue
Angie Dickinson
Tuesday Weld
Fabian
James Darren
George Hamilton

1961

Hayley Mills
Nancy Kwan
Horst Buchholtz
Carol Lynley
Delores Hart
Paula Prentiss
Jim Hutton
Juliet Prowse
Connie Stevens
Warren Beatty

1962

Bobby Darin
Ann-Margret
Richard Beymer
Suzanne Pleshette
Capucine
George Peppard
James MacArthur
Peter Falk
Michael Callan
Yvette Mimieux

1963

George Chakiris
Peter Fonda
Stella Stevens
Diane McBain
Pamela Tiffin
Pat Wayne
Dorothy Provine
Barbara Eden
Ursula Andress
Tony Bill

1964

Elke Sommer
Annette Funicello
Susannah York
Elizabeth Ashley
Stefanie Powers
Harve Presnell
Dean Jones
Keir Dullea
Nancy Sinatra
Joey Heatherton

1965

Rosemary Forsyth
Michael Anderson, Jr.
Michael Parks
Michael Caine
Mary Ann Mobley
Jocelyn Lane
Mia Farrow
Julie Christie
Richard Johnson
Senta Berger

1966

Elizabeth Hartman
George Segal
Alan Arkin
Raquel Welch
Geraldine Chaplin
Guy Stockwell
Robert Redford
Beverly Adams
Sandy Dennis
Chad Everett

1967

Lynn Redgrave
Faye Dunaway
James Caan
John Phillip Law
Michele Lee
Michael Sarrazin
Sharon Tate
Michael York
Hywell Bennett

David Hemmings

1968

Dustin Hoffman
Katharine Ross
Katharine Houghton
Estelle Parsons
Judy Geeson
Robert Drivas
Robert Blake
Jim Brown
Gayle Hunnicut
Carol White

1969

Jon Voight
Kim Darby
Glenn Campbell
Richard Benjamin
Mark Lester
Olivia Hussey
Leonard Whiting
Ali MacGraw
Barbara Hershey
Alan Alda

1970

Donald Sutherland
Liza Minnelli
Goldie Hawn
Jack Nicholson
Genevieve Bujold
Dyan Cannon
Marlo Thomas
Beau Bridges
Sharon Farrell
Peter Boyle

1971

Jennifer O'Neill
Karen Black
Gary Grimes
Sally Kellerman
Arthur Garfunkel
Bruce Davison
Richard Roundtree

Deborah Winters
Jane Alexander
Rosalind Cash

1972

Al Pacino
Edward Albert
Jeff Bridges
Joel Grey
Sandy Duncan
Timothy Bottoms
Madeline Kahn
Cybill Shepherd
Malcolm McDowell
Ron O'Neal

1973

Diana Ross
Michael Moriarty
Marsha Mason
Joe Don Baker
Jeannie Berlin
Candy Clark
Robert De Niro
Jan-Michael Vincent
Roy Scheider
Tatum O'Neal

1974

Valerie Perrine

Richard Dreyfuss
Randy Quaid
Deborah Raffin
Joseph Bottoms
Ron Howard
Sam Waterston
Linda Blair
Keith Carradine
Steven Warner

1975

Stockard Channing
Bo Svenson
Susan Blakely
William Atherton
Brad Dourif
Perry King
Bo Hopkins
Conny Van Dyke
Ronee Blakley
Paul Le Mat

1976

Sylvester Stallone
Talia Shire
Jessica Lange
Sissy Spacek
Robby Benson
Sam Elliott

Margaux Hemingway
Susan Sarandon
Ellen Greene
Lenny Baker

1977

John Travolta
Karen Lynn Gorney
Michael Ontkean
Mark Hamill
Harrison Ford
Carrie Fisher
Kathleen Quinlan
Peter Firth
Richard Gere
Melinda Dillon

1978

Christopher Reeve
John Belushi
Brad Davis
Amy Irving
John Savage
Brooke Adams
Gary Busey
Brooke Shields
Harry Hamlin
Tim Matheson

3/STARS' SALARIES

As MENTIONED, THE first film producers did not want to release the names of screen actors for fear an actor would demand a large salary should he grow famous. Those fears were well founded, of course, because actors did obtain exorbitant fees once their popularity became apparent. What those early producers did not realize, however, was that the very fact of large salaries could work for and not against them: large salaries make good news copy.

It would be impossible to deny that our fascination with screen stars stems both from an actor's very real talents and from the magical properties of movies. But it would be similarly foolish to deny that our star craziness does not owe something to our knowledge of their incomes. In a country charmed by rags-to-riches stories, Hollywood's fast money is bound to be paid attention. Stars give truth to American tales of unlimited social and economic mobility.

During the thirties and forties when the Secretary of the Treasury reported major incomes to the Ways and Means Committee, the reports were given wide press coverage: the film industry topped the country for the number of persons earning $75,000 a year or more. A star's income was public knowledge to be debated and discussed, a practice still evident today.

The salaries listed below are taken from trade publications, biographies and government reports. These should not be considered indisputable "facts"; wages have seldom been something about which studios or stars have been especially honest. As early as 1933 an essay in *Literary Digest* commented that "more fiction has been written about the pay envelopes of Hollywood than about the Wild West."

Two other cautions: when a star's salary is listed by the week, it should not be assumed that the salary was paid 52 weeks a year; and inflation has not been taken into account for any of the figures listed below.

Abbott and Costello:
$588,423 in 1941
$789,628 in 1942 (among the highest salaries that year)
Julie Andrews:
$125,000 for *Mary Poppins* (1964)
$700,000 for *Hawaii* (1966)
Fatty Arbuckle:
$3 a day as a Keystone Cop (1913)
$7,000 a week for Famous Players in late 1910s
Fred Astaire:
$150,000 per film in mid-1930s for RKO
Mary Astor:
$500 per week for Famous Players in early 1920s
$1,100 per week for *Beau Brummel* (1924)
$3,750 per week for 40 weeks for Fox in 1928-29
John Barrymore:
$76,250 per picture plus $7,625 per week over 7 weeks, plus all expenses for Warner Bros. in mid-1920s
$100,000 plus % per film for United Artists in late 1920s
$30,000 per week plus % for Warner Bros. in early 1930s
$150,000 per film at MGM in mid-1930s
Constance Bennett:
$30,000 per week for *Bought* (1931), one of the highest salaries up to that time.
$150,000 for 4½ week's work in *Two Against the World* (1932)
$10,000 for *Law of the Tropics* (1941)
Jack Benny:
$125,000 from 20th and $125,000 from Warner Bros. in 1941

Jacqueline Bisset:
$200,000 for *The Deep* (1977)
$500,000 for *Who's Killing the Great Chefs of Europe?* (1978)
Humphrey Bogart:
$750 per week from Fox in early 1930s
$96,525 from Warner Bros. in 1941
$114,125 from Warner Bros. in 1942
Charles Boyer:
$100,000 from Paramount,
$125,000 from Universal, and $125,000 from Warner Bros. in 1941: $350,000 total
Clara Bow:
$50 per week plus fare to Hollywood in 1923
$5,000 per week in 1929
$125,000 for *Call Her Savage* (1932)
Marlon Brando:
$50,000 for *The Men* (1950)
$75,000 for *Streetcar Named Desire* (1951)
$100,000 for *Viva Zapata!* (1952)
$300,000 plus % *Sayonara* (1957)
$1,250,000 for *Mutiny on the Bounty* (1962), including his %
Brando has said he received $250,000 plus % for *Godfather* (1972). *Variety* reported his fee was based entirely on %. Recent accounts have claimed his intake for the film has now passed $1,600,000.
$1,250,000 plus 11.3% of all gross receipts over $8,850,000 for *Missouri Breaks* (1976)
$2,225,000 for *Superman* (1978)
Charles Bronson:
$20,000 to $30,000 per shooting day plus $2,500 daily expenses in mid-1970s
Richard Burton:
$50,000 for *My Cousin Rachel* (1952)
$100,000 per film for Paramount in 1953
$500,000 for *The V.I.P.s* (1963)
$1,000,000 plus % for *Anne of the Thousand Days* (1970)
James Cagney:
$400 per week for Warner Bros. in 1930
$1,250 per week for Warner Bros. in 1932
$3,000 per week for Warner Bros. in 1933
$368,333 from Warner Bros. in 1939
Charlie Chaplin:
$150 per week for Keystone in 1913
$1,250 per week for Essanay plus bonuses in 1915
$10,000 per week plus $150,000 bonus for Mutual in 1916-17
$150,000 per film for First National in 1918-19
$152,000 from the Charlie Chaplin Film Corporation in 1939
Claudette Colbert:
$150,079 from RKO in 1939
$150,000 from RKO and $240,000 from Paramount in 1941
$360,000 in 1942 (among the highest salaries that year)

Sean Connery:
$1,200,000 for *Diamonds Are Forever* (1971)
Gary Cooper:
$311,000 in 1935
$295,106 from Goldwyn and $187,713 from Paramount in 1939
$299,177 from Goldwyn in 1941
$247,397 from Goldwyn in 1942
Joan Crawford:
$195,673 from MGM in 1941
$194,615 from MGM in 1943
Bing Crosby:
$318,907 in 1935
$336,111 in 1942 (among the highest salaries that year)
Bette Davis:
$300 per week at Universal in early 1930s
$129,750 from Warner Bros. in 1939
$252,333 from Warner Bros. in 1941
Goldwin had to pay $385,000 to Warner Bros. to borrow Davis for *The Little Foxes* (1941)
$365,000 in 1948 (among the highest salaries that year)
$25,000 plus % for *What Ever Happened to Baby Jane?* (1962). Davis is said to have eventually made over $1 million from the film.
Robert De Niro:
$200,000 plus $150,000 when film hits a profit for *The Last Tycoon* (1976)
Marlene Dietrich:
$125,000 per film for Paramount after *Morocco* (1930)
$200,000 for *The Garden of Allah* (1936)
$450,000 for Korda in England for *Knight Without Armour* (1937)
$200,000 from Universal in 1941
Kirk Douglas:
$175,000 for *20,000 Leagues Under the Sea* (1954)
$350,000 for *Paths of Glory* (1957)
$400,000 for *In Harm's Way* (1965)
Marie Dressler:
$1,500 per week for MGM in 1927
$5,000 per week for MGM in 1930
Deanna Durbin:
$3,000 per week plus $10,000 bonus per film for Universal in 1938
$112,125 from Universal in 1941
$282,250 from Universal in 1942-43
Clint Eastwood:
$150,000 for *Fistful of Dollars* (1964)
$50,000 plus % for *For a Few Dollars More* (1965)
$400,000 plus 25% of net for *Hang 'Em High* (1968)
Douglas Fairbanks:
$2,000 per week for Triangle in 1915
$10,000 per week for Triangle in 1916
$300,000 for *Reaching for the Moon* (1931)
Alice Faye:
$140,291 from 20th in 1939

$119,166 from 20th in 1941
W. C. Fields:
$5,000 per week for Mack Sennett in 1932
Errol Flynn:
$150 per week for Warner Bros. for *Murder in Monte Carlo* (1934)
$213,333 from Warner Bros. in 1939
$240,000 from Warner Bros. in 1941
Clark Gable:
$350 per week from MGM in 1931
$2,500 per week from MGM in 1933
$298,544 in 1940
$357,000 in 1941
$100,000 for *Soldier of Fortune* (1955)
$750,000 plus $58,000 for each week over-time for *The Misfits* (1961)
Greta Garbo:
$350 per week for MGM in 1926
$5,000 per week for MGM in 1927
$10,000 per week for MGM in 1933
$250,000 for *Anna Karenina* (1935)
$270,000 from MGM in 1938
Judy Garland:
$89,666 from MGM in 1942-43
Janet Gaynor:
$100 per week for 1926 for Fox
$1,500 per week in 1930
$169,750 in 1935
Cary Grant:
$450 per week for Paramount in 1932
$93,750 from RKO in 1939
$150,000 from Warner Bros., $100,000 from Columbia, and $101,562 from RKO in 1941: total $351,562
$150,000 for *Night and Day* (1946)
$300,000 for *People Will Talk* (1951)
Gene Hackman:
$1,250,000 *Lucky Lady*
$2,000,000 for *Superman* (1978)
Sonja Henie:
$244,166 plus $5,000 bonus from 20th in 1939
Katharine Hepburn:
$221,572 in 1935
$188,916 from MGM in 1941
$110,333 from MGM in 1942-43
$200,000 for *Guess Who's Coming to Dinner* (1967)
Dustin Hoffman:
$17,000 for *The Graduate* (1967)
$250,000 for *Midnight Cowboy* (1969)
$425,000 for *John and Mary* (1969)
William Holden:
10% of gross paid out at $50,000 per year for *The Bridge on the River Kwai* (1957)
$750,000 plus 20% profits for *The Horse Soldiers* (1959)
Bob Hope:
$204,166 from Paramount in 1941
Al Jolson:
$75,000 for *The Jazz Singer* (1927)

Buster Keaton:
$2,000 per week in 1923 plus %
$3,000 per week in 1928
$10,000 bonus from MGM in 1930
$15,000 for *Le Roi des Champs Elysées* in France (1934)
$2,500 per short for Educational (1935-37)
$100 per week as a gag man for MGM in 1940
Ruby Keeler:
$89,583 in 1935
$4,000 per week in 1937
Alan Ladd:
$290,00 for *Boy on a Dolphin* (1957)
Mario Lanza:
$800,000 in 1951
$150,000 for *Serenade* (1956)
Carole Lombard:
$75 per week in *Marriage in Transit* (1925)
$400 per week for *The Swim Princess* (1928)
$156,083 in 1935
$211,111 from RKO in 1939
Sophia Loren:
$25,000 for *Man of La Mancha* (1972)
Jeanette MacDonald:
$300,000 from MGM in 1941
Shirley MacLaine:
$600 per week for Hal Wallis in 1955
$800,000 plus % for *Sweet Charity* (1968)
Steve McQueen:
$19 per day as an extra in *Somebody Up There Likes Me* (1956)
$1,000,000 for *Bullitt* (1968)
Marilyn Monroe:
$125 per week for 20th in 1946
$500 per week for 20th in 1951
$1,200 per week for 20th in 1953
Monroe signed a contract with 20th in 1954 starting with $75,000 per film and going up to $100,000 per film after seven years. Another contract was signed in 1955 for $100,000 per film plus $500 weekly expenses.
Paul Newman:
$1,000 for Warner Bros. in 1954
$17,500 per film for Warner Bros. in late 1950s (at this time, however, Warner Bros. would charge $75,000 per film if another studio wanted him)
$200,000 for *Exodus* (1969)
$350,000 plus % for *Sweet Bird of Youth* (1962)
$750,000 plus 10% of gross and after that profit sharing in mid-1960s
$1,000,000 plus 10% gross (15% after film breaks even) for *The Towering Inferno* (1974)
Olivia Newton-John:
$125,000 for *Grease* (1978)
Jack Nicholson:
$1,250,000 plus 10% of all gross receipts over $12,500,000 for *Missouri Breaks*
Kim Novak:
$75 per week for Columbia in 1955

Preminger had to pay Columbia $100,000 for Novak's services in *The Man With the Golden Arm* (1956), although her salary at that time was only $100 per week
$13,000 for *Jeanne Eagels* (1957)
Ramon Novarro:
$125 per week for Rex Ingram in 1922-23
$10,000 per week for MGM in 1925
Al Pacino:
$500,000 plus 5% gross for *The Godfather Part II* (1974)
Gregory Peck:
$26,000 in 1944 (after taxes)
$48,000 in 1945 (after taxes)
$60,000 for *Only the Valiant* (1951), although Selznick charged $150,000 for Peck's services
$350,000 for two films: *The Million Pound Note* (1954) and *The Purple Plain* (1955), both made in England
Mary Pickford:
$10 per day for Biograph in 1909
$175 per week for Independent in 1910
$275 per week for Majestic in 1911
$500 per week for Famous Players in 1913
$1,000 per week for Famous Players in 1914
$2,000 per week for Famous Players in 1915
$10,000 per week for Famous Players in late 1915
$1,040,000 for two years plus bonuses starting in 1916
$250,000 for each of three pictures, plus $50,000 for her mother, plus a $100,000 bonus for each of the three films for First National: *Daddy Long Legs, The Hoodlum,* and *Heart o' the Hills*
Tyrone Power:
$151,250 in salary and $15,000 in other compensations from 20th in 1939
$203,125 from 20th in 1941
Christopher Reeve:
$250,000 plus $25,000 per/week after 52 weeks of shooting for *Superman* (1978)
Burt Reynolds:
$5,000,000 plus % for his next film, now titled *Cannonball*, the largest salary in film history.
Ginger Rogers:
$219,500 from RKO in 1939

$215,000 from 20th in 1941
$245,000 from Paramount in 1942
Mickey Rooney:
$158,083 from MGM in 1941
$156,166 from MGM in 1942-43
Rosalind Russell:
$100,000 from Columbia in 1941
George C. Scott:
$1,000,000 plus % of net profit for *Hindenburg* (1975)
Barbara Stanwyck:
$92,500 from Paramount in 1939
$90,000 from Columbia and $100,000 from Warner Bros. in 1941
Barbra Streisand:
$200,000 for *Funny Girl* (1968)
$350,000 for *On a Clear Day* (1970)
$750,000 for *Hello, Dolly!* (1969)
Elizabeth Taylor:
$1,500 per week for MGM in 1951
$5,000 per week for MGM in 1952
$500,000 for *Cat on a Hot Tin Roof* (1958)
$125,000 for sixteen weeks plus $50,000 for every week overtime, plus $3,000 a week expenses, plus 10% of the gross for *Cleopatra* (1963)
Spencer Tracy:
$233,461 from MGM in 1941
$219,871 from MGM in 1942-43
$165,000 plus % for *Broken Lance* (1954)
$300,000 for *Guess Who's Coming to Dinner* (1967)
Rudolph Valentino:
$5 per day for *Alimony* (1918)
$100 per week for Universal in 1919
$500 per week for Paramount in 1920
$10,000 per week plus % for United Artists in 1925
Mae West:
$5,000 per week for 10 weeks for Paramount in *Night after Night* (1932)
$480,833 in 1935 (highest paid woman in USA that year)
$350,000 for 10 days' work on *Myra Breckinridge* (1969)
Loretta Young:
$85,000 from Columbia in 1941

III. THE STUDIOS

1/HISTORIES OF STUDIOS

COLUMBIA PICTURES

Columbia Pictures had its beginnings in Harry Cohn, a producer of film shorts who in 1920 formed CBC Sales Corporation with his brother Jack and with Harry Brandt, both of whom left Universal to help start the new company. In 1924 CBC (or "Cornbeef and Cabbage," as it was nicknamed) expanded and was incorporated, changing its name to Columbia.

Cohn had unusual power over the studio, for from 1932 he was both its president and its production head, a rare phenomenon in Hollywood. Known for his autocratic personality, Cohn was reportedly the crassest, most demanding and hardest-to-please of all the studio moguls, not to mention the least popular. His unpleasantness was legendary.

Columbia began as a member of Poverty Row, that group of small B-movie studios on Gower Street always in the shadow of Hollywood's Big Five: MGM, RKO, Fox, Warner, and Paramount. But under Cohn's tough dictatorial rule, Columbia grew successful in the 1930s, when it produced most

of Frank Capra's popular social comedies —*Mr. Deeds Goes to Town, Mr. Smith Goes to Washington, You Can't Take It With You,* and *It Happened One Night,* the first movie to win the five major Academy Awards. (This feat wasn't repeated until *One Flew Over the Cuckoo's Nest* came along.) During the 1930s Columbia also succeeded with films directed by Howard Hawks and with movies starring Cary Grant.

During the 1940s Columbia produced largely unexceptional films—its main asset during this decade was Rita Hayworth. But the 1950s found the studio on the rebound: (1) in 1951 Columbia established a television division, Screen Gems, to produce television series and thus became one of the first studios to enter the TV Industry; and, (2) the studio started to back independent producers and directors like Sam Spiegel, David Lean, Elia Kazan, Otto Preminger and Fred Zinnemann who made such films for Columbia as *All the King's Men, Born Yesterday, From Here to Eternity, On the Waterfront, The Caine Mutiny* and *The Bridge on the River Kwai.* By the time Cohn died in 1958, Columbia had become a major studio.

Abe Schneider and Leo Jaffe were Cohn's successors, and under their leadership Columbia expanded their range of films, making large movies like *Lawrence of Arabia, A Man For All Seasons, Funny Girl* and *Oliver!* as well as smaller British films like *Georgy Girl, The Pumpkin Eater* and *The Go-Between.* In 1969 Columbia released the then controversial *Easy Rider.*

But in the early 1970s the studio declined rapidly, losing $30 million in 1971, $4 million in 1972 and some $50 million in 1973. In 1972 Columbia was forced to leave its studio and move its film and television facilities to the Warner Bros. lot. Columbia land is owned 55% by Warner and 45% by Columbia; and Warner land is owned 65% by Warner and 35% by Columbia. Columbia and Warner have formed a joint venture to continue for a minimum of seven years from April 1972, known as Burbank Studios. Both studios share in net profits of Burbank Studios in direct proportion to studio usage; net losses are shared in inverse proportion to studio usage.

During the past few years Columbia has recovered with such hit films as *Close Encounters, The Deep, The Way We Were,* and *Shampoo.* Profits have climbed steadily: $5,300,000 in 1975; $11,500,000 in 1976; and $29,800,000 in 1977. Columbia's best-known trademark is a woman obviously based on the Statue of Liberty.

METRO-GOLDWYN-MAYER

Metro-Goldwyn-Mayer had its origins in Marcus Loew, a shrewd pioneer during the nickelodeon era. Originally Loew's interest was in the exhibition of motion pictures and not in film production or distribution. Continually expanding his theaters in both their numbers and their locations, Loew organized his enterprises in 1919 as Loew's Inc.

At this time Loew and his associate Nicholas M. Schenck became interested in expanding their interests to include production as well as exhibition. In 1920 they acquired Metro Pictures Corp. and with their new facilities made two highly successful films, *The Four Horsemen of the Apocalypse* and *The Prisoner of Zenda.* Encouraged by success, Loew then purchased the Goldwyn Co. in 1924, but Samuel Goldwyn quickly left to establish his own independent organization. Later that same year Loew acquired the assets of Louis B. Mayer Pictures, and the triple merger took the name of Metro-Goldwyn-Mayer. Loew died in 1927.

Under the conservative economic policies of Nicholas Schenck in New York, the dominant force of Mayer as studio head in Hollywood, and the creative ideas of Irving Thalberg as executive producer, MGM developed through the late 1920s to become the most successful studio of the 1930s. (William Fox's attempt in 1929 to take over the studio had failed.) With "more stars than there are in the heavens," MGM had under contract such illuminaries as Greta Garbo, Joan Crawford, Clark Gable, Jean Harlow, the Barrymores and the Marx Brothers. And the studio's emblematic Leo the Lion could proudly roar with such directors as George Cukor, Mervyn LeRoy, Clarence Brown, Busby Berkeley and Vincente Minnelli. MGM made 40 to 50 films a year, with profits as high as $14 million in 1937, a record no other studio could then equal. MGM's films from the decade included such popular movies as *Grand Hotel, Dinner at Eight, Mutiny on the Bounty, The Wizard of Oz* and *Gone With the Wind.*

The studio continued its success in the early 1940s, when, having lost many of its male stars to the war effort, it turned to child stars and actresses in films like *Lassie*

Come Home and *Meet Me in St. Louis.* Dory Schary, who was the production head of RKO until Howard Hughes took over that studio in 1948, came to MGM in the late 1940s. But antagonism between Schary and Mayer grew so strong that in 1951 Mayer, once one of Hollywood's most powerful moguls, resigned, and Schenck appointed Schary studio head. During Schary's reign MGM, one of the first studios to use survey research techniques to learn what audiences wanted to see, made several fine musical comedies, most notably *Singin' in the Rain* and *The Band Wagon.*

But even such popular films could do little to fight MGM's two major problems in the early 1950s: television and the antitrust actions that forced the studio to divorce its production/distribution interests from its exhibition facilities. Although Schary's style in films was much more economical than the lavish tastes of Mayer, MGM started to decline, and in 1956 both Schary and Schenck lost their positions at the studio.

Under Joseph Vogel, MGM spent $15 million on *Ben-Hur,* which paid back its investment handsomely. But the studio's $27 million remake of *Mutiny on the Bounty* was financially disastrous: in 1963 the studio lost $17 million. In that year Robert O'Brien took over MGM, allowing the studio to invest $12 million in *Doctor Zhivago,* which made more money for the studio than any other film in its history, excepting *Gone With the Wind.* But the studio began to suffer declines again, and in an attempt to offset such losses, MGM changed management three times in 10 months.

In 1969 Kirk Kerkorian took power and within the next few years reduced the studio's film production, auctioned its costumes and properties, and invested the studio's money in a Las Vegas hotel—the MGM Grand, which cost approximately $125 million. In 1973 MGM stopped distributing, and its few current releases are now distributed by United Artists.

PARAMOUNT PICTURES

Paramount Pictures is largely the work of Adolph Zukor, whose interests, like those of so many other famous moguls, were initially confined to film exhibition. In 1912 Zukor expanded into distribution as well, acquiring the distributing rights to *La Reine Elizabeth,* a British/French movie starring Sarah Bernhardt. The success of the film—Zukor made $80,000 from it—encouraged Zukor to form his Famous Players Co., which was to feature famous players in famous plays, a policy that helped create the star system. In order to draw Mary Pickford away from Biograph in 1914, for example, Zukor had to offer Pickford a $2,000-a-week contract, and in order to re-sign that contract in 1916, Zukor had to give Pickford a two-year contract that guaranteed her over a million dollars.

In 1914 Famous Players merged with the Jesse Lasky Feature Play organization, which had been established by Lasky, Samuel Goldwyn and Cecil B. DeMille. The films produced by this merger were distributed through W. W. Hodkinson's Paramount Pictures distribution enterprise. Through a complicated series of mergers that included Paramount, Famous Players-Lasky and Artcraft Pictures, Zukor came out on top. Over the following years Zukor concentrated his energies both on acquiring a large number of theater chains and on expanding his stable of stars, which grew to include such players as William S. Hart, Dorothy Gish, Gloria Swanson, Rudolph Valentino and John Barrymore. The studio's early successes included *The Sheik* (1921), *The Covered Wagon* (1923) and DeMille's *The Ten Commandments* (1923). B. P. Schulberg was Paramount's general manager from 1925 to 1932.

Throughout the late 1920s and early 1930s, Paramount excelled in films made by European directors like Erich von Stroheim, Ernst Lubitsch, Josef von Sternberg and Rouben Mamoulian that featured European stars like Pola Negri, Marlene Dietrich and Maurice Chevalier.

Although the studio met trouble in the mid-1930s—Paramount Publix (as it was then called) went bankrupt in 1932 but was reorganized in 1935 as Paramount Pictures —it managed to survive. Under the new organization, Barney Balaban ran the studio, with Zukor as chairman of the board in an advisory capacity. During the late 1930s and the 1940s, Paramount's players included John Wayne, Bing Crosby, Bob Hope, Dorothy Lamour, Barbara Stanwyck, and Montgomery Clift.

In 1950 the federal government forced Paramount to separate its production/distribution facilities from its extensive exhibition services, resulting in two companies: Paramount Pictures Corp. to make and distribute movies, and United Paramount Theatres to exhibit them.

Although during the early 1950s the studio made such sccessful films as *Sunset Boulevard, A Place in the Sun* and *The Greatest Show on Earth,* it failed to use the wide-screen system developed by Twentieth Century-Fox: CinemaScope. Instead it was determined to develop its own system, called VistaVision, which later proved too expensive to be used. During the late 1950s and early 1960s many of Paramount's most popular films, like *Gunfight at the O.K. Corral* (1957) and *Becket* (1964), were produced by Hal Wallis.

In 1966 Paramount became a subsidiary of Gulf & Western. Like many of the other studios, Paramount encountered troubles in the late sixties, producing expensive but unsuccessful movies like *Paint Your Wagon* and *Darling Lili.* But under the guidance of such producers as Robert Evans and Frank Yablans, Paramount released some of the most successful films of all time: *Love Story* and *The Godfather.* The studio's most recent hits include the two John Travolta blockbusters *Grease* and *Saturday Night Fever.*

Paramount's best-known trademark is a snowcapped mountain peak encircled by stars.

RKO

RKO had its beginnings in the wheeling-dealings of Joseph P. Kennedy, the Irish immigrant who was, of course, to become the famous father of the Kennedy boys— John F., Robert, and Ted.

Before embarking on his career in banking and politics, the elder Kennedy had taken quite an interest in filmmaking, both as a distributor and producer. During the mid-1920s, Kennedy had managed a series of important deals that resulted in the merger of three film-related companies: the Film Booking Office of America, the production firm American Pathé, and the Keith, Albee, and Orpheum theater chain. In 1928 this group was joined by yet another company—the then young electronics conglomerate, Radio Corporation of America (RCA)—and this merger resulted in a film company to be known as Radio-Keith-Orpheum, or RKO.

Once the important merger had been made, Kennedy abandoned the film industry, having made five million dollars on his dealings with RKO. David Sarnoff, the young president of RCA, was named chairman of the board of RKO and one of Sarnoff's first moves was to create a strong production unit to turn out movies for the RKO theater chain.

Under the guidance of production head William LeBaron, RKO turned its attention to the then latest novelty in films— sound. *Rio Rita,* a film adaptation of a Ziegfeld stage musical, was the studio's first hit. And after the studio made the extravagant *Cimarron*—which captured three important Oscars in 1930/31—RKO was considered one of the five major Hollywood studios.

David O. Selznick took charge of production in 1931, trimming the studio's budgets, tightening its organization, and bringing in new talents in the fields of directing (George Cukor), writing (Ben Hecht, Dudley Nichols), and acting (Fred Astaire, Katharine Hepburn). During the early 1930s, RKO turned out what have since become some of Hollywood's most memorable movies, including *King Kong* (1933) and the first Astaire-Rogers musicals.

Selznick left RKO for MGM in 1933. Merian C. Cooper—who had produced and directed *Kong*—followed as head of production, and he in turn was followed by Pandro S. Berman in 1934. Despite the Berman touch, RKO was declared bankrupt in 1934. RCA sold most of its holdings to Floyd Odlum who, with Leo Spitz, re-vitalized the studio during the mid-1930s, with Berman still in charge of production. It was during these years that RKO made its most successful Astaire-Rogers vehicles, Katharine Hepburn's first films (*Christopher Strong, Alice Adams*), and one of John Ford's best-known works, *The Informer.* In addition to its production facilities, the studio had a strong distribution firm: for years RKO released all of the works of Walt Disney, Samuel Goldwyn, and David O. Selznick.

Berman left the studio in 1939 and RKO president George Schaefer began to rent out its production space to independent units, the most famous of which was Orson Welles' Mercury Theater. So it was RKO that in the early 1940s released Welles' first two masterpieces, *Citizen Kane* (1941) and *The Magnificent Ambersons* (1942).

When Charles Koerner took over production in 1942, however, the studio turned from quality productions like those of Welles' to more popular works like those of Val Lewton: *Cat People* (1942), *The Body Snatchers* (1945), and *Bedlam* (1946). Other hits during these years made at RKO included *The Spiral Staircase,* Hitchcock's *Notorious,* and Wyler's *The Best Years of Our Lives.*

After Koerner's early death in 1946, Dory Schary was named the new head of production and began working for RKO on Jan. 1, 1947. When eccentric millionaire Howard Hughes bought control of RKO in 1948, it was said to be the biggest cash deal in Hollywood history: Hughes gave Odlum a check for nearly nine million dollars. Under Hughes' often unpredictable leadership, RKO started to flounder: Schary quit, Hughes forced his own films on the company often with disastrous results, and television started to capture the American public. In 1953 RKO ceased production and two years later the studio was sold to General Teleradio. (Hughes managed to make a profit of 10 million dollars on the deal.) The RKO film library was then sold to the C&C Cola Co. for 15 million dollars; the Cola Co. then allowed television stations to air the old films free of charge . . . as long as the commercial breaks advertised the Cola. RKO made a handful of films in the mid-1950s, including two Fritz Lang works (*While the City Sleeps* and *Beyond a Reasonable Doubt*) and some of the early films by John Frankenheimer and Sidney Lumet. In 1958 the studio was sold to Desilu, and RKO came to its end.

RKO's trademark was a globe topped by a radio tower emitting airwaves.

TWENTIETH CENTURY-FOX

In the first years of this century William Fox, then in the garment trade, expanded his interests into the movie industry, establishing first a film-distribution branch in 1912 (the Greater New York Film Rental Company), and in 1913 a production facility (Box Office Attractions). Wishing to combine his organizations, Fox founded the Fox Film Company in 1915, moving its headquarters in 1917 from New York to Hollywood.

There the studio produced successful vamp pictures with Theda Bara and popular Westerns with Tom Mix and Buck Jones. In the 1920s the studio was among the first to pioneer sound films, using the discoveries of Theodore Case and Earl I. Sponable (whose sound-on-film process the studio renamed Fox Movietone) as well as acquiring the patent rights of the German Tri-Ergon sound process.

In 1929 Fox purchased control of Loew's Inc. (owner of MGM), but the federal government forced him to relinquish the Loew ownership, and in the reorganization Fox himself lost power in 1931. (Spending the rest of his life in retirement, he died in 1952). Sidney R. Kent replaced Fox in 1932, and in 1935 Fox Film merged with Twentieth Century Pictures, then headed by Darryl F. Zanuck and Joseph Schenck, whose brother Nicholas Schenck was one of the powers at Loew's/MGM. With his new merger, Twentieth Century-Fox was born: Darryl Zanuck took charge of production; Schenck became chairman of the board;

and Kent remained president until his death in 1942.

Following Kent's death, Spyros Skouras became president, and it was Skouras, along with Zanuck, who created the Fox image. Under their control the studio—with one of the largest back lots in Hollywood—made such films as *My Darling Clementine, The Song of Bernadette, The Snake Pit, David and Bathsheba* and *Gentleman's Agreement.* The studio's stars included Shirley Temple, Alice Faye, Betty Grable, Marilyn Monroe, Tyrone Power and Gregory Peck; and its roster of directors could boast of John Ford, Elia Kazan and Joseph L. Mankiewicz.

In an attempt to compete with television in the early fifties, the studio pioneered the use of the wide-screen process that had been invented by Henri Chrétien and which the studio called CinemaScope. The studio's first wide-screen film was the highly successful *The Robe* (1953), followed by such films as *There's No Business Like Show Business* (1954) and *The King and I* (1956).

In 1956 Zanuck left Twentieth Century-Fox to enter independent production, and he was succeeded first by Buddy Adler and then by Robert Goldstein and Peter G. Levathes. During the late 1950s and early 1960s the studio returned to spectaculars, disastrously investing some $40 million in the infamous *Cleopatra.* In an attempt to offset such losses (deficiencies of $23 million in 1962 and $40 million in 1963), the studio brought back Darryl Zanuck to take charge of the company. Along with his son, Richard, Zanuck reversed the company's fortunes: In 1965 the studio released *The Sound of Music,* the biggest hit in the studio's history and one of the most successful films of all time.

The studio then invested its gain in such ill-fated movies as *Doctor Dolittle* (1967) and *Star!* (1968) and began to lose overwhelming amounts of money: $37 million in 1969 and $77 million in 1970, although that year the studio did have popular films like *Patton* and *M*A*S*H*. Power changed hands once again in 1971, as the younger Zanuck was forced to go. Dennis C. Stanfill replaced Richard Zanuck as president and was later named chairman of the board. Several changes took place over the next few years.

In recent years the studio has once again turned to making large spectacular films like *The Towering Inferno* (which was made with Warner Bros.), *The Omen,* and *Star Wars*. Although the studio does not directly own any American theaters, it does have theaters in Australia, New Zealand, Egypt, Holland and other countries. Like many other studios, Twentieth Century-Fox is also active in television production.

The company's famous trademark is a large set of futuristic letters spelling the ccmpany's name as searchlights scan the sky.

UNITED ARTISTS

In 1919 Mary Pickford, Charles Chaplin, D. W. Griffith and Douglas Fairbanks organized United Artists, the first studio to be established by artists and not by businessmen. The function of United Artists was to finance and distribute movies independently of the Hollywood studio system in the hope of producing quality films.

United Artists owned no studio of its own, but rather rented facilities only when needed for each of its films, a policy that avoided the expensive overhead of the other major studios. Among United's first films were Fairbanks' *His Majesty The American* (1919), Griffith's *Broken Blossoms* (1919) and *Way Down East* (1920), Pickford's *Pol-*

lyanna (1920), and Chaplin's *A Woman of Paris* (1923) and *The Gold Rush* (1925).

The idea for United Artists came from Oscar Price, who had been assistant to William G. McAdoo when McAdoo was Secretary of the Treasury and Hollywood stars helped sell Liberty Loans. Price was named the first president of United Artists, but was soon succeeded by Hiram Abrahms.

Because Griffith left the company in 1924 and Chaplin made films so slowly, Joseph Schenck was brought in during the mid-twenties to replace Abrahms. Schenck (who later started Twentieth Century Pictures and whose brother, Nicholas, was a major power at Loew's/MGM) expanded the studio's talents to include Valentino, Gloria Swanson, Buster Keaton and Samuel Goldwyn. Howard Hughes contributed *Hell's Angels* in 1930 and *Scarface* in 1932.

During the 1930s United Artists established contracts with foreign filmmakers, adding director Alexander Korda to its roster. Nevertheless, the studio suffered losses into the early 1940s, undergoing continual changes in management: Schenck was replaced by Al Lichtman, who in turn was succeeded by Atillio H. Giannini and George Schaefer, who in turn were followed by Maurice Silverstone.

In 1941 Goldwyn sold his stock to the company, as did Korda in 1944. By 1950 both Pickford and Chaplin, the two remaining founders, had sold many of their shares to a syndicate headed by Paul V. McNutt. The following year another syndicate acquired the company. This syndicate—headed by Arthur B. Krim, Robert Benjamin, Matthew Fox, William J. Heineman, Max E. Youngstein and Arnold Picker—helped United Artists out of its decline. In 1952, the Krim Syndicate held 50% of the company's stock; the remaining 50% was shared by Chaplin and Pickford. Chaplin sold his 25 percent in 1955, and Pickford followed in 1956, giving total ownership to the Krim management. In 1957 United Artists became a public corporation, offering $17 million in stocks and debentures for sale.

The increase in independent production during the late 1950s and early 1960s put United Artists in an advantageous position. Through a contract with the Mirisch Brothers, United acquired directors like Billy Wilder, John Sturges, Robert Wise and Norman Jewison; and later Stanley Kramer, Fred Zinnemann and Richard Lester made films under UA. The company's films during these years included *Marty* (1955), *The Magnificent Seven* (1960), *The Apartment* (1960), *West Side Story* (1961) and the James Bond series starting with *Dr. No* (1962).

In 1967 United Artists became a subsidiary of the Transamerica Corp., a diversified organization known largely as a major insurance company. United Artists bought Warner Bros. pre-1948 films, and currently distributes MGM's films as well as its own.

UNIVERSAL PICTURES

Universal Pictures has its origins in Carl Laemmle, a pioneer in the film industry who, like many other famous producers, started out in the business as a film exhibitor, opening his first theater in Chicago in 1906. Later that year Laemmle expanded into distribution with the Laemmle Film Service, and in 1909 expanded into production with the Independent Motion Pictures Co. (IMP). In 1912 Laemmle merged IMP with several other smaller companies, like Nestor and Powers, to form one large organization: Universal.

Laemmle is often credited with launching the star system by hiring Florence Law-rence for $1,000 a week and identifying her by name—an unknown policy at that time. Because of the success of this practice and because of his own independent policies, Laemmle came into considerable conflict with the Motion Pictures Patents Co., which was basically a monopoly formed by most of the major studios. After years of fighting the Patents Co., Laemmle moved Universal to Hollywood, where he could be closer to the Mexican border to avoid prosecution for infringement of patent rights. In 1915 Universal acquired its present site, Universal City (then a chicken farm which Laemmle purchased for a down payment of $3,500), the first incorporated city to consist solely of a film studio.

Universal's first films included the early works of Erich von Stroheim *(Blind Husband, The Devil's Passage, Foolish Wives)*, the exotic films of Rudolph Valentino, and Westerns featuring popular stars like Ken Maynard and Harry Carey. In 1930 Universal released one of its most highly praised movies, *All Quiet on the Western Front.* In the following years the studio excelled in horror films, producing all the early classics directed by James Whale and starring Lon Chaney, Boris Karloff and Bela Lugosi.

In 1936 Laemmle lost Universal to J. Cheever Cowdin and Nate J. Blumberg. Under their direction the studio produced the low-budget movies of Abbott and Costello, Deanna Durbin and Frances the Talking Mule, but during these years Universal also made such interesting films as Hitchcock's *Shadow of a Doubt* and George Marshall's *Destry Rides Again,* which included Marlene Dietrich's famous rendition of "See What the Boys in the Back Room Will Have."

In 1946 Universal underwent several changes: the company merged with the International Pictures Corp. of Leo Spitz and William Goetz, both of whom became the studio's production heads; the studio acquired the distribution rights of the prestigious British films produced by the J. Arthur Rank Organization, which released films like Olivier's *Hamlet* and the Alec Guinness comedies *The Lavender Hill Mob* and *The Man in the White Suit;* and Universal established United World Pictures to produce and distribute nontheatrical films, acquiring the libraries of Bell & Howell and Castle Films.

In 1950 Cowdin resigned, with Blumberg assuming full command. And in 1952 Decca Records—through an extremely complicated arrangement that involved both the open-market sale of the company's stock and the purchase of J. Arthur Rank's holdings—became the controlling stockholders of Universal. The president of Decca, Milton J. Rackmil, became president of Universal later that year. When Decca was consolidated with Music Corporation of America in 1959, MCA, under the leadership of Jules Stein, became the new owner of Universal.

During the late 1950s and early 1960s the studio's greatest producer was Ross Hunter, who was responsible for the melodramatic films of Douglas Sirk *(Imitation of Life, Written on the Wind, The Tarnished Angels)* and the Rock Hudson/Doris Day comedies. During the mid-1960s Universal, under the guidance of Lew Wasserman, concentrated its energies on television, producing the first movie made for TV in 1966, *Fame is the Name of the Game.* Today Universal is the leading Hollywood studio in the field of television, having made such series as *Kojak, Marcus Welby, M.D., Baretta* and *The Sunday Night Mystery Movie.* Universal is also known for its conducted tours of the studio.

Today the studio is among the most powerful and wealthiest in Hollywood, having released such blockbusters as *Jaws, The Sting, American Graffiti, Airport, Smokey* *and the Bandit,* and *National Lampoon Animal House.* In recent years MCA has also sponsored development of phonograph records which will allow you to play complete movies on your television set.

WARNER BROS.

In 1917 Harry, Jack, Albert and Sam Warner established a film-distribution company in New York. Five years later they expanded into film production as well, forming Warner Bros. Pictures, Inc. Harry (the company's president) and Albert (its treasurer) managed the New York headquarters, while Jack and Sam ran the studio in Hollywood. Jack Warner was the most powerful of the four, running the studio under tight, economical policies.

Although the studio acquired the Vitagraph Co. in 1925, Warner Bros.' first years were nevertheless shaky. Its first great success did not come until the studio's introduction of sound in *The Jazz Singer* (1927). With Western Electric and Bell Laboratories, Sam Warner had invented the sound process, Vitaphone. (Sam died the day before *The Jazz Singer* opened, never knowing what a revolution he had helped to bring about in films.) Almost overnight Warner's rose to pre-eminence in Hollywood because of its early sound films. The company acquired the assets of other film-production firms like First National in 1929, purchased the vast Stanley theater chain in 1932 and established studios in England, acquiring a considerable share of Associated British Pictures Corp. in 1941.

During the 1930s and 1940s Warner's excelled in four types of films: (1) gangster movies (among the best: *Little Caesar, Public Enemy, Scarface*) that featured performers like Humphrey Bogart, James Cagney and Edward G. Robinson; (2) the Busby Berkeley musicals (the *Gold Diggers* series, *42nd Street, Footlight Parade*) that often starred Dick Powell and Ruby Keeler; (3) social-conscience films *(I Am a Fugitive from a Chain Gang, Confessions of a Nazi Spy* and *Mission to Moscow);* and (4) biographies of famous people like Zola, Pasteur and Reuter.

During these decades Warner's contract players included Bette Davis, Errol Flynn, Paul Muni and Olivia de Havilland. Its roster of directors included Michael Curtiz, Mervyn LeRoy, Raoul Walsh and Elia Kazan.

After unsuccessful ventures into the wide-screen process in the early 1950s, Jack Warner lost some control of the studio. During the latter part of the decade the company invested heavily in television series, with some degree of success. Since then the studio has dealt largely with independent producers for its feature films. Hence the studio's releases during the 1960s were more variable than they had previously been, ranging from large productions like *My Fair Lady, Camelot* and *The Great Race* to "risky" films like *Who's Afraid of Virginia Woolf?* and *Bonnie and Clyde.*

In 1967 Warner Bros. merged with the television company Seven Arts, and in 1969 was acquired by the conglomerate Kinney National Service. At that time Jack Warner retired from the board and was replaced by Ted Ashley. The studio changed its name to Warner Communications, sold its pre-1948 library to United Artists, and in 1972 started sharing its lot with Columbia. Ashley later resigned, and John Calley became president and production head.

During recent years Warner Bros. has made many popular films, including *The Exorcist, Towering Inferno* (which was made with Twentieth Century-Fox), *All the President's Men, Blazing Saddles, What's Up, Doc? The Goodbye Girl* and *A Star is Born.*

Warner's famous trademark is a badge bearing the initials WB.

2/THE NUMBER OF FEATURES RELEASED BY MAJOR STUDIOS EACH YEAR

Year	Columbia	MGM	Para-mount	RKO–Radio	20th Century–Fox	United Artists	Uni-versal	Warner
1927	25	51	78	—	50	11	66	43
1928	32	52	64	—	49	15	56	26
1929	22	52	68	35	53	17	41	36
1930	29	47	64	32	48	16	36	39
1931	31	46	62	33	48	13	23	24
1932	29	39	65	46	40	14	30	55
1933	32	42	58	48	50	16	37	55
1934	43	43	55	46	52	20	44	58
1935	49	47	63	40	52	19	37	49
1936	52	45	68	39	57	17	28	56
1937	52	51	61	53	61	25	37	68
1938	53	46	50	43	56	16	46	52
1939	55	50	58	49	59	18	46	53
1940	51	48	48	53	49	20	49	45
1941	61	47	45	44	50	26	58	48
1942	59	49	44	39	51	26	56	34
1943	47	33	30	44	33	28	53	21
1944	56	30	32	31	26	20	53	19
1945	38	33	23	33	27	17	46	19
1946	51	25	22	40	32	20	42	20
1947	49	29	29	36	27	26	33	20
1948	39	24	25	31	45	26	35	23

Year	Columbia	MGM	Para-mount	RKO–Radio	20th Century–Fox	United Artists	Uni-versal	Warner
1949	52	30	21	25	31	21	29	25
1950	59	38	23	32	32	18	33	28
1951	63	41	29	36	39	46	39	27
1952	48	38	24	32	37	34	39	26
1953	47	44	26	25	39	49	43	28
1954	35	24	17	16	29	52	32	20
1955	38	23	20	13	29	35	34	23
1956	40	24	17	20	32	48	33	23
1957	46	29	20	21	50	54	39	29
1958	38	29	25	—	42	44	35	24
1959	36	25	18	—	34	40	18	18
1960	35	18	22	—	49	23	20	17
1961	28	21	15	—	35	33	19	16
1962	30	21	17	—	25	36	18	15
1963	19	35	17	—	18	23	17	13
1964	19	30	16	—	18	18	25	18
1965	29	28	24	—	26	19	26	15
1966	29	24	22	—	21	18	23	12
1967	22	21	30	—	19	19	25	21
1968	20	27	33	—	21	23	30	23
1969	21	16	21	—	18	31	26	21
1970	29	23	15	—	15	39	16	16
1971	32	18	21	—	13	25	17	17
1972	26	24	14	—	25	22	16	18
1973	19	15	27	—	15	19	16	21
1974	19	•	25	—	20	26	12	22
1975	17	•	12	—	17	23	9	15
1976	15	•	19	—	20	23	12	15
1977	10	•	18	—	13	15	14	12
1978	14	•	15	—	7	19	23	19

• MGM's movies are now distributed through United Artists. Figures for United Artists Include MGM's releases.
Source: Through 1968, *Film Daily Yearbook.* From 1969 on, various annual industry reports.

3/ANNUAL PROFITS OF MAJOR STUDIOS

THE JULY 7, 1977, Issue of *The Economist* —the respected British Magazine—noted that many of America's film studios were about to celebrate 50th anniversaries. In honor of the occasion, *The Economist* compiled the annual profits and losses of the major Hollywood studios since 1932. The statistics were based on Moody's Industrial Manual and annual reports.

As the editors of *The Economist* commented, the only constant in this chart is change: boom and slump is the Hollywood way of life. The most recent slump came between 1969 and 1971, when most of the studios did the one thing that according to *The Economist* has made more businesses bankrupt than any other form of mismanagement: they overstocked. (As too many too-expensive films were being made in the hope of imitating the success of *The Sound of Music,* Hollywood inventory climbed to an astronomical $1.2 billion, although the world market for films was only $750 million.) The real miracle suggested by this chart is that so many of the original companies in this crazy extravagant industry have survived. This chart supplies some fascinating insights into the ups and downs of filmmaking: In 1969, for example, Warner lost $52 million. Yet its profits just the following year exceeded $33 million.

Although the industry throughout its history has attempted to find ways to reduce the horrible risks of spending millions of dollars up front without knowing whether a film will succeed or not, none of those ways have been foolproof. The star system has worked often, but not in a consistent or predictable fashion. Studio ownership of theaters was another way to reduce risk, but that policy was declared illegal almost 30 years ago. Stepping up investment to make films noticeably better than television fare has also failed to work regularly. Movie making remains a risky enterprise.

The Economist in 1973 claimed that diversification was the answer to filmmaking: the studios in the best shape were those that had been taken over by conglomerates during and after the 1969-71 slump. Many film buffs regret these takeovers: the conglomerates, they say, seem more interested in life insurance than in movies, and much of the unique flavor of the various studios has been lost. Nevertheless, many of the major studios have recovered under conglomerate management and the majors remain a powerful force: in 1972, for example, all but 6% of distributors' income was collected by the majors.

In *Gold Diggers of 1933,* Ginger Rogers —along with dozens of women holding giant silver coins—sings: "We're in the money, We're in the money. We've got a lot of what it takes to get along." It could serve as the theme song for any of the studios listed here.

The figures are in millions of dollars. Paramount's profits are not listed until 1936 because for the few years preceding that, the company was in reorganization. United Artists was not a listed corporation until 1950.

Year	Columbia	Loew's/ MGM	Para- mount	20th C–Fox	United Artists	Uni- versal	Warner	Disney
1932	0.6	8.0					(14.1)	
1933	0.7	4.3		1.7		(1.0)	(6.3)	
1934	1.0	8.6		1.3		(0.2)	(2.5)	
1935	1.8	7.5		3.1		(0.7)	0.7	
1936	1.6	10.6	4.0	7.7		(1.8)	3.2	
1937	1.3	14.3	6.0	8.6		(1.1)	5.9	
1938	0.2	9.9	2.8	7.2		(0.5)	1.9	
1939	0	9.5	2.8	4.2		1.2	1.7	
1940	0.5	8.7	6.4	(0.5)		2.4	2.7	
1941	0.6	11.0	9.2	4.9		2.7	5.5	(0.8)
1942	1.6	11.8	13.1	10.6		3.0	8.6	(0.2)
1943	1.8	13.4	14.6	10.9		3.8	8.3	0.4
1944	2.0	14.5	14.7	12.5		3.4	6.9	0.5
1945	1.9	12.9	15.4	12.7		4.0	9.9	0.4
1946	3.5	17.9	39.2	22.6		4.6	19.4	0.2
1947	3.7	10.5	28.2	14.0		3.2	22.0	0.3
1948	0.5	4.2	22.6	12.5		(3.2)	11.8	(0.1)
1949	1.0	6.0	20.8	12.4		(1.1)	10.5	(0.1)
1950	1.9	7.6	6.6	9.5		1.4	10.3	0.7
1951	1.5	7.8	5.5	4.3	0.3	2.3	9.4	0.4
1952	0.8	4.6	5.9	4.7	0.4	2.3	7.2	0.5
1953	0.9	4.5	6.7	4.8	0.6	2.6	2.9	0.5
1954	3.6	6.3	8.1	8.0	0.9	3.8	3.9	0.7
1955	4.9	5.0	9.4	6.0	2.7	4.0	4.0	1.4
1956	2.6	4.6	4.3	6.2	3.1	4.0	2.1	2.6
1957	2.3	(0.5)	5.4	6.5	3.3	2.8	3.4	3.6
1958	(5.0)	0.8	4.6	7.6	3.7	(2.0)	(1.0)	3.9
1959	(2.4)	7.7	4.4	2.3	4.1	4.7	9.4	3.4
1960	1.9	9.6	7.0	(2.9)	4.3	6.3	7.1	(1.3)
1961	(1.4)	12.7	5.9	(22.5)	4.0	7.5	7.2	4.5
1962	2.3	2.6	3.4	(39.8)	3.8	12.7	7.6	6.6
1963	2.6	(17.5)	5.9	9.1	(0.8)	13.6	5.7	7.0
1964	3.2	7.4	6.6	10.6	9.3	14.8	(3.9)	7.0
1965	2.0	7.8	6.3	11.7	12.8	16.2	4.7	11.0
1966	2.0	10.2	n.a.	12.5	13.6	13.6	6.5	12.4
1967	6.0	14.0	n.a.	15.4	15.5	16.5	3.0	11.3
1968	10.0	8.5	n.a.	13.7	19.5	13.5	10.0	13.1
1969	6.0	(35.0)	n.a.	(36.8)	16.2	2.5	(52.0)	15.8

Year	Columbia	Loew's/ MGM	Para- mount	20th C–Fox	United Artists	Uni- versal	Warner	Disney
1970	6.0	(8.2)	(2.0)	(77.4)	(45.0)	13.3	33.5	22.0
1971	(29.0)	7.8	(22.0)	6.5	1.0	16.7	41.6	26.7
1972	(4.0)	9.2	31.2	6.7	10.8	20.8	50.1	40.3
1973	(50.0)	2.1	38.7	7.7	14.0	25.6	51.2	47.8
1974	(2.3)	26.9	18.7	10.6	9.9	59.2	48.4	48.5
1975	5.3	31.9	29.9	17.4	11.5	95.5	9.1	61.4
1976	11.5	31.9	49.6	10.7	16.0	90.2	61.2	74.6
1977	29.8	33.2	n.a.	50.8	26.6	95.1	70.8	82.0

Note: Losses in parentheses. Figures after taxes and write-offs, before special credits.

a. Divorcement: United Paramount Theaters hived off, with profits of $16.7 million in 1948 and $17.6 million in 1949.
b. Divorcement: National Theaters hived off.
c. Divorcement: Loew's Theaters hived off.
d. Warner Bros. bought by Kinney Services, which changed its name to Warner Communications in 1971.

e. Bought by Gulf & Western: figures burned.
f. Bought by Transamerica Corporation.
g. Records & Music $23.8 million. Films $15.8 million.
Cable television $1.8 million. Total: $50.1 million.
h. Divorcement: Stanley Warner hived off.
i. $41 million reduction in carrying value of investment in National Kinney Corporation. Operating loss of profits.

4/Top Moneymaking Films of Each Major Studio

BUENA VISTA/DISNEY	Rank*
1. *Mary Poppins* (1964)	26
2. *Snow White* (1937) (released by RKO)	48
3. *The Jungle Book* (1967)	56
4. *The Love Bug* (1969)	76
5. *Swiss Family Robinson* (1960)	98
6. *Bambi* (1942) (released by RKO)	101
7. *Herbie Rides Again* (1974)	106
8. *Peter Pan* (1953) (released by RKO)	116
9. *The Apple Dumpling Gang* (1975)	122
10. *Pete's Dragon* (1977)	123

COLUMBIA	
1. *Close Encounters of the Third Kind* (1977)	8
2. *The Deep* (1977)	38
3. *Funny Girl* (1968)	50
4. *Guess Who's Coming To Dinner?* (1968)	54
5. *The Way We Were* (1973)	56
6. *Shampoo* (1975)	71
7. *Murder By Death* (1976)	71
8. *Cheap Detective* (1978)	91
9. *To Sir With Love* (1967)	96
10. *Easy Rider* (1969)	96

MGM	
1. *Gone With the Wind* (1939)	9
2. *Doctor Zhivago* (1965)	20
3. *Ben-Hur* (1959)	32
4. *2001: A Space Odyssey* (1968)	60
5. *The Dirty Dozen* (1967)	82
6. *Ryan's Daughter* (1970)	148
7. *Network* (1976)	153
8. *Coma* (1978)	157
9. *Quo Vadis* (1951)	185
10. *How The West Was Won* (1962) (made with Cinerama)	196

PARAMOUNT	Rank*
1. *The Godfather* (1972)	3
2. *Grease* (1978)	4
3. *Saturday Night Fever* (1977)	10
4. *Love Story* (1970)	16
5. *The Ten Commandments* (1956)	23
6. *Heaven Can Wait* (1978)	24
7. *King Kong* (1976)	30
8. *The Godfather, Part II* (1974)	40
9. *Foul Play* (1978)	55
10. *The Bad News Bears* (1976)	59

20TH CENTURY-FOX	
1. *Star Wars* (1977)	1
2. *The Sound of Music* (1965)	6
3. *The Towering Inferno* (1973) (made with Warner Bros.)	16
4. *Butch Cassidy and the Sundance Kid* (1969)	21
5. *The Poseidon Adventure* (1972)	25
6. *M*A*S*H* (1970)	31
7. *Young Frankenstein* (1975)	34
8. *Silver Streak* (1976)	42
9. *Patton* (1970)	45
10. *The Omen* (1976)	47

UNITED ARTISTS	
1. *One Flew Over the Cuckoo's Nest* (1975)	11
2. *Rocky* (1976)	14
3. *Fiddler on the Roof* (1971)	35
4. *Thunderball* (1965)	43
5. *Revenge of the Pink Panther* (1978)	56
6. *Around the World in 80 Days* (1956)	62
7. *Goldfinger* (1964)	65
8. *The Spy Who Loved Me* (1977)	71
9. *A Bridge Too Far* (1977)	76

* All-time moneymaking films regardless of studio, as of January 1979

UNITED ARTISTS	Rank*
10. *It's A Mad, Mad, Mad, Mad World* (1963)	79

UNIVERSAL

		Rank*
1.	*Jaws* (1975)	2
2.	*The Sting* (1973)	7
3.	*Smokey and the Bandit* (1977)	12
4.	*American Graffiti* (1973)	13
5.	*National Lampoon Animal House* (1978)	15
6.	*Jaws II* (1978)	18
7.	*Airport* (1970)	22
8.	*Earthquake* (1974)	33
9.	*Airport 1975* (1974)	53
10.	*Midway* (1976)	70

WARNER BROTHERS		Rank*
1.	*The Exorcist* (1973)	5
2.	*The Towering Inferno* (1975) (made with 20th C-F)	16
3.	*The Goodbye Girl* (1977)	26
4.	*Blazing Saddles* (1974)	28
5.	*A Star Is Born* (1976)	29
6.	*Billy Jack* (1971)	36
7.	*Hooper* (1978)	37
8.	*Oh, God!* (1977)	39
9.	*All the President's Men* (1976)	41
10.	*Trial of Billy Jack* (1974)	44

* All-time moneymaking films regardless of studio, as of January 1979

IV. THE FESTIVALS

1/VENICE FILM FESTIVAL PRIZES

THE VENICE FILM Festival is the oldest of all international cinema festivals. First held in 1932 under the auspices of the Venice Biennial, the first exhibition proved so popular that a second festival was held in 1934. After that time the festival became an annual event in its own right, independent of the Biennial. The goal of those early exhibitions was "to raise the new art of the film to the same level of the other arts," a relatively novel sentiment in those years when film was considered entertainment, not art.

Because of the continued success of the festival, a specially designed building—the Palace of Cinema—was constructed for the 1937 exhibition. At about that time, however, political controversy divided the festival. Many critics, disturbed by the preponderance of German and Italian films that were awarded prizes, claimed that the festival was run by Mussolini and his German allies. (Goebbels had visited the festival in 1936.) In order to counter such criticism, the festival announced that "the object of this Exhibition is to acknowledge and reward with public mention such films as aim at being genuine expressions of art, without any bias regarding nationalities or trends. The hospitality extended by the Exhibition to cinematographic art is such as to exclude political interference in the shows it organizes."

Despite the announcement, controversy continued. In 1937 Jean Renoir's pacifist film, *La Grande Illusion* (which the Italians had ironically translated as *The Impossible Illusion*) aroused considerable friction. And in 1938, when Leni Riefenstahl's *Olympia* won its award, British and American representatives argued that the film was a full-length political propaganda movie that glorified not sports but the Nazi Regime.

From 1940 to 1942 the festival continued, although the number of participating countries was of course drastically reduced because of the war. Finally, in 1943, the festival closed and remained closed for the remainder of the war. Under new regulations, the festival reopened in 1946. Under these new policies, retrospectives were added, short films and documentaries were included, and the artistic merits of movies (as opposed to the commercial standards of Cannes) were again emphasized.

In the 1960s the Venice Film Festival once again encountered trouble. Ernesto G. Laura replaced Dr. Luigi Chiarini, and under his direction, the jury and prize systems were abolished in 1969. In 1973 the festival was canceled altogether and was replaced by seven days of an Italian Film Review that did not take place in the Palace of Cinema. In 1975 the exhibition was called the Venice Biennial Cinema and returned to the Palace. The festival's existence has remained complicated ever since. Although the Biennial's budget was tripled in 1977 by an act of parliament, three of its chiefs resigned suddenly, including Giacomo Gambetti, head of the Biennial's cinema-TV section. With such constant changes and organization uncertainty, Venice had indeed lost its former prestige.

In recent years, however, attempts have been made to re-vitalize the Venice event. Carlo Lizzani, who succeeded Gambetti as director of the Venice Biennial's film section, has contacted filmmakers in 27 nations about returning to Venice. And Italian participation in the event—which in recent years had been haphazard and unenthusiastic at best—has greatly improved, now that political disagreements have been largely settled.

Although no official prizes were conferred at the 1979 festival, a number of awards—including an international film critics' prize and the Italian Film Journalists awards—were presented. Competitive prizes will be revived for the 1980 festival in three areas: best first film, best experimental film, and best film of international stature. And with those awards, Venice should once again be an international event.

The Venice Film Festival is held in late August-early September. Its chief prize is the famed Golden Lion of St. Mark. At one time the festival awarded more prizes than any other festival, including awards for scientific, experimental, children's educational and cultural films. Only the principal awards are listed below.

1932

NO OFFICIAL AWARDS: PUBLIC REFERENDUM

Favorite Actress:
Helen Hayes
Favorite Actor:
Fredric March
Best Director:
Nikolai Ekk, *The Road to Life*
Most Amusing Film:
A Nous la Liberté
Most Touching Film:
The Sin of Madelon Claudet
Most Original Film:
Dr. Jekyll and Mr. Hyde

1934

Best Foreign Film:
Man of Aran, Robert Flaherty
Best Italian Film:
Teresa Confalonieri, Guido Brignone
Best Direction:
Gustav Machaty, *Extase*; J. Rovensky, *Young Love*; Tomas Tinka, *Hurricane in the Tatras*; Karel Plicka, *Zem spieva*

Best State Entry:
USSR
Largest Industrial Entry:
Motion Picture Producers and Distributors of America
Best Photography:
Gerard Rutten, *Dood Water*
Best Actor:
Wallace Beery, *Viva Villa*
Best Actress:
Katharine Hepburn, *Little Women*
Best Animated Cartoon:
Three Little Pigs, Walt Disney
Best Documentary:
Manovre Navali
Best Story:
Maskarade, Willy Forst
Best First Screening:
Alexander Korda, *The Private Life of Don Juan*

1935

Best Foreign Film:
Anna Karenina, Clarence Brown
Best Italian Film:
Casta Diva, Carmine Gallone
Best Direction:
King Vidor, *Wedding Night*
Best Actor:
Pierre Blanchar, *Crime and Punishment*

Best Actress:
Paula Wessely, *Episode*
Best Screenplay:
The Informer, Dudley Nichols
Best Music:
Bozambo
Best Photography:
The Devil Is a Woman
Best Color Film:
Becky Sharp
Best Animated Cartoon:
Band Concert, Walt Disney

1936

Best Foreign Film:
Der Kaiser von Kalifornien, Luis Trenker
Best Italian Film:
Squadrone bianco, Augusto Genina
Best Direction:
Jacques Feyder, *La Kermesse Héroique* (Carnival in Flanders)
Best Actor:
Paul Muni, *The Story of Louis Pasteur*
Best Actress:
Anabella, *Veille d'Armes*

Best Cameraman:
M. Greenbaum, *Tudor Rose*
Best Musical:
Schussakkord, Detlef Slierck
Best Political/Social Film:
Il cammino degli eroi
Best Documentary:
Jugend der Welt, Hans
  Weidemann
Best Scientific Film:
Uno sguardo in fondo al mare

1937

Best Foreign Film:
Un Carnet de Bal, Julien
  Duvivier
Best Italian Film:
Scipione l'Africano, Carmine
  Gallone
Best Direction:
Robert Flaherty, Zoltan Korda,
  Elephant Boy
Best Italian Director:
Mario Camerini, *Il Signor Max*
Best Actor:
Emil Jannings, *Der Herrscher*
Best Actress:
Bette Davis, *Marked Woman*
  and *Kid Galahad*
Best Artistic Ensemble:
La Grande Illusion
**Best Film With Colonial
Subject:**
Sentinelle di Bronzo, Romolo
  Marcellini
Best Screenplay:
Sacha Guitry, *Les Perles de la
  Couronne*
Best Photography:
Peverell Marley, *Winterset*
Best Scientific Film:
Martin Rikli, *Röntgenstrahlen*
Best Animated Cartoon:
Walt Disney, *Hawaiian
  Holiday; Music Land; Old
  Mill; Alpine Climbers;
  Country Cousin; Mickey's
  Polo Team*
Best Documentary:
Walter Ruttman, *Mannesmann*
**Best Film Interpreting
Natural and Artistic
Beauties:**
Luis Trenker, *Condottieri*
Best First Screening:
Victoria the Great, Herbert
  Wilcox

1938

Best Foreign Film:
(ex-aequo)
Olympia, Leni Riefenstahl
Best Italian Film:
Lucianno Serra Pilota,
  Goffredo Alessandrini
Great Art Trophy:
Walt Disney, *Snow White and
  the Seven Dwarfs*
Best Actor:
Leslie Howard, *Pygmalion*
Best Actress:
Norma Shearer, *Marie
  Antoinette*
**Special Mention Medals
Artistic Ensemble:**
En kvinnas ansikte
Vivacious Lady
Alla en el Rancho Grande
Fahrendes Volk
Jezebel
Acting:
The Rage of Paris
Hanno Rapito Un Uomo
Der Mustergatte
Technique:
Goldwyn Follies
Sotto la Croce del Sud
Story:
Break the News
Geniusz Sceny
Direction:
Karl Ritter, *Urlaub auf
  Ehreuwort*
Marcel Carné, *Le Quai des
  Brumes*

1939

Best Foreign Film:
(Not awarded this year)
Best Italian Film:
Abuna Messias, Goffredo
  Alessandrini
Best Cameraman:
Ubaldo Arata, *Dernière
  Jeunesse*
Cups of the Biennial:
La Fin du Jour
*Robert Koch, der Bekämpfer
  des Todes*
The Four Feathers
Gläd dig i din ungdom and *En
  handfull Ris*

Selection of Swedish films as a
  whole
Special Mention Awards:
*Margarita, Armando y su
  Padre*
Tulak Macoun
Jeunes Filles en Détresse
Veertig Jaaren
Bors Istvan
*The Golden Harvest of the
  Wilwatersrand*
The Mikado

1940

Best Italian Film:
L'Asseido dell'Alcazar,
  Auguste Genina
Best Foreign Film:
Der Postmeister, Gustav
  Ucicky
(Only two prizes awarded this
year)

1941

Best Italian Film:
La Corona di Ferro,
  Alessandro Biasseti
Best Foreign Film:
Ohm Kruger, Hans Steinhoff
Best Actor:
Ermete Zacconi, *Don
  Buonaparte*
Best Actress:
Luise Ullrich, *Annelie*
Best Direction:
G. W. Pabst, *Komödianten*
Cups of the Biennial:
Lettre d'Amore Smarrite
Alter ego
Marianela
Ich klage an
I Mariti

1942

Best Italian Film:
Bengasi, Augusto Genina
Best Foreign Film:
Der grosse König, Veit Farlan

Best Actor:
Fosco Glachetti, *Un colpo di postola; Bengasi; Noi vivi*
Best Actress:
Kristina Soderbaum, *Der grosse König; Die goldene Stadt*
International Film Chamber Color Prize:
Die goldene Stadt
International Film Chamber Technique Prize:
Alfa Tan
Best Documentaries:
Comacchio (Italy)
Musica nel Tempo (Germany)
Der Seeadler (Germany)
Bunter Reigen (Germany)
La Drapeau de l'Humanité (Switzerland)
Soil of Rome (Rumania)
A Kis Katu (Hungary)
Rocciatori ed Aquile (Italy)
Erde auf Gewaltmärschen (Germany)
Mounting Guard on the Drina (Croatia)
Life and Death of Istvan Horthy (Hungary)
Best Animated Cartoons:
Anacleto e la Faina
Nel Paese dei Ranocchi

1943

(Festival not held)

1944

(Festival not held)

1945

(Festival not held)

1946

Best Film:
The Southerner (Jean Renoir, USA)
Special Mention:
Children of Paradise (Marcel Carné, France)
The Oath (Mikail Ciaureli, USSR)
Hangmen Also Die (Fritz Lang, USA)
Henry V (Laurence Olivier, England)
The Undaunted (Mark Donskoi, USSR)
Paisan (Roberto Rossellini, Italy)
Panique (Julien Duvivier, France)
Il Sole Sorge Ancora (Aldo Vergano, Italy)
Best Documentary:
In the Sands of Central Asia (Alexandr Zguridi, USSR)
Best Animated Cartoon:
Le Voleur de Paratonnères (Paul Grimault, France)

1947

Best Film, International Grand Prize:
Sirena (Karel Stekly, Czechoslovakia)
Best Original Contribution to Film Progress:
La Perla (Emilio Fernandez, Mexico)
Dreams That Money Can Buy (Hans Richter, USA)
Best Direction:
Henri-Georges Clouzot, *Quai des Orfèvres*
Most Original Story:
Vesna (Gregorij Alexandrov, USSR)
Best Actress:
Anna Magnani, *Honorable Angelina*
Best Actor:
Pierre Fresnay, *Monsieur Vincent*
Best Photography:
Gabriel Figuerosa, *La Perla* (Mexico)

Best Music:
E. F. Burian, *Sirena*
Best Feature Documentary:
On the Trail of the Animals (Boris Dolin, USSR)
Best Short Documentary:
Piazza San Marco, (Francisco Pasinetti, Italy)
Special Homage:
Carl Dreyer, *Dies irae*
Best Italian Film:
Caccia Tragica (Giuseppe De Sanctis)

1948

Best Film, International Grand Prize:
Hamlet (Laurence Olivier, England)
Best Direction:
G. W. Pabst, *Der Prozess* (Austria)
Best Actor:
Ernest Deutsch, *Der Prozess*
Best Actress:
Jean Simmons, *Hamlet*
Best Documentary:
Goemons (Yannick Bellon, France)
Best Animated Cartoon (ex aequo)
Melody Time (Walt Disney, USA)
Le petit Soldat (Paul Grimault, France)
Best Story and Screenplay:
Graham Greene, *The Fallen Idol*
Best Music:
Max Steiner, *Treasure of the Sierra Madre*
Best Photography:
Desmond Dickison, *Hamlet*
Best Scenography:
John Bryan, *Oliver Twist*
International Prizes:
John Ford, *The Fugitive* (for its drama)
Robert Flaherty, *Louisiana Story* (for its lyrical beauty)
Luchino Visconti, *La Terra Trema* (for its choral qualities and style)
Best Italian Film:
Sotto il sole di Roma (Renato Castellani)

1949

Best Film: Lion of St. Mark:
Manon (Henri-Georges Clouzot, France)
Best Direction:
Augusto Genina, *Cielo sulla Palude* (Italy)
Best Actor:
Joseph Cotton, *Portrait of Jennie*
Best Actress:
Olivia de Havilland, *The Snake Pit*
Best Scenario:
Jacques Tati, *Jour de Fête*
Best Photography:
Gabriel Figueroa, *La Malquerida* (Mexico)
Best Scenography:
William Kellner, *Kind Hearts and Coronets*
Best Music:
John Greenwood, *The Last Days of Dolwyn*
Best Documentary:
L'Equateur aux Cent Visages (Andre Cauvin, Belgium)
International Prizes:
Sidney Meyers, *The Quiet One*
Anatole Litvak, *The Snake Pit*
R. A. Stemmie, *Berliner Ballade*
Best Italian Film:
Cielo sulla (Augusto Genina)

1950

Best Film: Lion of St. Mark:
Justice is Done (Andre Cayatte, France)
Best Direction:
(Not awarded)
Best Actor:
Sam Jaffe, *The Asphalt Jungle*
Best Actress:
Eleanor Parker, *Caged*
Best Scenario:
Jacques Natanson, Max Ophuls, *La Ronde*
Best Photography:
Martin Bodin, *Bara en mor* (Sweden)

Best Music:
Brian Easdale, *Gone to Earth* (England)
Best Scenography:
D'Eaubonne, *La Ronde*
Best Documentary:
Paul Haesaert, *Visite à Picasso* (Belgium)
International Prizes:
Elia Kazan, *Panic in the Streets*
Jean Delannoy, *Dieu a Besoin des Hommes*
Alessandro Biassetti, *Prima Comunione*
Special Jury Prize:
Walt Disney, *Cinderella* and *Beaver Valley*
Best Italian Film:
Domani è troppo tardi (Leonide Moguy)

1951

Best Film: Lion of St. Mark:
Rashomon (Akira Kurosawa, Japan)
Best Direction:
(No longer awarded)
Best Actor:
Jean Gabin, *La Nuit est Mon Royaume*
Best Actress:
Vivien Leigh, *A Streetcar Named Desire*
Best Scenario:
T.E.B. Clarke, *The Lavender Hill Mob*
Best Photography:
L.H. Burel, *Le Journal d'un Curé de Campagne* (France)
Best Music:
Hugo Friedhofer, *Big Carnival* (USA)
Best Documentary:
Nature's Half Acre (Walt Disney, USA)
Special Jury Prize:
Elia Kazan, *A Streetcar Named Desire*
International Prizes
Robert Bresson, *Le Journal d'un Curé de Campagne*
Billy Wilder, *Big Carnival*
Jean Renoir, *The River*
Best Italian Film:
La Città si difende (Pietro Germi)

1952

Best Film: Lion of St. Mark:
Forbidden Games (Rene Clement, France)
Best Actor:
Fredric March, *Death of a Salesman*
Best Actress:
(*Not awarded this year*)
Best Scenario
Jean Negulesco, *Phone Call from a Stranger* (USA)
Best Music:
George Auric
Best Décor:
Carmen Dillon, *The Importance of Being Earnest*
Special Jury Prize:
Mendy (England)
International Prizes:
John Ford, *The Quiet Man*
Roberto Rossellini, *Europe 51*
K. Mizoguchi, *Life of Oharu*

1953

Best Film: Lion of St. Mark:
(*Not awarded this year*)
Best Actor:
Henri Vilbert, *Absolution Without Confession* (France)
Best Actress:
Lilli Palmer, *The Fourposter* (USA)
Silver Prize Winners:
Ugetsu Monogatari (Kenji Mizoguchi, Japan)
I Vitelloni (Federico Fellini, Italy)
The Little Fugitive (R. Ashley, USA)
Moulin Rouge (John Huston, England)
Thérèse Raquin (Marcel Carné, France)
Bronze Prize Winners:
War of God (Spain)
Les Orgueilleux (France)
Sinha Moca (Brazil)

1954

Best Film: Lion of St. Mark:
Romeo and Juliet (Renato Castellani, Italy-England)
Best Actor:
Jean Gabin, *Touchez par au Grisbi, The Air of Paris* (France)
Best Actress:
(*Not awarded this year*)
Silver Prize Winners:
On the Waterfront (Elia Kazan, USA)
Seven Samurai (Akira Kurosawa, Japan)
La Strada (Frederico Fellini, Italy)
Sansho the Bailiff (Kenji Mizoguchi, Japan)
Special Jury Prize for Ensemble Acting:
Executive Suite (with William Holden, June Allyson, Barbara Stanwyck, Fredric March, Walter Pidgeon, Shelley Winters)

1955

Best Film: Lion of St. Mark:
Ordet (Carl Dreyer, Denmark)
Best Actor:
Kenneth More, *The Deep Blue Sea* (England), Curt Jurgens, *The Devil's General* (Germany), and *Les Héros sont Fatigués* (France)
Best Actress:
(*Not awarded this year*)
Silver Prize Winners:
La Cicala (Samsonov, USSR)
The Big Knife (Robert Aldrich, USA)
Le Amiche (Michelangelo Antonioni, Italy)
Ciske de Rat (Wolfgang Staudte, Holland)
Most Promising New Directors:
Alexandre Astruc (France)
Vaclav Kraka (Czechoslovakia)
William Fairchild (England)
Francesco Maselli (Italy)
Andrzej Munk (Polland)

1956

Best Film: Lion of St. Mark:
(*Not awarded this year*)
Best Actor:
Bournvil, *La Traverse de Paris*
Best Actress:
Maria Schell, *Gervaise*
International Catholic Office Award:
Calabuch (Spain)
International Film Critics Award:
Gervaise
Calle Mayor
Italian Critics Award:
Attack! (Robert Aldrich, USA)
San Giorgio Prize:
Burma Harp (Kon Tchikawa, Japan)

1957

Best Film: Lion of St. Mark:
Aparajito (Satyajit Ray, India)
Best Actor:
Anthony Franciosa, *A Hatful of Rain* (USA)
Best Actress:
Dzidra Ritenberg, *Malva* (USSR)
Silver Prize Winner:
White Nights (Luchino Visconti, Italy)
Catholic Office Award:
A Hatful of Rain (USA)
International Film Critics Award:
A Hatful of Rain (USA)
Most Cooperative Performer at the Festival:
Esther Williams
San Giorgio Prize:
Something of Value (USA)

1958

Best Film: Lion of St. Mark:
Muhomatsu no Issho (Hiroshi Inagaki, Japan)
Best Actor:
Alec Guinness, *The Horse's Mouth* (England)

Best Actress:
Sophia Loren, *The Black Orchid* (USA)
Silver Prize Winner:
Les Amants (Malle, France)
Best Documentary:
The Last Day of Summer, (Tadeusz Konwicki & Jan Laskowski, Poland)

1959

Best Film: Lion of St. Mark:
Il Generale della Rovere (Roberto Rossellini, Italy)
La Grande Guerre (M. Monicelli, Italy)
Best Actor:
James Stewart, *Anatomy of a Murder* (USA)
Best Actress:
Madeline Robinson, *Double Tour* (France)
Special Jury Prize:
Ingmar Bergman, *The Magician*
Catholic Film Office:
Il Generale della Rovere
International Film Critics Prize:
Il Generale della Rovere

1960

Best Film: Lion of St. Mark:
Le Passage du Rhine (Andre Cayatte, France)
Best Actor:
John Mills, *Tunes of Glory* (England)
Best Actress:
Shirley MacLaine, *The Apartment* (USA)
Silver Prize Winner:
Rocco and His Brothers (Luchino Visconti, Italy)
Catholic Film Office Award:
Voyage In a Balloon (Albert Lamorisses, France)
International Film Critics Award:
The Motorcart (Spain)
Rocco and His Brothers (Italy)

Best First Feature:
Florestano Vancini, *That Long Night in '43* (Italy)

1961

Best Film: Lion of St. Mark:
Last Year at Marienbad (Alain Resnais, France)
Best Actor:
Toshiro Mifune, *Yojimbo* (Japan)
Best Actress:
Suzanne Flon, *Thou Shall Not Kill* (Yugoslavia)
Special Jury Prize:
Peace to All Who Enter (Alexander Alov, USSR)
Catholic Film Office Award:
Il Posto (Ermanno Olmi, Italy)
International Film Critics Award:
Il Brigante (Renato Castellani, Italy)
San Giorgio Prize:
Banditti a Orgasolo (Vittorio de Seta, Italy)

1962

Best Film: Lion of St. Mark:
Childhood of Ivan (Andrev Tarkovski, USSR)
Family Diary (Valerio Zurlini, Italy)
Best Actor:
Burt Lancaster, *Bird Man of Alcatraz*
Best Actress:
Emmanuelle Riva, *Thérèse Desqueyroux*
Special Jury Prize:
Vivre Sa Vie (Jean-Luc Godard, France)
Best First Film:
David and Lisa (Frank Perry, USA)
Los Innudados (Ferando Birri, Argentina)
Catholic Film Office Award:
Term of Trial (England)
International Film Critics Award:
Knife in the Water (Roman Polanski, Poland)

San Giorgio Prize:
Bird Man of Alcatraz

1963

Best Film: Lion of St. Mark:
Le Mani sulla città (Francesco Rosi, Italy)
Best Actor:
Albert Finney, *Tom Jones*
Best Actress:
Delphine Seyrig, *Muriel* (France)
Special Jury Prizes:
Le Feu Follet (Louis Malle, France)
Introduction to Life (Igor Talankine, USSR)
Best First Films:
A Sunday in September (Jorn Donner, Sweden)
Le Joli Mai (Chris Marker, France)
Catholic Film Office Award:
Hud (Martin Ritt, USA)
International Film Critics Award:
The Hangman (Luis Berlanga, Spain)

1964

Best Film: Lion of St. Mark:
Red Desert (Michelangelo Antonioni, Italy)
Best Actor:
Tom Courtenay, *King and Country* (England)
Best Actress:
Harriet Anderson, *To Love* (Sweden)
Special Jury Prizes:
Hamlet (Kosintzev, USSR)
Il Vangelo Secondo Matteo (Pier Paolo Pasolini, Italy)
Best First Film:
La Vie à l'Envers (Alain Jessua, France)
Catholic Film Office Award:
Il Vangelo Secondo Matteo (Italy)
International Film Critics Award:
Red Desert (Italy)

San Giorgio Prize:
Nothing but a Man (USA)

1965

Best Film: Lion of St. Mark:
Of a Thousand Delights (Luchino Visconti, Italy)
Best Actor:
Toshiro Mifune, *Akahige* (Japan)
Best Actress:
Annie Girardot, *Trois Chambres à Manhattan* (France)
Special Jury Prizes:
Simon of the Desert (Luis Buñuel, Mexico)
I'm Twenty (Marlen Koutziev, USSR)
Best First Film:
Faithfulness (Pietr Toderovski, USSR)
Catholic Film Office Award:
Akahige (Akira Kurosawa, Japan)
International Film Critics Award:
Simon of the Desert (Luis Buñuel, Mexico)
Gertrud (Carl Dreyer, Denmark)

1966

Best Film: Lion of St. Mark:
Battle of Algiers (Gillo Pontecorvo, Italy)
Best Actor:
Jacques Perrin, *Quest* (Spain) and *Half a Man* (Italy)
Best Actress:
Natalia Arinbasavora, *The First Schoolteacher* (USSR)
Special Jury Prizes:
Au Hasard Balthazar (Robert Bresson, France)
Abschied von Gestern (Alexander Kluge, Germany)
Chappaqua (Conrad Rooks, USA)

1967

Best Film: Lion of St. Mark:
Belle de Jour (Luis Buñuel,
France)
Best Actor:
Ljubisa Samardzic, *Dawn
(Yugoslavia)*
Best Actress:
Shirley Knight, *Dutchman*
(England)
Special Jury Prizes:
La Chinoise (Jean-Luc Godard,
France)
China Is Near (Marco
Bellocchio, Italy)
Opera Prima Prize:
Edgar Reitz, *Mahizelten*
(Germany)
Catholic Office Award:
Silent Voyage (Christian de
Chalone, France)

**International Film Critics
Award:**
China Is Near (Marco
Bellocchio, Italy) for films in
competition
Rebellion (Masaki Kobayashi,
Japan) for films not in
competition

1968

Best Film: Lion of St. Mark:
*Die Artisten in der
Zirkuskuppel* (Alexander
Kluge, Germany)
Best Actor:
John Morely, *Faces* (USA)
Best Actress:
Laura Betti, *Teorema* (Italy)
Special Jury Prize:
Le Socrate (Lapoujade, France)
Nostra Signora dei Turchi
(Bene, Italy)

1979

*(Jury and Award System
discontinued)*

**INTERNATIONAL CRITICS
(FIPRESCI) AWARD:**
(TIE)
La Nouba (Assia Djebbar,
Algeria)
Passe Montagne (Jean
Francois Stevenin, France)
**ITALIAN JOURNALIST
AWARDS:**
Best Film:
Saint Jack (Peter Bogdanovich,
U.S.)
Best Actor:
Evgeni Leonov, *Atumn
Marathon* (U.S.S.R.)
Best Actress:
Nobuko Otowa, *The Strangler*
(Japan)

2/CANNES FILM FESTIVAL PRIZES

CANNES IS THE best-known of all the International film festivals. Originally scheduled for 1939, the first exhibition at Cannes had to be postponed until 1946 due to the war. Despite its continued popularity, the festival has been cancelled three times during its history: in 1949 and 1950 owing to insufficient funds and to schisms within the French film industry, and in 1968 when political demonstrations led by such respected directors as Truffaut, Godard and Lelouch forced the festival to close in mid-progress.

The festival was quick to recover from the 1968 controversy, however, and has since regained its former prestige and attendant publicity. Cannes is now the largest of the film festivals: during the festival, as many as 600 films can be screened in the town, both at the festival itself and at the town's many local theaters. It's a 24-hour-a-day affair, attended by representatives from all aspects of the film industry—directors, producers, exhibitors, distributors, actors, writers, publicists and journalists. As a result, Cannes is famous for its wheeling-dealing marketplace atmosphere.

Although the structure of the festival continues to change, the exhibition mainly consists of three parts: (1) the competition itself, (2) the Critics' Week, and (3) the Directors' Fortnight. In the past few years, three noncompetitive segments were added to the festival: (1) "The Fertile Eyes," for films dealing in theatrical, dance or musical adaptation; (2) "The Air of the Times," with movies exploring important recent events; and (3) "The Composed Past," a look at classic works. Shortly after the 1977 festival, however, Gilles Jacob—the festival's director—announced that these three categories would be deleted from future festivals and that the rest of the festival would likewise be pared down to make it more manageable.

Unlike many of the other festivals that favor shorts and documentaries as well as feature-length films, Cannes concentrates largely on feature-length works.

Through 1950 the festival took place in the fall. But since 1951 it has been held in the spring, usually in May.

Canne's top prize (for best film) is the famed golden Palm.

1946

Best Films:
La Bataille du Rail (Rene Clément, France)
Symphonie Pastorale (Jean Delannoy, France)
The Lost Weekend (Billy Wilder, USA)
Brief Encounter (David Lean, England)
Open City (Roberto Rossellini, Italy)
Maria Candelaria (Emilio Fernandez, Mexico)
The Last Chance (Leopold Lindtberg, Switzerland)

Best Director:
René Clement, *La Bataille du Rail*

Best Actor:
Ray Milland, *The Lost Weekend*

Best Actress:
Michèle Morgan, *Symphonie Pastorale*

1947

Best Films:
Antoine et Antoinette (Jacques Becker, France)
Les Maudits (Rene Clément, France)
Crossfire (Edward Dmytryk, USA)
Dumbo (Walt Disney, USA)
Ziegfeld Follies (Vincente Minnelli, USA)
Best Director:
(not awarded)
Best Actor:
(not awarded)
Best Actress:
(not awarded)

1948

(No festival)

1949

Best Film:
The Third Man (Carol Reed, England)
Best Director:
René Clément, *Au Delà des Grilles*
Best Actor:
Edward G. Robinson, *House of Strangers*
Best Actress:
Isa Miranda, *Au Delà des Grilles*

1950

(No festival)

1951

Best Film:
Miracle in Milan (Vittorio De Sica, Italy) and *Miss Julie*
(Alf Sjöberg, Sweden) (tied; awarded *ex aequo*)
Best Director:
Luis Buñuel, *Los Olvidados*
Best Actor:
Michael Redgrave, *The Browning Version*
Best Actress:
Bette Davis, *All About Eve*
Special Jury Prize
All About Eve (Joseph Mankiewicz, USA)

1952

Best Film:
Othello (Orson Welles, Morocco) and *Two Cents Worth of Hope* (Renato Castellani, Italy) (tied; awarded *ex acquo*)
Best Director:
Christian-Jaque, *Fanfan la Tulipe*
Best Actor:
Marlon Brando, *Viva Zapatal*
Best Actress:
Lee Grant, *Detective Story*
Special Jury Prize:
Nous Sommes Tous des Assassins (Andre Cayatte, France)

1953

Best Film:
Wages of Fear (Henri-Georges Clouzot, *France*)
Best Director:
Walt Disney, for his work as a whole
Best Actor:
Charles Vanel, *Wages of Fear*
Best Actress:
Shirley Booth, *Come Back, Little Sheba*

1954

Best Film:
Gate of Hell (Teinosuke Kinugasa, Japan)

Best Director:
René Clément, *Monsieur Ripois*
Best Actor:
(Not awarded)
Best Actress:
(Not awarded)
Out of Competition Prize:
From Here to Eternity (Fred Zinnemann, USA)

1955

Best Film:
Marty (Delbart Mann, USA)
Best Director:
Jules Dassin, *Rififi*
Serge Vasiliev, *Heroes of Shipka*
Best Actor:
Spencer Tracy, *Bad Day at Black Rock*
Ernest Borgnine, *Marty*
Best Actress:
Betsy Blair, *Marty*
Special Prize:
The Lost Continent (Italy)
Best Documentary:
Isle of Fire (Italy)

1956

Best Film:
World of Silence (Louis Malle/Jacques-Yves Cousteau, France)
Best Director:
Serge Youtkevitch, *Othello*
Best Actor:
(Not awarded)
Best Actress:
Susan Hayward, *I'll Cry Tomorrow*
Special Prize:
Le Mystère Picasso (Henri-Georges Clouzot, France)
Most Poetic Humor:
Ingmar Bergman, *Smiles of a Summer Night*
Best Human Document:
Satyajit Ray, (Pather Panchali, USA)

1957

Best Film:
Friendly Persuasion (William Wyler, USA)
Best Director:
Robert Bresson, *A Condemned Man Escapes*
Best Actor:
John Kitzmiller, *Valley of Peace*
Best Actress:
Guilietta Massina, *Nights of Cabiria*
Special Prizes:
The Seventh Seal (Ingmar Bergman, Sweden)
Kanal (Andrzej Wajda, Poland)
Best Documentary:
The Roof of Japan (Japan) and *Qivitog* (Denmark) (tied)

1958

Best Film:
The Cranes Are Flying (Mikhail Kalatozov, USSR)
Best Director:
Ingmar Bergman, *Brink of Life*
Best Actor:
Paul Newman, *That Long Hot Summer*
Best Actress:
(collective prize)
Eva Dahlbeck, Ingrid Thulin, Bibi Andersson, Babro Ornas, *Brink of Life*
Special Prize:
Jacques Tati, *Mon Oncle*
Best Documentary:
Bronze Faces (Switzerland)
Best Script:
Mauro Bolognini, *Newlyweds*
International Critics Prize:
Juan Bardem, *Vengeance*

1959

Best Film:
Black Orpheus (Marcel Camus, France)

Best Director:
Francois Truffaut, *The 400 Blows*
Best Actor:
(collective prize)
Dean Stockwell, Bradford Dillman, Orson Welles, *Compulsion*
Best Actress:
Simone Signoret, *Room at the Top*
Special Jury Prize:
Stars (Burgaria)
Special Prize:
Luis Buñuel, *Nazarin*
International Critics Award:
Hiroshima Mon Amour and *Araya* (tied)
Catholic Film Office Award:
The 400 Blows
Film Writers Award:
Hiroshima Mon Amour

1960

Best Film
La Dolce Vita (Fredrico Fellini, Italy) (Ingmar Bergman, *The Virgin Spring* and Luis Buñuel *The Young One* were announced as too good to be judged)
Best Director:
(Not awarded)
Best Actor:
(Not awarded)
Best Actress:
Melina Mercouri, *Never on Sunday* and; Jeanne Moreau, *Moderato Cantabile*
Special Jury Prize:
Michelangelo Antonioni, *L'Avventura*
Special Prizes:
Ballad of a Soldier (USSR)
Lady with a Pet Dog (USSR)
Kaji (Japan)
International Critics Prize:
Ingmar Bergman, *The Virgin Spring*
Catholic Film Office Award:
Astrid Henning-Jensen, *Paw*

1961

Best Film:
Viridiana (Luis Buñuel, Spain) and *Une aussi longue absence* (Henri Colpi, France) (tied)
Best Director:
Yulia Solntzeva, *History of the Flaming Years*
Best Actor:
Anthony Perkins, *Goodbye Again*
Best Actress:
Sophia Loren, *Two Women*
Special Jury Prize:
Jerzy Kawalerowicz, *Mother Joan of the Angels*
International Critics prize:
Hands in the Trap, Torre Nilsson
Chronicle of a Summer, Jean Rouch
Gary Cooper Award for Human Values:
A Raisin in the Sun
Catholic Film Office Award:
Hoodlum Priest, Irvin Kershner

1962

Best Film:
The Given Word (Anselmo Duarte, Brazil)
Best Director:
(Not awarded)
Best Acting:
(given collectively to two films)
Katharine Hepburn, Ralph Richardson, Jason Robards Jr., Dean Stockwell, *Long Day's Journey Into Night*
Rita Tushingham, Murray Melvin, *A Taste of Honey*
Special Jury Prize:
Robert Bresson, Le Procès de *Jeanne D'Arc*
Michelangelo Antonioni, *L'Eclipse*
International Critics Prize:
Luis Buñuel,*The Exterminating Angel*
Catholic Film Office Award:
Michelangelo Antonioni, *L'Eclipse*

1963

Best Picture:
The Leopard (Luchino Visconti, Italy)
Best Director:
(Not awarded)
Best Actor:
Richard Harris, *This Sporting Life*
Best Actress:
Marina Vlady, *The Conjugal Bed* (a.k.a. *Queen Bee*)
Special Jury Prizes:
Harakiri, Setsuo V. Kobayashi (Japan)
One Day a Cat, V. Jasny (Czechoslovakia)
International Critics Prize:
This Sporting Life, Lindsay Anderson
Le Joli Mai, Chris Marker
Gary Cooper Award for Human Values:
To Kill a Mockingbird
Catholic Film Office Award:
The Fiancés, Ermanno Olmi

1964

Best Film:
The Umbrellas of Cherbourg (Jacques Demy, France)
Best Director:
(Not awarded)
Best Actor:
Antal Pager, *Pasirta*; and Saro Urzi, *Seduced and Abandoned* (tied)
Best Actress:
Anne Bancroft, *The Pumpkin Eater*; and, Barbara Barrie, *One Potato, Two Potato* (tied)
Special Jury Prize:
Hiroshi Teshigahara, *Woman of the Dunes*
International Critics Award:
The Passenger (Poland)
Catholic Film Office Award:
Umbrellas of Cherbourg (France)
Sterile Lives (Brazil)

1965

Best Film:
The Knack (Richard Lester, England)
Best Director:
L. Ciulei, *The Lost Forest*
Best Acting:
(awarded collectively)
Samantha Eggar and Terence Stamp, *The Collector*
Special Jury Prize:
Setsuo Kobayashi, *Kwaidan*
International Critics Award:
Tarahumara (Mexico)
Catholic Film Office Award:
Yoyo (France); *Tokyo Olympics* (Japan)

1966

Best Film:
A Man and a Woman (Claude Lelouch, France) and *Signore e Signori* (Pietro Germi, Italy) (tied)
Best Director:
Serge Youtkevitch, *Lenin in Poland*
Best Actor:
Per Oscarsson, *Hunger*
Best Actress:
Vanessa Redgrave, *Morgan*
Special Jury Prize:
Louis Gilbert, *Alfie*
20th Anniversary Tribute:
Orson Welles
International Critics Award:
Young Torless (Germany) and *La Guerre est finie* (France)
Catholic Film Office Award:
A Man and a Woman (France)

1967

Best Film:
Blow-Up (Michelangelo Antonioni, England)
Best Director:
Ferenc Kosa, *Ten Thousand Suns*
Best Actor:
Odded Kotler, *Three Days and a Child*
Best Actress:
Pia Degermark, *Elvira Madigan*
Special Jury Prize: (tie)
Alexender Petrovic, *Happy Gypsies* and; Joseph Losey, *Accident*

1968

(Festival closed)

1969

Best Film:
If (Lindsay Anderson, England)
Best Director:
Glauber Rocha, *Antonio Das Mortes* and; Vojtech Jasny, *My Dear* (tied)
Best Actor:
Jean-Louis Trintignant, *Z*
Best Actress:
Vanessa Redgrave, *Isadora*
Special Jury Award:
Adalen 31, Bo Widerberg
International Critics Award:
Andrei Roubloy (USSR)
Best First Film:
Easy Rider Dennis Hopper

1970

Best Film:
*M*A*S*H* (Robert Altman, USA)
Best Director:
John Boorman, *Leo the Last*
Best Actor:
Marcello Mastroianni, *Drama of Jealousy*
Best Actress:
Ottavio Piccolo, *Metelo*
Special Jury Prize:
Citizen Above Suspicion, Elio Petri
Jury Prizes:
The Balkans (Hungary)
Strawberry Statement (USA)
Best First Film:
Raoul Coutard, *Hoa Binh*

1971

Best Film:
The Go-Between (Joseph Losey, England)
Best Director:
(Not awarded)
Best Actor:
Ricardo Cucciola, *Sacco and Vanzetti*
Best Actress:
Kitty Winn, *Panic in Needle Park*
Special Jury Prize:
Taking Off, (Milos Foreman); and *Johnny Got His Gun* (Dalton Trumbo) (tied)
Special Prize:
Death in Venice, Luchino Visconti
Best First Film:
Nino Manfredi, *By Grace Received*

1972

Best Film:
The Working Class Goes to Paradise (Elio Petri, Italy) and *The Mattei Affair* (Francesco Rosi, Italy) (tied)
Best Director:
Miklós Jancsó, *The Red Psalm*
Best Actor:
Jean Yanne, *We Will Not Grow Old Together*
Best Actress:
Susannah York, *Images*
Special Jury Prize:
Solaris, Andrei Tarkovsky
Jury Prize:
Slaughterhouse Five, George Roy Hill

1973

Best Films:
Scarecrow, (Jerry Schatzberg, USA) and *The Hireling* (Alan Bridges, England) (tied)
Best Director:
(Not awarded)

Best Actor:
Giancarlo Giannini, *Love and Anarchy*
Best Actress:
Joanne Woodward, *The Effect of Gamma Rays . . .*
Grand Special Jury Prize:
The Mother and the Whore, Jean Eustache
Special Jury Prize:
Wild Planet, Laloux
Jury Prize:
The Invitation, Claude Goretta
Hourglass Sanatorium, Wojcelch Has
Best First Film:
Jeremy, Arthur Barron
International Critics Award:
La Grande Bouffe, Marco Ferreri
The Mother and the Whore, Jean Eustache

1974

Best Film:
The Conversation (Francis Ford Coppola, USA)
Best Director:
(Not awarded)
Best Actor:
Jack Nicholson, *The Last Detail*
Best Actress:
Marie-Jose Nat, *Les Violons du Bal*
Special Jury Prize:
Il Fiore delle Mille e una Notte, Pier Paolo Pasolini
Jury Prize:
La Prima Angelica, Carlos Saura
International Critics Award:
Lancelot du Lac, Robert Bresson
Fear Eats the Soul, Rainer Werner Fassbinder
Best Screenplay:
Hal Barwood, Matthew Robbins, *Sugarland Express*
Special Tribute:
Charles Boyer, *Stavisky*
Grand Prix de la Commission Superieure Technique du Cinéma Français:
Ken Russell, *Mahler*

1975

Best Film:
Chronicle of the Burning Years (Mohammed Lakhdar-Hamina, Algeria)
Best Director:
Constantine Costa-Gavras, *Section Spéciale* and; Michel Brault, *Les Ordes* (tied)
Best Actor:
Vittorio Gassman, *Scent of Woman*
Best Actress:
Valerie Perrine, *Lenny*
Special Jury Prize:
Werner Herzog, *Every Man for Himself* and *God Against All*
International Critics Award:
Every Man for Himself . . . (Werner Herzog, Germany)
Ecumenical Prize (Mixed Catholic and Protestant Jury):
Every Man for Himself

1976

Best Film:
Taxi Driver (Martin Scorsese, USA)
Best Director:
Ettore Scola, *Brutti, Sporchi, Cattivi*
Best Actor:
José-Luis Gómez, *La Familia de Pascual Duarte*
Best Actress:
Mari Torocsik, *Deryne, Hol Van*
Dominique Sanda, *L'Eredita Ferramonti*
Special Jury Prize:
Cria Cuervos (Carlos Saura, Spain)
The Marquise of O (Eric Rohmer, W. Germany)
International Critics Award:
Ferdinand the Strongman (Kluge, W. Germany)
Kings of the Road (Wim Wenders, W. Germany)

1977

Best Film:
Padre Padrone (Paolo and Vittorio Taviani, Italy)
Best Director:
(Not awarded this year)
Best Actor:
Fernando Rey, *Elisa My Love*
Best Actress:
Shelley Duvall, *Three Women*
Monique Mercure, *J.A. Martin, Photographer*
Best First Film:
Ridley Scott, *The Duellists*
Best Musical Score:
Norman Whitfield, *Car Wash*
Ecumenical Prize (mixed Catholic and Protestant jury):
The Lacemaker (Claude Goretta, Switzerland)
International Critics Prize:
Padre Padrone (Paolo and Vittorio Taviani, Italy)

1978

Best Film:
The Tree of Wooden Clogs (Ermanno Olmi, Italy)

Best Director:
Nagisa Oshima, *Empire of Passion*
Best Actor:
Jon Voight, *Coming Home*
Best Actress:
Jill Clayburgh, *An Unmarried Woman*
Isabelle Huppert, *Violette Noziere*
Special Jury Prize:
Bye Bye Monkey (Marco Ferreri, Italy)
The Shout (Jerzy Skolimowski Britain)
International Critics Prize:
Man of Marble (Andrzej Wajda, Poland)
Smell of Wild Flowers (Srdan Karanovic, Yugoslavia)
Ecumenical Prize:
The Tree of Wooden Clogs (Ermanno Olmi, Italy)
Best First Film:
Alambrista (Robert Young, USA)

1979

Best Film:
Apocalypse Now (Francis Ford Coppola, USA)

The Tin Drum (Volker Schloendorff, West Germany)
Best Director:
Terrence Malick, *Days of Heaven*
Best Actor:
Jack Lemmon, *The China Syndrome*
Best Actress:
Sally Field, *Norma Rae*
Best Supporting Actor:
Stefano Madia, *Caro Papa*
Best Supporting Actress:
Eva Mattes, *Woyzeck*
Special Jury Prize:
Siberiade (Andrei Mikhalov Konchalovsky, USSR)
International Critics Prize (for competed film):
Apocalypse Now
International Critics Prize (for noncompeted film):
Angi Vera (Pal Gabor, Hungary)
Black Jack (Ken Loach, Britain)
Ecumenical Prize:
Rough Treatment (Andrzej Wajda, Poland)
Special Prize:
Miklos Jancso for ensemble of his work
Grand Prix de la Commission Superieure Techniques du Cinema Francais:
Normae Rae (Martin Ritt, USA)
Camera D'Or:
Northern Lights (John Hanson & Rob Nilsson, USA)

3/BERLIN FILM FESTIVAL PRIZES

THE BERLIN FILM Festival was established in 1951 by Dr. Alfred Bauer. In its early years the festival, unlike many of its counterparts, allowed the audience as well as jury to determine awards. In 1956 the festival received "A" classification from the International Federation of Film Producers Association; and the following year, audience awards were no longer permitted.

It has often been said that the festival initially succeeded because of its location: it was one of the first European festivals to be held in a large city instead of in a small town or resort; and because of the political importance of Berlin, early festivals received world-wide attention, including the support of even the U.S. State Department. The festival has excelled in exhibiting independent films—unlike Cannes, which leans toward more commercial entries. Shorts and political cinema have been especially favored at Berlin. In 1970, political activists forced the festival to close.

In recent years the festival has been highly praised for its Forum of Young Films under the direction of Ulrich Gregor. Each year the forum is a series of films devoted to the young filmmakers of a specific country, and many people think the series has the potential of becoming as important as the Directors' Fortnight in Cannes. Each year the festival also holds highly respected Retrospectives and an International Film Fair. In 1977 Wolf Donner replaced Alfred Bauer as the festival's director and the festival changed. *Variety,* for example, reported that the 1977 festival took a slight turn to the left under Donner's direction: Russian and East German films were numerous; there was a forum dedicated to Lenin and the Soviet Revolution; and jurists included representatives from Russia and Cuba. Donner has also increased the number of sidebar events; some said to undermine Ulrich Gregor's Forum of Young Films.

Through 1977 the Berlin Film Festival was held in late June-early July. Beginning in 1978, however, the festival has been presented in late February-early March both to avoid overlap with the summer holidays and to come well in advance of the Cannes event.

Golden Bears are awarded in the best-film categories, Silver Bears in the direction and acting divisions.

1951

Dramatic Films:
1. *Four in a Jeep* (Switzerland)
2. *The Way of Hope* (Italy)
3. *The Browning Version* (England)

Comedies:
1. *Sans Lasser d'Advance* (France)
2. *Fahrt in Blanc* (Sweden)
3. *The Mating Season* (USA)

Crime and Adventure:
1. *Justice is Done* (France)
2. Award not given
3. *Destination Moon* (USA)

Musicals:
1. *Cinderella* (USA)
2. *Tales of Hoffmann* (Germany)
3. Award not given

Audience Awards:
1. *Cinderella* (USA)
2. *The Browning Version* (England)
3. *Justice is Done* (France)

1952

Audience Awards:
1. *She Danced for the Summer* (Sweden)
2. *Fanfan the Tulip* (France)
3. *Cry the Beloved Country* (England)

1953

Audience Awards:
1. *Wages of Fear* (France)
2. *The Green Secret* (Italy)
3. *Sie fanden eine Heimat* (Switzerland)

1954

Audience Awards:
1. *Hobson's Choice* (England)
2. *Bread, Love and Dreams* (Italy)
3. *Le Defreque* (France)

1955

Audience Awards:
1. *The Rats* (Germany)
2. *Marcellino* (Italy)
3. *Carmen Jones* (USA)

1956

Best Picture: First Prize:
Invitation to the Dance (Gene Kelly)
Best Picture: Second Prize:
Richard III (Laurence Olivier, England)
Best Direction:
Robert Aldrich, *Autumn Leaves*
Best Actor:
Burt Lancaster, *Trapeze*
Best Actress:
Elsa Martinelli, *Donatella*
Best Feature Documentaries:
1. *No Space for Wild Animals* (Germany)
2. *The African Lion* (Walt Disney, USA)
Best Short Documentaries:
1. *Paris La Nuit* (France)
2. *Spring Comes to Kashmir* (India)
   Hitit Gunesi (Turkey)
   Rhythmetic (Canada)
Audience Awards:
1. *Before Sunset* (Germany)
2. *Pepote* (Mexico)
3. *Trapeze* (USA)

1957

Best Picture:
Twelve Angry Men (Sidney Lumet, USA)
Best Direction:
Mario Monicelli, *Fathers and Sons*
Best Actor:
Pedro Infante, *Tizoc*
Best Actress:
Yvonne Mitchell, *Woman in a Dressing Gown*
Best Feature Documentaries:
Secrets of Life (Walt Disney, USA)
Best Short Documentaries:
1. *Far-Off People* (Italy)
2. *The Last Paradise* (Italy)
   One Thousand Small Characters (Germany)
   Plitvice Lakes (Yugoslavia)
Catholic Film Office Award:
Twelve Angry Men (Sidney Lumet, USA)

1958

Best Film:
The End of the Day (Sweden)
Best Direction:
Tadashi Ima, *Story of True Love*
Best Actor:
Sidney Poitier, *The Defiant Ones*
Best Actress:
Anna Magnani, *Wild is the Wind*
Best Feature Documentary:
Perri (Walt Disney, USA)
Best Short Documetary:
Olive Harvest in Calabria (Italy)

1959

Best Film:
The Cousins (Claude Chabrol, France)

Best Direction:
Akira Kurosawa, *The Hidden Fortress*
Best Actor:
Jean Gabin, *Archimede le Clochard*
Best Actress:
Shirley MacLaine, *Ask Any Girl*
Best Feature Documentary:
White Wilderness, (Walt Disney, USA)
Best Culture Film:
1. *Praise the Sea* (Holland)
2. *Hest pa ferie* (Denmark)
   Radha and Krishna (India)
   Das Knalleidoskop (Germany)
Special Prize:
Hayley Mills, *Tiger Bay*
International Critics Prize:
The Hidden Fortress (Akira Kurosawa, Japan)

1960

Best Film: First Prize:
Lazarillo de Tormes (Spain)
Best Film: Second Prize:
The Love Game (France)
Best Direction:
Jean-Luc Godard, *Breathless*
Best Actor:
Fredric March, *Inherit the Wind*
Best Actress:
Juliette Mayniel, *Country Fair*
Best Feature Documentary:
Faja Lobbi (Holland)
Best Short Documentary:
Les Songs des Chevaux Sauvages (France)
International Film Critics Prize:
Angry Silence (England)

1961

Best Film:
La Notte (Michelangelo Antonioni, Italy)
Best Direction:
Bernhard Wicki, *The Miracle of Father Malachias*

Best Actor:
Peter Finch, *No Love for Johnny*
Best Actress:
Anna Karina, *A Woman Is a Woman*
Best Documentary:
Description of a Struggle (Israel)

1962

Best Film:
A Kind of Loving (John Schlesinger, England)
Best Direction:
Francesco Rosi, *Salvatore Giuliano*
Best Actor:
James Stewart, *Mr. Hobbs Takes a Vacation*
Best Actress:
Rita Gam and Viveca Lindfors, *No Exit*
Best Documentary:
Galapagos (Germany)
Best Short Subject:
The Painter Karel Appel (Holland)
International Film Critics Prize:
Zoo (Holland)
Most Promising Newcomer:
Jon Young Sun, *To the Last Day* (Korea)

1963

Best Film:
Oath of Obedience (Germany) and *The Devil* (Italy)
Best Director:
Nikos Koundouros, *Little Aphrodite*
Best Actor:
Sidney Poitier, *Lilies of the Field*
Best Actress:
Bibi Andersson, *The Lovers*
Best Documentary:
The Great Atlantic (Germany)
Best Short Subject:
Bouwspelement (Holland)

International Film Critics Prize:
The Reunion (Italy)

1964

Best Film:
Dry Summer (Turkey)
Best Direction:
Satyajit Ray, *Mahanager*
Best Actor:
Rod Steiger, *The Pawnbroker*
Best Actress:
Sachiko Hidari, *She and He*
Other Awards:
Best Documentary:
Alleman (Holland)

1965

Best Film:
Alphaville (Jean-Luc Godard, France)
Best Direction:
Satyajit Ray, *Charulata*
Best Actor:
Lee Marvin, *Cat Ballou*
Best Actress:
Madhur Jaffrey, *Shakespeare Wallah*

1966

Best Film:
Cul de Sac (Roman Polanski, England)
Carlos Saura, *The Chase*
Jean-Pierre Léaud, *Masculin-Féminin*
Best Actress:
Lola Albright, *Lord Love a Duck*
Jury Awards:
Off-Season for Foxes (Germany)
Manhunt (Sweden)
Jury Tribute:
Satyajit Ray

1967

Best Film:
Le Départ (Jerzg Skolimowksi, Belgium)
Best Direction:
Zivojin Pavlovic, *The Rats Awaken*
Best Actor:
Michel Simon, *The Old Man and the Boy*
Best Actress:
Edith Evans, *The Whisperers*
Special Jury Prize:
La Collectionneuse (Eric Rohmer, France)
Best Screenplay:
Michael Lentz, *Every Year Again*
Best Short:
Through the Eyes of a Painter (India)
International Critics Prize:
Every Year Again (Germany)
Catholic Office Film Award:
The Whisperers (Byran Forbes England)

1968

Best Film: First Prize:
Ole Dole Doff (Jan Troell, Sweden)
Best Film: Second Prize:
Innocence Unprotected (Dustan Makavejev, Yugoslavia)
Come l'Amore (Mizui, Italy)
Best Direction:
Carlos Saura, *Peppermint Frappe*
Best Actor:
Jean-Louis Trintignant, *L'Homme Qui Ment*
Best Actress:
Stephane Audran, *Les Biches*

1969

Best Film: First Prize:
Early Years (Zelimir Zilnik, Yugoslavia)

Best Film: Second Prize:
Brazil Year 2000 (Lima, Brazil)
Made in Sweden (Bergenstrahle, Sweden)
I am a Elephant, Madame (Zadek, Germany)
Greetings (Brian De Palma, USA)
A Quiet Place in the Country (Petri, Italy)

1970

(Festival held, but prizes suspended)

1971

Best Film: First Prize:
The Garden of the Finzi-Continis (Vittorio De Sica, Italy)
Best Film: Second Prize:
Decameron (Pier Paolo Pasolini, Italy)
Best Actor:
Jean Gabin, *Le Chat*
Best Actress:
Shirley MacLaine, *Desperate Characters*
Simone Signoret, *Le Chat*
Best Camerawork:
Ragnar Lasse, *Love Is War* (Norway)
Best Short:
150½ (USA)
International Critics Prize:
Internationale Forum des jungen Films

1972

Best Film: First Prize:
The Canterbury Tales (Pier Paolo Pasolini, Italy)
Best Film: Second Prize:
The Hospital (Arthur Hiller, USA)
Best Direction:
Jean-Pierre Blanc, *The Spinster*

Best Actor:
Albert Sordi, *Detenuto in Attest di Giudizio*
Best Actress:
Elizabeth Taylor, *Hammersmith Is Out*
Special Prize:
Peter Ustinov
International Critics Federation Prize:
The Audience (Italy, Marco Ferreri)
Family Life (England, Ken Loach)

1973

Best Film: First Prize:
Distant Thunder (Satjayit Ray, India)
Best Film: Special Jury Prize:
Where There's Smoke There's Fire (Andre Cayatte, France)
Best Film: Second Prize:
The Revolution of the Seven Madmen (Leopoldo Torre Nilsson, Argentina)
The Tall Blond Man with One Black Shoe (Yves Robert, France)
The Experts (Norbert Kückelmann, West Germany)
All Nudity Will be Punished (Arnaldo Jabor, Brazil)
The 14 (Hemming, England)
International Critics Federation Prize:
Les Noces Rouges (Claude Chabrol, France) and *Lo Stagionale* (Italy)

1974

Best Film: First Prize:
The Apprenticeship of Duddy Kravitz (Ted Kotcheff, Canada)
Best Film: Special Jury Prize:
L'Horloger de St. Paul (France)
Best Films: Second Prize:
In the Name of the People (W. Germany)
Little Malcolm (England)
Still Life (Iran)

Bread and Chocolate (Italy)
Rebellion in Patagonia
(Argentina)
Best Actor:
Antonio Ferrandiz, *Next of Kin*
Best Actress:
Marta Vancourova, *The Lovers
of the Year 1*

1975

Best Film: First Prize:
Orkobefogadas (Marta
Meszaros, Hungary)
**Best Films: Special Jury
Prizes:**
Overlord (Cooper, England)
Dupont Lajoie (Boisset, France)
Best Direction:
Sergey Solovyov, *A Hundred
Days After Childhood*
Best Actor:
Vlastimil Brodsky, *Jakob der
Lügner*
Best Actress:
Kinuyo Tanaka, *Sandakan,
House #8*
Special Award:
Woody Allen
Best Short:
See (Lehman, USA)

1976

Best Film: First Prize:
Buffalo Bill and the Indians
(Robert Altman, USA) (award
declined)
**Best Films: Special Jury
Prize:**
Canoa (Cazals, Mexico)
Best Director:
Mario Monicelli, *Caro Michele*
Best Actor:
Gerhard Olschewski, *Lost Life*
Best Actress:
Jadwiga Baranska, *Night and
Days*
Best First Film:
Azonositas (Lugossy, Hungary)
Best Short:
Munakata, the Woodcarver
(Yanagawa, Japan)
International Critics Prize:
Long Vacations of '36 (Spain)

**Ecumenical Award (jury
consists of Catholic and
Protestant representatives):**
Loneliness of Konrad Steiner
(Switzerland)

1977

Best Film: First Prize:
The Ascent (Larissa Shepitko,
USSR)
Best Film: Second Prizes:
The Devil Probably (Robert
Bresson, France)
The Bricklayers (Jorge Fons,
Mexico)
A Strange Role (Pal Sandor,
Hungary)
Best Director:
Manuel Gutierrez, *Black Litter*
Best Actor:
Fernando Fernan Gomez, *The
Anchorite*
Best Actress:
Lily Tomlin, *The Late Show*
Best Short:
Not Known at This Address
(Hans Sachs, Rinneberg,
East Germany)
**International Federation of
Cinema Press:**
The Ascent (Larissa Shepitka,
USSR) Four members of the
jury—Derek Malcolm, Rainer
Werner Fassbinder, Basilio
Martin Patino and Helene
Vager—publicly stated that
they had voted against the
Russian film.

1978

Best Film: First Prize:
To "the entire Spanish
program" which includes
*Emilio Martinez Lazaro's
Max's Words* and *Jose Luis
Garcia Sanchez's The
Trouts.*
**Best Films: Special Jury
Prize:**
A Queda (Ray Guerra and
Nelson Xavier, Brazil)
Best Director:
Georgi Dyulgerov, *Advantage*

Best Actor:
Craig Russell, *Outrageous*
Best Actress:
Gena Rowlands, *Opening
Night*
Best First Film:
The Teacher (Octavio
Cortazar, Cuba)
Best Short:
*What Have We Done to the
Hens?* (Josef Hekrdla and
Vladimir Jiranek,
Czechoslovakia)
**For a Director's Complete
Oeuvre:**
Jerzy Kawalerowicz, Poland

1979

Best Film: First Prize:
David (Peter Lilienthal, West
Germany)
Best Film: Special Jury Prize:
Alexandria-Why (Youssef
Shahine, Egypt)
Best Director:
Astrid Henning Jensen,
Winter Children
Best Actor:
Michele Pacido, *Ernesto*
Best Actress:
Hanna Schygulla, *The
Marriage of Maria Braun*
Best Whole Technical Team:
The Marriage of Maria Braun
(West Germany)
Best Photography:
Sten Holmberg, *The Emperor*
Best Art Direction:
Henning Von Gierke,
Nosferatu
Best Short:
Ubu (Geoff Dunbar, Great
Britain)
International Critics Prize:
Albert-Why (Joseph Roedl,
West Germany)
My Way Home (Bill Douglas,
Britain)
Catholic Jury Prize:
Winter Children (Astrid
Henning-Jensen, Denmark)
Protesant Jury Prize:
Albert-Why (Youssef Shahine,
Egypt)

1980

Best Film: First Prize: (tie)
Heartland (Richard Pearce, U.S.A.)
Palermo Oder Wolfsburg (Werner Schroeter, West Germany)

Best Film: Special Jury Prize:
Chiedo Asilo (Marco Ferreri, Italy/France)
Best Director:
Istvan Szabo, *Bizalom*
Best Actor:
Andrzej Seweryn, *Dyrygent*
Best Actress:
Renate Krossner, *Solo Sunny*

Best Short: First Prize
Hlavy (Peter Sis, USSR)
Best Short: Second Prize
Rod Groth (Jorg Moser-Metius, West Germany)
International Critics Prize:
Solo Sunny (East Germany)

4/New York Film Festival Programs

THE NEW YORK Film Festival is now the most important of the American international festivals, although it is not the oldest. (The San Francisco International Film Festival began in 1957). Established in 1963, the New York Film Festival is presented under the auspices of the Film Society of Lincoln Center in cooperation with the International Film Importers and Distributors of America, Inc., and the Motion Picture Association of America. Richard Roud, the highly respected film critic, is the festival's director, and members of past program committees include such noted film scholars as Henri Langlois, Andrew Sarris, Susan Sontag and Richard Corliss.

The festival, however, has had its problems, foremost of which has been funding. Despite good attendances in its first years, the festival nevertheless lost money due to the high cost of running any festival in this country: in 1966, for example, the festival deficit ran $95,210. Contributions to the Film Society of Lincoln Center and support from the New York State Council on the Arts now make the festival possible.

The festival's second problem has been severe criticism from the New York film community. Despite its interesting programs, the festival is routinely attacked each year for any of several reasons: for favoring the films of one country over those of another, for slighting this director in-stead of that director, and even for the dress and life style of the festival's audience.

The most frequent complaint, however, has been the absence of American films. Although such films as *Five Easy Pieces, Bob & Carol & Ted & Alice, Funnyman, Mickey One, Portrait of Jason, Mean Streets, Badlands, Images, The Last Picture Show* and *A Woman Under the Influence* premiered at the festival, many critics have argued that American films have been consistently slighted. Festival directors have answered this argument by reminding the critics that it is after all, an international fetival. Richard Roud has pointed out that he wants to avoid concentrating on native products, unlike the practice of Cannes and Venice, which has so frequently led to accusations of chauvinistic favoritism. For a long time, moreover, American studios were reluctant to show their new films to an "art" audience and have only recently begun to realize that it might be worthwhile to hold off the release of a film in order for it to be showcased at the festival.

Because of its location, the New York Film Festival can expose a film to a wide audience of critics and potential distributors. The festival has introduced to this country such directors as Roman Polanski, Hiroshi Teshigara, Bo Wilderberg, Marco Bellocchio and recently many exciting new directors from West Germany. (The festival, moreover, has a strong influence on what foreign films will have commercial runs in New York: the festival, for example, exposed 20% of the foreign films that played in first-run commercial bookings in New York during 1977/78, a considerable percentage considering the festival's short two-week run.)

It's customary to question the worth— even the function—of film festivals. All film festivals, New York's or Cannes's, are imperfect. It's easy for the circumstances of the festival to take precedence over the content of the films. But the New York Film Festival has served an important function for the American film community. At its best, the festival allows us to remember the magic that attracted us to movies in the first place.

The New York Film Festival is held in the fall, usually in September-October. Short films are often screened before a feature at the fetival, but these are not listed below unless several shorts had been grouped to comprise a whole program.

1963

Jacques Bartier, *Dragées au Poivre*
Robert Bresson, *Le Procès de Jeanne d'Arc*
Luis Buñuel,*The Exterminating Angel*
Robert Enrico, *Au Coeur de la Vie*
Tamás Fejér,*Love in the Suburbs*
Jean-Luc Godard, Ugo Gregoretti, Pier Paolo Pasolini, Roberto Rossellini, *Rogopag*
Takis Kanelopoulos,*The Sky*
Masaki Kobayashi, *Harakiri*
Leacock/Pennebaker, *Crisis & the Chair*
Joseph Losey, *The Servant*
Chris Marker, *Le Joli Mai*
Adolfas Mekas, *Hallelujah the Hills*
Jean-Pierre Melville, *L'Aine des Ferchaux*
Takis Mouzenidis, *Elektra at Epidaurus*
Ermanno Olmi. *The Fiancés*
Yasujiro Ozu, *An Autumn Afternoon*
Giuseppe Patroni Griffi, *Il Mare*
Roman Polanski, *Knife in the Water*
Alain Resnais, *Muriel*
Glauber Rocha, *Barravento*
Alex Segal, *All the Way Home*
Leopoldo Torre Nilsson, *The Terrace*

1964

Ricardo Alventosa, *La Herencia*
Bernardo Bertolucci, *Before the Revolution*
Luis Buñuel, *L'Age d'Or*
Luis Buñuel, *Diary of a Chambermaid*
Jörn Donner, *To Love*
Abel Gance, *Cyrano et D'Artagnan*
Jean-Luc Godard, *Bande à Part*
Jean-Luc Godard, *Une Femme est une Femme*
Susumu Hani, *She and He*
Kon Ichikawa, *Conflagration*
Kon Ichikawa, *Alone on the Pacific*
Alain Jessua, *La Vie à l'Envers*
Grigori Kozintsev, *Hamlet*
Joseph Losey, *King and Country*
Sidney Lumet, *Fail Safe*
Adolfas and Jonas Mekas, *The Brig*
Kenji Mizoguchi, *The Taira Clan*
Andrzej Munk, *Passenger*
Don Owen, *Nobody Waved Good-bye*
Satyajit Ray, *The Great City*
Michael Roemer, *Nothing But a Man*
Francesco Rosi, *Le Mani sulla Città*
Francesco Rosi, *Salvatore Giuliano*
Robert Rossen, *Lilith*
Hiroshi Teshigahara, *Woman in the Dunes*

Andrzej Wajda, *Fury Is a Woman*

1965

Michelangelo Antonioni, *La Signora senza Camelie*
Marco Bellocchio, *I Pugni in Tasca*
Kevin Billington, *Twilight of Empire*
Claude Chabrol, Jean Douchet, Jean-Luc Godard, Jean-Daniel Pollet, Eric Rohmer, Jean Rouch, *Paris vu par. . .*
René Clement, *Knave of Hearts*
John Cromwell, *Of Human Bondage*
Carl Dreyer, *Gertrud*
Louis Feuillade, *Les Vampires*
Milos Forman, *Black Peter*
Georges Franju, *Thomas l'Imposteur*
Jean-Luc Godard, *Alphaville*
Jean-Luc Godard, *Le Petit Soldat*
James Ivory, *Shakespeare Wallah*
Jan Kadar, Elmar Klos, *The Shop on Main Street*
Buster Keaton, *Seven Chances*
Laurence L. Kent, *Caressed*
Akira Kurosawa, *Red Beard*
Chris Marker, *Le Mystère Koumiko*
Arthur Penn, *Mickey One*
Gerald Potterton, *The Railrodder*
Satyajit Ray, *Charulata*
Alan Schneider, *Film*

Jerzy Skolimowski, *Identification Marks: None*
Jerzy Skolimowski, *Walkover*
Jean-Marie Straub, *Unreconciled*
Erich von Stroheim, *The Wedding March*
Luchino Visconti, *Vaghe Stelle del'Orsa*
Bo Widerberg, *Raven's End*

1966

René Allio, *The Shameless Old Lady*
Gianni Amico, *Notes for a Film on Jazz*
Vera Chytilova, Jaromil Jires, Jan Nemec, Ewald Schorm, Jiri Menzel, *Pearls on the Ground*
Bernardo Bertolucci, *The Grim Reaper*
Robert Bresson, *Au Hasard, Balthazar*
Clarence Brown, *A Woman of Affairs*
Luis Buñuel, *Simon of the Desert*
Henning Carlsen, *Hunger*
André Delvaux, *The Man with the Shaven Head*
Cecil B. De Mille, *The Cheat*
Vittorio De Sica, *Un Uomo a Meta*
Milos Forman, *Loves of a Blonde*
Jean-Luc Godard, *Masculin-Féminin*
Jean-Luc Godard, *Pierrot le Fou*
Pavel Hobl, *Do You Keep a Lion at Home?*
Kon Ichikawa, *The Burmese Harp*
Miklós Jancsó, *The Roundup*
Robert Machover, Norm Fruchter, *Troublemakers*
Maysles Brothers, *Meet Marlon Brando*
Sergei Paradjhanov, *Shadows of Our Forgotten Ancestors*
Pier Paolo Pasolini, *Accattone*
Pier Paolo Pasolini, *The Hawks and the Sparrows*
Ivan Passer, *Intimate Lighting*
Aleksandar Petrovic, *Three*

Alain Resnais, *La Guerre est finie*
Carlos Saura, *The Hunt*
Leopoldo Torre Nilsson, *The Eavesdropper*
Agnès Varda, *Les Créatures*
Peter Watkins, *The War Game*
Peter Whitehead, *Wholly Communion*

1967

René Allio, *L'Une et l'Autre*
Donald Brittain, John Spotton, *Memorandum*
Shirley Clarke, *Portrait of Jason*
Jonas Cornell, *Hugs and Kisses*
Mark Donskoi, *Sons and Mothers*
Abel Gance, *Napoleon*
Jean-Luc Godard, *Les Carabiniers*
Jean-Luc Godard, Joris Ivens, William Klein, Claude Lelouch, Alain Resnais, Agnès Varda, *Far from Vietnam*
Jean-Luc Godard, *Made in USA*
Alexander Kluge, *Yesterday Girl*
Masaki Kobayashi, *Rebellion*
John Korty, *Funnyman*
Dragoslav Lazic, *The Feverish Years*
Dusan Makavejev, *An Affair of the Heart*
Rouben Mamoulian, *Applause*
Gillo Pontecorvo, *The Battle of Algiers*
Roberto Rossellini, *The Rise of Louis XIV*
Jean Rouch, *La Chasse au Lion a l'Arc*
Volker Schlöndorff, *Young Torless*
Jerzy Skolimowski, *Barbiera*
Jerzy Skolimowski, *Le Départ*
Istvan Szabo, *Father*
King Vidor, *Show People*
Peter Whitehead, *Tonite Let's All Make Love in London*
Peter Whitehead, *The Benefit of the Doubt*
Bo Widerberg, *Elvira Madigan*

1968

Gianni Amico, *Tropics*
Bernardo Bertolucci, *Partner*
Robert Bresson, *Mouchette*
John Cassavetes, *Faces*
Claude Chabrol, *Les Biches*
Dominique Delouche, *24 Heures de la Vie d'une Femme*
Milos Forman, *The Fireman's Ball*
Jean-Luc Godard, *Deux ou trois Choses que je sais d'elle*
Jean-Luc Godard, *Weekend*
Kjell Grede, *Hugo and Josefin*
Werner Herzog, *Signs of Life*
Miklós Jancsó, *The Red and the White*
Alexander Kluge, *Artists Under the Big Top: Perplexed*
Marcel L'Herbier, *L'Argent*
Norman Mailer, *Beyond the Law*
Jiri Menzel, *Capricious Summer*
Vatroslav Mimica, *Kaya*
Jan Nemec, *Report on the Party and the Guests*
Max Ophuls, *Lola Montes*
Maurice Pialat, *L'Enfance Nue*
Jean Renoir, *Toni*
Jacques Rivette, *Suzanne Simonin, La Religieuse de Diderot*
Jean-Marie Straub, *Chronicle of Anna Magdalena Bach*
Orson Welles, *Histoire Immortelle*

1969

René Allio, *Pierre and Paul*
Richard Attenborough, *Oh, What a Lovely War*
Ingmar Bergman, *The Ritual*
Walerian Borowczyk, *Goto, l'Ile d'Amour*
Robert Bresson, *Une Femme Douce*
Bill Duncalf, *The Epic That Never Was (I, Claudius)*
Marguerite Duras, *Détruire, Dit-Elle*

Judit Elek, *The Lady from Constantinople*
Jean-Luc Godard, *Le Gai Savior*
Juro Jakubisko, *The Deserter and the Nomads*
Jaromil Jires, *The Joke*
Paul Mazursky, *Bob & Carol & Ted & Alice*
Ermanno Olmi, *Un Certo Giorno*
Max Ophuls, *La Ronde*
Nagisa Oshima, *Boy*
Pier Paolo Pasolini, *Pigpen*
Eric Rohmer, *My Night at Maud's*
Ousmane Sembène, *Manadabi*
Victor Sjöstrom, *He Who Gets Slapped*
Susan Sontag, *Duet for Cannibals*
Erich von Stroheim, *The Merry Widow*
Agnès Varda, *Lions Love*
Bo Widerberg, *Adalen '31*

1970

Bernardo Bertolucci, *The Conformist*
Bernardo Bertolucci, *Strategia del Ragno*
Luis Buñuel, *Tristana*
Liliana Cavani, *I Cannibali*
Claude Chabrol, *Le Boucher*
Carlos Diegues, *The Inheritors*
Marguerite Duras, Paul Seban, *La Musica*
Dick Fontaine, *Double Pisces, Scorpio Rising*
Lasse Forsberg, *Mistreatment*
Hollis Frampton, *Zorns Lemma*
Jean-Luc Godard, *Wind from the East*
Kjell Grede, *Harry Munter*
Marcel Hanoun, *Une Simple Histoire*
Maurice Hatton, *Praise Marx and Pass the Ammunition*
Werner Herzog, *Even Dwarfs Started Small*
Marin Karmitz, *Camarades*
Ken Loach, *Kes*
Kenji Mizoguchi, *Chikamatzu Monogatari*
Ermanno Olmi, *I Recuperanti*

Bob Rafelson, *Five Easy Pieces*
Satyajit Ray, *Days and Nights in the Forest*
Alain Resnais, *Je t'aime, je t'aime*
Carlos Saura, *The Garden of Delights*
Martin Scorsese, *Street Scenes 1970*
Jean-Marie Straub, *Othon*
Francois Truffaut, *The Wild Child*
French Silent Cinema Program

1971

Marco Bellocchio, *In the Name of the Father*
Peter Bogdanovich, *Directed by John Ford*
Peter Bogdanovich, *The Last Picture Show*
Robert Bresson, *Four Nights of a Dreamer*
Rainer Werner Fassbinder, *Recruits in Ingolstadt*
Abel Gance, *Bonaparte and the Revolution*
Werner Herzog, *Fata Morgana*
Henry Jaglom, *A Safe Place*
Akira Kurosawa, *Dodes 'Ka-Den*
Dusan Makavejev, *WR-Mysteries of the Organism*
Louis Malle, *Murmur of the Heart*
Ermanno Olmi, *In the Summertime*
Marcel Ophuls, *The Sorrow and the Pity*
Gleb Panfilov, *The Debut*
Pier Paolo Pasolini, *Decameron*
Ivan Passer, *Born to Win*
Peter Watkins, *Punishment Park*
Krzysztof Zanussi, *Family Life*

1972

Robert Altman, *Images*
Robert Benton, *Bad Company*

Bernardo Bertolucci, *Last Tango in Paris*
Luis Buñuel, *The Discreet Charm of the Bourgeoisie*
Marguerite Duras, *Nathalie Granger*
Rainer Werner Fassbinder, *Merchant of Four Seasons*
Philippe Garrel, *Inner Scar*
Jean-Luc Godard and Jean-Pierre Gorin, *Tout Va Bien*
Miklós Jancsó, *Red Psalm*
Kenneth Loach, *Wednesday's Child*
Joseph Losey, *The Assassination of Trotsky*
Karoly Makk, *Love*
Adolfas Mekas, *Going Home*
Jonas Mekas, *Reminiscences of a Journey to Lithuania*
Paul Morrissey, *Heat*
Marcel Ophuls, *A Sense of Loss*
Maurice Pialat, *We Won't Grow Old Together*
Bob Rafelson, *The King of Marvin Gardens*
Satyajit Ray, *The Adversary*
Jacques Rivette, *L'Amour Fou*
Eric Rohmer, *Chlöe in the Afternoon*
Hiroshi Teshigahara, *Summer Soldiers*
Francois Truffaut, *Two English Girls*
Krzysztof Zanussi, *Behind the Wall*

NEW DIRECTORS / NEW FILMS

Tomas Guttierez Alea, *Memories of Underdevelopment*
Bata Cengic, *The Role of My Family in the World Revolution*
Edgardo Cozarinsky, *Dot Dot Dot*
Pal Gabor, *Horizon*
Claude Guillemot, *The Truce*
Barney Platts-Mills, *Private Road*
David Schickele, *Bushman*
Alain Tanner, *La Salamandre*
Christain Braad Thomsen, *Dear Irene*
Wim Wenders, *The Goalie's Anxiety at the Penalty Kick*

1973

Gianni Amico, *Return*
Denys Arcand, *Rejeanne Padovani*
Claude Chabrol, *Just Before Nightfall*
Claude Chabrol, *La Rupture*
Jean Eustache, *The Mother and the Whore*
Rainer Werner Fassbinder, *The Bitter Tears of Petra von Kant*
James Frawley, *Kid Blue*
Fritz Lang, *Doktor Mabuse*
Claude Lanzmann, *Israel Why*
Joseph Losey, *A Doll's House*
Terrence Malick, *Badlands*
Satyajit Ray, *Distant Thunder*
Martin Scorsese, *Mean Streets*
Jean-Marie Straub, *History Lessons*
Andrei Tarkovsky, *Andrei Rublev*
Francois Truffaut, *Day for Night*
Krzysztof Zanussi, *Illumination*

NEW DIRECTORS / NEW FILMS

Metodi Andonov, *The Goat Horn*
Niki de St. Phalle, Peter Whitehead, *Daddy*
Claude Faraldo, *Themroc*
Juraj Herz, *The Cremator*
Anthony Korner, *Helen, Queen of the Nautch Girls*
Paul Leduc, *John Reed (Mexican Insurgent)*
Toichiro Narushima, *Time Within Memory*
Shinsuke Ogawa, *Peasants of the Second Fortress*
Ababacar Samb, *Kodou*
Daniel Schmid, *Tonight or Never*
Pascal Thomas, *Les Zozos*

1974

Mirra Bank, *Yudie*
Robert Bresson, *Lancelot of the Lake*

Luis Buñuel, *Le Fantôme de la Liberté*
Luis Buñuel, Homage to Buñuel: *L'Age d'Or, The Exterminating Angel, The Milky Way, The Discreet Charm of the Bourgeoisie*
John Cassavetes, *A Woman Under the Influence*
Martha Coolidge, *An Old Fashioned Woman*
Rainer Werner Fassbinder, *All*
William Greaves, *From These Roots*
Jack Hazan, *A Bigger Splash*
Miklós Jancsó, *Rome Wants Another Caesar*
Alexander Kluge, *Part-Time Work of a Domestic Slave*
Louis Malle, *Lacombe, Lucien*
Jean-Pierre Melville, *Les Enfants Terribles*
Ermanno Olmi, *The Circumstance*
Max Ophuls, *Liebelei*
Alain Resnais, *Stavisky*
Sergio Ricardo, *The Night of the Scarecrow*
Jacques Rivette, *Celine and Julie Go Boating*
Jacques Rivette, *Out One Spectre*
Daniel Schmid, *La Paloma*
Martin Scorsese, *Italian-americans*
Alain Tanner, *The Middle of the World*
Pascal Thomas, *Don't Cry with Your Mouth Full*
Wim Wenders, *Alice in the Cities*

1975

Jean-Francois Davy, *Exhibition*
John Douglas and Robert Kramer, *Milestones*
Marguerite Duras, *India Song*
Rainer Werner Fassbinder, *Fist-Right of Freedom*
Claude Goretta, *The Wonderful Crook*
Werner Herzog, *Every Man for Himself and God Against All*
James Ivory, *Autobiography of a Princess*
Miklós Jancsó, *Elektreia*

Louis Malle, *Black Moon*
Maysles Brothers, *Grey Gardens*
Jean Renoir, *La Chienne*
Michael Ritchie, *Smile*
Volker Schlondorff and Margarethe von Trotta, *The Lost Honor of Katharina Blum*
Ousmane Sembene, *Xala*
Martin Smith, *Companero*
Jean-Marie Straub and Daniele Huillet, *Moses and Aaron*
Andre Techine, *French Provincial*
Francois Truffaut, *Story of Adele H*
Luchino Visconti, *Conversation Piece*
Orson Welles, *F for Fake*
Howard Zieff, *Hearts of the West*

1976

Walerian Borowczyk, *Story of a Sin*
Rainer Werner Fassbinder, *Fear of Fear*
Eduardo de Gregorio, *Serail*
King Hu, *Touch of Zen*
Ray Karp, *Sunday Funnies*
Alexander Kluge, *Strongman Ferdinand*
Barbara Kopple, *Harlan County, USA*
Akira Kurosawa, *Dersu Uzala*
Marcel Ophuls, *Memory of Justice*
Nagisa Oshima, *In the Realm of the Senses* (seized by customs, shown after festival)
Satyajit Ray, *The Middleman*
Jean Renoir, *Nana*
Jacques Rivette, *Duelle*
Eric Rohmer, *The Marquise of O*
Francesco Rosi, *Illustrious Corpses*
Joan Micklin Silver, *Bernice Bobs Her Hair*
Alain Tanner, *Jonah Who Will Be 25 in the Year 2000*
Francois Truffaut, *Small Change*
Luchino Visconti, *Ossessione*

Wim Wenders, *King of the Road*
Peter Werner, *In the Region of Ice*

1977

Merzak Allouache, *Omar Gatlato*
Bernardo Bertolucci, *1900*
Robert Bresson, *The Devil Probably*
Martin Brest, *Hot Tomorrows*
Noel Buchner, Mary Dore, Richard Broadman, and Al Gedicks, *Children of Labor*
Luis Buñuel, *That Obscure Object of Desire*
Rafael Corkidi, *Pufnucio Santo*
Jonathan Demme, *Handle With Care* (formerly Citizens Band)
Pereira dos Santos, *Tent of Miracles*
Marguerite Duras, *The Truck*
Claude Goretta, *The Lacemaker*
Werner Herzog, *Heart of Glass*
James Ivory, *Roseland*
Márta Mészáros, *Women*
Kote Mikaberitze, *My Grandmother*
Bill Miles, *Men of Bronze*
Pier Paolo Pasolini, *Salò*
Léonce Perret, *L'Enfant de Paris*
Paolo and Vittorio Taviani, *Padre Padrone*
Francois Truffaut, *L'Homme Qui Aimait les Femmes*
Agnés Varda, *One Sings, The Other Doesn't*
Robert M. Young, *Short Eyes*
Wim Wenders, *The American Friend*

SAVED (A retrospective of American films)

Clarence Badger, *It*
Monta Bell, *Downstairs*
Monta Bell, *The Letter*
Monta Bell, *The Torrent*
Frank Borzage, *Liliom*

William K. Howard, *Trans-atlantic*
F. W. Murnau, *City Girl*
Edward Sutherland, *It's the Old Army Game*
King Vidor, *Wild Oranges*
Raoul Walsh, *Regeneration*
Sam Wood, *Paid*
William Wyler, *Dodsworth*

1978

Robert Altman, *A Wedding*
Gianni Amico, *Elective Affinities*
Luc Béraud, *Like A Turtle on its Back*
Raymond Bernard, *The Miracle of the Wolves*
Bertrand Blier, *Get Out Your Handkerchiefs*
Claude Chabrol, *Violette*
Vera Chytilova, *The Apple Game*
Zale R. Dalen, *Skip Tracer*
Michel Deville, *Dossier 51*
Rainer Werner Fassbinder, *Despair*
Lorraine Gray, *With Babies and Banners: Story of the Women's Emergency Brigade*
Peter Handke, *The Left-Handed Woman*
Peter Hayden, *Movies Are My Life*
Saul Landau, *CIA: Case Officer*
Fritz Lang, *Spies*
Robin Lehman, *Manimals*
Errol Morris, *Gates of Heaven*
Robert Mulligan, *Bloodbrothers*
Margaret Murphy and Lucille Rhodes, *They are Their Own Gifts*
Phillip Noyce, *Newsfront*
Eric Rohmer, *Perceval*
Martin Scorsese, *American Boy*
Jerzy Skolimowski, *The Shout*
Francois Truffaut, *The Green Room*
Krzysztof Zanussi, *Camouflage*

New Currents In Japanese Cinema:

Yoichi Higashi, *Third Base*
Shohei Imamura, *The Pornographer*
Kazuo Kuroki, *Preparation for the Festival*
Shinsuke Ogawa, *Sanrizuka: The Skies of May*
Shuji Terayama, *Pastoral Hide-and-Seek*

1979

Gill Armstrong, *My Brilliant Career*
Carroll Ballard, *The Black Stallion*
Bernardo Bertolucci, *Luna*
Stewart Bird and Deborah Shaffer, *The Wobblies*
Youssef Chahine, *Alexandria . . . Why?*
Christian de Chalonge, *L'Argent des autres*
Rainer Werner Fassbinder, *In a Year of 13 Moons*
Rainer Werner Fassbinder, *The Marriage of Maria Braun*
Pal Gabor, *Angi Vera*
Eduardo de Gregorio, *La Memoire courte*
Howard Hawks, *Scarface*
Werner Herzog, *Nosferatu, The Vampyre*
John Huston, *Wise Blood*
James Ivory, *The Europeans*
Chuck Jones, *The Bugs Bunny/Road-Runner Movie*
Kenneth Loach, *Black Jack*
Ariane Mnouchkine, *Molière*
Anne Claire Poirier, *Mourir a Tue-Tete*
Michael Powell, *Peeping Tom*
Jean Renoir, *The Golden Coach*
Preston Sturges, *Mad Wednesday*
Andrzej Wajda, *Panny z Wilka*
Andrzej Wajda, *Without Anesthesia*
Ira Wohl, *Best Boy*

V. THE "TEN BEST" LISTS

1/BEST FILMS OF ALL TIME: DIRECTORS' CHOICES (1952 BELGIAN SURVEY) AND CRITICS' CHOICES (THE 1952, 1962, AND 1972 SIGHT AND SOUND SURVEYS)

IN 1952, THE committee of the *Festival Mondial du Film et des Beaux Arts de Belgique* asked more than a hundred film personalities (mainly directors) to select the Ten Best films of all time. Sixty-three answers were received: 26 from France; 10 from England; 10 from the United States; seven from Italy; six from Germany; one each from Austria, Denmark, Spain and Brazil; and none from India, Japan, China or Russia. Several directors, like Charles Chaplin, Erich von Stroheim, Rene Clair, Jean Cocteau, Alfred Hitchcock, and Laurence Olivier, did not wish to answer the questionnaire.

The committee asked each director to select *his own* favorites and not the films he thought would be preferred by academic orthodoxy. The results are, of course, interesting; who would have thought Carl Dreyer to be so fond of *The Petrified Forest,* or Buñuel of *Portrait of Jennie?* The absence of Jean Renoir's *Rules of the Game* was thought unusual, as were the generally low ratings for D. W. Griffith, Jean Vigo, and John Ford. Many directors voted for their own films: Cecil B. DeMille chose four of his own movies *(The Ten Commandments, King of Kings, The Sign of the Cross, Samson and Delilah)*; Luis Buñuel gave his *L'Age d'Or* a ninth-place vote; and King Vidor gave his *Big Parade* fourth place.

As a sequel to the 1952 Belgian survey in which approximately a hundred film directors voted for the Ten Best films of all time, *Sight and Sound* (the highly respected magazine published by the British Film Institute), the same year, conducted a survey in which critics were given their chance to select the Ten Best films. Eighty-five critics from Britain, France, the United States, Germany, Denmark, Sweden, Belgium, Czechoslovakia and Yugoslavia were asked; 63 answered. Surprisingly enough, the directors and the critics agreed on their top four choices, although not on the order of those choices.

Although most of the critics had several reservations about such a poll (their "favorite" films were not always the "best" films; the limitations of only listing 10 films were barbarous; the whole concept of the survey was ridiculous, etc.) the survey proved so interesting that it was repeated both in 1962 and 1972.

Between 1952 and 1962, cinema saw the rise of the French New Wave, the discovery of Japanese film, the growth of Italian cinema, as well as growing cinemas in Eastern Europe and Latin America. Some of these changes were reflected in the 1962 survey: only four of the Ten Best films in the 1952 poll remained in the top ten in 1962. The poll revealed several surprises: (1) the rise of *Citizen Kane* to first place—it hadn't even been a runner-up in 1952; (2) the decrease in the number of silent films selected—six in 1952 but only two in 1962; (3) the absence of Ingmar Bergman, who was then one of the most widely talked-about directors; and (4) the disappearance of any Chaplin film from the Ten Best.

The 1972 survey was sent to one hundred critics; 70 answered. Again, *Sight and Sound* asked the critics to select their personal choices, not those they believed others might choose. The majority of critics were British, French and American. Eighty-nine critics responded to the poll, and again the results were interesting: (1)

Ingmar Bergman finally entered the list with *Persona,* as did Frederico Fellini with *8½*; (2) Buster Keaton had been rediscovered, and Charlie Chaplin was almost forgotten; (3) Jean Vigo's popularity faded; and (4) there was little evidence of the underground's influence.

Only two films have remained on all three lists: *Potemkin* and *La Règle du Jeu (Rules of the Game).*

As the editors of *Sight and Sound* have noted, Top Ten lists are best approached with trepidation or amusement by compilers and with some skepticism by readers. Obviously one doesn't get an "objective" view of the best films ever made from such lists. These lists, however, do provide an important indication of how opinion changes, how international perspective shifts, whether the silent cinema still holds its ground, what cinema looked like in the perspective of 1952, 1962 and 1972. In short, Top Ten lists, despite their obvious limitations, give us vital—not to mention entertaining—information.

Whenever two or more films received the same number of votes in the following surveys, the tied movies are listed under the same numerical placement. The film receiving the next number of votes is then given a numerical placement that takes into account the preceding tie. For example, in the 1972 survey, *L'Avventura* and *Persona* tied for fifth place. *The Passion of Joan of Arc,* which received the next number of votes, is then said to occupy seventh place.

TEN BEST FILMS OF
ALL TIME

1952
CINEMATHEQUE BELGIQUE SURVEY

THE TEN BEST FILMS
1. *Battleship Potemkin* (Sergei Eisenstein, 1925)
2. *The Gold Rush* (Charlie Chaplin, 1925)
3. *The Bicycle Thief* (Vittorio De Sica, 1949)
4. *City Lights* (Charles Chaplin, 1930)
   La Grande Illusion (Jean Renoir, 1937)
   Le Million (René Clair, 1930)
7. *Greed* (Erich Von Stroheim, 1924)
8. *Hallelujah!* (King Vidor, 1929)
9. *Die Dreigroschenoper* (G. W. Pabst, 1931)
   Brief Encounter (David Lean, 1945)
   Intolerance (D. W. Griffith, 1916)
   Man of Aran (Robert Flaherty, 1934)

MAIN RUNNERS-UP
1. *The Passion of Joan of Arc* (Carl Dreyer, 1928)
2. *Les Enfants du Paradis* (Marcel Carné, 1944)
   Foolish Wives (Erich Von Stroheim, 1921)
   Storm Over Asia (V. Pudovkin, 1928)
5. *L'Age d'Or* (Buñuel, 1930)
   Birth of a Nation (D. W. Griffith, 1915)

1952
SIGHT AND SOUND SURVEY

TEN BEST
1. *The Bicycle Thief* (Vittorio De Sica, 1949)
2. *City Lights* (Charles Chaplin, 1930)
   The Gold Rush (Charles Chaplin, 1925)
4. *Battleship Potemkin* (Sergei Eisenstein, 1925)
5. *Louisiana Story* (Robert Flaherty, 1947)
   Intolerance (D. W. Griffith, 1916)
7. *Greed* (Erich Von Stroheim, 1924)
   Le Jour se lève (Marcel Carné, 1939)
   The Passion of Joan of Arc (Carl Dreyer, 1928)
10. *Brief Encounter* (David Lean, 1945)
    Le Million (René Clair, 1930)
    La Régle du Jeu (Jean Renoir, 1939)

RUNNERS-UP
1. *Citizen Kane* (Orson Welles, 1941)
   La Grande Illusion (Jean Renoir, 1937)
   The Grapes of Wrath (John Ford, 1940)
4. *The Childhood of Maxim Gorki* (Mark Donskoi, 1938)
   Monsieur Verdoux (Charles Chaplin, 1947)

1962
SIGHT AND SOUND SURVEY

TEN BEST
1. *Citizen Kane* (Orson Welles, 1941)
2. *L'Avventura* (Michelangelo Antonioni, 1960)
3. *La Règle du Jeu* (Jean Renoir, 1939)
4. *Greed* (Erich Von Stroheim, 1924)
   Ugetsu Monogatari (Kenji Mizoguchi, 1953)
6. *Battleship Potemkin* (Sergei Eisenstein, 1925)
   The Bicycle Thief (Vittorio De Sica, 1949)
   Ivan the Terrible (Sergei Eisenstein, 1943-46)
9. *La Terra Trema* (Luchino Visconti, 1948)
10. *L'Atalante* (Jean Vigo, 1933)

RUNERS-UP
1. *Hiroshima Mon Amour* (Alain Resnais, 1959)
   Pather Panchali (Satyajit Ray, 1955)
   Zéro de Conduite (Jean Vigo, 1933)
4. *City Lights* (Charles Chaplin, 1930)
   The Childhood of Maxim Gorki (Mark Donskoi, 1938)

1972
SIGHT AND SOUND SURVEY

TEN BEST
1. *Citizen Kane* (Orson Welles, 1941)
2. *La Règle du Jeu* (Jean Renoir, 1939)
3. *Battleship Potemkin* (Sergei Eisenstein, 1925)
4. *8½* (Federico Fellini, 1963)
5. *L'Avventura* (Michelangelo Antonioni, 1960)
   Persona (Ingmar Bergman, 1967)
7. *The Passion of Joan of Arc* (Carl Dreyer, 1928)
8. *The General* (Buster Keaton/Clyde Bruckman, 1926)
   The Magnificent Ambersons (Orson Welles, 1942)
10. *Ugetsu Monogatari* (Kenji Mizoguchi, 1953)
   Wild Strawberries (Ingmar Bergman, 1957)

RUNNERS-UP
1. *The Gold Rush* (Charles Chaplin, 1925)
   Hiroshima Mon Amour (Alain Resnais, 1959)
   Ikiru (Akira Kurosawa, 1952)
   Ivan the Terrible (Sergei Eisenstein, 1943-46)
   Pierrot le Fou (Jean-Luc Godard, 1965)
   Vertigo (Alfred Hitchcock, 1958)

1952
CINEMATHEQUE BELGIQUE SURVEY (CONTINUED)

Broken Blossoms (D. W. Griffith, 1919)
Devil in the Flesh (Claude Autant-Lara, 1946)

1952
SIGHT AND SOUND SURVEY (CONTINUED)

Que Viva Mexico (Sergei Eisenstein, 1931)
7. *Earth* (Alexander Dovzhenko, 1929)
Zéro de Conduite (Jean Vigo, 1933)
9. *Broken Blossoms* (D. W. Griffith, 1919)
Les Dames du Bois de Boulogne (Robert Bresson, 1945)
Hallelujah! (King Vidor, 1929)

VOTING BY DIRECTORS
(not calculated in 1952)

A SELECTION OF LISTS
Robert Bresson:
1. *The Gold Rush*
2. *City Lights*
3. *Potemkin*

A SELECTION OF LISTS
Lotte H. Eisner (France):
1. *Monsieur Verdoux*
2. *The Gold Rush*
3. *Birth of a Nation*

1962
**SIGHT AND SOUND
SURVEY (CONTINUED)**

The Gold Rush (Charles Chaplin, 1925)
7. *Sunrise* (F. W. Murnau, 1927)
8. *Earth* (Alexander Dovzhenko, 1930)
Monsieur Verdoux (Charles Chaplin, 1947)
10. *The General* (Buster Keaton, 1927)
La Grande Illusion (Jean Renoir, 1937)
Ikiru (Akira Kurosawa, 1952)
Nazarin (Luis Buñuel, 1958)
October (Sergei Eisenstein, 1928)
Umberto D. (Vittorio De Sica, 1951)

VOTING BY DIRECTORS
1. Sergei Eisenstein
2. Charles Chaplin
3. Jean Renoir
4. Orson Welles
5. Michelangelo Antonioni
6. Vittorio De Sica
7. Alain Resnais
   Jean Vigo
9. Kenji Mizoguchi
10. Erich Von Stroheim
11. Luis Buñuel
    Luchino Visconti

A SELECTION OF LISTS
Lotte H. Eisner (France):
1. *The Idiot* (Kurosawa)
2. *Ugetsu Monogatari*

1972
**SIGHT AND SOUND
SURVEY (CONTINUED)**

7. *La Grande Illusion* (Jean Renoir, 1937)
Mouchette (Robert Bresson, 1966)
The Searchers (John Ford, 1956)
Sunrise (F. W. Murnau, 1927)
2001: A Space Odyssey (Stanley Kubrick, 1968)
Viridiana (Luis Buñuel, 1961)

VOTING BY DIRECTORS
1. Orson Welles
2. Jean Renoir
3. Ingmar Bergman
4. Luis Buñuel
5. Sergei Eisenstein
6. John Ford
   Jean-Luc Godard
8. Buster Keaton
9. Federico Fellini
10. Michelangelo Antonioni
    Charles Chaplin
    Carl Dreyer

A SELECTION OF LISTS
Lotte H. Eisner (France):
1. *Earth*
2. *Greed*

1952
CINEMATHEQUE BELGIQUE SURVEY (CONTINUED)

4. *Brief Encounter*
5. *The Bicycle Thief*
6. *Man of Aran*
7. *Louisiana Story*

Elia Kazan:
1. *Potemkin*
2. *Aerograd* (Dovzhenko)
3. *The Gold Rush*
4. *Flesh and the Devil* (Brown)
5. *Open City*
6. *The Bicycle Thief*
7. *Shoulder Arms* (Chaplin)
8. *Target for Tonight* (Watt)
9. *Le Femme du Boulanger* (Pagnol)
10. *Marius, Fanny, Cesar* (Pagnol)

Carl Dreyer:
1. *Birth of a Nation*
2. *Arne's Treasure* (Stiller)
3. *Potemkin*
4. *The Gold Rush*
5. *Sous les Toits de Paris* (Clair)
6. *Quai des Brumes* (Carné)

1952
SIGHT AND SOUND SURVEY (CONTINUED)

4. *Potemkin*
5. *Greed*
6. *L'Age d'Or*
7. *Zéro de Conduite*
8. *Earth*
9. *Tabu* (Flaherty-Murnau)
10. *Louisiana Story*

Penelope Huston (England):
(alphabetical order)
1. *L'Atalante*
2. *Citizen Kane*
3. *City Lights*
4. *Les Dames du Bois de Boulogne*
5. *Earth*
6. *The General* (Keaton)
7. *The Grapes of Wrath*
8. *Greed*
9. *October*
10. *La Règle du Jeu*

Curtis Harrington (USA):
(not in order of preference)
1. *Greed*
2. *Zéro de Conduite*
4. *The Devil Is a Woman* (Sternberg)
5. *Vampyr* (Dreyer)
6. *L'Age d'Or*

1962
SIGHT AND SOUND
SURVEY (CONTINUED)

3. *Nazarin*
4. *Ivan the Terrible* (color sequence, Part II)
5. *Monsieur Verdoux*
6. *Fires on the Plain* (Ichikawa)
7. *Greed*
8. *Sunrise*
9. *Partie de Champagne* (Renoir)
10. *Zéro, de Conduite*

Penelope Houston (England):
(alphabetical order)
1. *L'Année dernière à Marienbad*
2. *L'Atalante*
3. *L'Avventura*
4. *Citizen Kane*
5. *The General*
6. *The Maltese Falcon*
7. *October*
8. *La Règle du Jeu*
9. *La Terra Trema*
10. *Ugetsu Monogatari*

Curtis Harrington (USA):
1. *Greed*
2. *Zéro de Conduite*
3. *La Règle du Jeu*
4. *The Devil Is a Woman*
5. *Dura Lex*
6. *Les Dames du Bois de Boulogne*
7. *Rashomon*
8. *I Vitelloni*

1972
SIGHT AND SOUND
SURVEY (CONTINUED)

3. *Ivan the Terrible* (color sequence, Part II)
4. *The Idiot*
5. *M*
6. *Monsieur Verdoux*
7. *The Passion of Joan of Arc*
8. *La Règle du Jeu*
9. *Senso* (Visconti)
10. *Sunrise*

Penelope Houston (England):
(alphabetical order)
1. *Au Hasard Balthazar* (Bresson)
2. *Charulata*
3. *Citizen Kane*
4. *The Eclipse*
5. *The General*
6. *Miracle of Morgan's Creek*
7. *Muriel*
8. *La Règle du Jeu*
9. *Silence and Cry* (Jancsó)
10. *2001: A Space Odyssey*

Peter Bogdanovich (USA):
(in chronological order)
1. *Only Angels Have Wings*
2. *Young Mr. Lincoln*
3. *The Magnificent Ambersons*
4. *Red River*
5. *She Wore a Yellow Ribbon*
6. *The Searchers*
7. *Rio Bravo*

1952
CINEMATHEQUE BELGIQUE SURVEY (CONTINUED)

7. *Brief Encounter*
8. *Henry V*
9. *The Petrified Forest* (Mayo)
10. *Open City*

David Lean:
1. *Intolerance*
2. *Variety* (Dupont)
3. *The Crowd* (Vidor)
4. *City Lights*
5. *White Shadows in the South Seas* (Van Dyke)
6. *A Nous la Libertél*
7. *La Grande Illusion*
8. *Les Enfants du Paradis*
9. *Le Jour se lève* (Carné)
10. *Citizen Kane*

Vittorio De Sica:
1. *Man of Aran*
2. *The Kid*
3. *La Chienne* (Renoir)
4. *Le Million*
5. *L'Atalante*
6. *Kameradschaft* (Pabst)
7. *Storm Over Asia*
8. *Potemkin*
9. *Hallelujahl*
10. *La Kermesse Héroique* (Feyder)

1952
SIGHT AND SOUND SURVEY (CONTINUED)

7. *Dura Lex* (Kuleshov)
8. *Never Give a Sucker an Even Break* (Cline)
9. *A Nous la Libertél*
10. *Les Dames du Bois de Boulogne*

Gavin Lambert (England):
1. *Greed*
2. *Earth*
3. *L'Age d'Or*
4. *La Règle du Jeu*
5. *The Kid*
6. *A Diary for Timothy* (Jennings)
7. *The Quiet Man* (Ford)
8. *Hallelujahl*
9. *Que Viva Mexico*
10. *Les Dames du Bois de Boulogne*

André Bazin (France):
1. *Les Vampires* (Fouillade)
2. *The Pilgrim* (Chaplin)
3. *Broken Blossoms*
4. *Sunrise*
5. *Greed*
6. *La Règle du Jeu*
7. *Le Jour se lève*
8. *The Little Foxes*
9. *Les Dames du Bois de Boulogne*
10. *The Bicycle Thief*

1962
**SIGHT AND SOUND
SURVEY (CONTINUED)**

9. *Citizen Kane*
10. *L'Avventura*

Gavin Lambert (England USA):
1. *L'Age d'Or*
2. *El* (Buñuel)
3. *Nazarin*
4. *Zéro de Conduite*
5. *Never Give A Sucker . . .*
6. *Ivan the Terrible*
7. *Modern Times*
8. *Moana* (Flaherty)
9. *Love of Jeanne Ney* (Pabst)
10. *Gone With the Wind*

Richard Roud (USA/England):
1. *L'Année dernière à Marienbad*
2. *L'Atalante*
3. *Citizen Kane*
4. *Cronaca di un Amore* (Antonioni)
5. *Les Dames du Bois de Boulogne*
6. *Hiroshima Mon Amour*
7. *La Notte*
8. *Pickpocket*
9. *La Règle du Jeu*
10. *Tokyo Story* (Ozu)

1972
**SIGHT AND SOUND
SURVEY (CONTINUED)**

8. *Touch of Evil*
9. *Vertigo*
10. *North by Northwest*

**Penelope Gilliatt
(England/USA):**
1. *The Navigator*
2. *La Règle du Jeu*
3. *8 ½*
4. *Persona*
5. *Ikiru*
6. *Citizen Kane*
7. *The Apu Trilogy*
8. *Battleship Potemkin*
9. *Jules et Jim*
10. *Weekend*

Richard Roud (USA/England):
1. *La Règle du Jeu*
2. *L'Atalante*
3. *Citizen Kane*
4. *Tokyo Story*
5. *Les Dames du Bois . . .*
6. *Deux ou trois Choses que je sais d'elle* (Godard)
7. *Not Reconciled*
8. *The Spider's Stratagem* (Bertolucci)
9. *The Go-Between* (Losey)
10. *Muriel*

1952
CINEMATHEQUE BELGIQUE SURVEY (CONTINUED)

Carol Reed:

1. *City Lights*
2. *Ninotchka* (Lubitsch)
3. *Les Enfants du Paradis*
4. *Gone With the Wind*
5. *La Ronde* (Ophuls)
6. *All Quiet on the Western Front*
7. *Le Kermesse Héroique*
8. *Variety*
9. *La Femme du Boulanger*
10. *Pygmalion* (Asquith)

King Vidor:
1. *Intolerance*
2. *Sunrise*
3. *Der letzte Mann* (Murnau)
4. *The Big Parade* (Vidor)
5. *Brief Encounter*
6. *Red Shoes* (Powell-Pressburger)
7. *Open City*
8. *City Lights*
9. *Citizen Kane*
10. *Best Years of Our Lives*

Billy Wilder:
1. *Potemkin*
2. *Greed*

1952
SIGHT AND SOUND SURVEY (CONTINUED)

Lindsay Anderson (England):

1. *Earth*
2. *They Were Expendable* (Ford)
3. *Zéro de Conduite*
4. *The Childhood of Maxim Gorki*
5. *The Grapes of Wrath*
   The Bicycle Thief
6. *Louisiana Story*
   The River
7. *Fires Were Started* (Jennings)
8. *La Règle du Jeu*
   Le Jour se lève
9. *Douce* (Autant-Lara)
   Antoine et Antoinette (Becker)
   Force of Evil (Polonsky)
10. *Meet Me in St. Louis*

Rudolf Arnheim (USA):
1. *The Wedding March*
2. *City Lights*
3. *The General*
4. *Potemkin*
5. *Road to Life* (Ekk)
6. *Our Daily Bread*
7. *Sous les Toits de Paris* (Clair)
8. *Man of Aran*
9. *The Bicycle Thief*
10. *Rashomon*

Henri Laglois (France):
1. *Chaplin's 1916 films*
2. *The Gold Rush*

1962
SIGHT AND SOUND SURVEY (CONTINUED)

Arthur Knight (USA):
1. *The Bicycle Thief*
2. *Citizen Kane*
3. *City Lights*
4. *Hiroshima Mon Amour*
5. *Ikiru*
6. *The Last Laugh* (Murnau)
7. *Moana*
8. *The Apu Trilogy*
9. *Battleship Potemkin*
10. *La Strada*

Dwight MacDonald (USA):
1. *Birth of a Nation*
2. *Intolerance*
3. *October*
4. *Sherlock Jr.* (Keaton)
5. *The Gorki Trilogy*
6. *La Grande Illusion*
7. *Citizen Kane*
8. *Les Enfants du Paradis*
9. *Hiroshima Mon Amour*
10. *L'Avventura*

Jonas Mekas (USA):
(alphabetical order)
1. *Battleship Potemkin*

1972
SIGHT AND SOUND SURVEY (CONTINUED)

Arthur Knight (USA):
1. *A Nous la Liberté*
2. *The Bicycle Thief*
3. *Citizen Kane*
4. *City Lights*
5. *Ikiru*
6. *La Notte*
7. *The Passion of Joan of Arc*
8. *Persona*
9. *Punishment* (Peter Watkins)
10. *Who's Afraid of Virginia Woolf?*

Richard Corliss (USA):
1. *Sunrise*
2. *La Règle du Jeu*
3. *His Girl Friday*
4. *The Lady Eve*
5. *Citizen Kane*
6. *Casablanca*
7. *Les Enfants du Paradis*
8. *Letter from an Unknown Woman*
9. *The Searchers*
10. *The Seventh Seal*
11. *Psycho*
12. *Chinese Firedrill* (Will Hindle)

Judith Crist (USA):
1. *City Lights*
2. *La Règle du Jeu*

1952
CINEMATHEQUE BELGIQUE SURVEY (CONTINUED)

3. *Variety*
4. *The Gold Rush*
5. *The Crowd*
6. *La Grande Illusion*
7. *The Informer* (Ford)
8. *Ninotchka*
9. *Best Years of Our Lives*
10. *The Bicycle Thief*

Luchino Visconti:
1. *La Grande Illusion*
2. *Greed*
3. *Potemkin*
4. *Que Viva Mexico* (Eisenstein)
5. *Hallelujah!*
6. *Stagecoach*
7. *Monsieur Verdoux*
8. *Tabu* (Murnau)
9. *The Lost Weekend*
10. *Les Enfants du Paradis*

Luis Buñuel:
1. *Underworld* (Sternberg)
2. *The Gold Rush*
3. *The Bicycle Thief*
4. *Potemkin*
5. *Portrait of Jennie* (Dieterle)
6. *Cavalcade* (Lloyd)
7. *White Shadows in the South Seas*
8. *Dead of Night* (Cavalcanti, etc.)
9. *L'Age d'Or*

1952
SIGHT AND SOUND SURVEY (CONTINUED)

3. *Intolerance*
4. *Birth of a Nation*
5. *Queen Kelly* (Von Stroheim)
6. *Potemkin*
7. *Que Viva Mexico*
8. *Monsieur Verdoux*

Siegfried Kracauer (USA):
1. *The Joyless Street*
2. *M*
3. *La Chienne*
4. *Le Million*
5. *Lonesome* (Fejos)
6. *Potemkin*
7. *Paisan*
8. *The Gold Rush*
9. *Louisiana Story*
10. *Los Olvidados*

Paul Rotha (England):
1. *Greed*
2. *Potemkin*
3. *The Gold Rush*
4. *The Italian Straw Hat*
5. *Turksib* (Turin)
6. *Earth*
7. *Kameradschaft*
8. *L'Atalante*
9. *Open City*
10. *The Bicycle Thief*

1962
**SIGHT AND SOUND
SURVEY (CONTINUED)**

2. Citizen Kane
3. The Gold Rush
4. Greed
5. Intolerance
6. Ivan the Terrible
7. Lola Montès
8. Nanook of the North
9. Le Sang d'un Poète
10. Zéro de Conduite

Jacques Rivette (France):
1. The Life of Oharu (Mizoguchi)
2. Germany Year Zero (Rossellini)
3. True Heart Susie (Griffith)
4. Sunrise
5. The River
6. Ivan the Terrible
7. L'Atalante
8. Day of Wrath
9. Monsieur Verdoux
10. Confidential Report (Welles)

Eric Rohmer (France):
(chronological order)
1. True Heart Susie
2. The General
3. Sunrise
4. La Règle du Jeu
5. Ivan the Terrible
6. Voyage en Italie
7. Red River
8. Vertigo
9. Pickpocket
10. La Pyramide Humaine

1972
**SIGHT AND SOUND
SURVEY (CONTINUED)**

3. Citizen Kane
4. La Grande Illusion
5. 8 ½
6. La Guerre est finie
7. Ikiru
8. Winter Light
9. War and Peace (Bondarchuk)
10. The Maltese Falcon

Stephen Farber (USA):
1. Citizen Kane
2. 8 ½
3. Jules et Jim
4. Lawrence of Arabia
5. The Manchurian Candidate
6. Masculin-Féminin
7. The Night of the Hunter
8. Performance
9. Persona
10. La Règle du Jeu

Stanley Kauffmann (USA):
1. The Gold Rush
2. Battleship Potemkin
3. The General
4. The Passion of Joan of Arc
5. La Grande Illusion
6. Citizen Kane
7. Rashomon
8. Tokyo Story
9. L'Avventura
10. Persona

1952
CINEMATHEQUE BELGIQUE
SURVEY (CONTINUED)

10.   *I Am a Fugitive from a Chain Gang*

Orson Welles:
1.   *City Lights*
2.   *Greed*
3.   *Intolerance*
4.   *Nanook*
5.   *Sciuscia* (De Sica)
6.   *Potemkin*
7.   *La Femme du Boulanger*
8.   *La Grande Illusion*
9.   *Stagecoach*
10.   *Our Daily Bread* (Vidor)

1952
SIGHT AND SOUND
SURVEY (CONTINUED)

Claude Mauriac (France):
1.   *Birth of a Nation*
2.   *The Gold Rush*
3.   *Que Viva Mexico*
4.   *The Magnificent Ambersons*
5.   *La Règle du Jeu*
6.   *Espoir* (Malraux)
7.   *The Bicycle Thief*
8.   *The Fallen Idol* (Reed)
9.   *Miss Julie* (Sjöberg)
10.   *The River* (Renoir)

Robin Wood (England):
1.   *Sansho Dayu*
2.   *Letter from an Unknown Woman*
3.   *A Passion*
4.   *La Règle du Jeu*
5.   *Rio Bravo*
6.   *Sunrise*
7.   *Vertigo*
8.   *Bigger Than Life* (Nicholas Ray)
9.   *Days and Nights in the Forest* (Satyajit Ray)
10.   *Viaggio in Italia*

BEST FILMS OF ALL TIME: DIRECTORS' CHOICES/137

1962
SIGHT AND SOUND
SURVEY (CONTINUED)

Colin Young (USA):

1. *Citizen Kane*
2. *The Gold Rush*
3. *Man of Aran*
4. *October*
5. *Song of Ceylon* (Wright)
6. *L'Avventura*
7. *Pather Panchali*
8. *Rashomon*
9. *The Seventh Seal*
10. *Umberto D.*

1972
SIGHT AND SOUND
SURVEY (CONTINUED)

Andrew Sarris (USA):

1. *Madame De*
2. *Lola Montès*
3. *Ugetsu Monogatari*
4. *La Règle du Jeu*
5. *Vertigo*
6. *The Searchers*
7. *Sherlock Jr.*
8. *Francesco Giullare di Dio* (Rossellini)
9. *The Magnificent Ambersons*
10. *Belle de Jour*

Jay Cocks (USA)

1. *The General*
2. *Jules et Jim*
3. *The Magnificent Ambersons*
4. *Persona*
5. *The Searchers*
6. *The Seven Samurai*
7. *The Third Man*
8. *2001: A Space Odyssey*
9. *The Wild Bunch*
10. *Zéro de Conduite*

Paul Schrader (USA):

1. *An Autumn Afternoon*
2. *Journal d'un Curé de Campagne*
3. *My Darling Clementine*
4. *The Passion of Joan of Arc*
5. *Masculin-Féminin*
6. *La Règle du Jeu*
7. *Viaggio in Italia*
8. *Kiss Me Deadly*
9. *Lolita*
10. *Performance*

1972
SIGHT AND SOUND
SURVEY (CONTINUED)

Paul D. Zimmerman (USA):

1. *A Nous la Liberté*
2. *Les Enfants du Paradis*
3. *Intolerance*
4. *Kind Hearts and Coronets*
5. *Modern Times*
6. *Zéro de Conduite*
7. *Olympic Games 1936*
8. *The Seven Samurai*
9. *The Lady Vanishes*
10. *La Grande Illusion*

2/BEST FILMS ABOUT WOMEN

THE WINTER 1975/76 issue of *Film Heritage* was devoted to the study of women and film. For this special issue, Karyn Kay and Gerald Peary asked several leading women film specialists to name the best ten films about women.

The most frequently listed films were George Cukor's *Adam's Rib* and Ingmar Berman's *Persona,* followed by Cukor's *Pat and Mike,* Jacques Rivette's *Céline and Julie Go Boating,* Luis Buñuel's *Belle de Jour,* Jill Godmilow-Judy Collins' *Antonia: Portrait of the Woman,* and Vittorio De Sica's *Brief Vacation.*

The polltakers noted several interesting results: (1) films made by men about women were selected much more frequently than those by women about women, a reflection of the obvious fact that there have been many more male directors; (2) television drama deserved "more notice for its women's roles"; and (3) the most highly publicized woman's pictures were not necessarily the most revered: *Alice Doesn't Live Here Anymore* wasn't on a single list, and *Woman Under the Influence* and *Scenes from a Marriage* were mentioned only once each, half as much as *National Velvet.*

List of Contributors:

Jan Dawson writes regularly for the British publication *Sight and Sound.*

Sybil Del Gaudio, a member of NOW's Images of Women in Film Committee, teaches film at Brooklyn College.

Patricia Erens, an editor of *The Northwestern Reader,* has written for *The Velvet Light Trap, Jump Cut,* and *Film Comment.*

Ellen Freyer is a filmmaker who has written for *The Velvet Light Trap, The Documentary Tradition* and reviewed films for *Craft Horizons.*

Molly Haskell, critic for *New York* and formerly for the *Village Voice,* is author of *From Reverence to Rape: The Treatment of Women in the Movies.*

Karyn Kay, lecturer in film at Livingston College, Rutgers, has written for *Film Quarterly, Jump Cut, Cinema* and *The Velvet Light Trap.*

Marsha Kinder, contributing editor of *Woman and Film* and co-author of *Close-Up: A Critical Perspective on Film,* is an associate professor of literature and film at Pitzer College. She is a contributor to *Film Heritage* and *Film Quarterly.*

Midge Kovacs, coordinator of the New York Chapter of NOW's Images of Women in Film Committee, has been appointed to the International Women's Year Committee on the Media, serving along with Alan Alda and Katharine Hepburn.

Julia Lesage, contributing editor of *Women and Film, Jump Cut* and

Cinéaste, teaches film at the University of Illinois, Chicago Circle.

Joan Mellen, associate professor at Temple University, is the author of *Women and their Sexuality in the New Film* and the recent *Voices from the Japanese Cinema.*

Eleanor Perry, screenwriter of *David and Lisa, The Swimmer, Last Summer, Diary of a Mad Housewife* and *The Man Who Loved Cat Dancing,* has completed the screenplay for *Blind Love.*

Amalie Rothschild, filmmaker of *Nana, Mom and Me, It Happens to Us* and *Woo Who, May Wilson,* and one of the founders of the New Day Films, is currently working on a feature script.

Nancy Schwartz, film critic for *The Soho Weekly News,* has written for *Film Comment* and *The Velvet Light Trap.*

Emily Sieger is research librarian for the Museum of Modern Art film division.

Elisabeth Weis, who teaches film at Brooklyn College, has written for *American Film* and the *Village Voice.*

JAN DAWSON

(listed alphabetically by director)
The Touch (Ingmar Bergman)
Last Tango in Paris (Bernado Bertolucci)
Adam's Rib (George Cukor)
India Song (Marguerite Duras)
Martha (Rainer Werner Fassbinder)
Two or Three Things I Know About Her (Jean-Luc Godard)
Part-time Work of a Domestic Slave (Alexander Kluge)
Muriel (Alain Resnais)
Céline and Julie Go Boating (Jacques Rivette)
Sunday Bloody Sunday (John Schlesinger)

SYBIL DEL GAUDIO

First Comes Courage (Dorothy Arzner)
Christopher Strong Dorothy Arzner)
Joyce at 34 (Joyce Chopra/Claudia Weill)
Antonia: Portrait of the Woman (Judy Collins/Jill Godmilow)
A Brief Vacation (Vittorio De Sica)
Holiday (George Cukor)
Adam's Rib (George Cukor)

National Velvet (Clarence Brown)
Persona (Ingmar Bergman)
So Proudly We Hail (Mark Sandrich)

PATRICIA ERENS

(in alphabetical order)
All About Eve (Joseph Mankiewicz)
Les Bonnes Femmes (Claude Chabrol)
Charulata (Satyajit Ray)
Dishonored (Josef von Sternberg)
His Girl Friday (Howard Hawks)
Jules and Jim (Francois Truffaut)
Legacy (Karen Arthur)
Persona (Ingmar Bergman)
Trouble in Paradise (Ernst Lubitsch)
A Very Curious Girl (Nelly Kaplan)

ELLEN FREYER

Love and Anarchy (Lina Wertmüller)
Bonnie and Clyde (Arthur Penn)
Persona (Ingmar Berman)
Meshes of the Afternoon (Maya Deren/Alexander Hammid)
The Blue Angel (Josef von Sternberg)
Dance, Girl, Dance (Dorothy Arzner)
I Am Somebody (Madeline Anderson)
Pat and Mike (George Cukor)
Lucia (Humberto Solas)
Claudine (John Berry)

MOLLY HASKELL

(films listed in no special order)
Orphans of the Storm (D. W. Griffith)
The Sternberg-Dietrich oeuvre
    Angel (Ernst Lubitsch)
The Major and the Minor (Billy Wilder)
Pat and Mike (George Cukor)
Gentlemen Prefer Blondes (Howard Hawks)
Stromboli (Roberto Rossellini)
Belle de Jour (Luis Buñuel)
My Night at Maud's (Eric Rohmer)
The Earrings of Madame de (Max Ophuls)
Gertrud (Carl Dreyer)

KARYN KAY

(limited to one film per director of fictional narratives)
Dance, Girl, Dance (Dorothy Arzner)
Marked Woman (Lloyd Bacon)
Marocco (Josef von Sternberg)
Tarnished Angels (Douglas Sirk)
Johnny Guitar (Nicholas Ray)
Mädchen in Uniform (Leontine Sagan)
Bed and Sofa (Abram Room)
Contempt (Jean-Luc Godard)
Persona (Ingmar Bergman)
Zambizanga (Sarah Muldorer)

MARSHA KINDER

Scenes from a Marriage (Ingmar Bergman)
Céline and Julie Go Boating (Jacques Rivette)
August and July (Murray Markowitz)
Old Acquaintance (Vincent Sherman)

Legacy (Karen Arthur)
Woman Under the Influence (John Cassavetes)
Antonia: Portrait of the Woman (Judy Collins/Jill Godmilow)
Persona (Ingmar Bergman)
Woman to Woman (Donna Deitch)
Mosori Monika (Chick Strand)

MIDGE KOVACS
(exclusively contemporary)
Happy New Year (Claude Lelouch)
Brief Vacation (Vittorio De Sica)
Middle of the World (Alain Tanner)
My Night at Maud's (Eric Rohmer)
Claudine (John Berry)
A Free Woman (Volker Schlondorff)

JULIA LESAGE
(no special order)
Janie's Janie (Geri Ashur)
Holding (Constance Beesons)
Parthogenesis (Michele Citron)
Women's Happy Time Commune (Sheila Page/Ariel Dougherty)
Self-Health (Catherine Allan/Judy Irola/Allie Light/Joan Musante)
The Women's Film (San Francisco Newsreel Collective)
Home Movie (Jan Oxenberg)
Persona (Ingmar Bergman)
Adam's Rib (George Cukor)
Salt of the Earth (Herbert Biberman)

JOAN MELLEN
Belle de Jour (Luis Buñuel)
The Life of Oharu (Kenji Mizoguchi)
She and He (Susumu Hani)
Untamed (Mikio Naruse)
Adam's Rib (George Cukor)
Forsaken (Mikio Naruse)
Osaka Elegy (Kenji Mizoguchi)
Gertrud (Carl Dreyer)
The Story of Adele H. (Francois Truffaut)
The Effects of Gamma Rays . . . (Paul Newman)

ELEANOR PERRY
Perry answered the survey by saying there weren't any great films for women, that most films—even those with spirited women like *Ninotchka, Casablanca, All About Eve* and *Sunday Bloody Sunday*—perpetuate the myth that a woman's only fulfillment is in her reflection in the eyes of a man. Perhaps, Perry said, only *A Touch of Class* is the halfway great movie for women.

AMALIE ROTHSCHILD
(limited to movies about women who defy stereotypes)
The Miracle Worker (Arthur Penn)
Rachel, Rachel (Paul Newman)
The Elizabeth Blackwell Story
Pat and Mike (George Cukor)
The Elizabeth R Series (BBC series)
Two Women (Vittorio De Sica)
Thank You All Very Much (Hussein)
The Notorious Woman: The Life of George Sand (Hussein, BBC series)
A Very Curious Girl (Nelly Kaplan)
Jenny (BBC series)

NANCY SCHWARTZ
The Model and the Marriage Broker (George Cukor)
Les Bonnes Femmes (Claude Chabrol)
The Earrings of Madame de (Max Ophuls)
Annie Oakley (George Stevens)
The Scarlet Empress (Josef von Sternberg)
Adam's Rib; Pat and Mike (George Cukor)
Antonia: Portrait of the Woman (Judy Collins/Jill Godmilow)
Belle de Jour (Luis Bunuel)
Persona (Ingmar Bergman)
Voyage to Italy (Roberto Rossellini)
Céline and Julie Go Boating (Jacques Rivette)

EMILY SIEGER
(in chronological order)
The Passion of Joan of Arc (Carl Dreyer)
Une Partie de Campagne (Jean Renoir)
Camille (George Cukor)
How Green Was My Valley (John Ford)
Letter From an Unknown Woman (Max Ophuls)
Yokihi (Kenji Mizoguchi)
Vertigo (Alfred Hitchcock)
Mouchette (Robert Bresson)
Seven Women (John Ford)
The Story of Adele H. (Francois Truffaut)

ELISABETH WEIS
Bed and Sofa (Abram Room)
Adam's Rib (George Cukor)
The Battle of Algiers (Gillo Pontecorvo)
Modern Times (Charles Chaplin)
National Velvet (Clarence Brown)
To Have and Have Not (Howard Hawks)
Yudi (Mirra Bank)
Dishonored (Josef von Sternberg)
Betty Boop for President (Max Fleischer)
A Brief Vacation (Vittorio De Sica)

3/AMERICAN FILM INSTITUTE SURVEY

To CELEBRATE ITS tenth anniversary, the American Film Institute in 1977 conducted the largest survey in the history of film studies. It asked each of its 35,000 members across the nation and around the world to select the greatest American films of all time.

Each member was asked to list his five choices in order of preference. Although any American movie could be named, a list of 341 films was compiled by the AFI staff to facilitate selection. Films were named by title and year only; directors were not cited.

The auditing firm of Laventhol and Horwath tabulated the balloting on a point system that reflected the order of each members' five choices. The response to the survey was extraordinary: more than 1,100 different film titles were included among the members' selections.

Because of the overwhelming response, a second ballot was compiled by AFI, listing in alphabetical order the 50 films that received the largest point totals. AFI members were then asked to make their final five choices from this list only.

This list of 50 films—reprinted here—is rather strange with regard to historical distribution. There is, I think, a surprising dearth of early films and an unusual excess of recent ones on the list. Almost 25% of the films cited have been released since 1970 alone, whereas only 6% of the movies chosen were made in the silent era. (It should be noted, however, that two of Chaplin's films on the list—*City Lights and Modern Times*—though made after 1930 did not have synchronized dialogue.)

Here is how the 50 films break down into decades:

1910-19: 2	**1950-59: 9**
1920-29: 1	**1960-69: 9**
1930-39: 9	**1970-77: 12**
1940-49: 8	

The preponderance of recent films suggests either that there has indeed been a deluge of good films in recent years (which is doubtful) or that AFI members don't have much sense of history, that they haven't seen or remain unimpressed by early movies. Hollywood has often slighted its own past. Studios, for example, have been reluctant to revise an old film's earnings, in the belief that once a movie has passed its first flush of success it no longer is important. And until quite recently, few theaters in Los Angeles exhibited older movies on a regular basis—classic films have been much more popular in cities like New York and San Francisco than in Los Angeles, where the main interest has been the current film crop.

The abundance of recent films in the second balloting of AFI's survey indicates that Hollywood's disregard for its earlier works is matched, at least to a certan extent, by AFI members. As a group, AFI members are much more impressed by films made in the past few years than those released in any other single period of time. Immediacy and not the "test of time" seems to be the standard in this survey.

It is difficult to discern many trends in the survey regarding directors. Only two directors—John Huston and William Wyler—had three of their films selected on this second ballot. Ten other directors had two of their films cited among the 50 movies: Frank Capra, Charles Chaplin, Francis Ford Coppola, Victor Fleming, D.W. Griffith, George Ray Hill, Elia Kazan, Stanley Kubrick, David Lean and Robert Wise. Several popular directors—like John Ford, Alfred Hitchcock and Orson Welles—had only one of their works chosen. And the films of several important directors—like Ernst Lubitsch, Howard Hawks, George Cukor, King Vidor, Rouben Mamoulian, Raoul Walsh, Preston Sturges, and Josef von Sternberg—were not mentioned at all. (Cukor did, however, direct portions of *Gone With the Wind,* which was of course on the list.)

Surprisingly, only two Westerns were selected: *High Noon* and *Butch Cassidy and the Sundance Kid.* Where, for heaven's sake, were *Stagecoach, My Darling Clementine, Rio Bravo, Red River, Shane,* and *The Wild Bunch*?

Musical fared slightly better: six were chosen. These included *Cabaret, Singin' in the Rain, The Sound of Music, West Side Story, The Wizard of Oz,* and—if you consider it a musical—*Nashville.* But there was no mention of such classics as *The Band Wagon, An American in Paris, Gigi, Meet Me in St. Louis, Love Me Tonight,* or of the Astaire-Rogers series.

Gangster films on the AFI Top 50 included *Chinatown, The Godfather I* and *II,* and *The Maltese Falcon.* But not a single James Cagney gangster movie like *White Heat* and *The Public Enemy* was mentioned.

Comedy seemed particularly slighted, as is often the case at the Oscars. Although works of Chaplin and Keaton made the list, the Marx Brothers, Laurel and Hardy, Harold Lloyd, Harry Langdon, W.C. Fields, and Mae West all failed to score.

And stars who failed to make the list included such luminaries as Gary Cooper, James Stewart, Bette Davis, Joan Crawford, Greta Garbo, Fred Astaire, Marlene Dietrich, Carole Lombard, Barbara Stanwyck, and James Cagney.

The Ten Greatest American Films of All Time selected from the second AFI balloting were announced at the Tenth Anniversary celebration at the JFK Center for the Performing Arts in Washington on November 17, 1977. The ceremony, with President Carter in attendance, was televised nationally a few days later.

The list of Ten Greatest American Films is, perhaps, even more surprising that the second ballot of 50 pictures: there is not a single silent film among the 10! In fact, none of the ten cited films was even made before 1939. Five of the 10 pictures were made within two years of 1940, a strange clustering. Even stranger: the list includes not a single Western, nor a single detective film, nor a real comedy. Only one director —Victor Fleming—had two of his films selected. The winner of the poll—*Gone With the Wind*—was a safe, predictable choice.

So it was no surprise that AFI's poll provoked counterattacks from columnists around the nation. *New York Times* writer Russell Baker, complaining that the decision about which movies are the greatest is too personal to be submitted to the democratic hordes, decided to compile his own "definitive" list of the truly great American films. Arthur Schlesinger, Jr. in *Saturday Review* noted the top choice—*Gone With the Wind*—"seemed to me a stately and sentimental pomposity when I saw it in 1939 and an interminable bore when I saw it again a year or two ago." And *Los Angeles Times* film critic Charles Champlin found some of the omissions on AFI's list so startling that he polled his own readers to see if they could come up with a better list. (Both Russell Baker's list and Charles Champlin survey are included in the "Ten Best Grabbag.") Perhaps, all this controversy proves Andrew Sarris's contention that any list on a subject of this magnitude is "hopelessly self-limiting."

THE TOP FIFTY

(in alphabetical order)
1. *The African Queen* (1952)
2. *All About Eve* (1950)
3. *All Quiet on the Western Front* (1930)
4. *All the President's Men* (1976)
5. *Ben-Hur* (1959)
6. *The Best Years of Our Lives* (1946)
7. *The Birth of a Nation* (1915)
8. *The Bridge on the River Kwai* (1957)
9. *Butch Cassidy and the Sundance Kid* (1969)
10. *Cabaret* (1972)
11. *Casablanca* (1942)
12. *Chinatown* (1974)
13. *Citizen Kane* (1941)
14. *City Lights* (1931)
15. *Dr. Strangelove* (1964)
16. *Fantasia* (1940)
17. *The General* (1927)
18. *The Godfather* (1972)
19. *The Godfather Part II* (1974)
20. *Gone With the Wind* (1939)
21. *The Graduate* (1967)
22. *The Grapes of Wrath* (1940)
23. *High Noon* (1952)
24. *Intolerance* (1916)
25. *It Happened One Night* (1934)
26. *It's a Wonderful Life* (1946)
27. *Jaws* (1976)
28. *King Kong* (1933)
29. *Lawrence of Arabia* (1962)
30. *The Maltese Falcon* (1941)
31. *Midnight Cowboy* (1969)
32. *Modern Times* (1936)
33. *Nashville* (1975)
34. *On the Waterfront* (1954)
35. *One Flew Over the Cuckoo's Nest* (1975)
36. *Psycho* (1960)
37. *Rocky* (1975)
38. *Singin' in the Rain* (1952)
39. *Snow White and the Seven Dwarfs* (1938)
40. *The Sound of Music* (1965)
41. *Star Wars* (1977)
42. *The Sting* (1973)
43. *A Streetcar Named Desire* (1951)
44. *Sunset Boulevard* (1950)
45. *To Kill a Mockingbird* (1962)
46. *Treasure of Sierra Madre* (1948)
47. *2001: A Space Odyssey* (1968)
48. *West Side Story* (1961)
49. *The Wizard of Oz* (1939)
50. *Wuthering Heights* (1939)

THE TOP TEN

(first three listed by number of votes; remaining seven listed alphabetically)
1. *Gone With the Wind* (1939)
2. *Citizen Kane* (1941)
3. *Casablanca* (1942)
4. *The African Queen* (1952)
5. *The Grapes of Wrath* (1940)
6. *One Flew Over the Cuckoo's Nest* (1975)
7. *Singin' In the Rain* (1952)
8. *Star Wars* (1977)
9. *2001: A Space Odyssey* (1968)
10. *The Wizard of Oz* (1939)

4/BEST OF THE SIXTIES

WHAT WERE THE best films, best starring and supporting performances, best directorial jobs, and best screenplays of the 1960s? Early in 1970, *Los Angeles Times* film columnist Joyce Haber decided to find out, polling first her readers and then a group of top filmmakers—directors, writers, producers, actors and actresses.

The results of Haber's two surveys—published in four consective Sunday editions of the *L.A. Times*, January 4 though January 23, 1970—were interesting, sometimes intriguing.

Both the 20 filmmakers polled by Haber and her readers selected the same film as Best Picture of the decade: *The Graduate.* Of the top 12 films chosen by the filmmakers, 7 were also on the readers' Best List. The main difference between the industry's favorite pics and the readers' was nationality: whereas the filmmakers elected 4 foreign-language films to their Best-of-the-Decade list, the readers named only movies in English.

Other identical choices? The readers and the filmmakers both named Mike Nichols as best comedy director for *The Graduate,* with Billy Wilder *(The Apartment)* and Stanley Kubrick *(Dr. Strangelove)* coming in second and third places respectively. Best

female performance in a comedy or musical was won by Barbra Streisand in *Funny Girl.* (In fact, in the readers' poll, Streisand received the largest single vote of the entire survey.) And Patty Duke was a favorite with both readers and filmmakers alike in the best dramatic supporting actress category.

The individual choices by the various filmmakers ran the gamut from predictable to provocative. Who would have thought Kirk Douglas to be so smitten by Vladimir Nabokov's screenplay for *Lolita*? Gene Kelly's vote for Paul Newman as the decade's best dramatic producer *(Rachel, Rachel)* might come as a bit of a surprise. And Raquel Welch's obvious interest in Jane Fonda's work—Welch named three of Fonda's films as her choice for the best comedy performance by an actress—is fascinating, especially considering how unpopular Fonda was in 1970.

Vincente Minnelli's vote for Luchino Visconti's *The Damned* as one of the decade's best five films would obviously interest any auteurist. His choice for the decade's best dramatic actress—Liza Minnelli in *The Sterile Cuckoo*—can perhaps only be forgiven as a father's perogative.

Here, then, is Haber's tally-sheet.

BEST FILMS

(Readers' choice)

1. *The Graduate*
2. *Bonnie and Clyde*
3. *The Sound of Music*
   Romeo and Juliet
4. *West Side Story*
5. *Who's Afraid of Virginia Woolf?*

6. *Lawrence of Arabia*
7. *Dr. Zhivago*
   My Fair Lady
8. *2001: A Space Odyssey*
9. *Midnight Cowboy*
   Funny Girl
10. *Tom Jones*

A Man for All Seasons
The Lion in Winter

BEST DRAMATIC DIRECTION

(Readers' choice)
1. Franco Zeffirelli, *Romeo and Juliet*
2. David Lean, *Dr. Zhivago*
   Arthur Penn, *Bonnie and Clyde*
   Mike Nichols, *Who's Afraid of Virginia Woolf?*
3. John Schlesinger, *Darling; Midnight Cowboy*
   David Lean, *Lawrence of Arabia*
   RUNNERS-UP:
   1. Roman Polanski, *Rosemary's Baby*
   2. Federico Fellini, *8 ½*
      Fred Zinnemann, *Man for All Seasons*

BEST COMEDY DIRECTION

(Readers' choice)
1. Mike Nichols, *The Graduate*
2. Billy Wilder, *The Apartment*
3. Stanley Kubrick, *Dr. Strangelove*
   Tony Richardson, *Tom Jones*
   RUNNERS-UP:
   1. Stanley Kramer, *It's a Mad, Mad, Mad, Mad World*
      Mel Brooks, *The Producers*

BEST FILMS

(Industry's choice)
1. *The Graduate*
2. *Bonnie and Clyde*
   Romeo and Juliet
   8 ½
3. *Midnight Cowboy*
   Lawrence of Arabia
4. *The Sound of Music*
   Battle of Algiers
   La Dolce Vita
   Dr. Strangelove
5. *A Man for All Seasons*
   Two Women

BEST DRAMATIC DIRECTION

(Industry's choice)
1. Federico Fellini, *8 ½; La Dolce Vita*
2. Gillo Pontecorvo, *Battle of Algiers*
3. Fred Zinnemann, *Man for All Seasons*

BEST COMEDY DIRECTION

(Industry's choice)
1. Mike Nichols, *The Graduate*
   Billy Wilder, *The Apartment; Some Like It Hot*
2. Stanley Kubrick, *Dr. Strangelove*

BEST DRAMATIC MALE PERFORMANCE

(Readers' choice)
1. Richard Burton, *Who's Afraid of Virginia Woolf?*
2. Peter O'Toole, *The Lion in Winter*
3. Rod Steiger, *Pawnbroker*
   RUNNER-UP:
   1. Paul Scofield, *Man for All Seasons*

BEST DRAMATIC FEMALE PERFORMANCE

(Readers' choice)
1. Elizabeth Taylor, *Who's Afraid of Virginia Woolf?*
2. Katharine Hepburn, *The Lion in Winter*
3. Audrey Hepburn, *Wait Until Dark*
   Anne Bancroft, *The Miracle Worker*
   RUNNERS-UP:
   1. Sophia Loren, *Two Women*
      Joanne Woodward, *Rachel, Rachel*
   2. Bette Davis, *What Ever Happened to Baby Jane?*

BEST COMEDY MALE PERFORMANCE

(Readers' choice)
1. Lee Marvin, *Cat Ballou*
2. Dustin Hoffman, *The Graduate*
3. Albert Finney, *Tom Jones*
   RUNNERS-UP:
   1. Peter Sellers, *Dr. Strangelove*
   2. Walter Matthau, *Odd Couple*
   3. Jack Lemmon, *The Apartment*

BEST DRAMATIC MALE PERFORMANCE

(Industry's choice)
1. Peter O'Toole, *The Lion in Winter; Lawrence of Arabia*
2. Dustin Hoffman, *The Graduate*
3. Anthony Quinn, *Zorba the Greek*
   Paul Scofield, *Man for All Seasons*
   Richard Burton, *Becket; Who's Afraid of Virginia Woolf?*

BEST DRAMATIC FEMALE PERFORMANCE

(Industry's choice)
1. Anne Bancroft, *The Pumpkin Eater; The Miracle Worker*
2. Audrey Hepburn, *Wait Until Dark; Two for the Road*
   Katharine Hepburn, *The Lion in Winter*
   Anna Magnani

BEST COMEDY MALE PERFORMANCE

(Industry's choice)
1. Walter Matthau, *Odd Couple*
2. Jack Lemmon, *Some Like It Hot; The Apartment*

3. Alan Arkin, *Popi*
    Peter Sellers, *Dr. Strangelove; Pink Panther*
    Dustin Hoffman, *The Graduate**

* Dustin Hoffman's performance in The Graduate *received 4 votes as the Best Dramatic Performance and 2 votes for the Best Comic Performance. If these votes were combined, Hoffman would have come in first place in either category.*

BEST FEMALE COMEDY PERFORMANCE

(Readers' choice)
1. Barbra Streisand, *Funny Girl*
2. Audrey Hepburn *Breakfast at Tiffany's*
3. Anne Bancroft, *The Graduate*
    Julie Andrews, *Sound of Music*
    RUNNERS-UP:
    1. Lynn Redgrave, *Georgy Girl*
        Shirley MacLaine, *The Apartment*

BEST DRAMATIC MALE SUPPORTING PERFORMANCE

(Readers' choice)
1. George Kennedy, *Cool Hand Luke*
2. Jack Albertson, *Subject Was Roses*
    Michael J. Pollard, *Bonnie and Clyde*
3. George C. Scott, *The Hustler*
    RUNNERS-UP
    1. Jack Nicholson, *Easy Rider*

BEST DRAMATIC FEMALE SUPPORTING PERFORMANCE

(Readers' choice)
1. Patty Duke, *The Miracle Worker*
2. Ruth Gordon, *Rosemary's Baby*
3. Estelle Parsons, *Bonnie and Clyde*
    RUNNERS-UP:
    1. Lila Kedrova, *Zorba the Greek*

BEST COMEDY MALE SUPPORTING PERFORMANCE

(Readers' choice)
1. Walter Matthau, *Fortune Cookie*
2. Hugh Griffith, *Tom Jones*
3. Jack Wild, *Oliver!*
    Gene Wilder, *The Producers*

BEST FEMALE COMEDY PERFORMANCE

(Industry's choice)
1. Barbra Streisand, *Funny Girl*
2. Shirley MacLaine, *The Apartment*
3. Marilyn Monroe, *Some Like It Hot*

BEST DRAMATIC MALE SUPPORTING PERFORMANCE

(Industry's choice)
1. Jack Nicholson, *Easy Rider*

BEST DRAMATIC FEMALE SUPPORTING PERFORMANCE

(Industry's choice)
1. Sandy Dennis, *Who's Afraid of Virginia Woolf?*
    Patty Duke, *The Miracle Worker*
    Estelle Parsons, *Bonnie and Clyde*

BEST COMEDY MALE SUPPORTING PERFORMANCE

(Industry's choice)
1. Hugh Griffith, *Tom Jones*
2. Walter Matthau, *Fortune Cookie; Guide for the Married Man*
    Gene Wilder, *Bonnie and Clyde*
    Martin Balsam, *A Thousand Clowns*
    RUNNERS-UP
    1. George C. Scott, *Dr. Strangelove*
        Peter Ustinov, *Topkapi*

BEST COMEDY FEMALE SUPPORTING PERFORMANCE

(Readers' choice)
1. Carol Channing, *Thoroughly Modern Millie*
2. Mildred Natwick, *Barefoot in the Park*
3. Margaret Rutherford, *The V.I.P.s*

BEST ORIGINAL SCREENPLAY

(Readers' choice)
1. Robert Benton and David Newman, *Bonnie and Clyde*
2. Billy Wilder and I.A.L. Diamond, *The Apartment*
3. Mel Brooks, *The Producers*
    RUNNERS-UP:
    1. Frederic Raphael, *Two for the Road*
    2. Peter Fonda, Terry Southern and Dennis Hopper, *Easy Rider*
        William Goldman, *Butch Cassidy and the Sundance Kid*
        Stanley Kubrick, Peter George, and Terry Southern, *Dr. Strangelove*
        William Rose, *Guess Who's Coming to Dinner?*

BEST ADAPTED SCREENPLAY

(Readers' choice)
1. Buck Henry, Calder Willingham, *The Graduate*
    James Goldman, *The Lion in Winter*
2. Robert Bolt, *Dr. Zhivago; A Man for All Seasons*
3. John Osborne, *Tom Jones*
    Horton Foote, *To Kill a Mockingbird*

RUNNERS-UP:
1.   Franco Zeffirelli, *Romeo and Juliet*
     Ernest Lehman, *Sound of Music; Who's Afraid of Virginia Woolf?*

BEST COMEDY FEMALE SUPPORTING PERFORMANCE

(Industry's choice)
(no actress received more than one vote in this category)

BEST ORIGINAL SCREENPLAY

(Industry's choice)
1.   Frederic Raphael, *Darling; Two for the Road*
2.   Federico Fellini, *8½*
     Robert Benton and David Newman, *Bonnie and Clyde*

BEST ADAPTED SCREENPLAY

(Industry's choice)
1.   Robert Bolt, *Dr. Zhivago; Lawrence of Arabia*
2.   Franco Zeffirelli, *Romeo and Juliet*
     Ernest Lehman, *Who's Afraid of Virginia Woolf?*

BEST DRAMATIC PRODUCER

(Readers' choice)
1.   Stanley Kubrick, *2001*
2.   Sam Spiegel, *Lawrence of Arabia*
3.   Warren Beatty, *Bonnie and Clyde*
     RUNNERS-UP:
     1.   Fred Zinnemann, *Man for All Seasons*
     2.   Carlo Ponti, *Dr. Zhivago*

BEST COMEDY PRODUCER

(Readers' choice)
1.   Tony Richardson, *Tom Jones*
2.   Billy Wilder, *The Apartment*
3.   Lawrence Turman, *The Graduate*
     RUNNERS-UP:
     1.   Robert Wise, *The Sound of Music*
     2.   Ross Hunter, *Thoroughly Modern Millie*
     3.   Stanley Kubrick, *Dr. Strangelove*

BEST DRAMATIC PRODUCER

(Industry's choice)
1.   Sam Spiegel, *Lawrence of Arabia*

BEST COMEDY PRODUCER

(Industry's choice)
1.   Lawrence Turman, *The Graduate*

BEST OF THE SIXTIES: THE INDIVIDUAL LISTS

Kirk Douglas

BEST MOVIES

Lawrence of Arabia
Dr. Strangelove
Battle of Algiers
Bonnie and Clyde
8½

BEST STARRING PERFORMANCES

Dramatic, Male:
Peter O'Toole, *Lawrence of Arabia*
Dramatic, Female:
Anne Bancroft, *The Pumpkin Eater*
Comedy, Male:
Jack Lemmon, *Some Like It Hot*
Comedy, Female:
Marilyn Monroe, *Some Like It Hot*

BEST SUPPORTING PERFORMANCES

Dramatic, Male:
Terence Stamp, *Billy Budd*
Dramatic, Female:
Sandy Dennis, *Who's Afraid of Virginia Woolf?*
Comedy, Male:
Hugh Griffith, *Tom Jones*
Comedy Female:
Geraldine Page, *You're a Big Boy Now*

BEST DIRECTION

Dramatic:
Gillo Pontecorvo, *The Battle of Algiers*
Comedy:
Tony Richardson, *Tom Jones*

BEST SCREENPLAY

Original:
Frederic Raphael, *Darling*
Adaptation:
Vladimir Nabokov, *Lolita*

BEST PRODUCER

Dramatic:
Sam Spiegel, *Lawrence of Arabia*
Comedy:
Tony Richardson, *Tom Jones*

Anthony Quinn

BEST MOVIES

(not necessarily in order of preference)
Easy Rider
Midnight Cowboy
Learning Tree
Medium Cool
Dream of Kings

BEST STARRING PERFORMANCES

Dramatic, Male:
Dustin Hoffman
Dramatic, Female:
Anna Magnani
Comedy, Male:
Woody Allen
Comedy, Female:
Shelley Winters

BEST SUPPORTING PERFORMANCES

Dramatic, Male:
Jack Nicholson
Dramatic, Female:
Irene Papas
Comedy, Male:
Elliott Gould
Comedy, Female:
Shelley Winters

BEST DIRECTION

Dramatic:
Daniel Mann
Comedy:
George Roy Hill

BEST SCREENPLAY

Adaptation:
Waldo Salt

BEST PRODUCER

Dramatic:
Stanley Kramer

Gene Kelly

BEST MOVIES (COMEDY OR MUSICAL)

The Apartment
Georgy Girl
Tom Jones
Sound of Music
West Side Story

BEST MOVIES (DRAMATIC)

Battle of Algiers
Rachel, Rachel
Lawrence of Arabia
Romeo and Juliet
A Man and a Woman

BEST STARRING PERFORMANCES

Dramatic, Male:
Peter O'Toole, *Lion in Winter*
Dramatic, Female:
Joanne Woodward, *Rachel, Rachel*
Comedy, Male:
Alan Bates, *Georgy Girl*
Comedy, Female:
Lynn Redgrave, *Georgy Girl*

BEST SUPPORTING PERFORMANCES

Dramatic, Male:
Philip Alford, *To Kill a Mockingbird*
Dramatic, Female:
Patty Duke, *The Miracle Worker*

BEST DIRECTION

Dramatic:
Federico Fellini, *8½*
Comedy:
Billy Wilder, *The Apartment*

BEST SCREENPLAY

Original:
Federico Fellini, *8½*
Adaptation:
Franco Zeffirelli, *Romeo and Juliet*

BEST PRODUCER

Dramatic:
Paul Newman, *Rachel, Rachel*
Comedy:
Lawrence Turman, *The Graduate*

Raquel Welch

BEST MOVIES (COMEDY)

The Graduate
Bob & Carol & Ted & Alice
Georgy Girl
Yesterday, Today and
*   Tomorrow*
Tom Jones

BEST MOVIES (DRAMATIC)

Bonnie and Clyde
Rosemary's Baby
Lion in Winter
Hud
Two Women

BEST STARRING
PERFORMANCES

Dramatic, Male:
Peter O'Toole
Dramatic, Female:
Katharine Hepburn
Comedy, Male:
Dustin Hoffman, *The Graduate*
Comedy, Female:
Jane Fonda, *Barefoot in the*
*   Park; Cat Ballou; Barbarella*

BEST SUPPORTING
PERFORMANCES

Dramatic, Male:
Robert Shaw, *Man for All*
*   Season*
Dramatic, Female:
Sandy Dennis, *Virginia Woolf*

BEST DIRECTION

Dramatic:
Roman Polanski
Comedy:
Mike Nichols

BEST SCREENPLAY

Original
James Goldman, *Lion in*
*   Winter*
Adaptation:
Ernest Lehman, *Who's Afraid*
of Virginia Woolf?

BEST PRODUCER

Dramatic:
Warren Beatty, *Bonnie and*
*   Clyde*
Comedy:
Lawrence Turman, *The*
*   Graduate*

Vincente Minnelli

BEST MOVIES

Lawrence of Arabia
8 ½
The Damned
Midnight Cowboy
Romeo and Juliet

BEST STARRING
PERFORMANCES

Dramatic Male:
Peter O'Toole, *Lion in Winter*
Dramatic, Female:
Liza Minnelli, *Sterile Cuckoo*
Comedy, Male:
Peter Sellers, *Dr. Strangelove*
Comedy, Female:
Barbra Streisand, *Funny Girl*
Dramatic, Male:
Jack Nicholson, *Easy Rider*
Dramatic, Female:
Estelle Parsons, *Bonnie and*
*   Clyde*
Comedy, Male:
Walter Matthau, *Fortune*
*   Cookie*
Comedy, Female:
Margaret Rutherford, *The*
*   V.I.P.'s*

BEST DIRECTION

Dramtic:
Federico Fellini, *La Dolce Vita*
Comedy:
Mike Nichols, *The Graduate*

BEST SCREENPLAY

Original:
Federico Fellini, *8 ½*
Adaptation:
Robert Benton, David
*   Newman, Bonnie and Clyde*

BEST PRODUCER

Dramatic:
Sam Spiegel, *Lawrence of*
*   Arabia*
Comedy:
Franco Cristaldi, *Divorce—*
*   Italian Style*

Jack Lemmon

BEST MOVIES

La Dolce Vita
Romeo and Juliet
A Man and a Woman
Some Like It Hot
Midnight Cowboy

BEST STARRING
PERFORMANCES

Dramatic, Male:
Laurence Olivier, *Othello*
Dustin Hoffman, Jon
*   Voight, Midnight Cowboy*
Dramatic, Female:
Rachel Roberts, *This Sporting*
*   Life*
Comedy, Male:
Walter Matthau, *The Odd*
*   Couple*

BEST SUPPORTING
PERFORMANCES

Dramatic, Male:
Jack Albertson

BEST DIRECTION

Dramatic:
Federico Fellini, *La Dolce Vita*
Comedy:
Billy Wilder, *Some Like It Hot*

BEST SCREEN PLAY

Original:
Billy Wilder, I.A.L. Diamond,
*   Some Like It Hot*

BEST PRODUCER

Dramatic:
Sam Spiegel, *Lawrence of*
*   Arabia*
Comedy:
Billy Wilder, for anything

Elizabeth Taylor & Richard Burton

BEST MOVIES

(not necessarily in order of preference)
The Hustler
The Graduate
The Heart is a Lonely Hunter
Psycho
Bonnie and Clyde

BEST STARRING PERFORMANCE

Dramatic, Male:
Dustin Hoffman, *The Graduate*
Dramatic, Female:
Audrey Hepburn, *Wait Until Dark*
Comedy, Male:
Lee Marvin, *Cat Ballou*

BEST PRODUCTION

Dramatic:
Mike Nichols, *The Graduate*
Comedy:
Mike Nichols, *The Graduate*

Walter Matthau

BEST MOVIES

Oh, What a Lovely War!

Special Note: "I cannot in good faith fill the best performances categories because so many were so good, and I don't feel that competitiveness in artistic achievement is fair. The same goes for directorial, screenplay, and producer categories. Also, the division of comedy and dramatic is naive. True, comedic drama is much more difficult to achieve, but why penalize people who can only do straight drama?"

Richard Zanuck

BEST MOVIES

Sound of Music
Who's Afraid of Virginia Woolf?
Dr. Strangelove
La Dolce Vita
Zorba the Greek

BEST STARRING PERFORMANCES

Dramatic, Male:
Anthony Quinn, *Zorba the Greek*
Dramatic, Female:
Katharine Hepburn, *The Lion in Winter*
Comedy, Male:
Walter Matthau, *Odd Couple*
Comedy, Female:
Julie Andrews, *Mary Poppins*

BEST DIRECTION

Dramatic:
Fred Zinnemann, *A Man for All Seasons*
Comedy:
Stanley Kubrick, *Dr. Strangelove*

BEST SCREENPLAY

Original:
William Goldman, *Butch Cassidy and the Sundance Kid*
Adaptation:
William Lehman, *Who's Afraid of Virginia Woolf?*

BEST PRODUCER

Dramatic:
Robert Wise
Comedy:
Ross Hunter

Mike Nichols

BEST MOVIES

8½
2001: A Space Odyssey
Jules and Jim
Persona
The Silence

BEST STARRING PERFORMANCES

Dramatic, Male:
Richard Burton
Oskar Werner
Dramatic, Female:
Jeanne Moreau
Bibi Anderson

BEST SUPPORTING PERFORMANCE

Dramatic, Male:
Jack Nicholson, *Easy Rider*
Dramatic, Female:
Liv Ullmann
Comedy, Male:
Gene Wilder, *Bonnie and Clyde*

BEST DIRECTION

Federico Fellini
Ingmar Bergman
Stanley Kubrick

BEST SCREENPLAY

Ingmar Bergman

Robert Wise

The Battle of Algiers
Romeo and Juliet
8½
The Hustler
The Graduate

BEST STARRING PERFORMANCES

Dramatic, Male:
Rod Steiger
Dramatic, Female:
Deborah Kerr
Comedy, Male:
Jack Lemmon
Comedy, Female:
Shirley MacLaine

BEST SUPPORTING PERFORMANCE

Dramatic, Male:
Gene Hackman
Dramatic, Female:
Lila Kedrova
Comedy, Male:
Hugh Griffith
Gene Wilder

BEST DIRECTION

Dramatic:
Gillo Pontecorvo
Comedy:
Billy Wilder

BEST SCREENPLAY

Original:
Franco Solinas, *Battle of Algiers*
Adaptation:
Robert Bolt, *Man for All Seasons*

BEST PRODUCER

Dramatic:
Franco Zeffirelli
Comedy:
Lawrence Turman

Robert Evans

BEST MOVIES

Romeo and Juliet
Darling
The Graduate
Elmer Gantry
Two for the Road

BEST STARRING PERFORMANCES

Dramatic, Male:
Burt Lancaster, *Elmer Gantry*
Dramatic, Female:
Audrey Hepburn, *Two for the Road*
Comedy, Male:
Walter Matthau, *Odd Couple*
Comedy, Female:
Barbra Streisand, *Funny Girl*

BEST DIRECTION

Dramatic:
David Lean, *Lawrence of Arabia*
Comedy:
Mike Nichols, *The Graduate*

BEST PRODUCER

Dramatic:
Sam Spiegel, *Lawrence of Arabia*

Edward Anhalt

(Screenwriter, *Panic in the Streets, Becket, The Young Lions*)

BEST MOVIES

La Dolce Vita
Doctor Zhivago
Dr. Strangelove
Battle of Algiers
Lawrence of Arabia

BEST STARRING PERFORMANCES

Dramatic, Male:
Peter O'Toole, *Lawrence of Arabia*
Dramatic, Female:
Piper Laurie, *The Hustler*
Comedy, Male:
Dustin Hoffman, *The Graduate*
Comedy, Female:
Marilyn Monroe, *Some Like It Hot*

BEST SUPPORTING PERFORMANCES

Dramatic, Male:
Michael J. Pollard, *Bonnie and Clyde*
Dramatic, Female:
Estelle Parsons, *Bonnie and Clyde*
Comedy, Male:
Hugh Griffith, *Tom Jones*
Comedy, Female:
Joyce Redman, *Tom Jones*

BEST DIRECTION

Dramatic:
Gillo Pontecorvo, *Battle of Algiers*
Comedy:
Stanley Kubrick, *Dr. Strangelove*

BEST SCREENPLAY

Original:
Frederic Raphael, *Darling*
Adaptation:
Robert Bolt, *Dr. Zhivago*

BEST PRODUCER

Dramatic:
Franco Zeffirelli, *Romeo and Juliet*
Comedy:
John Woolf, *Oliver!*

Joseph E. Levine

BEST MOVIES

The Graduate
Lion in Winter
8 ½
Two Women
Yesterday, Today and Tomorrow

Ray Stark

BEST MOVIES

La Dolce Vita
The Graduate
Man for All Seasons
Persona
2001: A Space Odyssey

BEST STARRING PERFORMANCES

Dramatic, Male:
Richard Burton, *Becket*
Dramatic, Female:
Anna Magnani
Comedy, Female:
Shirley MacLaine
Barbra Streisand

Lawrence Turman

(Producer, *The Graduate, Pretty Poison, The Great White Hope*)

BEST MOVIES

8 ½
Dr. Strangelove
Bonnie and Clyde

> SPECIAL NOTE: "Sorry, but I just hate to answer some of these and, indeed do not feel there is 'one best' is any category."

Robert Fryer

(Producer, *Prime of Miss Jean Brodie, Myra Breckingridge*)

BEST MOVIES

Two Women
My Fair Lady
Sound of Music
Midnight Cowboy
A Man for All Seasons

BEST STARRING PERFORMANCES

Dramatic, Male:
Paul Scofield, *Man for All Seasons*
Dramatic, Female:
Anne Bancroft, *Miracle Worker*
Comedy, Male:
Jack Lemmon, *The Apartment*
Comedy, Female:
Shirley MacLaine, *The Apartment*

BEST SUPPORTING PERFORMANCES

Dramatic, Male:
Martin Balsam, *A Thousand Clowns*
Dramatic, Female:
Maggie Smith, *The V.I.P.'s*
Comedy, Male:
Walter Matthau, *Guide for the Married Man*
Comedy, Female:
Estelle Parsons, *Rachel, Rachel*

BEST DIRECTION

Dramatic:
John Schlesinger, *Midnight Cowboy*
Comedy:
George Cukor, *My Fair Lady*

BEST SCREENPLAY

Original:
Frederic Raphael, *Two for the Road*
Adaptation:
Edward Anhalt, *Becket*

BEST PRODUCER

Dramatic:
Hal Willis
Comedy:
Lawrence Turman, *The Graduate*

Ross Hunter

(Producer, *Magnificent Obsession, Pillow Talk, Thoroughly Modern Millie*)

BEST MOVIES

Man for All Seasons
Sound of Music
The Graduate
Romeo and Juliet
Bonnie and Clyde

BEST STARRING PERFORMANCES

Dramatic, Male:
Paul Scofield, *Man for All Seasons*
Dramatic, Female:
Anne Bancroft, *Miracle Worker*
Comedy, Male:
Walter Matthau, *Odd Couple*
Alan Arkin, *Popi*
Comedy, Female:
Barbra Streisand, *Funny Girl*
Lucille Ball, *Yours, Mine and Ours*

BEST SUPPORTING PERFORMANCES

Dramatic, Male:
George Kennedy, *Cool Hand Luke*
Dramatic, Female
Brenda Vaccaro, *Midnight Cowboy*
Comedy, Male:
Martin Balsam, *A Thousand Clowns*
Comedy, Female:
Lee Grant, *Buona Sera, Mrs. Campbell*

BEST DIRECTION

Dramatic:
Fred Zinnemann, *Man for All Seasons*
Comedy:
Billy Wilder, *The Apartment*

BEST SCREENPLAY

Original:
Robert Benton, David Newman, *Bonnie and Clyde*
Adaptation:
Franco Zeffirelli, *Romeo and Juliet*

BEST PRODUCER

Dramatic:
Mike Frankovich, *Man for All Seasons*
Comedy:
Howard W. Koch, *Odd Couple*

James H. Nicholson

(Co-Founder of
   American-International
   Pictures)

BEST MOVIES

Alice's Restaurant
Marooned
Midnight Cowboy
Last Summer
Easy Rider

BEST STARRING PERFORMANCE

Dramatic, Male:
Dustin Hoffman
Dramatic, Female:
Sandy Dennis
Comedy, Male:
Alan Arkin

BEST SUPPORTING PERFORMANCES

Dramatic, Female:
Cathy Burns
Comedy, Male:
Arthur Hiller, *Popi*

BEST SCREENPLAY

Original:
Paul Mazursky and Larry
   Tucker, *Bob & Carol & Ted
   & Alice*
Adaptation:
Mayo Simon, *Marooned*

BEST PRODUCER

Dramatic:
Mike Frankovich, *Marooned*
Comedy:
Herbert B. Leonard, *Popi*

Stirling Silliphant

(Screenwriter, *In the Heat of
   the Night, Shaft, The
   Poseidon Adventure, The
   Towering Inferno*)

BEST MOVIES

(not necessarily in order of
preference)
Zorba the Greek
On the Beach
Lawrence of Arabia
Bonnie and Clyde
Shoot the Piano Player

BEST STARRING PERFORMANCES

Dramatic, Male:
Anthony Quinn, *Zorba the
   Greek*
Dramatic, Female:
Anne Bancroft, *The Miracle
   Worker*
Comedy, Male:
Peter Sellers, *The Pink
   Panther*

BEST SUPPORTING PERFORMANCES

Dramatic, Male:
Melvyn Douglas, *Hud*
Dramatic, Female:
Patty Duke, *The Miracle
   Worker*
Comedy, Male:
William Daniels, *Two for the
   Road*, and others

BEST DIRECTION

Dramatic:
Michelangelo Antonioni,
   L'Avventura
Comedy:
Mel Brooks, *The Producers*

BEST SCREENPLAY

Original:
Frederick Raphael, *Two for
   the Road*
Adaptation:
Robert Bolt, *Lawrence of
   Arabia*

BEST PRODUCER

Dramatic:
Sam Spiegel, *Lawrence of
   Arabia*
Comedy:
Mel Brooks, *The Producers*

5/BEST OF THE SEVENTIES

FOR THEIR JULY 1978 issue, the editors of the film magazine *Take One* asked 20 leading film critics to choose the best films of the decade running from Jan. 1 1968 to Dec. 31, 1977. ("Cultural patterns don't fit neat chronological patterns anyway," the editors said, defending their "unusual" demarcation of the decade.)

The critics were asked to select 10 movies in each of the Best American and Best European categories and five films in the Best Third World division. The American category included Canada. Japan, Australia, and the USSR were included in he European slot. Black American and Québécois films were allowed under either American or Third World categories. Critics were permitted to decide whether directors like Stanley Kubrick and John Schlesinger were American or European.

James Monaco, the magazine's editor who conducted the survey, expressed surprise over the critics' response to the Third World films: over half of the critics surveyed ignored the category or named fewer than the requested five films.

Surprises in the American division? The strong showings of films like *Petulia, Badlands,* and *Barry Lyndon* were unexpected, and the considerable presence of director Alan Pakula—two of whose films ranked in the top 21 films—was a surprise, according to Monaco.

The European category produced fewer surprises: the critics' choices here seem strongly influenced by the auteur policy; it's a directors list.

Special Note: *The Godfather* is treated as a single work in two parts in this survey. Eleven critics voted for one or both parts of the film: eight voted for the film as a whole, two for Part I and four for Part II. If the films had been ranked separately, *Godfather II* would have been tie with *Nashville* as the Best American Film of the decade.

BEST OF THE DECADE, 1968-1977. (*TAKE ONE* SURVEY)

BEST AMERICAN FILMS

1. *The Godfather* .... 14pts.
(Francis Ford Coppola, 1971, 74)
2. *Nashville* 12
(Robert Altman, 1975)
3. *Petulia* 9
(Richard Lester, 1968)

BEST EUROPEAN FILMS

1. *My Night at Maud's*
.... 7pts.
(Eric Rohmer, 1968)
    Scenes From a Marriage 7
(Ingmar Bergman, 1973)

BEST THIRD WORLD FILMS

1. *Memories of Underdevelopment* .. 6
(Tomas Gutierrez Alea, 1968)
2. *The Hour of the Furnaces* 5
(Fernando Solanas, Octavio Getino, 1968)

BEST AMERICAN FILMS

4. *Annie Hall* 9
(Woody Allen, 1977)
5. *Mean Streets* 7
(Martin Scorsese, 1973)
6. *2001: A Space
Odyssey* 6
(Stanley Kubrick, 1968)
7. *The Wild Bunch* 6
(Sam Peckinpah, 1969)
Badlands 5
(Terrence Malick, 1973)
Taxi Driver 5
(Martin Scorsese, 1976)
*McCabe and Mrs.
Miller* 5
(Robert Altman, 1971)
Chinatown 5
(Roman Polanski, 1974)
Barry Lyndon 5
(Stanley Kubrick, 1975)
13. *Blume in Love* 4
(Paul Mazursky, 1973)
The Conversation 4
(Francis Ford
Coppola, 1974) *Midnight
Cowboy* 4
(John Schlesinger, 1969)
*All the President's
Men* 4
(Alan Pakula, 1976)
17. *The Man Who Would
Be King* 3
(John Huston, 1975)
Klute 3
(Alan Pakula, 1971)
Five Easy Pieces 3
(Bob Rafelson, 1970)
*The Last Picture
Show* 3
(Peter Bogdanovich, 1971)
21. *The Shootist* 2
(George Siegel, 1976)
*One Flew Over the
Cuckoo's Nest* 2
(Milos Forman, 1975)
Fat City 2
(John Huston, 1972)
*Beyond the Valley of
the Dolls* 2
(Russ Meyer, 1970)
The Parallax View 2
(Alan Pakula, 1974)
Rosemary's Baby 2
(Roman Polanski, 1968)

BEST EUROPEAN FILMS

3. *Claire's Knee* 6
(Eric Rohmer, 1970)
The Conformist 6
(Bernardo Bertolucci, 1970)
Amarcord 6
(Federico Fellini, 1973)
*The Sorrow and the
Pity* 6
(Max Ophuls, 1971)
7. *Lancelot du Lac* 5
(Robert Bresson, 1974)
*The Mother and the
Whore* 5
(Jean Eustache, 1973)
*The Discreet Charm of
The Bourgeoisie* 5
(Luis Buñuel, 1972)
Le Boucher 5
(Claude Chabrol, 1970)
The Passenger 5
(Michelangelo Antonioni,
1975)
12. *Aguirre: The Wrath of
God* 4
(Werner Herzog, 1972)
Two English Girls 4
(Francois Truffaut, 1971)
Day for Night 4
(Francois Truffaut, 1973)
The Wild Child 4
(Francois Truffaut, 1969)
Last Tango in Paris .. 4
(Bernardo Bertolucci, 1972)
Performance 4
(Nicholas Roeg/Donald Cam-
mell, 1968)
*The Merchant of Four
Seasons* 4
(Rainer Werner Fassbinder,
1971)
19. *The Legend of
Kaspar Hauser* 3
(Werner Herzog, 1974)
*Once Upon a Time in
the West* 3
(Serge Leone, 1969)
Weekend 3
(Jean-Luc Godard, 1967)
*Jonah Who Will Be 25
In the Year 2000* 3
(Alain Tanner, 1976)

BEST THIRD WORLD FILMS

3. *The Harder They
Come* 4
(Peter Henzell, 1973)
Lucia 4
(Humberto Solas, 1969)
Distant Thunder 4
(Satyajit Ray, 1973)
6. *A Touch of Zen* 3
(King Hu, 1975)
Antonio das Mortes 3
(Rocha, 1969)
The Battle of Chile 3
(Guzman, 1973-76)
*Days and Nights In the
Forest* 3
10. *Xala* 2
(Ousmane Sembene, 1974)
Emitai 2
(Ousmane Sembene, 1971)
Black Girl 2
(Ousmane Sembene, 1965)
Charulata 2
(Satyajit Ray, 1964)
The Promised Land .. 2
(Littin, 1973)

BEST AMERICAN FILMS

*Sweet Sweetback's
Badass Song* 2
(Melvin Van Peebles, 1971)
Ganja & Hess 2
(Bill Gunn, 1973)
Harlan County, USA 2
(Barbara Kopple, 1976)
*Pat Garrett and Billy
The Kid* 2
(Sam Peckinpah, 1973)
*The Night of the Living
Dead* 2
(George Romero, 1968)
*The King of Marvin
Gardens* 2
(Bob Rafelson, 1972)
Madigan 2
(George Siegel, 1968)
Alice's Restaurant 2
(Arthur Penn, 1968)
Star Wars 2
(George Lucas, 1977)
Deliverance 2
(John Boorman, 1972)
*Close Encounters of
The Third Kind* 2
(Steven Spielberg, 1977)

BEST EUROPEAN FILMS

The Passion of Anna
.... 3
(Ingmar Bergman, 1970)
A Piece of Pleasure .. 3
(Claude Chabrol, 1970)
The Marquise of O 3
(Eric Rohmer, 1976)
Stolen Kisses 3
(Francois Truffaut, 1968)
*The Emmigrants/The
New Land* 3
(Jan Troell, 1972, 73)
*In the Realm of the
Senses* 2
(Nagisa Oshima, 1976)
If 2
(Lindsay Anderson, 1968)
1900 2
(Bernardo Bertolucci, 1976)
The Spider's Strategem
.... 2
(Bernardo Bertolucci, 1970)
Dersu Uzala 2
(Akira Kurosawa, 1975)
Tout va bien 2
(Jean-Luc Godard, 1972)
Belle de Jour 2
(Luis Buñuel, 1967)
Deep End 2
(Jerzy Skolimowski, 1971)
The Touch 2
(Ingmar Bergman, 1971)
Effi Briest 2
(Rainer Werner Fassbinder,
1974)
The Last Woman 2
(Marco Fererri, 1976)
Tristana 2
(Luis Buñuel, 1970)
The Rise of Louis XIV 2
(Roberto Rossellini, 1966)
This Man Must Die .. 2
(Claude Chabrol, 1969)
Cries and Whispers .. 2
(Ingmar Bergman, 1972)
The Devil Probably .. 2
(Robert Bresson, 1977)
*The Red and the
White* 2
(Miklos Jancso, 1967)

BEST THIRD WORLD FILMS

BEST AMERICAN FILMS BY DIRECTOR	BEST EUROPEAN FILMS BY DIRECTOR	BEST THIRD WORLD FILMS BY DIRECTOR
1. Robert Altman (for 6 films) .... 21pts.	**1.** Ingmar Bergman (for 6 films) .... 16pts.	**1.** Satyajit Ray (for 4 films) 10pts
2. Francis Coppola (for 3 films) 18	Francois Truffaut (for 5 films) 16	**2.** Ousmane Sembene (for 4 films) 7
3. Martin Scorsese (for 3 films) 13	Eric Rohmer (for 3 films) 16	**3.** Tomas Gutierrez Alea (for 1 film) 6
4. Richard Lester (for 3 films) 11	**4.** Bernardo Bertolucci (for 4 films) 14	Fernando Solanas/Octavio Getino (for 1 film) 6
Stanley Kubrick (for 2 films) 11	**5.** Luis Buñuel (for 6 films) 12	Henzell (for 1 film) 6
6. Alan Pakula (for 3 films) ,................ 9	Chabrol (for 5 films) 12	Solas (for 1 film) 6
Sam Peckinpah (for 3 films) 9	**7.** Fellini (for 4 films) 7	
8. George Lucas (for 2 films) 7	**8.** Fassbinder (for 3 films) 7	
Roman Polanski (for 2 films) 7	Herzog (for 2 films) 7	
10. Don Siegel (for 4 films) 6	Bresson (for 2 films) 7	
11. Steven Spielberg (for 4 films) 5	Ophuls (for 2 films) 7	
John Schlesinger (for 2 films) 5	**12.** Godard (for 3 films) 7	
John Huston (for 2 films) 5	Roeg (for 3 films) 7	
Bob Rafelson (for 2 films) 5	Antonioni (for 2 films) 7	
Paul Mazursky (for 2 films) 5	**15.** Tanner (for 3 films) 5	
Terrence Malick (for 1 film) 5	Eustache (for 1 film) 5	

THE INDIVIDUAL LISTS

PETER BISKIND (an editor on the staff of *Seven Days* and a freelance film critic):

BEST AMERICAN FILMS	BEST EUROPEAN FILMS	BEST THIRD WORLD FILMS
1. *Godfather I*	1. *Tout va bien*	1. *The Promised Land*
2. *Jaws*	2. *Weekend*	2. *Hour of the Furnaces*
3. *Godfather II*	3. *The Conformist*	3. *Battle of Chile*
4. *Annie Hall*	4. *Passion of Anna*	4. *Ceddo*
5. *Pat Garrett and Billy the Kid*	5. *Swept Away . . .*	5. *Lucia*
6. *Klute*	6. *Wild Child*	
7. *Night of the Living Dead*	7. *1900*	
8. *Midnight Cowboy*	8. *The Mattei Affair*	
9. *French Connection I*	9. *WR: Mysteries of the Organism*	
10. *Chinatown*	10. *Middle of the World*	

VICENT CANBY (the film critic for *The New York Times* and an occasional novelist):

Method of Evaluation: "Whim"

BEST AMERICAN FILMS	BEST EUROPEAN FILMS	BEST THIRD WORLD FILMS
(in no particular order)	*(in no particular order)*	*(in no particular order)*
1. *2001: A Space Odyssey*	1. *Stolen Kisses*	1. *Memories of Underdevelopment*
2. *Alice's Restaurant*	2. *Claire's Knee*	2. *Distant Thunder*
3. *True Grit*	3. *Tristana*	3. *Hour of the Furnaces-Part I*
4. *The Wild Bunch*	4. *The Rise of Louis XIV*	4. *Lucia*
5. *Mean Streets*	5. *Sunday Bloody Sunday*	5. *Xala*
6. *Nashville*	6. *Playtime*	
7. *Milestones*	7. *Amarcord*	
8. *Annie Hall*	8. *Lancelot du Lac*	
9. *Star Wars*	9. *Face to Face*	
10. *The Godfather*	10. *Effi Briest*	

RICHARD CORLISS (editor of *Film Comment*):

BEST AMERICAN FILMS	BEST EUROPEAN FILMS	BEST THIRD WORLD FILMS
1. *Petulia*	1. *Claire's Knee*	(Corliss did not compile a list in this category)
2. *Blume in Love*	2. *Aguirre: The Wrath of God*	
3. *Carnal Knowledge*	3. *Padre, Padrone*	
4. *Beyond the Valley of the Dolls*	4. *Two English Girls*	
5. *Badlands*	5. *The Go-Between*	
6. *The Parallax View*	6. *Scenes From a Marriage*	
7. *Alice Doesn't Live Here Anymore*	7. *In the Realm of the Senses*	
8. *The Conversation*	8. *The Mother and the Whore*	
9. *The Way We Were*	9. *The Vertical Smile*	
10. *Schoolgirl*	10. *The Spider's Stratagem*	

PETER COWIE (the editor of *International Film Guide* and the author of books on Scandinavian cinema and general world cinema):

BEST AMERICAN FILMS	BEST EUROPEAN FILMS	BEST THIRD WORLD FILMS
1. *The Godfather* ("The only $70 million-plus film of any lasting value.")	1. *Last Tango in Paris* ("Quite simply the most inspired film of the entire period.")	1. *Days and Nights in the Forest* ("The most complex and profound of recent films by the greatest director of the Third World.")
2. *Five Easy Pieces* ("The best film about the mood of the declining sixties.")	2. *The Passenger* ("Antonioni's best film since *The Eclipse*.")	2. *The Postman*
3. *2001* ("The best-ever sci-fi movie.")	3. *Scenes from a Marriage* (Bergman's most sustained achievement of the Seventies.")	3. *A Touch of Zen*
4. *Deliverance* ("The most terrifying film of the decade.")	4. *My Night at Maud's* ("The finest conversation piece of the decade.")	4. *Antonio Das Mortes*
		5. *The Castle of Purity*

BEST AMERICAN FILMS	BEST EUROPEAN FILMS	BEST THIRD WORLD FILMS
5. *Midnight Cowboy* ("The most haunting of all recent films about Manhattan; warmer than *Taxi Driver*.")	5. *Roma* (Original Version —"A dazzling tribute to the Italy that Fellini represents for us all.")	
6. *American Graffiti* ("The most engaging and most vulnerable in its feelings, of all the 'youth movies.' ")	6. *Illumination* ("The most disquieting film made about the clash between science, art, and mysticism.")	
7. *A Woman Under the Influence* ("The best 'experimental-commerical' movie of the period.")	7. *Everything for Sale* ("The best film [since Bergman's *Persona*] about the dilemmas of the movie director.")	
8. *Annie Hall* ("The funniest film of the decade.")	8. *Don't Look Now* 9. *If . . .* 10. *Day for Night* ("Truffaut's most sparkling movie in years.")	
9. *Play Misty for Me* ("The most obsessive of Eastwood's films as star or director.")		
10. *Fat City* ("The best film about boxing since *The Harder They Fall*, and a million times better than *Rocky*.")		

Method of Evaluation: "Priority given to films that are clearly an urgent, personal act of expression by their makers, in however commerical a context that may be."

JAN DAWSON (freelance critic and journalist and author of a book on new German cinema):

BEST AMERICAN FILMS	BEST EUROPEAN FILMS	BEST THIRD WORLD FILMS
(in no particular order)	*(in no particular order)*	*(in no particular order)*
1. *McCabe and Mrs. Miller*	1. *The Cermony*	1. *The Adversary*
2. *Mean Streets*	2. *Last Tango in Paris*	2. *Hour of the Furnaces*
3. *David Holzman's Diary*	3. *Out One Spectre*	3. *Lucia*
4. *Zabriskie Point*	4. *Wrong Movement*	4. *The Perfumed Nightmare*
5. *Annie Hall*	5. *The Sorrow and the Pity*	5. *Emitai*
6. *The King of Marvin Gardens*	6. *The Mother and the Whore*	
7. *Le vieux pays où Rimbaud est mort*	7. *Performance*	
8. *Inserts*	8. *Wild Child*	
9. *Nashville*	9. *Artistes at the Top of the Big Top: Disorientated*	
10. *Night of the Living Dead*	10. *Aguirre: The Wrath of God*	
	11. *Le Diable, probablement*	

Method of Evaluation: "Purely subjective."

STEPHEN FARBER (movie critic for *New West* and writer for a wide variety of other publications):

BEST AMERICAN FILMS	**BEST EUROPEAN FILMS**	**BEST THIRD WORLD FILMS**
(in chronological order)	*(in chronological order)*	

BEST AMERICAN FILMS	**BEST EUROPEAN FILMS**
1. Petulia	1. Shame
2. The Wild Bunch	2. Performance
3. Five Easy Pieces	3. This Man Must Die
4. Deliverance	4. The Music Lovers
5. American Graffiti	5. The Conformist
6. Badlands	6. Walkabout
7. The Conversation	7. The Sorrow and the Pity
8. Nashville	8. The Emigrants and The New Land
9. Dog Day Afternoon	9. Day For Night
10. Carrie	10. Amarcord

Method of Evaluation: "I tried to choose films that seemed to have the most historical importance— cultural and aesthetic. There were films I enjoyed more on a first viewing, but they haven't held up as well. I wanted to include a broad range of films and major filmmakers. I haven't seen enough Third World films to complete that category."

MICHAEL GOODWIN (a San Francisco-based freelancer and an associate editor of *Take One*):

BEST AMERICAN FILMS	**BEST EUROPEAN FILMS**	**BEST THIRD WORLD FILMS**
(in no particular order)	*(in no particular order)*	*(in no particular order)*
1. Coogan's Bluff	1. Claire's Knee	1. The Hour of the Furnaces
2. Beyond the Valley of the Dolls	2. A Very Curious Girl	2. The Harder They Come
3. 2001: A Space Odyssey	3. Aguirre: The Wrath of God	3. Heroes Two
4. Petulia	4. Dead Pigeon on Beethoven Street	4. The Battle of Chile
5. The Last Movie	5. The Immortal Story	5. Antonio das Mortes
6. The Last Picture Show	6. Performance	
7. Mean Streets	7. Le Boucher	
8. The Legend of Lylah Clare	8. Jonah, Who Will Be 25 In the Year 2000	
9. The Texas Chainsaw Massacre	9. Scenes From a Marriage	
10. The Shootist	10. Juggernaut	

Method of Evaluation: "Collective and idiosyncratic."

MOLLY HASKELL (author of *From Reverence to Rape: The Treatment of Women in the Movies*):

BEST AMERICAN FILMS	**BEST EUROPEAN FILMS**	**BEST THIRD WORLD FILMS**
1. Nashville	1. Belle de Jour	1. Charulata
2. Petulia	2. Once Upon a Time in the West	2. Memories of Underdevelopment
3. Barry Lyndon	3. Le Boucher	3. Black Girl
4. Blume in Love	4. La Marquise d'O	
5. Annie Hall	5. The Last Woman	
6. All the President's Men	6. The Merchant of Four Seasons	
7. The Godfather I, Godfather II	7. Deep End	
8. Klute		

BEST AMERICAN FILMS	BEST EUROPEAN FILMS	BEST THIRD WORLD FILMS
9. Faces	8. My Night at Maud's	
10. Madigan	9. A Piece of Pleasure	
11. Mean Streets	10. The Touch	
	11. The Sorrow and the Pity	

Method of Evaluation: "These are the pictures I have taken the most pleasure in, that I have been impatient to see more than once; that I consider the richest expression of directors I most admire and, in their idiosyncratic way, of the last decade."

DIANE JACOBS (freelance critic and author of *Hollywood Renaisance*):

BEST AMERICAN FILMS	BEST EUROPEAN FILMS	BEST THIRD WORLD FILMS
1. American Graffiti	1. Amarcord	1. Days and Nights in the Forest
2. Annie Hall	2. Claire's Knee	2. Distant Thunder
3. Badlands	3. Lancelot du Lac	3. Memories of Underdevelopment
4. The Godfather	4. Le Boucher	
5. Harry and Tonto	5. The Merchant of Four Seasons	
6. The Man Who Would Be King	6. The Mother and the Whore	
7. McCabe and Mrs. Miller	7. The Passenger	
8. Mean Streets	8. Scenes From a Marriage	
9. Midnight Cowboy	9. The Spider's Stratagem	
10. Smile	10. Two English Girls	

RICHARD T. JAMESON (editor of the Seattle Film Society's magazine *Movietone News* and teacher of film at the University of Washington):

BEST AMERIAN FILMS	BEST EUROPEAN FILMS	BEST THIRD WORLD FILMS
1. 2001: A Space Odyssey	1. My Night at Maud's	1. Bring Me the Head Of Alfredo Garcia
2. Petulia	2. Once Upon a Time in the West	
3. The Wild Bunch	3. Le Boucher	
4. Topaz	4. The Conformist	
5. Performance	5. Red Psalm	
6. The Private Life of Sherlock Holmes	6. The Discreet Charm of the Bourgeoisie	
7. Chinatown	7. The Merchant of Four Seasons	
8. The Parallax View	8. Lancelot du Lac	
9. Nashville	9. The Legend of Kaspar Hauser	
10. The Man Who Would Be King	10. Kings of the Road	

Method of Evaluation: "Within each category I determined to limit directors to a single film. Criteria were more intuitive than rational or specific. Autumnal masterpieces are as valuable to their time as more explicitly contemporaneous works that herald the arrival of important new talents, visions, and styles. It mattered a lot to me in the seventies that Sam Peckinpah could be so intransigently personal, and fashionability of outlook be damned; that Alan Pakula could be so awesomely classical while a lot of neoclassicalists were beginning to give the *hommage* a bad name; that Lester and Roeg could translate the fragmentation of modern life into a challenging, illuminating form and grammar; that Eric Rohmer could make literate conversation cinematically viable; that Altman, Jancso, and Leone could disclose new horizons within known movie spaces; that all of these directors made the films that only they could have made and kept film alive and growing, no matter how hard the industry, an unadventurous public, and 90% of the new academicians labored to kill it off."

STANLEY KAUFFMANN (film critic for *The New Republic* and author and editor of numerous books on film):

BEST AMERICAN FILMS	BEST EUROPEAN FILMS	BEST THIRD WORLD FILMS
1. *Close Encounters of the Third Kind*	1. *Amarcord*	1. *Blood of the Condor*
2. *The Conversation*	2. *The Goalie's Anxiety at the Penalty Kick*	2. *Hour of the Furnaces*
3. *Desperate Characters*	3. *How I Won the War*	3. *Memories of Underdevelopment*
4. *Harlan County, U.S.A.*	4. *The Marquise of O*	4. *Ramparts of Clay*
5. *The Hired Hand*	5. *The Milky Way*	
6. *Midnight Cowboy*	6. *The Passion of Anna*	
7. *Mikey and Nicky*	7. *The Red and the White*	
8. *Payday*	8. *The Rise of Louis XIV*	
9. *Wanda*	9. *La Salamandre*	
10. *The Wild Bunch*	10. *The Sorrow and the Pity*	

Method of Evaluation: "These are favorite films, not necessarily 'best.'"

GREIL MARCUS (author of *Mystery Train: Images of America in Rock 'n' Roll Music*; writes about books for *Rolling Stone*):

BEST AMERICAN FILMS	BEST EUROPEAN FILMS	BEST THIRD WORLD FILMS
1. *The Godfather, II* ("lacks the control of the first movie, but it also withholds the forgiveness the first movie offered to its characters and to its audience.")	1. *Weekend* ("prophecy for the seventies")	(Marcus did not compile a list in this category)
2. *The Godfather, I* ("may be the most exciting melodrama ever made")	2. *The Battle of Chile* ("the only film I've ever seen that can be compared with *Intolerance*")	
3. *Thieves Like Us*	3. *Vladimir and Rosa* ("the most honest film anyone has made about sixties and seventies realities")	
4. *The Man Who Would Be King* ("is not only spookier than *The Treasure of the Sierra Madre*, it's more fun")	4. *Burn!* ("the colonialist version of the same vision as *Across 110th Street*")	
5. *Across 110th Street* ("you can see it as a black footnote to *The Godfather, II*, or you can suffer it on its own terms, as the most violent commercial movie of the decade")	5. *Jonah, Who Will Be 25 in the Year 2000*	
6. *The Autobiography of Miss Jane Pittman*	6. *The Wild Child*	
7. *McCabe and Mrs. Miller*	7. *The Harder They Come*	
8. *Spend It All* ("shows how Cajuns spend it mostly on food")	8. *Scenes from a Marriage*	
9. *Mean Streets*	9. *We All Loved Each Other So Much*	
10. *Chinatown*	10. *Last Tango in Paris*	

Preferential ratings really apply to only the first two choices in each category.

JANET MASLIN (reviews film for *The New York Times*):

BEST AMERICAN FILMS

(in no particular order)

1. Nashville
2. Taxi Driver
3. Bad Company
4. Blume in Love
5. September 30, 1955
6. The Last American Hero
7. Annie Hall
8. Rosemary's Baby
9. Dirty Harry
10. Sugarland Express

BEST EUROPEAN FILMS

(in no particular order)

1. The Discreet Charm of the Bourgeoisie
2. Day for Night
3. Scenes from a Marriage
4. Le Boucher
5. Two English Girls
6. The Devils
7. Petulia
8. Z
9. The Legend of Kaspar Hauser
10. The Bitter Tears of Petra Von Kant

BEST THIRD WORLD FILMS

(Maslin did not compile a list in this category)

JAMES MONACO (author of several books on films):

BEST AMERICAN FILMS

1. Petulia
2. Medium Cool
3. The Godfather
4. Blume in Love
5. Hearts and Minds
6. Nashville
7. Downhill Racer
8. All the President's Men
9. 2001: A Space Odyssey
10. Barry Lyndon

BEST EUROPEAN FILMS

1. Stolen Kisses
2. The Wild Child
3. Fellini Satyricon
4. The Sorrow and the Pity
5. Tout va bien
6. Emigrants/The New Land
7. The Mother and the Whore
8. Jonah, Who Will be 25 in the Year 2000
9. Ca va, ca vient
10. Praise Marx and Pass the Ammunition

BEST THIRD WORLD FILMS

1. Sweet Sweetback's Baadass's Song
2. Ganja and Hess
3. The Harder They Come
4. A Touch of Zen
5. The Promised Land

GENE MOSKOWITZ (based in Paris for *Variety*, one of the most quoted film critics in the business):

BEST AMERICAN FILMS

(in no particular order)

1. American Graffiti
2. Easy Rider
3. The Wild Bunch
4. The Shootist
5. One Flew Over the Cuckoo's Nest
6. The Godfather, II
7. Fat City
8. Taxi Driver
9. Duel
10. Nashville

BEST EUROPEAN FILMS

(in no particular order)

1. In the Realm of the Senses
2. Love (Szerelèm)
3. If . . .
4. Lancelot du Lac
5. Conversation Piece
6. Providence
7. The Phantom of Liberty
8. The Legend of Kaspar Hauser
9. La Grande Bouffe
10. 1900

BEST THIRD WORLD FILMS

(in no particular order)

1. Distant Thunder
2. Xala
3. A Touch of Zen
4. Antonio das Mortes
5. Chronicle of the Year of Embers

Method of Evaluation: "First those that have stayed with me and then I weeded some out. Also, those films reflecting the 70s got preference."

FRANK RICH (currently film and television critic for *Time*. He previously wrote for the *New York Post* and *New Times*):

BEST AMERICAN FILMS *(in alphabetical order)*	BEST EUROPEAN FILMS *(in alphabetical order)*	BEST THIRD WORLD FILMS *(in alphabetical order)*
1. *Alice's Restaurant*	1. *Amarcord*	1. *Days and Nights in the Forest*
2. *Badlands*	2. *The Conformist*	2. *Distant Thunder*
3. *Barry Lyndon*	3. *The Discreet Charm of the Bourgeoisie*	3. *Memories of Underdevelopment*
4. *The Godfather, II*	4. *Lacombe, Lucien*	
5. *McCabe and Mrs. Miller*	5. *My Night at Maud's*	
6. *The Memory of Justice*	6. *Murmur of the Heart*	
7. *Nashville*	7. *Scenes from a Marriage*	
8. *Petulia*	8. *The Sorrow and the Pity*	
9. *Taxi Driver*	9. *Stolen Kisses*	
10. *2001: A Space Odyssey*	10. *The Story of Adele H.*	

CLAYTON RILEY (freelance writer and playwright who has written for numerous publications including *The New York Times, Black Sports, Amsterdam News*):

BEST AMERICAN FILMS	BEST EUROPEAN FILMS	BEST THIRD WORLD FILMS
1. *Sweet Sweetback's Badass Song*	1. *The Conformist*	1. *The Harder They Come*
2. *The Long Goodbye*	2. *Duelle*	2. *Emitai*
3. *Chinatown*	3. *Barocco*	3. *Lucia*
4. *Julia*	4. *Maternale (Mother and Daughter)*	4. *The Battle of Algiers*
5. *Ganja and Hess*	5. *Derzu Uzala*	5. *Bush Mama*
6. *The Godfather*	6. *Last Tango in Paris*	
7. *The Conversation*	7. *Lumière*	
8. *Taxi Driver*	8. *The Passenger*	
9. *Harlan County, U.S.A.*	9. *Amarcord*	
10. *The Fortune*	10. *Weekend*	

ANDREW SARRIS (film critic for *The Village Voice*, teacher of film at Columbia University, and the author of many books on film):

BEST AMERICAN FILMS	BEST EUROPEAN FILMS	BEST THIRD WORLD FILMS
1. *Petulia*	1. *Belle de Jour*	1. *Mon Oncle Antoine*
2. *Love among the Ruins*	2. *The Merchant of Four Seasons*	2. *Charulata*
3. *Three Women*	3. *Once Upon a Time in the West*	3. *Black Girl*
4. *The Passenger*	4. *La Rupture*	4. *Memories of Underdevelopment*
5. *Barry Lyndon*	5. *Deep End*	5. *How Tasty Was My Little Frenchman*
6. *All the President's Men*	6. *Claire's Knee*	
7. *Nashville*	7. *The Touch*	
8. *McCabe and Mrs. Miller*	8. *A Piece of Pleasure*	
9. *Annie Hall*	9. *My Night at Maud's*	
10. *Madigan*	10. *Effi Briest*	
	11. *The Last Woman*	
	12. *The Discreet Charm of the Bourgeoisie*	

Method of Evalutation: "The films above represent to me the most interesting work done during the decade. They stick in my mind because of some intuitive blend of forms and feelings. All films reflect an unresolved tension between art and life."

RICHARD SCHICKEL (film critic for *Time*, producer of a television series on movies):

BEST AMERICAN FILMS	**BEST EUROPEAN FILMS**	**BEST THIRD WORLD FILMS**
(in alphabetical order)	*(in alphabetical order)*	(Schickel did not compile a list in this category)

BEST AMERICAN FILMS	**BEST EUROPEAN FILMS**
1. *American Graffiti*	1. *Day for Night*
2. *Badlands*	2. *The Emigrants*
3. *Barry Lyndon*	3. *The Marquise of O*
4. *Five Easy Pieces*	4. *My Night at Maud's*
5. *The Godfather, I; Godfather II*	5. *That Obscure Object of Desire*
6. *Klute*	6. *The Passion of Anna*
7. *M*A*S*H*	7. *The Red and the White*
8. *Nashville*	8. *This Man Must Die*
9. *The Wild Bunch*	9. *Wedding in Blood*
10. *Star Wars*	10. *A Piece of Pleasure*

Method of Evaluation: "Very simple. The ones that linger in the mind, recalled with pleasure and easily. They are all movies I would happily see again."

DAVID THOMSON (teaches film at Dartmouth, is film critic for *The Real Paper* in Boston and author of *Biographical Dictionary of Film*):

BEST AMERICAN FILMS	**BEST EUROPEAN FILMS**	**BEST THIRD WORLD FILMS**
(in alphabetical order)	*(in alphabetical order)*	(Thomson did not compile a list in this category)

BEST AMERICAN FILMS	**BEST EUROPEAN FILMS**
1. *Chinatown*	1. *Two English Girls*
2. *Close Encounters of the Third Kind*	2. *Céline and Julie Go Boating*
3. *The Godfather I; Godfather II*	3. *Claire's Knee*
4. *The King of Marvin Gardens*	4. *The Conformist*
5. *The Last Picture Show*	5. *Cries and Whispers*
6. *Mean Streets*	6. *The Discreet Charm of the Bourgeoisie*
7. *Nashville*	7. *Lancelot du Lac*
8. *Pat Garrett and Billy the Kid*	8. *The Mother and the Whore*
9. *Taxi Driver*	9. *The Passenger*
10. *Trash*	10. *Stavisky*

Method of Evaluation: "I simply listed the films that gave me most enjoyment in repeated viewings; I tried to name no more than one film by any director, but failed with Scorsese and would still like *New York, New York*."

FRANCOIS TRUFFAUT (the famous French film director):

BEST AMERICAN FILMS	**BEST EUROPEAN FILMS**	**BEST THIRD WORLD FILMS**
(in chronological order)	*(in chronological order)*	

BEST AMERICAN FILMS	**BEST EUROPEAN FILMS**
1. *Rosemary's Baby* ("un film réellement gracieux")	1. *My Night at Maud's* ("suspense de dialogue")
2. *The Honeymoon Killers* ("100% réaliste")	2. *Marie pour mémoire* ("le fils de Godard")

BEST AMERICAN FILMS	BEST EUROPEAN FILMS	BEST THIRD WORLD FILMS
3. *Johnny Got His Gun* ("un cas extrême de survie")	3. *Le petit théâtre de Jean Renoir* ("Renoir working")	
4. *The Last Picture Show* ("de vrais caractères")	4. *Tristana* ("la vérité sur la vieilesse")	
5. *Rio Lobo* ("magistrale direction")	5. *Cries and Whispers* ("la mort rouge et la musique")	
6. *One Flew Over the Cuckoo's Nest* ("Puissance de Forman")	6.	
7. *All the President's Men* ("un film moral")	7. *Derzu Uzala* ("la mort et le vent")	
8. *Family Plot* ("Hitch working")	8. *Aguirre: The Wrath of God* ("le travelling en radeau")	
9. *F for Fake* ("l'ivresse of the cutting")	9. *Le Diable, probablement* ("la beauté de la jeunesse")	
10. *Annie Hall* ("vive le cinéma autobiographique")	10. *Casanova* ("la poesie anti-Hollywood")	

Method of Evaluation: "J'ai choisi les films que j'ai en envie de voir plusiers fois."

6/THE *NEW YORK TIMES* ANNUAL "TEN BEST" LISTS

THE NEW YORK Times has reviewed a considerable portion of the films released in New York during the past 60 years. In fact, between 1913, when the *Times* decided to cover movies, and 1970, when it reviews were collected and indexed, the *Times* published nearly 19,000 reviews.

Movies were at least 15 years old by 1913, but the first *Times'* writers did not yet know quite what to make of the new medium. There were no film specialists in those days, just trained journalists trying to come to terms with a new and hybrid art form. But as George Amberg comments in his introduction to the one-volume selection of *The New York Film Reviews,* eventually some reviewers went beyond the safe limits of mere reporting into the more perilous arena of critical analysis. This transition from content analysis and performance appraisal to the realization that film is a unique and complicated art in its own right happened not only in the *Times,* of course, but in the art world at large.

The collected *Times* film reviews reflect, then, the writing styles, the moral and cultural stances, and the political and social prejudices—in short, the tastes and attitudes of four generations of moviegoers. And many of those attitudes and tastes can be discerned in the Ten Best Lists printed below.

Mordaunt Hall was the *Times'* principal film reviewer when the newspaper began compiling its annual Ten Best lists in 1924. Andre Sennwald was his successor from 1934 to 1936, and he in turn was replaced by Frank S. Nugent. Bosley Crowther took over in 1940 and retained the position through 1967, proving to be one of America's most durable and influential reviewers. Renata Adler held the post during 1968, and in 1969 Vincent Canby became the *Times'* first-string film critic, a position he still holds.

Through 1968 the films are listed in order of preference. In 1969 Canby began citing his choices alphabetically. Between 1956 and 1961, foreign-language films are considered separately from English-language films. (Between 1956 and 1961, *Time* also made the same distinction.)

1924

The Dramatic Life of Abraham
  Lincoln
The Thief of Bagdad
Beau Brummel
Merton of the Movies
The Sea Hawk
He Who Gets Slapped
The Marriage Circle
In Hollywood With Potash and
  Perlmutter
Peter Pan
Isn't Life Wonderful

1925

The Big Parade
The Last Laugh
The Unholy Three
The Gold Rush
The Merry Widow
The Dark Angel
Don Q, Son of Zorro
Ben-Hur
Stella Dallas
A Kiss for Cinderella

1926

Variety
Beau Geste
What Price Glory
Potemkin
The Grand Duchess and the
  Waiter
The Black Pirate
Old Ironsides
Moana
La Bohème
So This is Paris

1927

The King of Kings
Chang
The Way of All Flesh
Wings
Seventh Heaven
Sunrise

Service for Ladies
Quality Street
Underworld
Stark Love

1928

The Circus
Street Angel
Czar Ivan the Terrible
The Last Command
White Shadows of the South
  Sea
The Patriot
The End of St. Petersburg
Show People
Homecoming
Four Devils

1929

The Love Parade
Disraeli
Hallelujah!
The Passion of Joan of Arc
The Taming of the Shrew
Bulldog Drummond
They Had to See Paris
The Sky Hawk
The Virginian
Sally

1930

With Byrd at the South Pole
All Quiet on the Western
  Front
Journey's End
Lightnin'
The Devil to Pay
Outward Bound
Tom Sawyer
Holiday
Abraham Lincoln
Anna Christie

1931

The Guardsman
City Lights

The Smiling Lieutenant
Arrowsmith
Tabu
Bad Girl
Frankenstein
Skippy
Private Lives
A Connecticut Yankee

1932

Mädchen in Uniform
Trouble in Paradise
Der Raub der Mona Lisa
Grand Hotel
Dr. Jekyll and Mr. Hyde
The Mouthpiece
One Hour with You
A Bill of Divorcement
The Doomed Battalion
Reserved for Ladies

1933

Cavalcade
Reunion in Vienna
Morgenroth
State Fair
Dinner at Eight
Berkeley Square
The Private Life of Henry VIII
Little Women
The Invisible Man
His Double Life

1934

It Happened One Night
The House of Rothschild
The Battle
The Thin Man
Catherine the Great
The First World War
One Night of Love
The Lost Patrol
Man of Aran
Our Daily Bread

1935

The Informer
Ruggles of Red Gap
David Copperfield
Lives of a Bengal Lancer
Les Misérables
The Scoundrel
Chapayev
The Man Who Knew Too
   Much
Sequoia
Love Me Forever

1936

(Eleven films this year)
La Kermesse Héroique
(Carnival in Flanders)
Fury
Dodsworth
Mr. Deeds Goes to Town
Winterset
Romeo and Juliet
The Green Pastures
The Ghost Goes West
The Story of Louis Pasteur
These Three
The Great Ziegfeld

1937

The Life of Emile Zola
The Good Earth
Stage Door
Captains Courageous
They Won't Forget
Make Way for Tomorrow
I Met Him in Paris
A Star Is Born
Camille
Lost Horizon

1938

Snow White and the Seven
   Dwarfs
The Citadel
To the Victor
Pygmalion

A Slight Case of Murder
Three Comrades
The Lady Vanishes
The Adventures of Robin
   Hood
A Man to Remember
Four Daughters

1939

Made for Each Other
Stagecoach
Wuthering Heights
Dark Victory
Juárez
Goodbye, Mr. Chips
The Women
Mr. Smith Goes to
   Washington
Ninotchka
Gone With the Wind

1940

The Grapes of Wrath
The Baker's Wife
Rebecca
Our Town
The Mortal Storm
Pride and Prejudice
The Great McGinty
The Long Voyage Home
The Great Dictator
Fantasia

1941

The Lady Eve
Citizen Kane
Major Barbara
Sergeant York
The Stars Look Down
Here Comes Mr. Jordan
Target for Tonight
Dumbo
How Green Was My Valley
One Foot in Heaven

1942

In Which We Serve
Journey for Margaret
Casablanca
One of Our Aircraft Is Missing
Wake Island
Mrs. Miniver
Yankee Doodle Dandy
The Gold Rush
Woman of the Year
Sullivan's Travels

1943

Air Force
Desert Victory
The Ox-Bow Incident
The More the Merrier
For Whom the Bell Tolls
Report from the Aleutians
Watch on the Rhine
Corvette K-225
Sahara
Madame Curie

1944

Destination Tokyo
The Miracle of Morgan's
   Creek
The Purple Heart
Going My Way
Wilson
Hail the Conquering Hero
Thirty Seconds Over Tokyo
None But the Lonely Heart
Meet Me in St. Louis
National Velvet

1945

A Tree Grows in Brooklyn
The Way Ahead
Anchors Aweigh
Pride of the Marines
The House on Ninety-Second
   Street
Story of G.I. Joe
Spellbound

The Last Chance
The Lost Weekend
They Were Expendable

1946

Open City
Road to Utopia
The Green Years
Henry V
Notorious
Brief Encounter
The Well-Digger's Daughter
The Best Years of Our Lives
My Darling Clementine
Stairway to Heaven

1947

The Yearling
Great Expectations
Miracle on 34th Street
Crossfire
Life with Father
Shoe Shine
Gentleman's Agreement
To Live in Peace
The Bishop's Wife
The Fugitive

1948

Treasure of Sierra Madre
The Pearl
The Search
A Foreign Affair
Louisiana Story
Hamlet
Johnny Belinda
Apartment for Peggy
The Red Shoes
The Snake Pit

1949

Command Decision
A Letter to Three Wives
The Quiet One
Lost Boundaries
Pinky

The Heiress
All the King's Men
Battleground
The Fallen Idol
Intruder in the Dust

1950

The Titan—Story of
    Michelangelo
Twelve O'Clock High
Father of the Bride
The Asphalt Jungle
Destination Moon
The Men
Sunset Boulevard
Trio
All About Eve
Born Yesterday

1951

Fourteen Hours
The Brave Bulls
Oliver Twist
A Place in the Sun
People Will Talk
A Streetcar Named Desire
An American in Paris
Detective Story
Death of a Salesman
Decision Before Dawn
Best Foreign: Rashomon
    (Japan)

1952

The Greatest Show on Earth
Cry, The Beloved Country
Viva Zapatal
Five Fingers
High Noon
Ivanhoe
The Quiet Man
Limelight
Breaking the Sound
    Barrier
Come Back, Little Sheba

1953

Moulin Rouge
Lili
Shane
Julius Caesar
Man on a Tightrope
Stalag 17
From Here to Eternity
Roman Holiday
Martin Luther
The Conquest of Everest

1954

The Glenn Miller Story
Genevieve
Knock on Wood
Mr. Hulot's Holiday
Seven Brides for Seven
    Brothers
On the Waterfront
The Little Kidnappers
Sabrina
The Country Girl
Romeo and Juliet

1955

The Bridges at Toko-Ri
Bad Day at Black Rock
A Man Called Peter
Marty
The Great Adventure
Mister Roberts
The Phoenix City Story
It's Always Fair Weather
Oklahomal
The Prisoner

1956

Richard III
The King and I
Moby Dick
Bus Stop
Lust for Life
The Silent World
Giant
Around the World in 80 Days

Friendly Persuasion
Anastasia
BEST FOREIGN FILMS

The Proud and the Beautiful
  (France)
Rififi (France)
La Strada (Italy)
The Grand Maneuver (France)
The Magnificent Seven
  (Japan)

1957

The Great Man
Funny Face
Twelve Angry Men
The Green Man
A Hatful of Rain
Silk Stockings
Love in the Afternoon
Les Girls
Sayonara
The Bridge on the River Kwai
BEST FOREIGN FILMS

We Are All Murderers (France)
Gold of Naples (Italy)
The Red Balloon (France)
Torerol (Mexico)
Passionate Summer (France)
The Last Bridge (Germany)
Cabiria (Italy)
Gervaise (France)
Ordet (Denmark)
Smiles of a Summer Night
  (Sweden)

1958

Teacher's Pet
Gigi
The Goddess
God's Little Acre
Cat on a Hot Tin Roof
The Defiant Ones
Damn Yankees
The Horse's Mouth
I Want to Live!
A Night to Remember
BEST FOREIGN FILMS

Gates of Paris (France)
Rouge et Noir (France)
Case of Dr. Laurent (France)

The Captain from Koepenick
  (Germany)
Pather Panchali (India)
Inspector Maigret (France)
The Seventh Seal (Sweden)
My Uncle (France)
Witches of Salem (France)
He Who Must Die (France)

1959

The Diary of Anne Frank
Room at the Top
The Nun's Story
Porgy and Bess
Anatomy of a Murder
A Hole in the Head
North by Northwest
Pillow Talk
Ben-Hur
On the Beach
BEST FOREIGN FILMS

The Devil Strikes at Night
  (Germany)
Forbidden Fruit (France)
Aparajito (India)
The Roof (Italy)
Wild Strawberries (Sweden)
The Magician (Sweden)
The Lovers (France)
The 400 Blows (France)
The Cousins (France)
Black Orpheus (France/Brazil)

1960

I'm All Right, Jack
The Apartment
Psycho
Elmer Gantry
Sunrise at Campobello
The Entertainer
Inherit the Wind
The Angry Silence
Exodus
Tunes of Glory
BEST FOREIGN FILMS

Rosemary (Germany)
Ikiru (Japan)
The Cranes Are Flying (Russia)
Hiroshima Mon Amour
  (France)
The World of Apu (India)
Never on Sunday (Greece)

The Virgin Spring (Sweden)
General della Rovere (Italy)
The Big Deal on Madonna
  Street (Italy)
The Ballad of a Soldier
  (Russia)

1961

The Facts of Life
A Raisin in the Sun
Saturday Night and Sunday
  Morning
Fanny
The Hustler
Splendor in the Grass
West Side Story
El Cid
Judgment at Nuremberg
One, Two, Three
BEST FOREIGN FILMS

Don Quixote (Russia)
Breathless (France)
La Dolce Vita (Italy)
The Bridge (Germany)
Two Women (Italy)
Ashes and Diamonds (Poland)
Rocco and His Brothers (Italy)
Purple Noon (France)
Girl with a Suitcase (Italy)
A Summer to Remember
  (Russia)

1962

Lover Come Back
Last Year at Marienbad
Whistle Down the Wind
A Taste of Honey
Divorce—Italian Style
The Longest Day
Long Day's Journey Into Night
Sundays and Cybele
Freud
Electra

1963

Heavens Abovel
The L-Shaped Room
Hud
Cleopatra

8 ½
Tom Jones
Any Number Can Win
The Sound of Trumpets
It's a Mad, Mad, Mad, Mad World
America, America

1964

Dr. Strangelove
The Servant
That Man from Rio
One Potato, Two Potato
A Hard Day's Night
Woman in the Dunes
Mary Poppins
My Fair Lady
The Americanization of Emily
Marriage Italian Style

1965

The Pawnbroker
Ship of Fools
Darling
Repulsion
Juliet of the Spirits
The Eleanor Roosevelt Story
Red Desert
Kwaidan
To Die in Madrid
Thunderball

1966

The Shop on Main Street
The Gospel According to St. Matthew
Dear John
Morgan!
The Russians Are Coming, The Russians Are Coming
Who's Afraid of Virginia Woolf?
Georgy Girl
Loves of a Blonde
A Man for All Seasons
Blow-up

1967

La Guerre 'est finie
Ulysses
The Hunt
In the Heat of the Night
Father
Elvira Madigan
Closely Watched Trains
Cool Hand Luke
In Cold Blood
The Graduate

1968

Charlie Bubbles
The Two of Us
Belle de Jour
Faces
Les Carabiniers
The Bride Wore Black
The Fifth Horseman Is Fear
Petulia
Rosemary's Baby
A Report on the Party and the Guests

1969

(listed alphabetically)
Alice's Restaurant
The Damned
If . . .
La Femme Infidèle
Midnight Cowboy
Stolen Kisses
Topaz
True Grit
The Wild Bunch
Z

1970

(listed alphabetically)
The Ballad of Cable Hogue
Catch-22
Fellini Satyricon
Little Big Man
Loving
*M*A*S*H*

My Night at Maud's
The Passion of Anna
Tristana
The Wild Child

1971

(listed alphabetically)
Bed and Board
Carnal Knowledge
Claire's Knee
A Clockwork Orange
The Conformist
Derby
The French Connection
The Last Picture Show
Le Boucher
Sunday Bloody Sunday

1972

(listed alphabetically)
Chloë in the Afternoon
Cries and Whispers
The Discreet Charm of the Bourgeoisie
Fat City
Frenzy
The Godfather
The Heartbreak Kid
Tokyo Story
Traffic
Two English Girls

1973

(listed alphabetically)
American Graffiti
Day for Night
Heavy Traffic
Last Tango in Paris
The Long Goodbye
Love
Mean Streets
Memories of Underdevelopment
Playtime
Sleeper

1974

(eleven films listed alphabetically)
Amarcord
Badlands
California Split
Claudine
Daisy Miller
Harry and Tonto
Lacombe, Lucien
Man Is Not a Bird
Le Petit Théâtre de Jean
   Renoir
Phantom of Liberté
Scenes from a Marriage

1975

(listed alphabetically)
Alice Doesn't Live Here
   Anymore
Barry Lyndon
Distant Thunder
Hearts and Minds
Love and Death
The Magic Flute
Nashville
Shampoo
The Story of Adele H.
Swept Away . . .

1976

(eight films listed alphabetically)
Seven Beauties
All the President's Men

Face to Face
La Chienne
Network
The Seven-Per-Cent Solution
Memory of Justice
Taxi Driver

1977

(listed alphabetically)
Annie Hall
Close Encounters of the Third
   Kind
Effi Briest
The Goalie's Anxiety at the
   Penalty Kick
Handle With Care
The Late Show
The Man Who Loved Women
Star Wars
Stroszek
That Obscure Object of Desire

1978

(listed alphabetically)
California Suite
Days of Heaven
The Deer Hunter
A Geisha
Movie Movie
Perceval
Pretty Baby
A Slave of Love
Straight Time
Violette
   (special mention, in no special
   order)
The Duellists
The Buddy Holly Story

The Chess Players
F.I.S.T.
Joseph Andrews
An Unmarried Woman
Landscape After the Battle
Death on the Nile
Autumn Sonata
Interiors

1979

(in alphabetical order)
Breaking Away
Escape from Alcatraz
Fedora
Hair
Kramer vs. Kramer
Love on the Run
Manhattan
The Marriage of Maria Braun
10
The Tree of Wooden Clogs
   Runners-up
   (in no special order)
Being There
Apocalypse Now
Moonraker
The Electric Horseman
Monty Phython's Life of Brian
Woyzeck
Norma Rae
The China Syndrome
All That Jazz
The Muppet Movie

7/*TIME* MAGAZINE'S ANNUAL "TEN BEST" LISTS

1945

(in chronological order)

The Fighting Lady
A Tree Grows in Brooklyn
Colonel Blimp
The Clock
San Pietro
The Southerner
Anchors Aweigh
The True Glory
The House on 92nd Street
The Lost Weekend

1946

(in chronological order)

Open City
Henry V
Anna and the King of Siam
Brief Encounter
The Killers
The Jolson Story
Margie
My Darling Clementine
The Best Years of Our Lives
It's A Wonderful Life

1947

(in chronological order)

Odd Man Out

Boomerang!
Ivan the Terrible
Monsieur Verdoux
Great Expectations
Crossfire
Shoe Shine
Gentleman's Agreement
Man About Town
To Live in Peace

1948

(List not compiled this year)

1949

(List not compiled this year)

1950

(in chronological order)

Tight Little Island
The Titan
The Third Man
The Hasty Heart
Cinderella
Kind Hearts and Coronets
The Men

Sunset Boulevard
The Breaking Point
All About Eve

1951

(in chronological order)

Isle of Sinners
Oliver Twist
A Place in the Sun
A Streetcar Named Desire
An American in Paris
The Red Badge of Courage
The Lavender Hill Mob
La Ronde
Detective Story
Miracle in Milan

1952

(in chronological order)

The African Queen
The Man in the White Suit
The Story of Robin Hood
High Noon
The Strange Ones
Ivanhoe
Flowers of St. Francis
Breaking the Sound Barrier
Forbidden Games
Come Back, Little Sheba
The Member of the Wedding
Moulin Rouge

1953

(in chronological order)
Lili
Call Me Madam
Shane
Fanfan the Tulip
From Here to Eternity
The Cruel Sea
Roman Holiday
The Captain's Paradise
The Living Desert
The Conquest of Everest

1954

(in chronological order)
Beat the Devil
Genevieve
*Seven Brides for Seven
 Brothers*
The Earrings of Madame de
On the Waterfront
High and Dry
The Little Kidnappers
Ugetsu
Carmen Jones
Gate of Hell

1955

(eight films in chronological order)
Game of Love
Wages of Fear
Marty
The Great Adventure
Summertime
The Desperate Hours
Umberto D.
The Man with the Golden Arm

1956

(in chronological order)
AMERICAN
The King and I
Somebody Up There Likes Me
Lust for Life

Giant
Around the World in 80 Days
Secrets of the Reef
FOREIGN
Richard III
The Grand Maneuver
I Vitelloni
Marcelino

1957

(12 films in chronological order)
AMERICAN
Full of Life
Twelve Angry Men
Sweet Smell of Success
Love in the Afternoon
A Hatful of Rain
The Pajama Game
Les Girls
Paths of Glory
The Bridge on the River Kwai
FOREIGN
Gold of Naples
The Devil's General
The Last Bridge

1958

(12 films in chronological order)
AMERICAN
The Enemy Below
The High Cost of Living
The Hot Spell
The Goddess
The Key
The Defiant Ones
Me and the Colonel
The Big Country
Damn Yankees

FOREIGN
Pather Panchali
The Horse's Mouth
He Who Must Die

1959

(13 films in chronological order)
AMERICAN
Some Like It Hot
The Diary of Anne Frank
Pork Chop Hill
Middle of the Night
Ben-Hur
FOREIGN
The Mistress
Aparajito
Room at the Top
The Roof
Wild Strawberries
Black Orpheus
The 400 Blows
Ivan the Terrible, Part II

1960

(17 films in chronological order)
AMERICAN
The Apartment
Come Back, Africa
Elmer Gantry
Sons and Lovers
Sunrise at Campobello
Spartacus
Weddings and Babies
Exodus
FOREIGN
Ikiru
A Lesson in Love
Dreams
The Virgin Spring
I'm All Right, Jack
Hiroshima Mon Amour
The World of Apu
General della Rovere
The Loving Game

1961

(19 films in chronological order)

AMERICAN

Facts of Life
101 Dalmatians
Shadows
Cold Wind in August
The Honeymoon Machine
Homicidal
The Hustler
The Mark
El Cid

FOREIGN

A Midsummer Night's Dream
Ballad of a Soldier
Breathless
Saturday Night and Sunday
  Morning
L'Avventura
La Dolce Vita
Rocco and His Brothers
The Kitchen
The Five-Day Lover
Throne of Blood

1962-1968

(Lists not compiled these years)

1969

(Top of the Decade)

Godard's Breathless and
  Fellini's La Dolce Vita open
  in the U.S., 1961
Dr. No is released, starting the
  James Bondwagon, 1963
A Hard Day's Night brings the
  Beatles to the screen, 1964
Dr. Strangelove, 1964
The Sound of Music spawns
  endless expensive musicals,
  1974
Bonnie and Clyde, 1967
The Graduate alerts filmmakers
  to the news that more than
  60 percent of their audience
  is thirty or under, 1967

GMRX ratings begin, 1968
Easy Rider establishes a trend
  toward the low-budget,
  personal movie, 1969
I Am Curious (Yellow) makes
  the X-rated, sex-sated movie
  a nationwide phenomenon,
  1969

1970

(in alphebetical order)

Catch-22
Husbands
Joe
Little Big Man
A Married Couple
M*A*S*H
The Passion of Anna
Patton
Satyricon
Woodstock

1971

(in alphabetical order)

A Clockwork Orange
The Clowns
The Conformist
Dirty Harry
The French Connection
Glen and Randa
The Last Picture Show
Minnie and Moskowitz
Straw Dogs
Sunday Bloody Sunday

1972

(14 films in alphabetical order)

Chloë in the Afternoon
Cries and Whispers
Deliverance
The Discreet Charm of the
  Bourgeoisie
Frenzy
The Godfather
Greaser's Palace
The Great Northfield,
  Minnesota Raid

The Heartbreak Kid
The King of Marvin Gardens
My Uncle Antoine
A Sense of Loss
The Sorrow and the Pity
Why

1973

(11 films in alphabetical order)

American Graffiti
An Autumn Afternoon
Day for Night
Don't Look Now
Last Tango in Paris
Love
Mean Streets
O Lucky Man!
Pat Garrett and Billy the Kid
Pulp
The Spider's Stratagem

1974

(in alphabetical order)

Amarcord
Antonia: A Portait of the
  Woman
Badlands
Chinatown
The Conversation
The Godfather, Part II
The Little Theater of Jean
  Renoir
The Seduction of Mimi
The Phantom of Liberté
The Three Musketeers

1975

(in alphabetical order)

Alice Doesn't Live Here
  Anymore
Barry Lyndon
Jaws
Just Before Nightfall
The Magic Flute
The Man Who Would Be King
Nashville
The Passenger
Tommy
The Wind and the Lion

1976

(in alphabetical order)
All the President's Men
Buffalo Bill and the Indians
Carrie
Face to Face
The Marquise of O
Obsession
The Outlaw Josey Wales
Small Change
Seven Beauties
Une Partie de Plaisir

1977

(in alphabetical order)
Annie Hall
Black and White in Color
Close Encounters of the Third
   Kind
Handle With Care
High Anxiety
1900
That Obscure Object of Desire

*Dated by U.S. release.

The Late Show
Semi-Tough
Star Wars

1978

(in alphabetical order)
Bread and Chocolate
Cat and Mouse
Days of Heaven
Get Out Your Handkerchiefs
Heaven Can Wait
Movie Movie
National Lampoon's Animal
   House
Summer Paradise
The Deer Hunter
Watership Down

1979

AMERICAN

Five Easy Pieces (1970)
M*A*S*H (1970)

Godfather I and II (1972,
   1974)
American Graffiti (1973)
Badlands (1974)
Barry Lyndon (1975)
Nashville (1975)
Annie Hall (1977)
Star Wars (1977)
Manhattan (1979)

FOREIGN*

My Night at Maud's (1970)
Murmur of the Heart (1971)
Last Tango in Paris (1972)
The Discreet Charm of the
   Bourgeoisie (1972)
The Sorrow and the Pity
   (1972)
Day for Night (1973)
Amarcord (1974)
Distant Thunder (1975)
Just Before Nightfall (1975)
That Obscure Object of Desire
   (1977)

8/"TEN BEST" GRAB BAG

A. TOP TEN EDITORS

The March-April 1977 issue of *Film Comment* was devoted largely to a study of film editing. A highlight of the issue was a survey of more than 100 editors in which the film editors were asked to choose the editors and directors whose editing is consistently outstanding. The winners were as follows:

BEST EDITORS		Number of votes	BEST DIRECTORS		Number of votes
1.	William Hornbeck	19	1.	David Lean	14
2.	David Lean	9	2.	Robert Wise	12
3.	Margaret Booth	7	3.	William Wyler	8
	William Reynolds	7	4.	John Ford	6
	Ralph Winters	7		Alfred Hitchcock	6
6.	Dede Allen	6		Orson Welles	6
	Daniel Mandell	6	7.	Frank Capra	5
	Merrill C. White	6	8.	Ingmar Bergman	4
	Robert Wise	6		Jean-Luc Godard	4
10.	Jack Harris	5		George Stevens	4

B. BRITISH CRITICS' FAVORITE DIRECTORS

The editors of the British film magazine *Cinema* asked 17 of their contributors to select their 10 best films and 10 best directors. The critics were urged to be "as eclectic as possible" in order to overcome the restrictions of established taste and fashionability. The lists were published in the October 1969 issue of *Cinema*. Based on the results, a *Cinema* "Pantheon" and "Second Line" of directors was compiled. A "Third Line" was added, but the directors in this group were the selections of the editors along. Critics included: Bruce Beresford, Ian Christie, Stephen Crofts, David Curtis, Raymond Durgnat, Roger Huss, Paul Joannides, Karlos Kondzialki, Alan Lovell, Colin McArthur, Robert Mundy, Tom Nairn, Glynne Parker, Noel Purdon, Tony Rayns, Mike Wallington, and Peter Wollen.

Pantheon	Second Line	Third Line
(in alphabetical order)	*(in alphabetical order)*	*(in alphabeticl order)*
1. Kenneth Anger	1. Georges Franju	1. Walerian Borowczyk
2. Luis Buñuel	2. Samuel Fuller	2. John Huston
3. Carl Dreyer	3. Jean-Luc Godard	3. Stanley Kubrick
4. Sergei Eisenstein	4. Buster Keaton	4. Joseph Losey
5. Federico Fellini	5. Kenji Mizoguchi	5. Pier Paolo Pasolini
6. John Ford	6. Sam Peckinpah	6. Roman Polanski
7. Alfred Hitchcock	7. Jean Vigo	7. Michael Powell
8. Fritz Lang	8. Josef Von Sternberg	8. Don Siegel
9. Jean Renoir	9. Andrzej Wajda	9. Glauber Rocha
10. Billy Wilder	10. Orson Welles	10. Robert Rossen

C. MY FAVORITE FILMS/TEXTS/THINGS

Jonathan Rosenbaum—an assistant editor of the *Monthly Film Bulletin*—asked 35 filmpersons in the United Kingdom for two lists: 12 film titles and six texts or authors relevant to cinema. Rosenbaum encouraged idiosyncracy and permitted "cheating" (via ties, alternate choices, and the like). He did not include among his group of filmpersons any of the critics who had published 10 best lists in the 1972 *Sight and Sound* survey or the October 1969 *Cinema* Poll (both of which are included in *Film Facts*). Twenty-nine of the people responded. The results were published in the November-December 1976 issue of *Film Comment.*

FILMS	NUMBER OF VOTES
1. *L'Atalante* (Jean Vigo)	4
2. *The Magnificent Ambersons* (Orson Welles)	3.5
Penthesilea: Queen of the Amazons (Laura Mulvey and Peter Wollen)	3.5
4. *The Searchers* (John Ford)	3.33
5. *Madame de...* (Max Ophuls)	3
The Nightcleaners (Berwick Street Collective)	3
Pursued (Raoul Walsh)	3
The Rules of the Game (Jean Renoir)	3
Sansho the Bailiff (Kenji Mizoguchi)	3
Strike (Sergei Eisenstein)	3

FILMMAKERS	NUMBER OF VOTES
1. Jean-Luc Godard	15.5
2. Orson Welles	11
3. Alfred Hitchcock	10.25
4. Jean Renoir	9
5. John Ford	8
6. Michael Snow	7.5
7. Kenji Mizoguchi	7
8. Howard Hawks	6.5
9. Carl-Theodor Dreyer	6
10. Robert Bresson	5.5
Max Ophuls	5.5

Texts (included only those dealing with film)   **NUMBER OF VOTES**

1. **Peter Wollen** (author of Signs and Meaning in the Cinema) 9
2. **Raymond Durgnat** 7
   Robin Wood 7
4. **Noel Burch** (including votes for his collaboration with Jorge Dana)....................................6
   Jean-Luc Godard 6
6. **Andre Bazin** 5
   V.F. Perkins 5

A special citation to *Screen* magazine and to the *Cahiers du cinema* analysis of *Mr. Lincoln.*

D. BEST OF THE HALF CENTURY

In 1971 *Daily Variety* asked 200 filmmakers to name the best achievements in American cinema's first 50 years. Each of the 200 people polled had worked in the film industry for at least 25 years. The nominations were divided into three categories: The Silent Era; Sound; and Silent and Sound Eras. The results came up looking like this:

SILENT

Best film:
  Birth of a Nation
Best actor:
  Charlie Chaplin
Best actress:
  Greta Garbo

SOUND

Best film:
  Gone with the Wind
Best actor:
  Spencer Tracy
Best actress:
  Ingrid Bergman
Best producer:
  Samuel Goldwyn

OVERALL

Best film:
  Gone with the Wind
Best actor:
  Charlie Chaplin
Best actress:
  Greta Garbo
Best producer:
  Irving Thalberg
Best director:
  D.W. Griffith

E. COLLEGE FAVORITES

Has television changed the younger generation's moviegoing habits? In late 1978, the *Minneapolis Star* and *Tribune* interviewed 949 college students at six Minneapolis and St. Paul campuses to determine what films and stars attract today students. And according to the poll, movies remain the most popular form of entertainment outside the home: 86% of the students questioned said they had seen a film within the last three months, as opposed to 59% who had listened to live music in bars or dancehalls, 52% who had attended a live theater performance, 52% who had gone to musical concerts at which admissions were charged, and 30% who had attended free concerts. The students' favorites stars and films line up this way:

	FAVORITE STARS	Number of Votes
1.	Barbara Streisand	124
2.	Robert Redford	71
3.	Jane Fonda	70
4.	Katharine Hepburn	64
5.	Richard Dreyfuss	62

6.	Diane Keaton	59
7.	Dustin Hoffman	58
8.	Clint Eastwood	55
9.	Paul Newman	38
10.	Woody Allen	34

FAVORITE FILMS   **Number of Votes**

1.	*Gone With the Wind*	75
2.	*Star Wars*	64
3.	*The Sound of Music*	50
4.	*Rocky*	38
5.	*The Goodbye Girl*	35

F. FAVORITE FLICKS OF THE FRENCH

To celebrate the 80th anniversary of cinema, the Association of French Film Critics and the Theaters of Art and Experiment polled local French critics in 1975 to determine their all-time favorite films. Forty-five works were selected and then screened at Parisian theaters. American response to the poll? What, no Chaplin or Keaton?

The critics' choices came up this way:

(in no special order)

1. *L'Avventura* (Michelangelo Antonioni, Italy, 1960).
2. *My Night at Maud's* (Eric Rohmer, France, 1968).
3. *Strike* (Sergei Eisenstein, USSR, 1924).
4. *Pierrot Le Fou* (Jean-Luc Godard, France, 1965).
5. *Roma* (Federico Fellini, Italy, 1972).
6. *Lola Montes* (Max Ophuls, France, 1955).
7. *Paisan* (Roberto Rossellini, Italy, 1947).
8. *Tristana* (Luis Bunuel, Spain-France, 1970).
9. *The Scarlet Empress* (Josef Von Sternberg, USA, 1934).
10. *Greed* (Erich Von Stroheim, USA, 1923).
11. *Meet Me in St. Louis* (Vincente Minnelli, USA, 1944).
12. *A Nous La Liberte* (Rene Clair, France, 1931).
13. *Jules and Jim* (Francois Truffaut, France, 1961).
14. *Muriel* (Alain Resnais, France, 1963).
15. *Kiss Me Deadly* (Robert Aldrich, USA, 1955).
16. *Paradise Lost* (Abel Gance, France, 1939).
17. *The Lady From Shanghai* (Orson Welles, USA, 1948).
18. *The Passion of Joan of Arc* (Carl Dreyer, Denmark, 1928).
19. *Night and Fog* (Alain Resnais, France, 1955).
20. *Paris 1900* (Nicole Vedres, France, 1948).
21. *A Star is Born* (George Cukor, USA, 1954).
22. *Zero for Conduct* (Jean Vigo, France, 1932).
23. *Un Chien Andalou* (Luis Bunuel, France, 1928).
24. *Nothing But the Hours* (Alberto Cavalcanti, France, 1926).
25. *Farrebique* (Georges Ruquier, France, 1946).
26. *Orpheus* (Jean Cocteau, France, 1950).
27. *Hour of the Wolf* (Ingmar Bergman, Sweden, 1968).
28. *Knife in the Water* (Roman Polanski, Poland, 1962).
29. *Hallelujah* (King Vidor, USA, 1929).
30. *The Golden Coach* (Jean Renoir, France-Italy, 1953).

31. *The Cabinet of Dr. Caligari* (Robert Wiene, Germany, 1919).
32. *Storm Over Asia* (Vsevolod Pudovkin, USSR, 1928).
33. *Accident* (Joseph Losey, Great Britain, 1967).
34. *Letter from an Unknown Woman* (Max Ophuls, USA, 1948).
35. *The Big Sleep* (Howard Hawks, USA, 1946).
36. *Jesus Christ Superstar* (Norman Jewison, USA, 1973).
37. *Duck Soup* (Leo McCarey, USA, 1933).
38. *A Walk with Love and Death* (John Huston, USA, 1969).
39. *Pickpocket* (Robert Bresson, France, 1959).
40. *Salvatore Giuliano* (Francesco Rosi, Italy, 1962).
41. *M.* (Fritz Lang, Germany, 1931).
42. *Seven Women* (John Ford, USA, 1966).
43. *Brigadoon* (Vincente Minnelli, USA, 1954).
44. *The Last Laugh* (F.W. Murnau, 1924, Germany).
45. *The Children of Paradise* (Marcel Carne, France, 1945).

G. HEDDA HOPPER'S BEST AND WORST

In the January 3, 1957 *Los Angeles Times*, Hedda Hopper—one of the most powerful and best-known columnists in Hollywood's history—revealed her choices for the 10 best and worst films of all time.

TEN BEST
1. *The Birth of a Nation*
2. *Big Parade*
3. *Gone With the Wind*
4. *Wuthering Heights*
5. *Going My Way*
6. *A Man Called Peter*
7. *Snow White and the Seven Dwarfs*
8. *The King and I*
9. *The Best Years of Our Lives*
10. *Around the World in 80 Days*

TEN WORST
1. *Next Voice You Hear*
2. *Parnell*
3. *Vagabond King*
4. *Night in Harlem*
5. *Inferno*
6. *Horn Blows at Midnight*
7. *Proud and Profane*
8. *Catered Affair*
9. *Knights of the Round Table*
10. *Moby Dick*

H. THE "DEFINITIVE LIST OF TRULY GREAT AMERICAN MOVIES"

When the American Film Institute (AFI) polled its members to elect the 10 greatest American films of all time, the results were so startling that columnists across the nation couldn't refrain from attacking the survey. *New York Times* writer Russell Baker argued that the AFI poll only proved how gravely you can err "when you submit art to democracy." In a moment of churlish whimsy, Baker decided to compile his own "definitive list of the truly Greatest American movies":

The Greatest Weeper:
Imitation of Life (Claudette Colbert version)
The Greatest War Movie:
Paths of Glory
The Greatest Detective Movie:
The Maltese Falcon
The Greatest Propaganda Movie:
Yankee Doodle Dandy
The Greatest Western:
Stagecoach
The Greatest Horror Film:
Frankenstein

The Greatest Comedy:
Gunga Din
The Greatest Musical:
The Wizard of Oz
The Greatest Chase Movie:
The 39 Steps
The Greatest Movie-You-Can-See-Every-Week
Casablanca
The Greatest Movie Starring Marlon Brando:
On the Waterfront

I. TEN BEST DIRECTORIAL ACHIEVEMENTS

In 1950 the Screen Directors Guild of America (now the Directors Guild of America) polled 100 entertainment editors around the nation to determine the 10 best achievements in film directing from 1900 to 1950. Seventy-four films were cited in the poll; of the top 10 films, six were made in the silent era.

TEN BEST DIRECTORIAL ACHIEVEMENTS, 1900-1950
(in no special order)

1. King Vidor, *Big Parade*
2. James Cruze, *The Covered Wagon*
3. Cecil B. DeMille, *The Ten Commandments*
4. Frank Capra, *It Happened One Night*
5. D.W. Griffith, *Birth of a Nation*
6. William Wyler, *The Best Years of Our Lives*
7. John Ford, *The Informer*
8. D.W. Griffith, *Intolerance*
9. Frank Lloyd, *Cavalcade*
10. King Vidor, *The Crowd*

J. BEST COMEDY FILMS OF ALL TIME

In 1967 the Canadian Centennial Commission polled film historians and critics in 40 nations to determine the best comedy films of all time.

	FILM (DIRECTOR, DATE)	NUMBER OF VOTES
1.	*The Gold Rush* (Chaplin, 1925)	40
2.	*The General* (Keaton, 1926)	33
3.	*Modern Times* (Chaplin, 1936)	22
4.	*A Night at the Opera* (Wood, 1935, starring the Marx Brothers)	22
5.	*Monsieur Hulot's Holiday* (Tati, 1952)	18
6.	*Duck Soup* (McCarey, 1933, starring the Marx Brothers)	17
7.	*Le Million* (Clair, 1930)	16
	Kind Hearts and Coronets (Hamer, 1949)	16
9.	*The Italian Straw Hat* (Clair, 1927)	15
10.	*Safety Last* (Taylor, 1923, starring Harold Lloyd)	14

11.	*Some Like It Hot* (Wilder, 1959) 13
12.	*Divorce, Italian Style* (Germi, 1962) 10
	City Lights (Chaplin, 1931) 10
	Monsieur Verdoux (Chaplin, 1947) 10
	It Happened One Night (Capra, 1934) 10

TEN RUNNERS UP:
1.	*A Nous La Liberte* (Clair, 1931)
2.	*Hellzapoppin* (Potter, 1941)
3.	*Ninotchka* (Lubitsch, 1939)
4.	*La Kermesse Heroique* (Feyder, 1935)
5.	*The Navigator* (Keaton/Crisp, 1924)
6.	*Sherlock Jr.* (Keaton, 1924)
7.	*Shoulder Arms* (Chaplin, 1918)
8.	*Big Deal on Madonna Street* (Monicelli, 1958)
9.	*The Three Must-Get-Theres*
10.	*To Be or Not To Be* (Lubitsch, 1942)

K. TOP EXECUTIVES' TOP FILMS

In late 1975 the Broadcast Information Bureau polled more than 1500 top executives in the film and television industries to determine the executives' favorite films of all time. Each executive was asked to name his/her top 10 films. To the Bureau's surprise not a single vote was cast for Griffith's *Birth of a Nation*. Six films that had won Best Movie Oscars were also without a single nomination from the industry execs: *In the Heat of the Night; Cavalcade; Broadway Melody; Greatest Show on Earth; Wings;* and *Marty*. The results of the survey:

TOP TEN
1.	The Best Years of Our Lives
2.	Casablanca
3.	Gone With the Wind
4.	All About Eve
5.	The Wizard of Oz
6.	Citizen Kane
7.	Lost Horizon (the original)
8.	Top Hat
9.	Wuthering Heights
10.	The Maltese Falcon

RUNNERS UP:
11.	Dinner at Eight
12.	A Night at the Opera
	Psycho
14.	Philadelphia Story

15.	Naughty Marietta
16.	African Queen
17.	Ninotchka
18.	Singing in the Rain
19.	Love Affair
20.	San Francisco
21.	42nd Street
22.	Rebecca
23.	A Star is Born (with Janet Gaynor)
24.	Great Expectations
25.	Mrs. Miniver
26.	The Great Ziegfeld
27.	My Fair Lady
28.	City Lights
29.	Pride and Prejudice
30.	Grand Illusion

L. FIFTY MOST SIGNIFICANT AMERICAN FILMS

In late 1972 the Performing Arts Council of the University of Southern California asked a panel of film producers and critics to name the most significant movies in American cinema history. The producers and critics were requested to cite those films which gave new concepts and advanced the art and technique of filmmaking.

Nine silent films were nominated (only three silent films were cited on American Film Institute's similar poll in 1977); and only 13 of the mentioned films were Oscar winners.

1.	*Citizen Kane*		*The Wizard of Oz*
	Gone With the Wind		*The Graduate*
3.	*The Birth of a Nation*	29.	*Nanook of the North*
4.	*All Quiet on the Western Front*		*Little Caesar*
5.	*The Best Years of Our Lives*		*The Bridge on the River Kwai*
	Midnight Cowboy		*The Sound of Music*
	Stagecoach	33.	*City Lights*
8.	*High Noon*		*Ben Hur* (1925)
	On the Waterfront		*Forty Second Street*
10.	*2001: A Space Odyssey*		*The Maltese Falcon*
11.	*The Treasure of the Sierra Madre*		*Public Enemy*
12.	*The Jazz Singer*		*Dr. Strangelove*
	The Informer	39.	*Ben-Hur* (1959)
	West Side Story		*A Streetcar named Desire*
	The Grapes of Wrath		*An American in Paris*
16.	*The Gold Rush*		*The Robe*
	It Happened One Night		*I Am a Fugitive from a Chain Gang*
18.	*The Big Parade*		*The Lost Weekend*
	Casablanca		*Easy Rider*
	Fantasia		*Bonnie and Clyde*
21.	*Greed*	47.	*Covered Wagon*
	Intolerance		*Snow White and the Seven Dwarfs*
	King Kong		*The 39 Steps*
24.	*The Great Train Robbery*		*The General*
	Who's Afraid of Virginia Woolf?		*Shane*
	Sunset Boulevard		*The Godfather*
			Lost Horizon

M. BEST AT BRUSSELS

During the film festival held at the Brussels World Fair in 1958, 12 films were screened as the Best Films of All Time. The selection was made by a jury of 117 film historians from 26 countries and contained few if any individual surprises, consisting largely of conventional "classics." As a group, however, the 12 films surprisingly contained only three sound films. And many people thought it strange that no Rene Clair or John Ford film got on the list, even though Clair was third and Ford was sixth on a list obtained by combining the number of votes each director received for all of his films mentioned on the ballot.

The list of 12 films was then given to a second jury of young filmmakers to classify the films "according to their present-day value." After 10 hours of debate, the jurors (Robert Aldrich, Alexander Mackendrick, Alexandre Astruc, Juan-Antonio Bardem, Francesco Maselli, Michael Cacoyannis and Satyajit Ray) announced that the films "should not be measured against each other." They also expressed their dismay over the preponderance of silent films and the absence of certain very important schools of filmmaking like the Japanese. Nevertheless, this second jury said that after lengthy discussion, six films emerged as having "a living and lasting value": *The Battleship Potemkin, The Gold Rush, La Grande Illusion, The Bicycle Thief, Mother* and *The Passion of Joan of Arc.* (When this list was read to the audience, several people shouted "And where is *Kane?*")

A third jury, displeased by the decisions of the first two juries, then organized itself to give recognition to the important films that the festival had neglected. This jury's list included: *L'Atalante, L'Age d'Or, La Terra Trema, Sherlock Jr,. Rashomon, Hôtel des Invalides, The Grapes of Wrath, The Childhood of Maxim Gorki, Underworld, Die Dreigroschenoper, Peter Ibbetson* and *Smiles of a Summer Night.* During this film festival, Eisenstein's *Ivan the Terrible, Part II* had its Western premiere.

BEST FILMS OF ALL TIMES

Rank	Film	Votes
1.	*Battleship Potemkin* (Eisenstein, 1925)	100
2.	*The Gold Rush* (Chaplin, 1925)	85
	The Bicycle Thief (De Sica, 1948)	85
4.	*The Passion of Joan of Arc* (Dreyer, 1928)	78
5.	*La Grande Illusion* (Renoir, 1937)	72
6.	*Greed* (Von Stroheim, 1924)	71
7.	*Intolerance* (Griffith, 1916)	61
8.	*Mother* (Pudovkin, 1926)	54
9.	*Citizen Kane* (Welles, 1941)	40
10.	*Earth* (Dovzhenko, 1930)	47
11.	*The Last Laugh* (Murnau, 1924)	45
12.	*The Cabinet of Dr. Caligari* (Wiene, 1919)	43

By combining the number of votes obtained by each director for all of his films mentioned in the ballot, the following top twelve emerged:

BEST DIRECTORS

Rank	Director	Votes
1.	Chaplin	250
2.	Eisenstein	168
3.	Clair	135
4.	De Sica	125
5.	Griffith	123
6.	Ford	107
7.	Renoir	105
8.	Dreyer	99
9.	Von Stroheim	93
10.	Pudovkin	91
11.	Murnau	90
12.	Flaherty	82

N. TOPS IN LOS ANGELES

In the July 23, 1967 *Los Angeles Times*, first-string film critic Charles Champlin asked his readers to name their favorite ten films of all time, their By-Damn'I'd-Like-To-See-That-One-Again movies. The response to Champlin's request was overwhelming: more than 2,000 cards were received, and in several cases entire families sat down together to prepare their lists.

Prompted by the American Film Institute's Best-American-Films-of-All-Time survey in 1977 (included in *Film Facts*), Champlin once again polled his readers in late 1977 and the results appeared in the *L.A. Times* of March 5, 1978. Whereas readers in the 1967 poll could cite their "favorite" American *and* European films, the 1977 *L.A.Times* survey was restricted to the "best" or "greatest" American pictures. More than 2,500 cards were received in the 1977 survey; in all, some 1,597 different films were nominated, including five votes for *Deep Throat*.

Champlin noted that his readers' tastes had changed remarkably over the decade: only six of the twenty favorite films from 1967 made it to the top in 1977. The preferences of Champlin's readers, however, did coincide with those of AFI's *American Film: Gone With the Wind* was the winner in both polls; the two runners-up were identical in both surveys; and forty-six movies showed up on both of the top fifty lists.

READERS' TOP TEN IN 1967	READERS' TOP TEN IN 1977
1. The African Queen	1. Gone With the Wind
2. Gone With the Wind	2. Casablanca
3. Citizen Kane	3. Citizen Kane
4. Treasure of the Sierra Madre	4. The Wizard of Oz
5. Wuthering Heights	5. The African Queen
6. Streetcar Named Desire	6. The Sound of Music
7. Rebecca	7. One Flew Over the Cuckoo's Nest
8. Casablanca	8. The Grapes of Wrath
9. Ben-Hur	9. The Godfather
10. Lawrence of Arabia	10. Star Wars
RUNNERS UP IN 1967	**RUNNERS UP IN 1977**
11. The Red Shoes	11. 2001: A Space Odyssey
12. High Noon	12. Singing in the Rain
13. Lili	13. Rocky
14. To Kill a Mockingbird	14. The Graduate
15. All About Eve	15. Fantasia
16. An American In Paris	16. Ben-Hur
17. Around the World in 80 Days	17. It Happened One Night
18. Brief Encounter	18. Treasure of the Sierra Madre
19. Shane	19. Best Years of Our Lives
20. Stagecoach	20. On the Waterfront

O. TEN "MOST WANTED" MOVIES

Early in 1980 the preservation staff of The American Film Institute compiled a "Ten Most Wanted" list of lost films, which included some of the most historically and artistically significant films archivists continue to search for:

(in no particular order)
1.   *Cleopatra* (1917) starring Theda Bara
2.   *That Royale Girl*, a D. W. Griffth silent with W.C. Fields
3.   *The Kaiser, Beast of Berlin*, a World War I anti-German film
4.   *The Rogue Song* (1930), an early Technicolr film directed by Lionel Barrymore and featuring Laurel and Hardy
5.   *Greed*, Erich von Stroheim's 40-reel version
6.   *Little Red Riding Hood* (1922), an early Walt Disney cartoon, pre-Hollywood.
7.   *Frankenstein (1910), made by Edision, the earliest film version of the famous Mary Shelley story.*
8.   *London After Midnight* (1927), directed by Tod Browning and starring Lon Chaney
9.   *Camille* (1927), starring Norma Talmadge
10.   *The Divine Woman* starring Greta Garbo.

P. TEN BEST "OSCARLESS" MOVIES

Before the 1979 Oscars were announced, social historian and film buff Arthur Schlesinger Jr. noted that the Academy can often be fallible in its choices: Greata Garbo never won an award for best performance, nor did Charlie Chaplin.

Schlesinger suggested that a list of ten movies denied the Best Picture award would be quite as impressive as any 10 best Oscar pictures:

1.   *Citizen Kane* (1941), lost to *How Green Was My Valley*
2.   *Modern Times* (1936), lost of *The Great Ziegfeld*
3.   *2001: A Space Odyssey* (1968), lost to *Oliver*
4.   *High Noon* (1952), lost to *The Greatest Show on Earth*
5.   *Nashville* (1975), lost to *xx One Flew Over the Cuckoo's Nest*
6.   *The Grapes of Wrath* (1940) lost to *Rebecca*
7.   *The Wizard of Ox* (1939), lost to *Gone with the Wind*
8.   *The Front Page* (1931/32) lost to *Grand Hotel*
9.   *King Kong* (1932/33), lost to *Cavalcade*
10.   *To Be or Not To Be* (1942), lost to *Mrs. Miniver.*

VI. THE AWARDS

1/THE ACADEMY AWARDS

FROM THERE VERY beginnings at the turn of the century down to the present day, movies have frequently been attacked for corrupting American morals and ideals. Rather than face government regulations or further public criticism that could be financially disastrous, the film industry has invariably handled such attacks by trying to take matters into its own hands: internal control has always been preferred to external intervention.

In 1909, for example, when more and more outside groups were calling for film censorship, key figures in the movie industry established the National Board of Censorship (later renamed the National Board of Review) to preview films and to provide guidelines for possible necessary changes. In 1922, during the Fatty Arbuckle scandal and continued calls for censorship, Hollywood moguls formed the Motion Picture Producers and Distributors Association to placate their critics: Will H. Hays, a conservative former member of Harding's Cabinet, was the organization's first president.

And in 1927, when Hollywood's reputation was once again suffering, the industry founded the Academy of Motion Picture Arts and Sciences to raise the "cultural, educational, and scientific standards" of film. Even the association's name was calculated to enhance the industry's status: an "academy" suggested refined activity, and "arts and sciences" were hardly conducive to immorality. The new organization's title conveniently contained no suggestion of the two things for which Hollywood was best known: mass entertainment and big business.

There were 36 charter members of the Academy; Douglas Fairbanks was its first president; and one of the Academy's first functions was to give annual achievement awards. Thus, the Academy Awards were born. To be eligible for an award, a film must be shown in a commercial theater in the Los Angeles area for at least a week during the previous year. For the first six annual presentations, the awards were based on seasonal, not calendar years; that is, on the period from August 1 of one year to July 31 of the next year. Since 1934, however, the calendar year has been used.

Only a handful of Academy members determined the awards for 1927/28 and 1928/29. But in 1929/30 the entire Academy was allowed to vote for the nominees and the winners. For the 1937 prizes, the final voting was further expanded to include some 15,000 people in the movie industry, although the nominations had been limited to Academy members only. Later the procedure was reversed and the film industry at large selected the nominations, but only the Academy decided the winners. For the 1957 awards, voting policies changed once again, so that all voting was —and is—confined to the Academy.

The Academy is divided into several branches, such as the acting branch, the editing branch, the writing branch, the directing branch, etc. All branches determine the five nominees for Best Picture but the nominations for all other regular categories are selected by each specific branch. For example, the nominations for writing awards are made by the Academy Writers Branch, for directing awards by the Academy Directors Branch. All Academy members are then allowed to vote for the final winners.

The honorary and special awards, such as the Thalberg Memorial Award and the Jean Hersholt Humanitarian Award, are chosen by the Academy's Board of Governors. The nominations in the documentary categories are voted by the Documentary Awards Committee, but the Academy at large decides the winner.

The numerous scientific and technical awards are voted by the Board of Governors based on recommendations made by the Scientific or Technical Awards Committee. These technical awards are given in three categories. From 1930/31 to 1937, the technical awards in Class I received an Academy statuette and plaque, Class II winners received a certificate of honorable mention, and Class III and honorable mention in the report of the Board of Judges. From 1938 to 1977, Class I winners received a statuette, Class II a plaque, and Class III a certificate. Beginning with the 1978 awards, the Academy altered the wording of the scientific and technical awards. Rather than Class I, II, and III, the awards are now conferred as Academy Awards of Merit (a stattuette), Scientific and Engineering Awards (a plaque), and Technical Achievement Awards (a certificate).

Prior to 1956, the Best Foreign-Lan-guage Film was an honorary award voted by the Board of Governors. But beginning in 1956, the vote was opened to the entire Academy membership. The five nominations in this category are selected by a special Foreign-Language Film Awards Committee. Every country is invited to submit films to this committee, but only one film from any one nation can be nominated in any particular year. Unlike the awards in most of the Academy's other categories, a movie does not have to be released commercially in Los Angeles to be eligible for the Best Foreign-Language Film. This special eligibility explains why a film may be nominated for Best Foreign-Language Film one year, while its cast and crew may be nominated in other categories the following year. In 1973, for example, *Day for Night* won the Best Foreign-Language Film Award before it had been commercially released in the Los Angeles area, but in 1974, after its commercial showing, both its director (Francois Truffaut) and supporting actress (Valentina Cortese) were nominated in those respective categories. For the 1976 Best Foreign-Language Film, an Academy member had to have seen all five nominated movies before voting. Many people said this particular requirement was responsible for the little-known film *Black-and-White in Color* winning the award over the more popular movies *Cousin, Cousine* and *Seven Beauties.*

Originally the awards were presented at small banquets held in one of Hollywood's hotels, like the Ambassador or the Biltmore. Due to increasing attention, the presentations moved in 1944 to the large Grauman's Chinese Theatre, and in 1947 to the even larger Shrine Auditorium, where the public was allowed to attend. When the major studios refused to continue to pay for the presentations in 1949, the awards were held at the Academy's own small theater. The RKO Pantages Theatre in Hollywood was the site of the presentations from 1950 to 1959. In 1961 the vast Santa Monica Civic Auditorium was needed to house the event. In 1969 they moved once again, this time to the present home of the awards presentation, the Dorothy Chandler Pavilion of the Los Angeles Music Center.

The winners of the first awards in 1927/28 had been known some three months before the night of the banquet. During the next several years, prizes were announced a week prior to their presentation; later the names of the winners were released on the morning of the presentation. In 1941 the policy of sealed envelopes was initiated, and it remains in effect today.

The Oscar statuette was designed by MGM art director Cedric Gibbons in 1928 and has always been manufactured by the Dodge Trophy Company of Crystal Lake, Illinois. (The awards were made at the company's California plant until the 1969 earthquake when the manufacturing of the famous statuette was moved to the firm's home office in Illinois.) The 8 lb. 13" statuette has a 24kt gold exterior with an interior made from a mixture of metals the formula of which is known only to the Dodge Trophy officials. (During World War II the figure was made from plaster in order to conserve precious metals.) The price of the Oscar is also kept secret: Dodge Trophy president Paul Feltrinelli will only reveal that the statuette's material worth is "minimal" when compared to the prestige of winning it. The awards hold up remarkably well over the years, says Feltrinelli. The most frequent problem has come from winners like the late Spencer Tracy and Francis Coppola who kept their Oscars in beach homes where the damp salt air corroded the statuettes and turned them green. (The Dodge Company can repair the Oscar in such cases.)

There is still some uncertainty over the origin of the statuette's name: Oscar. Some say that when Academy librarian Margret Herrick first saw the statuette, she exclaimed, "Why it looks just like my Uncle Oscar." Supposedly a reporter overheard the remark, printed the story, and the name stuck. Others claim that Bette Davis nicknamed the figure after her first husband, Harmon Oscar Nelson, Jr.

The 1928/29 awards were carried live by a local Los Angeles radio station. In 1945, national radio broadcast the event. Television coverage began in 1953: the first color broadcast was in 1966. The presentation of the 1978 awards (aired that is, in April 1979) was seen by some 70 million Americans and by 350 million people in 54 other nations.

Arthur Freed, former Academy president, once said that the Oscars "honor artistic achievement, with little regard for popularity, box-office success or other yardsticks applied by critics or the general public." But the awards have been repeatedly criticized for having virtually no connection whatsoever to artistic achievement. Even as early as the 1928/29 awards, when Mary Pickford was selected Best Actress for her role in *Coquette*, people began complaining that the prizes were given on a political or social rather than artistic basis. Since then, the Academy's "poor" judgments have become legendary: almost everyone has his favorite example of the Academy's strange choices. Many people, for example, like to point out that *Citizen Kane*, one of the most important films ever made, won only a single Oscar in 1941—for Best Original Screenplay.

The Academy's popular and sentimental standards of selection do work, I think, to the Academy's advantage in the long run. The Academy's habit of awarding sentimental favorites, for example, might give Hollywood the image of being emotional, human, kind-hearted, even soft-headed, but such an image advantageously counteracts

Hollywood's other image of being a cold, calculating, and cynically ruthless town. And the Academy's predilection for selecting the most popular and not necessarily the "best" film each year reinforces one of Hollywood's most cherished beliefs: that the average filmgoer who makes those films popular *does* have good taste, and that the people and not the critics *do* know what's best.

Thus, the Academy's selections may be questionable at best, ridiculous at worst, but even so, such inadequacies can work for and not against Hollywood. The Oscars give Hollywood a sense of community, a sense that Hollywood "takes care of its own kind"—a sentiment most Americans understand. On Oscar night Hollywood has the intimacy of a community, the importance of international attention—and the combination is hard to beat. Hollywood As Global Village is almost impossible to resist.

Do studios try to "buy" Oscars? A Universal executive told the Los Angeles Advertising Club that for the 1978 Academy Awards, each of the six major studios spent approximately $300,000 mounting awards advertising campaigns. Since there are 3,600 voting members of the Academy, that comes down to $500 a vote.

Why spend so much money? Supposedly, a Best Picture Oscar can easily generate from 2 million dollars to 10 million dollars in additional revenues for its studio. For example: in just the ten-to-twelve day period following its Best Picture Oscar, *Annie Hall* gathered $4,745,000 in grosses. And it has been claimed that *The Sting* stayed in release nine more months because of its Best Picture Oscar, earning more than $10,000,000 in that time.

Academy Presidents include: Douglas Fairbanks, Sr. (May 1927-1929); William C. DeMille (October 1929-October 1931); M.C. Levee (October 1931-October 1932); Conrad Nagel (October 1932-April 1933, resigned); J. Theodore Reed (April 1933-October 1934); Frank Lloyd (October 1934-October 1935); Frank Capra (October 1935-December 1939); Walter Wanger (December 1939-October 1941); Bette Davis (October 1941-December 1941, resigned); Walter Wanger (December 1941-October 1945); Jean Hersholt (October 1945-May 1949); Charles Brackett (May 1949-May 1955); George Seaton (June 1955-May 1958); George Stevens (June 1958-May 1959); B.B. Kahane (June 1959-September 1960); Valentine Davies (September 1960-July 1961); Wendell R. Corey (August 1961-June 1963); Arthur Freed (June 1963-May 1967); Gregory Peck (June 1967-May 1970); Daniel Taradash (June 1970-June 1973); Walter Mirisch (June 1973-May 1977); Howard W. Koch (June 1977-   ).

Both nominees and winners are given below in the categories of directing, acting, writing, cinematography, Best Picture and Best Foreign-Language Picture. In all other categories, only the winners are listed. In the listings of the Special Effects category, the photography technicians (mentioned first) are separated from the sound technicians by a semicolon whenever the Academy made such a distinction. Similarly, in the listings for Interior Decoration, the art designers (cited first) are separated from the set designers by a semicolon whenever that distinction was made by the Academy. (Until 1955, art designers were given Oscars; the set designers were awarded plaques.) In the Best Song category, the composer is listed first, followed by the lyricist.

1927/28

BEST PICTURE

☐ *Wings* (Paramount)
The Last Command (Paramount)
The Racket (Paramount)
Seventh Heaven (Fox)
The Way of All Flesh (Paramount)

BEST DIRECTOR

☐ Frank Borzage, *Seventh Heaven*
Herbert Brenon, *Sorrell and Son*
King Vidor, *The Crowd*

BEST COMEDY DIRECTOR

☐ Lewis Milestone, *Two Arabian Knghts*
Ted Wilde, *Speedy*
Charles Chaplin, *The Circus*

BEST ACTOR

☐ Emil Jannings, *The Last Command; The Way of All Flesh*
Richard Barthelmess, *The Noose*
Richard Barthelmess,*The Patent Leather Kid*
Charles Chaplin, *The Circus*

BEST ACTRESS

☐ Janet Gaynor, *Seventh Heaven; Street Angel; Sunrise*
Gloria Swanson, *Sadie Thompson*
Louise Dresser, *A Ship Comes In*

WRITING (ADAPTATION)

☐ Benjamin Glazer, *Seventh Heaven*
Anthony Coldeway, *Glorious Betsy*
Alfred Cohn, *The Jazz Singer*

WRITING (ORIGINAL STORY)

☐ Ben Hecht, *Underworld*
Lajos Biro, *The Last Command*
Rupert Hughes, *The Patent Leather Kid*

CINEMATOGRAPHY

☐ Charles Rosher, Karl Struss, *Sunrise*
George Barnes, *Devil Dancer*
Karl Struss, *Drums of Love*

☐ Indicates winner

George Barnes, *Magic Flame*
Charles Rosher, *My Best Girl*
George Barnes, *Sadie Thompson*
Charles Rosher, *The Tempest*

TITLE WRITING

☐ Joseph Farnham, *The Fair Co-Ed*
Joseph Farnham, *Laugh, Clown, Laugh*
Joseph Farnham, *Telling the World*

ENGINEERING EFFECTS

☐ Roy Pomeroy, *Wings*

ARTISTIC QUALITY OF PRODUCTION

☐ Fox, *Sunrise*

INTERIOR DECORATION

☐ William Cameron Menzies, *The Dove*
William Cameron Menzies, *The Tempest*

SPECIAL AWARDS

☐ Warner Bros.,*The Jazz Singer*, the pioneer talking picture, which has revolutionized the industry
☐ Charles Chaplin, *The Circus*, for versatility and genius in writing, acting, directing and producing

1928/29

BEST PICTURE

☐ *The Broadway Melody* (MGM)
Alibi (United Artists)
Hollywood Revue (MGM)
In Old Arizona (Fox)
The Patriot (Paramount)

BEST DIRECTOR

☐ Frank Lloyd, *The Divine Lady*
Lionel Barrymore, *Madame X*
Harry Beaumont, *Broadway Melody*
Irving Cummings, *In Old Arizona*
Frank Lloyd, *Weary River*
Frank Lloyd, *Drag*
Ernst Lubitsch, *The Patriot*

BEST ACTOR

☐ Warner Baxter, *In Old Arizona*
Chester Morris, *Alibi*
Paul Muni, *The Valiant*
George Bancroft, *Thunderbolt*
Lewis Stone, *The Patriot*

BEST ACTRESS

☐ Mary Pickford, *Coquette*
Ruth Chatterton, *Madame X*
Betty Compson, *The Barker*
Jeanne Eagles, *The Letter*
Bessie Love, *Broadway Melody*

WRITING

☐ Hans Kraly, *The Patriot*
Tom Barry, *In Old Arizona*
Elliott Clawson, *The Leatherneck*
Josephine Lovett, *Our Dancing Daughters*
Tom Barry, *The Valiant*
Bess Meredyth, *Wonder of Women*

CINEMATOGRAPHY

☐ Clyde De Vinna, *White Shadows in the South Seas*
John Seitz, *The Divine Lady*
Ernest Palmer, *Four Devils*
Arthur Edeson, *In Old Arizona*
George Barnes, *Our Dancing Daughters*
Ernest Palmer, *Street Angel*

INTERIOR DECORATION

☐ Cedric Gibbons, *The Bridge of San Luis Rey*

1929/30

BEST PICTURE

☐ *All Quiet on the Western Front* (Universal)
The Big House (MGM)
Disraeli (Warner Bros.)
The Divorcee (MGM)
The Love Parade (Paramount)

BEST DIRECTOR

☐ Lewis Milestone, *All Quiet on the Western Front*
Clarence Brown, *Anna Christie*
Clarence Brown, *Romance*
Robert Leonard, *The Divorcee*
Ernst Lubitsch, *The Love Parade*
King Vidor, *Hallelujah*

BEST ACTOR

☐ George Arliss, *Disraeli*
George Arliss, *The Green Goddess*
Wallace Beery, *The Big House*
Maurice Chevalier, *The Love Parade*
Maurice Chevalier, *The Big Pond*

Ronald Colman, *Bulldog Drummond*
Ronald Colman, *Condemned*
Lawrence Tibbett, *The Rogue Song*

BEST ACTRESS
□ Norma Shearer, *The Divorcee*
Nancy Carroll, *The Devil's Holiday*
Ruth Chatterton, *Sarah and Son*
Greta Garbo, *Anna Christie*
Greta Garbo, *Romance*
Norma Shearer, *Their Own Desire*
Gloria Swanson, *The Trespasser*

WRITING
□ Francis Marion, *The Big House*
Julian Josephson, *Disraeli*
John Meehan, *The Divorcee*
Howard Estabrook, *Street of Chance*
George Abbott, Maxwell Anderson, Dell Andrews, *All Quiet on the Western Front*

CINEMATOGRAPHY
□ Joseph T. Rucker, William Van Der Veer, *With Byrd at the South Pole*
Arthur Edeson, *All Quiet on the Western Front*
William Daniels, *Anna Christie*
Gaetano Gaudio, Harry Perry, *Hell's Angels*
Victor Milner, *The Love Parade*

INTERIOR DECORATION
□ Herman Rosse, *King of Jazz*

SOUND RECORDING
□ Douglas Shearer, *The Big House*

1930/31

BEST PICTURE
□ *Cimarron* (RKO Radio)
East Lynne (Fox)
The Front Page (United Artists)
Skippy (Paramount)
Trader Horn (MGM)

BEST DIRECTOR
□ Norman Taurog, *Skippy*
Clarence Brown, *A Free Soul*

Lewis Milestone, *The Front Page*
Wesley Ruggles, *Cimarron*
Josef von Sternberg, *Morocco*

BEST ACTOR
□ Lionel Barrymore, *A Free Soul*
Jackie Cooper, *Skippy*
Richard Dix, *Cimarron*
Fredric March, *The Royal Family of Broadway*
Adolphe Menjou, *The Front Page*

BEST ACTRESS
□ Marie Dressler, *Min and Bill*
Marlene Dietrich, *Morocco*
Irene Dunne, *Cimarron*
Ann Harding, *Holiday*
Norma Shearer, *A Free Soul*

WRITING (ADAPTATION)
□ Howard Estabrook, *Cimarron*
Seton Miller, Fred Niblo Jr.,, *Criminal Code*
Horace Jackson, *Holiday*
Francis Faragoh, Robert N. Lee, *Little Caesar*
Joseph Mankiewicz, Sam Mintz, *Skippy*

WRITING (ORIGINAL STORY)
□ John Monk Saunders, *The Dawn Patrol*
Rowland Brown, *Doorway to Hell*
Harry d'Abbadie d'Arrast, Douglas Doty, Donald Ogden Stewart, *Laughter*
John Bright, Kubec Glasmon, *Public Enemy*
Lucien Hubbard, Joseph Jackson, *Smart Money*

CINEMATOGRAPHY
□ Floyd Crosby, *Tabu*
Edward Cronjager, *Cimarron*
Lee Garmes, *Morocco*
Charles Lang, *The Right to Love*
Barney McGill, *Svengali*

INTERIOR DECORATION
□ Max Ree, *Cimarron*

SOUND RECORDING
□ Paramount Studio Sound Dept.

SCIENTIFIC OR TECHNICAL AWARDS

Class I:
□ Electrical Research Products, Inc., RCA and RKO Radio Pictures, Inc., for

noise-reduction recording equipment
□ Du Pont Film Manufacturing Corporation and Eastman Kodak, for super-sensitive panchromatic film

Class II:
□ Fox Film Corp., for effective use of synchro-projection composite photography

Class III:
□ Electrical Research Products, for moving coil microphone transmitters
□ RKO, for reflex type microphone concentrators
□ RCA, for ribbon microphone transmitters

1931/32

BEST PICTURE
□ *Grand Hotel* (MGM)
Arrowsmith (Goldwyn-UA)
Bad Girl (Fox)
The Champ (MGM)
Five Star Final (First National)
One Hour with You (Paramount)
Shanghai Express (Paramount)
Smiling Lieutenant (Paramount)

DIRECTING
□ Frank Borzage, *Bad Girl*
King Vidor, *The Champ*
Josef von Sternberg, *Shanghai Express*

BEST ACTOR
□ Wallace Beery, *The Champ*
□ Fredric March, *Dr. Jekyll and Mr. Hyde*
Alfred Lunt, *The Guardsman*

BEST ACTRESS
□ Helen Hayes, *The Sin of Madelon Claudet*
Marie Dressler, *Emma*
Lynn Fontanne, *The Guardsman*

WRITING (ADAPTATION)
□ Edwin Burke, *Bar Girl*
Sidney Howard, *Arrowsmith*
Percy Heath, Samuel Hoffenstein, *Dr. Jekyll and Mr. Hyde*

WRITING (ORIGINAL STORY)
□ Frances Marion, *The Champ*

Grover Jones, William
Slavens McNutt, *Lady and
Gent*
Lucien Hubbard, *Star Witness*
Adela Rogers St. John, *What
Price Hollywood*

CINEMATOGRAPHY
☐ Lee Garmes, *Shanghai
Express*
Ray June, *Arrowsmith*
Karl Struss, *Dr. Jekyll and Mr.
Hyde*

INTERIOR DECORATION
☐ Gordon Wiles, *Transatlantic*

SOUND RECORDING
☐ Paramount Studio

SHORT SUBJECTS
Cartoons:
☐ Walt Disney (UA), *Flowers and
Trees*
Comedy:
☐ Hal Roach (MGM), *The Music
Box*
Novelty:
☐ Mack Sennett (Educational),
Wrestling Swordfish

SPECIAL AWARD
☐ Walt Disney, for creation of
Mickey Mouse

**SCIENTIFIC OR TECHNICAL
AWARDS**
Class II:
☐ Technicolor M.P. Corp., for
color cartoon process
Class III:
☐ Eastman Kodak, for the type
Two-B sensitometer

1932/33

BEST PICTURE
☐ *Cavalcade* (Fox)
A Farewell to Arms
(Paramount)
Forty-Second Street (Warner
Bros.)
*I Am A Fugitive from a Chain
Gang* (Warner Bros.)
Lady for a Day (Columbia)
Little Women (RKO Radio)
The Private Life of Henry VIII
(UA)
She Done Him Wrong
(Paramount)
Smilin' Through (MGM)
State Fair (Fox)

DIRECTING
☐ Frank Lloyd, *Cavalcade*
Frank Capra, *Lady for a Day*
George Cukor, *Little Women*

BEST ACTOR
☐ Charles Laughton, *Private Life
of Henry VIII*
Leslie Howard, *Berkeley
Square*
Paul Muni, *I Am a Fugitive
from a Chain Gang*

BEST ACTRESS
☐ Katharine Hepburn, *Morning
Glory*
May Robson, *Lady for a Day*
Diana Wynward, *Cavalcade*

WRITING (ADAPTATION)
☐ Victor Heerman, Sarah Y.
Mason, *Little Women*
Robert Riskin, *Lady for a Day*
Paul Green, Sonya Levien,
State Fair

**WRITING (ORIGINAL
STORY)**
☐ Robert Lord, *One Way
Passage*
Francis Marion, *The
Prizefighter and the Lady*
Charles MacArthur, *Rasputin
and the Empress*

CINEMATOGRAPHY
☐ Charles Bryant Lang, Jr., *A
Farewell to Arms*
George J. Folsey, Jr., *Reunion
in Vienna*
Karl Struss, *The Sign of the
Cross*

INTERIOR DECORATION
☐ William S. Darling, *Cavalcade*

SOUND RECORDING
☐ Harold C. Lewis, *A Farewell to
Arms*

SHORT SUBJECTS
Cartoons:
☐ Walt Disney (UA), *Three Little
Pigs*
Comedy:
☐ RKO Radio, *So This Is Harris*
Novelty:
☐ Educational, *Krakatoa*

ASSISTANT DIRECTOR
☐ Charles Barton (Paramount)
Scott Beal (Universal)
Charles Dorian (MGM)
Fred Fox (UA)
Gordon Hollingshead (Warner
Bros.)
☐ Dewey Starkey (RKO Radio)

☐ William Tummel (Fox)

**SCIENTIFIC OR TECHNICAL
AWARDS**
Class II:
☐ Electrical Research Products,
for wide range recording/
reproducing system
☐ RCA, for high-fidelity
recording/reproducing
system
Class III:
☐ Fox Film Corp., Fred Jackman,
and Warner Bros. Pictures,
and Sidney Sanders of RKO,
for development and
effective use of translucent
cellulose screen in composite
photography

1934

BEST PICTURE
☐ *It Happened One Night*
(Columbia)
*The Barretts of Wimpole
Street* (MGM)
Cleopatra (Paramount)
Flirtation Walk (First National)
The Gay Divorcee (RKO Radio)
Here Comes the Navy
(Warner Bros.)
The House of Rothschild (20th
Century-UA)
Imitation of Life (Universal)
One Night Of Love (Columbia)
The Thin Man (MGM)
Viva Villa (MGM)
The White Parade (Fox)

BEST DIRECTOR
☐ Frank Capra, *It Happened One
Night*
Victor Schertzinger, *One Night
of Love*
W. S. Van Dyke, *The Thin
Man*

BEST ACTOR
☐ Clark Gable, *It Happened One
Night*
Frank Morgan, *Affairs of
Cellini*
William Powell, *The Thin Man*

BEST ACTRESS
☐ Claudette Colbert, *It
Happened One Night*
Grace Moore, *One Night of
Love*

Norma Shearer, *The Barretts of Wimpole Street*

WRITING (ADAPTATION)
☐ Robert Riskin, *It Happened One Night*
Frances Goodrich, Albert Hackett, *The Thin Man*
Ben Hecht, *Viva Villa*

WRITING (ORIGINAL STORY)
☐ Arthur Caesar, *Manhattan Melodrama*
Mauri Grashin, *Hide-Out*
Norman Krasna, *Richest Girl in the World*

CINEMATOGRAPHY
☐ Victor Milner, *Cleopatra*
Charles Rosher, *Affairs of Cellini*
George Folsey, *Operator 13*

INTERIOR DECORATION
☐ Cedric Gibbons, Frederic Hope, *The Merry Widow*

SOUND RECORDING
☐ Paul Neal, *One Night of Love*

SHORT SUBJECTS

Cartoons:
☐ Walt Disney, *The Tortoise and the Hare*
Comedy:
☐ RKO Radio, *La Cucaracha*
Novelty:
☐ Educational, *City of Wax*

MUSIC

Best Song:
☐ Con Conrad, Herb Magidson, "Continental" (*The Gay Divorcee*)
Best Score:
☐ Louis Silvers, *One Night of Love*

FILM EDITING
☐ Conrad Nervig, *Eskimo*

ASSISTANT DIRECTOR
☐ John Waters, *Viva Villa*

SPECIAL AWARD
☐ Shirley Temple, in grateful recognition of her outstanding contribution to screen entertainment during the year 1934

SCIENTIFIC OR TECHNICAL AWARDS

Class II:
☐ Electrical Research Products, Inc., for development of the

vertical cut disc method of recording sound (hill and dale recording)
Class III:
☐ Columbia Pictures Corp., for their application of the vertical cut disc method to actual studio production, with their recording of the sound on *One Night of Love*
☐ Bell & Howell Co., for development of the Bell & Howell fully automatic sound and picture printer

---

1935

BEST PICTURE
☐ *Mutiny on the Bounty* (MGM)
Alice Adams (RKO Radio)
Broadway Melody of 1936 (MGM)
Captain Blood (Cosmopolitan-Warner Bros.)
David Copperfield (MGM)
The Informer (RKO Radio)
Les Misérables (20th Century-UA)
The Lives of a Bengal Lancer (Paramount)
A Midsummer Night's Dream (Warner Bros.)
Naughty Marietta (MGM)
Ruggles of Red Gap (Paramount)
Top Hat (RKO Radio)

BEST DIRECTOR
☐ John Ford, *The Informer*
Henry Hathaway, *The Lives of a Bengal Lancer*
Frank Lloyd, *Mutiny on the Bounty*

BEST ACTOR
☐ Victor McLaglen, *The Informer*
Clark Gable, *Mutiny on the Bounty*
Charles Laughton, *Mutiny on the Bounty*
Franchot Tone, *Mutiny on the Bounty*

BEST ACTRESS
☐ Bette Davis, *Dangerous*
Elisabeth Bergner, *Escape Me Never*
Claudette Colbert, *Private Worlds*

Katharine Hepburn, *Alice Adams*
Miriam Hopkins, *Becky Sharp*
Merle Oberon, *The Dark Angel*

WRITING (ORIGINAL STORY)
☐ Ben Hecht, Charles MacArthur *The Scoundrel*
Moss Hart, *Broadway Melody of 1936*
Don Hartman, Stephen Avery, *The Gay Deception*

WRITING (SCREENPLAY)
☐ Dudley Nichols, *The Informer*
Achmed Abdullah, John L. Balderston, Grover Jones, William Slavens McNutt, Waldemar Young, *The Lives of a Bengal Lancer*
Jules Furthman, Talbot Jennings, Carey Wilson, *Mutiny on the Bounty*

CINEMATOGRAPHY
☐ Hal Mohr, *A Midsummer Night's Dream*
Ray June, *Barbary Coast*
Victor Milner, *The Crusades*
Gregg Toland, *Les Misérables*

INTERIOR DECORATION
☐ Richard Day, *The Dark Angel*

SOUND RECORDING
☐ Douglas Shearer, *Naughty Marietta*

SHORT SUBJECTS

Cartoons:
☐ Walt Disney (UA), *Three Orphan Kittens*
Comedy:
☐ MGM, *How to Sleep*
Novelty:
☐ Educational, *Wings Over Mt. Everest*

FILM EDITING
☐ Ralph Dawson, *A Midsummer Night's Dream*

MUSIC

Best Song:
☐ Harry Warren, Al Dubin, "Lullaby of Broadway" (*Gold Diggers of 1935*)
Best Score:
☐ Max Steiner, *The Informer*

ASSISTANT DIRECTOR
☐ Clem Beauchamp, *The Lives of a Bengal Lancer*

Paul Wing, *The Lives of a Bengal Lancer*

DANCE DIRECTION

Dave Gould, " I've Got a Feeling You're Fooling" (*Broadway Melody*) and "Straw Hat" (*Folies Bergère*)

SPECIAL AWARD

D. W. Griffith, for his distinguished achievements as director and producer and his invaluable initiative and lasting contributions to the progress of the motion picture arts

SCIENTIFIC OR TECHNICAL AWARDS

Class II:

AGFA Ansco Corp., for development of the Agfa infra-red film

Eastman Kodak Co., for development of Eastman Pola-Screen

Class III:

MGM Studio, for development of anti-directional negative and positive development by means of jet turbulation, and the application of the method to all negative and print processing of the entire product of a major producing company

William A. Mueller of Warner Bros.-First National Studio Sound Dept., for his method of dubbing, in which the level of the dialogue automatically controls the level of the accompanying music and sound effects

Mole-Richardson Co., for development of the "Solar-spot" spot lamps

Douglas Shearer and MGM Studio Sound Dept., for their automatic control system for cameras and sound-recording machines and auxiliary stage equipment

Electrical Research Products, Inc., for their study and development of equipment to analyze and measure flutter resulting from the travel of film through the mechanisms used in the recording and reproduction of sound

Paramount Productions, Inc., for the design and construction of the Paramount transparency air turbine developing machine

Nathan Levinson, director of Sound Recording for Warner Bros.-First National Studio, for the method of intercutting variable density and variable area sound tracks to secure an increase in the effective volume range of sound recorded for motion pictures

1936

BEST PICTURE

The Great Ziegfeld (MGM)
Anthony Adverse (Warner Bros.)
Dodsworth (Goldwyn-UA)
Libeled Lady (MGM)
Mr. Deeds Goes to Town (Columbia)
Romeo and Juliet (MGM)
San Francisco (MGM)
The Story of Louis Pasteur (Warner Bros.)
A Tale of Two Cities (MGM)
Three Smart Girls (Universal)

BEST DIRECTOR

Frank Capra, *Mr. Deeds Goes to Town*
Gregory La Cava, *My Man Godfrey*
Robert Z. Leonard, *The Great Ziegfeld*
W. S. Van Dyke, *San Francisco*
William Wyler, *Dodsworth*

BEST ACTOR

Paul Muni, *The Story of Louis Pasteur*
Gary Cooper, *Mr. Deeds Goes to Town*
William Powell, *My Man Godfrey*
Walter Huston, *Dodsworth*
Spencer Tracy, *San Francisco*

BEST ACTRESS

Luise Rainer, *The Great Ziegfeld*
Irene Dunne, *Theodora Goes Wild*

Gladys George, *Valiant Is the Word for Carrie*
Carole Lombard, *My Man Godfrey*
Norma Shearer, *Romeo and Juliet*

BEST SUPPORTING ACTOR

Walter Brennan, *Come and Get It*
Mischa Auer, *My Man Godfrey*
Stuart Erwin, *Pigskin Parade*
Basil Rathbone, *Romeo and Juliet*
Akim Tamiroff, *The General Died at Dawn*

BEST SUPPORTING ACTRESS

Gale Sondergaard, *Anthony Adverse*
Beulah Bondi, *The Gorgeous Hussy*
Alice Brady, *My Man Godfrey*
Bonita Granville, *These Three*
Maria Ouspenskaya, *Dodsworth*

WRITING (ORIGINAL STORY)

Pierre Collings, Sheridan Gibney, *The Story of Louis Pasteur*
Norman Krasna, *Fury*
William Anthony McGuire, *The Great Ziegfeld*
Robert Hopkins, *San Francisco*

Adele Commandini, *Three Smart Girls*

WRITING (SCREENPLAY)

Pierre Collings, Sheridan Gibney, *The Story of Louis Pasteur*
Frances Goodrich, Albert Hackett, *After the Thin Man*
Sidney Howard, *Dodsworth*
Robert Riskin, *Mr. Deeds Goes to Town*
Eric Hatch, Morris Ryskind, *My Man Godfrey*

CINEMATOGRAPHY

Gaetano Gaudio, *Anthony Adverse*
Victor Milner, *The General Died at Dawn*
George Folsey, *The Gorgeous Hussy*

INTERIOR DECORATION

Richard Day, *Dodsworth*

SOUND RECORDING
☐ Douglas Shearer, *San Francisco*

SHORT SUBJECTS
Cartoons:
☐ Walt Disney (UA), *Country Cousin*
One-Reel:
☐ Hal Roach (MGM), *Bored of Education*
Two-Reel:
☐ MGM, *The Public Pays*
Color:
☐ Warner Bros., *Give Me Liberty*

MUSIC
Best Song:
☐ Jerome Kern, Dorothy Fields, "The Way You Look Tonight" (*Swing Time*)
Best Score:
☐ Leo Forbstein, *Anthony Adverse*

FILM EDITING
☐ Ralph Dawson, *Anthony Adverse*

ASSISTANT DIRECTOR
☐ Jack Sullivan, *The Charge of the Light Brigade*

DANCE DIRECTION
☐ Seymour Felix, "A Pretty Girl Is Like a Melody" (*The Great Ziegfeld*)

SPECIAL AWARDS
☐ The March of Time, for its significance to motion pictures and for having revolutionized one of he most important branches of the industry—the newsreel
☐ W. Howard Greene and Harold Rosson, for the color cinematography of *The Garden of Allah* (Selznick Intern.)

SCIENTIFIC OR TECHNICAL AWARDS
Class I:
☐ Douglas Shearer and MGM Studio Sound Dept., for development of a practical two-way horn system, and a biased Class A push-pull recording system
Class II:
☐ E.C. Wente and Bell Telephone Laboratories, for multicellular high-frequency horn and receiver

☐ RCA Manufacturing Co., Inc., for their rotary stabilizer sound head
Class III:
☐ RCA Manufacturing Co., Inc., for development of a method of recording and printing sound records utilizing a restricted spectrum (known as ultraviolet light recording)
☐ Electrical Research Products, Inc., for the ERPI "Type Q" portable recording channel
☐ RCA Manufacturing Co., Inc., for furnishing a practical design and specifications for a nonslip printer
☐ United Artists Studio Corp., for development of a practical, efficient and quiet wind machine

---

1937

BEST PICTURE
☐ *The Life of Emile Zola* (Warner Bros.)
The Awful Truth (Columbia)
Captains Courageous (MGM)
Dead End (Goldwyn-UA)
The Good Earth (MGM)
In Old Chicago (20th Century-Fox)
Lost Horizon (Columbia)
100 Men and a Girl (Universal)
Stage Door (RKO Radio)
A Star Is Born (Selznick-UA)

BEST DIRECTOR
☐ Leo McCarey, *The Awful Truth*
Sidney Franklin, *The Good Earth*
William Dieterle, *The Life of Emile Zola*
Gregory La Cava, *Stage Door*
William Wellman, *A Star Is Born*

BEST ACTOR
☐ Spencer Tracy, *Captains Courageous*
Charles Boyer, *Conquest*
Fredric March, *A Star Is Born*
Robert Montgomery, *Night Must Fall*
Paul Muni, *The Life of Emile Zola*

BEST ACTRESS
☐ Luise Rainer, *The Good Earth*
Irene Dunne, *The Awful Truth*
Greta Garbo, *Camille*
Janet Gaynor, *A Star Is Born*
Barbara Stanwyck, *Stella Dallas*

BEST SUPPORTING ACTOR
☐ Joseph Schildkraut, *The Life of Emile Zola*
Ralph Bellamy, *The Awful Truth*
Thomas Mitchell, *Hurricane*
H.B. Warner, *Lost Horizon*
Roland Young, *Topper*

BEST SUPPORTING ACTRESS
☐ Alice Brady, *In Old Chicago*
Andrea Leeds, *Stage Door*
Anne Shirley, *Stella Dallas*
Claire Trevor, *Dead End*
Dame May Whitty, *Night Must Fall*

WRITING (ORIGINAL STORY)
☐ William A. Wellman, Robert Carson, *A Star Is Born*
Robert Lord, *Black Legion*
Niven Busch, *In Old Chicago*
Heinz Herald, Geza Herczeg, *The Life of Emile Zola*
Hans Kraly, *100 Men and a Girl*

WRITING (SCREENPLAY)
☐ Heinz Herald, Geza Herczeg, Norman Reilly Raine, *The Life of Emile Zola*
Vina Delmar, *The Awful Truth*
Marc Connolly, John Lee Mahin, Dale Van Every, *Captains Courageous*
Morris Ryskind, Anthony Veiller, *Stage Door*
Alan Campbell, Robert Carson, Dorothy Parker, *A Star Is Born*

CINEMATOGRAPHY
☐ Karl Freund, *The Good Earth*
Gregg Toland, *Dead End*
Joseph Valentine, *Wings Over Honolulu*

INTERIOR DECORATION
☐ Stephen Goosson, *Lost Horizon*

SOUND RECORDING
☐ Thomas Moulton, *The Hurricane*

SHORT SUBJECTS

Cartoons:
- Walt Disney (RKO), *The Old Mill*

One-Reel:
- Educational, *Private Life of the Gannets*

Two-Reel:
- MGM, *Torture Money*

Color:
- Pete Smith (MGM), *Penny Wisdom*

MUSIC

Best Song:
- Harry Owens, "Sweet Leilani" (*Waikiki Wedding*)

Best Score:
- Charles Previn, *100 Men and a Girl*

FILM EDITING
- Gene Havlick, Gene Milford, *Lost Horizon*

ASSISTANT DIRECTOR
- Robert Webb, *In Old Chicago*

DANCE DIRECTION
- Hermes Pan, "Fun House" (*Damsel in Distress*)

SPECIAL AWARDS
- Mack Sennett, for his lasting contribution to the comedy technique of the screen, the basic principles of which are as important today as when they were first put into practice, the Academy presents a Special Award to that master of fun, discoverer of stars, sympathetic, kindly, understanding comedy genius
- Edgar Bergen for his outstanding comedy creation, Charlie McCarthy
- The Museum of Modern Art Film Library for its significant work in collecting films dating from 1895 to the present and for the first time making available to the public the means of studying the historical and aesthetic development of the motion picture as one of the major arts
- W. Howard Greene for the color photography of *A Star Is Born*. (This Award was recommended by a committee of leading cinematographers after viewing all the color pictures made during the year.)

IRVING G. THALBERG MEMORIAL AWARD
- Darryl F. Zanuck

SCIENTIFIC OR TECHNICAL AWARDS

Class I:
- AGFA Ansco Corp., for Agfa Supreme and Agfa Ultra Speed pan motion picture negatives

Class II:
- Walt Disney Prods. Ltd., for design and application to production of the Multi-Plane Camera
- Eastman Kodak Co., for two fine-grain duplicating film stocks
- Farciot Edourat and Paramount Pictures, Inc., for development of the Paramount dual screen transparency camera setup
- Douglas Shearer and MGM Studio Sound Dept., for a method of varying the scanning width of variable density sound tracks (squeeze tracks) for the purpose of obtaining an increased amount of noise reduction

Class III:
- John Arnold and MGM Studio Camera Dept., for their improvement of the semi-automatic follow focus device and its application to all of the cameras used by MGM Studio
- John Livadary, director of Sound Recording for Columbia Pictures Corp., for the application of the bi-planar light value to motion picture sound recording
- Thomas T. Moulton and the United Artists Studio Sound Dept., for the application to motion picture sound recording of volume indicators which have peak-reading response and linear decibel scales
- RCA Manufacturing Co., Inc., for introduction of the modulated high-frequency method of determining optimum photographic processing conditions for variable width sound tracks
- Joseph E. Robbins and Paramount Pictures, Inc., for an exceptional application of acoustic principles to the sound proofing of gasoline generator and water pumps
- Douglas Shearer and MGM Studio Sound Dept., for the design of the film mechanism incorporated in the ERPI 1010 reproducer

1938

BEST PICTURE
- *You Can't Take It With You* (Columbia)
- *The Adventures of Robin Hood* (Warner Bros.)
- *Alexander's Ragtime Band* (20th Century-Fox)
- *Boys Town* (MGM)
- *The Citadel* (MGM)
- *Four Daughters* (Warners-First National)
- *Grand Illusion* (R.A.C.-World Pictures)
- *Jezebel* (Warner Bros.)
- *Pygmalion* (MGM)
- *Test Pilot* (MGM)

BEST DIRECTOR
- Frank Capra, *You Can't Take It with You*
- Michael Curtiz, *Angels with Dirty Faces*
- Michael Curtiz, *Four Daughters*
- Norman Taurog, *Boys Town*
- King Vidor, *The Citadel*

BEST ACTOR
- Spencer Tracy, *Boys Town*
- Charles Boyer, *Algiers*
- James Cagney, *Angels with Dirty Faces*
- Robert Donat, *The Citadel*
- Leslie Howard, *Pygmalion*

BEST ACTRESS
- Bette Davis, *Jezebel*
- Fay Bainter, *White Banners*
- Wendy Hiller, *Pygmalion*
- Norma Shearer, *Marie Antoinette*

Margaret Sullavan, *Three Comrades*

BEST SUPPORTING ACTOR
☐ Walter Brennan, *Kentucky*
John Garfield, *Four Daughters*
Gene Lockhart, *Algiers*
Robert Morley, *Marie Antoinette*
Basil Rathbone, *If I Were King*

BEST SUPPORTING ACTRESS
☐ Fay Bainter, *Jezebel*
Beulah Bondi, *Of Human Hearts*
Billie Burke, *Merrily We Live*
Spring Byington, *You Can't Take It With You*
Miliza Korjus, *The Great Waltz*

WRITING (ADAPTATION)
☐ Ian Dalrymple, Cecil Lewis, W. P. Lipscomb, *Pygmalion* (Only nomination)

WRITING (ORIGINAL STORY)
☐ Eleanore Griffin, Dore Schary, *Boys Town*
Irving Berlin, *Alexander's Ragtime Band*
Rowland Brown, *Angels with Dirty Faces*
John Howard Lawson, *Blockade*
Marcella Burke, Frederick Kohner, *Mad About Music*
Frank Wead, *Test Pilot*

WRITING (SCREENPLAY)
☐ George Bernard Shaw, *Pygmalion*
John Meehan, Dore Schary, *Boys Town*
Ian Dalrymple, Elizabeth Hill, Frank Wead, *The Citadel*
Lenore Coffee, Julius J. Epstein, *Four Daughters*
Robert Riskin, *You Can't Take It with You*

CINEMATOGRAPHY
☐ Joseph Ruttenberg, *The Great Waltz*
James Wong Howe, *Algiers*
Ernest Miller, Harry Wild, *Army Girl*
Victor Milner, *The Buccaneer*
Ernest Haller, *Jezebel*
Joseph Valentine, *Mad About Music*
Norbert Brodine, *Merrily We Live*
Peverell Marley, *Suez*

Robert de Grasse, *Vivacious Lady*
Joseph Walker, *You Can't Take It with You*
Leon Shamroy, *The Young at Heart*

INTERIOR DECORATION
☐ Carl J. Weyl, *The Adventures of Robin Hood*

SOUND RECORDING
☐ Thomas Moulton, *The Cowboy and the Lady*

SHORT SUBJECTS

Cartoons:
☐ Walt Disney (RKO), *Ferdinand the Bull*
One-Reel:
☐ MGM, *That Mothers Might Live*
Two-Reel:
☐ Warner Bros., *Declaration of Independence*

MUSIC

Best Song:
☐ Ralph Rainger, Leo Robin, "Thanks for the Memory," *The Big Broadcast of 1938*
Best Score:
☐ Alfred Newman, *Alexander's Ragtime Band*
Original Score:
☐ Erich Wolfgang Korngold, *The Adventures of Robin Hood*

FILM EDITING
☐ Ralph Dawson, *The Adventures of Robin Hood*

SPECIAL AWARDS
☐ Deanna Durbin and Mickey Rooney for their significant contribution in bringing to the screen the spirit and personification of youth, and as juvenile players setting a high standard of ability and achievement
☐ Harry M. Warner in recognition of patriotic service in the production of historical short subjects presenting significant episodes in the early struggle of the American people for liberty
☐ Walt Disney for *Snow White and the Seven Dwarfs*, recognized as a significant screen innovation which has charmed millions and

pioneered a great new entertainment field for the motion picture cartoon
☐ Oliver Marsh and Allen Davey for the color cinematography of the MGM production, *Sweethearts*
☐ For outstanding achievement in creating Special Photographic and Sound Effects in the Paramount production, *Spawn of the North*. Special effects by Gordon Jennings, assisted by Jan Domela, Dev Jennings, Irmin Roberts and Art Smith. Transparencies by Farciot Edouart, assisted by Loyal Griggs. Sound Effects by Loren Ryder, assisted by Harry Mills, Louis H. Mesenkop and Walter Oberst
☐ J. Arthur Ball for his outstanding contributions to the advancement of color in picture motion photography

IRVING G. THALBERG MEMORIAL AWARD
☐ Hal B. Wallis

SCIENTIFIC OR TECHNICAL AWARDS

Class III:
☐ John Aalberg and RKO Studio Sound Dept., for application of compression to variable area recording in motion picture production
☐ Byron Haskin and Special Effects Dept. of **Warner Bros. Studio**, for pioneering the development and the first practical application to motion picture production of the triple head background projector

---

1939

BEST PICTURE
☐ *Gone With the Wind* (MGM)
Dark Victory (Warner Bros.)
Goodbye, Mr. Chips (MGM)
Love Affair (RKO Radio)
Mr. Smith Goes to Washington (Columbia)
Ninotchka (MGM)

Of Mice and Men (Ral Roach-UA)
Stagecoach (Walter Wanger-UA)
The Wizard of Oz (MGM)
Wuthering Heights (Goldwyn-UA)

BEST DIRECTOR

☐ Victor Fleming, *Gone With the Wind*
Frank Capra, *Mr. Smith Goes to Washington*
John Ford, *Stagecoach*
Sam Wood, *Goodbye, Mr. Chips*
William Wyler, *Wuthering Heights*

BEST ACTOR

☐ Robert Donat, *Goodbye, Mr. Chips*
Clark Gable, *Gone With the Wind*
Laurence Olivier, *Wuthering Heights*
Mickey Rooney, *Babes in Arms*
James Stewart, *Mr. Smith Goes to Washington*

BEST ACTRESS

☐ Vivien Leigh, *Gone With the Wind*
Bette Davis, *Dark Victory*
Irene Dunne, *Love Affair*
Greta Garbo, *Ninotchka*
Greer Garson, *Goodbye, Mr. Chips*

BEST SUPPORTING ACTOR

☐ Thomas Mitchell, *Stagecoach*
Brian Aherne, *Juarez*
Harry Carey, *Mr. Smith Goes to Washington*
Brian Donlevy, *Beau Geste*
Claude Rains, *Mr. Smith Goes to Washington*

BEST SUPPORTING ACTRESS

☐ Hattie McDaniel, *Gone With the Wind*
Olivia de Havilland, *Gone With the Wind*
Geraldine Fitzgerald, *Wuthering Heights*
Edna May Oliver, *Drums Along the Mohawk*

Maria Ouspenskaya, *Love Affair*

WRITING (ORIGINAL STORY)

☐ Lewis R. Foster, *Mr. Smith Goes to Washington*
Felix Jackson, *Bachelor Mother*
Mildred Cram, Leo McCarey, *Love Affair*
Melchior Lengyel, *Ninotchka*
Lamar Trotti, *Young Mr. Lincoln*

WRITING (SCREENPLAY)

☐ Sidney Howard, *Gone with the Wind*
Eric Maschwitz, R. C. Sheriff, Claudine West, *Goodbye, Mr. Chips*
Sidney Buchman, *Mr. Smith Goes to Washington*
Charles Brackett, Walter Reisch, Billy Wilder, *Ninotchka*
Ben Hecht, Charles MacArthur, *Wuthering Heights*

CINEMATOGRAPHY (BLACK-AND-WHITE)

☐ Gregg Toland, *Wuthering Heights*
☐ Bert Glennon, *Stagecoach*

CINEMATOGRAPHY (COLOR)

☐ Ernest Haller, Ray Rennahan, *Gone With the Wind*
Sol Polito, W. Howard Greene, *The Private Lives of Elizabeth and Essex*

INTERIOR DECORATION

☐ Lyle Wheeler, *Gone With the Wind*

SOUND RECORDING

☐ Bernard B. Brown, *When Tomorrow Comes*

SHORT SUBJECTS

Cartoons:
☐ Walt Disney (RKO Radio), *The Ugly Duckling*
One-Reel:
☐ Paramount, *Busy Little Bears*
Two-Reel:
☐ Warner Bros., *Sons of Liberty*

MUSIC

Best Song:
☐ Harold Arlen, E.Y. Harburg,

"Over the Rainbow," *The Wizard of Oz*

Best Score:
☐ Richard Hageman, Franke Harling, John Leipold, Leo Shuken, *Stagecoach*
Original Score:
☐ Herbert Stothart, *The Wizard of Oz*

FILM EDITING

☐ Hal C. Kern, James E. Newcom, *Gone With the Wind*

SPECIAL EFFECTS

☐ E.H. Hansen, Fred Sersen, *The Rains Came*

SPECIAL AWARDS

☐ Douglas Fairbanks (Commemorative Award). Recognizing the unique and outstanding contribution of Douglas Fairbanks, first President of the Academy, to the international development of the motion picture
☐ The Motion Picture Relief Fund, acknowledging the outstanding services to the industry during the past year of the Motion Picture Relief Fund and its progressive leadership. Presented to Jean Hersholt, President; Ralph Morgan, Chairman of the Executive Committee; Ralph Block, First Vice-President; Conrad Nagle
☐ Technicolor Company, for its contributions in successfully bringing three-color feature production to the screen
☐ Judy Garland, for her outstanding performance as a screen juvenile during the past year
☐ William Cameron Menzies, for outstanding achievement in the use of color for the enhancement of dramatic mood in the production, *Gone With the Wind*

SCIENTIFIC OR TECHNICAL AWARDS

Class III:
☐ George Anderson of Warner

Bros. Studio, for an improved positive head for sun arcs

☐ John Arnold of MGM Studio, for the MGM mobile camera crane

☐ Thomas T. Moulton, Fred Albin and Sound Dept. of the Samuel Goldwyn Studio, for the origination and application of the Delta db test to sound recording in motion pictures

☐ Farciot Edouart, Joseph E. Robbins, William Rudolph and Paramount Pictures, Inc., for the design and construction of a quiet portable treadmill

☐ Emery Huse and Ralph B. Atkinson of Eastman Kodak Co., for their specifications for chemical analysis of photographic developers and fixing baths

☐ Harold Nye of Warner Bros. Studio, for a miniature incandescent spot lamp

☐ A.J. Tondreau of Warner Bros. Studio, for the design and manufacture of an improved sound track printer

Multiple Award for important contributions in cooperative development of new improved Process Projection Equipment:

☐ F.R. Abbott, Haller Belt, Alan Cook and Bausch & Lomb Optical Co., for faster projection lens

☐ Mitchell Camera Co., for a new type process projection head

☐ Mole-Richardson Co., for a new type automatically controlled projection arc lamp

☐ Charles Handley, David Joy and National Carbon Co., for improved and more stable high-intensity carbons

☐ Winton Hoch and Technicolor Motion Picture Corp., for an auxiliary optical system

☐ Don Musgrave and Selznick International Pictures, Inc. for pioneering in the use of coordinated equipment in the production *Gone With the Wind*

1940

BEST PICTURE

☐ *Rebecca* (Selznick-UA)
All This, and Heaven Too (Warner Bros.)
Foreign Correspondent (Wanger-UA)
The Grapes of Wrath (20th Century-Fox)
The Great Dictator (Chaplin-UA)
Kitty Foyle (RKO Radio)
The Letter (Warner Bros.)
The Long Voyage Home (Wanger-UA)
Our Town (Lesser-UA)
The Philadelphia Story (MGM)

BEST DIRECTOR

☐ John Ford, *The Grapes of Wrath*
George Cukor, *The Philadelphia Story*
Alfred Hitchcock, *Rebecca*
Sam Wood, *Kitty Foyle*
William Wyler, *The Letter*

BEST ACTOR

☐ James Stewart, *The Philadelphia Story*
Charles Chaplin, *The Great Dictator*
Henry Fonda, *The Grapes of Wrath*
Raymond Massey, *Abe Lincoln in Illinois*
Laurence Olivier, *Rebecca*

BEST ACTRESS

☐ Ginger Rogers, *Kitty Foyle*
Bette Davis, *The Letter*
Joan Fontaine, *Rebecca*
Katharine Hepburn, *The Philadelphia Story*
Martha Scott. *Our Town*

BEST SUPPORTING ACTOR

☐ Walter Brennan, *The Westerner*
Albert Basserman, *Foreign Correspondent*
William Gargan, *They Knew What They Wanted*
Jack Oakie, *The Great Dictator*
James Stephenson, *The Letter*

BEST SUPPORTING ACTRESS

☐ Jane Darwell, *The Grapes of Wrath*
Judith Anderson, *Rebecca*

Ruth Hussey, *The Philadelphia Story*
Barbara O'Neil, *All This, and Heaven Too*
Marjorie Rambeau, *Primrose Path*

WRITING (ORIGINAL STORY)

☐ Benjamin Glazer, John S. Toldy, *Arise, My Love*
Walter Reisch, *Comrade X*
Hugo Butler, Dory Schary, *Edison the Man*
Leo McCarey, Bella Spewack, Samuel Spewack, *My Favorite Wife*
Stuart N. Lake, *The Westerner*

WRITING (ORIGINAL SCREENPLAY)

☐ Preston Sturges, *The Great McGinty*
Ben Hecht, *Angels Over Broadway*
Norman Burnside, Heinz Herald, John Huston, *Dr. Ehrlich's Magic Bullet*
Charles Bennett, Joan Harrison, *Foreign Correspondent*
Charles Chaplin, *The Great Dictator*

WRITING (SCREENPLAY)

☐ Donald Ogden Stewart, *The Philadelphia Story*
Nunnally Johnson, *The Grapes of Wrath*
Dalton Trumbo, *Kitty Foyle*
Dudley Nichols, *The Long Voyage Home*
Robert E. Sherwood, Joan Harrison, *Rebecca*

CINEMATOGRAPHY (BLACK-AND-WHITE)

☐ George Barnes, *Rebecca*
James Wong Howe, *Abe Lincoln in Illinois*
Ernest Haller, *All This, and Heaven Too*
Charles B. Lang, Jr., *Arise, My Love*
Harold Rosson, *Boom Town*
Rudolph Mate, *Foreign Correspondent*
Gaetano Gaudio, *The Letter*
Gregg Toland, *The Long Voyage Home*
Joseph Valentine, *Spring Parade*
Joseph Ruttenberg, *Waterloo Bridge*

CINEMATOGRAPHY (COLOR)

☐ George Perinal, *The Thief of Bagdad*
Oliver T. Marsh, Allen Davey, *Bitter Sweet*
Arthur Miller, Ray Rennahan, *The Blue Bird*
Leon Shamroy, Ray Rennahan, *Down Argentine Way*
Victor Milner, W. Howard Greene, *North West Mounted Police*
Sidney Wagner, William V. Skall, *Northwest Passage*

INTERIOR DECORATION

Black-and-White:
☐ Paul Groesse, Cedric Gibbons, *Pride and Prejudice*
Color:
☐ Vincent Korda, *The Thief of Bagdad*

SOUND RECORDING

☐ Douglas Shearer, *Strike Up the Band*

SHORT SUBJECTS

Cartoons:
☐ MGM, *Milky Way*
One-Reel:
☐ Pete Smith (MGM), *Quicker 'n a Wink*
Two-Reel:
☐ Warner Bros., *Teddy, the Rough Rider*

MUSIC

Best Song:
☐ Leigh Harline, Ned Washington, "When You Wish Upon a Star," *Pinocchio*
Best Score:
☐ Alfred Newman, *Tin Pan Alley*
Original Score:
☐ Leigh Harline, Paul J. Smith, Ned Washington, *Pinocchio*

FILM EDITING

☐ Anne Bauchens, *North West Mounted Police*

SPECIAL EFFECTS

☐ Lawrence Butler, Jack Whitney, *The Thief of Bagdad*

SPECIAL AWARDS

☐ Bob Hope, in recognition of his unselfish services to the motion picture industry
☐ Colonel Nathan Levinson, for his outstanding service to the

industry and the Army during the past nine years, which has made possible the present efficient mobilization of the motion picture industry facilities for the production of Army Training Films

SCIENTIFIC OR TECHNICAL AWARDS

Class I:
☐ 20th Century-Fox Film Corp., for the design and construction of the 20th Century Silenced Camera, developed by Daniel Clark, Grover Laube, Charles Miller, and Robert W. Stevens
Class III:
☐ Warner Bros. Studio Art Dept. and Anton Grot, for the design and perfection of the Warner Bros. water ripple and wave illusion machine

1941

BEST PICTURE

☐ *How Green Was My Valley* (20th Century-Fox)
Blossoms in the Dust (MGM)
Citizen Kane (Mercury-RKO Radio)
Here Comes Mr. Jordan (Columbia)
Hold Back the Dawn (Paramount)
The Little Foxes (Goldwyn-RKO Radio)
The Maltese Falcon (Warner Bros.)
One Foot in Heaven (Warner Bros.)
Sergeant York (Warner Bros.)
Suspicion (RKO Radio)

BEST DIRECTOR

☐ John Ford, *How Green Was My Valley*
Alexander Hall, *Here Comes Mr. Jordan*
Howard Hawks, *Sergeant York*
Orson Welles, *Citizen Kane*
William Wyler, *The Little Foxes*

BEST ACTOR

☐ Gary Cooper, *Sergeant York*

Cary Grant, *Penny Serenade*
Walter Huston, *All That Money Can Buy*
Robert Montgomery, *Here Comes Mr. Jordan*
Orson Welles, *Citizen Kane*

BEST ACTRESS

☐ Joan Fontaine, *Suspicion*
Bette Davis, *The Little Foxes*
Greer Garson, *Blossoms in the Dust*
Olivia de Havilland, *Hold Back the Dawn*
Barbara Stanwyck, *Ball of Fire*

BEST SUPPORTING ACTOR

☐ Donald Crisp, *How Green Was My Valley*
Walter Brennan, *Sergeant York*
Charles Coburn, *The Devil and Miss Jones*
James Gleason, *Here Comes Mr. Jordan*
Sydney Greenstreet, *The Maltese Falcon*

BEST SUPPORTING ACTRESS

☐ Mary Astor, *The Great Lie*
Sara Allgood, *How Green Was My Valley*
Patricia Collinge, *The Little Foxes*
Teresa Wright, *The Little Foxes*
Margaret Wycherly, *Sergeant York*

WRITING (ORIGINAL STORY)

☐ Harry Segall, *Here Comes Mr. Jordan*
Thomas Monroe, Billy Wilder, *Ball of Fire*
Monckton Hoffe, *The Lady Eve*
Richard Connell, Robert Presnell, *Meet John Doe*
Gordon Wellesley, *Night Train*

WRITING (ORIGINAL SCREENPLAY)

☐ Herman J Mankiewicz, Orson Welles, *Citizen Kane*
Norman Krasna, *The Devil and Miss Jones*
Harry Chandlee, Abem Finkel, John Huston, Howard Koch, *Sergeant York*
Karl Tunberg, Darrell Ware, *Tall, Dark and Handsome*

Paul Jarrico, *Tom, Dick and Harry*

WRITING (SCREENPLAY)

☐ Sidney Buchman, Seton I. Miller, *Here Comes Mr. Jordan*
Charles Brackett, Billy Wilder, *Hold Back the Dawn*
Philip Dunne, *How Green Was My Valley*
Lillian Hellman, *The Little Foxes*
John Huston, *The Maltese Falcon*

CINEMATOGRAPHY (BLACK-AND-WHITE)

☐ Arthur Miller, *How Green Was My Valley*
Karl Freund, *The Chocolate Soldier*
Gregg Toland, *Citizen Kane*
Joseph Ruttenberg, *Dr. Jekyll and Mr. Hyde*
Leo Tover, *Hold Back the Dawn*
Sol Polito, *Sergeant York*
Edward Cronjager, *Sun Valley Serenade*
Charles Lang, *Sundown*
Rudolph Mate, *That Hamilton Woman*
Joseph Walker, *Here Comes Mr. Jordan*

CINEMATOGRAPHY (COLOR)

☐ Ernest Palmer, Ray Rennahan, *Blood and Sand*
Wildred M. Cline, Karl Struss, William Synder, *Aloma of the South Seas*
William V. Skall, Leonard Smith, *Billy the Kid*
Karl Freund, W. Howard Greene, *Blossoms in the Dust*
Bert Glennon, *Dive Bomber*
Harry Hallenberger, Ray Rennahan, *Louisiana Purchase*

INTERIOR DECORATION

Black-and-White:
☐ Richard Day, Nathan Juran Thomas Little, *How Green Was My Valley*
Color:
☐ Cedric Gibbons, Urie McCleary; Edwin B. Willis, *Blossoms in the Dust*

SOUND RECORDING

☐ Jack Whitney (General Service), *That Hamilton Woman*

SHORT SUBJECTS

Cartoons:
☐ Walt Disney (RKO), *Lend a Paw*
One-Reel:
☐ MGM, *Of Pups and Puzzles*
Two-Reel:
☐ MGM, *Main Street on the March*

DOCUMENTARY

☐ UA, *Churchill's Island*

MUSIC

Best Song:
☐ Jerome Kern, Oscar Hammerstein II, "The Last Time I Saw Paris," *Lady Be Good*
Scoring of a Dramatic Picture:
☐ Bernard Herrmann, *All That Money Can Buy*
Scoring of a Musical Picture:
☐ Frank Churchill, Oliver Wallace, *Dumbo*

FILM EDITING

☐ William Holmes, *Sergeant York*

SPECIAL EFFECTS

☐ Farciot Edouart, Gordon Jennings; Louis Mesenkop, *I Wanted Wings*

SPECIAL AWARDS

☐ *Churchill's Island*, Canadian National Film Board. Citation for distinctive achievement in short subjects Documentary production
☐ Rey Scott, for his extraordinary achievement in producing *Kuhan*, the film record of China's struggle, including its photography with a 16mm camera under the most difficult and dangerous conditions
☐ The British Ministry of Information, for its vivid and dramatic presentation of the heroism of the R.A.F. in the documentary film, *Target for Tonight*
☐ Walt Disney, William Garity, John N.A. Hawkins and RCA, for their outstanding contribution to the advancement of the use of sound in motion pictures through the production of *Fantasia*
☐ Leopold Stokowski and his associates, for their unique achievement in the creation of a new form of visualized music in Walt Disney's production *Fantasia*, thereby widening the scope of the motion picture as entertainment and as an art form

IRVING G. THALBERG MEMORIAL AWARD

☐ Walt Disney

SCIENTIFIC OR TECHNICAL AWARDS

Class II:
☐ Electrical Research Products Division of Western Electric Co., Inc. for the development of the precision integrating sphere densitometer
☐ RCA Manufacturing Co., for the design and development of the MI-3043 Unidirectional microphone
Class III:
☐ Ray Wilkson and Paramount Studio Laboratory, for pioneering in the use of and for the first application to release printing of fine grain positive stock
☐ Charles Lootens and the Republic Studio Sound Dept., for pioneering the use of and the first practical application to motion picture production of Class B push-pull variable area recording
☐ Wilbur Silvertooth and Paramount Studio Engineering Dept., for the design and computation of a relay condenser system applicable to transparency process projection, delivering considerably more usable light
☐ Paramount Pictures, Inc., and 20th Century-Foxfilm Corp., for the development and first practical application to motion picture production of

an automatic scene slating device
- Douglas Shearer and MGM Studio Sound Dept., and Loren Ryder and the Paramount Studio Sound Dept., for pioneering the development of fine grain emulsions for variable density original sound recording in studio production

1942

BEST PICTURE
- Mrs. Miniver (MGM)
  The Invaders (Columbia)
  The Magnificent Ambersons (Mercury-RKO)
  The Pied Piper (20th Century-Fox)
  Pride of the Yankees (Goldwyn-RKO)
  Random Harvest (MGM)
  Talk of the Town (Columbia)
  Wake Island (Paramount)
  Yankee Doodle Dandy (Warner Bros.)

BEST DIRECTOR
- William Wyler, Mrs. Miniver
  Michael Curtiz, Yankee Doodle Dandy
  John Farrow, Random Harvest
  Sam Wood, Kings Row

BEST ACTOR
- James Cagney, Yankee Doodle Dandy
  Ronald Colman, Random Harvest
  Gary Cooper, Pride of the Yankees
  Walter Pidgeon, Mrs. Miniver
  Monty Woolley, The Pied Piper

BEST ACTRESS
- Greer Garson, Mrs. Miniver
  Bette Davis, Now, Voyager
  Katharine Hepburn, My Sister Eileen
  Teresa Wright, Pride of the Yankees

BEST SUPPORTING ACTOR
- Van Heflin, Johnny Eager
  William Bendix, Wake Island
  Walter Huston, Yankee Doodle Dandy
  Frank Morgan, Tortilla Flat

Henry Travers, Mrs. Miniver

BEST SUPPORTING ACTRESS
- Teresa Wright, Mrs. Miniver
  Gladys Cooper, Now, Voyager
  Agnes Moorehead, The Magnificent Ambersons
  Susan Peters, Random Harvest
  Dame May Whitty, Mrs. Miniver

WRITING (ORIGINAL STORY)
- Emeric Pressburger, The Invaders
  Irving Berlin, Holiday Inn
  Paul Gallico, Pride of the Yankees
  Sidney Harmon, Talk of the Town
  Robert Buckner, Yankee Doodle Dandy

WRITING (ORIGINAL SCREENPLAY)
- Michael Kanin, Ring Lardner Jr., Woman of the Year
  Michael Powell, Emeric Pressburger, One of Our Aircraft is Missing
  Frank Butler, Don Hartman, Road to Morocco
  W.R. Burnett, Frank Butler, Wake Island
  George Oppenheimer, The War Against Mrs. Hadley

WRITING (SCREENPLAY)
- George Froeschel, James Hilton, Claudine West, Arthur Wimperis, Mrs. Miniver
  Rodney Ackland, Emeric Pressburger, The Invaders
  Herman J. Mankiewicz, Joe Swerling, Pride of the Yankees
  George Froeschel, Claudine West, Arthur Wimperis, Random Harvest
  Sidney Buchman, Irwin Shaw, Talk of the Town

CINEMATOGRAPHY (BLACK AND WHITE)
- Joseph Ruttenberg, Mrs. Miniver
  James Wong Howe, Kings Row
  Stanley Cortez, The Magnificent Ambersons
  Charles Clarke, Moontide

Edward Cronjager, The Pied Piper
Rudolph Mate, Pride of the Yankees
John Mescall, Take a Letter, Darling
Ted Tetzlaff, Talk of the Town
Leon Shamroy, Ten Gentlemen from West Point
Arthur Miller, This Above All

CINEMATOGRAPHY (COLOR)
- Leon Shamroy, The Black Swan
  Milton Krasner, William V. Skall, W. Howard Greene, Arabian Nights
  Sol Polito, Captains of the Clouds
  W. Howard Greene, Jungle Book
  Victor Milner, William V. Skall, Reap the Wild Wind
  Edward Crongajer, William V. Skall, To the Shores of Tripoli

INTERIOR DECORATION

Black-and-White:
- Richard Day, Joseph Wright, Thomas Little, This Above All

Color:
- Richard Day, Joseph Wright, Thomas Little, My Gal Sal

SOUND RECORDING
- Nathan Levinson, Yankee Doodle Dandy

SHORT SUBJECTS

Cartoons:
- Walt Disney-RKO, Der Fuehrer's Face

One-Reel:
- Paramount, Speaking of Animals and Their Families

Two-Reel:
- Warner Bros., Beyond the Line of Duty

DOCUMENTARY
- 20th Century-Fox, Battle of Midway

MUSIC

Best Song
- Irving Berlin, "White Christmas," Holiday Inn
Best score of a Dramatic or Comedy Picture
- Max Steiner, Now, Voyager

Best Score of a Musical Picture:

☐ Ray Heindorf, Heinz Roemheld, *Yankee Doodle Dandy*

FILM EDITING

☐ Daniel Mandell, *Pride of the Yankees*

SPECIAL EFFECTS

☐ Farciot Edouart, Gordon Jannings, William L Pereira; Louis Mesenkop, *Reap the Wild Wind*

SPECIAL AWARDS

☐ Charles Boyer, for his progressive cultural achievement in establishing the French research Foundation in Los Angeles as a source of reference for the Hollywood Motion Picture Industry

☐ Noël Coward, for his outstanding production achievement, *In Which We Serve*

☐ MGM Studio, for its achievement in representing the American Way of Life in the production of the "Andy Hardy" series of films

IRVING G. THALBERT MEMORIAL AWARD

☐ Sidney Franklin

SCIENTIFIC OR TECHNICAL AWARDS

Class II:

☐ Carroll Clark, F. Thomas Thompson and RKO Radio Studio Art and Miniature Depts., for the design and construction of a moving cloud and horizon machine

☐ Daniel B. Clark and 20th Century-Fox Film Corp., for the development of a lens calibration system and the application of this system to exposure control in cinematography

Class III:

☐ Robert Henderson and Paramount Studio Engineering and Transparency depts., for the design and construction of adjustable light bridges and frames for transparency process photography

☐ Daniel J Bloomberg and Republic Studio Sound Dept., for the design and appliction to motion picture production of a device for marking action negative for pre-selection purposes

---

1943

BEST PICTURE

☐ *Casablanca* (Warner Bros.)
For Whom the Bell Tolls (Paramount)
Heaven Can Wait (20th Century-Fox)
The Human Comedy (MGM)
In Which We Serve (United Artists)
Madame Curie (MGM)
The More the Merrier (Columbia)
The Ox-Bow Incident (20th Century-Fox)
The Song of Bernadette (20th Century-Fox)
Watch on the Rhine (Warner Bros.)

BEST DIRECTOR

☐ Michael Curtiz, *Casablanca*
Clarence Brown, *The Human Comedy*
Henry King, *The Song of Bernadette*
Ernest Lubitsch, *Heaven Can Wait*
George Stevens, *The More the Merrier*

BEST ACTOR

☐ Paul Lukas, *Watch on the Rhine*
Humphrey Bogart, *Casablanca*
Gary Cooper, *For Whom the Bell Tolls*
Walter Pidgeon, *Madame Curie*
Mickey Rooney, *The Human Comedy*

BEST ACTRESS

☐ Jennifer Jones, *The Song of Bernadette*
Jean Arthur, *The More the Merrier*
Ingrid Bergman, *For Whom the Bell Tolls*
Joan Fontaine, *The Constant Nymph*
Greer Garson, *Madame Curie*

BEST SUPPORTING ACTOR

☐ Charles Coburn, *The More the Merrier*
Charles Bickford, *The Song of Bernadette*
J. Carroll Naish, *Sahara*
Claude Rains, *Casablanca*
Akim Tamiroff, *For Whom the Bell Tolls*

BEST SUPPORTING ACTRESS

☐ Katina Paxinou, , *For Whom the Bell Tolls*
Gladys Cooper, *The Song of Bernadette*
Paulette Goddard, *So Proudly We Hail*
Anne Revere, *The Song of Bernadette*
Lucile Watson, *Watch on the Rhine*

WRITING (ORIGINAL STORY)

☐ William Saroyan, *The Human Comedy*
Guy Gilpatric, *Action in the North Atlantic*
Steve Fisher, *Destination Tokyo*
Frank Ross, Robert Russell, *The More the Merrier*
Gordon McDonell, *The Shadow of a Doubt*

WRITING (ORIGINAL SCREENPLAY)

☐ Norman Krasna, *Princess O'Rourke*
Dudley Nichols, *Air Force*
Noel Coward, *In Which We Serve*
Allan Scott, *So Proudly We Serve*
Lillian Hellman, *The North Star*

WRITING (SCREENPLAY)

☐ Julius J. Epstein, Philip G. Epstein, Howard Koch, *Casablanca*
Nunnally Johnson, *Holy Matrimony*
Richard Flournoy, Lewis R. Foster, Frank Ross, Robert Russell, *The More the Merrier*
George Seaton, *The Song of Bernadette*
Dashiell Hammett, *Watch on the Rhine*

CINEMATOGRAPHY (BLACK-AND-WHITE)

- Arthur Miller, *The Song of Bernadette*
  James Wong Howe, Elmer Dyer, Charles Marshall, *Air Force*
  Arthur Edeson, *Casablanca*
  Tony Gaudio, *Corvette K-225*
  John Seitz, *Five Graves to Cairo*
  Harry Stradling, *The Human Comedy*
  Joseph Ruttenberg, *Madame Curie*
  James Wong Howe, *The North Star*
  Rudolph Mate, *Sahara*
  Charles Lang, *So Proudly We Hail*

CINEMATOGRAPHY (COLOR)

- Hal Mohr, W. Howard Greene, *The Phantom of the Opera*
  Ray Rennahan, *For Whom the Bell Tolls*
  Edward Cronjager, *Heaven Can Wait*
  Charles G. Clarke, Allen Davey, *Hello, Frisco, Hello*
  Leonard Smith, *Lassie Come Home*
  George Folsey, *Thousands Cheer*

INTERIOR DECORATION

- James Basevi, William Darling; Thomas Little, *The Song of Bernadette*

Color:
- Alexander Golitzen, John B. Goodman; Russell A. Gausman, Ira S. Webb, *The Phantom of the Opera*

SOUND RECORDING

- Stephen Dunn, *The Land Is Mine*

SHORT SUBJECTS

Cartoons:
- MGM, *Yankee Doodle Mouse*

One-Reel:
- Paramount, *Amphibious Fighters*

Two-Reel:
- MGM, *Heavenly Music*

DOCUMENTARY

Short Subjects:
- U.S. Navy, *December 7th*

Features:
- British Ministry of Information, *Desert Victory*

MUSIC

Best Song:
- Harry Warren, Mack Gordon, "You'll Never Know," *Hello, Frisco, Hello*

Best Score of a Dramatic or Comedy Picture:
- Alfred Newman, *The Song of Bernadette*

Best Score of a Musical Picture:
- Ray Heindorf, *This Is the Army*

FILM EDITING

- George Amy, *Air Force*

SPECIAL EFFECTS

- Fred Sersen; Roger Heman, *Crash Dive*

SPECIAL AWARDS

- George Pal, for the development of novel methods and techniques in the production of short subjects known as Puppetoons

IRVING G. THALBERG MEMORIAL AWARD

- Hal B. Wallis

SCIENTIFIC OR TECHNICAL AWARDS

Class II:
- Farciot Edouart, Earle Morgan, Barton Thompson and Paramount Studio Engineering and Transparency Depts., for the development and practical application to motion picture production of a method of duplicating and enlarging natural color photographs, transferring the image emulsions to glass plates and projecting these slides by especially designed stereopticon equipment
- Photo Products Dept., E.I. du Pont de Nemours and Co., Inc., for the development of fine-grain motion picture films

Class III:
- Daniel J. Bloomberg and Republic Studio Sound Dept., for the design and development of an inexpensive method of converting Movieolas to Class B push-pull reproduction
- Charles Galloway Clarke and 20th Century-Fox Studio Camera Dept., for the development and practical application of a device for composing artificial clouds into motion picture scenes during production photography
- Farciot Edouart and Paramount Studio Transparency Dept., for an automatic electric transparency cueing timer
- Willard H. Turner and RKO Studio Sound Dept., for design and construction of the phono-cue starter

---

1944

BEST PICTURE

- *Going My Way* (Paramount)
  Double Indemnity (Paramount)
  Gaslight (MGM)
  Since You Went Away (Selznick-UA)
  Wilson (20th Century-Fox)

BEST DIRECTOR

- Leo McCarey, *Going My Way*
  Alfred Hitchcock, *Lifeboat*
  Henry King, *Wilson*
  Otto Preminger, *Laura*
  Billy Wilder, *Double Indemnity*

BEST ACTOR

- Bing Crosby, *Going My Way*
  Charles Boyer, *Gaslight*
  Barry Fitzgerald, *Going My Way*
  Cary Grant, *None But the Lonely Heart*
  Alexander Knox, *Wilson*

BEST ACTRESS

- Ingrid Bergman, *Gaslight*
  Claudette Colbert, *Since You Went Away*
  Bette Davis, *Mr. Skeffington*
  Greer Garson, *Mrs. Parkington*
  Barbara Stanwyck, *Double Indemnity*

BEST SUPPORTING ACTOR

- Barry Fitzgerald, *Going My Way*

Hume Cronyn, *The Seventh Cross*
Claude Rains, *Mr. Skeffington*
Clifton Webb, *Laura*
Monty Woolley, *Since You Went Away*

BEST SUPPORTING ACTRESS

☐ Ethel Barrymore, *None But the Lonely Heart*
Jennifer Jones, *Since You Went Away*
Angela Lansbury, *Gaslight*
Aline MacMahon, *Dragon Seed*
Agnes Moorehead, *Mrs. Parkington*

WRITING (ORIGINAL STORY)

☐ Leo McCarey, *Going My Way*
David Boehm, Chandler Sprague, *A Guy Named Joe*
John Steinbeck, *Lifeboat*
Alfred Neumann, Joseph Than, *None Shall Escape*
Edward Doherty, Jules Schermer, *The Sullivans*

WRITING (ORIGINAL SCREENPLAY)

☐ Lamar Trotti, *Wilson*
Preston Sturges, *Hail the Conquering Hero*
Richard Connell, Gladys Lehman, *Two Girls and a Sailor*
Jerome Cady, *Wing and a Prayer*
Preston Sturges, *The Miracle of Morgan's Creek*

CINEMATOGRAPHY (BLACK AND WHITE)

☐ Joseph LaShelle, *Laura*
John Seitz, *Double Indemnity*
Sidney Wagner, *Dragon Seed*
Joseph Ruttenberg, *Gaslight*
Lionel Lindon, *Going My Way*
Glen MacWilliams, *Lifeboat*
Stanley Cortez, Lee Garmes, *Since You Went Away*
Robert Surtees, Harold Rosson, *Thirty Seconds Over Tokyo*
Charles Lang, *The Uninvited*
George Folsey, *The White Cliffs of Dover*

CINEMATOGRAPHY (COLOR)

☐ Leon Shamroy, *Wilson*

Rudy Mate, Allen M. Davey *Cover Girl*
Edward Cronjager, *Home in Indiana*
Charles Rosher, *Kismet*
Ray Rennahan, *Lady in the Dark*
George Folsey, *Meet Me in St. Louis*

INTERIOR DECORATION

Black-and-White:
☐ Cedric Gibbons, William Ferrari; Edwin B. Willis, Paul Huldschinsky, *Gaslight*
Color:
☐ Wiard Ihnen; Thomas Little, *Wilson*

SOUND RECORDING

☐ E. H. Hansen, *Wilson*

SHORT SUBJECTS

Cartoons:
☐ MGM, *Mouse Trouble*
One-Reel:
☐ Paramount, *Who's Who in Animal Land*
Two-Reel:
☐ Warner Bros., *I Won't Play*

DOCUMENTARY

Short Subjects:
☐ U.S. Marine Corps, *With the Marines at Tarawa*
Features:
☐ 20th Century-Fox, U.S. Navy, *The Fighting Lady*

MUSIC

Best Song:
☐ James Van Heusen, Johnny Burke, "Swinging on a Star," *Going My Way*
Best Score of a Dramatic or Comedy Picture:
☐ Max Steiner, *Since You Went Away*
Best Score of a Musical Picture:
☐ Carmen Dragon, Morris Stoloff, *Cover Girl*

FILM EDITING

☐ Barbara McLean, *Wilson*

SPECIAL EFFECTS

☐ A. Arnold Gillespie, Donald Jahraus, Warren Newcombe Jahraus, Douglas Shearer, *Thirty Seconds Over Tokyo*

SPECIAL AWARDS

☐ Margaret O'Brien, for

outstanding child actress of 1944
☐ Bob Hope, for his many services to the Academy

IRVING G. THALBERT MEMORIAL AWARD

☐ Darryl F. Zanuck

SCIENTIFIC OR TECHNICAL AWARDS

Class II:
☐ Stephen Dunn and RKO Studio Sound Dept. and RCA, for the design and development of the electronic compressor-limiter
Class III:
☐ Linwood Dunn, Cecil Love and Acme Tool Manufacturing Co., for the design and construction of the Acme-Dunn Optical Printer
☐ Grover Laube and 20th Century-Fox Studio Camera Dept., for the development of a continuous loop projection device
☐ Western Electric Co., for the design and construction of the 1126A Limiting Amplifier for variable density sound recording
☐ Russell Brown, Ray Hinsdale and Joseph E. Robbins, for the development and production use of the Paramount floating hydraulic boat rocker
☐ Gordon Jennings, for the design and construction of the Paramount nodal point tripod
☐ RCA and RKO Radio Studio Sound Dept., for the design and construction of the RKO reverberation chamber
☐ Daniel J. Bloomberg and the Republic Studio Sound Dept., for the design and development of a multi-interlock selector switch
☐ Bernard B. Brown and John P. Livadary, for the design and engineering of a separate soloist and chorus recording room
☐ Paul Zeff, S. J. Twining and George Seid of the Columbia Studio Laboratory, for the formula and application to production of

a simplified variable area sound negative developer
☐ **Paul Lerpae**, for the design and construction of the Paramount traveling matte projection and photographing device

---

1945

BEST PICTURE

☐ *The Lost Weekend* (Paramount)
Anchors Aweigh (MGM)
The Bells of St. Mary's (Rainbow-RKO)
Mildred Pierce (Warner Bros.)
Spellbound (Selznick-UA)

BEST DIRECTOR

☐ Billy Wilder, *The Lost Weekend*
Clarence Brown, *National Velvet*
Alfred Hitchcock, *Spellbound*
Leo McCarey, *The Bells of St. Mary's*
Jean Renoir, *The Southerner*

BEST ACTOR

☐ Ray Milland, *The Lost Weekend*
Bing Crosby, *The Bells of St. Mary's*
Gene Kelly, *Anchors Aweigh*
Gregory Peck, *The Keys of the Kingdom*
Cornel Wilde, *A Song to Remember*

BEST ACTRESS

Joan Crawford, *Mildred Pierce*
Ingrid Bergman, *The Bells of St. Mary's*
Greer Garson, *The Valley of Decisions*
Jennifer Jones, *Love Letters*
Gene Tierney, *Leave Her to Heaven*

BEST SUPPORTING ACTOR

☐ James Dunn, *A Tree Grows in Brooklyn*
Michael Chekhov, *Spellbound*
John Dail, *The Corn Is Green*
Robert Mitchum, *G.I. Joe*
J. Carroll Naish, *A Medal for Benny*

BEST SUPPORTING ACTRESS

☐ Anne Revere, *National Velvet*
Eve Arden, *Mildred Pierce*
Ann Blyth, *Mildred Pierce*
Angela Lansbury, *The Picture of Dorian Gray*
Joan Lorring, *The Corn Is Green*

WRITING (ORIGINAL STORY)

☐ Charles G. Booth, *The House on 92nd Street*
Laszlo Gorog, Thomas Monroe, *The Affairs of Susan*
John Steinbeck, Jack Wagner, *A Medal for Benny*
Alvah Bessie, *Objective— Burma*
Ernst Marischka, *A Song to Remember*

WRITING (ORIGINAL SCREENPLAY)

☐ Richard Schweizer, *Marie Louise*
Philip Yordan, *Dillinger*
Myles Connolly, *Music for Millions*
Milton Holmes, *Salty O'Rourke*
Harry Kurnitz, *What Next, Corporal Hargrove?*

WRITING (SCREENPLAY)

☐ Charles Brackett, Billy Wilder, *The Lost Weekend*
Leopold Atlas, Guy Endore, Philip Stevenson, *G.I. Joe*
Ronald MacDougall, *Mildred Pierce*
Albert Maltz, *Pride of the Marines*
Frank Davis, Tess Slesinger, *A Tree Grows in Brooklyn*

CINEMATOGRAPHY (BLACK-AND-WHITE)

☐ Harry Stradling, *The Picture of Dorian Gray*
Arthur Miller, *The Keys of the Kingdom*
John F Seitz, *The Lost Weekend*
Ernest Haller, *Mildred Pierce*
George Barnes, *Spellbound*

CINEMATOGRAPHY (COLOR)

☐ Leon Shamroy, *Leave Her to Heaven*
Robert Planck, Charles Boyle, *Anchors Aweigh*

Leonard Smith, *National Velvet*
Tony Gaudio, Allen M. Davey, *A Song to Remember*
George Barnes, *The Spanish Main*

INTERIOR DECORATION

Black-and-White:
☐ Wiard Ihnen: A. Ronald Fields, *Blood on the Sun*
Color:
☐ Hans Dreier, Ernest Fegte; Sam Comer, *Frenchman's Creek*

SOUND RECORDING

☐ Stephen Dunn, *The Bells of St. Mary's*

SHORT SUBJECTS

Cartoons:
☐ MGM, *Please*
One-Reel:
☐ MGM, *Stairway to Light*
Two-Reel:
☐ Warner Bros., *Star in the Night*

DOCUMENTARY

Short Subjects:
☐ Warner Bros., *Hitler Lives*
Features:
☐ England and the U.S., *The True Glory*

MUSIC

Best Song:
☐ Richard Rodgers, Oscar Hammerstein II, "It Might As Well Be Spring," *State Fair*
Best Score of a Dramatic or Comedy Picture:
☐ Miklos Rozsa, *Spellbound*
Best Score of a Musical Picture:
☐ Georgie Stoll, *Anchors Aweigh*

FILM EDITING

☐ Robert J. Kern, *National Velvet*

SPECIAL EFFECTS

☐ John Fulton; A.W. Johns, *Wonder Man*

SPECIAL AWARDS

☐ Walter Wanger, for his six years service as president of the Academy
☐ Peggy Ann Garner, outstanding child actress of 1945
☐ *The House I Live In*, tolerance

short subject; produced by Frank Ross and Mervyn LeRoy; directed by Mervyn LeRoy; screenplay by Albert Maltz; song "The House I Live In," music by Earl Robinson, lyrics by Lewis Allen; starring Frank Sinatra; released by RKO Radio

☐ Republic Studios, Daniel J. Bloomberg and the Republic Studio Sound Dept., for the building of an outstanding musical scoring auditorium which provides optimum recording conditions and combines all elements of acoustic and engineering design

SCIENTIFIC OR TECHNICAL AWARDS

Class III:

☐ Loren L. Ryder, Charles R. Daily and the Paramount Studio Sound Dept., for the design, construction and use of the first dial-controlled step-by-step sound channel line-up and test circuit

☐ Michael S. Leshing, Benjamin C. Robinson, Arthur B. Chatelain and Robert C. Stevens of 20th Century-Fox Studio, and John G. Capstaff of Eastman Kodak Co., for the 20th Century-Fox film processing machine

1946

BEST PICTURE

☐ *The Best Years of Our Lives* (Samuel Goldwyn-RKO)
☐ *Henry V* (United Artists)
☐ *It's a Wonderful Life* (Liberty-RKO)
☐ *The Razor's Edge* (20th Century-Fox)
☐ *The Yearling* (MGM)

BEST DIRECTOR

☐ William Wyler, *The Best Years of Our Lives*
Clarence Brown, *The Yearling*
Frank Capra, *It's a Wonderful Life*
David Lean, *Brief Encounter*
Robert Siodmak, *The Killers*

BEST ACTOR

☐ Fredric March, *The Best Years of Our Lives*
Laurence Olivier, *Henry V*
Larry Parks, *The Jolson Story*
Gregory Peck, *The Yearling*
James Stewart, *It's a Wonderful Life*

BEST ACTRESS

☐ Olivia de Havilland, *To Each His Own*
Celia Johnson, *Brief Encounter*
Jennifer Jones, *Duel In the Sun*
Rosalind Russell, *Sister Kenny*
Jane Wyman, *The Yearling*

BEST SUPPORTING ACTOR

☐ Harold Russell, *The Best Years of Our Lives*
Charles Coburn, *The Green Years*
William Demarest, *The Jolson Story*
Claude Rains, *Notorious*
Clifton Webb, *The Razor's Edge*

BEST SUPPORTING ACTRESS

☐ Anne Baxter, *The Razor's Edge*
Ethel Barrymore, *The Spiral Staircase*
Lillian Gish, *Duel in the Sun*
Flora Robson, *Saratoga Trunk*
Gale Sondergaard, *Anna and the King of Siam*

WRITING (ORIGINAL STORY)

☐ Clemence Dane, *Vacation from Marriage*
Vladimir Pozner, *The Dark Mirror*
Jack Patrick, *The Strange Love of Martha Ivers*
Victor Trivas, *The Stranger*
Charles Brackett, *To Each His Own*

WRITING (ORIGINAL SCREENPLAY)

☐ Muriel Box, Sydney Box, *The Seventh Veil*
Raymond Chandler, *The Blue Dahlia*
Jacques Prevert, *Children of Paradise*
Ben Hecht, *Notorious*
Norman Panama, Melvin Frank, *The Road to Utopia*

WRITING (SCREENPLAY)

Robert E. Sherwood, *The Best Years of Our Lives*
Sally Benson, Talbot Jennings, *Anna and the King of Siam*
Anthony Havelock-Allan, David Lean, Ronald Neame, *Brief Encounter*
Anthony Veiller, *The Killers*
Sergio Amidei, Federico Fellini, *Open City*

CINEMATOGRAPHY (BLACK-AND-WHITE)

☐ Arthur Miller, *Anna and the King of Siam*
George Folsey, *The Green Years*

CINEMATOGRAPHY (COLOR)

☐ Charles Rosher, Leonard Smith, Arthur Arling, *The Yearling*
Joseph Walker, *The Jolson Story*

INTERIOR DECORATION

Black-and-White:

☐ Lyle Wheeler, William Darling; Thomas Little, Frank E. Hughes, *Anna and the King of Siam*

Color:

☐ Cedric Gibbons, Paul Groesse; Edwin B. Willis, *The Yearling*

SOUND RECORDING

☐ John Livadary, *The Jolson Story*

SHORT SUBJECTS

Cartoons:

☐ MGM, *The Cat Concerto*

One-Reel:

☐ Warner Bros., *Facing Your Danger*

Two-Reel:

☐ Warner Bros., *A Boy and His Dog*

DOCUMENTARY

Short Subjects:

☐ U.S. War Dept., *Seeds of Destiny*

Features:

(none nominated this year)

MUSIC

Best Song:

☐ Harry Warren, Johnny Mercer, "On the Atchison Topeka

and the Santa Fe," *The Harvey Girls*

Best Score of a Dramatic or Comedy Picture:
Hugo Friedhofer, *The Best Years of Our Lives*

Best Score of a Musical Picture:
☐ Morris Stoloff, *The Jolson Story*

FILM EDITING
☐ Daniel Mandell, *The Best Years of Our Lives*

SPECIAL EFFECTS
☐ Thomas Howard, *Blithe Spirit*

SPECIAL AWARDS
☐ Laurence Olivier, for his outstanding achievement as actor, producer and director in bringing *Henry V* to the screen
☐ Harold Russell, for bringing hope and courage to his fellow veterans through his appearance in *The Best Years of Our Lives*
☐ Ernst Lubitsch, for his distinguished contributions to the art of the motion picture
☐ Claude Jarman Jr., outstanding child actor of 1946

IRVING G. THALBERG MEMORIAL AWARD
☐ Samuel Goldwyn

SCIENTIFIC OR TECHNICAL AWARDS
Class III:
☐ Harlan L. Baumbach and Paramount West Coast Laboratory, for an improved method for the quantitiative determination of hydroquinone and metol in photographic developing baths
☐ Herbert E. Britt for the development and application of formulas and equipment for producing cloud and smoke effects
☐ Burton F. Miller, and the Warner Bros. Studio Sound and Electrical Depts., for the design and construction of a motion picture arc lighting generator filter
☐ Carl Faulkner of the 20th Century-Fox Studio Sound

Dept., for the reversed bias method, including a double bias method for light valve and galvanometer density recording
☐ Mole-Richardson Co., for the Type 450 super high intensity carbon arc lamp
☐ Arthur F. Blinn, Robert O. Cook, C. O. Slyfield and Walt Disney Studio Sound Dept., for the design and development of an audio finder and track viewer for checking and locating noise in sound tracks
☐ Burton F. Miller and Warner Bros. Studio Sound dept., for the design and application of an equalizer to eliminate relative spectral energy distortion in electronic compressors
☐ Marty Martin and Hal Adkins of RKO Radio Studio Miniature Dept., for the design and construction of equipment providing visual bullet effects
☐ Harold Nye and Warner Bros. Electrical Dept., for development of the electronically controlled fire and gaslight effect

---

1947

BEST PICTURE
☐ *Gentleman's Agreement* (20th Century-Fox)
The Bishop's Wife (Goldwyn-RKO)
Crossfire (RKO)
Great Expectations (Universal-International)
Miracle on 34th Street (20th Century-Fox)

BEST DIRECTOR
☐ Elia Kazan, *Gentleman's Agreement*
George Cukor, *A Double Life*
Edward Dmytrik, *Crossfire*
Henry Koster, *The Bishop's Wife*
David Lean, *Great Expectations*

BEST ACTOR
☐ Ronald Colman, *A Double Life*

John Garfield, *Body and Soul*
Gregory Peck, *Gentleman's Agreement*
William Powell, *Life with Father*
Michael Redgrave, *Mourning Becomes Electra*

BEST ACTRESS
☐ Loretta Young, *The Farmer's Daughter*
Joan Crawford, *Possessed*
Susan Hayward, *Smash Up— The Story of a Woman*
Dorothy McGuire, *Gentleman's Agreement*
Rosalind Russell, *Mourning Becomes Electra*

BEST SUPPORTING ACTOR
☐ Edmund Gwenn, *Miracle on 34th Street*
Charles Bickford, *The Farmer's Daughter*
Thomas Gomez, *Ride the Pink Horse*
Robert Ryan, *Crossfire*
Richard Widmark, *Kiss of Death*

BEST SUPPORTING ACTRESS
☐ Celeste Holm, *Gentleman's Agreement*
Ethel Barrymore, *The Paradine Case*
Gloria Grahame, *Crossfire*
Marjorie Main, *The Egg and I*
Anne Revere, *Gentleman's Agreement*

WRITING (ORIGINAL STORY)
☐ Valentine Davies, *Miracle on 34th Street*
Georges Chaperot, Rene Wheeler, *A Cage of Nightingales*
Herbert Clyde Lewis, Frederic Stephani, *It Happened on Fifth Avenue*
Eleazar Lipsky, *Kiss of Death*
Dorothy Parker, Frank Cavett, *Smash Up—The Story of a Woman*

WRITING (ORIGINAL SCREENPLAY)
☐ Sidney Sheldon, *The Bachelor and the Bobbysoxer*
Abraham Polonsky, *Body and Soul*
Ruth Gordon, Garson Kanin, *A Double Life*

Charles Chaplin, *Monsieur Verdoux*
Sergio Amidei, Adolfo Franci, C. G. Viola, Cesare Zavaittini, *Shoeshine*

WRITING (SCREENPLAY)

George Seaton, *Miracle on 34th Street*
Richard Murphy, *Boomerang*
John Paxton, *Crossfire*
Moss Hart, *Gentleman's Agreement*
David Lean, Ronald Neame, Anthony Havelock-Allan, *Great Expectations*

CINEMATOGRAPHY (BLACK-AND-WHITE)

☐ Guy Green, *Great Expectations*
Charles Lang, Jr., *The Ghost of Mrs. Muir*
George Folsey, *Green Dolphin Street*

CINEMATOGRAPHY (COLOR)

☐ Jack Cardiff, *Black Narcissus*
Peverell Marley, William V. Skall, *Life With Father*
Harry Jackson, *Mother Wore Tights*

ART DIRECTION/SET DECORATION

Black-and-White:
☐ John Bryan; Wilfred Shingleton, *Great Expectations*
Color:
☐ Alfred Junge, *Black Narcissus*

SOUND RECORDING

☐ Goldwyn Sound Dept., *The Bishop's Wife*

SHORT SUBJECTS

Cartoons:
☐ Warner Bros., *Tweetie Pie*
One-Reel:
☐ MGM, *Goodbye Miss Turlock*
Two-Reel:
☐ Monogram, *Climbing the Matterhorn*

DOCUMENTARY

Short Subjects:
☐ U.N. Films and Visual Education, *First Steps*
Features:
☐ RKO, *Design for Death*

MUSIC

Best Song:
☐ Allie Wrubel, Ray Gilbert,

"Zip-a-dee-doo-dah," *Song of the South*
Best Score of a Dramatic or Comedy Picture:
☐ Miklos Rozsa, *A Double Life*
Best Score of a Musical Picture:
☐ Alfred Newman, *Mother Wore Tights*

FILM EDITING

☐ Francis Lyon, Robert Parrish, *Body and Soul*

SPECIAL EFFECTS

☐ A. Arnold Gillespie, Warner Newcombe; Douglas Shearer, Michael Steinore, *Green Dolphin Street*

SPECIAL AWARDS

☐ James Baskette, for his characterization of Uncle Remus in *Song of the South*
☐ *Bill and Coo*, for a novel and entertaining use of the motion picture
☐ *Shoeshine*, an Italian production of superlative quality made under adverse circumstances
☐ Colonel William N. Selig, Albert E. Smith, Thomas Armat and George K. Spoor, as pioneers whose belief in a new medium blazed the trail along which the motion picture has progressed

SCIENTIFIC OR TECHNICAL AWARDS

Class II:
☐ C.C. Davis and Electrical Research Products, Division of Western Electric Co., for the development and application of an improved film drive filter mechanism
☐ C. R. Daily and Paramount Studio Film Laboratory, Still and Engineering Dept., for the development and first practical application to motion picture and still photograhy of a method of increasing film speed as first suggested to the industry by E.I. du Pont de Nemours & Co.

Class III:
☐ Nathan Levinson and Warner Bros. Studio Sound Dept., for the design and

construction of a constant-speed sound editing machine
☐ Farciot Edouart, C. R. Daily, Hal Corl, H.G. Cartwright and the Paramount Studio Transparency and Engineering Depts., for the first application of a special anti-solarizing glass to high intensity background and spot arc projectors
☐ Fred Ponedel of Warner Bros. Studio, for pioneering the fabrication and practical application to motion picture color photography of large translucent photographic backgrounds
☐ Kurt Singer and RCA-Victor Division of RCA, for the design and development of a continuously variable band elimination filter
☐ James Gibbons of Warner Bros. Studio, for development and production of large dyed plastic filters for motion picture photography

---

1948

BEST PICTURE

☐ *Hamlet* (Universal-International)
Johnny Belinda (Warner Bros.)
The Red Shoes (Eagle Lion)
The Snake Pit (20th Century-Fox)
Treasure of Sierra Madre (Warner Bros.)

BEST DIRECTOR

☐ John Huston, *Treasure of Sierra Madre*
Anatole Litvak, *The Snake Pit*
Jean Negulesco, *Johnny Belinda*
Laurence Olivier, *Hamlet*
Fred Zinnemann, *The Search*

BEST ACTOR

☐ Laurence Olivier, *Hamlet*
Lew Ayres, *Johnny Belinda*
Montgomery Clift, *The Search*
Dan Dailey, *When My Baby Smiles at Me*
Clifton Webb, *Sitting Pretty*

BEST ACTRESS

☐ Jane Wyman, *Johnny Belinda*
Ingrid Bergman, *Joan of Arc*
Olivia de Havilland, *The Snake Pit*
Irene Dunne, *I Remember Mama*
Barbara Stanwyck, *Sorry, Wrong Number*

BEST SUPPORTING ACTOR

☐ Walter Huston, *Treasure of Sierre Madre*
Charles Bickford, *Johnny Belinda*
José Ferrer, *Joan of Arc*
Oscar Homolka, *I Remember Mama*
Cecil Kellaway, *The Luck of the Irish*

BEST SUPPORTING ACTRESS

☐ Claire Trevor, *Key Largo*
Barbara Bel Geddes, *I Remember Mama*
Ellen Corby, *I Remember Mama*
Agnes Moorehead, *Johnny Belinda*
Jean Simmons, *Hamlet*

WRITING (MOTION PICTURE STORY)

☐ Richard Schweizer, David Wechsler, *The Search*
Frances Flaherty, Robert Flaherty, *The Louisiana Story*
Malvin Wald, *The Naked City*
Borden Chase, *Red River*
Emeric Pressburger, *The Red Shoes*

WRITING (SCREENPLAY)

☐ John Huston, *Treasure of Sierra Madre*
Charles Brackett, Billy Wilder, Richard L. Breen, *A Foreign Affair*
Irmgard Von Cube, Allen Vincent, *Johnny Belinda*
Richard Schweizer, David Wechsler, *The Search*
Frank Partos, Millen Brand, *The Snake Pit*

CINEMATOGRAPHY (BLACK-AND-WHITE)

■ William Daniels, *The Naked City*
Charles B. Lang, Jr., *A Foreign Affair*

Nicholas Musuraca, *I Remember Mama*
Ted McCord, *Johnny Belinda*
Joseph August, *Portrait of Jennie*

CINEMATOGRAPHY (COLOR)

☐ Joseph Valentine, William V. Skall, Winton Hoch, *Joan of Arc*
Charles G. Clarke, *Green Grass of Wyoming*
William Snyder, *The Loves of Carmen*
Robert Planck, *The Three Musketeers*

ART DIRECTION/SET DIRECTION

Black-and-White:
☐ Roger K. Furse; Carmen Dillon, *Hamlet*
Color:
☐ Hein Heckroth; Arthur Lawson, *The Red Shoes*

SOUND RECORDING

☐ 20th Century-Fox Sound Dept., *The Snake Pit*

DOCUMENTARY

Short Subjects:
☐ U.S. Army, *Toward Independence*
Features:
☐ U.S. Navy, MGM, *The Secret Land*

SHORT SUBJECTS

Cartoons:
☐ MGM, *The Lttle Orphan*
One-Reel:
☐ 20th Century-Fox, *Symphony of a City*
Two-Reel:
☐ Walt Disney-RKO, *Seal Island*

MUSIC

Best Song:
☐ Jay Livingston, Ray Evans, "Buttons and Bows," *Paleface*
Best Score of a Dramatic or Comedy Picture:
☐ Brian Easdale, *The Red Shoes*
Best Score of a Musical Picture:
☐ Johnny Green, Roger Edens, *Easter Parade*

FILM EDITING

☐ Paul Weatherwax, *The Naked City*

SPECIAL EFFECTS

☐ Paul Eagler, J. McMillan Johnson, Russell Shearman, Clarence Slifer; Charles Freeman, James G. Stewart, *Portrait of Jennie*

COSTUME DESIGN

Black-and-White:
☐ Roger K. Furse, *Hamlet*
Color:
☐ Dorothy Jeakins, Karinska, *Joan of Arc*

SPECIAL AWARDS

☐ Monsieur Vincent, as the most outstanding foreign film of 1948
☐ Ivan Jandl, for outstanding juvenile performance in *The Search*
☐ Sid Grauman, who raised the standard of motion picture exhibition
☐ Adolph Zukor, for services over forty years to the industry
☐ Walter Wanger, for distinguished service to the industry by adding to its moral stature in the world community by his production of *Joan of Arc*

IRVING G. THALBERG AWARD

☐ Jerry Wald

SCIENTIFIC OR TECHNICAL AWARDS

Class II:
Victor Caccialanza, Maurice Ayers and Paramount Studio Set Construction Dept., for the development and application of "Paralite" a new lightweight plaster process for set construction
☐ Nick Kalton, Louis J. Witti and 20th Century-Fox Studio Mechanical Effects Dept., for a process of preserving a flame-proofing foliage
Class III:
☐ Marty Martin, Jack Lannon, Russell Sherman and RKO Radio Studio Special Effects Dept., for development of a new method of simulating falling snow on motion picture sets
☐ A.J. Moran and Warner Bros. Studio Electrical Dept., for a

method of remote control for shutters on motion picture arc lighting equipment

1949

BEST PICTURE
☐ *All the King's Men* (Columbia)
Battleground (MGM)
The Heiress (Paramount)
A Letter to Three Wives (20th Century-Fox)
Twelve O'Clock High (20th Century-Fox)

BEST DIRECTOR
☐ Joseph L. Mankiewicz, *A Letter to Three Wives*
Carol Reed, *The Fallen Idol*
Robert Rossen, *All the King's Men*
William A. Wellman, *Battleground*
William Wyler, *The Heiress*

BEST ACTOR
☐ Broderick Crawford, *All the King's Men*
Kirk Douglas, *Champion*
Gregory Peck, *Twelve O'Clock High*
Richard Todd, *The Hasty Heart*
John Wayne, *Sands of Iwo Jima*

BEST ACTRESS
☐ Olivia de Havilland, *The Heiress*
Jeanne Crain, *Pinky*
Susan Hayward, *My Foolish Heart*
Deborah Kerr, *Edward My Son*
Loretta Young, *Come to the Stable*

BEST SUPPORTING ACTOR
☐ Dean Jagger, *Twelve O'Clock High*
John Ireland, *All the King's Men*
Arthur Kennedy, *Champion*
Ralph Richardson, *The Heiress*
James Whitmore, *Battleground*

BEST SUPPORTING ACTRESS
☐ Mercedes McCambridge, *All the King's Men*

Ethel Barrymore, *Pinky*
Celeste Holm, *Come to the Stable*
Elsa Lanchester, *Come to the Stable*
Ethel Waters, *Pinky*

WRITING (MOTION PICTURE STORY)
☐ Douglas Morrow, *The Stratton Story*
Clare Boothe Luce, *Come to the Stable*
Shirley W. Smith, Valentine Davies, *It Happens Every Spring*
Harry Brown, *Sands of Iwo Jima*
Virginia Kellogg, *White Heat*

WRITING (SCREENPLAY)
☐ Joseph L. Mankiewicz, *A Letter to Three Wives*
Robert Rossen, *All the King's Men*
Cesare Zavattini, *The Bicycle Thief*
Carl Foreman, *Champion*
Graham Greene, *The Fallen Idol*

WRITING (STORY AND SCREENPLAY)
☐ Robert Pirosh, *Battleground*
Sidney Buchman, *Jolson Sings Again*
Alfred Hayes, Federico Fellini, Sergio Amidei, Marcello Pagliero, Roberto Rossellini, *Paisan*
T.E.B. Clark, *Passport to Pimlico*
Helen Leyitt, Janice Loeb, Sidney Meyers, *The Quiet One*

CINEMATOGRAPHY (BLACK-AND-WHITE)
☐ Paul C. Vogel, *Battleground*
Frank Planer, *Champion*
Joseph LaShelle, *Come to the Stable*
Leo Tover, *The Heiress*
Leon Shamroy, *Prince of Foxes*

CINEMATOGRAPHY (COLOR)
☐ Winton Hoch, *She Wore a Yellow Ribbon*
Harry Stradling, *The Barkleys of Broadway*

William Snyder, *Jolson Sings Again*
Robert Planck, Charles Schoenbaum, *Little Women*
Charles G. Clarke, *Sand*

ART DIRECTION/SET DIRECTION
Black-and-White:
☐ John Meehan, Harry Horner; Emile Kuri, *The Heiress*
Color:
☐ Cedric Gibbons, Paul Groesse; Edwin B. Willis, Jack D. Moore, *Little Women*

SOUND RECORDING
☐ 20th Century-Fox Sound Dept., *Twelve O'Clock High*

SHORT SUBJECTS
Cartoons:
☐ Warner Bros., *For Scentimental Reasons*
One-Reel:
☐ Paramount, *Aquatic House-Party*
Two-Reel:
☐ Canton-Weiner, *Van Gogh*

DOCUMENTARY
Short Subjects:
☐ 20th Century-Fox, *A Chance to Live*
Features:
British Information Services, *Daybreak in Udi*

MUSIC
Best Song:
☐ Frank Loesser, "Baby, It's Cold Outside," *Neptune's Daughter*
Best Scoring of a Dramatic or Comedy Picture:
☐ Aaron Copland, *The Heiress*
Best Scoring of a Musical Picture:
☐ Roger Edens, Lennie Hayton, *On the Town*

FILM EDITING
☐ Harry Gerstad, *Champion*

SPECIAL EFFECTS
☐ RKO-Radio, *Mighty Joe Young*

COSTUME DESIGN
Black-and-White:
☐ Edith Head, Gille Steele, *The Heiress*
Color:
☐ Leah Rhodes, Travilla, Marjorie Best, *Adventures of Don Juan*

SPECIAL AWARDS

- *The Bicycle Thief*, as most outstanding foreign film
- Bobby Driscoll, as outstanding juvenile actor of 1949
- Fred Astaire, for his contributions to the technique of musical pictures and unique artistry
- Jean Hersholt, for distinguished service to the industry
- Cecil B. DeMille, distinguished motion picture pioneer, for 37 years of brilliant showmanship

SCIENTIFIC OR TECHNICAL AWARDS

Class I:

- Eastman Kodak Co., for development and introduction of an improved safety base motion picture film

Class III:

- Loren L. Ryder, Bruce H. Denney, Robert Carr and Paramount Studio Sound Dept., for the development and application of the supersonic playback and public address system
- M.B. Paul for the first successful large-area seamless translucent backgrounds
- Herbert Britt, for development and application of formulas and equipment producing artificial snow and ice for dressing motion picture sets
- André Coutant and Jacques Mathot, for the design of the Eclair Camerette
- Charles R. Daily, Steve Csillag and Paramount Studio Engineering, Editorial and Music Depts., for a new precision method of computing variable tempo-click tracks
- International Projector Corp., for a simplified and self-adjusting take-up device for projection machines
- Alexander Velcoff, for the application to production of the infra-red photographic evaluator

1950

BEST PICTURE

- *All About Eve* (20th Century-Fox)
- *Born Yesterday* (Columbia)
- *Father of the Bride* (MGM)
- *King Solomon's Mines* (MGM)
- *Sunset Boulevard* (Paramount)

BEST DIRECTOR

- Joseph L. Mankiewicz, *All About Eve*
- George Cukor, *Born Yesterday*
- John Huston, *The Asphalt Jungle*
- Carol Reed, *The Third Man*
- Billy Wilder, *Sunset Boulevard*

BEST ACTOR

- José Ferrer, *Cyrano de Bergerac*
- Louis Calhern, *The Magnificent Yankee*
- William Holden, *Sunset Boulevard*
- James Stewart, *Harvey*
- Spencer Tracy, *Father of the Bride*

BEST ACTRESS

- Judy Holliday, *Born Yesterday*
- Anne Baxter, *All Aboue Eve*
- Bette Davis, *All About Eve*
- Eleanor Parker, *Caged*
- Gloria Swanson, *Sunset Boulevard*

BEST SUPPORTING ACTOR

- George Sanders, *All About Eve*
- Jeff Chandler, *Broken Arrow*
- Edmund Gwenn, *Mister 880*
- Sam Jaffe, *The Asphalt Jungle*
- Erich von Stroheim, *Sunset Boulevard*

BEST SUPPORTING ACTRESS

- Josephine Hull, *Harvey*
- Hope Emerson, *Caged*
- Celeste Holm, *All About Eve*
- Nancy Olson, *Sunset Boulevard*
- Thelma Ritter, *All About Eve*

WRITING (MOTION PICTURE STORY)

- Edna Anhalt, Edward Anhalt, *Panic in the Streets*
- Guiseppe De Santis, Carlo Lizzani, *Bitter Rice*

Leonard Spigelgass, *Mystery Street*

William Bowers, André de Toth, *The Gunfighter*

Sy Gomberg, *When Willie Comes Marching Home*

WRITING (SCREENPLAY)

- Joseph L. Mankiewicz, *All About Eve*
- Ben Maddow, John Huston, *The Asphalt Jungle*
- Albert Mannheimer, *Born Yesterday*
- Michael Blankfort, *Broken Arrow*
- Frances Goodrich, Albert Hackett, *Father of the Bride*

WRITING (STORY AND SCREENPLAY)

- Charles Brackett, Billy Wilder, D.M. Marshman, Jr., *Sunset Boulevard*
- Ruth Gordon, Garson Kanin, *Adam's Rib*
- Virginia Kellogg, Bernard C. Schoenfeld, *Caged*
- Carl Foreman, *The Men*
- Joseph L. Mankiewicz, Lesser Samuels, *No Way Out*

CINEMATOGRAPHY (BLACK-AND-WHITE)

- Robert Krasker, *The Third Man*
- Milton Krasner, *All About Eve*
- Harold Rosson, *The Asphalt Jungle*
- Victor Milner, *The Furies*
- John F. Seitz, *Sunset Boulevard*

CINEMATOGRAPHY (COLOR)

- Robert Surtees, *King Solomon's Mines*
- Charles Rosher, *Annie Get Your Gun*
- Ernest Palmer, *Broken Arrow*
- Ernest Haller, *The Flame and the Arrow*
- George Barnes, *Samson and Delilah*

ART DIRECTION/SET DIRECTION

Black-and-White:

- Hans Dreier, John Meehan; Sam Comer, Ray Moyer, *Sunset Boulevard*

Color:

- Hans Dreier, Walter Tyler; Sam Comer, Ray Moyer, *Samson and Delilah*

SOUND RECORDING
☐ 20th Century-Fox, Sound Dept., *All About Eve*

SHORT SUBJECTS
Cartoons:
☐ UPA-Columbia, *Gerald McBoing-Boing*
One-Reel:
☐ Warner Bros., *Grandad of Races*
Two-Reel:
☐ Walt Disney, RKO, *In Beaver Valley*

DOCUMENTARY
Short Subjects:
☐ 20th Century-Fox, *Why Korea?*
Features:
☐ Classics Pictures, *The Titan: Story of Michelangelo*

MUSIC
Best Song:
☐ Jay Livingston, Ray Evans, "Mona Lisa," *Captain Carey, USA*
Best Score of a Dramatic or Comedy Picture:
☐ Franz Waxman, *Sunset Boulevard*
Best Score of a Musical Picture:
☐ Adolph Deutsch, Roger Edens, *Annie Get Your Gun*

FILM EDITING
☐ Ralph E. Winters, Conrad A. Nervig, *King Solomon's Mines*

SPECIAL EFFECTS
☐ Eagle-Lion, *Destination Moon*

COSTUME DESIGN
Black-and-White:
☐ Edith Head, Charles LeMaire, *All About Eve*
Color:
☐ Edith Head, Dorothy Jeakins, Eloise Jenssen, Gille Steele, Gwen Wakeling, *Samson and Delilah*

HONORARY AND OTHER AWARDS
☐ George Murphy, for services in interpreting the industry to the country at large
☐ Louis B. Mayer, for distinguished service to the industry
☐ *The Walls of Malapaga* (Franco-Italian), voted by the Board of Governors as the most outstanding foreign-language film released in the United States in 1950

IRVING G. THALBERG MEMORIAL AWARD
☐ Darryl F. Zanuck

SCIENTIFIC OR TECHNICAL AWARDS
Class II:
☐ James B. Gordon and 20th Century-Fox Studio Camera Dept., for the design and development of a multiple-image film viewer
☐ John Paul Livadary, Floyd Campbell, L.W. Russell and Columbia Studio Sound Dept., for the development of a multi-track magnetic re-recording system
☐ Loren L. Ryder and Paramount Studio Sound Dept., for the first studio-wide application of magnetic sound recording to motion picture production

---

1951

BEST PICTURE
☐ *An American in Paris* (MGM)
Decision Before Dawn (20th Century-Fox)
A Place in the Sun (Paramount)
Quo Vadis (MGM)
A Streetcar Named Desire (Feldman-Warner Bros.)

BEST DIRECTOR
☐ George Stevens, *A Place in the Sun*
John Huston, *The African Queen*
Elia Kazan, *A Streetcar Named Desire*
Vincente Minnelli, *An American in Paris*
William Wyler, *Detective Story*

BEST ACTOR
☐ Humphrey Bogart, *The African Queen*
Marlon Brando, *A Streetcar Named Desire*
Montgomery Clift, *A Place in the Sun*
Arthur Kennedy, *Bright Victory*
Fredric March, *Death of a Salesman*

BEST ACTRESS
☐ Vivien Leigh, *A Streetcar Named Desire*
Katharine Hepburn, *The African Queen*
Eleanor Parker, *Detective Story*
Shelley Winters, *A Place in the Sun*
Jane Wyman, *The Blue Veil*

BEST SUPPORTING ACTOR
☐ Karl Malden, *A Streetcar Named Desire*
Leo Genn, *Quo Vadis*
Kevin McCarthy, *Death of a Salesman*
Peter Ustinov, *Quo Vadis*
Gig Young, *Come Fill the Cup*

BEST SUPPORTING ACTRESS
☐ Kim Hunter, *A Streetcar Named Desire*
Joan Blondell, *The Blue Veil*
Mildred Dunnock, *Death of a Salesman*
Lee Grant, *Detective Story*
Thelma Ritter, *The Mating Season*

WRITING (MOTION PICTURE STORY)
☐ Paul Dehn, James Bernard, *Seven Days to Noon*
Budd Boetticher, Ray Nazzaro, *The Bullfighter and the Lady*
Oscar Millard, *The Frogmen*
Robert Riskin, Liam O'Brien, *Here Comes the Groom*
Alfred Hayes, Stewart Stern, *Teresa*

WRITING (SCREENPLAY)
☐ Michael Wilson, Harry Brown, *A Place in the Sun*
James Agee, John Huston, *The African Queen*
Philip Yordan, Robert Wyler, *Detective Story*
Jacques Natanson, Max Ophuls, *La Ronde*
Tennessee Williams, *A Streetcar Named Desire*

WRITING (STORY AND SCREENPLAY)
☐ Alan Jay Lerner, *An American in Paris*
Billy Wilder, Lesser Samuels, Walter Newman, *The Big Carnival*

Philip Dunne, *David and Bathsheba*
Robert Pirosh, *Go For Broke*
Clarence Greene, Russell Rouse, *The Well*

CINEMATOGRAPHY (BLACK-AND-WHITE)

☐ William C. Mellor, *A Place in the Sun*
Frank Planer, *Death of a Salesman*
Norbert Brodine, *The Frogmen*
Robert Burks, *Strangers on a Train*
Harry Stradling, *A Streetcar Named Desire*

CINEMATOGRAPHY (COLOR)

☐ Alfred Gilks, John Alton, *An American In Paris*
Leon Shamroy, *David and Bathsheba*
Robert Surtees, William V. Skall, *Quo Vadis*
Charles Rosher, *Show Boat*
John F. Seitz, W. Howard Greene, *When Worlds Collide*

ART DIRECTION/SET DIRECTION

Black-and-White:
☐ Richard Day; George James Hopkins, *A Streetcar Named Desire*
Color:
☐ Cedric Gibbons, Preston Ames; Edwin B. Willis, Keogh Gleason, *An American in Paris*

SOUND RECORDING

☐ Douglas Shearer, *The Great Caruso*

SHORT SUBJECTS

Cartoons:
☐ MGM, *Two Mousketeers*
One-Reel:
☐ Warner Bros., *World of Kids*
Two-Reel:
☐ Walt Disney, RKO, *Nature's Half Acre*

DOCUMENTARY

Short Subjects:
☐ Fred Zinnemann, *Benjy*
Features:
☐ RKO Radio, *Kon-Tiki*

MUSIC

Best Song:
☐ Hoagy Carmichael, Johnny Mercer, "In the Cool, Cool, Cool of the Evening," *Here Comes the Groom*
Best Score of a Dramatic or Comedy Picture:
☐ Franz Waxman, *A Place in the Sun*
Best Score of a Musical Picture:
☐ Johnny Green, Saul Chaplin, *An American in Paris*

FILM EDITING

■ William Hornbeck, *A Place in the Sun*

SPECIAL EFFECTS

(1951 through 1953 classified as an "other" award; thus no nominations)
☐ Paramount, *When Worlds Collide*

COSTUME DESIGN

Black-and-White:
☐ Edith Head, *A Place in the Sun*
Color:
☐ Orry Kelly, Walter Plunkett, Irene Sharaff, *An American in Paris*

HONORARY AND OTHER AWARDS

☐ Gene Kelly, in appreciation of his versatility as actor, singer, director and dancer, and specifically for his brilliant achievements in the art of choreography on film
☐ *Rashomon* (Japanese), voted by the Board of Governors as the most outstanding foreign-language film released in the United States during 1951

IRVING G. THALBERG MEMORIAL AWARD

☐ Arthur Freed

SCIENTIFIC OR TECHNICAL AWARDS

Class II:
☐ Gordon Jennings, S.L. Stancliffe and Paramount Studio Special Photographic and Engineering Depts., for the design, construction and application of a servo-operated recording and repeating device
☐ Olin L. Dupy of MGM Studio, for the design, construction and application of a motion picture reproducing system
☐ RCA, Victor Division, for pioneering direct positive recording with anticipatory noise reduction
Class III:
☐ Richard N. Haff, Frank P. Hernfeld, Garland C. Misener and the Ansco Film Division of General Aniline and Film Corp., for the development of the Ansco color scene tester
☐ Fred Ponedel, Ralph Ayres and George Brown of Warner Bros. Studio, for an air-driven water motor to provide flow, wake, and white water for marine sequences in motion pictures
☐ Glen Robinson and MGM Studio Construction dept., for the development of a new music wire and cable cutter
☐ Jack Gaylord and MGM Studio Construction Dept., for development of balsa falling snow
☐ Carlos Rivas of MGM Studio, for the development of an automatic magnetic film splicer

1952

BEST PICTURE

☐ *The Greatest Show on Earth* (DeMille-Paramount)
High Noon (Kramer-UA)
Ivanhoe (MGM)
Moulin Rouge (Romulus-UA)
The Quiet Man (Argosy-Republic)

BEST DIRECTOR

☐ John Ford, *The Quiet Man*
Cecil B. DeMille, *The Greatest Show on Earth*
John Huston, *Moulin Rouge*
Joseph L. Mankiewicz, *Five Fingers*
Fred Zinnemann, *High Noon*

BEST ACTOR

- [ ] Gary Cooper, *High Noon*
  Marlon Brando, *Viva Zapata!*
  Kirk Douglas, *The Bad and the Beautiful*
  José Ferrer, *Moulin Rouge*
  Alec Guinness, *The Lavender Hill Mob*

BEST ACTRESS

- [ ] Shirley Booth, *Come Back, Little Sheba*
  Joan Crawford, *Sudden Fear*
  Bette Davis, *The Star*
  Julie Harris, *The Member of the Wedding*
  Susan Hayward, *With a Song in My Heart*

BEST SUPPORTING ACTOR

- [ ] Anthony Quinn, *Viva Zapata!*
  Richard Burton, *My Cousin Rachel*
  Arthur Hunnicutt, *The Big Sky*
  Victor McLaglen, *The Quiet Man*
  Jack Palance, *Sudden Fear*

BEST SUPPORTING ACTRESS

- [ ] Gloria Grahame, *The Bad and the Beautiful*
  Jean Hagen, *Singin' in the Rain*
  Colette Marchand, *Moulin Rouge*
  Terry Moore, *Come Back, Little Sheba*
  Thelma Ritter, *With a Song in My Heart*

WRITING (MOTION PICTURE STORY)

- [ ] Frederic M. Frank, Theodore St. John, Frank Cavett, *The Greatest Show on Earth*
  Leo McCarey, *My Son John*
  Martin Goldsmith, Jack Leonard, *The Narrow Margin*
  Guy Trosper, *The Pride of St. Louis*
  Edna Anhalt, Edward Anhalt, *The Sniper*

WRITING (SCREENPLAY)

- [ ] Charles Schnee, *The Bad and the Beautiful*
  Michael Wilson, *Five Fingers*
  Carl Foreman, *High Noon*
  Roger MacDougall, John Dighton, Alexander Mackendrick, *The Man in the White Suit*

Frank S. Nugent, *The Quiet Man*

WRITING (STORY AND SCREENPLAY)

- [ ] T.E.B. Clarke, *The Lavender Hill Mob*
  Sidney Boehm, *The Atomic City*
  Terence Rattigan, *Breaking the Sound Barrier*
  Ruth Gordon, Garson Kanin, *Pat and Mike*
  John Steinbeck, *Viva Zapata!*

CINEMATOGRAPHY (BLACK-AND-WHITE)

- [ ] Robert Surtees, *The Bad and the Beautiful*
  Russell Harlan, *The Big Sky*
  Joseph LaShelle, *My Cousin Rachel*
  Virgil E. Miller, *Navajo*
  Charles B. Lang, Jr., *Sudden Fear*

CINEMATOGRAPHY (COLOR)

- [ ] Winton C. Hoch, Archie Stout, *The Quiet Man*
  Harry Stradling, *Hans Christian Andersen*
  F.A. Young, *Ivanhoe*
  George J. Folsey, *Million Dollar Mermaid*
  Leon Shamroy, *The Snows of Kilimanjaro*

ART DIRECTION/SET DIRECTION

Black-and-White:

- [ ] Cedric Gibbons, Edward Carfagno; Edwin B. Willis, Keogh Gleason, *The Bad and the Beautiful*

Color:

- [ ] Paul Sheriff; Marcel Vertes, *Moulin Rouge*

SOUND RECORDING

- [ ] London Film Sound Dept., *Breaking the Sound Barrier*

SHORT SUBJECTS

Cartoons:

- [ ] MGM, *Johann Mouse*

One-Reel:

- [ ] 20th Century-Fox, *Light in the Window*

Two-Reel:

- [ ] Walt Disney, RKO, *Water Birds*

DOCUMENTARY

Short Subjects:

- [ ] National Film Board of Canada, *Neighbours*

Features:

- [ ] RKO Radio, *The Sea Around Us*

MUSIC

Best Songs:

- [ ] Dimitri Tiomkin, Ned Washington, "High Noon," *High Noon*

Best Scoring of a Dramatic or Comedy Picture:

- [ ] Dimitri Tiomkin, *High Noon*

Best Scoring of a Musical Picture:

- [ ] Alfred Newman, *With a Song in My Heart*

FILM EDITING

- [ ] Elmo Williams, Harry Gerstad, *High Noon*

SPECIAL EFFECTS

(1951-1953 classified as an "other" award; hence no nominations)

- [ ] MGM, *Plymouth Adventure*

COSTUME DESIGN

Black-and-White:

- [ ] Helen Rose, *The Bad and the Beautiful*

Color:

- [ ] Marcel Vertes, *Moulin Rouge*

HONORARY AND OTHER AWARDS

- [ ] George Alfred Mitchell, for design/development of the camera which bears his name and for his continued and dominant presence in the field of cinematography
- [ ] Joseph M. Schenck, for long and distinguished service to motion picture industry
- [ ] Merian C. Cooper, for his many innovations and contributions to the art of motion pictures
- [ ] Harold Lloyd, master comedian and good citizen
- [ ] Bob Hope, for his contribution to laughter, his service to the industry; and his devotion to the American premise
- [ ] *Forbidden Games* (France), for best foreign-language film, first released in the United States during 1952

IRVING G. THALBERG MEMORIAL AWARD
□ Cecil B. DeMille

SCIENTIFIC OR TECHNICAL AWARDS

Class I:
□ Eastman Kodak Co., for the introduction of Eastman color negative and Eastman color print film
□ Ansco Division, General Aniline and Film Corp., for introduction of Ansco color negative and Ansco color print film

Class II:
□ Technicolor Motion Picture Corp., for an improved method of color motion picture photography under incandescent light

Class III:
□ Projection, Still Photographic and Development Engineering Depts. of MGM Studio, for an improved method of projecting photographic backgrounds
□ John G. Frayne and R.R. Scoville and Westrex Corp., for a method of measuring distortion in sound reproduction
□ Photo Research Corp., for creating the Spectra color temperature meter
□ Gustav Jirouch, for the design of the Robot automatic film splicer
□ Carlos Rivas of MGM Studio, for the development of a sound reproducer for magnetic film

---

1953

BEST PICTURE
□ *From Here to Eternity* (Columbia)
Julius Caesar (MGM)
The Robe (20th Century-Fox)
Roman Holiday (Paramount)
Shane (Paramount)

BEST DIRECTOR
□ Fred Zinnemann, *From Here to Eternity*
George Stevens, *Shane*

Charles Walters, *Lili*
Billy Wilder, *Stalag 17*
William Wyler, *Roman Holiday*

BEST ACTOR
William Holden, *Stalag 17*
Marlon Brando, *Julius Caesar*
Richard Burton, *The Robe*
Montgomery Clift, *From Here to Eternity*
Burt Lancaster, *From Here to Eternity*

BEST ACTRESS
Audrey Hepburn, *Roman Holiday*
Leslie Caron, *Lili*
Ava Gardner, *Mogambo*
Deborah Kerr, *From Here to Eternity*
Maggie McNamara, *The Moon Is Blue*

BEST SUPPORTING ACTOR
□ Frank Sinatra, *From Here to Eternity*
Eddie Albert, *Roman Holiday*
Brandon De Wilde, *Shane*
Jack Palance, *Shane*
Robert Strass, *Stalag 17*

BEST SUPPORTING ACTRESS
□ Donna Reed, *From Here to Eternity*
Grace Kelly, *Mogambo*
Geraldine Page, *Hondo*
Marjorie Rambeau, *Torch Song*
Thelma Ritter, *Pickup on South Street*

WRITING (MOTION PICTURE STORY)
□ Ian McLellan Hunter, *Roman Holiday*
□ Beirne Lay, Jr., *Above and Beyond*
Alec Coppel, *The Captain's Paradise*
Joseph Burstyn, Ray Ashley, Morris Engel, Ruth Orkin, *The Little Fugitive*
Hondo (writer not eigible under Academy laws, since story was not an original)

WRITING (SCREENPLAY)
□ Daniel Taradash, *From Here to Eternity*
Eric Ambler, *The Cruel Sea*
Helen Deutsch, *Lili*
Ian McLellan Hunter, John Dighton, *Roman Holiday*

A.B. Guthrie, Jr., *Shane*

WRITING (STORY AND SCREENPLAY)
□ Charles Brackett, Walter Reisch, Richard Breen, *Titanic*
Betty Comden, Adolph Green, *The Band Wagon*
Richard Murphy, *The Desert Rats*
Sam Rolfe, Harold Jack Bloom, *The Naked Spur*
Millard Kaufman, *Take the High Ground*

CINEMATOGRAPHY (BLACK-AND-WHITE)
Burnett Guffey, *From Here to Eternity*
Hal Mohr, *The Four Poster*
Joseph Ruttenberg, *Julius Caesar*
Joseph C. Brun, *Martin Luther*
Frank Planer, Henry Alekan, *Roman Holiday*

CINEMATOGRAPHY (COLOR)
□ Loyal Griggs, *Shane*
George Folsey, *All the Brothers Were Valiant*
Edward Cronjager, *Beneath the Twelve-Mile Reef*
Robert Planck, *Lili*
Leon Shamroy, *The Robe*

ART DIRECTION/SET DIRECTION

Black-and-White:
□ Cedric Gibbons, Edward Carfagno; Edwin B. Willis, Hugh Hunt, *Julius Caesar*

Color:
□ Lyle Wheeler, George W. Davis; Walter M. Scott, Paul S. Fox, *The Robe*

SOUND RECORDING
□ Columbia Sound Dept., *From Here to Eternity*

SHORT SUBJECTS

Cartoons:
□ Walt Disney, Buena Vista, *Toot, Whistle, Plunk and Boom*

One-Reel:
□ MGM, *The Merry Wives of Windsor Overture*

Two-Reel:
□ Walt Disney, RKO, *Bear Country*

DOCUMENTARY

Short Subjects:
- [ ] Walt Disney, RKO, *The Alaskan Eskimo*

Features:
- [ ] Walt Disney, Buena Vista, *The Living Desert*

MUSIC

Best Song:
- [ ] Sammy Fain, Paul Francis Webster, "Secret Love," *Calamity Jane*

Best Scoring of a Dramatic or Comedy Picture:
- [ ] Bronislau Kaper, *Lili*

Best scoring of a Musical Picture:
- [ ] Alfred Newman, *Call Me Madam*

FILM EDITING
- [ ] William Lyon, *From Here to Eternity*

SPECIAL EFFECTS

(from 1951-1953 given as an "other" award; hence no nominations)
- [ ] Paramount, *The War of the Worlds*

COSTUME DESIGN

Black-and-White:
- [ ] Edith Head, *Roman Holiday*

Color:
- [ ] Charles LeMaire, Emile Santiago, *The Robe*

HONORARY AND OTHER AWARDS
- [ ] Pete Smith, for his witty and pungent observations on the American Scene in "Pete Smith Specialties"
- [ ] 20th Century-Fox Corp., in recognition of their imagination, showmanship and foresight in introducing CinemaScope
- [ ] Joseph I. Breen, for his conscientious, open-minded and dignified management of the Motion Picture Production Code
- [ ] Bell & Howell Co., for their pioneering achievements in advancing the motion picture industry

IRVING G. THALBERG MEMORIAL AWARD
- [ ] George Stevens

SCIENTIFIC OR TECHNICAL AWARDS

Class I:
- [ ] Professor **Henri Chretien** and Earl Sponable, Sol Halprin, Lorin Grignon, Herbert Bragg and Carl Faulkner of 20th Century-Fox Studios, for creating, developing, and engineering the equipment, processes and techniques known as CinemaScope
- [ ] Fred Waller, for designing and developing the multiple photographic and projection systems which culminated in Cinerama

Class II:
- [ ] Reeves Soundcraft Corp., for their development of a process of applying stripes of magnetic oxide to motion picture film for sound recording and reproduction

Class III:
- [ ] Westrex Corp., for the design and contruction of a new film-editing machine

1954

BEST PICTURE
- [ ] *On the Waterfront* (Columbia)
  The Caine Mutiny (Kramer-Columbia)
  The Country Girl (Paramount)
  Seven Brides for Seven Brothers (MGM)
  Three Coins in the Fountain (20th Century-Fox)

BEST DIRECTOR
- [ ] Elia Kazan, *On the Waterfront*
  Alfred Hitchcock, *Rear Window*
  George Seaton, *The Country Girl*
  William Wellman, *The High and the Mighty*
  Billy Wilder, *Sabrina*

BEST ACTOR
- [ ] Marlon Brando, *On the Waterfront*
  Humphrey Bogart, *The Caine Mutiny*
  Bing Crosby, *The Country Girl*
  James Mason, *A Star Is Born*

Dan O'Herlihy, *Adventures of Robinson Crusoe*

BEST ACTRESS
- [ ] Grace Kelly, *The Country Girl*
  Dorothy Dandridge, *Carmen Jones*
  Judy Garland, *A Star Is Born*
  Audrey Hepburn, *Sabrina*
  Jane Wyman, *Magnificent Obsession*

BEST SUPPORTING ACTOR
- [ ] Edmond O'Brien, *The Barefoot Contessa*
  Lee J. Cobb, *On the Waterfront*
  Karl Malden, *On the Waterfront*
  Rod Steiger, *On the Waterfront*
  Tom Tully, *The Caine Mutiny*

BEST SUPPORTING ACTRESS
- [ ] Eva Marie Saint, *On The Waterfront*
  Nina Foch, *Executive Suite*
  Katy Jurado, *Broken Lance*
  Jan Sterling, *The High and the Mighty*
  Claire Trevor, *The High and the Mighty*

WRITING (MOTION PICTURE STORY)
- [ ] Philip Yordan, *Broken Lance*
  Ettore Margadonna, *Bread, Love and Dreams*
  François Boyer, *Forbidden Games*
  Jed Harris, Tom Reed, *Night People*
  Lamar Trotti, *There's No Business Like Show Business*

WRITING (SCREENPLAY)
- [ ] George Seaton, *The Country Girl*
  Stanley Roberts, *The Caine Mutiny*
  John Michael Hayes, *Rear Window*
  Billy Wilder, Samuel Taylor, Ernest Lehman, *Sabrina*
  Albert Hackett, Frances Goodrich, Dorothy Kingsley, *Seven Brides for Seven Brothers*

WRITING (STORY AND SCREENPLAY)
- [ ] Budd Schulberg, *On the Waterfront*

Joseph L. Mankiewicz, *The Barefoot Contessa*
William Rose, *Genevieve*
Valentine Davies, Oscar Brodney, *The Glenn Miller Story*
Norman Panama, Melvin Frank, *Knock on Wood*

CINEMATOGRAPHY (BLACK-AND-WHITE)

☐ Boris Kaufman, *On the Waterfront*
George Folsey, *Executive Suite*
John F. Warren, *The Country Girl*
John Seitz, *Rogue Cop*
Charles Lang, Jr., *Sabrina*

CINEMATOGRAPHY (COLOR)

■ Milton Krasner, *Three Coins in the Fountain*
Leon Shamroy, *The Egyptian*
Robert Burks, *Rear Window*
George Folsey, *Seven Brides for Seven Brothers*
William V. Skall, *The Silver Chalice*

ART DIRECTION/SET DIRECTION

Black-and-White:
☐ Richard Day, *On the Waterfront*
Color:
☐ John Meehan; Emile Kuri, *20,000 Leagues under the Sea*

SOUND RECORDING

☐ Leslie I. Carey, *The Glenn Miller Story*

SHORT SUBJECTS

Cartoons:
☐ UPA, Columbia, *When Magoo Flew*
One-Reel:
☐ Warner Bros., *This Mechnical Age*
Two-Reel:
☐ Carnival Productions, *A Time Out of War*

DOCUMENTARY

Short Subjects:
☐ British Information Services, *Thursday's Children*
Features:
☐ Walt Disney, Buena Vista, *The Vanishing Prairie*

MUSIC

Best Song:
☐ Jule Styne, Sammy Cahn, "Three Coins in the Fountain," *Three Coins in the Fountain*
Best Scoring of a Dramatic or Comedy Picture:
☐ Dimitri Tiomkin, *The High and the Mighty*
Best Scoring of a Musical Picture:
☐ Adolph Deutsch, Saul Chaplin, *Seven Brides for Seven Brothers*

FILM EDITING

☐ Gene Milford, *On the Waterfront*

SPECIAL EFFECTS

☐ Walt Disney, *20,000 Leagues under the Sea*

COSTUME DESIGN

Black-and-White:
☐ Edith Head, *Sabrina*
Color:
☐ Sanzo Wada, *Gate of Hell*

HONORARY AND OTHER AWARDS

☐ Bausch & Lomb Optical Co., for their contributions to the advancement of the motion picture industry
☐ Kemp R. Niver, for development of Renovare Process, which has made possible restoration of Library of Congress Paper Film Collection
☐ Greta Garbo, for her unforgetable screen performances
☐ Danny Kaye, for his unique talents, service to the Academy, the industry, and the American people
☐ Jon Whitely, for his outstanding juvenile performance in *The Little Kidnappers*
☐ Vincent Winter, for his outstanding juvenile performance in *The Little Kidnappers*
☐ *Gate of Hell* (Japan), for best foreign film released in the United States during 1954

SCIENTIFIC OR TECHNICAL AWARDS

Class I:
☐ Paramount Pictures, Inc., Loren L. Ryder, John R. Bishop, and all the members of the technical and engineering staff, for developing a method of producing and exhibiting motion pictures known as VistaVision
Class III:
☐ David S. Horsley and the Universal-International Studio Special Photographic Dept., for a portable remote-control device for process projectors
☐ Karl Freund and Frank Crandell of Photo Research Corp., for the design and development of a direct reading brightness meter
☐ Wesley C. Miller, J.W. Stafford, K.M. Frierson and MGM Studio Sound Dept., for an electronic sound-printing comparison device
☐ John P. Livadary, Lloyd Russell and the Columbia Studio Sound Dept., for an improved limiting amplifier as applied to sound level comparison devices
☐ Roland Miller and Max Goeppiger of Magnascope Corp., for the design and development of a cathode ray magnetic soundtrack viewer
☐ Carlos Rivas, G.M. Sprague and MGM Studio Sound Dept., for the design of a magntic sound editing machine
☐ Fred Wilson of the Samuel Goldwyn Studio Sound Dept., the design of a variable multi-band equalizer
☐ P.C. Young of the MGM Studio Sound Production Dept., for the Practical application of a variable focal length attachment of motion picture projection lenses
☐ Fred Knoth and Orien Ernest of the Universal-International Studio Technical Dept., for the

development of a
hand-portable, electric, dry
oil-fog machine

1955

BEST PICTURE
- *Marty* (Hecht-Lancaster, UA)
  Love Is a Many-Splendored Thing (20th Century-Fox)
  Mister Roberts (Warner Bros.)
  Picnic (Columbia)
  The Rose Tattoo (Wallis, Paramount)

BEST DIRECTOR
- Delbert Mann, *Marty*
  Elia Kazan, *East of Eden*
  David Lean, *Summertime*
  Joshua Logan, *Picnic*
  John Sturges, *Bad Day at Black Rock*

BEST ACTOR
- Ernest Borgnine, *Marty*
  James Cagney, *Love Me or Leave Me*
  James Dean, *East of Eden*
  Frank Sinatra, *The Man with the Golden Arm*
  Spencer Tracy, *Bad Day at Black Rock*

BEST ACTRESS
- Anna Magnani, *The Rose Tattoo*
  Susan Hayward, *I'll Cry Tomorrow*
  Katharine Hepburn, *Summertime*
  Jennifer Jones, *Love Is a Many-Splendored Thing*
  Eleanor Parker, *Interrupted Melody*

BEST SUPPORTING ACTOR
- Jack Lemmon, *Mister Roberts*
  Arthur Kennedy, *Trial*
  Joe Mantell, *Marty*
  Sal Mineo, *Rebel Without a Cause*
  Arthur O'Connell, *Picnic*

BEST SUPPORTING ACTRESS
- Jo Van Fleet, *East of Eden*
  Betsy Blair, *Marty*
  Peggy Lee, *Pete Kelly's Blues*
  Marisa Pavan, *The Rose Tattoo*
  Natalie Wood, *Rebel Without a Cause*

WRITING (MOTION PICTURE STORY)
- Daniel Fuchs, *Love Me or Leave Me*
  Joe Connelly, Bob Mosher, *The Private War of Major Benson*
  Nicholas Ray, *Rebel Without a Cause*
  Jean Marsan, Henry Troyat, Jacques Perrat, Henri Verneuil, Raoul Ploquin, *The Sheep Has Five Legs*
  Beirne Lay, Jr., *Strategic Air Command*

WRITING (SCREENPLAY)
- Paddy Chayefsky, *Marty*
  Millard Kaufman, *Bad Day at Black Rock*
  Richard Brooks, *The Blackboard Jungle*
  Paul Osborn, *East of Eden*
  Daniel Fuchs, Isobel Lennart, *Love Me or Leave Me*

WRITING (STORY AND SCREENPLAY)
- William Ludwig, Sonya Levien, *Interrupted Melody*
  Milton Sperling, Emmett Lavery, *The Court Martial of Billy Mitchell*
  Betty Comden, Adolph Green, *It's Always Fair Weather*
  Jacques Tati, Henri Marquet, *Mr. Hulot's Holiday*
  Melville Shavelson, Jack Rose, *The Seven Little Foys*

CINEMATOGRAPHY (BLACK-AND-WHITE)
- James Wong Howe, *The Rose Tattoo*
  Russell Harlan, *Blackboard Jungle*
  Arthur E. Arling, *I'll Cry Tomorrow*
  Joseph LaShelle, *Marty*
  Charles Lang, *Queen Bee*

CINEMATOGRAPHY (COLOR)
- Robert Burks, *To Catch a Thief*
  Harry Stradling, *Guys and Dolls*
  Leon Shamroy, *Love Is a Many-Splendored Thing*
  Harold Lipstein, *A Man Called Peter*
  Robert Surtees, *Oklahoma!*

ART DIRECTION/SET DIRECTION
Black-and-White:
- Hal Pereira, Tambi Larsen; Sam Comer, Arthur Krams, *The Rose Tattoo*
Color:
- William Flannery, Joe Mielziner; Robert Priestley, *Picnic*

SOUND RECORDING
- Todd-AO Sound Dept., *Oklahoma!*

SHORT SUBJECTS
Cartoons:
- Warner Bros., *Speedy Gonzales*
One-Reel:
- 20th Century-Fox, *Survival City*
Two-Reel:
- University of Southern California, *The Face of Lincoln*

DOCUMENTARY
Short Subjects:
- Walt Disney, Buena Vista, *Men Against the Arctic*
Features:
- Nancy Hamilton, *Helen Keller in Her Story*

MUSIC
Best Song:
- Sammy Fain, Paul Francis Webster, "Love Is a Many-Splendored Thing," *Love is a Many-Splendored Thing*
Best Scoring of a Dramatic or Comedy Picture:
- Alfred Newman, *Love is a Many-Splendored Thing*
Best Scoring of a Musical Picture:
- Robert Russell Bennett, Jay Blackton, Adolph Deutsch, *Oklahoma!*

FILM EDITING
- Charles Nelson, William A. Lyon, *Picnic*

SPECIAL EFFECTS
- Paramount, *The Bridges at Toko-Ri*

COSTUME DESIGN
Black-and-White:
- Helen Rose, *I'll Cry Tomorrow*

Color:
- Charles LeMaire, *Love is a Many-Splendored Thing*

HONORARY AND OTHER AWARDS
- *Samurai (Japan) for best foreign-language film, first released in the United States during 1955*

SCIENTIFIC OR TECHNICAL AWARDS

Class I:
- National Carbon Co., for the development and production of a high-efficiency yellow flame carbon for motion picture color photography

Class II:
- Eastman Kodak Co., for Eastman Tri-X panchromatic negative film
- Farciot Edouart, Hal Corl and Paramount Studio Transparency Dept., for the engineering and development of a double-frame, triple-head background projector

Class III:
- 20th Century-Fox Studio and Bausch & Lomb Co., for the new combination lenses for CinemaScope photography
- Walter Jolley, Maurice Larson, and R.H. Spies of 20th Century-Fox Studio for a spraying process which creates simulated metallic surfaces
- Steve Krilanovich, for an improved camera dolly incorporating multidirectional steering
- David Anderson of 20th Century Studio, for an improved spotlight capable of maintaining a fixed circle of light at constant intensity over varied distances
- Loren L. Ryder, Charles West, Henry Fracker and Paramount Studio, for a projection film index to establish proper framing for various aspect ratios
- Farciot Edouart, Hal Corl and Paramount Studio Transparency Dept., for an improved dual stereopticon background projector

1956

BEST PICTURE
- *Around the World in 80 Days* (Todd-UA)
  Friendly Persuasion (Allied Artists)
  Giant (Warner Bros.)
  The King and I (20th Century-Fox)
  The Ten Commandments (DeMille-Paramount)

BEST DIRECTOR
- George Stevens *Giant*
  Michael Anderson, *Around the World in 80 Days*
  Walter Lang, *The King and I*
  King Vidor, *War and Peace*
  William Wyler, *Friendly Persuasion*

BEST ACTOR
- Yul Brynner, *The King and I*
  James Dean, *Giant*
  Kirk Douglas, *Lust for Life*
  Rock Hudson, *Giant*
  Sir Laurence Olivier, *Richard III*

BEST ACTRESS
- Ingrid Bergman, *Anastasia*
  Carroll Baker, *Baby Doll*
  Katharine Hepburn, *The Rainmaker*
  Nancy Kelly, *The Bad Seed*
  Deborah Kerr, *The King and I*

BEST SUPPORTING ACTOR
- Anthony Quinn, *Lust for Life*
  Don Murray, *Bus Stop*
  Anthony Perkins, *Friendly Persuasion*
  Mickey Rooney, *The Bold and the Brave*
  Robert Stack, *Written on the Wind*

BEST SUPPORTING ACTRESS
- Dorothy Malone, *Written on the Wind*
  Mildred Dunnock, *Baby Doll*
  Eileen Heckart, *The Bad Seed*
  Mercedes McCambridge, *Giant*
  Patty McCormack, *The Bad Seed*

WRITING (MOTION PICTURE STORY)
- *The Brave One* (At the time of the award, writer credit had

not been established. The story was attributed to "Robert Rich," pseudonym for Dalton Trumbo, one of the blacklisted Hollywood Ten. In May 1975 Trumbo at last received the award.)
  Leo Katcher, *The Eddy Duchin Story*
  Edward Bernds, Elwood Ullman (withdrawn from final ballot), *High Society*
  Jean-Paul Sartre, *The Proud and the Beautiful*
  Cesare Zavattini, *Umberto D.*

WRITING (BEST SCREENPLAY—ADAPTED)
- James Poe, John Farrow, S.J. Perelman, *Around the World in 80 Days*
  Tennessee Williams, *Baby Doll*
  Fred Guiol, Ivan Moffat, *Giant*
  Norman Corwin, *Lust for Life*, *Friendly Persuasion* (Writer ineligible for nomination under Academy bylaws which forbid any person who is a professed Communist or who refuses to deny such to receive an Academy Award. This bylaw was in effect from February 1957 to January 1959.)

WRITING (BEST SCREENPLAY—ORIGINAL)
- Albert Lamorisse, *The Red Balloon*
  Robert Lewin, *The Bold and the Brave*
  Federico Fellini, Tullio Pinelli, *La Strada*
  William Rose, *The Lady Killers*
  Andrew L. Stone, *Julie*

CINEMATOGRAPHY (BLACK-AND-WHITE)
- Joseph Ruttenberg, *Somebody Up There Likes Me*
  Boris Kaufman, *Baby Doll*
  Hal Rosson, *The Bad Seed*
  Burnett Guffey, *The Harder They Fall*
  Walter Strenge, *Stagecoach to Fury*

CINEMATOGRAPHY (COLOR)
- Lionel Lindon, *Around the World in 80 Days*

Harry Stradling, *The Eddy Duchin Story*
Leon Shamroy, *The King and I*
Loyal Griggs, *The Ten Commandments*
Jack Cardiff, *War and Peace*

FOREIGN-LANGUAGE FILM
(first year of nomination)

□ *La Strada* (Italy)
The Captain of Koepenick (Germany)
Gervaise (France)
Harp of Burma (Japan)
Quivitoq (Denmark)

ART DIRECTION/SET DIRECTION

Black-and-White:
□ Cedric Gibbons, Malcolm F. Brown; Edwin B. Willis, F. Keogh Gleason, *Somebody Up There Likes Me*
Color:
□ Lyle R. Wheeler, John DeCuir; Walter M. Scott, Paul S. Fox, *The King and I*

SOUND RECORDING

□ 20th Century-Fox Sound Dept., *The King and I*

SHORT SUBJECTS

Cartoons:
□ UPA, Columbia, *Mister Magoo's Puddle Jumper*
One-Reel:
□ Warner Bros., *Crashing the Water Barrier*
Two-Reel:
□ George K. Arthur, *The Bespoke Overcoat*

DOCUMENTARY

Short Subjects:
□ Camera Eye Pictures, *The True Story of the Civil War*
Features:
□ Cousteau-Columbia, *The Silent World*

MUSIC

Best Song:
□ Jay Livingston, Ray Evans, "Whatever Will Be, Will Be," *The Man Who Knew Too Much*
Best Scoring of a Dramatic or Comedy Picture:
□ Victor Young, *Around the World in 80 Days*

Best Scoring of a Musical Picture:
□ Alfred Newman, Ken Darby, *The King and I*

FILM EDITING

Gene Ruggiero, Paul Weatherwax, *Around the World in 80 Days*

SPECIAL EFFECTS

□ John Fulton, *The Ten Commandments*

COSTUME DESIGN

Black-and-White:
□ Jean Louis, *The Sold Gold Cadillac*
Color:
□ Irene Sharaff, *The King and I*

HONORARY AND OTHER AWARDS

□ Eddie Cantor, for distinguished service to the film industry

IRVING G. THALBERG MEMORIAL AWARD

□ Buddy Adler

JEAN HERSHOLT HUMANITARIAN AWARD

□ Y. Frank Freeman

SCIENTIFIC OR TECHNICAL AWARDS

Class III:
□ Richard H. Ranger of Rangertone Inc., for the development of a synchronous recording and reproducing system for quarter-inch magnetic tape
□ Ted Hirsch, Carl Hauge and Edward Reichard of Consolidated Film Industries, for an automatic scene counter for laboratory projection rooms
□ Technical Depts. of Paramount Pictures Corp., for the engineering and development of the Paramount lightweight horizontal-movement VistaVision camera
□ Roy C. Stewart and Sons of Stewart-Trans Lux Corp., Dr. C. R. Daily and the Transparency Dept. of Paramount Pictures Corp., for the engineering and development of the HiTrans and Para-HiTrans rear projection screens

□ Construction Dept. of MGM Studio, for a new hand-portable fog machine
□ Daniel J. Bloomberg, John Pond, William Wade and the Engineering and Camera Depts. of Republic Studio, for the Naturama adaptation to the Mitchell camera

1957

BEST PICTURE

□ *The Bridge on the River Kwai* (Columbia)
Peyton Place (20th Century-Fox)
Sayonara (Warner Bros.)
Twelve Angry Men (UA)
Witness for the Prosecution (UA)

BEST DIRECTOR

□ David Lean, *The Bridge on the River Kwai*
Joshua Logan, *Sayonara*
Sidney Lumet, *Twelve Angry Men*
Mark Robson, *Peyton Place*
Billy Wilder, *Witness for the Prosecution*

BEST ACTOR

□ Alec Guinness, *The Bridge on the River Kwai*
Marlon Brando, *Sayonara*
Anthony Franciosa, *A Hatful of Rain*
Charles Laughton, *Witness for the Prosecution*
Anthony Quinn, *Wild Is the Wind*

BEST ACTRESS

□ Joanne Woodward, *The Three Faces of Eve*
Deborah Kerr, *Heaven Knows, Mr. Allison*
Anna Magnani, *Wild is the Wind*
Elizabeth Taylor, *Raintree County*
Lana Turner, *Peyton Place*

BEST SUPPORTING ACTOR

□ Red Buttons, *Sayonara*
Vittorio De Sica, *A Farewell to Arms*
Sessue Hayakawa, *The Bridge on the River Kwai*
Arthur Kennedy, *Peyton Place*

Russ Tamblyn, *Peyton Place*

BEST SUPPORTING ACTRESS

- [ ] Miyoshi Jmeki, *Sayonara*
  Carolyn Jones, *The Bachelor Party*
  Elsa Lanchester, *Witness for the Prosecution*
  Hope Lange, *Peyton Place*
  Diane Varsi, *Peyton Place*

BEST SCREENPLAY (BASED ON MATERIAL FROM ANOTHER MEDIUM)

- [ ] Pierre Boulle, *The Bridge on the River Kwai*
  John Lee Mahin, John Huston, *Heaven Knows, Mr. Allison*
  John Michael Hayes, *Peyton Place*
  Paul Osborn, *Sayonara*
  Reginald Rose, *Twelve Angry Men*

BEST STORY AND SCREENPLAY (WRITTEN DIRECTLY FOR THE SCREEN)

- [ ] George Wells, *Designing Woman*
  Leonard Gershe, *Funny Face*
  Ralph Wheelright, R. Right Campbell, Ivan Goff, Ben Roberts, *Man of a Thousand Faces*
  Barney Slater, Joel Kane, Dudley Nichols, *The Tin Star*
  Federico Fellino, Ennio Flaiano, Tullio Pinelli, *I Vitelloni*

CINEMATOGRAPHY

(not separated this year into black-and-white and color)

- [ ] Jack Hildyard, *The Bridge on the River Kwai*
  Milton Krasner, *An Affair to Remember*
  Ray June, *Funny Face*
  William Mellor, *Peyton Place*
  Ellsworth Fredericks, *Sayonara*

FOREIGN-LANGUAGE FILM

- [ ] *The Nights of Cabiria* (Italy)
  The Devil Came at Night (Germany)
  Gates of Paris (France)
  Mother India (India)
  Nine Lives (Norway)

ART DIRECTION/SET DIRECTION

(awards not separated this year into black-and-white and color)

- [ ] Ted Haworth; Robert Priestley, *Sayonara*

SOUND RECORDING

- [ ] Warner Bros. Sound Dept., *Sayonara*

SHORT SUBJECTS

(rules changed this year to two awards instead of three)

Cartoons:
- [ ] Warner Bros., *Birds Anonymous*

Live Action Subjects:
- [ ] Walt Disney, Buena Vista, *The Wetback Hound*

DOCUMENTARY

(no short subject voted this year)

Features:
- [ ] Hill and Anderson, Louis de Rochemont, *Albert Schweitzer*

MUSIC

Best Song:
- [ ] James Van Heusen, Sammy Cahn, "All the Way," *The Joker is Wild*

Best Score:
(awards not divided this year into "dramatic or comedy" and "musical" categories)
- [ ] Malcolm Arnold, *The Bridge on the River Kwai*

FILM EDITING

- [ ] Peter Taylor, *The Bridge on the River Kwai*

SPECIAL EFFECTS

- [ ] Walter Rossi, *The Enemy Below*

COSTUME DESIGN

(one award given this year instead of the previous two)
- [ ] Orry-Kelly, *Les Girls*

HONORARY AND OTHER AWARDS

- [ ] Charles Brackett, for outstanding service to the Academy
- [ ] B.B. Kahane, for distinguished service to the motion picture industry
- [ ] Gilbert M. ("Broncho Billy") Anderson, for his contributions to development of movies as entertainment

- [ ] Society of Motion Picture and Television Engineers, for their contributions to the advancement of the industry

JEAN HERSHOLT HUMANITARIAN AWARD

- [ ] Samuel Goldwyn

SCIENTIFIC OR TECHNICAL AWARDS

Class I:
- [ ] Todd-AO Corp. and Westrex Corp., for developing a method of producing and exhibiting wide-film motion pictures known as the Todd-AO System
- [ ] Motion Picture Research Council, for the design and development of a high-efficiency projection screen for drive-in theaters

Class II:
- [ ] The Société d'Optique et de Mécanique de Haute Précision for the development of a high-speed vari-focal photographic lens
- [ ] Harlan L. Baumbach, Lorand Wargo, Howard M. Little and Unicorn Engineering Corp., for the development of an automatic printer light selector

Class III:
- [ ] Charles E. Sutter, William B. Smith, Paramount Pictures Corp. and Genral Cable Corp., for the engineering and application to studio use of aluminum lightweight electrical cable and connectors

1958

BEST PICTURE

- [ ] *Gigi* (MGM)
  Auntie Mame (Warner Bros.)
  Cat on a Hot Tin Roof (MGM)
  The Defiant Ones (Kramer-UA)
  Separate Tables (Hecht-Hill-Lancaster-UA)

BEST DIRECTOR

- [ ] Vincente Minnelli, *Gigi*
  Richard Brooks, *Cat on a Hot Tin Roof*

Stanley Kramer, *The Defiant Ones*
Mark Robson, *The Inn of the Sixth Happiness*
Robert Wise, *I Want to Live!*

BEST ACTOR

□ David Niven, *Separate Tables*
Tony Curtis, *The Defiant Ones*
Paul Newman, *The Cat on a Hot Tin Roof*
Sidney Poitier, *The Defiant Ones*
Spencer Tracy, *The Old Man and the Sea*

BEST ACTRESS

□ Susan Hayward, *I Want to Live!*
Deborah Kerr, *Separate Tables*
Shirley MacLaine, *Some Came Running*
Rosalind Russell, *Auntie Mame*
Elizabeth Taylor, *Cat on a Hot Tin Roof*

BEST SUPPORTING ACTOR

□ Burl Ives, *The Big Country*
Theodore Bikel, *The Defiant Ones*
Lee J Cobb, *The Brothers Karamazov*
Arthur Kennedy, *Some Came Running*
Gig Young, *Teacher's Pet*

BEST SUPPORTING ACTRESS

□ Wendy Hiller, *Separate Tables*
Peggy Cass, *Auntie Mame*
Martha Hyer, *Some Came Running*
Maureen Stapleton, *Lonelyhearts*
Cara Williams, *The Defiant Ones*

BEST SCREENPLAY (BASED ON MATERIAL FROM ANOTHER MEDIUM)

□ Alan Jay Lerner, *Gigi*
Richard Brooks, James Poe, *Cat on a Hot Tin Roof*
Alec Guinness, *The Horse's Mouth*
Nelson Gidding, Don Mankiewicz, *I Want to Live!*
Terence Rattigan, John Gay, *Separate Tables*

BEST STORY AND SCREENPLAY (WRITING DIRECTLY FOR THE SCREEN)

□ Nathan E. Douglas, Harold Jacob Smith, *The Defiant Ones*
Paddy Chayefsky, *The Goddess*
Melville Shavelson, Jack Rose, *Houseboat*
James Edward Grant (story); William Bowers and James Edward Grant (screenplay), *The Sheepmen*
Fay Kanin and Michael Kanin, *Teacher's Pet*

CINEMATOGRAPHY (BLACK-AND-WHITE)

□ Sam Leavitt, *The Defiant Ones*
Daniel L. Fapp, *Desire Under the Elms*
Lionel Lindon, *I Want to Live!*
Charles Lang, Jr., *Separate Tables*
Joe MacDonald, *The Young Lions*

CINEMATOGRAPHY (COLOR)

□ Joseph Ruttenberg, *Gigi*
Harry Stradling, *Auntie Mame*
William Daniels, *Cat on a Hot Tin Roof*
James Wong Howe, *The Old Man and the Sea*
Leon Shamroy, *South Pacific*

FOREIGN-LANGUAGE FILM

□ *My Uncle* (France)
Arms and the Man (Germany)
La Venganza (Spain)
The Road a Year Long (Yugoslavia)
The Usual Unidentified Thieves (Italy)

ART DIRECTION/SET DIRECTION

□ William A. Horning, Preston Ames; Henry Grace, Keogh Gleason, *Gigi*

SOUND

□ Todd-AO Sound Dept., *South Pacific*

SHORT SUBJECTS

Cartoons:
□ Warner Bros., *Knighty Knight Bugs*
Live Action Subjects:
□ Walt Disney, Buena Vista, *Grand Canyon*

DOCUMENTARY

Short Subjects:
Walt Disney, Buena Vista, *Ama Girls*
Features:
□ Walt Disney, Buena Vista, *White Wilderness*

MUSIC

Best Song:
□ Frederick Loewe, Alan Jay Lerner, "Gigi," *Gigi*
Best Scoring of a Dramatic or Comedy Picture:
□ Dimitri Tiomkin, *The Old Man and the Sea*
Best Scoring of a Musical Picture:
□ André Previn, *Gigi*

FILM EDITING

□ Adrienne Fazan, *Gigi*

SPECIAL EFFECTS

□ Tom Howard, *Tom Thumb*

COSTUME DESIGN

Black-and-White or Color:
□ Cecil Beaton, *Gigi*

HONORARY AND OTHER AWARDS

□ Maurice Chevalier, for his contributions to world of entertainment for more than half a century

IRVING G. THALBERG MEMORIAL AWRD

□ Jack L. Warner

SCIENTIFIC OR TECHNICAL AWARDS

Class II:
□ Don W. Prideaux, LeRoy G. Leighton and the Lamp Division of General Electric Co., for the development and production of an improved 10-kilowatt lamp for motion picture set lighting
□ Panavision, Inc., for the design and development of the Auto Panatar anamorphic photographic lens for 35mm CinemaScope photography
Class III:
□ Willy Borberg of the General Precision Laboratory, Inc, for the development of a high-speed intermittent movement for 35mm motion picture theater projection equipment

Fred Ponedel, George Brown and Conrad Boye of the Warner Bros. Special Effects Dept., for the design and fabrication of a new rapid-fire marble gun

1959

BEST PICTURE
- *Ben-Hur* (MGM)
  Anatomy of a Murder (Preminger-Columbia)
  The Diary of Anne Frank (Stevens-20th Century-Fox)
  The Nun's Story (Zinnemann-Warner Bros.)
  Room at the Top (Continental)

BEST DIRECTOR
- William Wyler, *Ben-Hur*
  Jack Clayton, *Room at the Top*
  George Stevens, *The Diary of Anne Frank*
  Billy Wilder, *Some Like It Hot*
  Fred Zinnemann, *The Nun's Story*

BEST ACTOR
- Charlton Heston, *Ben-Hur*
  Laurence Harvey, *Room at the Top*
  Jack Lemmon, *Some Like It Hot*
  Paul Muni, *The Last Angry Man*
  James Stewart, *Anatomy of a Murder*

BEST ACTRESS
- Simone Signoret, *Room at the Top*
  Doris Day, *Pillow Talk*
  Audrey Hepburn, *The Nun's Story*
  Katharine Hepburn, *Suddenly, Last Summer*
  Elizabeth Taylor, *Suddenly, Last Summer*

BEST SUPPORTING ACTOR
- Hugh Griffith, *Ben-Hur*
  Arthur O'Connell, *Anatomy of Murder*
  George C. Scott, *Anatomy of Murder*
  Robert Vaughn, *The Young Philadelphians*
  Ed Wynn, *The Diary of Anne Frank*

BEST SUPPORTING ACTRESS
- Shelley Winters, *The Diary of Anne Frank*
  Hermione Baddeley, *Room at the Top*
  Juanita Moore, *Imitation of Life*
  Susan Kohner, *Imitation of Life*
  Thelma Ritter, *Pillow Talk*

BEST SCREENPLAY (BASED ON MATERIAL FROM ANOTHER MEDIUM)
- Neil Paterson, *Room at the Top*
  Wendell Mayes, *Anatomy of a Murder*
  Karl Tunberg, *Ben-Hur*
  Robert Anderson, *The Nun's Story*
  Billy Wilder, I.A.L. Diamond, *Some Like It Hot*

BEST STORY AND SCREENPLAY (WRITTEN DIRECTLY FOR THE SCREEN)
- Russell Rouse, Clarence Greene (story); Stanley Shapiro, Maurice Richlin (screenplay), *Pillow Talk*
  François Truffaut, Marcel Moussy, *The 400 Blows*
  Ernest Lehman, *North by Northwest*
  Paul King, Joseph Stone (story); Stanley Shapiro, Maurice Richlin (screenplay), *Operation Petticoat*
  Ingmar Bergman, *Wild Strawberries*

CINEMATOGRAPHY (BLACK-AND-WHITE)
- William C. Mellor, *The Diary of Anne Frank*
  Sam Leavitt, *Anatomy of a Murder*
  Joseph LaShelle, *Career*
  Charles Lang, Jr., *Some Like It Hot*
  Harry Stradling, *The Young Philadelphians*

CINEMATOGRAPHY (COLOR)
- Robert L. Surtees, *Ben-Hur*
  Lee Garmes, *The Big Fisherman*
  Daniel L. Fapp, *The Five Pennies*
  Franz Planer, *The Nun's Story*

Leon Shamroy, *Porgy and Bess*

FOREIGN-LANGUAGE FILM
- *Black Orpheus* (France)
  The Bridge (Germany)
  The Great War (Italy)
  Paw (Denmark)
  The Village on the River (The Netherlands)

ART DIRECTION/SET DIRECTION
Black-and-White:
- Lyle R. Wheeler, George W. Davis; Walter M. Scott, Stuart A. Reiss, *The Diary of Anne Frank*

Color:
- William A. Horning, Edward Carfagno; Hugh Hunt, *Ben-Hur*

SOUND
- MGM Sound Dept., *Ben-Hur*

SHORT SUBJECTS
Cartoons:
- Storybook, Inc., *Moonbird*

Live Action Subjects:
- Jacques-Yves Cousteau, *The Golden Fish*

DOCUMENTARY
Short Subjects:
- George K. Arthur, Netherlands govn, *Glass*

Feature:
- Okapia-Film Prod., Transocean-Film, *Serengeti Shall Not Die*

MUSIC
Best Song:
- James Van Heusen, Sammy Cahn, "High Hopes," *A Hole in the Head*

Best Scoring of a Dramatic or Comedy Picture:
- Miklos Rozsa, *Ben-Hur*

Best Scoring of a Musical Picture:
- André Previn, Ken Darby, *Porgy and Bess*

FILM EDITING
- Ralph E. Winters, John D. Dunning, *Ben-Hur*

SPECIAL EFFECTS
- A. Arnold Gillespie, Robert MacDonald, Milo Lory, *Ben-Hur*

COSTUME DESIGN

Black-and-White:
- Orry-Kelly, *Some Like It Hot*
Color:
- Elizabeth Haffenden, *Ben-Hur*

HONORARY AND OTHER AWARDS

- Lee De Forest, for his pioneering inventions which brough sound to the motion picture
- Buster Keaton, for his unique talents which brought immortal comedies to the screen

JEAN HERSHOLT HUMANITARIAN AWARD
- Bob Hope

SCIENTIFIC OR TECHNICAL AWARDS

Class II:
- Douglas G. Shearer of MGM, Inc., and Robert E. Gottschalk and John R. Moore of Panavision Inc., for the development of a system of producing and exhibiting wide-film motion pictures known as Camera 65
- Wadsworth E. Pohl, William Evans, Werner Hopf, S.E. Howse, Thomas P. Dixon, Stanford Research Institute and Technicolor Corp., for the design and development of the Technicolor electronic printing timer
- Wadsworth E. Pohl, Jack Alford, Henry Imus, Joseph Schmidt, Paul Fassnacht, Al Lofquist and Technicolor Corp., for the development and practical application of equipment for wet printing
- Dr. Howard S. Coleman, Dr. A. Francis Turner, Harold H. Schroeder, James R. Benford and Harold E. Rosenberger of the Bausch & Lomb Optical Co., for the design and development of the Balcold projection mirror
- Robert P. Gutterman of General Kinetics, Inc., and Lipsner-Smith Corp., for the design and development of the CF-2 Ultra-sonic Film Cleaner

Class III:
- Ub Iwerks of Walt Disney Prods., for the design of an improved optical printer for special effects and matte shots
- E.L. Stones, Glen Robinson, Winfield Hubbard and Luther Newman of MGM Studio Construction Dept., for the design of a multiple-cable remote-control winch

---

1960

BEST PICTURE
- *The Apartment* (Mirisch-UA)
  The Alamo (UA)
  Elmer Gantry (UA)
  Sons and Lovers (Wald-20th Century-Fox)
  The Sundowners (Warner Bros.)

BEST DIRECTOR
- Billy Wilder, *The Apartment*
  Jack Cardiff, *Sons and Lovers*
  Jules Dassin, *Never on Sunday*
  Alfred Hitchcock, *Psycho*
  Fred Zinnemann, *The Sundowners*

BEST ACTOR
- Burt Lancaster, *Elmer Gantry*
  Trevor Howard, *Sons and Lovers*
  Jack Lemmor *The Apartment*
  Laurence Oli ier, *The Entertainer*
  Spencer Tracy, *Inherit the Wind*

BEST ACTRESS
- Elizabeth Taylor, *Butterfield 8*
  Greer Garson, *Sunrise at Campobello*
  Deborah Kerr, *The Sundowners*
  Shirley MacLaine, *The Apartment*
  Melina Mercouri, *Never on Sunday*

BEST SUPPORTING ACTOR
- Peter Ustinov, *Spartacus*
  Peter Falk, *Murder, Inc.*
  Jack Kruschen, *The Apartment*
  Sal Mineo, *Exodus*

Chill Wills, *The Alamo*

BEST SUPPORTING ACTRESS
- Shirley Jones, *Elmer Gantry*
  Glynis Johns, *The Sundowners*
  Shirley Knight, *The Dark at the Top of the Stairs*
  Janet Leigh, *Psycho*
  Mary Ure, *Sons and Lovers*

BEST SCREENPLAY (BASED ON MATERIAL FROM ANOTHER MEDIUM)
- Richard Brooks, *Elmer Gantry*
  Nathan E. Douglas, Harold Jacob Smith, *Inherit the Wind*
  Gavin Lambert, T.E.B. Clarke, *Sons and Lovers*
  Isobel Lennart, *The Sundowners*
  James Kennaway, *Tunes of Glory*

BEST STORY AND SCREENPLAY (WRITTEN DIRECTLY FOR THE SCREEN)
- Billy Wilder, I.A.L. Diamond, *The Apartment*
  Richard Gregson, Michael Craig, Bryan Forbes, *The Angry Silence*
  Norman Panama, Melvin Frank, *The Facts of Life*
  Marguerite Duras, *Hiroshima, Mon Amour*
  Jules Dassin, *Never on Sunday*

CINEMATOGRAPHY (BLACK-AND-WHITE)
- Freddie Francis, *Sons and Lovers*
  Joseph LaShelle, *The Apartment*
  Charles B. Lang, Jr., *The Facts of Life*
  Ernest Laszlo, *Inherit the Wind*
  John L. Russell, *Psycho*

CINEMATOGRAPHY (COLOR)
- Russell Metty, *Spartacus*
  William H. Clothier, *The Alamo*
  Joseph Ruttenberg, Charles Harten, *Butterfield 8*
  Sam Leavitt, *Exodus*
  Joe MacDonald, *Pepe*

FOREIGN-LANGUAGE FILM
- *The Virgin Spring* (Sweden)

Kapo (Italy)
La Vérité (France)
Macario (Mexico)
The Ninth Circle (Yugoslavia)

ART DIRECTION/SET DIRECTION

Black-and-White:
☐ Alexander Trauner; Edward G. Boyle, *The Apartment*

Color:
☐ Alexander Golitzen, Eric Orbom; Russell A. Gausman, Julia Heron, *Spartacus*

SOUND

☐ Samuel Goldwyn Studio Sound Dept., and Todd-AO Sound Dept., *The Alamo*

SHORT SUBJECTS

Cartoons:
☐ Rembrandt Films, Film Representations, Inc., *Munro*
Live Action Subjects:
☐ Kingsley-Union Films, *Day of the Painter*

DOCUMENTARY

Short Subjects:
☐ James Hill Prod., Lester A. Schoenfeld Films, *Giuseppina*
Features:
☐ Walt Disney, Buena Vista, *The Horse with the Flying Tail*

MUSIC

Best Song:
☐ Manos Hadjidakis, "Never on Sunday," *Never on Sunday*
Best Scoring of a Dramatic or Comedy Picture:
☐ Ernest Gold, *Exodus*
Best Scoring of a Musical Picture:
☐ Morris Stoloff, Harry Sukman, *Song Without End*

FILM EDITING

☐ Daniel Mandell, *The Apartment*

SPECIAL EFFECTS

☐ Gene Warren, Tim Baar, *The Time Machine*

COSTUME DESIGN

Black-and-White:
☐ Edith Head, Edward Stevenson, *The Facts of Life*
Color:
☐ Valles, Bill Thomas, *Spartacus*

HONORARY AND OTHER AWARDS

☐ Gary Cooper, for his many memorable performances and the international recognition he, as an individual, has gained for the industry
☐ Stan Laurel, for his creative pioneering in the field of cinema comedy
☐ Hayley Mills, for *Pollyanna*, the most outstanding juvenile performance during 1960

JEAN HERSHOLT HUMANITARIAN AWARD

☐ Sol Lesser

SCIENTIFIC OR TECHNICAL AWARDS

Class II:
☐ Ampex Professional Products Co., for the production of a well-engineered multipurpose sound system combining high standards of quality with convenience of control, dependable operation and simplified emergency provisions
Class III:
☐ Arthur Holcomb, Petro Vlahos and Columbia Studio Camera Dept., for the camera flicker indicating device
☐ Anthony Paglia and 20th Century-Fox Studio Mechanical Effects Dept., for the design and construction of a miniature flak gun and ammunition
☐ Carl Hauge, Robert Grubel and Edward Reichard of Consolidated Film Industries, for the development of an automatic developer replenisher system

---

1961

BEST PICTURE

☐ *West Side Story* (Mirisch-UA)
Fanny (Logan-Warner Bros.)
The Guns of Navarone (Foreman-Columbia)
The Hustler (Rossen-20th Century-Fox)
Judgment at Nuremberg (Kramer-UA)

BEST DIRECTOR

☐ Robert Wise, Jerome Robbins, *West Side Story*
Federico Fellini, *La Dolce Vita*
Stanley Kramer, *Judgment at Nuremburg*
Robert Rossen, *The Hustler*
J. Lee Thompson, *The Guns of Navarone*

BEST ACTOR

☐ Maximilian Schell, *Judgment at Nuremberg*
Charles Boyer, *Fanny*
Paul Newman, *The Hustler*
Spencer Tracy, *Judgment at Nuremberg*
Stuart Whitman, *The Mark*

BEST ACTRESS

☐ Sophia Loren, *Two Women*
Audrey Hepburn, *Breakfast at Tiffany's*
Piper Laurie, *The Hustler*
Geraldine Page, *Summer and Smoke*
Natalie Wood, *Splendor in the Grass*

BEST SUPPORTING ACTOR

☐ George Chakiris, *West Side Story*
Montgomery Clift, *Judgment at Nuremberg*
Peter Falk, *Pocketful of Miracles*
Jackie Gleason, *The Hustler*
George C. Scott, *The Hustler* (nomination refused)

BEST SUPPORTING ACTRESS

☐ Rita Moreno, *West Side Story*
Fay Bainter, *The Children's Hour*
Judy Garland, *Judgment at Nuremberg*
Lotte Lenya, *The Roman Spring of Mrs. Stone*
Una Merkel, *Summer and Smoke*

BEST SCREENPLAY (BASED ON MATERIAL FROM ANOTHER MEDIUM)

☐ Abby Mann, *Judgment at Nuremberg*
George Axelrod, *Breakfast at Tiffany's*
Carl Foreman, *The Guns of Navarone*

Sidney Carroll, Robert Rossen,
The Hustler
Ernest Lehman, *West Side
Story*

BEST STORY AND SCREENPLAY (WRITTEN DIRECTLY FOR THE SCREEN)

☐ William Inge, *Splendor in the
Grass*
Valentin Yoshov, Grigori
Chukhrai, *Ballad of a Soldier*
Sergio Amidei, Diego Fabbri,
Indro Montanelli, *General
della Rovere*
Federico Fellini, Tullio Pinelli,
Ennio Flaiano, Brunello
Rondi, *La Dolce Vita*
Stanley Shapiro, Paul
Henning, *Lover Come Back*

CINEMATOGRAPHY (BLACK-AND-WHITE)

☐ Eugen Shuftan, *The Hustler*
Edward Colman, *The
Absent-Minded Professor*
Franz F. Planer, *The Children's
Hour*
Ernest Laszlo, *Judgment at
Nuremberg*
Daniel L. Fapp, *One, Two,
Three*

CINEMATOGRAPHY (COLOR)

☐ Daniel L. Fapp, *The West Side
Story*
Jack Cardiff, *Fanny*
Russell Metty, *Flower Drum
Song*
Harry Stradling, *A Majority of
One*
Charles Lang, Jr., *One-Eyed
Jacks*

FOREIGN-LANGUAGE FILM

☐ *Through a Glass Darkly*
(Sweden)
Harry and the Butler
(Denmark)
Immortal Love (Japan)
The Important Man (Mexico)
Placido (Spain)

ART DIRECTION/SET DIRECTION

Black-and-White:
☐ Harry Horner; Gene Callahan,
The Hustler
Color:
☐ Boris Leven; Victor Gangelin,
West Side Story

SOUND

☐ Todd-AO Sound Dept. **Samuel
Goldwyn** Sound Dept., *West
Side Story*

SHORT SUBJECTS

Cartoons:
☐ Zagreb Film, *Erstaz*
Live Action Subjects:
☐ Templar Film Studios,
Seawards the Great Ships

DOCUMENTARY

Short Subjects:
☐ Klaeger Film, *Project Hope*
Features:
☐ Ardennes Films and **Michael
Arthur** Film Prods., **Rank
Film** Distributors, *Le Ciel et
la Boue* (The Sky Above and
the Mud Below)

MUSIC

Best Song:
☐ Henry Mancini, Johnny
Mercer, "Moon River,"
Breakfast at Tiffany's
**Best Scoring of a Dramatic
or Comedy Picture:**
☐ Henry Mancini, *Breakfast at
Tiffany's*
**Best Scoring of a Musical
Picture:**
☐ Saul Chaplin, Johnny Green,
Sid Ramin, Irwin Kostal,
West Side Story

FILM EDITING

☐ Thomas Stanford, *West Side
Story*

SPECIAL EFFECTS

☐ Bil Warrington, Vivian C.
Greeham, *The Guns of
Navarone*

COSTUME DESIGN

Black-and-White:
☐ Piero Gherardi, *La Dolce Vita*
Color:
☐ Irene Sharaff, *West Side Story*

HONORARY AND OTHER AWARDS

☐ William L. Hendricks, for his
outstanding patriotic service
in the Marine Corps Film *A
Force In Readiness* which
has brought honor to the
Academy and the industry
☐ Fred L. Metzler, for his
dedication and outstanding
service to the Academy
☐ Jerome Robbins, for his

brilliant achievements in film
choreography

IRVING G. THALBERG MEMORIAL AWARD

☐ Stanley Kramer

JEAN HERSHOLT HUMANITARIAN AWARD

☐ George Seaton

SCIENTIFIC OR TECHNICAL AWARDS

Class II:
☐ Sylvania Electric Products,
Inc., for the development of
a hand-held high-power
photographic lighting unit
known as the Sun Gun
Professional
☐ James Dale, S. Wilson, H.E.
Rice, John Rude, Laurie
Atkin, Wadsworth E. Pohl,
H. Peasgood and
Technicolor Corp., for a
process of automatic
selective printing
☐ 20th Century-Fox Research
Dept., under the direction of
E.I. Sponable and Herbert E.
Bragg, DeLuxe Laboratories,
Inc., with assistance of F.D.
Leslie, R.D. Whitmore, A.A.
Alden, Endel Pool and
James B. Gordon, for a
system of decompressing
and recomposing
CinemaScope pictures for
conventional aspect ratios
Class III:
☐ Hurletron, Inc. Electric Eye
Equipment Division, for an
automatic light changing
system for motion picture
printers
☐ Wadsworth E. Pohl and
Technicolor Corp., for an
integrated sound and picture
transfer process

1962

BEST PICTURE

☐ *Lawrence of Arabia*
(Horizon-Columbia)
The Longest Day
(Zanuck-20th Century-Fox)
The Music Man (Warner Bros.)
Mutiny on the Bounty (MGM)

To Kill a Mockingbird
(Universal-International)

BEST DIRECTOR

☐ David Lean, *Lawrence of Arabia*
Pietro Germi, *Divorce—Italian Style*
Robert Mulligan, *To Kill a Mockingbird*
Arthur Penn, *The Miracle Worker*
Frank Perry, *David and Lisa*

BEST ACTOR

☐ Gregory Peck, *To Kill a Mockingbird*
Burt Lancaster, *Birdman of Alcatraz*
Jack Lemmon, *Days of Wine and Roses*
Marcello Mastroianni, *Divorce—Italian Style*
Peter O'Toole, *Lawrence of Arabia*

BEST ACTRESS

☐ Anne Bancroft, *The Miracle Worker*
Bette Davis, *What Ever Happened to Baby Jane?*
Katharine Hepburn, *Long Day's Journey Into Night*
Geraldine Page, *Sweet Bird of Youth*
Lee Remick, *Days of Wine and Roses*

BEST SUPPORTING ACTOR

☐ Ed Begley, *Sweet Bird of Youth*
Victor Buono, *What Ever Happened to Baby Jane?*
Telly Savalas, *Birdman of Alcatraz*
Omar Sharif, *Lawrence of Arabia*
Terence Stamp, *Billy Budd*

BEST SUPPORTING ACTRESS

☐ Patty Duke, *The Miracle Worker*
Mary Badham, *To Kill a Mockingbird*
Shirley Knight, *Sweet Bird of Youth*
Angela Lansbury, *The Manchurian Candidate*
Thelma Ritter, *Birdman of Alcatraz*

BEST SCREENPLAY (BASED ON MATERIAL FROM ANOTHER MEDIUM)

☐ Horton Foote, *To Kill a Mockingbird*
Eleanor Perry, *David and Lisa*
Robert Bolt, *Lawrence of Arabia*
Vladimir Nabokov, *Lolita*
William Gibson, *The Miracle Worker*

BEST STORY AND SCREENPLAY (WRITTEN DIRECTLY FOR THE SCREEN)

☐ Ennio de Concini, Alfredo Giannetti, Pietro Germi, *Divorce—Italian Style*
Charles Kaufman, Wolfgang Reinhardt, *Freud*
Alain Robbe-Grillet, *Last Year at Marienbad*
Stanley Shapiro, Nate Monaster, *That Touch of Mink*
Ingmar Bergman, *Through a Glass Darkly*

CINEMATOGRAPHY (BLACK-AND-WHITE)

☐ Jean Bourgoin, Henri Persin, Walter Wottitz, *The Longest Day*
Burnett Guffey, *Birdman of Alcatraz*
Russell Harlan, *To Kill a Mockingbird*
Ted McCord, *Two for the Seesaw*
Ernest Haller, *What Ever Happened to Baby Jane?*

CINEMATOGRAPHY (COLOR)

☐ Fred A. Young, *Lawrence of Arabia*
Harry Stradling, *Gypsy*
Robert L. Surtees, *Mutiny on the Bounty*
Russell Harlan, *Hatari!*
Paul C. Vogel, *The Wonderful World of the Brothers Grimm*

FOREIGN-LANGUAGE FILM

☐ *Sundays and Cybele* (France)
Electra (Greece)
Four Days of Naples (Italy)
Keeper of Promises (The Given word) (Brazil)
Tlayucan (Mexico)

OTHER AWARDS:

ART DIRECTION/SET DIRECTION

Black-and-White:
☐ Alexander Golitzen, Henry Bumstead; Oliver Emert, *To Kill a Mockingbird*
Color:
☐ John Box, John Stroll; Dario Simoni, *Lawrence of Arabia*

SOUND
☐ Shepperton Studio Sound Dept., *Lawrence of Arabia*

SHORT SUBJECTS

Cartoons:
☐ Brandon Films, *The Hole*
Live Action Subjects:
☐ CAPAC Prods., Atlantic Pictures Corp., TWW Ltd., Janus Films, *Heureux Anniversaire*

DOCUMENTARY

Short Subjects:
(Welsh) *Dylan Thomas*
Features:
☐ Astor Pictures, *Black Fox*

MUSIC

Best Song:
☐ Henry Mancini, Johnny Mercer, "Days of Wine and Roses," *Days of Wine and Roses*
Best Music Score—Substantially Original:
(new classification this year)
☐ Maurice Jarre, *Lawrence of Arabia*
Best Music Score—Adaptation or Treatment:
(new classification this year)
☐ Ray Heindorf, *The Music Man*

FILM EDITING
☐ Anne Coates, *Lawrence of Arabia*

SPECIAL EFFECTS
☐ Robert MacDonald; Jacques Maumont, *The Longest Day*

COSTUME DESIGN

Black-and-White:
☐ Norman Koch, *What Ever Happened to Baby Jane?*

JEAN HERSHOLT HUMANITARIAN AWARD
☐ Steve Broidy

SCIENTIFIC OR TECHNICAL AWARDS

Class II:
- Ralph Chapman, for the design and development of an advanced motion picture camera crane
- Albert S. Pratt, James L. Wassell and Hans C. Wohlrab of the Professional Division, Bell & Howell Co., for the design and development of a new and improved automatic motion picture additive color printer
- North American Philips Co., Inc., for the design and engineering of the Norelco Universal 70/35mm motion picture projector
- Charles E. Sutter, William Bryson Smith and Louis C. Kennell of Paramount Pictures Corp., for the engineering and application to motion picture production of a new system of electric power distribution

Class III:
- Electro-Voice, Inc., for a highly directional dynamic line microphone
- Louis G. MacKenzie, for a selective sound effects repeater

1963

BEST PICTURE
- *Tom Jones* (Lopert-UA)
  America America (Kazan-Warner Bros.)
  Cleopatra (20th Century-Fox)
  How the West Was Won (MGM, Cinerama)
  Lilies of the Field (UA)

BEST DIRECTOR
- Tony Richardson, *Tom Jones*
  Federico Fellini, *8½*
  Elia Kazan, *America America*
  Otto Preminger, *The Cardinal*
  Martin Ritt, *Hud*

BEST ACTOR
- Sidney Poitier, *Lilies of the Field*
  Albert Finney, *Tom Jones*

Richard Harris, *This Sporting Life*
Rex Harrison, *Cleopatra*
Paul Newman, *Hud*

BEST ACTRESS
- Patricia Neal, *Hud*
  Leslie Caron, *The L-Shaped Room*
  Shirley MacLaine, *Irma La Douce*
  Rachel Roberts, *This Sporting Life*
  Natalie Wood, *Love with the Proper Stranger*

BEST SUPPORTING ACTOR
- Melvyn Douglas, *Hud*
  Nick Adams, *Twilight of Honor*
  Bobby Darin, *Captain Newman, M.D.*
  Hugh Griffith, *Tom Jones*
  John Huston, *The Cardinal*

BEST SUPPORTING ACTRESS
- Margaret Rutherford, *The V.I.P.s*
  Diane Cilento, *Tom Jones*
  Edith Evans, *Tom Jones*
  Joyce Redman, *Tom Jones*
  Lilia Skala, *Lilies of the Field*

BEST SCREENPLAY (BASED ON MATERIAL FROM ANOTHER MEDIUM)
- John Osborne, *Tom Jones*
  Richard L. Breen, Phoebe and Henry Ephron, *Captain Newman, M.D.*
  Irving Ravetch, Harriet Frank Jr., *Hud*
  James Poe, *Lilies of the Field*
  Serge Bourguignon, Antonio Tudal, *Sundays and Cybele*

BEST STORY AND SCREENPLAY (WRITTEN DIRECTLY FOR THE SCREEN)
- James R. Webb, *How the West Was Won*
  Elia Kazan, *America America*
  Federico Fellini, Tullio Pinelli, Ennio Flaiano, Brunello Rondi, *8½*
  Pasquale Festa Campanile, Massimo Franciosa, Nanni Loy, Vasco Pratolini, Carlo Bernari, *Four Days of Naples*
  Arnold Schulman, *Love with the Proper Stranger*

CINEMATOGRAPHY (BLACK-AND-WHITE)
- James Wong Howe, *Hud*
  George Folsey, *The Balcony*
  Lucien Ballard, *The Caretakers*
  Ernest Haller, *Lilies of the Field*
  Milton Krasner, *Love with the Proper Stranger*

CINEMATOGRAPHY (COLOR)
- Leon Shamroy, *Cleopatra*
  Leon Shamroy, *The Cardinal*
  William H. Daniels, Milton Krasner, Charles Lang Jr., Joseph LaShelle, *How the West Was Won*
  Joseph LaShelle, *Irma La Douce*
  Ernest Laszlo, *It's a Mad, Mad, Mad, Mad World*

FOREIGN-LANGUAGE FILM
- *8½* (Italy)
  Knife in the Water (Poland)
  Los Tarantos (Spain)
  The Red Lanterns (Greece)
  Twin Sisters of Kyoto (Japan)

ART DIRECTION/SET DIRECTION

Black-and-White
- Gene Callahan, *America America*

Color:
John DeCuir, Jack Martin Smith, Hilyard Brown, Herman Blumenthal, Elven Webb, Maurice Pelling, Boris Juraga; Walter M. Scott, Paul S. Fox, Ray Moyer, *Cleopatra*

SOUND
- MGM Sound Dept., *How the West Was Won*

SHORT SUBJECTS
Cartoons:
- Columbia, *The Critic*

Live Action Subjects:
- Janus Films, *An Occurrence at Owl Creek Bridge*

DOCUMENTARY

Short Subjects:
- Auerbach-Flag Films, *Chagall*

Features:
- WGBH Educational Foundation, *Robert Frost: A Lover's Quarrel with the World*

MUSIC

Best Song:
☐ James Van Heusen, Sammy Cahn, *"Call Me Irresponsible,"* Papa's Delicate Condition

Best Musical Score—Substantially Original:
☐ John Addison, *Tom Jones*

Best Musical Score—Adaptation or Treatment:
☐ André Previn, *Irma La Douce*

FILM EDITING
☐ Harold F. Kress, *How the West Was Won*

SPECIAL EFFECTS
☐ Emile Kosa, Jr., *Cleopatra*

SOUND EFFECTS
(new category this year)
☐ Walter G. Elliott, *It's a Mad, Mad, Mad, Mad World*

COSTUME DESIGN

Black-and-White:
☐ Piero Gherardi, *8½*
Color:
☐ Irene Sharaff, Vittorio Nino Novarese, Renie, *Cleopatra*

IRVING G. THALBERG MEMORIAL AWARD
☐ Sam Spiegel

SCIENTIFIC OR TECHNICAL AWARDS

Class III:
☐ Douglas A. Shearer and A. Arnold Gillespie of MGM Studios, for the engineering of an improved Background Process Project System

---

1964

BEST PICTURE
☐ *My Fair Lady* (Warner Bros.)
Becket (Wallis-Paramount)
Dr. Strangelove (Kubrick-Columbia)
Mary Poppins (Disney-Buena Vista)
Zorba the Greek (Intern'l Classics-20th Century-Fox)

BEST DIRECTOR
☐ George Cukor, *My Fair Lady*
Michael Cacoyannis, *Zorba the Greek*

Peter Glenville, *Becket*
Stanley Kubrick, *Dr. Strangelove*
Robert Stevenson, *Mary Poppins*

BEST ACTOR
☐ Rex Harrison, *My Fair Lady*
Richard Burton, *Becket*
Peter O'Toole, *Becket*
Anthony Quinn, *Zorba the Greek*
Peter Sellers, *Dr. Strangelove*

BEST ACTRESS
☐ Julie Andrews, *Mary Poppins*
Anne Bancroft, *The Pumpkin Eater*
Sophia Loren, *Marriage Italian Style*
Debbie Reynolds, *The Unsinkable Molly Brown*
Kim Stanley, *Séance on a Wet Afternoon*

BEST SUPPORTING ACTOR
☐ Peter Ustinov, *Topkapi*
John Gielgud, *Becket*
Stanley Holloway, *My Fair Lady*
Edmond O'Brien, *Seven Days in May*
Lee Tracy, *The Best Man*

BEST SUPPORTING ACTRESS
☐ Lila Kedrova, *Zorba the Greek*
Gladys Cooper, *My Fair Lady*
Edith Evans, *The Chalk Garden*
Grayson Hall, *The Night of the Iguana*
Agnes Moorehead, *Hush . . . Hush, Sweet Charlotte*

BEST SCREENPLAY (BASED ON MATERIAL FROM ANOTHER MEDIUM)
☐ Edward Anhalt, *Becket*
Stanley Kubrick, Peter George, Terry Southern, *Dr. Strangelove*
Bill Walsh, Don DaGradi, *Mary Poppins*
Alan Jay Lerner, *My Fair Lady*
Michael Cacoyannis, *Zorba the Greek*

BEST STORY AND SCREENPLAY (WRITTEN DIRECTLY FOR THE SCREEN)
☐ S.H. Barnett (story); Peter Stone, Frank Tarloff (screenplay), *Father Goose*

Alun Owen, *A Hard Day's Night*
Orville H. Hampton, Raphael Hayes, *One Potato, Two Potato*
Age (a.k.a. "Agenore Incrocci"), Scapelli (a.k.a. "Furio Scarpelli"), Mario Monicelli, *The Organizer*
J.P. Rapeneau, Ariane Mnouchkine, Daniel Boulager, Philippe De Broca, *That Man from Rio*

CINEMATOGRAPHY (BLACK-AND-WHITE)
☐ Walter Lassally, *Zorba the Greek*
Philip H. Lathrop, *The Americanization of Emily*
Milton Krasner, *Fate Is the Hunter*
Joseph Biroc, *Hush . . . Hush, Sweet Charlotte*
Gabriel Figueroa, *The Night of the Iguana*

CINEMATOGRAPHY (COLOR)
☐ Harry Stradling, *My Fair Lady*
Geoffrey Unsworth, *Becket*
William Clothier, *Cheyenne Autumn*
Edward Colman, *Mary Poppins*
Daniel L. Fapp, *The Unsinkable Molly Brown*

FOREIGN-LANGUAGE FILM
☐ *Yesterday, Today, and Tomorrow* (Italy)
Raven's End (Sweden)
Sallah (Israel)
The Umbrellas of Cherbourg (France)
Woman in the Dunes (Japan)

ART DIRECTION/SET DIRECTION

Black-and-White:
☐ Vassilis Photopoulos, *Zorba the Greek*
Color:
☐ Gene Allen, Cecil Beaton; George James Hopkins, *My Fair Lady*

SOUND
☐ Warner Bros. Sound Dept., *My Fair Lady*

SHORT SUBJECTS

Cartoons:
☐ Mirisch-United Artists, *The Pink Phink*

Live Action Subjects:
☐ Thalia-Beckman Corp., *Casals Conducts: 1964*

DOCUMENTARY

Short Subjects:
☐ Guggenheim Productions, *Nine from Little Rock*
Features:
☐ Columbia, *Jacques-Yves Cousteau's World Without Sun*

MUSIC

Best Song:
☐ Richard M. Sherman, Robert B. Sherman, "Chim-Chim Cher-ee," *Mary Poppins*
Best Musical Scoring—Substantially Original Music:
☐ Richard M. Sherman, Robert B. Sherman, *Mary Poppins*
Best Musical Scoring—Adaptation or Treatment:
☐ André Previn, *My Fair Lady*

FILM EDITING
☐ Cotton Warburton, *Mary Poppins*

SOUND EFFECTS
☐ Norman Wanstall, *Goldfinger*

VISUAL EFFECTS
(new classification)
☐ Peter Ellenshaw, *Mary Poppins*

COSTUME DESIGN

Black-and-White:
☐ Dorothy Jeakins, *The Night of the Iguana*
Color:
Cecil Beaton, *My Fair Lady*

HONORARY AND OTHER AWARDS
☐ William Tuttle, for his outstanding make-up achievement for *The Seven Faces of Dr. Lao*

SCIENTIFIC OR TECHNICAL AWARDS

Class I:
☐ Petro Vlahos, Wadsworth E. Pohl and Ub Iwerks, for the conception and perfection of techniques for Color Traveling Matte Composite Cinematography
Class II:
☐ Sidney P. Solow, Edward H. Reichard, Carl W. Hauge and Job Sanderson, of

Consolidated Film Industries, for the design and development of versatile Automatic 35mm Composite Color Printer
☐ Pierre Angenieux, for the development of a ten-to-one Zoom Lens for cinematography
Class III:
☐ Milton Forman, Richard B. Glickman and Daniel J. Pearlman of Color Tran Industries, for advancements in the design and application to motion picture photography of lighting units using quartz iodine lamps
☐ Stewart Filmscreen Corporation, for a seamless translucent Blue Screen for Traveling Matte Color Cinematography
☐ Anthony Paglia and the 20th Century-Fox Studio Mechanical Effects Dept., for an improved method of production Explosion Flash Effects for motion pictures
☐ Edward H. Reichard and Carl W. Hauge of Consolidated Film Industries, for the design of a Proximity Cue Detector and its application to motion picture printers
☐ Edward H. Reichard, Leonard L. Sokolow and Carl W. Hauge of Consolidated Film Industries, for the design and application to motion picture laboratory practice of a Stroboscopic Scene Tester for color and black-and-white film
☐ Nelson Tyler, for the design and construction of an improved Helicopter Camera System

1965

BEST PICTURE
☐ *The Sound of Music* (20th Century-Fox)
Darling (Embassy)
Doctor Zhivago (Ponti-MGM)
Ship of Fools (Kramer-Columbia)

A Thousand Clowns (UA)

BEST DIRECTOR
☐ Robert Wise, *The Sound of Music*
David Lean, *Doctor Zhivago*
Hiroshi Teshigahara, *Woman in the Dunes*
John Schlesinger, *Darling*
William Wyler, *The Collector*

BEST ACTOR
☐ Lee Marvin, *Cat Ballou*
Richard Burton, *The Spy Who Came In from the Cold*
Laurence Olivier, *Othello*
Rod Steiger, *The Pawnbroker*
Oskar Werner, *Ship of Fools*

BEST ACTRESS
☐ Julie Christie, *Darling*
Julie Andrews, *The Sound of Music*
Samantha Eggar, *The Collector*
Elizabeth Hartman, *A Patch of Blue*
Simone Signoret, *Ship of Fools*

BEST SUPPORTING ACTOR
☐ Martin Balsam, *A Thousand Clowns*
Ian Bannen, *The Flight of the Phoenix*
Tom Courtenay, *Doctor Zhivago*
Michael Dunn, *Ship of Fools*
Frank Finlay, *Othello*

BEST SUPPORTING ACTRESS
☐ Shelley Winters, *A Patch of Blue*
Ruth Gordon, *Inside Daisy Clover*
Joyce Redman, *Othello*
Maggie Smith, *Othello*
Peggy Wood, *The Sound of Music*

BEST SCREENPLAY (BASED ON MATERIAL FROM ANOTHER MEDIUM)
☐ Robert Bolt, *Doctor Zhivago*
Walter Newman, Frank R. Pierson, *Cat Ballou*
Stanley Mann, John Kohn, *The Collector*
Abby Mann, *Ship of Fools*
Herb Gardner, *A Thousand Clowns*

BEST STORY AND SCREENPLAY (WRITTEN DIRECTLY FOR THE SCREEN)

□ Frederic Raphael, *Darling*
Age (a.k.a. "Agenore Incrocci"), Scarpelli (a.k.a. "Furio Scarpelli"). Mario Monicelli, Tonino Guerra, Giorgio Salvioni, Suso Cecchi D'Amico, *Casanova '70*
Jack Davies, Ken Annakin, *Those Magnificent Men in Their Flying Machines*
Franklin Coen, Frank Davis, *The Train*
Jacques Demy, *The Umbrellas of Cherbourg*

CINEMATOGRAPHY (BLACK-AND-WHITE)

□ Ernest Laszlo, *Ship of Fools*
Loyal Griggs, *In Harm's Way*
Burnett Guffey, *King Rat*
Robert Burks, *A Patch of Blue*
Conrad Hall, *Morituri*

CINEMATOGRAPHY (COLOR)

□ Freddie Young, *Doctor Zhivago*
Leon Shamroy, *The Agony and the Ecstasy*
Russell Harlan, *The Great Race*
William C. Mellor, Loyal Griggs, *The Greatest Story Ever Told*
Ted McCord, *The Sound of Music*

FOREIGN-LANGUAGE FILM

□ *The Shop on Main Street* (Czechoslovakia)
Blood on the Land (Greece)
Dear John (Sweden)
Kwaidan (Japan)
Marriage Italian Style (Italy)

ART DIRECTION/SET DIRECTION

Black-and-White:
□ Robert Clatworthy; Joseph Kish, *Ship of Fools*
Color:
□ John Box, Terry March; Dario Simoni, *Doctor Zhivago*

SOUND

□ 20th Century-Fox Sound Dept., *The Sound of Music*

SHORT SUBJECTS

Cartoons:
□ MGM, *The Dot and the Line*
Live Action Subjects:
□ Renn-Pathé Contemporary, *The Chicken* (Le Poulet)

DOCUMENTARY

Short Subjects:
□ Johnson's Wax, *To Be Alive!*
Features:
□ Glazier-American International, *The Eleanor Roosevelt Story*

MUSIC

Best Song:
□ Johnny Mandel, Paul Francis Webster, "The Shadow of Your Smile." *The Sandpiper*
Best Musical Scoring— Substantially Original:
□ Maurice Jarre, *Doctor Zhivago*
Best Musical Scoring— Adaptation or Treatment:
Irwin Kostal, *The Sound of Music*

FILM EDITING

□ William Reynolds, *The Sound of Music*

SOUND EFFECTS

□ Tregoweth Brown, *The Great Race*

VISUAL EFFECTS

□ John Stears, *Thunderball*

COSTUME DESIGN

Black-and-White:
□ Julie Harris, *Darling*
Color:
□ Phyllis Dalton, *Doctor Zhivago*

HONORARY AND OTHER AWARDS

□ Bob Hope, for unique and distinguished service to the industry and the Academy

IRVING G. THALBERG MEMORIAL AWARD

□ William Wyler

JEAN HERSHOLT HUMANITARIAN AWARD

□ Edmond L. DePatie

SCIENTIFIC OR TECHNICAL AWARDS

Class II:
□ Arthur J. Hatch of the Strong Electric Corp., subsidiary of General Precision Equipment Corp., for the design and development of an Air Blown Carbon Arc Projection Lamp
□ Stefan Kudelski, for the design and development of the Nagra portable quarter-inch tape-recording system for motion picture sound recording

---

1966

BEST PICTURE

□ *A Man for All Seasons* (Columbia)
Alfie (Paramount)
The Russians Are Coming, The Russians Are Coming (UA)
The Sand Pebbles (20th Century-Fox)
Who's Afraid of Virginia Woolf? (Warner Bros.)

BEST DIRECTOR

□ Fred Zinnemann, *A Man for All Seasons*
Michelangelo Antonioni, *Blow-Up*
Richard Brooks, *The Professionals*
Claude Lelouch, *A Man and a Woman*
Mike Nichols, *Who's Afraid of Virginia Woolf?*

BEST ACTOR

□ Paul Scofield, *A Man for All Seasons*
Alan Arkin, *The Russians Are Coming, The Russians Are Coming*
Richard Burton, *Who's Afraid of Virginia Woolf?*
Michael Caine, *Alfie*
Steve McQueen, *The Sand Pebbles*

BEST ACTRESS

□ Elizabeth Taylor, *Who's Afraid of Virginia Woolf?*
Anouk Aimée, *A Man and a Woman*
Ida Kaminska, *The Shop on Main Street*
Lynn Redgrave, *Georgy Girl*
Vanessa Redgrave, *Morgan!*

BEST SUPPORTING ACTOR

□ Walter Matthau, *The Fortune Cookie*

Mako, *The Sand Pebbles*
James Mason, *Georgy Girl*
George Segal, *Who's Afraid of Virginia Woolf?*
Robert Shaw, *A Man for All Seasons*

BEST SUPPORTING ACTRESS
□ Sandy Dennis, *Who's Afraid of Virginia Woolf?*
Wendy Hiller, *A Man for All Seasons*
Jocelyn Lagarde, *Hawaii*
Vivien Merchant, *Alfie*
Geraldine Page, *You're a Big Boy Now*

BEST SCREENPLAY (BASED ON MATERIAL FROM ANOTHER MEDIUM)
□ Robert Bolt, *A Man for All Seasons*
Richard Brooks, *The Professionals*
William Rose, *The Russians Are Coming, The Russians Are Coming*
Ernest Lehman, *Who's Afraid of Virginia Woolf?*
Bill Naughton, *Alfie*

BEST STORY AND SCREENPLAY (WRITTEN DIRECTLY FOR THE SCREEN)
□ Claude Lelouch (story); Pierre Uytterhoeven and Claude Lelouch (screenplay), *A Man and a Woman*
Michelangelo Antonioni, Tonino Guerra, Edward Bond, *Blow-Up*
Billy Wilder, I.A.L. Diamond , *The Fortune Cookie*
Clint Johnston, Don Peters, *The Naked Prey*
Robert Ardrey, *Khartoum*

CINEMATOGRAPHY (BLACK-AND-WHITE)
□ Haskell Wexler, *Who's Afraid of Virginia Woolf?*
Joseph LaShelle, *The Fortune Cookie*
Ken Higgings, *Georgy Girl*
Marcel Grignon, *Is Paris Burning?*
James Wong Howe, *Seconds*

CINEMATOGRAPHY (COLOR)
□ Ted Moore, *A Man for All Seasons*

Ernest Laszlo, *Fantastic Voyage*
Russell Harlan, *Hawaii*
Conrad Hall, *The Professionals*
Joseph MacDonald, *The Sand Pebbles*

FOREIGN-LANGUAGE FILM
□ *A Man and a Woman* (France)
The Battle of Algiers (Italy)
Loves of a Blonde (Czechoslovakia)
Pharaoh (Poland)
Three (Yugoslavia)

ART DIRECTION/SET DIRECTION
Black-and-White:
□ Richard Sylbert; George James Hopkins, *Who's Afraid of Virginia Woolf?*
Color:
□ Jack Martin Smith, Dale Hennesy; Walter M. Scott, Stuart A. Reiss, *Fantastic Voyage*

SOUND
□ MGM Sound Dept., *Grand Prix*

SHORT SUBJECTS
Cartoons:
□ Hubley-Paramount, *Herb Alpert and the Tijuana Brass Double Feature*
Live Action Subjects:
□ British Transport Films, Manson Distributing, *Wild Wings*

DOCUMENTARY
Short Subjects:
□ Office of Economic Opportunity, *A Year Toward Tomorrow*
Features:
□ Pathé Contemporary Films, *The War Game*

MUSIC
Best Song:
□ John Barry, Don Black, "Born Free," *Born Free*
Best Original Score:
(for which only composer shall be eligible)
□ John Barry, *Born Free*
Best Scoring—Adaptation or Treatment:
□ Ken Thorne, *A Funny Thing Happened on the Way to the Forum*

FILM EDITING
□ Fredric Steinkamp, Henry Berman, Stewart Linder, Frank Santillo, *Grand Prix*

SOUND EFFECTS
□ Gordon Daniel, *Grand Prix*

SPECIAL VISUAL EFFECTS
□ Art Cruickshank, *Fantastic Voyage*

COSTUME DESIGN
Black-and-White:
□ Irene Sharaff, *Who's Afraid of Virginia Woolf?*
Color:
□ Elizabeth Haffenden, Joan Bridge, *A Man for All Seasons*

HONORARY AND OTHER AWARDS
□ Y. Frank Freeman, for unusual and outstanding service to the Academy during his 30 years in Hollywood
□ Yakima Canutt, for pioneering film stunt work

IRVING G. THALBERG MEMORIAL AWARD
□ Robert Wise

JEAN HERSHOLT HUMANITARIAN AWARD
□ George Bagnall

SCIENTIFIC OR TECHNICAL AWARDS
Class II:
□ Mitchell Camera Corporation, for the design and development of the Mitchell Mark II 35mm Portable Motion Picture Reflex Camera
□ Arnold & Richter KG, for the design and development of the Arriflex 35mm Portable Motion Picture Reflex Camera
Class III:
□ Panavision, Inc., for the design of the Panatron Power Inverter and its application to motion picture camera operation
□ Carroll Knudson for the production of a Composers Manual for Motion Picture Music Synchronization
□ Ruby Raksin for the production of a Composers Manual for

Motion Picture Music
Synchronization

1967

BEST PICTURE

☐ *In the Heat of the Night* (Mirisch-UA)
Bonnie and Clyde (Warner Bros.-Seven Arts)
Doctor Dolittle (20th Centry-Fox)
The Graduate (Embassy)
Guess Who's Coming to Dinner (Kramer-Columbia)

BEST DIRECTOR

☐ Mike Nichols, *The Graduate*
Richard Brooks, *In Cold Blood*
Norman Jewison, *In the Heat of the Night*
Stanley Kramer, *Guess Who's Coming to Dinner*
Arthur Penn, *Bonnie and Clyde*

BEST ACTOR

☐ Rod Steiger, *In the Heat of the Night*
Warren Beatty, *Bonnie and Clyde*
Dustin Hoffman, *The Graduate*
Paul Newman, *Cool Hand Luke*
Spencer Tracy, *Guess Who's Coming to Dinner*

BEST ACTRESS

☐ Katharine Hepburn, *Guess Who's Coming to Dinner*
Anne Bancroft, *The Graduate*
Faye Dunaway, *Bonnie and Clyde*
Dame Edith Evans, *The Whisperers*
Audrey Hepburn, *Wait Until Dark*

BEST SUPPORTING ACTOR

☐ George Kennedy, *Cool Hand Luke*
John Cassavetes, *The Dirty Dozen*
Gene Hackman, *Bonnie and Clyde*
Cecil Kellaway, *Guess Who's Coming to Dinner*
Michael J. Pollard, *Bonnie and Clyde*

BEST SUPPORTING ACTRESS

☐ Estelle Parsons, *Bonnie and Clyde*
Carol Channing, *Thoroughly Modern Millie*
Mildred Natwick, *Barefoot in the Park*
Beah Richards, *Guess Who's Coming to Dinner?*
Katharine Ross, *The Graduate*

BEST SCREENPLAY (BASED ON MATERIAL FROM ANOTHER MEDIUM)

☐ Stirling Silliphant, *In the Heat of the Night*
Don Pearce, Frank R. Pierson, *Cool Hand Luke*
Calder Willingham, Buck Henry, *The Graduate*
Richard Brooks, *In Cold Blood*
Joseph Strick, Fred Haines, *Ulysses*

BEST STORY AND SCREENPLAY (WRITTEN DIRECTLY FOR THE SCREEN)

☐ William Rose, *Guess Who's Coming to Dinner*
David Newman, Robert Benton, *Bonnie and Clyde*
Robert Kaufman, Norman Lear, *Divorce American Style*
Jorge Semprun, *La Guerre Est Finie*
Frederic Raphael, *Two for the Road*

CINEMATOGRAPHY

(rules changed to one award; no longer separate awards for black-and-white and color)
☐ Burnett Guffey, *Bonnie and Clyde*
Richard H. Kline, *Camelot*
Robert Surtees, *Doctor Dolittle*
Robert Surtees, *The Graduate*
Conrad Hall, *In Cold Blood*

FOREIGN-LANGUAGE FILM

☐ *Closely Watched Trains* (Czechoslovakia)
El Amor Brujo (Spain)
I Never Met Happy Gypsies (Yugoslavia)
Live for Life (France)
Portrait of Chieko (Japan)

ART DIRECTION/SET DIRECTION

(rules changed to only one award; no longer separate color and black-and-white awards)
☐ John Truscott, Edward Carrere; John W. Brown, *Camelot*

SOUND

☐ Samuel Goldwyn Studio Sound Dept., *In the Heat of the Night*

SHORT SUBJECTS

Cartoons:
☐ Murakami Wolf-Brandon, *The Box*
Live Action Subjects:
☐ A.T.D.F.-Columbia, *A Place to Stand*

DOCUMENTARY

Short Subjects:
☐ King Screen Productions, *The Redwoods*
Features:
☐ French Broadcasting System, *The Anderson Platoon*

MUSIC

Best Song:
☐ Leslie Bricusse, "Talk to the Animals," *Doctor Dolittle*
Best Original Score:
(for which only the composer shall be eligible)
☐ Elmer Bernstein, *Thoroughly Modern Millie*
Best Scoring of Music— Adaptation or Treatment:
(for which only the adapter and/or music director shall be eligible)
☐ Alfred Newman, Ken Darby, *Camelot*

FILM EDITING

☐ Hal Ashby, *In the Heat of the Night*

SOUND EFFECTS

☐ John Poyner, *The Dirty Dozen*

SPECIAL VISUAL EFFECTS

☐ L.B. Abbott, *Doctor Dolittle*

COSTUME DESIGN

(rules changed this year to only one award; no longer separate categories)
☐ John Truscott, *Camelot*

HONORARY AND OTHER AWARDS

☐ Arthur Freed, for distinguished service to the Academy and the production of six top-rated Awards telecasts

IRVING G. THALBERG MEMORIAL AWARD

☐ Alfred Hitchcock

JEAN HERSHOLT HUMANITARIAN AWARD

☐ Gregory Peck

SCIENTIFIC OR TECHNICAL AWARDS

Class III:

☐ Electro-Optical Division of the Kollmorgen Corp., for the design and development of a series of Motion Picture Projection Lenses

☐ Panavision, Inc,, for a Variable Speed Motor for Motion Picture Cameras

☐ Fred R. Wilson of the **Samuel Goldwyn Studio** Sound Dept., for an Audio Level Clamper

☐ Waldon O. Watson and the Universal City Studio Sound Dept., for new concepts in the design of a Music Scoring Stage

1968

BEST PICTURE

☐ *Oliver!* (Romulus-Columbia)
Funny Girl (Rastar-Columbia)
The Lion in Winter (Avco-Embassy)
Rachel, Rachel (Warner Bros.-Seven Arts)
Romeo and Juliet (Zeffirelli-Paramount)

BEST DIRECTOR

☐ Carol Reed, *Oliver!*
Anthony Harvey, *The Lion in Winter*
Stanley Kubrick, *2001: A Space Odyssey*
Gillo Pontecorvo, *The Battle of Algiers*
Franco Zeffirelli, *Romeo and Juliet*

BEST ACTOR

☐ Cliff Robertson, *Charly*

Alan Arkin, *The Heart Is a Lonely Hunter*
Ron Moody, *The Fixer*
Peter O'Toole, *The Lion in Winter*

BEST ACTRESS

☐ Katharine Hepburn, *The Lion in Winter*
☐ Barbra Streisand, *Funny Girl*
Patricia Neal, *The Subject Was Roses*
Vanessa Redgrave, *Isadora*
Joanne Woodward, *Rachel, Rachel*

BEST SUPPORTING ACTOR

☐ Jack Albertson, *The Subject Was Roses*
☐ Seymour Cassel, *Faces*
Daniel Massey, *Star!*
Jack Wild, *Oliver!*
Gene Wilder, *The Producers*

BEST SUPPORTING ACTRESS

☐ Ruth Gordon, *Rosemary's Baby*
Lynn Carlin, *Faces*
Sondra Locke, *The Heart Is a Lonely Hunter*
Kay Medford, *Funny Girl*
Estelle Parsons, *Rachel, Rachel*

BEST SCREENPLAY (BASED ON MATERIAL FROM ANOTHER MEDIUM)

☐ James Goldman, *The Lion in Winter*
Neil Simon, *The Odd Couple*
Vernon Harris, *Oliver!*
Stewart Stern, *Rachel, Rachel*
Roman Polanski, *Rosemary's Baby*

BEST STORY AND SCREENPLAY (WRITTEN DIRECTLY FOR THE SCREEN)

☐ Mel Brooks, *The Producers*
Franco Solinas, Gillo Pontecorvo, *The Battle of Algiers*
John Cassavetes, *Faces*
Ira Wallach, Peter Ustinov, *Hot Millions*
Stanley Kubrick, Arthur C. Clarke, *2001: A Space Odyssey*

CINEMATOGRAPHY

☐ Pasquale De Santis, *Romeo and Juliet*
Harry Stradling, *Funny Girl*

Daniel L. Fapp, *Ice Station Zebra*
Oswald Morris, *Oliver!*
Ernest Laszlo, *Star!*

FOREIGN-LANGUAGE FILM

☐ *War and Peace* (Russia)
The Boys of Paul Street (Hungary)
The Firemen's Ball (Czechoslovakia)
The Girl with the Pistol (Italy)
Stolen Kisses (France)

ART DIRECTION/SET DIRECTION

☐ John Box, Terence Marsh; Vernon Dixon, Ken Muggleston, *Oliver!*

SOUND

☐ Shepperton Studio Sound Dept., *Oliver!*

SHORT SUBJECTS

Cartoons:
☐ Walt Disney, *Winnie the Pooh and the Blustery Day*
Live Action Subjects
☐ Guggenheim-National General, *Robert Kennedy Remembered*

DOCUMENTARY

Short Subjects:
☐ Saul Bass, *Why Man Creates*
Features:
☐ Western Behavioral Sciences Institute. *Journey Into Self* (Columbia's Young Americans *was originally voted the award but on May 7, 1969, declared ineligible when it was learned that the film had been shown in 1967 and hence was ineligible for a 1968 award.)*

MUSIC

Best Song:
☐ Michel Legrand, Alan and Marilyn Bergman, "The Windmills of Your Mind," *The Thomas Crown Affair*
Best Original Score for a Non-Musical Picture:
(for which only the composer shall be eligible)
☐ John Barry, *The Lion in Winter*

Best Score of a Musical Picture, Original or Adaptation:

(for which the composer, lyricist and the adapter shall be eligible if the music score was written directly for the screen, but only the adapter if the score was adapted from another medium)

☐ John Green, *Oliver!*

FILM EDITING
☐ Frank P. Keller, *Bullitt*

SPECIAL VISUAL EFFECTS
☐ Stanley Kubrick, *2001: A Space Odyssey*

COSTUME DESIGN
☐ Danilo Donati, *Romeo and Juliet*

HONORARY AND OTHER AWARDS
☐ Onna White, for her outstanding choreography of *Oliver!*
☐ John Chambers, for his make-up design for *Planet of the Apes*

JEAN HERSHOLT HUMANITARIAN AWARD
☐ Martha Raye

SCIENTIFIC OR TECHNICAL AWARDS

Class I:
☐ Philip V. Palmquist of Minnesota Mining and Manufacturing Co.; Dr. Herbert Meyer of the Motion Picture and Television Research Center; and Charles D. Staffell of the Rank Organisation, for the development of a successful embodiment of the reflex background projection system for composite cinematography
☐ Eastman Kodax Company, for the development and introduction of a color reversal intermediate film for motion pictures.

Class II:
☐ Donald W. Norwood, for the design and development of the Norwood Photographic Exposure Meters
☐ Eastman Kodak Company and Producers Service Company,

for the development of a new high-speed stereoptical reduction printer
☐ Edmund M. DiGiulio, Niels G. Petersen and Norman S. Hughes of the Cinema Product Development Company, for the design and application of a conversion which makes available the reflex viewing system for motion picture cameras
☐ Optical Coating Laboratory, Inc., for the development of an improved antireflection coating for photographic and projection lens systems
☐ Eastman Kodak Company, for the introduction of a new high-speed motion picture color negative film
☐ Panavision, Inc., for the conception, design and introduction of a 65mm hand-held motion picture camera
☐ Todd-AO Company and the Mitchell Camera Company, for the design and engineering of the Todd-AO hand-held motion picture camera

Class III:
☐ Carl W. Hauge and Edward H. Reichard of Consolidated Film Industries and E. Michael Meahl and Roy J. Ridenour of Ramtronics, for engineering an automatic exposure control for printing-machine lamps
☐ Eastman Kodak Company, for a new direct positive film, and Consolidated Film Industries, for the application of this film to the making of post-production work prints

1969

BEST PICTURE
☐ *Midnight Cowboy* (UA)
Anne of the Thousand Days (Wallis-Universal)
Butch Cassidy and the Sundance Kid (20th Century-Fox)

Hello, Dolly! (Chenault-20th Century-Fox)
Z (Cinema V)

BEST DIRECTOR
☐ John Schlesinger, *Midnight Cowboy*
Costa-Gavras, *Z*
Arthur Penn, *Alice's Restaurant*
Sydney Pollack, *They Shoot Horses, Don't They?*
George Roy Hill, *Butch Cassidy and the Sundance Kid*

BEST ACTOR
☐ John Wayne, *True Grit*
Richard Burton, *Anne of the Thousand Days*
Dustin Hoffman, *Midnight Cowboy*
Peter O'Toole, *Goodbye, Mr. Chips*
Jon Voight, *Midnight Cowboy*

BEST ACTRESS
☐ Maggie Smith, *The Prime of Miss Jean Brodie*
Genevieve Bujold, *Anne of the Thousand Days*
Jane Fonda, *They Shoot Horses, Don't They*
Liza Minnelli, *The Sterile Cuckoo*
Jean Simmons, *The Happy Ending*

BEST SUPPORTING ACTOR
☐ Gig Young, *They Shoot Horses, Don't They?*
Rupert Crosse, *The Reivers*
Elliott Gould, *Bob & Carol & Ted & Alice*
Jack Nicholson, *Easy Rider*
Anthony Quayle, *Anne of the Thousand Days*

BEST SUPPORTING ACTRESS
☐ Goldie Hawn, *Cactus Flower*
Catherine Burns, *Last Summer*
Dyan Cannon, *Bob & Carol & Ted & Alice*
Sylvia Miles, *Midnight Cowboy*
Susannah York, *They Shoot Horses, Don't They?*

BEST SCREENPLAY (BASED ON MATERIAL FROM ANOTHER MEDIUM)
☐ Waldo Salt, *Midnight Cowboy*
John Hale, Bridget Boland,

Richard Sokolove, *Anne of the Thousand Days*

Arnold Schulman, *Goodbye, Columbus*

James Poe, Robert E. Thompson, *They Shoot Horses, Don't They?*

Jorge Semprun, Costa-Gavras, *Z*

BEST STORY AND SCREENPLAY (BASED ON MATERIAL NOT PREVIOUSLY PUBLISHED OR PRODUCED)

- □ William Goldman, *Butch Cassidy and the Sundance Kid*

Paul Mazursky , Larry Tucker, *Bob & Carol & Ted & Alice*

Nicola Badalucco, Enrico Medioli, Luchino Visconti, *The Damned*

Peter Fonda, Dennis Hopper, Terry Southern, *Easy Rider*

Walon Green, Roy N. Sickner, Sam Peckinpah, *The Wild Bunch*

CINEMATOGRAPHY

- □ Conrad Hall, *Butch Cassidy and the Sundance Kid*

Arthur Betson, *Anne of the Thousand Days*

Charles B. Lang, *Bob & Carol & Ted & Alice*

Harry Stradling, *Hello, Dolly!*

Daniel Fapp, *Marooned*

FOREIGN-LANGUAGE FILM

- □ *Z* (Algeria)

Adalen '31 (Sweden)

The Battle of Neretva (Yugoslavia)

The Brothers Karamazov (Russia)

My Night at Maud's (France)

ART DIRECTION/SET DIRECTION

- □ John DeCuir, Jack Martin Smith, Herman Blumenthal; Walter M. Scott, George Hopkins, Raphael Bretton, *Hello, Dolly!*

SOUND

- □ Jack Solomon, Murray Spivack, *Hello, Dolly!*

SHORT SUBJECTS

Cartoons:

- □ Walt Disney, Buena Vista, *It's Tough to Be a Bird*

Live Action Subjects:

- □ Fly-By-Night Productions-Manson, *The Magic Machines*

DOCUMENTARY

Short Subjects:

- □ Sanders-Fresco-USIA, *Czechoslvakia 1968*

Features:

- □ Midem Production, *Artur Rubinstein—The Love of Live*

MUSIC

Best Song:

- □ Burt Bacharach, Hal David, "Raindrops Keep Fallin' on My Head," *Butch Cassidy and the Sundance Kid*

Best Original Score of a Nonmusical Picture:

(for which only the composer shall be eligible)

- □ Burt Bacharach, *Butch Cassidy and the Sundance Kid*

Best Scoring of a Musical Picture—Original or Adaptation:

(for which the composer, lyricist, and adapter shall be eligible if the music was written directly for the screen, but only adapter shall be eligible if score is an adaptation)

- □ Lennie Hayton, Lionel Newman, *Hello, Dolly!*

FILM EDITING

- □ Francoise Bonnot, *Z*

SPECIAL VISUAL EFFECTS

- □ Robbie Robertson, *Marooned*

COSTUME DESIGN

- □ Margaret Furse, *Anne of the Thousand Days*

HONORARY AND OTHER AWARDS

- □ Cary Grant, for his unique mastery of the art of screen acting, with the respect and affection of his colleagues

JEAN HERSHOLT HUMANITARIAN AWARD

- □ George Jessel

SCIENTIFIC OR TECHNICAL AWARDS

Class II:

- □ Hazeltine Corporation, for the design and development of the Hazeltine Color Film Analyzer
- □ Fouad Said, for the design and introduction of the Cinemobile series of equipment trucks for location motion picture production
- □ Juan De La Cierva and Dynasciences Corporation, for the design and development of the Dynalens optical image motion compensator

Class III:

- □ Otto Popelka of Magna-Tech Electronic Co., Inc., for the development of an Electronically Controlled Looping System
- □ Fenton Hamilton of MGM Studios, for the concept and engineering of a mobile battery power unit for location lighting
- □ Panavision, Inc., for the design and development of the Panaspeed Motion Picture Camera Motor
- □ Robert M. Flynn and Russell Flynn of Universal City Studios, Inc., for a machine-gun modification for motion picture photography

---

1970

BEST PICTURE

- □ *Patton* (20th Century-Fox)

Airport (Hunter-Universal)

Five Easy Pieces (BBS-Columbia)

Love Story (Paramount)

*M*A*S*H* (20th Century-Fox)

BEST DIRECTOR

- □ Franklin J. Schaffner, *Patton*

Robert Altman, *M*A*S*H*

Federico Fellini, *Satyricon*

Arthur Hiller, *Love Story*

Ken Russell, *Women in Love*

BEST ACTOR

- □ George C. Scott, *Patton (award declined)*

Melvyn Douglas, *I Never Sang for My Father*

James Earl Jones, *The Great White Hope*

Jack Nicholson, *Five Easy Pieces*
Ryan O'Neal, *Love Story*

BEST ACTRESS
☐ Glenda Jackson, *Women in Love*
Carrie Snodgrass, *Diary of a Mad Housewife*
Jane Alexander, *The Great White Hope*
Ali MacGraw, *Love Story*
Sarah Miles, *Ryan's Daughter*

BEST SUPPORTING ACTOR
☐ John Mills, *Ryan's Daughter*
Richard Castellano, *Lovers and Other Strangers*
Chief Dan George, *Little Big Man*
Gene Hackman, *I Never Sang for My Father*
John Marley, *Love Story*

BEST SUPPORTING ACTRESS
☐ Helen Hayes, *Airport*
Karen Black, *Five Easy Pieces*
Lee Grant, *The Landlord*
Sally Kellerman, *M*A*S*H*
Maureen Stapleton, *Airport*

BEST SCREENPLAY (BASED ON MATERIAL FROM ANOTHER MEDIUM)
☐ Ring Lardner, Jr., *M*A*S*H*
George Seaton, *Airport*
Robert Anderson, *I Never Sang for My Father*
Renée Taylor, Joseph Bologna, David Zelag Goodman, *Lovers and Other Strangers*
Larry Kramer, *Women in Love*

BEST STORY AND SCREENPLAY (BASED ON FACTUAL MATERIAL OR MATERIAL NOT PREVIOUSLY PUBLISHED)
☐ Francis Ford Coppola, Edmund H. North, *Patton*
Bob Rafelson, Adrien Joyce, *Five Easy Pieces*
Norman Wexler, *Joe*
Erich Segal, *Love Story*
Eric Rohmer, *My Night at Maud's*

CINEMATOGRAPHY
☐ Freddie Young, *Ryan's Daughter*
Ernest Laszlo, *Airport*
Fred Koenekamp, *Patton*
Charles F. Wheeler, Osami

Furuya, Sinsaku Himeda, Masamichi Satoh, *Toral Toral Toral*
Billy Williams, *Women in Love*

FOREIGN-LANGUAGE FILM
☐ *Investigation of a Citizen Above Suspicion* (Italy)
First Love (Switzerland)
Hoa-Binh (France)
Paix sur les champs (Belguim)
Tristana (Spain)

ART DIRECTION/SET DIRECTION
☐ Urie McCleary, Gil Parrondo, Antonio Mateos, Pierre-Louis Thevenet, *Patton*

SOUND
☐ Douglas Williams, Don Bassman, *Patton*

SHORT SUBJECTS
Cartoons:
☐ Stephen Bosustow Prod., Schoenfeld Films, *Is It Always Right to be Right?*
Live Action Subjects:
☐ USC Dept. of Cinema, Universal, *The Resurrection of Broncho Billy*

DOCUMENTARY
Short Subjects:
☐ Laser Film Corp., *Interviews with My Lai Veterans*
Features:
☐ Wadleigh-Maurice, Warner Bros., *Woodstock*

MUSIC
Best Song:
☐ Fred Karlin, Robb Wilson, Arthur James, "For All We Know," *Lovers and Other Strangers*
Best Original Score:
(for which the composer and collaborator, if any, shall be eligible)
☐ Francis Lai, *Love Story*
Best Original Song Score:
(for which the song writer or writers and adapter, if any, shall be eligible)
☐ The Beatles, *Let It Be*

FILM EDITING
☐ Hugh S. Fowler, *Patton*

SPECIAL VISUAL EFFECTS
☐ A.D. Flowers, L.B. Abbott, *Toral Toral Toral*

COSTUME DESIGN
☐ Nino Novarese, *Cromwell*

HONORARY AND OTHER AWARDS
☐ Lillian Gish, for superlative artistry and for distinguished contribution to the progress of motion pictures
☐ Orson Welles, for superlative artistry and versatility in the creation of motion pictures

IRVING G. THALBERG MEMORIAL AWARD
☐ Ingmar Bergman

JEAN HERSHOLT HUMANITARIAN AWARD
☐ Frank Sinatra

SCIENTIFIC OR TECHNICAL AWARDS
Class II:
☐ Leonard Sokolow and Edward H. Reichard of Consolidated Film Industries, for the concept and engineering of the Color Proofing Printer for motion pictures
Class III:
☐ Sylvania Electric Product, Inc., for the development and introduction of a series of compact tungsten halogen lamps for motion picture production
☐ B.J. Losmandy, for the concept, design and application of micro-miniature solid-state amplifier modules used in motion picture recording equipment
☐ Eastman Kodak Company and Photo Electronics Corp., for the design and engineering of an improved video color analyzer for motion picture laboratories
☐ Electro Sound Inc., for the design and introduction of the Series 8000 Sound System for motion picture theaters

1971

BEST PICTURE
☐ *The French Connection* (20th Century-Fox)

A Clockwork Orange (Warner Bros.)
Fiddler on the Roof (Mirisch-UA)
The Last Picture Show (BBS-Columbia)
Nicholas and Alexandra (Horizon-Columbia)

BEST DIRECTOR
☐ William Friedkin, The French Connection
Peter Bogdanovich, The Last Picture Show
Norman Jewison, Fiddler on the Roof
Stanley Kubrick, A Clockwork Orange
John Schlesinger, Sunday Bloody Sunday

BEST ACTOR
☐ Gene Hackman, The French Connection
Peter Finch, Sunday Bloody Sunday
Walter Matthau, Kotch
George C. Scott, The Hospital
Topol, Fiddler on the Roof

BEST ACTRESS
☐ Jane Fonda, Klute
Julie Christie, McCabe & Mrs. Miller
Glenda Jackson, Sunday Bloody Sunday
Vanessa Redgrave, Mary, Queen of Scots
Janet Suzman, Nicholas and Alexandra

BEST SUPPORTING ACTOR
☐ Ben Johnson, The Last Picture Show
Jeff Bridges, The Last Picture Show
Leonard Frey, Fiddler on the Roof
Richard Jaeckel, Sometimes a Great Notion
Roy Scheider, The French Connection

BEST SUPPORTING ACTRESS
☐ Cloris Leachman, The Last Picture Show
Ellen Burstyn, The Last Picture Show
Barbara Harris, Who Is Harry Kellerman and Why Is He Saying All Those Terrible Things About Me?

Margaret Leighton, The Go-Between
Ann-Margret, Carnal Knowledge

BEST SCREENPLAY (BASED ON MATERIAL FROM ANOTHER MEDIUM)
☐ Ernest Tidyman, The French Connection
Stanley Kubrick, A Clockwork Orange
Bernardo Bertolucci, The Conformist
Ugo Pirro, Vittorio Bonicelli, The Garden of the Finzi-Continis
Larry McMurtry, Peter Bogdanovich, The Last Picture Show

BEST STORY AND SCREENPLAY (BASED ON FACTUAL MATERIAL OR MATERIAL NOT PREVIOUSLY PUBLISHED)
☐ Paddy Chayefsky, The Hospital
Elio Petri, Ugo Pirro, Investigation of a Citizen Above Suspicion
Andy and Dave Lewis, Klute
Herman Raucher, Summer of '42
Penelope Gilliatt, Sunday Bloody Sunday

CINEMATOGRAPHY
☐ Oswald Morris, Fiddler on the Roof
Owen Roizman, The French Connection
Robert Surtees, The Last Picture Show
Freddie Young, Nicholas and Alexandra
Robert Surtees, Summer of '42

FOREIGN-LANGUAGE FILM
☐ The Garden of the Finzi-Continis (Italy)
Dodes 'Ka-Den (Japan)
The Emigrants (Sweden)
The Policeman (Israel)
Tchaikovsky (USSR)

ART DIRECTION/SET DIRECTION
☐ John Box, Ernest Archer, Jack Maxsted, Gil Parrondo; Vernon Dixon, Nicholas and Alexandra

SOUND
☐ Gordon K. McCallum, David Hildyard, Fiddler on the Roof

SHORT SUBJECTS
Cartoons:
☐ Maxwell-Petok Prod., Regency Films, The Crunch Bird
Live Action Subjects:
☐ Producciones Concord, Paramount, Sentinels of Silence

DOCUMENTARY
Short Subjects:
☐ Producciones Concord, Paramount, Sentinels of Silence
Features:
☐ David Wolper-Cinema 5, Hellstrom Chronicle

MUSIC
Best Song:
☐ Isaac Hayes, "Theme from Shaft," Shaft
Best Original Score:
(for which only the composer shall be eligible)
☐ Michel Legrand, Summer of '42
Best Scoring: Adaptation and Original Song Score:
(for which the composer, lyricist and adapter shall be eligible if the material was written for or first used in an eligible motion picture, but only the adapter shall be eligible if the material is an adaptation or has been previously used)
☐ John Williams, Fiddler on the Roof

FILM EDITING
☐ Jerry Greenberg, The French Connection

SPECIAL VISUAL EFFECTS
☐ Danny Lee, Eustace Lycett, Alan Maley, Bedknobs and Broomsticks

COSTUME DESIGN
☐ Yvonne Blake, Antonio Castillo, Nicholas and Alexandra

HONORARY AND OTHER AWARDS
☐ Charles Chaplin, for the incalculable effect he has had in in making motion

pictures the art form of this country

SCIENTIFIC OR TECHNICAL AWARDS

Class II:
☐ John N. Wilkinson of Optical Radiation Corp., for the development and engineering of a system of xenon arc lamphouses for motion picture projection

Class III:
☐ Thomas Jefferson Hutchinson, James R. Rochester and Fenton Hamilton, for the development and introduction of the Sunbrute system of xenon arc lamps for location lighting in motion picture projection
☐ Photo Research, a division of Kollmorgen Corp., for the development and introduction of the film-lens balanced Three Color Meter
☐ Robert D. August and Cinema Products Company, for the development and introduction of a new crystal-controlled lightweight motor for the Arriflex 35mm motion picture camera
☐ Producers Service Corp. and Consolidated Film Industries, and Cinema Research Corp. and Research Products, Inc., for the engineering and implementation of fully automated blowup motion picture printing systems
☐ Cinema Products Company, for a control motor to actuate zoom lenses on motion picture cameras

---

1972

BEST PICTURE

☐ *The Godfather* (Paramount)
Cabaret (ABC Pictures, Allied Artists)
Deliverance (Warner Bros.)
The Emigrants (Warner Bros.)
Sounder (Radnitz, Mattel, 20th Century-Fox)

BEST DIRECTOR

☐ Bob Fosse, *Cabaret*
John Boorman, *Deliverance*
Francis Ford Coppola, *The Godfather*
Joseph L. Mankiewicz, *Sleuth*
Jan Troell, *The Emigrants*

BEST ACTOR

☐ Marlon Brando, *The Godfather* (award declined)
Michael Caine, *Sleuth*
Laurence Olivier, *Sleuth*
Peter O'Toole, *The Ruling Class*
Paul Winfield, *Sounder*

BEST ACTRESS

☐ Liza Minnelli, *Cabaret*
Diana Ross, *Lady Sings the Blues*
Maggie Smith, *Travels with My Aunt*
Cicely Tyson, *Sounder*
Liv Ullmann, *The Emigrants*

BEST SUPPORTING ACTOR

☐ Joel Grey, *Cabaret*
Eddie Albert, *The Heartbreak Kid*
James Caan, *The Godfather*
Robert Duvall, *The Godfather*
Al Pacino, *The Godfather*

BEST SUPPORTING ACTRESS

☐ Eileen Heckart, *Butterflies Are Free*
Jeannie Berlin, *The Heartbreak Kid*
Geraldine Page, *Pete 'n' Tillie*
Susan Tyrrell, *Fat City*
Shelley Winters, *The Poseidon Adventure*

BEST SCREENPLAY (BASED ON MATERIAL FROM ANOTHER MEDIUM)

☐ Mario Puzo, Francis Ford Coppola, *The Godfather*
Jan Troell, Bengt Forslund, *The Emigrants*
Jay Allen, *Cabaret*
Julius J. Epstein, *Pete 'n' Tillie*
Lonne Elder III, *Sounder*

BEST STORY AND SCREENPLAY (BASED ON FACTUAL MATERIAL OR MATERIAL NOT PREVIOUSLY PUBLISHED)

☐ Jeremy Larner, *The Candidate*
Luis Buñuel, *The Discreet Charm of the Bourgeoisie*
Terence McCloy, Chris Clark,

Suzanne de Passe, *Lady Sings the Blues*
Louis Malle, *Mumur of the Heart*
Carl Foreman, *Young Winston*

CINEMATOGRAPHY

☐ Geoffrey Unsworth, *Cabaret*
Charles B. Lang, *Butterflies Are Free*
Harold E. Stine, *The Poseidon Adventure*
Harry Stradling, Jr., *1776*
Douglas Slocombe, *Travels with My Aunt*

FOREIGN-LANGUAGE FILM

☐ *The Discreet Charm of the Bourgeoisie* (France)
The Dawns Here Are Quiet (USSR)
I Love You Rosa (Israel)
My Dearest Señorita (Spain)
The New Land (Sweden)

ART DIRECTION/SET DIRECTION

☐ Rolf Zehetbauer, Jurgen Kiebach; Herbert Strabl, *Cabaret*

SOUND

☐ Robert Knudson, David Hildyard, *Cabaret*

SHORT SUBJECTS

Cartoons:
☐ Richard Williams (ABC), *A Christmas Carol*
Live Action Subjects:
☐ Concepts Unlimited Production-United Artists, *Norman Rockwell's World . . . An American Dream*

DOCUMENTARY

Short Subjects:
☐ Charles Huguenot van der Linden Productions, *This Tiny World*
Features:
☐ Cinema X, Cinema 5, Ltd., *Marjoe*

MUSIC

Best Song:
☐ Al Kasha, Joel Hirschhorn, "The Morning After," *The Poseidon Adventure*
Best Original Dramatic Score:
(*for which only the composer shall be eligible*)
☐ Charles Chaplin, Raymond

Rasch, Larry Russell, *Limelight*

Best Scoring:

(*for which the composer, the lyricist and the adapter shall be eligible if the score was written or first used for an eligible picture, but only the adapter shall be eligible if the material is an adaptation*)

- Ralph Burns, *Cabaret*

FILM EDITING

- David Bretherton, *Cabaret*

COSTUME DESIGN

- Anthony Powell, *Travels with My Aunt*

HONORARY AND OTHER AWARDS

- Edward G. Robinson, who achieved greatness as a player, a patron of the arts and a dedicated citizen . . . in sum, a Renaissance Man
- Charles Boren, leader for 38 years of the industry's enlightened labor relations and architect of its policy of non-discrimination
- L.B. Abbott and A.D. Flowers for their special visual effects in *The Poseidon Adventure*

The Godfather Score, composed by Nino Rota, was originally announced as one of the five nominees, but was later declared ineligible when it was discovered that portions of the composition had been used in Rota's score for a 1958 Italian film, *Fortunella*.

JEAN HERSHOLT HUMANITARIAN AWARD

- Rosalind Russell

SCIENTIFIC OR TECHNICAL AWARDS

Class II:

- Joseph E. Bluth, for research and development in the field of electronic photography and transfer of video tape to motion picture film
- Edward H. Reichard and Howard T. Lazare of Consolidated Film Industries, and Edward Efron of IBM, for the engineering of a computerized light valve

monitoring system for motion picture printing

- Panavision, Inc., for the development and engineering of a Panaflex motion picture camera

Class III:

- Photo Research, a division of Kollmorgen Corp., and Producers Service for the Spectra Film Gate Photometer, for motion picture printers
- Carter Equipment Company and Ramtronics, for the Ramtronics light-value photometer for motion picture printers
- David Degenkolb, Harry Larson, Manfred Michelson, and Fred Scobey of Deluxe General, for the development of a computerized motion picture printer and process control system
- Jiro Mukai and Ryusho Hirose of Canon, Inc., and Wilton R. Holm of the AMPTP Motion Picture and Television Research Center, for development of the Canon Macro Zoom Lens for motion picture photography
- Philip V. Palmquist and Leonard I. Olson of the 3M Company and Frank P. Clark of the AMPTP Research Center, for development of the Nextel simulated blood for motion picture color photography
- E.H. Geissler and G.M. Berggren of Wil-Kin, Inc., for engineerng of the Ultra-Vision Motion Picture Theater Projection System

---

1973

BEST PICTURE

- *The Sting* (Zanuck-Brown-Universal)
  American Graffiti (Universal)
  Cries and Whispers (New World)
  The Exorcist (Warner Bros.)
  A Touch of Class (Brut-Avco Embassy)

BEST DIRECTOR

- George Roy Hill, *The Sting*
  Ingmar Bergman, *Cries and Whispers*
  Bernardo Bertolucci, *Last Tango in Paris*
  William Friedkin, *The Exorcist*
  George Lucas, *American Graffiti*

BEST ACTOR

- Jack Lemmon, *Save the Tiger*
  Marlon Brando, *Last Tango in Paris*
  Jack Nicholson, *The Last Detail*
  Al Pacino, *Serpico*
  Robert Redford, *The Sting*

BEST ACTRESS

- Glenda Jackson, *A Touch of Class*
  Ellen Burstyn, *The Exorcist*
  Marsha Mason, *Cinderella Liberty*
  Barbra Streisand, *The Way We Were*
  Joanne Woodward, *Summer Wishes, Winter Dreams*

BEST SUPPORTING ACTOR

- John Houseman, *The Paper Chase*
  Vincent Gardenia, *Bang the Drum Slowly*
  Jack Gilford, *Save the Tiger*
  Jason Miller, *The Exorcist*
  Randy Quaid, *The Last Detail*

BEST SUPPORTING ACTRESS

- Tatum O'Neal, *Paper Moon*
  Linda Blair, *The Exorcist*
  Candy Clark, *American Graffiti*
  Madeline Kahn, *Paper Moon*
  Sylvia Sidney, *Summer Wishes, Winter Dreams*

BEST SCREENPLAY (BASED ON MATERIAL FROM ANOTHER MEDIUM)

- William Peter Blatty, *The Exorcist*
  Robert Towne, *The Last Detail*
  James Bridges, *The Paper Chase*
  Alvin Sargent, *Paper Moon*
  Waldo Salt, Norman Wexler, *Serpico*

BEST STORY AND SCREENPLAY (BASED ON FACTUAL MATERIAL OR MATERIAL NOT PREVIOUSLY PUBLISHED)

☐ David S. Ward, *The Sting*
George Lucas, Gloria Katz, Willard Huyck, *American Graffiti*
Ingmar Bergman, *Cries and Whispers*
Steve Shagan, *Save the Tiger*
Melvin Frank, Jack Rose, *A Touch of Class*

CINEMATOGRAPHY

☐ Sven Nykvist, *Cries and Whispers*
Owen Roizman, *The Exorcist*
Jack Couffer, *Jonathan Livingston Seagull*
Robert Surtees, *The Sting*
Harry Stradling, Jr., *The Way We Were*

FOREIGN-LANGUAGE FILM

☐ *Day for Night* (France)
The House on Chelouche Street (Israel)
L'Invitation (Switzerland)
The Pedestrian (West Germany)
Turkish Delight (The Netherlands)

ART DIRECTION/SET DIRECTION

☐ Henry Bumstead; James Payne, *The Sting*

MUSIC

Best Song:
☐ Marvin Hamlisch, Alan and Marilyn Bergman, "The Way We Were," *The Way We Were*
Best Original Dramatic Score:
☐ Marvin Hamlisch, *The Way We Were*
Best Scoring—Original Song Score and Adaptation; or Best Scoring—Adaptation:
☐ Marvin Hamlisch, *The Sting*

SOUND

☐ Robert Knudson, Chris Newman, *The Exorcist*

SHORT SUBJECTS

Cartoons:
☐ Frank Mouris Production, *Frank Film*

Live Action Subjects:
☐ Allan Miller Production, *The Bolero*

DOCUMENTARY

Short Subjects:
☐ Krainin-Sage Productions, *A Search for Answers*
Features:
☐ Kieth Merrill, Rodeo Films, *The Great American Cowboy*

FILM EDITING

☐ William Reynolds, *The Sting*

COSTUME DESIGN

☐ Edith Head, *The Sting*

HONORARY AND OTHER AWARDS

☐ Groucho Marx, for his brilliant creativity and unequaled achievements of the Marx Brothers in the art of motion picture comedy
☐ Henri Langlois, for his untiring devotion to the art of film, for his massive contributions toward preserving its historical part and his unswerving faith in its future

IRVING G. THALBERG MEMORIAL AWARD

☐ Lawrence Weingarten

JEAN HERSHOLT HUMANITARIAN AWARD

☐ Lew Wasserman

SCIENTIFIC OR TECHNICAL AWARDS

Class II:
☐ Joachim Gerb and Erich Kastner of the Arnold and Richter Company, for the development and engineering of the Arriflex 35BL motion picture camera
☐ Magna-Tech Electronic Company, for the engineering and development of a high-speed re-recording system for motion picture production
☐ William W. Vallant of PSC Technology, Inc., Howard F. Ott of Eastman Kodak Company and Gerry Diebold of the Richmark Camera Service, Inc., for the development of a liquid-gate system for motion picture printers
☐ Harold A. Scheib, Clifford H.

Ellis and Roger W. Banks of Research Products, Incorporated, for the concept and engineering of the model 2101 optical printer for motion picture optical effects
Class III:
☐ Rosco Laboratories, Inc., for the technical advances and development of a complete system of light-control materials for motion picture photography
☐ Richard H. Vetter of the Todd-AO Corporation, for the design of an improved anamorphic focusing system for motion picture photography

---

1974

BEST PICTURE

☐ *The Godfather, Part II* (Paramount)
Chinatown (Paramount)
The Conversation (Paramount)
Lenny (UA)
The Towering Inferno (20th Century-Fox–Warner Bros.)

BEST DIRECTOR

☐ Francis Ford Coppola, *The Godfather, Part II*
John Cassavetes, *A Woman Under the Influence*
Bob Fosse, *Lenny*
Roman Polanski, *Chinatown*
Francois Truffaut, *Day for Night*

BEST ACTOR

☐ Art Carney, *Harry and Tonto*
Albert Finney, *Murder on the Orient Express*
Dustin Hoffman, *Lenny*
Jack Nicholson, *Chinatown*
Al Pacino, *The Godfather, Part II*

BEST ACTRESS

☐ Fllen Burstyn, *Alice Doesn't Live Here Anymore*
Diahann Carroll, *Claudine*
Faye Dunaway, *Chinatown*
Valerie Perrine, *Lenny*
Gena Rowlands, *A Woman Under the Influence*

BEST SUPPORTING ACTOR

- Robert De Niro, *The Godfather Part, II*
  Fred Astaire, *The Towering Inferno*
  Jeff Bridges, *Thunderbolt and Lightfoot*
  Michael V. Gasso, *The Godfather, Part II*
  Lee Strasberg, *The Godfather, Part II*

BEST SUPPORTING ACTRESS

- Ingrid Bergman, *Murder on the Orient Express*
  Valentina Cortese, *Day for Night*
  Madeline Kahn, *Blazing Saddles*
  Diane Ladd, *Alice Doesn't Live Here Anymore*
  Talia Shire, *The Godfather, Part II*

BEST SCREENPLAY (ADAPTED FROM OTHER MATERIAL)

- Francis Ford Coppola, Mario Puzo, *The Godfather, Part II*
  Mordecai Richler, Lionel Chetwynd, *The Apprenticeship of Duddy Kravitz*
  Julian Barry, *Lenny*
  Paul Dehn, *Murder on the Orient Express*
  Gene Wilder, Mel Brooks, *Young Frankenstein*

BEST ORIGINAL SCREENPLAY

- Robert Towne, *Chinatown*
  Robert Getchell, *Alice Doesn't Live Here Anymore*
  Francis Ford Coppola, *The Conversation*
  Francois Truffaut, Jean-Louis Richard, Suzanne Schiffman, *Day for Night*
  Paul Mazursky, Josh Greenfeld, *Harry and Tonto*

CINEMATOGRAPHY

- Fred Koenekamp, Joseph Biroc, *The Towering Inferno*
  John A. Alonzo, *Chinatown*
  Philip Lathrop, *Earthquake*
  Bruce Surtees, *Lenny*
  Geoffrey Unsworth, *Murder on the Orient Express*

FOREIGN-LANGUAGE FILM

- *Amarcord* (Italy)

Catsplay (Hungary)
The Deluge (Poland)
Lacombe, Lucien (France)
The Truce (Argentina)

ART DIRECTION/SET DIRECTION

- Dean Tavoularis, Angelo Graham; George R. Nelson, *The Godfather, Part II*

SOUND

- Ronald Pierce, Melvin Metcalfe, Sr., *Earthquake*

SHORT SUBJECTS

Cartoons:
- Lighthouse Productions, *Closed Mondays*

Live Action:
- C.A.P.A.C. (Paris), *One-Eyed Men Are Kings*

DOCUMENTARY

Short Subjects:
- R. A. Films, *Don't*

Features:
- BBS-Rainbow Pictures, *Hearts and Minds*

MUSIC

Best Song:
- Al Kasha, Joel Hirschhorn, "We May Never Love Like This Again," *The Towering Inferno*

Best Original Dramatic Score:
- Nino Rota, Carmine Coppola, *The Godfather, Part II*

Best Scoring: Original Song Score and/or Adaptation:
- Nelson Riddle, *The Great Gatsby*

FILM EDITING

- Harold F. Kress, Carl Kress, *The Towering Inferno*

COSTUME DESIGN

- Theoni V. Aldredge, *The Great Gatsby*

HONORARY AND OTHER AWARDS

- Howard Hawks, as a giant of the American cinema whose pictures, taken as a whole, represent one of the most consistent, vivid and varied bodies of work in world cinema
- Jean Renoir, as a filmmaker who has worked with grace, responsibility and enviable

competence through silent film, sound film, feature documentary and television
- *Earthquake*, a special achievement award for visual effects to Frank Brendel, Albert Whitlock, and Glen Robinson

JEAN HERSHOLT HUMANITARIAN AWARD

- Arthur Krim

SCIENTIFIC OR TECHNICAL AWARDS

Class II:
- Joseph D. Kelly of Glen Glenn Sound, for designing new audio control consoles for film sound recording and re-recording
- Quad-Eight Sound Corp., for engineering and constructing new audio control consoles designed by Burbank Studios Sound and Goldwyn Sound Dept.
- Waldon O Watson, Richard J. Stumpf, Robert J. Leonard and the Universal Studios Sound Dept., for their development and engineering of the "Sensurround" system
- Burbank Studios Sound Dept., for the design of new audio control consoles engineered and constructed by Quad-Eight Sound Corp.
- Samuel Goldwyn Studios Sound Dept., for the design of new audio control consoles engineered and constructed by Quad-Eight Sound Corp.

Class III:
- Elemack Company, for the introduction of the Spyder camera dolly
- Louis Ami of Universal Studios, for designing and constructing a reciprocating camera platform used for filming special visual effects

---

1975

BEST PICTURE

- *One Flew Over the Cuckoo's Nest* (Fantasy-UA)

Barry Lyndon (Warner Bros.)
Dog Day Afternoon (Warner Bros.)
Jaws (Universal)
Nashville (ABC—Paramount)

BEST DIRECTOR

☐ Milos Forman, *One Flew Over the Cuckoo's Nest*
  Robert Altman, *Nashville*
  Federico Fellini, *Amarcord*
  Stanley Kubrick, *Barry Lyndon*
  Sidney Lumet, *Dog Day Afternoon*

BEST ACTOR

☐ Jack Nicholson, *One Flew Over the Cuckoo's Nest*
  Walter Matthau, *The Sunshine Boys*
  Al Pacino, *Dog Day Afternoon*
  Maximilian Schell, *The Man in the Glass Booth*
  James Whitmore, *Give 'em Hell, Harry!*

BEST ACTRESS

☐ Louise Fletcher, *One Flew Over the Cuckoo's Nest*
  Isabelle Adjani, *The Story of Adele H.*
  Ann-Margret, *Tommy*
  Glenda Jackson, *Hedda*
  Carol Kane, *Hester Street*

BEST SUPPORTING ACTOR

☐ George Burns, *The Sunshine Boys*
  Brad Dourif, *One Flew Over the Cuckoo's Nest*
  Burgess Meredith, *The Day of the Locust*
  Chris Sarandon, *Dog Day Afternoon*
  Jack Warden, *Shampoo*

BEST SUPPORTING ACTRESS

☐ Lee Grant, *Shampoo*
  Ronee Blakley, *Nashville*
  Sylvia Miles, *Farewell, My Lovely*
  Lily Tomlin, *Nashville*
  Brenda Vaccaro, *Once Is Not Enough*

BEST SCREENPLAY (ADAPTED FROM ANOTHER MEDIUM)

☐ Laurence Hauben, Bo Goldman, *One Flew Over the Cuckoo's Nest*
  Stanley Kubrick, *Barry Lyndon*
  John Huston, Gladys Hill, *The Man Who Would Be King*

Ruggero Maccari, Dino Risi, *Scent of a Woman*
Neil Simon, *The Sunshine Boys*

BEST ORIGINAL SCREENPLAY

☐ Frank Pierson, *Dog Day Afternoon*
☐ Federico Fellini, Tonino Guerra, *Amarcord*
  Claude Lelouch, Pierre Uytterhoeven, *And Now My Love*
  Ted Allan, *Lies My Father Told Me*
  Robert Towne, Warren Beatty, *Shampoo*

CINEMATOGRAPHY

  John Alcott, *Barry Lyndon*
  Conrad Hall, *The Day of the Locust*
  James Wong Howe, *Funny Lady*
  Robert Surtees, *The Hindenburg*
  Haskell Wexler, Bill Butler, *One Flew Over the Cuckoo's Nest*

FOREIGN-LANGUAGE FILM

☐ *Dersu Uzala* (USSR)
  Land of Promise (Poland)
  Letters from Marusia (Mexico)
  Sandakan House #8 (Japan)
  Scent of a Woman (Italy)

ART DIRECTION/SET DIRECTION

☐ Ken Adam, Roy Walker; Vernon Dixon, *Barry Lyndon*

SOUND

☐ Robert L. Hoyt, Roger Heman, Earl Madery, John Carter, *Jaws*

SHORT SUBJECTS

Cartoons:
☐ Granstern Ltd./British Lion, *Great*
Live Action:
☐ Bert Salzman Productions, *Angel and Big Joe*

DOCUMENTARY

Short Subjects:
☐ Opus Films, Ltd., *The End of the Game*
Features:
☐ Crawley Films, *The Man Who Skied Down Everest*

MUSIC

Best Song:
☐ Keith Carradine, "I'm Easy," *Nashville*
Best Original Score:
☐ John Williams, *Jaws*
Best Original Song Score and Adaptation; or Best Scoring, Adaptation only:
  Leonard Rosenman, *Barry Lyndon*

FILM EDITING

☐ Verna Fields, *Jaws*

COSTUME DESIGN

☐ Ulla-Britt Soderlund, Milena Canonero, *Barry Lyndon*

HONORARY AND OTHER AWARDS

☐ Mary Pickford, in recognition of her unique contributions to the industry and the development of film as an artistic medium
☐ The Hindenburg, for its visual effects by Albert Whitlock and Glen Robinson and its sound effects by Peter Berkos

IRVING G. THALBERG MEMORIAL AWARD

☐ Mervyn LeRoy

JEAN HERSHOLT HUMANITARIAN AWARD

☐ Jules Stein

SCIENTIFIC OR TECHNICAL AWARDS

Class II:
☐ Chadwell O'Connor of the O'Connor Engineering Laboratories, for the concept and engineering of a fluid-damped camera-head for motion picture photography
☐ William F. Miner of Universal City Studios, for the development and engineering of a solid-state, 500-kilowatt, direct-current static rectifier for motion picture lighting
Class III:
☐ Lawrence W. Butler and Roger Banks, for the concept of applying low inertia and stepping electric motors to film transport systems and optical printers for motion picture production

☐ David J. Degenkolb and Fred Scobey of Deluxe General Incorprated, and John C. Dolan and Richard Dubois of the Akwaklame Company, for the development of a technique for silver recovery from photographic wash-waters by ion exchange

☐ Joseph Westheimer, for the development of a device to obtain shadowed titles on motion picture film

☐ The Carter Equipment Co., Inc. and Ramtronics, for the engineering and manufacture of a computerized tape punching system for programming laboratory printing machines

☐ Bell & Howell, for the engineering and manufacture of a computerized tape punching system for programming laboratory printing machines

☐ Fredrik Schlyter, for the engineering and manufacture of a computerized tape punching system for programming laboratory printing machines

☐ Hollywood Film Co., for the engineering and manufacture of a computerized tape punching system for programming laboratory printing machines

1976

BEST PICTURE
☐ Rocky (Chartoff—Winkler-UA)
All the President's Men (Wildwood-Warner)
Bound for Glory (UA)
Network (MGM-UA)
Taxi Driver (Columbia)

BEST DIRECTOR
☐ John G. Avildsen, Rocky
Alan J. Pakula, All the President's Men
Ingmar Bergman, Face to Face
Sidney Lumet, Network
Lina Wertmüller, Seven Beauties

BEST ACTOR
☐ Peter Finch, Network

Robert De Niro, Taxi Driver
Giancarlo Giannini, Seven Beauties
William Holden, Network
Sylvester Stallone, Rocky

BEST ACTRESS
☐ Faye Dunaway, Network
Marie-Christine Barrault, Cousin, Cousine
Talia Shire, Rocky
Sissy Spacek, Carrie
Liv Ullmann, Face to Face

BEST SUPPORTING ACTOR
☐ Jason Robards, All the President's Men
Ned Beatty, Network
Burgess Meredith, Rocky
Laurence Olivier, Marathon Man
Burt Young, Rocky

BEST SUPPORTING ACTRESS
☐ Beatrice Straight, Network
Jane Alexander, All the President's Men
Jodie Foster, Taxi Driver
Lee Grant, Voyage of the Damned
Piper Laurie, Carrie

BEST SCREENPLAY ADAPTATION
☐ William Goldman, All the President's Men
Robert Getchell, Bound for Glory
Federico Fellini, Bernardino Zapponi, Casanova
Nicholas Meyer, The Seven-Per-Cent Solution
Steve Shagan, David Butler, Voyage of the Damned

BEST ORIGINAL SCREENPLAY
☐ Paddy Chayefsky, Network
Jean-Charles Tacchella, Daniele Thompson, Cousin, Cousine
Walter Bernstein, The Front
Sylvester Stallone, Rocky
Lina Wertmüller, Seven Beauties

CINEMATOGRAPHY
☐ Haskell Wexler, Bound for Glory
Richard H Kline, King Kong
Ernest Laszlo, Logan's Run
Owen Roizman, Network
Robert Surtees, A Star Is Born

FOREIGN-LANGUAGE FILM
☐ Black and White in Color (Ivory Coast)
Cousin, Cousine (France)
Jacob, the Liar (German Democratic Republic)
Nights and Days (Poland)
Seven Beauties (Italy)

ART DIRECTION/SET DIRECTION
☐ George Jenkins; George Gaines, All the President's Men

SOUND
☐ Arthur Piantadosi, Les Fresholtz, Dick Alexander, Jim Webb, All the President's Men

SHORT SUBJECTS

Cartoons:
☐ Suzanne Baker, Film Australian Prod., Leisure
Live Action:
☐ André Guttfreund Production, In the Region of Ice

DOCUMENTARY

Short Subjects:
☐ Community Television of Southern California, Number Our Days
Features:
☐ Cabin Creek Films, producer, Harlan County U.S.A.

MUSIC

Best Song:
☐ Paul Williams, Barbra Streisand, "Evergreen," A Star Is Born
Best Original Score:
☐ Jerry Goldsmith, The Omen
Best Original Song Score:
☐ Leonard Rosenman, Bound for Glory

FILM EDITING
☐ Richard Halsey, Scott Conrad, Rocky

COSTUME DESIGN
☐ Danilo Donati, Fellini's Casanova

IRVING G. THALBERG MEMORIAL AWARD
☐ Pandro S. Berman

HONORARY AND OTHER AWARDS
☐ Carlo Rambaldi, Glen Robinson and Frank Van Der

Veer, for the visual effects of *King Kong*

☐ L.B. Abbott, Glen Robinson and Matthew Yuricich, for visual effects of *Logan's Run*

SCIENTIFIC OR TECHNICAL AWARDS

Class II:

☐ Consolidated Film Industries and the Barnebey-Cheney Co., for the development of a system for the recovery of film-cleaning solvent vapors in a motion picture laboratory

☐ William L. Graham, Manfred G. Michelson, Geoffrey F. Norman and Siegfried Seiber of Technicolor, for the development and engineering of a Continuous, High-Speed, Color Motion Picture Printing System

Class III:

☐ Fred Bartscher of the Kollmorgen Corp. and Glenn Berggren of the Schneider Corp., for the design and development of a single-lens magnifier for motion picture projection lenses

☐ Panavision, Inc., for the design and development of super-speed lenses for motion picture photography

☐ Hiroshi Suzukawa of Canon and Wilton R. Holm of the AMPTP Motion Picture and Television Research Center, for the design and development of super-speed lenses for motion picture photography

☐ Carl Zeiss Company, for the design and development of super-speed lenses for motion picture photography

☐ Photo Research Division of the Kollmorgen Corp., for the engineering and manufacture of the Spectra TriColor Meter

1977

BEST PICTURE

☐ *Annie Hall* (Rollins-Joffe,UA)

The Goodbye Girl (MGM-Warner Bros.)
Julia (20th Century-Fox)
Star Wars (20th Century-Fox)
The Turning Point (20th Century-Fox)

BEST DIRECTOR

☐ Woody Allen, *Annie Hall*
George Lucas, *Star Wars*
Herbert Ross, *The Turning Point*
Steven Spielberg, *Close Encounters of the Third Kind*
Fred Zinnemann, *Julia*

BEST ACTOR

☐ Richard Dreyfuss, *The Goodbye Girl*
Woody Allen, *Annie Hall*
Richard Burton, *Equus*
Marcello Mastroianni, *A Special Day*
John Travolta, *Saturday Night Fever*

BEST ACTRESS

☐ Diane Keaton, *Annie Hall*
Anne Bancroft, *The Turning Point*
Jane Fonda, *Julia*
Shirley MacLaine, *The Turning Point*
Marsha Mason, *The Goodbye Girl*

BEST SUPPORTING ACTOR

☐ Jason Robards, *Julia*
Mikhail Baryshnikov, *The Turning Point*
Peter Firth, *Equus*
Alec Guinness, *Star Wars*
Maximilian Schell, *Julia*

BEST SUPPORTING ACTRESS

☐ Vanessa Redgrave, *Julia*
Leslie Browne, *The Turning Point*
Quinn Cummings, *The Goodbye Girl*
Melinda Dillon, *Close Encounters of the Third Kind*
Tuesday Weld, *Looking for Mr. Goodbar*

BEST ORIGINAL SCREENPLAY

Woody Allen, Marshall Brickman, *Annie Hall*
Neil Simon, *The Goodbye Girl*
Robert Benton, *The Late Show*
George Lucas, *Star Wars*

Arthur Laurents, *The Turning Point*

BEST SCREENPLAY ADAPTATION

☐ Alvin Sargent, *Julia*
Peter Shaffer, *Equus*
Gavin Lambert, Lewis John Carlino, *I Never Promised You a Rose Garden*
Larry Gelbart, *Oh, God!*
Luis Buñuel, Jean-Claude Carriere, *That Obscure Object of Desire*

CINEMATOGRAPHY

☐ Vilmos Zsigmond, *Close Encounters of the Third Kind*
Fred J. Loenekamp, *Islands in the Stream*
Douglas Slocombe, *Julia*
William A. Fraker, *Looking for Mr. Goodbar*
Robert Surtees, *The Turning Point*

FOREIGN-LANGUAGE FILM

☐ *Madame Rosa* (France)
Iphigenia (Greece)
Operation Tunderbolt (Israel)
A Special Day (Italy)
That Obscure Object of Desire (Spain)

ART DIRECTION/SET DIRECTION

☐ Norman Reynolds and Leslie Dilley; Roger Christian, *Star Wars*

SOUND

☐ Don MacDougall, Ray West, Bob Minkler, and Derek Ball, *Star Wars*

SHORT SUBJECTS

Cartoons:
National Film Board of Canada, *Sand Castle*
Live Action:
National Film Board of Canada, *I'll Find a Way*

DOCUMENTARY

Short Subjects:
☐ Joseph Productions, *Gravity Is My Enemy*
Features:
☐ Korty Films, *Who Are the DeBolts? And Where Did They Get Nineteen Kids?*

MUSIC

Best Song:

☐ Joseph Brooks, "You Light Up My Life," *You Light Up My Life*

Best Original Score:

☐ John Williams, *Star Wars*

Best Original Song Score and Its Adaptation or Best Adaptation Score:

☐ Jonathan Tunick, *A Little Night Music*

FILM EDITING

☐ Paul Hirsch, Marcia Lucas, and Richard Chew, *Star Wars*

COSTUME DESIGN

☐ John Mollo, *Star Wars*

VISUAL EFFECTS

☐ John Stears, John Dykstra, Richard Edlund, Grant McCune and Robert Blalack, *Star Wars*

IRVING G. THALBERG MEMORIAL AWARD

☐ Walter Mirisch

JEAN HERSHOLT HUMANITARIAN AWARD

☐ Charlton Heston

SPECIAL ACHIEVEMENT AWARDS

☐ Frank Warner, for sound effects editing, *Close Encounters of the Third Kind*

☐ Benjamin Burtt, Jr., for sound effects, *Star Wars*

HONORARY AND OTHER AWARDS

☐ Margaret Booth for her exceptional contribution to the art of film editing in the motion picture industry

☐ Gordon E. Sawyer and Sidney P. Solow in appreciation for outstanding service and dedication in upholding the high standards of the Academy of Motion Picture Arts and Sciences (medal of commendation)

SCIENTIFIC OR TECHNICAL AWARDS

Class I:

☐ Garrett Brown and the Cinema Products Corp. Engineering Staff under the supervision of John Jurgens for the invention and development of Steadicam

Class II:

☐ Joseph D. Kelly, Emory M. Cohen, Barry K. Henley, Hammond H. Holt and Joseph Agalsoff of Glen Glenn Sound for the concept and development of a post-production audio processing system for motion picture films.

☐ Panavision, Inc. for the concept and engineering of the improvements incorporated in the Panaflex Motion Picture Camera.

☐ N. Paul Kenworthy, Jr and William R. Latady for the invention and development of the Kenworthy Snorkel Camera System for motion picture photography.

☐ John C. Dykstra for the development of the Dykstraflex Camera and Alvah J. Miller and Jerry Jeffress for the engineering of the Electronic Motion Control System used in concert for multiple exposure visual effects motion picture photography.

☐ Eastman Kodak Co. for the development and introduction of a new duplicating film for motion pictures.

☐ Stefan Kudelski for Nagra Magnetic Recorders, Inc for the engineering of the improvements incorporated in the Nagra 4.2L sound recorder for motion picture production.

Class III:

☐ Ernest Nettmann of the Astrovision Division of Continental Camera Systems, Inc., for the engineering of its Periscope Aerial Camera System.

☐ Electronic Engineering Co. of California for developing a method for interlocking non-sprocketed film and tape media used in motion picture production.

☐ Dr Bernhard Kuhl and Werner Block of OSRAM for the development of the HMI high-efficiency discharge lamp for motion picture lighting.

☐ Panavision, Inc., for the design of Panalite, a camera-mounted controllable light for motion picture photography.

☐ Panavision, Inc., for the enginering of the Panahead gearhead for motion picture cameras.

☐ Piclear, Inc., for originating and developing an attachment to motion picture projectors to improve screen image quality.

1978

BEST PICTURE

☐ *The Deer Hunter* (EMI/Cimino, Universal)
Coming Home (Hellman, United Artists)
Heaven Can Wait (Paramount)
Midnight Express (Columbia)
An Unmarried Woman (Twentieth Century-Fox)

BEST DIRECTOR

☐ Michael Cimino, *The Dear Hunter*
Woody Allen, *Interiors*
Hal Ashby, *Coming Home*
Warren Beatty and Buck Henry, *Heaven Can Wait*
Alan Parker, *Midnight Express*

BEST ACTOR

☐ Jon Voight, *Coming Home*
Warren Beatty, *Heaven Can Wait*
Gary Busey, *The Buddy Holly Story*
Robert De Niro, *The Deer Hunter*
Laurence Olivier, *The Boys from Brazil*

BEST ACTRESS

☐ Jane Fonda, *Coming Home*
Ingrid Bergman, *Autumn Sonata*
Ellen Burstyn, *Same Time Next Year*
Jill Clayburgh, *An Unmarried Woman*
Geraldine Page, *Interiors*

BEST SUPPORTING ACTOR

☐ Christopher Walken, *The Deer Hunter*
Bruce Dern, *Coming Home*
Richard Farnsworth, *Comes a Horseman*
John Hurt, *Midnight Express*
Jack Warden, *Heaven Can Wait*

BEST SUPPORTING ACTRESS

☐ Maggie Smith, *California Suite*
Dyan Cannon, *Heaven Can Wait*
Penelope Milford, *Coming Home*
Maureen Stapleton, *Interiors*
Meryl Streep, *The Deer Hunter*

BEST ORIGINAL SCREENPLAY

☐ Nancy Dowd (story), Waldo Salt and Robert Jones (screenplay), *Coming Home*
Woody Allen, *Interiors*
Ingmar Bergman, *Autumn Sonata*
Michael Cimino, Louis Garfinkle and Quinn K. Redeker (story) and Deric Washburn (story and screenplay), *The Deer Hunter*
Paul Mazursky, *An Unmarried Woman*

BEST SCREENPLAY ADAPTATION

☐ Oliver Stone, *Midnight Express*
Elaine May and Warren Beatty, *Heaven Can Wait*
Walter Newman, *Bloodbrothers*
Neil Simon, *California Suite*
Bernard Slade, *Same Time Next Year*

CINEMATOGRAPHY

☐ Nestor Almendros, *Days of Heaven*
Oswald Morris, *The Wiz*
William Fraker, *Heaven Can Wait*
Robert Surtees, *Same Time Next Year*
Vilmos Zsigmond, *The Deer Hunter*

FOREIGN-LANGUAGE FILM

Get Out Your Handkerchiefs (France)
The Glass Cell (West Germany)
Hungarians (Hungary)

Viva Italia! (Italy)
White Bim, The Black Ear (Soviet Union)

ART DIRECTION/SET DIRECTION

☐ Paul Sylbert, Edwin O'Donovan, George Gaines, *Heaven Can Wait*

SOUND

☐ Richard Portman, William McCaughey, Aaron Rochin, Darrin Knight, *The Deer Hunter*

SHORT SUBJECTS

Animated:
☐ National Film Board of Canada, *Special Delivery*
Live Action:
☐ New Visions, Inc. for the Children's Home Society of California, *Teenage Father*

DOCUMENTARY

Short Subjects:
☐ Shedd Production, *The Flight of the Gossamer Condor*
Features:
☐ Golden West Television Production, *Scared Straight*

MUSIC

Best Song:
☐ Paul Jabara, "Last Dance," *Thank God, It's Friday*
Best Original Score:
☐ Giorgio Moroder, *Midnight Express*
Best Original Song Score and Its Adaptation, or Best Adaptation Score:
☐ Joe Renzetti, *The Buddy Holly Story*

FILM EDITING

☐ Peter Zinner, *The Deer Hunter*

COSTUME DESIGN

☐ Anthony Powell, *Death on the Nile*

JEAN HERSHOLT HUMANITARIAN AWARD

☐ Leo Jaffe

SPECIAL ACHIEVEMENT

☐ Les Bowie, Colin Chilvers, Denys Coops, Roy Field, Derek Meddings, and Zoran Perisic for the visual effects in *Superman*

HONORARY AND OTHER AWARDS

☐ The Museum of Modern Art, for its inestimable service to the motion picture industry in its recognition of film as an art form and its continuing archival activity in the preservation and presentation of historic films.
☐ King Vidor, for his incomparable achievements as a cinematic creator and innovator.
☐ Walter Lanz, for bringing joy and laughter to every part of the world through his unique animated motion pictures.
☐ Sir Laurence Olivier, for the full body of his work, for the unique achievement of his entire career, and his lifetime contribution to the art of film.

SCIENTIFIC OR TECHNICAL AWARDS

Academy Award of Merit:
☐ Eastman Kodak Co., for the research and development of a Duplicating Color Film for motion pictures
☐ Stefan Kudelski of Nagra Magnetic Recorders, Inc., for the continuing research, design and development of the Nagra Production Sound Recorder for motion pictures.
☐ Panavision, Inc., and its engineering staff under the direction of Robert E. Gottschalk, for the concept, design and continuous development of the Panaflex Motion Picture Camera System
Scientific and Engineering Award:
☐ Ray M. Dolby, Ioan R. Allen, David P. Robinson, Stephen M. Katz, and Philip S. J. Boole of Dolby Laboratories, Inc., for the development and implementation of an improved Sound Recording and Reproducing System for motion picture production and exhibition.
Technical Achievement Award:
☐ Karl Macher and Glenn M. Berggren of Isco Optische Werke for the development and introduction of the

Cinelux-ULTRA Lens for 35mm motion picture projection.

☐ David J. Degenkolb, Arthur L. Ford, and Fred J. Scobey of DeLuxe General, Inc., for the development of a method to recycle motion picture laboratory photographic wash waters by ion exchange.

☐ Kiichi Sekiguchi of CINE-FI International for the development of the CINE-FI Auto Radio Sound System for drive-in theaters.

☐ Leonard Chapman of Leonard Equipment Co., for the design and manufacture of a small, mobile, motion picture camera platform known as Chapman Hustler Dolly.

☐ James L. Fisher of J.L. Fisher, Inc., for the design and manufactre of a small, mobile, motion picture camera platform known as the Fisher Model Ten Dolly.

☐ Robert Stindt of Production Grip Equipment Co., for the design and manufacture of a small, mobile, motion picture camera platform known as the Stindt Dolly.

1979

BEST PICTURE

☐ *Kramer vs. Kramer* (Columbia)
All That Jazz (Columbia/20th Century-Fox)
Apocalypse Now (UA)
Breaking Away (20th Century-Fox)
Norma Rae (20th Century-Fox)

BEST DIRECTOR

☐ Robert Benton, *Kramer vs. Kramer*
Bob Fosse, *All That Jazz*
Peter Yates, *Breaking Away*
Francis Ford Coppola, *Apocalypse Now*
Edouard Molinaro, *La Cage aux Folles*

BEST ACTOR

☐ Dustin Hoffman, *Kramer vs. Kramer*

Jack Lemmon, *The China Syndrome*
Al Pacino, *And Justice For All*
Roy Scheider, *All That Jazz*
Peter Sellers, *Being There*

BEST ACTRESS

☐ Sally Field, *Norma Rae*
Jill Clayburgh, *Starting Over*
Jane Fonda, *The China Syndrome*
Marsha Mason, *Chapter Two*
Bette Midler, *The Rose*

BEST SUPORTING ACTOR

☐ Melvyn Douglas, *Being There*
Robert Duvall, *Apocalypse Now*
Frederic Forrest, *The Rose*
Justin Henry, *Kramer vs. Kramer*
Mickey Rooney, *The Black Stallion*

BEST SUPPORTING ACTRESS

☐ Meryl Streep, *Kramer vs. Kramer*
Barbara Barrie, *Breaking Away*
Candice Bergen, *Starting Over*
Mariel Hemingway, *Manhattan*
Jane Alexander, *Kramer vs. Kramer*

BEST SCREENPLAY (ADAPTED FROM ANOTHER MEDIUM)

☐ Robert Benton, *Kramer vs. Kramer*
John Milius, Francis Ford Coppola, *Apocalypse Now*
Francis Veber, Edouard Molinaro, Marcello Danon, Jean Poiret, *La Cage aux Folles*
Allan Burns, *A Little Romance*
Irving Ravetch, Harriet Frank, Jr., *Norma Rae*

BEST SCREENPLAY (WRITTEN DIRECTLY FOR THE SCREEN)

☐ Steve Tesich, *Breaking Away*
Robert Alan Arthur, Bob Fosse, *All That Jazz*
Valerie Curtin, Barry Levinson, *And Justice For All*
Mike Gray, T.S. Cook, James Bridges, *The China Syndrome*
Woody Allen, Marshall Brickman, *Manhattan*

CINEMATOGRAPHY

☐ Vittorio Storaro, *Apocalypse Now*
Giuseppe Rotunno, *All That Jazz*
Frank Phillips, *The Black Hole*
Nestor Almendros, *Kramer vs. Kramer*
William A. Fraker, *1941*

FOREIGN-LANGUAGE FILM

☐ *The Tin Drum* (West Germany)
The Maids of Wilko (Poland)
A Simple Story (France)
Mama Turns a Hundred (Spain)
To Forget Venice (Italy)

ART DIRECTION

☐ Philip Rosenberg, Tony Walton; Edward Stewart, Gary Brink, *All That Jazz*

SOUND

☐ Walter Murch, Mark Berger, Richard Beggs, Nat Boxer, *Apocalypse Now*

SHORT SUBJECT

Animated:
☐ National Film Board of Canada, *Every Child*
Live:
☐ Ron Ellis Films, *Board and Care*

DOCUMENTARY

Short Subject:
☐ Janus Films, *Paul Robeson: Tribute to an Artist*
Features:
☐ Ira Wohl, *Best Boy*

MUSIC

Best Song:
☐ David Shire; Norman Gimbel, "It Goes Like It Goes" *Norma Rae*
Best Original Score:
☐ George Delerue, *A Little Romance*
Best Original Song Score and its Adaptation, or Best Adaptation Score:
☐ Ralph Burns, *All That Jazz*

FILM EDITING

☐ Alan Heim, *All That Jazz*

COSTUME DESIGN

☐ Albert Wolsky, *All That Jazz*

VISUAL EFFECTS

☐ H.R. Giger, Carlo Rambaldi, Brian Johnson, Nick Allder, Denys Aling, *Alien*

HONORARY AND OTHER AWARDS

- Alec Guinness for advancing the art of screen acting through a host of memorable and distinguished performances.
- Hal Elias for unswerving dedication and distinguished and continued service to the Academy.
- Alan Splet, special achievement award, for sound effects editing, *The Black Stallion*

IRVING G. THALBERG MEMORIAL AWARD

- Ray Stark

JEAN HERSHOLT HUMANITARIAN AWARD

- Robert S. Benjamin

ACADEMY AWARD OF MERIT

- Mark Serrurier, for progressive development of the Moviola

to the present Series 20 film editing equipment.

SCIENTIFIC AND ENGINEERING AWARD

- Neiman-Tillar Associates for the creative development, and to Mini-Micro Systems, Inc. for design and engineering of an Automated Computer Controlled Editing Sound System (ACCESS) for motion picture production.

TECHNICAL ACHIEVEMENT AWARD

- A.D. Flowers and Logan R. Frazee for development of a device to control flight patterns of miniature airplane during motion picture photography.
- Photo Reserch Division of Kollmorgen Corp. for development of Spectra II Cine Special Exposure Meter for film photography.
- Michael V. Chewey, Walter G. Eggers, and Allen Hecht of MGM Laboratories and Irwing Young, Paul Kaufman and Fredrik Schlyter of DuArt Laboratories for computer-contolled paper tape programmer systems and their application in film labs.
- Paul Trester and James Stanfield for developing and manufacturing of device to repair or protect sprocket holes in films.
- Zoran Perisic of Courier Films, Ltd. for Zeptic Special Optical Effects Device for film photography.
- Bruce Lyon and John Lamb for developing Video Animation System for testing picture animation sequences.
- Rose Lowel of Lowel-Light Manufacturing Company, Inc. for developing compact light equipment for film photography.

ACADEMY RECORD-BREAKERS

MOST OSCAR-WINNING FILM:
1. *Ben-Hur* (1959), 11 awards
2. *West Side Story* (1961), 10 awards
   Gone With the Wind (1939), 10 awards including one special award.
4. *Gigi* (1958), 9 awards
5. *From Here to Eternity* (1953), 8 awards
   On the Waterfront (1954), 8 awards
   Cabaret (1972), 8 awards
8. *Bridge on the River Kwai* (1957), 7 awards
   My Fair Lady (1964), 7 awards
   Patton (1970), 7 awards
   Lawrence of Arabia (1962), 7 awards
   The Sting (1973), 7 awards

MOST NOMINATED FILM:
1. *All About Eve* (1950), 14 nominations

MOST NOMINATED FILM NOT TO WIN A SINGLE OSCAR:
1. *The Turning Point* (1977), 11 nominations, 0 Oscars
2. *The Little foxes* (1941), 9 nominations, 0 Oscars
3. *Quo Vadis* (1951), 8 nominations, 0 Oscars
   The Nun's Story (1959), 8 nominations, 0 Oscars

CLEAN-SWEEP FILMS (BEST PICTURE, BEST DIRECTOR, BEST ACTOR, AND BEST ACTRESS):
1. *It Happened One Night* (1934)
2. *One Flew Over the Cuckoo's Nest* (1975)

ONLY SHAKESPEARE FILM TO WIN BEST PICTURE:
1. *Hamlet* (1948)

ONLY WESTERN TO WIN BEST PICTURE:
1. *Cimarron* (1931/32)

FIRST REMAKE TO WIN BEST PICTURE:
1. *Ben-Hur* (1959)

FIRST SEQUEL TO WIN BEST PICTURE:
1. *The Godfather, Part II* (1974)

FIRST HORROR FILM TO BE NOMINATED FOR BEST PICTURE:
1. *The Exorcist* (1973)

FILM WITH MOST ACTING NOMINATIONS:
1. *All About Eve* (1950), 5 acting nominations
   From Here to Eternity (1953), 5 acting nominations
   On the Waterfront (1954), 5 acting nominations
   Mrs. Miniver (1942), 5 acting nominations
   Tom Jones (1963), 5 acting nominations
   Bonnie and Clyde (1967), 5 acting nominations
   The Godfather Part, II (1974), 5 acting nominations
   Network (1976), 5 acting nominations

FILM WITH MOST BEST SUPPORTING ACTRESS NOMINATIONS:
1. *Tom Jones* (1963), 3 Best Supporting Actress Nominations

FILM WITH MOST BEST SUPPORTING ACTOR NOMINATIONS:
1. *On the Waterfront* (1954), 3 Best Supporting Actor nominations
   Godfather (1972), 3 Best Supporting Actor nominations
   Godfather, Part II (1974), 3 Best Supporting Actor nominations

FILM WITH MOST BEST ACTOR NOMINATIONS:
1. *Mutiny on the Bounty* (1935), 3 Best Actor nominations

MOST OSCAR-WINNING BEST ACTRESS:
1. Katharine Hepburn, 3 Oscars: *Morning Glory* (1932/33), *Guess Who's Coming to Dinner* (1967), *The Lion in Winter* (1968)
2. Luise Rainer, 2 Oscars: *The Great Ziegfeld* (1936) and *The Good Earth* (1937)
   Bette Davis, 2 Oscars: *Dangerous* (1935) and *Jezebel* (1938)
   Vivien Leigh, 2 Oscars: *Gone With the Wind* (1939) and *Streetcar Named Desire* (1951)

Olivia De Havilland, 2 Oscars: *To Each His Own (1946) and The Heiress* (1949)

Ingrid Bergman, 2 Best Actress Oscars: *Gaslight* (1944) and *Anastasia* (1956)

Elizabeth Taylor, 2 Best Actress Oscars: *Butterfield 8* (1960) and *Who's Afraid of Virginia Woolf?* (1966)

Glenda Jackson, 2 Best Actress Oscars: *Women in Love* (1970) and *A Touch of Class* (1973)

Jane Fonda, 2 Best Actress Oscars: *Klute* (1971) and *Coming Home* (1978)

ONLY TIE FOR BEST ACTRESS:
1. 1968—Katharine Hepburn (*Lion in Winter*) and Barbra Streisand *(Funny Girl)*

MOST NOMINATED BEST ACTRESS:
1. Katharine Hepburn, 11 nominations
2. Bette Davis, 10 nominations
3. Greer Garson, 7 nominations

ONLY ACTRESSES TO WIN 2 CONSECUTIVE BEST ACTRESS OSCARS:
1. Katharine Hepburn, 1967 (*Guess Who's Coming to Dinner*) and 1968 (*Lion in Winter*)
2. Luise Rainer, 1936 (*The Great Ziegfeld*) and 1937 (*The Good Earth*)

ONLY ACTRESS TO WIN BEST ACTRESS OSCAR IN A FOREIGN-LANGUAGE FILM:
1. Sophia Loren, *Two Women* (1961)

MOST CONSECUTIVE BEST ACTRESS NOMINATIONS:
1. Bette Davis, 5 consecutive Best Actress nominations (1938-1942)

   Greer Garson, 5 consecutive Best Actress nominations (1941-1945)

MOST NOMINATED BEST ACTRESS NEVER TO WIN OSCAR:
1. Deborah Kerr, 6 Best Actress nominations, 0 Best Actress Oscars

SISTERS WHO COMPETED FOR BEST ACTRESS OSCAR:
1. Olivia De Havilland (*Hold Back the Dawn*) and Joan Fontaine (*Suspicion*) in 1941—Fontaine won.
2. Lynn Redgrave (*Georgy Girl*) and Vanessa Redgrave (*Morgan!*) in 1966—neither won

MOST OSCAR-WINNING BEST SUPPORTING ACTRESS:
1. Shelley Winters, 2 Best supporting Oscars: *Diary of Anne Frank* (1959) and *A Patch of Blue* (1965)

ACTRESSES WHO HAVE WON BOTH BEST ACTRESS AND BEST SUPPORTING ACTRESS OSCARS:
1. Ingrid Bergman: 2 Best Actress (*Gaslight*, 1944 and *Anastasia*, 1956) and 1 Best Supporting Actress (*Murder on the Orient Express*, 1974)
2. Helen Hayes: 1 Best Actress (*The Sin of Madelon Claudet*, 1931/32) and 1 Best Supporting Actress (*Airport*, 1970)
3. Maggie Smith: 1 Best Actress (*The Prime of Miss Jean Brodie*, 1969) and 1 Best Supporting Actress (*California Suite*, 1978).

ACTRESSES NOMINATED FOR BEST ACTRESS AND BEST SUPPORTING ACTRESS IN SAME YEAR:
1. Fay Bainter, nominated for Best Actress (*White Banners*) and Best Supporting Actress *(Jezebel)* in 1938—won for *Jezebel.*
2. Teresa Wright, nominated for Best Actress (*Pride of the Yankees*) and Best Supporting Actress (*Mrs. Miniver*) in 1942—won for *Mrs. Miniver.*

MOST NOMINATED BEST SUPPORTING ACTRESS:
1. Thelma Ritter, 7 Best Supporting Actress nominations

MOST NOMINATED BEST ACTOR:
1. Laurence Olivier, 9 nominations
   Spencer Tracy, 9 nominations
2. Marlon Brando, 7 nominations

MOST OSCAR-WINNING BEST ACTOR:
1. Spencer Tracy, 2 Best Actor Oscars: *Captains Courageous* (1937) and *Boys Town* (1938).

   Fredric March, 2 Best Actor Oscars: *Dr. Jekyll and Mr. Hyde* (1931/32) and *Best Years of Our Lives* (1946).

   Gary Cooper, 2 Best Actor Oscars: *Sergeant York* (1941) and *High Noon* (1952).

   Marlon Brando, 2 Best Actor Oscars: *On the Waterfront* (1952) and *Godfather* (1972).

ONLY TIE FOR BEST ACTOR:
1. 1931/32—Fredric March (*Dr. Jekyll and Mr. Hyde*) and Wallace Berry (*The Champ*)

ONLY ACTOR TO BE NOMINATED FOR BEST ACTOR AND BEST SUPPORTING ACTOR FOR SAME ROLE:
1. Barry Fitzgerald, *Going My Way* (1944). Academy rules prohibit this now.

ONLY ACTOR TO WIN TWO CONSECUTIVE BEST ACTOR OSCARS:
1. Spencer Tracy, 1937 *(Captains Courageous)* and 1938 (*Boys Town*)

ONLY ACTORS TO BE NOMINATED FOR BEST ACTOR AND BEST WRITING OSCARS:

1. Charlie Chaplin, *The Great Dictator* (1940)—didn't win either award that year.
2. Orson Welles, *Citizen Kane* (1941)—won (with Herman J. Mankiewicz) the writing award that year.
3. Sylvester Stallone, *Rocky* (1976)—didn't win either award that year.

FILM BRITISH ACTOR IN A BRITISH FILM TO WIN BEST ACTOR:

1. Charles Laughton, *The Private Life of Henry VIII* (1932/33)

ACTORS TO WIN POSTHUMOUS BEST ACTOR NOMINATIONS:

1. James Dean, *East of Eden* (1955) and *Giant* (1956)—was not awarded for either year
2. Spencer Tracy, *Guess Who's Coming to Dinner* (1967)—was not awarded for that year.
3. Peter Finch, *Network* (1976)—only posthumous Best Actor Oscar.

MOST OSCAR-WINNING BEST SUPPORTING ACTOR:

1. *Walter Brennan, 3 Best Supporting Actor Oscars: Come and Get It* (1936), *Kentucky* (1938), and *The Westerner* (1940)

MOST OSCAR-WINNING BEST DIRECTOR:

1. John Ford, 4 Best Director Oscars: *The Informer* (1935), *The Grapes of Wrath* (1940), *How Green Was My Valley* (1941), and *The Quiet Man* (1952).
2. Frank Capra, 3 Best Director Oscars: *It Happened One Night* (1934), *Mr. Deeds Goes to Town* (1936), *You Can't Take It With You* (1938).
   William Wyler, 3 Best Director Oscars: *Mrs. Miniver* (1942), *The Best Years of Our Lives* (1946), and *Ben-Hur* (1959).

DIRECTORS TO WIN BEST DIRECTING AND BEST WRITING FOR SAME FILM:

1. Joseph L. Mankiewicz, *All About Eve* (1950)
2. Joseph L. Mankiewicz, *Letter to Three Wives* (1949)
3. Billy Wilder, *The Apartment* (1960)
4. Francis Coppola, *Godfather II* (1974)
5. Woody Allen, *Annie Hall* (1977)
6. John Huston, *Treasure of Sierre Madre* (1948)
7. Billy Wilder, *The Lost Weekend* (1945)
8. Leo McCarey, *Going My Way* (1944)

DIRECTORS TO WIN TWO CONSECUTIVE BEST ACTOR OSCARS:

1. John Ford, 1940 *(Grapes of Wrath)* and 1941 (*How Green Was My Valley*)
2. Joseph L. Mankiewicz, 1949 (*Letter to Three Wives*) and 1950 (*All About Eve*)

ONLY SHARED BEST DIRECTOR OSCAR:

1. 1961, Jerome Robbins and Robert Wise, co-directors of *West Side Story*

MOST OSCAR-WINNING ART DIRECTOR:

1. Cedric Gibbons, 11 Oscars

MOST OSCAR-WINNING SET DECORATOR:

1. Edwin B. Willis, 8 Oscars

MOST OSCAR-WINNING COSTUME DESIGNER:

1. Edith Head, 8 Oscars and 34 Nominations

YOUNGEST PERSON TO WIN OSCAR:

1. Tatum O'Neal, 10 years old when she won Best Supporting Actress in 1973 for *Paper Moon*.

STUDIOS WITH MOST OSCARS FOR BEST PICTURE:

1. United Artists, 11
2. Columbia, 9
   MGM, 9
4. Twentieth Century-Fox, 7
5. *Paramount, 6*
6. Universal, 4
7. Warner Brothers, 3
8. RKO, 2

2/THE NATIONAL SOCIETY OF FILM CRITICS AWARDS

WHEN THE NATIONAL Society of Film Critics was founded in late 1966, its pronounced function was fourfold: first, to give annual recognition to the best work in films of the preceding year without distinction of nationality; second, to promote throughout the year films the Society deemed worthy of support; third, to register protest against any practice in film production, distribution or exhibition that the Society thought injurious to films or the public interest; and fourth, to serve fraternal purposes among filmmakers and film critics, American and foreign.

During its first years the National Society stressed that although its members held widely divergent views and practiced considerably different critical methods, all its members took films seriously and deemed them worthy of the highest standards of criticism. The seriousness of the Society's standards was obvious in its first awards: whereas older organizations like the New York Film Critics Circle, the National Board of Review and the Academy selected *A Man for All Seasons* as the Best Picture of 1966, the newly formed National Society chose the much more interesting and much more complicated *Blow-Up*. And in 1967, while those older groups honored films like in the *Heat of the Night* and *Far from the Madding Crowd*, the National Society gave its accolade to *Persona*. Whether the National Society was being eccentric or

avant-garde, more perceptive or more obscurantist, remained—as John Simon said in his introduction to the 1967 awards—a question for each viewer to answer.

Although the Society claimed its purpose was not to combat any previously existing series of awards, many critics believed that it was founded to counter the "middle-brow" propensities of such groups as the New York Film Critics Circle, which had for some time demonstrated the same tastes as the Academy. (Later the New York Film Critics Circle changed its membership, voting procedures and award categories to come closer to those of the National Society.)

In 1966 the National Society consisted of 11 voting members. Most of these members —despite the "National" in the Society's name—lived in New York. In 1972 the Society became a more truly national group, as the membership grew to 24 with the addition of several critics from Los Angeles, San Francisco and Chicago. These additions, however, caused John Simon to withdraw from the group as many of the newly elected fell "far below the minimal requirements of critical competence." Stanley Kauffmann also left the Society that year. The Society has continued to elect new members.

Besides Simon (*New Leader*), the original members were Hollis Alpert (*Saturday Review*); Brad Darrach (*Time*); Brendan Gill

(*The New Yorker*); Philip T. Hartung (*Commonweal*); Pauline Kael (then for *New Republic*, soon to write for *The New Yorker*); Stanley Kauffmann (then for Channel 13, soon to write for *New Republic*); Arthur Knight (*Saturday Review*); Joseph Morgenstern (*Newsweek*); Andrew Sarris (*Village Voice*); Richard Schickel (*Life*).

The voting procedure for the Society is simple and direct: on the first ballot, each critic has one vote in each category. If no candidate wins a simple majority on that first ballot, each critic then lists his or her top three choices, giving them three points, two points, and one point respectively. A simple plurality establishes the winner. The votes are not secret: for seven years the complete tabulations were published in the Society's annual anthologies, *Film 67/68*, *Film 68/69*, etc.

1966

Best Picture:
Blow Up
Best Director:
Michelangelo Antonioni
Best Actor:
Michael Caine, *Alfie*
Best Actress:
Sylvie, *The Shameless Old Lady*

1967

Best Picture:
Persona
Best Director:
Ingmar Bergman, *Persona*
Best Actor:
Rod Steiger, *In the Heat of the Night*
Best Actress:
Bibi Andersson, *Persona*
Best Supporting Actor:
Gene Hackman, *Bonnie and Clyde*
Best Supporting Actress:
Marjorie Rhodes, *The Family Way*
Best Screenplay:
David Newman and Robert Benton, *Bonnie and Clyde*
Best Cinematography:
Haskell Wexler, *In the Heat of the Night*

1968

Best Picture:
Shame
Best Director:
Ingmar Bergman, *Shame; Hour of the Wolf*
Best Actor:
Per Oscarsson, *Hunger*
Best Actress:
Liv Ullmann, *Shame*
Best Supporting Actor:
Seymour Cassel, *Faces*
Best Supporting Actress:
Billie Whitelaw, *Charlie Bubbles*
Best Cinematography:
William A. Fraker, *Bullitt*
Best Screenplay:
John Cassavetes, *Faces*
Special Awards:
Allan King's *Warrendale* and Eugene S. Jones's *A Face of War* for feature-length documentary
Yellow Submarine for feature-length animation

1969

Best Picture:
Z
Best Director:
Francois Truffaut, *Stolen Kisses*
Best Actor:
Jon Voight, *Midnight Cowboy*
Best Actress:
Vanessa Redgrave, *The Loves of Isadora*
Best Supporting Actor:
Jack Nicholson, *Easy Rider*
Best Supporting Actress:
Sian Phillips, *Goodbye, Mr. Chips*
Best Screenplay:
Paul Mazursky and Larry Tucker, *Bob & Carol & Ted & Alice*
Best Cinematography:
Lucien Ballard, *The Wild Bunch*
Special Awards:
Ivan Passer, for *Intimate Lighting*, a first film of great originality
Dennis Hopper, for *Easy Rider* as director, co-writer and co-star

1970

Best Picture:
*M*A*S*H*
Best Director:
Ingmar Bergman, *The Passion of Anna*
Best Actor:
George C. Scott, *Patton*
Best Actress:
Glenda Jackson, *Women in Love*
Best Supporting Actor:
Chief Dan George, *Little Big Man*
Best Supporting Actress:
Lois Smith, *Five Easy Pieces*

Best Screenplay:
Eric Rohmer, *My Night at Maud's*
Best Cinematography:
Nestor Almendros, *The Wild Child*; *My Night at Maud's*
Special Awards:
Donald Richie and the Film Dept. of the Museum of Modern Art, for the three-month retrospective of Japanese films
Daniel Talbot of the New Yorker Theatre, for the contribution he has made to the cinema by showing films that otherwise might not have been available to the public

1971

Best Picture:
Claire's Knee
Best Director:
Bernardo Bertolucci, *The Conformist*
Best Actor:
Peter Finch, *Sunday Bloody Sunday*
Best Actress:
Jane Fonda, *Klute*
Best Supporting Actor:
Bruce Dern, *Drive, He Said*
Best Supporting Actress:
Ellen Burstyn, *The Last Picture Show*
Best Screenplay:
Penelope Gilliatt, *Sunday Bloody Sunday*
Best Cinematography:
Vittorio Storaro, *The Conformist*
Special Award:
The Sorrow and the Pity, directed by Marcel Ophuls, a film of extraordinary public interest and distinction

1972

Best Picture:
The Discreet Charm of the Bourgeoisie

Best Director:
Luis Buñuel, *The Discreet Charm . . .*
Best Actor:
Al Pacino, *The Godfather*
Best Actress:
Cicely Tyson, *Sounder*
Best Supporting Actor:
Joel Grey, *Cabaret*
Eddie Albert, *The Heartbreak Kid*
Best Supporting Actress:
Jeannie Berlin, *The Heartbreak Kid*
Best Screenplay:
Ingmar Bergman, *Cries and Whispers*
Best Cinematography:
Sven Nykvist, *Cries and Whispers*
Richard and Hinda Rosenthal Foundation Awards:
My Uncle Antoine, directed by Claude Jutra (for a film which, although not sufficiently recognized by public attendance, has nevertheless been an outstanding cinematic achievement)
Ivan Passer, director of *Intimate Lighting*, and Robert Kaylor, director of *Derby* (for a person working in cinema whose contribution to film art has not yet received due public recognition)

1973

Best Pictures:
Day for Night
Best Director:
Francois Truffaut, *Day for Night*
Best Actor:
Marlon Brando, *Last Tango in Paris*
Best Actress:
Liv Ullmann, *The New Land*
Best Supporting Actor:
Robert De Niro, *Mean Streets*
Best Supporting Actress:
Valentina Cortese, *Day for Night*

Best Screenplay:
George Lucas, Gloria Katz and Willard Huyck, *American Graffiti*
Best Cinematography:
Vilmos Zsigmond, *The Long Goodbye*
Richard and Hinda Rosenthal Foundation Awards:
Memories of Underdevelopment, directed by Tomás Gutiérrez Alea (for a film which, although not sufficiently recognized by public attendance has nevertheless been an outstanding cinematic achievement)
Daryl Duke, director of *Payday* (to a person working in cinema whose contribution to film art has not yet received due public recognition)
Special Award:
Robert Ryan (awarded posthumously), for his performance in *The Iceman Cometh*

1974

Best Picture:
Scenes from a Marriage
Best Director:
Francis Ford Coppola, *The Conversation* and *The Godfather Part II*
Best Actor:
Jack Nicholson, *The Last Detail*; and *Chinatown*
Best Actress:
Liv Ullmann, *Scenes from a Marriage*
Best Supporting Actor:
Holger Lowenadler, *Lacombe, Lucien*
Best Supporting Actress:
Bibi Andersson, *Scenes from a Marriage*
Best Screenplay:
Ingmar Bergman, *Scenes from a Marriage*
Best Cinematography:
Gordon Willis, *The Godfather Part II* and *The Parallax View*

Special Award:
Jean Renoir

1975

Best Picture:
Nashville
Best Director:
Robert Altman, Nashville
Best Actor:
Jack Nicholson, One Flew
Over the Cuckoo's Nest
Best Actress:
Isabelle Adjani, The Story of
Adele H.
Best Supporting Actor:
Henry Gibson, Nashville
Best Supporting Actress:
Lily Tomlin, Nashville
Best Screenplay:
Robert Towne, Warren Beatty,
Shampoo
Best Cinematography:
John Alcott, Barry Lyndon
Special Award:
Ingmar Bergman's The Magic
Flute, for demonstrating
how pleasurable opera can
be on film

1976

Best Picture:
All the President's Men
Best Director:
Martin Scorsese, Taxi Driver
Best Actor:
Robert De Niro, Taxi Driver
Best Actress:
Sissy Spacek, Carrie

Best Supporting Actor:
Jason Robards, All the
President's Men
Best Supporting Actress:
Jodie Foster, Taxi Driver
Best Screenplay:
Alain Tanner, John Berger,
Jonah, Who Will Be 25 in
the Year 2000
Best Cinematography:
Haskell Wexler, Bound for
Glory

1977

Best Picture:
Annie Hall
Best Director:
Luis Buñuel, That Obscure
Object of Desire
Best Actor:
Art Carney, The Late Show
Best Actress:
Diane Keaton, Annie Hall
Best Supporting Actor:
Edward Fox, A Bridge Too Far
Best Supporting Actress:
Ann Wedgeworth, Handle
with Care
Best Screenplay:
Woody Allen and Marshall
Brickman, Annie Hall
Best Cinematography:
Thomas Mauch, Aquirre, The
Wrath of God

1978

Best Picture:
Get Out Your Handkerchiefs
Best Director:
Terrence Malick, Days of
Heaven

Best Actor:
Gary Busey, The Buddy Holly
Story
Best Actress:
Ingrid Bergman, Autumn
Sonata
Best Supporting Actor:
Richard Farnsworth, Comes A
Horseman
Robert Morley, Who's Killing
the Great Chefs of Europe?
Best Supporting Actress:
Meryl Streep, The Deer Hunter
Best Screenplay:
Paul Mazursky, An Unmarried
Woman
Best Cinematography:
Nestor Almendros, Days of
Heaven
Special Award:
Battle of Chile

1979

Best Picture:
Breaking Away
Best Director: tie
Robert Benton, Kramer vs.
Kramer
Woody Allen, Manhattan
Best Actor:
Dustin Hoffman, Kramer vs.
Kramer, Agatha
Best Actress:
Sally Field, Norma Rae
Best Supporting Actor:
Frederic Forrest, The Rose;
Apocalypse Now
Best Supporting Actress:
Meryl Streep, Kramer vs.
Kramer; Manhattan;
Seduction of Joe Tynan
Best Screenplay:
Steve Tesich, Breaking Away
Best Cinematography: tie
Caleb Sechanel, The Black
Stallion; Being There

3/THE NEW YORK FILM CRITICS AWARDS

THE NEW YORK Film Critics was founded in 1935 to recognize the finest achievements in motion pictures and to maintain the importance of film criticism. A few years after it was established, the organization came under the strong influence of Bosley Crowther, the first-string film critic of the *New York Times* who for nearly three decades was the most powerful movie reviewer in America. Crowther supported films that dealt with "significant" social issues, films like *The Lost Weekend* and *Gentleman's Agreement* that espoused general liberal causes. And unlike many of today's critics, Crowther favored Hollywood's BIG BIG products adapted from other media, films like *Ben Hur*, *Gigi*, and *West Side Story*.

Crowther's taste for serious humanism and faithful adaptation was certainly reflected in the New York Film Critics annual prizes: *Going My Way, The Best Years of Our Lives, All the King's Men, Marty* and *On the Waterfront* all won Best Picture awards during his tenure at the *Times*. Hollywood, which liked to think of itself as an active force in the betterment of America, shared Crowther's penchant for honoring its more "serious" movies: 18 of the Best Picture choices during Crowther's 28 year membership in the New York Film Critics also won the Academy vote.

In 1969, one year after Crowther left the *Times*, the New York Film Critics underwent radical changes: it invited several new critics to join (including some from the recently established National Society of Film Critics); it employed new voting procedures; it dropped the foreign-versus-domestic distinction that had hitherto been used in the Best Picture voting; and it added some new categories. These changes have made the New York Film Critics awards more similar to those of the National Society, and less like those of the Academy—since 1969 the Academy and the New York Film Critics have only agreed three times on their respective choices for Best Picture: in 1977 (*Annie Hall*), in 1978 (*The Deer Hunter*), and in 1979 (*Kramer vs. Kramer*).

The original voting procedure was this: each member voted for one nominee in each category. If on the first ballot no nominee had received two thirds of the votes of the members present or those presented by proxy, another ballot was cast. After the first two ballots, only nominees who had received two or more votes were retained for following ballots. If no nominee had received the required two-thirds majority by the sixth ballot, the winner was established by a plurality of votes. The voting was by secret ballot—only the totals given the various nominees were officially announced.

In 1969 the procedure changed to one very similar to the National Society's: on the first ballot, each critic has one vote in each category. If no candidate wins a simple majority, a second ballot is held whereby each critic lists his or her top three choices, alloting them three points, two points, and one point respectively.

1935

Best Motion Picture:
The Informer
Best Actor:
Charles Laughton, *Mutiny on the Bounty; Ruggles of Red Gap*
Best Actress:
Greta Garbo, *Anna Karenina*
Best Direction:
John Ford, *The Informer*

1936

Best Motion Picture:
Mr. Deeds Goes to Town
Best Actor:
Walter Huston, *Dodsworth*
Best Actress:
Luise Rainer, *The Great Ziegfeld*
Best Direction:
Rouben Mamoulian, *The Gay Desperado*
Best Foreign Film:
La Kermesse Héroique (France)

1937

Best Motion Picture:
The Life of Emile Zola
Best Actor:
Paul Muni, *The Life of Emile Zola*
Best Actress:
Greta Garbo, *Camille*
Best Direction:
Gregory La Cava, *Stage Door*
Best Foreign Film:
Mayerling (France)

1938

Best Motion Picture:
The Citadel
Best Actor:
James Cagney, *Angels with Dirty Faces*
Best Actress:
Margaret Sullavan, *Three Comrades*
Best Direction:
Alfred Hitchcock, *The Lady Vanishes*
Best Foreign Film:
La Grande Illusion (France)
Special Award:
Snow White and the Seven Dwarfs

1939

Best Motion Picture:
Wuthering Heights
Best Actor:
James Stewart, *Mr. Smith Goes to Washington*
Best Actress:
Vivien Leigh, *Gone With the Wind*
Best Direction:
John Ford, *Stagecoach*
Best Foreign Film:
Harvest (France)

1940

Best Motion Picture:
The Grapes of Wrath
Best Actor:
Charles Chaplin, *The Great Dictator* (award refused)
Best Actress:
Katharine Hepburn, *The Philadelphia Story*

Best Direction:
John Ford, *The Grapes of Wrath; The Long Voyage Home*
Best Foreign Film:
The Baker's Wife (France)
Special Award:
Walt Disney, *Fantasia*

1941

Best Picture:
Citizen Kane
Best Actor:
Gary Cooper, *Sergeant York*
Best Actress:
Joan Fontaine, *Suspicion*
Best Direction:
John Ford, *How Green Was My Valley*

1942

Best Motion Picture:
In Which We Serve
Best Actor:
James Cagney, *Yankee Doodle Dandy*
Best Actress:
Agnes Moorehead, *The Magnificent Ambersons*
Best Direction:
John Farrow, *Wake Island*

1943

Best Motion Picture:
Watch on the Rhine
Best Actor:
Paul Lukas, *Watch on the Rhine*
Best Actress:
Ida Lupino, *The Hard Way*
Best Direction:
George Stevens, *The More the Merrier*

1944

Best Motion Picture:
Going My Way
Best Actor:
Barry Fitzgerald, *Going My Way*
Best Actress:
Tallulah Bankhead, *Lifeboat*
Best Direction:
Leo McCarey, *Going My Way*

1945

Best Motion Picture:
The Lost Weekend
Best Actor:
Ray Milland, *The Lost Weekend*
Best Actress:
Ingrid Bergman, *Spellbound*; *The Bells of St. Mary's*
Best Direction:
Billy Wilder, *The Lost Weekend*
Special Awards:
The True Glory; The Fighting Lady (U.S. documentaries)

1946

Best Motion Picture:
The Best Years of Our Lives
Best Actor:
Laurence Olivier, *Henry V*
Best Actress:
Celia Johnson, *Brief Encounter*
Best Direction:
William Wyler, *The Best Years of Our Lives*
Best Foreign Film:
Open City (Italy)

1947

Best Motion Picture:
Gentleman's Agreement
Best Actor:
William Powell, *Life with Father; The Senator Was Indiscreet*
Best Actress:
Deborah Kerr, *Black Narcissus; The Adventuress*
Best Direction:
Elia Kazan, *Gentleman's Agreement; Boomerang*
Best Foreign Film:
To Live in Peace (Italy)

1948

Best Motion Picture:
Treasure of Sierra Madre
Best Actor:
Laurence Olivier, *Hamlet*
Best Actress:
Olivia de Havilland, *The Snake Pit*
Best Direction:
John Huston, *Treasure of Sierra Madre*
Best Foreign Film:
Paisan (Italy)

1949

Best Motion Picture:
All the King's Men
Best Actor:
Broderick Crawford, *All the King's Men*
Best Actress:
Olivia de Havilland, *The Heiress*
Best Direction:
Carol Reed, *The Fallen Idol*
Best Foreign Film:
The Bicycle Thief (Italy)

1950

Best Motion Picture:
All About Eve
Best Actor:
Gregory Peck, *Twelve O'Clock High*
Best Actress:
Bette Davis, *All About Eve*
Best Direction:
Joesph L. Mankiewicz, *All About Eve*

Best Foreign Film:
Ways of Love (Italy/France)

1951

Best Motion Picture:
A Streetcar Named Desire
Best Actor:
Arthur Kennedy, *Bright Victory*
Best Actress:
Vivien Leigh, *A Streetcar Named Desire*
Best Direction:
Elia Kazan, *A Streetcar Named Desire*
Best Foreign Film:
Miracle in Milan (Italy)

1952

Best Motion Picture:
High Noon
Best Actor:
Ralph Richardson, *Breaking the Sound Barrier*
Best Actress:
Shirley Booth, *Come Back, Little Sheba*
Best Direction:
Fred Zinnemann, *High Noon*
Best Foreign Film:
Forbidden Games (France)

1953

Best Motion Picture:
From Here to Eternity
Best Actor:
Burt Lancaster, *From Here to Eternity*
Best Actress:
Audrey Hepburn, *Roman Holiday*
Best Direction:
Fred Zinnemann, *From Here to Eternity*
Best Foreign Film:
Justice is Done (France)

1954

Best Motion Picture:
On the Waterfront
Best Actor:
Marlon Brando, *On the Waterfront*
Best Actress:
Grace Kelly, *The Country Girl; Rear Window; Dial M for Murder*
Best Direction:
Elia Kazan, *On the Waterfront*
Best Foreign Film:
Gate of Hell (Japan)

1955

Best Motion Picture:
Marty
Best Actor:
Ernest Borgnine, *Marty*
Best Actress:
Anna Magnani, *The Rose Tattoo*
Best Direction:
David Lean, *Summertime*
Best Foreign Film:
a tie between *Umberto D.* (Italy) and *Diabolique* (France)

1956

Best Motion Picture:
Around the World in 80 Days
Best Actor:
Kirk Douglas, *Lust for Life*
Best Actress:
Ingrid Bergman, *Anastasia*
Best Direction:
John Huston, *Moby Dick*
Best Foreign Film:
La Strada (Italy)
Best Writing:
S.J.Perelman, *Around the World in 80 Days*

1957

Best Motion Picture:
The Bridge on the River Kwai
Best Actor:
Alec Guinness, *The Bridge on the River Kwai*
Best Actress:
Deborah Kerr, *Heaven Knows, Mr. Allison*
Best Direction:
David Lean, *The Bridge on the River Kwai*
Best Foreign Film:
Gervaise (France)

1958

Best Motion Picture:
The Defiant Ones
Best Actor:
David Niven, *Separate Tables*
Best Actress:
Susan Hayward, *I Want to Live!*
Best Direction:
Stanley Kramer, *The Defiant Ones*
Best Foreign Film:
My Uncle (France)
Best Writing:
Nathan E. Douglas, Harold Jacob Smith, *The Defiant Ones*

1959

Best Motion Picture:
Ben-Hur
Best Actor:
James Stewart, *Anatomy of a Murder*
Best Actress:
Audrey Hepburn, *The Nun's Story*
Best Direction:
Fred Zinnemann, *The Nun's Story*
Best Foreign Film:
The 400 Blows (France)
Best Writing:
Wendell Mayes, *Anatomy of a Murder*

1960

Best Motion Picture:
a tie between *The Apartment* and *Sons and Lovers*
Best Actor:
Burt Lancaster, *Elmer Gantry*
Best Actress:
Deborah Kerr, *The Sundowners*
Best Direction:
a tie between Billy Wilder (*The Apartment*) and Jack Cardiff (*Sons and Lovers*)
Best Foreign Film:
Hiroshima, Mon Amour (France/Japan)
Best Writing:
Billy Wilder, I.A.L. Diamond, *The Apartment*

1961

Best Motion Picture:
West Side Story
Best Actor:
Maximilian Schell, *Judgment at Nuremberg*
Best Actress:
Sophia Loren, *Two Women*
Best Direction:
Robert Rossen, *The Hustler*
Best Foreign Film:
La Dolce Vita (Italy)

1962

(None)

1963

Best Motion Picture:
Tom Jones
Best Actor:
Albert Finney, *Tom Jones*
Best Actress:
Patricia Neal, *Hud*
Best Direction:
Tony Richardson, *Tom Jones*

Best Foreign Film:
8 ½ (Italy)

1964

Best Motion Picture:
My Fair Lady
Best Actor:
Rex Harrison, My Fair Lady
Best Actress:
Kim Stanley, Séance on a
Wet. Afternoon
Best Direction:
Stanley Kubrick, Dr.
Strangelove
Best Foreign Film:
That Man from Rio (France)
Best Screenwriting:
Harold Pinter, The Servant
Special Citation:
To Be Alive! (Johnson's Wax)

1965

Best Motion Pictures:
Darling
Best Actor:
Oskar Werner, Ship of Fools
Best Actress:
Julie Christie, Darling
Best Direction:
John Schlesinger, Darling
Best Foreign Film:
Juliet of the Spirits (Italy)

1966

Best Motion Picture:
A Man for All Seasons
Best Actor:
Paul Scofield, A Man for All
Seasons
Best Actress:
a tie between Elizabeth Taylor
(Who's Afraid of Virginia
Woolf?) and Lynn Redgrave
(Georgy Girl)
Best Direction:
Fred Zinnemann, A Man for
All Seasons
Best Foreign Film:
The Shop on Main Street
(Czechoslovakia)

Best Screenwriting:
Robert Bolt, A Man for All
Seasons

1967

Best Motion Picture:
In the Heat of the Night
Best Actor:
Rod Steiger, In the Heat of the
Night
Best Actress:
Edith Evans, The Whisperers
Best Direction:
Mike Nichols, The Graduate
Best Foreign Film:
La Guerre Est Finie (France)
Best Screenwriting:
David Newman, Robert
Benton, Bonnie and Clyde
Special Award:
Bosley Crowther

1968

Best Motion Picture:
The Lion in Winter
Best Actor:
Alan Arkin, The Heart is a
Lonely Hunter
Best Actress:
Joanne Woodward, Rachel,
Rachel
Best Direction:
Paul Newman, Rachel, Rachel
Best Foreign Film:
War and Peace (Russia)
Best Screenwriting:
Lorenzo Semple, Jr., Pretty
Poison

1969

Best Motion Picture:
Z
Best Actor:
Jon Voight, Midnight Cowboy
Best Actress:
Jane Fonda, They Shoot
Horses, Don't They?
Best Supporting Actor:
Jack Nicholson, Easy Rider

Best Supporting Actress:
Dyan Cannon, Bob & Carol &
Ted & Alice
Best Direction:
Costa-Gavras, Z
Best Screenwriting:
Bob & Carol & Ted & Alice (as
film, not to the individual
writers)

1970

Best Motion Picture:
Five Easy Pieces
Best Actor:
George C. Scott, Patton
Best Actress:
Glenda Jackson, Women in
Love
Best Supporting Actor:
Chief Dan George, Little Big
Man
Best Supporting Actress:
Karen Black, Five Easy Pieces
Best Direction:
Bob Rafelson, Five Easy
Pieces
Best Screenwriting:
Eric Rohmer, My Night at
Maud's

1971

Best Motion Picture:
A Clockwork Orange
Best Actor:
Gene Hackman, The French
Connection
Best Actress:
Jane Fonda, Klute
Best Supporting Actor:
Ben Johnson, The Last Picture
Show
Best Supporting Actress:
Ellen Burstyn, The Last Picture
Show
Best Direction:
Stanley Kubrick, A Clockwork
Orange
Best Screenwriting:
a tie between Peter
Bogdanovich and Larry
McMurtry for The Last
Picture Show and Penelope

Gilliatt for *Sunday Bloody Sunday*

1972

Best Motion Picture:
Cries and Whispers
Best Actor:
Laurence Olivier, *Sleuth*
Best Actress:
Liv Ullmann, *Cries and Whispers; The Emigrants*
Best Supporting Actor:
Robert Duvall, *The Godfather*
Best Supporting Actress:
Jeannie Berlin, *The Heartbreak Kid*
Best Direction:
Ingmar Bergman, *Cries and Whispers*
Best Screenwriting:
Ingmar Bergman, *Cries and Whispers*
Special Citation:
The Sorrow and the Pity, as the years's best documentary

1973

Best Motion Picture:
Day for Night
Best Direction:
Francois Truffaut, *Day for Night*
Best Actor:
Marlon Brando, *Last Tango in Paris*
Best Actress:
Joanne Woodward, *Summer Wishes, Winter Dreams*
Best Supporting Actor:
Robert De Niro, *Bang the Drum Slowly*
Best Supporting Actress:
Valentina Cortese, *Day for Night*
Best Screenwriting:
George Lucas, Gloria Katz, Willard Huyck, *American Graffiti*

1974

Best Motion Picture:
Amarcord
Best Direction:
Federico Fellini, *Amarcord*
Best Actor:
Jack Nicholson, *Chinatown* and *The Last Detail*
Best Actress:
Liv Ullmann, *Scenes from a Marriage*
Best Supporting Actor:
Charles Boyer, *Stavisky*
Best Supporting Actress:
Valerie Perrine, *Lenny*
Best Screenwriting:
Ingmar Bergman, *Scenes from a Marriage*
Special Award:
Fabiano Canosa, for his innovative programs at the First Ave.Screening Room

1975

Best Motion Picture:
Nashville
Best Direction:
Robert Altman, *Nashville*
Best Actor:
Jack Nicholson, *One Flew Over the Cuckoo's Nest*
Best Actress:
Isabelle Adjani, *The Story of Adele H.*
Best Supporting Actor:
Alan Arkin, *Hearts of the West*
Best Supporting Actress:
Lily Tomlin, *Nashville*
Best Screenwriting:
Francois Truffaut, Jean Gruault, Suzanne Schiffman, *The Story of Adele H.*

1976

Best Motion Picture:
All the President's Men

Best Direction:
Alan Pakula, *All the President's Men*
Best Actor:
Robert De Niro, *Taxi Driver*
Best Actress:
Liv Ullmann, *Face to Face*
Best Supporting Actor:
Jason Robards, *All the President's Men*
Best Supporting Actress:
Talia Shire, *Rocky*
Best Screenwriting:
Paddy Chayefsky, *Network*

1977

Best Motion Picture:
Annie Hall
Best Director:
Woody Allen, *Annie Hall*
Best Actor:
John Gielgud, *Providence*
Best Actress:
Diane Keaton, *Annie Hall*
Best Supporting Actor:
Maximilian Schell, *Julia*
Best Supporting Actress:
Sissy Spacek, *Three Women*
Best Screenplay:
Woody Allen, Marshall Brickman, *Annie Hall*

1978

Best Motion Picture:
The Deer Hunter
Best Foreign-Language Motion Picture:
Bread and Chocolate
Best Director:
Terrence Malick, *Days of Heaven*
Best Actor:
Jon Voight, *Coming Home*
Best Actress:
Ingrid Bergman, *Autumn Sonata*
Best Supporting Actor:
Christopher Walken, *The Deer Hunter*
Best Supporting Actress:
Colleen Dewhurst, *Interiors*

Best Screenwriting:
Paul Mazursky, *An Unmarried Woman*

1979

Best Motion Picture:
Kramer vs. Kramer

Best Director:
Woody Allen, *Manhattan*
Best Actor:
Dustin Hoffman, *Kramer vs. Kramer*
Best Actress:
Sally Field, *Norma Rae*
Best Supporting Actor:
Melvyn Douglas, *Being There*

Best Supporting Actress:
Meryl Strepp, *Kramer vs. Kramer; Seduction of Joe Tynan*
Best Screenplay:
Steve Tesich, *Breaking Away;*
Best Foreign Film:
The Tree of Wooden Clogs
(Ermanno Olmi, Italy)

4/THE NATIONAL BOARD OF REVIEW AWARDS

ALMOST FROM THEIR beginnings, movies were attacked for their alleged immorality. Religious and reform groups, quick to realize the seductive powers of cinema, strongly criticized the motion picture's influence on American morals and ideals. The film industry, understandably fearful of government regulations, often chose voluntary regulation rather than federal intervention. In 1908, for example, representatives of the industry asked Dr. Charles Sprague Smith (the head of a social research bureau) to establish a citizen's committee to preview films before they were exhibited in theaters. Smith's committee was founded in March 1909 and was initially named the National board of Censorship of Motion Pictures.

Through the work of a large number of volunteers in various parts of the country, the National Board examined new films and gave its opinions, suggesting possible changes whenever it thought changes necessary. Because the Board could not legally censor but merely suggest and advise, its official title was changed in 1915 to the National Board of Review of Motion Pictures.

Although the National Board was praised at first as a valuable method of avoiding official censorship through a voluntary public committee, it soon came under attack, most particularly for the fact that it was financially dependent upon the film industry itself. (A fee was required to review each film and this fee was paid by the film's producer.) In order to counter such criticism, the Board expanded its attempts to improve the artistic, moral and educational values of film patrons and producers alike.

Among these attempts was the creation in 1916 of the National Committee for Better Films, whose function was "to both liberate and formulate thought regarding motion pictures, their uses and possibilities, and the best way to achieve a free screen of the most desirable kind." The Committee issued lists of approved movies—"Pictures Boys Want and Grown-Ups Endorse," "Monthly List of Selected Pictures," "Motion Picture Aids to Sermons," etc.—in order to improve the public's taste. (Many scholars later criticized the National Board for trying to influence the public's taste instead of the studios'.) These lists were both widely distributed and used.

Although the power of the National Board was considerably diminished in 1922 when the firm industry established its own self-regulatory board under the leadership of Will H. Hays (the Motion Picture Producers and Distributors of America, Inc., now called the Motion Picture Association of America), the National Board continued its work. According to its own bylines, the National Board of Review maintains that "responsibility for good motion pictures is not the industry's alone, but is also the public's. Therefore the National Board reviews films, classifies them, disseminates information about them, and organizes audience support for them. The National Board further assists the development of the motion picture as entertainment, as education, and as art, by providing media for the expression of the public's opinions about films and their cultural and social effects."

In 1920 the Board started to award Best Film prizes in order "to increase public awareness of the meritorious aspects of movies." Later its annual awards were expanded to include lists of best American films and of best foreign movies. The Board has continued to award these prizes to the present day and is now considered the oldest of the "best picture" polls.

The awards are voted by the Board's Committee on Exceptional Films and are usually the first of the many movie prizes to be selected each year, the winners being announced in late December or early January. In 1930 and 1931 the committee listed its choices for the 10 best films alphabetically.

From 1932 to 1935 it selected one Best Film of the year and announced its nine other choices alphabetically. The following year the Board began citing the films according to the number of votes each film received.

The awards were expanded in 1937 to include acting awards, in 1943 to include directing citations, and in 1948 to include writing prizes. (Screenplay awards were later dropped.) From 1945 to 1949 the Board did not use separate categories for American and foreign films, and it has often changed its policy regarding American versus English-language movies. (These distinctions are given in the listings below.)

The Academy and the National Board have seldom seen eye to eye. Since 1934, when the Academy began using the calendar year, the Academy and the National Board have only agreed nine times on their choice for Best Film. Starting with the 1979 awards, winners were presented with a David Wark Griffith trophy.

1930

Best American Films:
All Quiet on the Western
   Front
Holiday
Laughter
The Man from Blankely's
Men Without Women
Morocco
Outward Bound
Romance
The Street of Chance
Tol'able David
Best Foreign Films:
High Treason
Old and New
Soil
Storm Over Asia
Zwei Herzen im ¾ Takt

1931

Best American Films:
Cimarron

City Lights
City Streets
Dishonored
The Front Page
The Guardsman
Quick Millions
Rango
Surrender
Tabu
Best Foreign Films:
Die Dreigroschenoper
Das Lied vom Leben
Le Million
Sous les Toits de Paris
Vier von der Infanterie

1932

Best American Films:
I Am a Fugitive from a Chain
   Gang
As You Desire Me
A Bill of Divorcement
A Farewell to Arms
Madame Racketeer
Payment Deferred

Scarface
Tarzan the Ape Man
Trouble in Paradise
Two Seconds
Best Foreign Films:
A Nous la Liberté
Der Andere
The Battle of Gallipoli
Golden Mountains
Kameradschaft
Mädchen in Uniform
Der Raub der Mona Lisa
Reserved for Ladies
Road to Life
Zwei Menschen

1933

Best American Films:
Topaz
Berkeley Square
Cavalcade
Little Women
Mama Loves Papa
The Pied Piper

She Done Him Wrong
State Fair
Three-Cornered Moon
Zoo in Budapest
Best Foreign Films:
Hertha's Erwachen
Ivan
M
Morgenroth
Niemandsland
Poil de Carotte
The Private Life of Henry VIII
Quatorze Juillet
Rome Express
Le Sang d'un Poète

1934

Best American Films:
It Happened One Night
The Count of Monte Cristo
Crime Without Passion
Eskimo
The First World War
The Lost Patrol
Lot in Sodom (a short)
No Greater Glory
The Thin Man
Viva Villa!
Best Foreign Films:
Man of Aran
The Blue Light
Catherine the Great
The Constant Nymph
Madame Bovary

1935

Best American Films:
The Informer
Alice Adams
Anna Karenina
David Copperfield
The Gilded Lily
Les Misérables
The Lives of a Bengal Lancer
Mutiny on the Bounty
Ruggles of Red Gap
Who Killed Cock Robin?
Best Foreign Films:
Chapayev
Crime and Punishment
Le Dernier Milliardaire
The Man Who Knew Too
   Much

Marie Chapdelaine
La Maternelle
The New Gulliver
Peasants
Thunder in the East
The Youth of Maxim

1936

Best American Films:
Mr. Deeds Goes to Town
The Story of Louis Pasteur
Modern Times
Fury
Winterset
The Devil Is a Sissy
Ceiling Zero
Romeo and Juliet
The Prisoner of Shark Island
Green Pastures
Best Foreign Films:
Carnival in Flanders (La
   Kermesse Héroique)
The New Earth
Rembrandt
The Ghost Goes West
Nine Days a Queen
We are from Kronstadt
Son of Mongolia
The Yellow Cruise
Les Misérables
The Secret Agent

1937

Best American Films:
Night Must Fall
The Life of Emile Zola
Black Legion
Camille
Make Way for Tomorrow
The Good Earth
They Won't Forget
Captains Courageous
A Star Is Born
Stage Door
Best Foreign Films:
The Eternal Mask
The Lower Depths
Baltic Deputy
Mayerling
The Spanish Earth
Golgotha
Elephant Boy
Rembrandt

Janosik
The Wedding of Palo
Best Acting:
   (listed alphabetically)
Harry Baur, The Golem
Humphrey Bogart, Black
   Legion
Charles Boyer, Conquest
Nikolai Cherkassov, Baltic
   Deputy
Danielle Darrieux, Mayerling
Greta Garbo, Camille
Robert Montgomery, Night
   Must Fall
Maria Ouspenskaya, Conquest
Luise Rainer, The Good Earth
Joseph Schildkraut, The Life
   of Emile Zola
Mathias Wieman, The Eternal
   Mask
Dame May Whitty, Night Must
   Fall

1938

Best English-Language Films:
The Citadel
Snow White and the Seven
   Dwarfs
The Beachcomber
To the Victor
Sing You Sinners
The Edge of the World
Of Human Hearts
Jezebel
South Riding
Three Comrades
Best Foreign Films:
La Grande Illusion
Ballerina
Un Carnet de Bal
Generals Without Buttons
Peter the First
Best Acting:
   (alphabetically)
Lew Ayres, Holiday
Pierre Blanchar, Harry Baur,
   Louis Jouvet; Raimu, Un
   Carnet de Bal
James Cagney, Angels with
   Dirty Faces
Joseph Calleia, Algiers
Chico, The Adventures of
   Chico
Robert Donat, The Citadel
Will Fyffe, To the Victor
Pierre Fresnay, Jean Gabin,
   Dita Parlo; Erich von

Stroheim, *La Grande Illusion*
John Garfield, *Four Daughters*
Wendy Hiller, *Pygmalion*
Charles Laughton; Elsa Lanchester, *The Beachcomber*
Robert Morley, *Marie Antoinette*
Ralph Richardson, *South Riding; The Citadel*
Margaret Sullavan, *Three Comrades*
Spencer Tracy, *Boys Town*

1939

Best English-Language Films:
Confessions of a Nazi Spy
Wuthering Heights
Stagecoach
Ninotchka
Young Mr. Lincoln
Crisis
Goodbye, Mr. Chips
Mr. Smith Goes to Washington
The Roaring Twenties
U-Boat 29
Best Foreign Films:
Port of Shadows
Harvest
Alexander Nevsky
The End of a Day
Robert Koch
Best Acting:
(alphabetically)
James Cagney, *The Roaring Twenties*
Bette Davis, *Dark Victory; The Old Maid*
Geraldine Fitzgerald, *Dark Victory, Wuthering Heights*
Henry Fonda, *Young Mr. Lincoln*
Jean Gabin, *Port of Shadows*
Greta Garbo, *Ninotchka*
Francis Lederer, Paul Lukas, *Confessions of a Nazi Spy*
Thomas Mitchell, *Stagecoach*
Laurence Olivier, *Wuthering Heights*
Flora Robson, *We Are Not Alone*
Michel Simon, *Port of Shadows; The End of a Day*

1940

Best American Films:
The Grapes of Wrath
The Great Dictator
Of Mice and Men
Our Town
Fantasia
The Long Voyage Home
Foreign Correspondent
The Biscuit Eater
Gone With the Wind
Rebecca
Best Foreign Film:
The Baker's Wife
Best Acting:
(alphabetically)
Jane Bryan, *We Are Not Alone*
Charles Chaplin, *The Great Dictator*
Jane Darwell, *The Grapes of Wrath*
Betty Field, *Of Mice and Men*
Henry Fonda, *The Grapes of Wrath; Return of Frank James*
Joan Fontaine, *Rebecca*
Greer Garson, *Pride and Prejudice*
William Holden, *Our Town*
Vivien Leigh, *Gone With the Wind; Waterloo Bridge*
Thomas Mitchell, *The Long Voyage Home*
Raimu, *The Baker's Wife*
Ralph Richardson, *The Fugitive*
Ginger Rogers, *The Primrose Path*
George Sanders, *Rebecca*
Martha Scott, *Our Town*
James Stewart, *The Shop Around the Corner*
Conrad Veidt, *Escape*
Best Documentary:
The Fight for Life

1941

Best American Films:
Citizen Kane
How Green Was My Valley
The Little Foxes
The Stars Look Down
Dumbo

High Sierra
Here Comes Mr. Jordan
Tom, Dick and Harry
The Road to Zanzibar
The Lady Eve
Best Foreign Film:
Pépé le Moko
Best Documentaries:
Target for Tonight
The Forgotten Village
Ku Kan
The Land
Best Acting:
(alphabetically)
Sara Allgood, *How Green Was My Valley*
Mary Astor, *The Great Lie; The Maltese Falcon*
Ingrid Bergman, *Rage in Heaven*
Humphrey Bogart, *High Sierra; The Maltese Falcon*
Gary Cooper, *Sergeant York*
Donald Crisp, *How Green Was My Valley*
Bing Crosby, *The Road to Zanzibar, Birth of the Blues*
George Coulouris, *Citizen Kane*
Patricia Collinge and Bette Davis, *The Little Foxes*
Isobel Elsom, *Ladies in Retirement*
Joan Fontaine, *Suspicion*
Greta Garbo, *Two-Faced Woman*
James Gleason, *Meet John Doe, Here Comes Mr. Jordan*
Walter Huston, *All That Money Can Buy*
Ida Lupino, *High Sierra; Ladies in Retirement*
Roddy McDowall, *How Green Was My Valley*
Robert Montgomery, *Rage in Heaven; Here Comes Mr. Jordan*
Ginger Rogers, *Kitty Foyle; Tom, Dick and Harry*
James Stephenson, *The Letter; Shining Victory*
Orson Welles, *Citizen Kane*

1942

Best English-Language Films:
In Which We Serve

One of Our Aircraft Is Missing
Mrs. Miniver
Journey for Margaret
Wake Island
The Male Animal
The Major and the Minor
Sullivan's Travels
The Moon and Sixpence
The Pied Piper
Best Foreign Films:
(none cited this year)
Best Documentary:
Moscow Strikes Back
Best Acting:
(alphabetically)
Ernest Anderson, *In This Our Life*
Florence Bates, *The Moon and Sixpence*
James Cagney, *Yankee Doodle Dandy*
Jack Carson, *The Male Animal*
Charles Coburn, *H. M. Pulham Esq.; In This Our Life; Kings Row*
Greer Garson, *Mrs. Miniver; Random Harvest*
Sydney Greenstreet, *Across the Pacific*
William Holden, *The Remarkable Andrew*
Tim Holt, *The Magnificent Ambersons*
Glynis Johns, *The Invaders*
Gene Kelly, *For Me and My Gal*
Diana Lynn, *The Major and the Minor*
Ida Lupino, *Moontide*
Bernard Miles, John Mills, *In Which We Serve*
Agnes Moorehead, *The Magnificent Ambersons*
Hattie McDaniel, *In This Our Life*
Thomas Mitchell, *Moontide*
Margaret O'Brien, *Journey for Margaret*
Susan Peters, *Random Harvest*
Edward G. Robinson, *Tales of Manhattan*
Ginger Rogers, *Roxie Hart; The Major and the Minor*
George Sanders, *The Moon and Sixpence*
Ann Sheridan, *Kings Row*
William Severn, *Journey for Margaret*
Rudy Vallee, *The Palm Beach Story*
Anton Walbrook, *The Invaders*

Googie Withers, *One of Our Aircraft Is Missing*
Monty Woolley, *The Pied Piper*
Teresa Wright, *Mrs. Miniver*
Robert Young, *H. M. Pulham, Esq.; Joe Smith; American; Journey for Margaret*

1943

Best English-Language Films:
The Ox-Bow Incident
Watch on the Rhine
Air Force
Holy Matrimony
The Hard Way
Casablanca
Lassie Come Home
Bataan
The Moon Is Down
The Next of Kin
Best Foreign Films:
(none cited this year)
Best Documentaries:
Desert Victory
Battle of Russia
Prelude to War
Saludos Amigos
The Silent Village
Best Director:
William A. Wellman, *The Ox-Bow Incident*
Tay Garnett, *Bataan; The Cross of Lorraine*
Michael Curtiz, *Casablanca; This is the Army*
Best Actresses:
Gracie Fields, *Holy Matrimony*
Katina Paxinou, *For Whom the Bell Tolls*
Teresa Wright, *Shadow of a Doubt*
Best Actors:
Paul Lukas, *Watch on the Rhine*
Henry Morgan, *The Ox-Bow Incident; Happy Land*
Cedric Hardwicke, *The Moon Is Down; The Cross of Lorraine*

1944

Best English-Language Films:
None But the Lonely Heart
Going My Way

The Miracle of Morgan's Creek
Hail the Conquering Hero
The Song of Bernadette
Wilson
Meet Me in St. Louis
Thirty Seconds Over Tokyo
Thunder Rock
Lifeboat
Best Foreign Films:
(none cited this year)
Best Documentaries:
The Memphis Belle
Attack! The Battle for New Britain
With the Marines at Tarawa
Battle for the Marianas
Tunisian Victory
Best Acting:
(alphabetically)
Ethel Barrymore, *None But the Lonely Heart*
Ingrid Bergman, *Gaslight*
Eddie Bracken, *Hail the Conquering Hero*
Humphrey Bogart, *To Have and Have Not*
Bing Crosby, *Going My Way*
June Duprez, *None But the Lonely Heart*
Barry Fitzgerald, *Going My Way*
Betty Hutton, *The Miracle of Morgan's Creek*
Margaret O'Brien, *Meet Me in St. Louis*
Franklin Pangborn, *Hail the Conquering Hero*

1945

Best Film:
The True Glory
Best Director:
Jean Renoir, *The Southerner*
Best Actress:
Joan Crawford, *Mildred Pierce*
Best Actor:
Ray Milland, *The Lost Weekend*
Best Foreign Films:
(none cited)
Ten Best Films:
(including documentaries as well as English-language features)
The True Glory

The Lost Weekend
The Southerner
The Story of G.I. Joe
The Last Chance
Colonel Blimp
A Tree Grows in Brooklyn
The Fighting Lady
The Way Ahead
The Clock

1946

Best Picture:
Henry V
Best Director:
William Wyler, *The Best Years of Our Lives*
Best Actress:
Anna Magnani, *Open City*
Best Actor:
Laurence Olivier, *Henry V*
Ten Best Films:
(including foreign)
Henry V
Open City (also voted Best Foreign-Language Film)
The Best Years of Our Lives
Brief Encounter
A Walk in the Sun
It Happened at the Inn
My Darling Clementine
The Diary of a Chambermaid
The Killers
Anna and the King of Siam

1947

Best Picture:
Monsieur Verdoux
Best Director:
Elia Kazan, *Boomerang; Gentleman's Agreement*
Best Actress:
Celia Johnson, *This Happy Breed*
Best Actor:
Michael Redgrave, *Mourning Becomes Electra*
Ten Best Films:
(including foreign)
Monsieur Verdoux
Great Expectations
Shoeshine
Crossfire
Boomerang

Odd Man Out
Gentleman's Agreement
To Live in Peace
It's a Wonderful Life
The Overlanders

1948

Best Picture:
Paisan
Best Director:
Roberto Rossellini, *Paisan*
Best Actress:
Olivia de Havilland, *The Snake Pit*
Best Actor:
Walter Huston, *Treasure of Sierra Madre*
Best Script:
John Huston, *Treasure of Sierra Madre*
Ten Best Films:
(including foreign)
Paisan
Day of Wrath
The Search
Treasure of Sierra Madre
Louisiana Story
Hamlet
The Snake Pit
Johnny Belinda
Joan of Arc
The Red Shoes

1949

Best Picture:
The Bicycle Thief
Best Director:
Vittorio De Sica, *The Bicycle Thief*
Best Actress:
(none cited this year)
Best Actor:
Ralph Richardson, *The Heiress; The Fallen Idol*
Best Script:
Graham Greene, *The Fallen Idol*
Ten Best Films:
(including foreign)
The Bicycle Thief
The Quiet One
Intruder in the Dust

The Heiress
Devil in the Flesh
Quartet
Germany
Year Zero
Home of the Brave
Letter to Three Wives
The Fallen Idol

1950

Best American Film:
Sunset Boulevard
Best Foreign Film:
The Titan
Best Director:
John Huston, *The Asphalt Jungle*
Best Actress:
Gloria Swanson, *Sunset Boulevard*
Best Actor:
Alec Guinness, *Kind Hearts and Coronets*
Best American Films:
Sunset Boulevard
All About Eve
The Asphalt Jungle
The Men
Edge of Doom
Twelve O'Clock High
Panic in the Streets
Cyrano de Bergerac
No Way Out
Stage Fright
Best Foreign Films:
The Titan
Tight Little Island
The Third Man
Kind Hearts and Coronets
Paris 1900

1951

Best American Film:
A Place in the Sun
Best Foreign Film:
Rashomon
Best Director:
Akira Kurosawa, *Rashomon*
Best Actress:
Jan Sterling, *The Big Carnival*
Best Actor:
Richard Basehart, *Fourteen Hours*

Best Script:
T. E. B. Clarke, *The Lavender Hill Mob*
Best American Films:
A Place in the Sun
Red Badge of Courage
An American in Paris
Death of a Salesman
Detective Story
A Streetcar Named Desire
Decision Before Dawn
Strangers on a Train
Quo Vadis
Fourteen Hours
Best Foreign Films:
Rashomon
The River
Miracle in Milan
Kon-Tiki
The Browning Version

1952

Best American Film:
The Quiet Man
Best Foreign Film:
Breaking the Sound Barrier
Best Director:
David Lean, *Breaking the Sound Barrier*
Best Actress:
Shirley Booth, *Come Back, Little Sheba*
Best Actor:
Ralph Richardson, *Breaking the Sound Barrier*
Best American Films:
The Quiet Man
High Noon
Limelight
Five Fingers
The Snows of Kilimanjaro
The Thief
The Bad and the Beautiful
Singin' in the Rain
Above and Beyond
My Son John
Best Foreign Films:
Breaking the Sound Barrier
The Man in the White Suit
Forbidden Games
Beauty and the Devil
Ivory Hunter

1953

Best American Picture:
Julius Caesar
Best Foreign Picture:
A Queen is Crowned
Best Director:
George Stevens, *Shame*
Best Actress:
Jean Simmons, *Young Bess; The Robe; The Actress*
Best Actor:
James Mason, *Face to Face; The Desert Rats; The Man Between; Julius Caesar*
Best American Films:
Julius Caesar
Shame
From Here to Eternity
Martin Luther
Lili
Roman Holiday
Stalag 17
Little Fugitive
Mogambo
The Robe
Best Foreign Films:
A Queen Is Crowned
Moulin Rouge
The Little World of Don Camillo
Strange Deception
Conquest of Everest

1954

Best American Picture:
On the Waterfront
Best Foreign Picture:
Romeo and Juliet
Best Director:
Renato Castellani, *Romeo and Juliet*
Best Actress:
Grace Kelly, *The Country Girl; Dial M for Murder; Rear Window*
Best Actor:
Bing Crosby, *The Country Girl*
Best Supporting Actress:
Nina Foch, *Executive Suite*
Best Supporting Actor:
John Williams, *Sabrina; Dial M for Murder*
Special Citations:
For the choreography of Michael Kidd in *Seven Brides for Seven Brothers*
For the modernization of traditional Japanese acting by Machiko Kyo in *Gate of Hell* and *Ugetsu*
For the new methods of moving puppets in *Hansel and Gretel*
Best America Films:
On the Waterfront
Seven Brides for Seven Brothers
The Country Girl
A Star Is Born
Executive Suite
The Vanishing Prince
Sabrina
20,000 Leagues Under the Sea
The Unconquered
Beat the Devil
Best Foreign Films:
Romeo and Juliet
The Heart of the Matter
Gate of Hell
Diary of a Country Priest
The Little Kidnappers
Genevieve
Beauties of the Night
Mr. Hulot's Holiday
The Detective
Bread, Love and Dreams

1955

Best American Picture:
Marty
Best Foreign Picture:
The Prisoner
Best Director:
William Wyler, *The Desperate Hours*
Best Actress:
Anna Magnani, *The Rose Tattoo*
Best Actor:
Ernest Borgnine, *Marty*
Best Supporting Actress:
Marjorie Rambeau, *A Man Called Peter; The View from Pompey's Head*
Best Supporting Actor:
Charles Bickford, *Not as a Stranger*
Special Citation:
For aerial photography in *Strategic Air Command*
Best American Films:
Marty
East of Eden

Mister Roberts
Bad Day at Black Rock
Summertime
The Rose Tattoo
A Man Called Peter
Not as a Stranger
Picnic
The Affrican Lion
Best Foreign Films:
The Prisoner
The Great Adventure
The Divided Heart
Diabolique
The End of the Affair

1956

Best American Picture:
Around the World in 80 Days
Best Foreign Picture:
The Silent World
Best Director:
John Huston, Moby Dick
Best Actress:
Dorothy McGuire, Friendly
    Persuasion
Best Actor:
Yul Brynner, The King and I;
    Anastasia; The Ten
    Commandments
Best Supporting Actress:
Debbie Reynolds, The Catered
    Affair
Best Supporting Actor:
Richard Basehart, Moby Dick
Best American Films:
Around the World in 80 Days
Moby Dick
The King and I
Lust for Life
Friendly Persuasion
Somebody Up There Likes Me
The Catered Affair
Anastasia
The Man Who Never Was
Bus Stop
Best Foreign Films:
The Silent World
War and Peace
Richard III
La Strada
Rififi

1957

Best American Picture:
The Bridge on the River Kwai
Best Foreign Picture:
Ordet
Best Director:
David Lean, The Bridge on the
    River Kwai
Best Actress:
Joanne Woodward, The Three
    Faces of Eve; No Down
    Payment
Best Actor:
Alec Guinness, The Bridge on
    The River Kwai
Best Supporting Actress:
Dame Sybil Thorndike, The
    Prince and the Showgirl
Best Supporting Actor:
Sessue Hayakawa, The Bridge
    on the River River Kwai
Special Citation:
For the photographic
    innovations in Funny Face
Best American Films:
The Bridge on the River Kwai
Twelve Angry Men
The Spirit of St. Louis
The Rising of the Moon
Albert Schweitzer
Funny Face
The Bachelor Party
Enemy Below
A Hatful of Rain
A Farewell to Arms
Best Foreign Films:
Ordet
Gervaise
Torerol
The Red Balloon
A Man Escaped

1958

Best American Picture:
The Old Man and the Sea
Best Foreign Picture:
Pather Panchali
Best Director:
John Ford, The Last Hurrah
Best Actress:
Ingrid Bergman, The Inn of
    the Sixth Happiness
Best Actor:
Spencer Tracy, The Old Man
    and the Sea; The Last
    Hurrah
Best Supporting Actress:
Kay Walsh, The Horse's Mouth

Best Supporting Actor:
Albert Salmi, The Brothers
    Karamazov; The Bravados
Special Citation:
For the valor of Robert
    Donat's last performance in
    The Inn of the Sixth
    Happiness
Best American Films:
The Old Man and the Sea
Separate Tables
The Last Hurrah
The Long Hot Summer
Windjammer
Cat on a Hot Tin Roof
The Goddess
The Brothers Karamazov
Me and the Colonel
Gigi
Best Foreign Films:
Pather Panchali
Rouge et Noir
The Horse's Mouth
My Uncle
A Night to Remember

1959

Best American Picture:
The Nun's Story
Best Foreign Picture:
Wild Strawberries
Best Director:
Fred Zinnemann, The Nun's
    Story
Best Actress:
Simone Signoret, Room at the
    Top
Best Actor:
Victor Seastrom, Wild
    Strawberries
Best Supporting Actress:
Dame Edith Evans, The Nun's
    Story
Best Supporting Actor:
Hugh Griffith, Ben-Hur
Special Citations:
To Ingmar Bergman for the
    body of his work
To Andrew Marton; and
    Yakima Canutt for their
    direction of the chariot race
    in Ben-Hur
Best American Films:
The Nun's Story
Ben-Hur
Anatomy of a Murder

The Diary of Anne Frank
Middle of the Night
The Man Who Understood
  Women
Some Like It Hot
Suddenly, Last Summer
On the Beach
North by Northwest
Best Foreign Films:
Wild Strawberries
Room at the Top
Aparajito
The Roof
Look Back In Anger

1960

Best American Picture:
Sons and Lovers
Best Foreign Picture:
The World of Apu
Best Director:
Jack Cardiff, Sons and Lovers
Best Actress:
Greer Garson, Sunrise at
  Campobello
Best Actor:
Robert Mitchum, Home from
  the Hill; The Sundowners
Best Supporting Actress:
Shirley Jones, Elmer Gantry
Best Supporting Actor:
George Peppard, Home from
  the Hill
Best American Films:
Sons and Lovers
The Alamo
The Sundowners
Inherit the Wind
Sunrise at Campobello
Elmer Gantry
Home from the Hill
The Apartment
Wild River
The Dark at the Top of the
  Stairs
Best Foreign Films:
The World of Apu
General della Rovere
The Angry Silence
I'm All Right, Jack
Hiroshima, Mon Amour

1961

Best American Picture:
Question 7
Best Foreign Picture:
The Bridge
Best Director:
Jack Clayton, The Innocents
Best Actress:
Geraldine Page, Summer and
  Smoke
Best Actor:
Albert Finney, Saturday Night
  and Sunday Morning
Best Supporting Actress:
Ruby Dee, A Raisin in the Sun
Best Supporting Actor:
Jackie Gleason, The Hustler
Best American Films:
Question 7
The Hustler
West Side Story
The Innocents
The Hoodlum Priest
Summer and Smoke
The Young Doctors
Judgment at Nuremberg
One, Two, Three
Fanny
Best Foreign Films:
The Bridge
La Dolce Vita
Two Women
Saturday Night and Sunday
  Morning
A Summer to Remember

1962

**Best English-Language
Picture:**
The Longest Day
**Best Foreign-Language
Picture:**
Sundays and Cybele
Best Director:
David Lean, Lawrence of
  Arabia
Best Actress:
Anne Bancroft, The Miracle
  Worker
Best Actor:
Jason Robards, Long Day's
  Journey into Night and
  Tender Is the Night
Best Supporting Actress:
Angela Lansbury, The
  Manchurian Candidate and
  All Fall Down

Best Supporting Actor:
Burgess Meredith, Advise and
  Consent
Best English-Language Films:
The Longest Day
Billy Budd
The Miracle Worker
Lawrence of Arabia
Long Day's Journey Into Night
Whistle Down the Wind
Requiem for a Heavyweight
A Taste of Honey
Birdman of Alcatraz
War Hunt
**Best Foreign-Language
Films:**
Sundays and Cybele
Barabbas
Divorce—Italian Style
The Island
Through a Glass Darkly

1963

**Best English-Language
Picture:**
Tom Jones
**Best Foreign-Language
Picture:**
8½
Best Director:
Tony Richardson, Tom Jones
Best Actress:
Patricia Neal, Hud
Best Actor:
Rex Harrison, Cleopatra
Best Supporting Actress:
Margaret Rutherford, The
  V.I.P.s
Best Supporting Actor:
Melvyn Douglas, Hud
Best English-Language Films:
Tom Jones
Lilies of the Field
All the Way Home
Hud
This Sporting Life
Lord of the Flies
The L-Shaped Room
The Great Escape
How the West Was Won
The Cardinal
**Best Foreign-Language
Films:**
8½
The Four Days of Naples

Winter Light
The Leopard
Any Number Can Win

1964

Best English-Language Picture:
Becket
Best Foreign-Language Picture:
World Without Sun
Best Director:
Desmond Davis, *The Girl with Green Eyes*
Best Actress:
Kim Stanley, *Séance on a Wet Afternoon*
Best Actor:
Anthony Quinn, *Zorba the Greek*
Best Supporting Actress:
Edith Evans, *The Chalk Garden*
Best Supporting Actor:
Martin Balsam, *The Carpetbaggers*
Best English-Language Films:
Becket
My Fair Lady
The Girl with Green Eyes
The World of Henry Orient
Zorba the Greek
Topkapi
The Chalk Garden
The Finest Hours
Four Days in November
Séance on a Wet Afternoon
Best Foreign-Language Films:
World Without Sun
The Organizer
Anatomy of a Marriage
Seduced and Abandoned
Yesterday, Today and Tomorrow

1965

Best English-Language Picture:
The Eleanor Roosevelt Story
Best Foreign-Language Story:
Juliet of the Spirits
Best Director:
John Schlesinger, *Darling*

Best Actress:
Julie Christie, *Darling; Doctor Zhivago*
Best Actor:
Lee Marvin, *Cat Ballou; Ship of Fools*
Best Supporting Actress:
Joan Blondell, *The Cincinnati Kid*
Best Supporting Actor:
Harry Andrews, *The Agony and the Ecstasy; The Hill*
Best English-Language Films:
The Eleanor Roosevelt Story
The Agony and the Ecstasy
Doctor Zhivago
Ship of Fools
The Spy Who Came In From the Cold
Darling
The Greatest Story Ever Told
A Thousand Clowns
The Train
The Sound of Music
Best Foreign-Language Films:
Juliet of the Spirits
The Overcoat
La Bohème
La Tia Tula
Gertrud

1966

Best English-Language Picture:
A Man for All Seasons
Best Foreign-Language Picture:
The Sleeping Car Murders
Best Director:
Fred Zinnemann, *A Man for All Seasons*
Best Actress:
Elizabeth Taylor, *Who's Afraid of Virginia Woolf?*

Best Actor:
Paul Scofield, *A Man for All Seasons*
Best Supporting Actress:
Vivien Merchant, *Alfie*
Best Supporting Actor:
Robert Shaw, *A Man for All Seasons*
Best English-Language Films:
A Man for All Seasons
Born Free
Alfie

Who's Afraid of Virginia Woolf?
The Bible
Georgy Girl
Years of Lightning, Day of Drums
It Happened Here
The Russians Are Coming, The Russians Are Coming
Shakespeare Wallah
Best Foreign-Language Films:
The Sleeping Car Murders
The Gospel According to St. Matthew
The Shameless Old Lady
A Man and a Woman
Hamlet

1967

Best English-Language Picture:
Far from the Madding Crowd
Best Foreign-Language Picture:
Elvira Madigan
Best Director:
Richard Brooks, *In Cold Blood*
Best Actress:
Edith Evans, *The Whisperers*
Best Actor:
Peter Finch, *Far from the Madding Crowd*
Best Supporting Actress:
Marjorie Rhodes, *The Family Way*
Best Supporting Actor:
Paul Ford, *The Comedians*
Best English-Language Films:
Far from the Madding Crowd
The Whisperers
Ulysses
In Cold Blood
The Family Way
The Taming of the Shrew
Doctor Dolittle
The Graduate
The Comedians
Accident
Best Foreign-Language Films:
Elvira Madigan
The Hunt
Africa Addio
Persona
The Great British Train Robbery

1968

Best English-Language Picture:
The Shoes of the Fisherman
Best Foreign-Language Picture:
War and Peace
Best Director:
Franco Zeffirelli, *Romeo and Juliet*
Best Actress:
Liv Ullmann, *Hour of the Wolf* and *Shame*
Best Actor:
Cliff Robertson, *Charly*
Best Supporting Actress:
Virginia Maskell, *Interlude*
Best Supporting Actor:
Leo McKern, *The Shoes of the Fisherman*
Best English-Language Films:
The Shoes of the Fisherman
Romeo and Juliet
Yellow Submarine
Charly
Rachel, Rachel
The Subject Was Roses
The Lion in Winter
Planet of the Apes
Oliver
2001: A Space Odyssey
Best Foreign-Language Films:
War and Peace
Hagbard and Signo
Hunger
The Two of Us
The Bride Wore Black

1969

Best English-Language Picture:
They Shoot Horses, Don't They?
Best Foreign-Language Picture:
Shame
Best Director:
Alfred Hitchcock, *Topaz*
Best Actress:
Geraldine Page, *Trilogy*
Best Actor:
Peter O'Toole, *Goodbye, Mr. Chips*

Best Supporting Actress:
Pamela Franklin, *The Prime of Miss Jean Brodie*
Best Supporting Actor:
Philippe Noiret, *Topaz*
Best English-Language Films:
They Shoot Horses, Don't They?
Ring of Bright Water
Topaz
Goodbye, Mr. Chips
Battle of Britain
The Loves of Isadora
The Prime of Miss Jean Brodie
Support Your Local Sheriff
True Grit
Midnight Cowboy
Best Foreign-Language Films:
Shame
Stolen Kisses
The Damned
La Femme Infidèle
Adalen '31

1970

Best English-Language Picture:
Patton
Best Foreign-Language Picture:
The Wild Child
Best Director:
Francois Truffaut, *The Wild Child*
Best Actress:
Glenda Jackson, *Women in Love*
Best Actor:
George C. Scott, *Patton*
Best Supporting Actress:
Karen Black, *Five Easy Pieces*
Best Supporting Actor:
Frank Langella, *Diary of a Mad Housewife*; *The Twelve Chairs*
Best English-Language Films:
Patton
Kes
Women in Love
Five Easy Pieces
Ryan's Daughter
I Never Sang for My Father
Diary of a Mad Housewife
Love Story
The Virgin and the Gypsy
Toral Toral Toral

Best Foreign-Language Films:
The Wild Child
My Night at Maud's
The Passion of Anna
The Confession
This Man Must Die

1971

Best English-Language Picture:
Macbeth
Best Foreign-Language Picture:
Claire's Knee
Best Director:
Ken Russell, *The Devils and The Boy Friend*
Best Actress:
Irene Papas, *The Trojan Women*
Best Actor:
Gene Hackman, *The French Connection*
Best Supporting Actress:
Cloris Leachman, *The Last Picture Show*
Best Supporting Actor:
Ben Johnson, *The Last Picture Show*
Best English-Language Films:
Macbeth
The Boy Friend
One Day in the Life of Ivan Denisovich
The French Connection
The Last Picture Show
Nicholas and Alexandra
Best Actor:
Gene Hackman, *The French Connection*
Best Supporting Actress:
Cloris Leachman, *The Last Picture Show*
Best Supporting Actor:
Ben Johnson, *The Last Picture Show*
Best English-Language Films:
Macbeth
The Boy Friend
One Day in the Life of Ivan Denisovich
The French Connection
The Last Picture Show
Nicholas and Alexandra
The Go-Between
King Lear

*Peter Rabbit and Tales of
  Beatrix Potter*
**Best Foreign-Language
Films:**
*Claire's Knee
Bed and Board
The Clowns
The Garden of the
  Finzi-Continis
The Conformist*

1972

**Best English-Language
Picture:**
Cabaret
**Best Foreign-Language
Picture:**
The Sorrow and the Pity
Best Director:
Bob Fosse, *Cabaret*
Best Actress:
Cicely Tyson, *Sounder*
Best Actor:
Peter O'Toole, *The Ruling
  Class; Man of La Mancha*
Best Supporting Actress:
Marisa Berenson, *Cabaret*
Best Supporting Actor:
Joel Grey, *Cabaret*
Al Pacino, *The Godfather*
Best English-Language Films:
*Cabaret
Man of La Mancha
The Godfather
Sounder
1776
The Effect of Gamma Rays on
  Man-in-the-Moon Marigolds
Deliverance
The Ruling Class
The Candidate
Frenzy*
**Best Foreign-Language
Films:**
*The Sorrow and the Pity
The Emigrants
The Discreet Charm of the
  Bourgeoisie
Chloë in the Afternoon
Uncle Vanya*

1973

**Best English-Language
Picture:**
The Sting

**Best Foreign-Language
Picture:**
Cries and Whispers
Best Director:
Ingmar Bergman, *Cries and
  Whispers*
Best Actress:
Liv Ullmann, *The New Land*
Best Actor:
Al Pacino, *Serpico*
Robert Ryan, *The Iceman
  Cometh*
Best Supporting Actress:
Sylvia Sidney, *Summer
  Wishes, Winter Dreams*
Best Supporting Actor:
John Houseman, *The Paper
  Chase*
Special Citations:
American Film Theatre; Ely
  Landau
Woody Allen for his script
  Sleeper
Walt Disney Productions for
  Robin Hood
Paramount for *Charlotte's
  Web*
Best English-Language Films:
*The Sting
Paper Moon
The Homecoming
Bang the Drum Slowly
Serpico
O Lucky Man
The Last American Hero
The Hireling
The Day of the Dolphin
The Way We Were*
**Best Foreign-Language
Films:**
*Cries and Whispers
Day for Night
The New Land
The Tall Blond Man with One
  Black Shoe
Alfredo, Alfredo
Traffic*

1974

**Best English-Language
Picture:**
The Conversation
**Best Foreign-Language
Picture:**
Amarcord
Best Director:
Francis Ford Coppola, *The
  Conversation*

Best Actress:
Gena Rowlands, *A Woman
  Under the Influence*
Best Actor:
Gene Hackman, *The
  Conversation*
Best Supporting Actress:
Valerie Perrine, *Lenny*
Best Supporting Actor:
Holger Lowenadler, *Lacombe,
  Lucien*
Best English-Language Films:
*The Conversation
Murder on the Orient Express
Chinatown
The Last Detail
Harry and Tonto
A Woman Under the
  Influence
Thieves Like Us
Lenny
Daisy Miller
The Three Musketeers*
**Best Foreign-Language
Films:**
*Amarcord
Lacombe, Lucien
Scenes from a Marriage
The Phantom of Liberté
The Pedestrian*
Special Citations:
Special effects in *The Golden
  Voyage of Sinbad;
  Earthquake; Towering
  Inferno*
The film industry for increasing
  care in subsidiary casting of
  many films
Robert G. Youngson for his
  twenty-five-year work with
  tasteful and intelligent
  compilation of films

1975

**Best English-Language
Picture:**
*Nashville
Barry Lyndon*
**Best Foreign-Language
Picture:**
The Story of Adele H.
Best Director:
Robert Altman, *Nashville*
Stanley Kubrick, *Barry Lyndon*
Best Actress:
Isabelle Adjani, *The Story of
  Adele H.*

Best Actor:
Jack Nicholson, *One Flew Over the Cuckoo's Nest*
Best Supporting Actress:
Ronee Blakley, *Nashville*
Best Supporting Actor:
Charles Durning, *Dog Day Afternoon*
Special Citation:
Ingmar Bergman's *The Magic Flute*, outstanding in its translation of opera to screen
Best English-Language Films:
Barry Lyndon
Nashville
Conduct Unbecoming
One Flew OVer the Cuckoo's Nest
Lies My Father Told Me
Dog Day Afternoon
Day of the Locust
The Passenger
Hearts of the West
Farewell, My Lovely
Alice Doesn't Live Here Anymore
Best Foreign-Language Films:
The Story of Adele H.
A Brief Vacation
A Special Section
Stavisky
Swept Away

1976

Best English-Language Picture:
All the President's Men
Best Foreign-Language Picture:
The Marquise of O
Best Director:
Alan Pakula, *All the President's Men*
Best Actress:
Liv Ullmann, *Face to Face*
Best Actor:
David Carradine, *Bound for Glory*
Best Supporting Actress:
Talia Shire, *Rocky*
Best Supporting Actor:
Jason Robards, *All the President's Men*

Best English-Language Films
All the President's Men
Network
Rocky
The Last Tycoon
The Seven-Per-Cent Solution
The Front
The Shootist
Family Plot
Silent Movie
Obsession
Best Foreign-Language Films
The Marquise of O
Face to Face
Small Change
Cousin, Cousine
The Clockmaker

1977

Best English-Language Picture:
The Turning Point
Best Foreign-Language Picture:
That Obscure Object of Desire
Best Director:
Luis Buñuel, *That Obscure Object of Desire*
Best Actress:
Anne Bancroft, *The Turning Point*
Best Actor:
John Travolta, *Saturday Night Fever*
Best Supporting Actress:
Diane Keaton, *Annie Hall*
Best Supporting Actor:
Tom Skerritt, *The Turning Point*
Best English-Language Films:
The Turning Point
Annie Hall
Julia
Star Wars
Close Encounters of the Third Kind
The Late Show
Saturday Night Fever
Equus
The Picture Show Man
Harlan County, U.S.A.
Best Foreign-Language Films:
That Obscure Object of Desire
The Man Who Loved Women

A Special Day
Cria
The American Friend
Special Awards:
Walt Disney Studios for restoring and upgrading animation in *The Rescuers*
Columbia Pictures for special effects in *Close Encounters of the Third Kind*

1978

Best English-Language Picture:
Days of Heaven
Best Foreign-Language Picture:
Autumn Sonata
Best Director:
Ingmar Bergman, *Autumn Sonata*
Best Actress:
Ingrid Bergman, *Autumn Sonata*
Best Actor:
Laurence Olivier, *The Boys From Brazil*
Jon Voight, *Coming Home*
Best Supporting Actress:
Angela Lansbury, *Death on the Nile*
Best Supporting Actor:
Richard Farnsworth, *Comes A Horseman*
Best English-Language Films:
Days of Heaven
Coming Home
Interiors
Superman
Movie Movie
Midnight Express
An Unmarried Woman
Pretty Baby
Girl Friends
Comes A Horseman
Best Foreign-Language Films:
Autumn Sonata
Dear Detective
Madame Rosa
A Slave of Love
Bread and Chocolate

1979

Best English-Language Picture:
Manhattan
Best Foreign-Language Picture:
La Cage Aux Folles
Best Director:
John Schlesinger, *Yanks*
Best Actress:
Sally Field, *Norma Rae*
Best Actor:
Peter Sellers, *Being There*

Best Supporting Actress:
Meryl Streep, *Manhattan*;
  Kramer vs. Kramer;
  Seduction of Joe Tynan
Best Supporting Actor:
Paul Dooley, *Breaking Away*
Best English-Language Films:
Manhattan
Yanks
The Europeans
The China Syndrome
Breaking Away
Apocalypse Now
Being There
Time After Time
North Dallas Forty
Kramer vs. Kramer

Best Foreign-Language Films:
La Cage Aux Folles
The Tree of Wooden Clogs
The Marriage of Maria Braun
Nosferatu
Peppermint Soda
Special Awards:
Ira Wohl, *Best Boy*, "for his extraordinary moving film about family love and sacrifice, his feature-length directorial debut."
Myrna Loy, in "grateful recognition for her outstanding contribution to the art of screen acting."

5/THE GOLDEN GLOBE AWARDS

THE HOLLYWOOD FOREIGN PRESS Association, established in 1940, is an association of foreign journalists who cover the entertainment industries in Los Angeles. In 1944 the association presented its first Golden Globe Awards, honoring film achievements of 1943, and the awards have been presented annually ever since.

There are now more than 80 active members in the association, representing some 100 million readers in over 50 countries. All members vote both for the nominees and winners in the various categories.

Although modeled on the Academy Awards, the Golden Globe categories do differ in several respects. For one thing, the Best Film and Best Actor/Actress categories are subdivided into one award for Drama and another for Comedy/Musical. (Many feel this is a legitimate distinction and have urged the Academy to make a similar division.) Secondly, film Golden Globes are given in several popular categories for which there are no corresponding prizes in the Oscars: starting with the 1949 awards, for example, promising newcomers have been honored; and since the 1950 prizes, World Film Favorites have been selected. And thirdly, since 1955 the Golden Globes have honored achievements in television as well as cinema. (Television Golden Globes are not listed here. For a few years the Association announced awards for achievements in the recording industry. Like the TV prizes, there are not listed below.)

The Golden Globes and the Academy Awards have coincided regularly in their selections. In its choice for Best Film, for example, the Golden Globes in 37 years of awards have only disagreed 10 times with the Academy. For Best Actor, the Golden Globes and the Oscars have concurred on 29 occasions; for Best Actress, on 21. (These statistics take into account the Golden Globe's subdivided categories.)

The Golden Globes are usually announced in late January-early February.

1943

Best Motion Picture—Drama:
The Song of Bernadette
Best Actress:
Jennifer Jones, *The Song of Bernadette*
Best Actor:
Paul Lukas, *Watch on the Rhine*

1944

Best Motion Picture—Drama:
Going My Way
Best Actress:
Ingrid Bergman, *The Bells of St. Mary's*
Best Actor:
Alexander Knox, *President Wilson*

1945

Best Motion Picture—Drama:
The Lost Weekend
Best Actress:
Ingrid Bergman, *Gaslight*
Best Actor:
Ray Milland, *The Lost Weekend*
Best Supporting Actress:
Angela Lansbury, *Gaslight*

Best Supporting Actor:
J. Carroll Naish, *Gaslight*

1946

Best Motion Picture—Drama:
The Best Years of Our Lives
Best Director:
Frank Capra, *It's a Wonderful Life*
Best Actress:
Rosalind Russell, *Sister Kenny*
Best Actor:
Gregory Peck, *The Yearling*
Best Supporting Actress:
Anne Baxter, *The Razor's Edge*
Best Supporting Actor:
Clifton Webb, *The Razor's Edge*
Best Film Promoting International Understanding:
The Last Chance (Switzerland)
Award for Best Nonprofessional Acting:
Harold Russell, *The Best Years of Our Lives*

1947

Best Motion Picture—Drama:
Gentleman's Agreement
Best Director:
Elia Kazan, *Gentleman's Agreement*
Best Actress:
Rosalind Russell, *Mourning Becomes Electra*
Best Actor:
Ronald Colman, *A Double Life*
Best Supporting Actress:
Celeste Holm, *Gentleman's Agreement*
Best Supporting Actor:
Edmund Gwenn, *Miracle on 34th Street*
Most Promising Female Newcomer:
Lois Maxwell, *That Hagen Girl*
Most Promising Male Newcomer:
Richard Widmark, *Kiss of Death*
Best Screenplay:
George Seaton, *Miracle on 34th Street*
Best Score:
Max Steiner, *Life with Father*

Best Cinematography:
Jack Cardiff, *Black Narcissus*
Special Award to Best Juvenile Actor:
Dean Stockwell, *Gentleman's Agreement*
Special Award for Furthering the Influence of the Screen:
Walt Disney, *Bambi* (the Hindustani version)

1948

Best Motion Picture—Drama:
Treasure of Sierra Madre
Johnny Belinda
Best Motion Picture—Foreign:
Hamlet (England)
Best Director:
John Huston, *Treasure of Sierra Madre*
Best Actress:
Jane Wyman, *Johnny Belinda*
Best Actor:
Laurence Olivier, *Hamlet*
Best Supporting Actress:
Ellen Corby, *I Remember Mama*
Best Supporting Actor:
Walter Huston, *Treasure of Sierra Madre*
Best Screenplay:
Richard Schweizer, *The Search*
Best Score:
Brian Easdale, *The Red Shoes*
Best Cinematograpy:
Gabriel Figueroa, *The Pearl*
Best Film Promoting International Understanding:
The Search
Special Award to Best Juvenile Actor:
Ivan Yandl, *The Search*

1949

Best Motion Picture—Drama:
All the King's Men
Best Foreign Film:
The Bicycle Thief (Italy)
Best Director:
Robert Rossen, *All the King's Men*

Best Actress:
Olivia de Havilland, *The Heiress*
Best Actor:
Broderick Crawford, *All the King's Men*
Best Supporting Actress:
Mercedes McCambridge, *All the King's Men*
Best Supporting Actor:
James Whitmore, *Battleground*
Most Promising Female Newcomer:
Mercedes McCambridge, *All the King's Men*
Most Promising Male Newcomer:
Richard Todd, *The Hasty Heart*
Best Screenplay:
Robert Pirosh, *Battleground*
Best Score:
Johnny Green, *The Inspector General*
Best Cinematography—Black-and-White:
Frank Planer, *Champion*
Best Cinematography—Color:
Walt Disney Studios, *Ichabod & Mr. Toad*
Best Film Promoting International Understanding:
The Hasty Heart

1950

Best Motion Picture—Drama:
Sunset Boulevard
Best Director:
Billy Wilder, *Sunset Boulevard*
Best Actress—Drama:
Gloria Swanson, *Sunset Boulevard*
Best Actor—Drama:
Jose Ferrer, *Cyrano de Bergerac*
Best Actress—Musical/Comedy:
Judy Holliday, *Born Yesterday*
Best Actor—Musical/Comedy:
Fred Astaire, *Three Little Words*
Best Supporting Actress:
Josephine Hull, *Harvey*
Best Supporting Actor:
Edmund Gwenn, *Mister 880*

Most Promising Newcomer:
Gene Nelson, *Tea for Two*
Best Screenplay:
Joseph Mankiewicz, *All About Eve*
Best Score:
Franz Waxman, *Sunset Boulevard*
Best Cinematography—Black-and-White:
Frank Planer, *Cyrano de Bergerac*
Best Cinematography—Color:
Robert Surtees, *King Solomon's Mines*
Best Film Promoting International Understanding:
Broken Arrow
World Film Favorite—Female:
Jane Wyman
World Film Favorite—Male:
Gregory Peck

1951

Best Motion Picture—Drama:
A Place in the Sun
Best Motion Picture—Musical/Comedy:
An American in Paris
Best Director:
Laslo Benedek, *Death of a Salesman*
Best Actress—Drama:
Jane Wyman, *The Blue Veil*
Best Actor—Drama:
Fredric March, *Death of a Salesman*
Best Actress—Musical/Comedy:
June Allyson, *Too Young to Kiss*
Best Actor—Musical/Comedy:
Danny Kaye, *On the Riviera*
Best Supporting Actress:
Kim Hunter, *A Streetcar Named Desire*
Best Supporting Actor:
Peter Ustinov, *Quo Vadis*
Most Promising Newcomers:
Pier Angeli, *Teresa*
Kevin McCarthy, *Death of a Salesman*
Best Screenplay:
Robert Buckner, *Bright Victory*

Best Score:
Victor Young, *September Affair*
Best Cinematography—Black-and-White:
Frank Planer, *Death of a Salesman*
Best Cinematography—Color:
Robert Surtees, William V. Skall, *Quo Vadis*
Best Film Promoting International Understanding:
The Day the Earth Stood Still
Cecil B. DeMille Award:
Cecil B. DeMille

1952

Best Motion Picture—Drama:
The Greatest Show on Earth
Best Motion Picture—Musical/Comedy:
With a Song in My Heart
Best Director:
Cecil B. DeMille, *The Greatest Show on Earth*
Best Actress—Drama:
Shirley Booth, *Come Back, Little Sheba*
Best Actor—Drama:
Gary Cooper, *High Noon*
Best Actress—Musical/Comedy:
Susan Hayward, *With a Song in My Heart*
Best Actor—Musical/Comedy:
Donald O'Connor, *Singin' in the Rain*
Best Supporting Actress:
Katy Jurado, *High Noon*
Best Supporting Actor:
Millard Mitchell, *My Six Convicts*
Most Promising Newcomers:
Colette Marchand, *Moulin Rouge*
Richard Burton, *My Cousin Rachel*
Best Screenplay:
Michael Wilson, *Five Fingers*
Best Score:
Dimitri Tiomkin, *High Noon*
Best Cinematography—Black-and-White:
Floyd Crosby, *High Noon*

Best Cinematography—Color:
George Barnes, J. Peverell Marley, *The Greatest Show on Earth*
Best Film Promoting International Understanding:
Anything Can Happen
Cecil B. DeMille Award:
Walt Disney
World Film Favorite—Female:
Susan Hayward
World Film Favorite—Male:
John Wayne
Special Award for Best Juvenile Actor:
Brandon DeWilde, *Member of the Wedding*
Francis Kee Teller, *Navajo*

1953

Best Motion Picture—Drama:
The Robe
Best Director:
Fred Zinnemann, *From Here to Eternity*
Best Actress—Drama
Audrey Hepburn, *Roman Holiday*
Best Actor—Drama
Spencer Tracy, *The Actress*
Best Actress—Musical/Comedy:
Ethel Merman, *Call Me Madam*
Best Actor—Musical/Comedy:
David Niven, *The Moon Is Blue*
Best Supporting Actress:
Grace Kelly, *Mogambo*
Best Supporting Actor:
Frank Sinatra, *From Here to Eternity*
Most Promising Newcomers—Female:
Pat Crowley, Bella Darvi, Barbara Rush
Most Promising Newcomers—Male:
Hugh O'Brian, Steve Forrest, Richard Egan
Best Screenplay:
Helen Deutsch, *Lili*

Best Film Promoting International Understanding:
Little Boy Lost
Cecil B. DeMille Award:
Darryl Zanuck
World Film Favorite—Female:
Marilyn Monroe
World Film Favorite—Male:
Robert Taylor
Alan Ladd
Best Documentary of Historical Interest:
A Queen Is Crowned
Best Western Star:
Guy Madison
Special Award:
Walt Disney, *The Living Desert*
Honor Award:
Jack Cummings (producer for 30 years at MGM)

1954

Best Motion Picture—Drama:
On the Waterfront
Best Motion Picture—Musical/Comedy:
Carmen Jones
Best Foreign Films:
Genevieve (England), *No Way Back* (Germany), *Twenty-four Eyes* (Japan), *La Mujer de las Camelias* (Argentina)
Best Director:
Elia Kazan, *On the Waterfront*
Best Actress—Drama:
Grace Kelly, *The Country Girl*
Best Actor—Drama:
Marlon Brando, *On the Waterfront*
Best Actress—Musical/Comedy:
Judy Garland, *A Star Is Born*
Best Actor—Musical/Comedy:
James Mason, *A Star Is Born*
Best Supporting Actress:
Jan Sterling, *The High and the Mighty*
Best Supporting Actor:
Edmond O'Brien, *The Barefoot Contessa*

Most Promising Newcomers —Female:
Shirley MacLaine, Kim Novak, Karen Sharpe
Most Promising Newcomers —Male:
Joe Adams, George Nader, Jeff Richards
Best Screenplay:
Billy Wilder, Samuel Taylor, Ernest Lehman, *Sabrina*
Best Cinematography—Black-and-White:
Boris Kaufman, *On the Waterfront*
Best Cinematography—Color:
Joseph Ruttenberg, *Brigadoon*
Best Film Promoting International Understanding:
Broken Lance
Cecil B. DeMille Award:
Jean Hersholt
World Film Favorite—Female:
Audrey Hepburn
World Film Favorite—Male:
Gregory Peck
Pioneer Award:
John Ford
Pioneer Award for Color:
Dr. Herbert Kalmus
Special Award for Creative Musical Contribution:
Dimitri Tiomkin
Special Award for Experimental Film:
Anywhere in Our Time (Germany)

1955

Best Motion Picture—Drama:
East of Eden
Best Motion Picture—Musical/Comedy:
Guys and Dolls
Best Foreign Films:
Ordet (Denmark), *Stella* (Greece), *Eyes of Children* (Japan), *Sons, Mothers, and a General* (Germany), *Dangerous Curves* (Brazil)
Best Outdoor Drama:
Wichita
Best Director:
Joshua Logan, *Picnic*

Best Actress—Drama:
Anna Magnani, *The Rose Tattoo*
Best Actor—Drama:
Ernest Borgnine, *Marty*
Best Actress—Musical/Comedy:
Jean Simmons, *Guys and Dolls*
Best Actor/Musical/Comedy:
Tom Ewell, *The Seven-Year Itch*
Best Support Actress:
Marisa Pavan, *The Rose Tattoo*
Best Supporting Actor:
Arthur Kennedy, *The Trial*
Most Promising Newcomers —Female:
Anita Ekberg, Virginia Shaw, Dana Wynter
Most Promising Newcomers —Male:
Ray Danton, Russ Tamblyn
Best Film Promoting International Understanding:
Love Is a Many-Splendored Thing
Cecil B. DeMill Award:
Jack Warner
World Film Favorite—Female:
Grace Kelly
World Film Favorite—Male:
Marlon Brando
Hollywood Citizenship Award:
Esther Williams
Posthumous Award for Best Dramatic Actor:
James Dean

1956

Best Motion Picture—Drama:
Around the World in 80 Days
Best Motion Picture—Musical/Comedy:
The King and I
Best English-Language Foreign Film:
Richard III
Best Foreign-Language Foreign Film:
The White Reindeer (Finland)
Before Sundown (Germany)
The Girls in Black (Greece)
Rose on the Arm (Japan)

War and Peace (Italy)
Best Director:
Elia Kazan, *Baby Doll*
Best Actress—Drama:
Ingrid Bergman, *Anastasia*
Best Actor—Drama:
Kirk Douglas, *Lust for Life*
**Best Actress—
Musical/Comedy:**
Deborah Kerr, *The King and I*
**Best Actor—
Musical/Comedy:**
Cantinflas, *Around the World in 80 Days*
Best Supporting Actress:
Eileen Heckart, *The Bad Seed*
Best Supporting Actor:
Earl Holliman, *The Rainmaker*
Most Promising Newcomers—Female:
Carroll Baker, Jayne Mansfield, Natalie Wood
Most Promising Newcomers—Male:
John Kerr, Paul Newman, Tony Perkins
Foreign Newcomer Award—Female:
Taina Elg (Finland)
Foreign Newcomer Award—Male:
Jacques Bergerac (France)
Best Film Promoting International Understanding:
Battle Hymn
Recognition Award for Music:
Dimitri Tiomkin
Cecil B. DeMille Award:
Mervyn LeRoy
World Film Favorite—Female:
Kim Novak
World Film Favorite—Male:
James Dean
Special Award for Advancing Film Industry:
Edwin Schallert
Hollywood Citizenship Award:
Ronald Reagan
Special Award for Consistent Performance:
Elizabeth Taylor

1957

Best Motion Picture—Drama:
The Bridge on the River Kwai
Best Motion Picture—Musical/Comedy:
Les Girls
Best English-Language Foreign Film:
Woman in a Dressing Gown
Best Foreign-Language Foreign Film:
The Confessions of Felix Krull (Germany), *Yellow Crow* (Japan), *Tizok* (Mexico)
Best Director:
David Lean, *The Bridge on the River Kwai*
Best Actress—Drama:
Joanne Woodward, *Three Faces of Eve*
Best Actor—Drama:
Alec Guinness, *The Bridge on the River Kwai*
Best Actress—Musical/Comedy:
Kay Kendall, *Les Girls*
Best Actor—Musical/Comedy:
Frank Sinatra, *Pal Joey*
Best Supporting Actress:
Elsa Lanchester, *Witness for the Prosecution*
Best Supporting Actor:
Red Buttons, *Sayonara*
Most Promising Newcomers—Female:
Sandra Dee, Carolyn Jones, Diane Varsi
Most Promising Newcomers—Male:
James Garner, John Saxon, Pat Wayne
Best Film Promoting International Understanding:
The Happy Road
Special Award for Bettering the Standard of Motion Picture Music:
Hugo Friedhofer
Cecil B. DeMille Award:
Buddy Adler
World Film Favorite—Female:
Doris Day
World Film Favorite—Male:
Tony Curtis
Best Film Choreography:
Le Roy Prinz

Best World Entertainment through Musical Films:
George Sidney
Most Versatile Actress:
Jean Simmons
Most Glamorous Actress:
Zsa Zsa Gabor
Ambassador of Good Will:
Bob Hope

1958

Best Motion Picture—Drama:
The Defiant Ones
Best Motion Picture—Comedy:
Auntie Mame
Best Motion Picture—Musical:
Gigi
Best English-Language Foreign Film:
A Night to Remember
Best Foreign-Language Foreign Film:
The Road a Year Long (Yugoslavia), *The Girl and the River* (France), *The Girl Rose Marie* (Germany)
Best Director:
Vincente Minnelli, *Gigi*
Best Actress—Drama:
Susan Hayward, *I Want to Live!*
Best Actor—Drama:
David Niven, *Separate Tables*
Best Actress—Comedy/Musical:
Rosalind Russell, *Auntie Mame*
Best Actor—Comedy/Musical:
Danny Kaye, *Me and the Colonel*
Best Supporting Actress:
Hermione Gingold, *Gigi*
Best Supporting Actor:
Burl Ives, *The Big Country*
Most Promising Newcomers—Female:
Linda Cristal, Susan Kohner, Tina Louise
Most Promising Newcomers—Male:
Bradford Dillman, John Gavin, Efrem Zimbalist, Jr.
Samuel Goldwyn Award:
Two Eyes, Twelve Hands (Italy)

Cecil B. DeMille Award:
Maurice Chevalier
World Film Favorite—Female:
Deborah Kerr
World Film Favorite—Male:
Rock Hudson
Best Film Promoting International Understanding:
The Inn of the Sixth Happiness
Special Award to Best Juvenile:
David Ladd
Special Award to Most Versatile Actress:
Shirley MacLaine

1959

Best Motion Picture—Drama:
Ben-Hur
Best Motion Picture—Comedy:
Some Like It Hot
Best Motion Picture—Musical:
Porgy and Bess
Best Foreign Films:
Black Orpheus (France), Odd Obsession (Japan), The Bridge (Germany), Wild Strawberries (Sweden), Aren't We Wonderful? (Germany)
Best Director:
William Wyler, Ben-Hur
Best Actress—Drama:
Elizabeth Taylor, Suddenly, Last Summer
Best Actor—Drama:
Anthony Franciosa, Career
Best Actress—Musical/Comedy:
Marilyn Monroe, Some Like It Hot
Best Actor—Musical/Comedy:
Jack Lemmon, Some Like It Hot
Best Supporting Actress:
Susan Kohner, Imitation of Life
Best Supporting Actor:
Stephen Boyd, Ben-Hur
Most Promising Newcomers—Female:
Tuesday Weld, Angie

Dickenson, Janet Munro, Stella Stevens
Most Promising Newcomers—Male:
James Shigata, Barry Coe, Troy Donahue, George Hamilton
Special Award for Directing the Chariot Race in Ben-Hur:
Andrew Morton
Best Score:
Ernest Gold, On the Beach
Best Film Promoting International Understanding:
The Diary of Anne Frank
Cecil B. DeMille Award:
Bing Crosby
Samuel Goldwyn Award:
Room at the Top
World Film Favorite—Female:
Doris Day
World Film Favorite—Male:
Rock Hudson
Outstanding Merit:
The Nun's Story
Journalistic Merit Awards:
Hedda Hopper, Louella Parsons
Special Awards to Famous Silent Film Stars:
Francis X. Bushman, Ramon Navarro

1960

Best Motion Picture—Drama:
Spartacus
Best Motion Picture—Comedy:
The Apartment
Best Motion Picture—Musical:
Song Without End
Best English-Language Foreign Film:
The Man with the Green Carnation
Best Foreign-Language Foreign Film:
La Vérité (France), The Virgin Spring (Sweden)
Best Director:
Jack Cardiff, Sons and Lovers
Best Actress—Drama:
Greer Garson, Sunrise at Campobello

Best Actor—Drama:
Burt Lancaster, Elmer Gantry
Best Actress—Musical/Comedy:
Shirley MacLaine, The Apartment
Best Actor—Musical/Comedy:
Jack Lemmon, The Apartment
Best Supporting Actress:
Janet Leigh, Psycho
Best Supporting Actor:
Sal Mineo, Exodus
Most Promising Newcomers—Female:
Ina Balin, Nancy Kwan, Hayley Mills
Most Promising Newcomers—Male:
Michael Callan, Mark Kamon, Brett Halsey
Best Score:
Dimitri Tiomkin, Alamo
Samuel Goldwyn Award:
Never on Sunday (Greece)
Cecile B. DeMille Award:
Fred Astaire
Best Film Promoting International Understanding:
Hand in Hand
World Film Favorite—Female:
Gina Lollobrigida
World Film Favorite—Male:
Rock Hudson, Tony Curtis
Special Award for Comedy:
Cantinflas
Special Award for Artistic Integrity:
Stanley Kramer
Merit Award:
The Sundowners

1961

Best Motion Picture—Drama:
The Guns of Navarone
Best Motion Picture—Comedy:
A Majority of One
Best Motion Picture—Musical:
West Side Story
Best Foreign-Language Foreign Film:
Two Women (Italy)
Silver Globes: Animas Trujano (Mexico)

The Good Soldier Schweik
(Germany)
Best Director:
Stanley Kramer, *Judgment at Nuremberg*
Best Actress—Drama:
Geraldine Page, *Summer and Smoke*
Best Actor—Drama:
Maximilian Schell, *Judgment at Nuremberg*
Best Actress—Musical/Comedy:
Rosalind Russell, *A Majority of One*
Best Actor—Musical/Comedy:
Glenn Ford, *Pocketful of Miracles*
Best Supporting Actress:
Rita Moreno, *West Side Story*
Best Supporting Actor:
George Chakiris, *West Side Story*
Most Promising Newcomers—Female:
Christine Kaufmann, Ann-Margret, Jane Fonda
Most Promising Newcomers-Male:
Richard Beymer, Bobby Darin, Warren Beatty
Best Song:
Dimitri Tiomkin, Ned Washington, "Town Without Pity," *Town Without Pity*
Best Score:
Dimitri Tiomkin, *The Guns of Navarone*
Samuel Goldwyn Award for Best English Film:
The Mark
Cecil B. DeMille Award:
Judy Garland
World Film Favorite—Female:
Marilyn Monroe
World Film Favorite—Male:
Charlton Heston
Best Film Promoting International Understanding:
A Majority of One
Special Merit Award:
Samuel Bronston, *El Cid*
Special Journalistic Merit Awards:
Army Archerd (Daily Variety)
Mike Connolly (Hollywood Reporter)

1962

Best Motion Picture—Drama:
Lawrence of Arabia
Best Motion Picture—Comedy:
That Touch of Mink
Best Motion Picture—Musical:
The Music Man
Best Foreign-Language Foreign Film:
Divorce—Italian Style (Italy), *Best of Enemies* (Italy)
Best Director:
David Lean, *Lawrence of Arabia*
Best Actress—Drama:
Geraldine Page, *Sweet Bird of Youth*
Best Actor—Drama:
Gregory Peck, *To Kill a Mockingbird*
Best Actress—Musical/Comedy:
Rosalind Russell, *Gypsy*
Best Actor—Musical/Comedy:
Marcello Mastroianni, *Divorce—Italian Style*
Best Supporting Actress:
Angela Lansbury, *The Manchurian Candidate*
Best Supporting Actor:
Omar Sharif, *Lawrence of Arabia*
Most Promising Newcomers—Female:
Patty Duke, Sue Lyon, Rita Tushingham
Most Promising Newcomers—Male:
Keir Dullea, Omar Sharif, Terence Stamp
Best Original Score:
Elmer Bernstein, *To Kill a Mockingbird*
Best Film Promoting International Understanding:
To Kill a Mockingbird
Cecil B. DeMille Award:
Bob Hope
World Film Favorite—Female:
Doris Day
World Film Favorite—Male:
Rock Hudson
Samuel Goldwyn Award:
Sundays and Cybele (France)

Best Cinematography—Black-and-White:
Henri Persin, Walter Wottitz, Jean Bourgoin, *The Longest Day*
Best Cinematography—Color:
F.A. Young, *Lawrence of Arabia*

1963

Best Motion Picture—Drama:
The Cardinal
Best Motion Picture—Musical/Comedy:
Tom Jones:
Best English-Language Foreign Film:
Tom Jones
Best Foreign-Language Foreign Film:
Any Number Can Win (France)
Best Director:
Elia Kazan, *America, America*
Best Actress—Drama:
Leslie Caron, *The L-Shaped Room*
Best Actor—Drama:
Sidney Poitier, *Lilies of the Field*
Best Actress—Musical/Comedy:
Shirley MacLaine, *Irma La Douce*
Best Actor—Musical/Comedy:
Alberto Sordi, *To Bed or Not to Bed*
Best Supporting Actress:
Margaret Rutherford, *The V.I.P.s*
Best Supporting Actor:
John Huston, *The Cardinal*
Most Promising Newcomers—Female:
Ursula Andress, Tippi Hedren, Elke Sommer
Most Promising Newcomers—Male:
Albert Finney, Robert Walker, Stathis Giallelis
Best Motion Picture Promoting International Understanding:
Lilies of the Field

**Samuel Goldwyn
International Award:**
*Yesterday, Today and
Tomorrow*
Cecil B. DeMille Award:
Joseph E. Levine
**World Film Favorite—
Female:**
Sophia Loren
World Film Favorite—Male:
Paul Newman

Washington, "Circus
World," *Circus World*
Cecil B. DeMille Award:
James Stewart
**World Film Favorite—
Female:**
Sophia Loren
World Film Favorite—Male:
Marcello Mastroianni

Cecil B. DeMille Award:
John Wayne
**World Film Favorite—
Female:**
Natalie Wood
World Film Favorite—Male:
Paul Newman

1964

Best Motion Picture—Drama:
Becket
**Best Motion Picture—
Musical/Comedy:**
My Fair Lady
Best English-Language Film:
The Girl with Green Eyes
**Best Foreign-Language
Foreign Film:**
Marriage Italian Style (Italy),
Sallah (Israel)
Best Director:
George Cukor, *My Fair Lady*
Best Actress—Drama:
Anne Bancroft, *The Pumpkin
Eater*
Best Actor—Drama:
Peter O'Toole, *Becket*
**Best Actress—
Musical/Comedy:**
Julie Andrews, *Mary Poppins*
**Best Actor—
Musical/Comedy:**
Rex Harrison, *My Fair Lady*
Best Supporting Actress:
Agnes Moorehead, *Hush . . .
Hush, Sweet Charlotte*
Best Supporting Actor:
Edmond O'Brien, *Seven Days
in May*
**Most Promising Newcomers
—Female:**
Mia Farrow, Celia Kaye, Mary
Ann Mobley
**Most Promising Newcomers
—Male:**
Harv Presnell, George Segal,
Chaim Topol
Best Original Score:
Dimitri Tiomkin, *The Fall of
the Roman Empire*
Best Song:
Dimitri Tiomkin, Ned

1965

Best Motion Picture—Drama:
Doctor Zhivago
**Best Motion Picture—
Musical/Comedy:**
The Sound of Music
**Best English-Language
Foreign Film:**
Darling
**Best Foreign-Language
Foreign Film:**
Juliet of the Spirits (Italy)
Best Director:
David Lean, *Doctor Zhivago*
Best Actress—Drama:
Samantha Eggar, *The
Collector*
Best Actor—Drama:
Omar Sharif, *Doctor Zhivago*
**Best Actress—
Musical/Comedy:**
Julie Andrews, *The Sound of
Music*
**Best Actor—
Musical/Comedy:**
Lee Marvin, *Cat Ballou*
Best Supporting Actres:
Ruth Gordon, *Inside Daisy
Clover*
Best Supporting Actor:
Oskar Werner, *The Spy Who
came in from the Cold*
**Most Promising Newcomer—
Female:**
Elizabeth Hartman, *A Patch of
Blue*
**Most Promising Newcomer—
Male:**
Robert Redford, *Inside Daisy
Clover*
Best Screenplay:
Robert Bolt, *Doctor Zhivago*
Best Original Score;
Maurice Jarre, *Doctor Zhivago*
Best Original Song:
"Forget Domani," *The Yellow
Rolls Royce*

1966

Best Motion Picture—Drama:
A Man for All Seasons
**Best Motion Picture—
Musical/Comedy:**
*The Russians Are Coming,
The Russians Are Coming*
**Best English-Language
Foreign Film:**
Alfie
**Best Foreign-Language
Foreign Film:**
A Man and a Woman (France)
Best Director:
Fred Zinnemann, *A Man for
All Seasons*
Best Actress—Drama:
Anouk Aimée, *A Man and a
Woman*
Best Actor—Drama:
Paul Scofield, *A Man for All
Seasons*
**Best Actress—
Musical/Comedy:**
Lynn Redgrave, *Georgy Girl*
**Best Actor—
Musical/Comedy:**
Alan Arkin, *The Russians Are
Coming, The Russians Are
Coming*
Best supporting Actress;
Jocelyn La Garde, *Hawaii*
Best Supporting Actor:
Richard Attenborough, *The
Sand Pebbles*
**Most Promising Newcomer—
Female:**
Camilla Spary, *Dead on a
Merry Go Round*
**Most Promising Newcomer—
Male:**
James Farentino, *The Pad*
Best Screenplay:
Robert Bolt, *A Man for All
Seasons*
Best Original Score:
Elmer Bernstein, *Hawaii*

Best Original Song:
"Strangers in the Night," *A Man Could Get Killed*
Cecil B. DeMille Award:
Charlton Heston
World Film Favorite—Female:
Julie Andrews
World Film Favorite—Male:
Steve McQueen

1967

Best Motion Picture—Drama:
In the Heat of the Night
Best Motion Picture—Musical/Comedy:
The Graduate
Best English-Language Foreign Film:
The Fox (Canada)
Best Foreign-Language Foreign Film:
Live for Life (France)
Best Director:
Mike Nichols, *The Graduate*
Best Actress—Drama:
Dame Edith Evans, *The Whisperers*
Best Actor—Drama:
Rod Steiger, *In the Heat of the Night*
Best Actress—Musical/Comedy:
Anne Bancroft, *The Graduate*
Best Actor—Musical/Comedy:
Richard Harris, *Camelot*
Best Supporting Actress:
Carol Channing, *Thoroughly Modern Millie*
Best Supporting Actor:
Richard Attenborough, *Doctor Dolittle*
Most Promising Newcomer—Female:
Katharine Ross, *The Graduate*
Most Promising Newcomer—Male:
Dustin Hoffman, *The Graduate*
Best Screenplay:
Stirling Silliphant, *In the Heat of the Night*
Best Original Score;
Frederick Loewe, *Camelot*
Best Original Song:
"If Ever I Should Leave You," *Camelot*

Cecil B. DeMille Award:
Kirk Douglas
World Film Favorite—Female:
Julie Andrews
World Film Favorite—Male:
Paul Newman

1968

Best Motion Picture—Drama:
The Lion in Winter
Best Motion Picture—Musical/Comedy:
Oliver!
Best English-Language Foreign Film:
Romeo and Juliet ✓
Best Foreign-Language Foreign Film:
War and Peace (Russia)
Best Director:
Paul Newman, *Rachel, Rachel*
Best Actress—Drama:
Joanne Woodward, *Rachel, Rachel*
Best Actor—Drama:
Peter O'Toole, *The Lion In Winter*
Best Actress—Musical/Comedy:
Barbra Streisand, *Funny Girl*
Best Actor—Musical/Comedy:
Ron Moody, *Oliver!*
Best Supporting Actress:
Ruth Gordon, *Rosemary's Baby*
Best Supporting Actor:
Daniel Massey, *Star!*
Most Promising Newcomer—Female:
Olivia Hussey, *Romeo and Juliet* ✓
Most Promising Newcomer—Male:
Leonard Whiting, *Romeo and Juliet* ✓
Best Screenplay:
Stirling Silliphant, *Charly*
Best Original Score:
Alex North, *The Shoes of the Fisherman*
Best Original Song:
Michel Legrand, Alan Bergman and Marilyn Bergman, "The Windmills of

Your Mind," *The Thomas Crown Affair*
Cecil B. DeMille Award:
Gregory Peck
World Film Favorite—Female:
Sophia Loren
World Film Favorite—Male:
Sidney Poitier

1969

Best Motion Picture—Drama:
Anne of the Thousand Days
Best Motion Picture—Musical/Comedy:
The Secret of Santa Vittoria
Best English-Language Foreign Film:
Oh, What a Lovely War!
Best Foreign-Language Foreign Film:
Z (Algeria)
Best Director:
Charles Jarrott, *Anne of the Thousand Days*
Best Actress—Drama:
Genevieve Bujold, *Anne of the Thousand Days*
Best Actor—Drama:
John Wayne, *True Grit*
Best Actress—Musical/Comedy:
Patty Duke, *Me, Natalie*
Best Actor—Musical/Comedy:
Peter O'Toole, *Goodbye, Mr. Chips*
Best Supporting Actress:
Goldie Hawn, *Cactus Flower*
Best Supporting Actor:
Gig Young, *They Shoot Horses, Don't They?*
Most Promising Newcomer—Female:
Ali MacGraw, *Goodbye, Columbus*
Most Promising Newcomer—Male:
Jon Voight, *Midnight Cowboy*
Best Screenplay:
John Hale, Bridget Boland, Richard Sokolove, *Anne of the Thousand Days*
Best Original Score;
Burt Bacharach, *Butch Cassidy and the Sundance Kid*

Best Original Song:
Rod McKuen, "Jean," *The Prime of Miss Jean Brodie*
Cecil B. DeMille Award:
Joan Crawford
World Film Favorite—Female:
Barbra Streisand
World Film Favorite—Male:
Steve McQueen

CeciL B: DeMille Award:
Frank Sinatra
World Film Favorite—Female:
Barbra Streisand
World Film Favorite—Male:
Clint Eastwood

CeciL B. DeMille Award:
Alfred Hitchcock
World Film Favorite—Female:
Ali MacGraw
World Film Favorites—Male:
Charles Bronson
Sean Connery

1970

Best Motion Picture—Drama:
Love Story
Best Motion Picture—Musical/Comedy:
*M*A*S*H*
Best English-Language Foreign Film:
Women in Love
Best Foreign-Language Foreign Film:
Rider on the Rain (France)
Best Director:
Arthur Hiller, *Love Story*
Best Actress—Drama:
Ali MacGraw, *Love Story*
Best Actor—Drama:
George C. Scott, *Patton*
Best Actress—Musical/Comedy:
Carrie Snodgrass, *Diary of a Mad Housewife*
Best Actor—Musical/Comedy:
Albert Finney, *Scrooge*
Best Supporting Actress:
Karen Black, *Five Easy Pieces*
Maureen Stapleton, *Airport*
Best Supporting Actor:
John Mills, *Ryan's Daughter*
Most Promising Newcomer—Female:
Carrie Snodgrass, *Diary of a Mad Housewife*
Most Promising Newcomer—Male:
James Earl Jones, *The Great White Hope*
Best Screenplay:
Erich Segal, *Love Story*
Best Original Score:
Francis Lai, *Love Story*
Best Original Song:
Henry Mancini, Johnny Mercer, "Whistling Away the Dark," *Darling Lili*

1971

Best Motion Picture—Drama:
The French Connection
Best Motion Picture—Musical/Comedy:
Fiddler on the Roof
Best English-Language Foreign Film:
Sunday Bloody Sunday
Best Foreign-Language Foreign Film:
The Policeman (Israel)
Best Director:
William Friedkin, *The French Connection*
Best Actress—Drama:
Jane Fonda, *Klute*
Best Actor—Drama:
Gene Hackman, *The French Connection*
Best Actress—Musical/Comedy:
Twiggy, *The Boy Friend*
Best Actor—Musical/Comedy:
Topol, *Fiddler on the Roof*
Best Supporting Actress:
Ann-Margret, *Carnal Knowledge*
Best Supporting Actor:
Ben Johnson, *The Last Picture Show*
Most Promising Newcomer—Female:
Twiggy, *The Boy Friend*
Most Promising Newcomer—Male:
Desi Arnaz, Jr., *Red Sky at Morning*
Best Screenplay:
Paddy Chayefsky, *The Hospital*
Best Original Score:
Isaac Hayes, *Shaft*
Best Original Song:
Marvin Hamlisch, Johnny Mercer, "Life Is What You Make It,"*Kotch*

1972

Best Motion Picture—Drama:
The Godfather
Best Motion Picture—Musical/Comedy:
Cabaret
Best English-Language Foreign Film:
Young Winston
Best Foreign-Language Foreign Films:
The Emigrants (Sweden)
The New Land (Sweden)
Best Director:
Francis Ford Coppola, *The Godfather*
Best Actress—Drama:
Liv Ullmann, *The Emigrants*
Best Actor—Drama:
Marlon Brando, *The Godfather*
Best Actress—Musical/Comedy:
Liza Minnelli, *Cabaret*
Best Actor—Musical/Comedy:
Jack Lemmon, *Avanti*
Best Supporting Actress:
Shelley Winters, *The Poseidon Adventure*
Best Supporting Actor:
Joel Grey, *Cabaret*
Most Promising Newcomer—Female:
Diana Ross, *Lady Sings the Blues*
Most Promising Newcomer—Male:
Edward Albert, *Butterflies Are Free*
Best Screenplay:
Francis Ford Coppola, Mario Puzo, *The Godfather*
Best Original Score:
Nino Rota, *The Godfather*
Best Original Song:
Walter Scharf, Don Black, "Ben," *Ben*

Best Documentary Films:
Elvis on Tour
Walls of Fire
Cecil B. DeMille Award;
Samuel Goldwyn
World Film Favorite—Female:
Jane Fonda
World Film Favorite—Male:
Marlon Brando

"The Way We Were," *The Way We Were*
Best Documentary Film:
Visions of Eight
Cecil B. DeMille Award:
Bette Davis
World Film Favorite—Female:
Elizabeth Taylor
World Film Favorite—Male:
Marlon Brando

Cecil B. DeMille Award:
Hal B. Wallis
World Film Favorite—Female:
Barbra Streisand
World Film favorite—Male;
Robert Redford

1975

Best Motion Picture—Drama:
One Flew Over the Cuckoo's Nest
Best Motion Picture—Musical/Comedy:
The Sunshine Boys
Best Foreign Film:
Lies My Father Told Me (Canada)
Best Director:
Milos Forman, *One Flew Over the Cuckoo's Nest*
Best Actress—Drama:
Louise Fletcher, *One Flew Over the Cuckoo's Nest*
Best Actor—Drama:
Jack Nicholson, *One Flew Over the Cuckoo's Nest*
Best Actress—Musical/Comedy:
Ann-Margret, *Tommy*
Best Actor—Musical/Comedy:
Walter Matthau, *The Sunshine Boys*
Best Supporting Actress:
Brenda Vaccaro, *Once is Not Enough*
Best Supporting Actor:
Richard Benjamin, *The Sunshine Boys*
Best Acting Debut—Female:
Marilyn Hassett, *The Other Side of the Mountain*
Best Acting Debut—Male:
Brad Dourif, *One Flew Over the Cuckoo's Nest*
Best Screenplay:
Laurence Hauben, Bo Goldman, *One Flew Over the Cuckoo's Nest*
Best Original Score:
John Williams, *Jaws:*
Best Original Song;
Keith Carradine, "I'm Easy," *Nashville*
Best Documentary Film:
Youthquake

1973

Best Motion Picture—Drama:
The Exorcist
Best Motion Picture—Musical/Comedy:
American Graffiti
Best Foreign-Language Foreign Film:
The Pedestrian (West Germany)
Best Director:
William Friedkin, *The Exorcist*
Best Actress—Drama:
Marsha Mason, *Cinderella Liberty*
Best Actor—Drama:
Al Pacino, *Serpico*
Best Actress—Musical/Comedy:
Glenda Jackson, *A Touch of Class*
Best Actor—Musical/Comedy:
George Segal, *A Touch of Class*
Best Supporting Actress:
Linda Blair, *The Exorcist*
Best Supporting Actor:
John Houseman, *The Paper Chase*
Most Promising Newcomer—Female:
Tatum O'Neal, *Paper Moon*
Most Promising Newcomer—Male;
Paul Le Mat, *American Graffiti*
Best Screenplay;
William Peter Blatty, *The Exorcist*
Best Original Score:
Neil Diamond, *Jonathan Livingston Seagull*
Best Original Song:
Marvin Hamlisch, Alan Bergman, Marilyn Bergman,

1974

Best Motion Picture—Drama:
Chinatown
Best Motion Picture—Musical/Comedy:
The Longest Yard
Best Foreign Film:
Scenes from a Marriage (Sweden)
Best Director:
Roman Polanski, *Chinatown*
Best Actress—Drama:
Gena Rowlands, *A Woman Under the Influence*
Best Actor—Drama:
Jack Nicholson, *Chinatown*
Best Actress—Musical/Comedy:
Raquel Welch, *The Three Musketeers*
Best Actor—Musical/Comedy:
Art Carney, *Harry and Tonto*
Best Supporting Actress:
Karen Black, *The Great Gatsby*
Best Supporting Actor:
Fred Astaire, *The Towering Inferno*
Most Promising Newcomer—Female:
Susan Flannery, *The Towering Inferno*
Most Promising Newcomer—Male:
Joseph Bottoms, *The Dove*
Best Screenplay:
Robert Towne, *Chinatown*
Best Original Score:
Alan Jay Lerner, Frederick Loewe, *The Little Prince*
Best Original Song:
Eul Box and Betty Box, "I Feel Love," *Benjy*
Best Documentary Film:
Beautiful People

1976

Best Motion Picture—Drama:
Rocky
Best Motion Picture—Musical/Comedy:
A Star Is Born
Best Foreign Film:
Face to Face (Sweden)
Best Director:
Sidney Lumet, *Network*
Best Actress—Drama:
Faye Dunaway, *Network*
Best Actor—Drama:
Peter Finch, *Network*
Best Actress—Musical/Comedy:
Barbra Streisand, *A Star Is Born*
Best Actor—Musical/Comedy:
Kris Kristofferson, *A Star Is Born*
Best Supporting Actress:
Katharine Ross, *Voyage of the Damned*
Best Supporting Actor:
Laurence Olivier, *Marathon Man*
Best Acting Debut—Female:
Jessica Lange, *King Kong*
Best Acting Debut—Male:
Arnold Schwarzenegger, *Stay Hungry*
Best Screenplay:
Paddy Chayefsky, *Network*
Best Original Score:
Paul Williams, Kenny Ascher, *A Star Is Born*
Best Original Song:
Paul Williams, Barbra Streisand, "Evergreen," *A Star Is Born*
Best Documentary Film:
Altars of the World
Cecil B. DeMille Award:
Walter Mirisch
World Film Favorite—Female:
Sophia Loren
World Film Favorite—Male:
Robert Redford

1977

Best Motion Picture—Drama:
The Turning Point

Best Motion Picture—Musical/Comedy:
The Goodbye Girl
Best Foreign Film;
A Special Day
Best Director:
Herbert Ross, *The Turning Point*
Best Actress—Drama:
Jane Fonda, *Julia*
Best Actor—Drama:
Richard Burton, *Equus*
Best Actress—Musical/Comedy:
Marsha Mason, *The Goodbye Girl*; Diane Keaton, *Annie Hall*
Best Actor—Musical/Comedy:
Richard Dreyfuss, *The Goodbye Girl*
Best Supporting Actress:
Vanessa Redgrave, *Julia*
Best Supporting Actor:
Peter Firth, *Equus*
Best Acting Debut—Female:
Not given this year
Best Acting Debut—Male:
(Not given this year)
Best Screenplay
Neil Simon, *The Goodbye Girl*
Best Original Score:
John Williams, *Star Wars*
Best Original Song:
Joseph Brooks, "You Light Up My Life," *You Light Up My Life*
Best Documentary:
(Not given this year)
Cecil B. De Mille Award:
Red Skelton
World Film Favorite—Female:
Barbra Streisand
World Film Favorite—Male:
Robert Redford

1978

Best Motion Picture—Drama:
Midnight Express
Best Motion Picture—Musical/Comedy:
Heaven Can Wait
Best Foreign Film
Autumn Sonata
Best Director:
Michael Cimino, *The Deer Hunter*

Best Actress—Drama:
Jane Fonda, *Coming Home*
Best Actor—Drama:
Jon Voight, *Coming Home*
Best Actress—Musical/Comedy:
Maggie Smith, *California Suite*
Ellen Burstyn, *Same Time Next Year*
Best actor—Musical/Comedy:
Warren Beatty, *Heaven Can Wait*
Best Supporting Actress:
Dyan Cannon, *Heaven Can Wait*
Best Supporting Actor:
John Hurt, *Midnight Express*
Best Acting Debut—Female:
Irene Miracle, *Midnight Express*
Best Acting Debut—Male:
Brad Davis, *Midnight Express*
Best Screenplay:
Oliver Stone, *Midnight Express*
Best Original Score:
Giorgio Moroder, *Midnight Express*
Best Original Song:
Paul Jabara, "Last Dance," *Thank God It's Friday*
Best Documentary:
(Not given this year)
Cecil B. DeMille Award:
Lucille Ball
World Film Favorite—Female:
Jane Fonda
World Film Favorite—Male:
John Travolta

1979

Best Motion Picture—Drama:
Kramer vs. Kramer
Best Motion Picture—Musical/Comedy:
Breaking Away
Best Foreign Film:
La Cage aux Folles
Best Director:
Francis Coppola, *Apocalypse Now*
Best Actress—Drama:
Sally Field, *Norma Rae*

Best Actor—Drama:
Dustin Hoffman, *Kramer vs. Kramer*
Best Actress— Musical/Comedy:
Bette Midler, *The Rose*
Best Actor— Musical/Comedy:
Peter Sellers, *Being There*
Best Supporting Actress:
Meryl Streep, *Kramer vs. Kramer*

Best Supporting Actor: (tie)
Robert Duvall, *Apocalypse Now*
Melvyn Douglas, *Being There*
Best New Female Star of the Year:
Bette Midler, *The Rose*
Best New Male Star of the Year:
Ricky Shroder, *The Champ*
Best Original Song:
Amanda McBroom, "The Rose," *The Rose*

Best Original Score:
Carmine Coppola, *The Black Stallion*
Best Screenplay:
Robert Benton, *Kramer vs. Kramer*
Cecil B. DeMille Award:
Henry Fonda
World Film Favorite— Female:
Jane Fonda
World Film Favorite—Male:
Roger Moore

6/THE BRITISH ACADEMY AWARDS

THE BRITISH FILM Academy (BFA) was founded in September 1948 to promote and improve creative work among persons engaged in filmmaking. The noted film critic and historian Roger Manvell was the Academy's first president. In 1959 the BFA merged with the Guild of Television Producers and Directors to form a new organization: the Society of Film and Television Arts (SFTA). Through 1967 the Guild and the Academy presented separate awards, but since 1968, the awards have been presented annually for achievements in the various areas of film and television. (The television awards are not included in *Film Facts.*) In 1975, SFTA was re-organized once again and is now known as the British Academy of Film and Television Arts (BAFTA).

The membership in the Academy's first days was small, and the awards—by the organization's own admission—were not especially well-organized. Today, membership of the Academy is by election: senior creative workers in British film and television are eligible. In addition to its annual awards, BAFTA holds meetings, organizes discussions and screenings, publishes books and magazines, and maintains a library.

Beginning with the 1967 awards, the Academy's statuette has been called the "Stella," as result of the competition in the *TV Times.*

The United Nations Award has been given to that film which best embodies one or more of the principles of the U.N. charter.

The President of the Academy is H.R.H. Princess Anne.

1947

Best Film:
Best Years of Our Lives
Best British Film:
Odd Man Out
Best Documentary:
The World Is Rich

1948

Best Film:
Hamlet
Best British Film:
The Fallen Idol

Best Documentary:
The Louisiana Story
Best Specialized Film:
Atomic Physics

1949

Best Film:
Bicycle Thieves
Best British Film:
The Third Man
Best Documentary:
Daybreak in Udi
United Nations Award:
The Search

Best Specialized Film:
La Famille Martin

1950

Best Film:
All About Eve
Best British Film:
The Blue Lamp
United Nations Award:
Intruder in the Dust
Best Documentary
The Undefeated
Best Specialized Film:
The True Face of Japan

1951

Best Film:
La Ronde
Best British Film:
The Lavender Hill Mob
United Nations Award:
Four in a Jeep
Best Documentary:
Beaver Valley
Best Specialized Film:
Gerald McBoing Boing

1952

Best Film:
The Sound Barrier
Best British Film:
The Sound Barrier
United Nations Award:
Cry, The Beloved Country
Best British Actress:
Vivien Leigh, *A Streetcar Named Desire*
Best British Actor:
Ralph Richardson, *The Sound Barrier*
Best Foreign Actress:
Simone Signoret, *Casque d'Or*
Best Foreign Actor:
Marlon Brando, *Viva Zapata!*
Best Promising Newcomer:
Claire Bloom, *Limelight*
Best Documentary:
Royal Journey
Best Specialized Film:
Animated Genesis

1953

Best Film:
Jeux Interdits
Best British Film:
Genevieve
United Nations Award:
World Without End
Best British Actress:
Audrey Hepburn, *Roman Holiday*
Best British Actor:
John Gielgud, *Julius Caesar*

Best Foreign Actress:
Leslie Caron, *Lili*
Best Foreign Actor:
Marlon Brando, *Julius Caesar*
Most Promising Newcomer:
David Kossoff, *The Young Lovers*
Best Documentary:
Conquest of Everest
Best Specialized Film:
Romance of Transportation

1954

Best Film:
The Wages of Fear
Best British Film:
Hobson's Choice
United Nations Award:
The Divided Heart
Best British Actress:
Yvonne Mitchell, *The Divided Heart*
Best British Actor:
Kenneth More, *Doctor in the House*
Best Foreign Actress:
Cornell Borchers, *The Divided Heart*
Best Foreign Actor:
Marlon Brando, *On the Waterfront*
Most Promising Newcomer:
Norman Wisdom, *Trouble in Store*
Best Documentary:
The Great Adventure
Best Animated Film:
Song on the Prairie
Best Screenplay (British Film):
George Tabori, Robin Estrdige, *The Young Lovers*

1955

Best Film:
Richard III
Best British Film:
Richard III
United Nations Award:
Children of Hiroshima
Best British Actress:
Kate Johnson, *The Ladykillers*

Best British Actor:
Laurence Olivier, *Richard III*
Best Foreign Actress:
Betsy Blair, *Marty*
Best Foreign Actor:
Ernest Borgnine, *Marty*
Most Promising Newcomer:
Paul Scofield, *That Lady*
Best Documentary:
The Vanishing Prairie
Best Specialized Film:
The Bespoken Overcoat
Best Animated Film:
Blinkity Blank
Best Screenplay (British Film):
William Rose, *The Ladykillers*

1956

Best Film:
Gervaise
Best British Film:
Reach for the Sky
United Nations Award:
Race for Life
Best British Actress:
Virginia McKenna, *A Town Like Alice*
Best British Actor:
Peter Finch, *A Town Like Alice*
Best Foreign Actress:
Anna Magnani, *The Rose Tattoo*
Best Foreign Actor:
Francois Perier, *Gervaise*
Most Promising Newcomer:
Eli Wallach, *Baby Doll*
Best Documentary:
On the Bowery
Best Specialized Film:
The Red Balloon
Best Animated Film:
Gerald McBoing Boing on Planet Moo
Best Screenplay (British Film):
Nigel Balchin, *The Man Who Never Was*

1957

Best Film:
The Bridge on the River Kwai

Best British Film:
The Bridge on the River Kwai
Best British Actress:
Heather Sears, *The Story of Esther Costello*
Best British Actor:
Alec Guinness, *The Bridge on the River Kwai*
Best Foreign Actress:
Simone Signoret, *Witches of Salem*
Best Foreign Actor:
Henry Fonda, *Twelve Angry Men*
Most Promising Newcomer:
Eric Barker, *Brothers in Law*
Best Documentary:
Journey Into Spring
Best Specialized Film:
A Chairy Tale
Best Animated Film:
Pan-Tele-Tron
Best Screenplay (British Film):
Pierre Boulle, *The Bridge on the River Kwai*

1958

Best Film:
Room at the Top
Best British Film:
Room at the Top
United Nations Award:
The Defiant Ones
Best British Actress:
Irene Worth, *Orders to Kill*
Best British Actor:
Trevor Howard, *The Key*
Best Foreign Actress:
Simone Signoret, *Room at the Top*
Best Foreign Actor:
Sidney Poitier, *The Defiant Ones*
Most Promising Newcomer:
Paul Massie, *Orders to Kill*
Best Documentary:
Glass
Best Specialized Film:
The Children's Film Foundation
Best Animated Film:
The Little Island
Best Screenplay (British Film):
Paul Dehn, *Orders to Kill*

1959

Best Film:
Ben-Hur
Best British Film:
Sapphire
United Nations Award:
On the Beach
Best British Actress:
Audrey Hepburn, *The Nun's Story*
Best British Actor:
Peter Sellers, *I'm All Right, Jack*
Best Foreign Actress:
Shirley MacLaine, *Ask Any Girl*
Best Foreign Actor:
Jack Lemmon, *Some Like It Hot*
Most Promising Newcomer:
Hayley Mills, *Tiger Bay*
Robet Flaherty Award (Best Feature Length Documentary):
The Savage Eye
Best Short Film:
Seven Cities of Antarctica
Best Specialized Film:
This is the BBC
Best Animated Film:
The Violinist
Best Screenplay (British Film):
Frank Harvey, John Boulting, Alan Hackney, *I'm All Right, Jack*

1960

Best Film:
The Apartment
Best British Film:
Saturday Night and Sunday Morning
United Nations Award:
Hiroshima, Mon Amour
Best British Actress:
Rachel Roberts, *Saturday Night and Sunday Morning*
Best British Actor:
Peter Finch, *The Trials of Oscar Wilde*
Best Foreign Actress:
Shirley MacLaine, *The Apartment*

Best Foreign Actor:
Jack Lemmon, *The Apartment*
Most Promising Newcomer:
Albert Finney, *Saturday Night and Sunday Morning*
Robert Flaherty Award (Best Feature-Length Documentary):
(Not awarded this year)
Best Short Film:
High Journey
Best Specialized Film:
Dispute
Best Animated Film:
Universe
Best Screenplay:
Bryan Forbes, *The Angry Silence*

1961

Best Film:
Ballad of a Soldier
The Hustler
Best British Film:
A Taste of Honey
United Nations Award:
Let My People Go
Best British Actress:
Bora Bryan, *A Taste of Honey*
Best British Actor:
Peter Finch, *No Love for Johnny*
Best Foreign Actress:
Sophia Loren, *Two Women*
Best Foreign Actor:
Paul Newman, *The Hustler*
Most Promising Newcomer:
Rita Tushingham, *A Taste of Honey*
Robert Flaherty Award (Best Feature-Length Documentary):
Volcano
Best Short Film:
Terminus
Best Animated Film:
101 Dalmations
Best Screenplay (British Film):
Val Guest, Wolf Mankowaitz, *The Day the Earth Caught Fire*
Shelagh Delaney, Tony Richardson, *A Taste of Honey*

1962

Best Film:
Lawrence of Arabia
Best British Film:
Lawrence of Arabia
United Nations Award:
Reach for Glory
Best British Actress:
Leslie Caron, *The L-Shaped Room*
Best British Actor:
Peter O'Toole, *Lawrence of Arabia*
Best Foreign Actress:
Anne Bancroft, *The Miracle Worker*
Best Foreign Actor:
Burt Lancaster, *The Bird Man of Alcatraz*
Most Promising Newcomer:
Tom Courtenay, *The Long Distance Runner*
Robert Flaherty Award (Best Feature-Length Documentary):
(Not awarded this year)
Best Short Film:
Incident at Owl Creek
Best Animated Film:
The Apple
Best Specialized Film:
Four Line Conics
Best Screenplay (British Film):
Robert Bolt, *Lawrence of Arabia*

1963

Best Film:
Tom Jones
Best British Film:
Tom Jones
United Nations Award:
Inheritance
Best British Actress:
Rachel Roberts, *This Sporting Life*
Best British Actor:
Dirk Bogarde, *The Servant*
Best Foreign Actress:
Patricia Neal, *Hud*
Best Foreign Actor:
Marcello Mastroianni, *Divorce, Italian Style*

Most Promising Newcomer:
James Fox, *The Servant*
Robert Flaherty Award (Best Feature-Length Documentary):
(Not awarded this year)
Best Specialized Film:
(Not awarded this year)
Best Animated Film:
The Critic
Automania 2000
Best Short Film:
Happy Anniversary
Best Screenplay (British Film):
John Osborne, *Tom Jones*
Best Cinematography (British Film):
  Black and White:
  Douglas Slocombe, *The Servant*
  Color:
  Ted Moore, *From Russia With Love*

1964

Best Film:
Dr. Strangelove
Best British Film:
Dr. Strangelove
United Nations Award:
Dr. Strangelove
Best British Actress:
Audrey Hepburn, *Charade*
Best British Actor:
Richard Attenborough, *Guns at Batasi; Séance on a Wet Afternoon*
Best Foreign Actress:
Anne Bancroft, *The Pumpkin Eater*
Best Foreign Actor:
Marcello Mastroianni, *Yesterday, Today and Tomorrow*
Most Promising Newcomer:
Julie Andrews, *Mary Poppins*
Robert Flaherty Award (Best Feature-Length Documentary):
Nobody Waved Goodbye
Best Short:
Kenojuak
Best Animated Film:
The Insects

Best Specialized Film:
Driving Technique—Passenger Trains
Best Screenplay (British Film):
Harold Pinter, *The Pumpkin Eater*
Best Cinematography (British Film):
  Black and White:
  Oswald Morris, *The Pumpkin Eater*
  Color:
  Geoffrey Unsworth, *Becket*
Best Art Direction (British Film):
  Black and White:
  Ken Adam, *Dr. Strangelove*
  Color:
  John Bryan, *Beckett*
Best Costume Design (British Film):
  Black and White:
  Motley, *The Pumpkin Eater*
  Color:
  Margaret Furse, *Becket*

1965

Best Film:
My Fair Lady
Best British Film:
The Ipcress File
United Nations Award:
Tokyo Olympiad
Best British Actress:
Julie Christie, *Darling*
Best British Actor:
Dirk Bogarde, *Darling*
Best Foreign Actress:
Patricia Neal, *In Harm's Way*
Best Foreign Actor:
Lee Marvin, *The Killers; Cat Ballou*
Most Promising Newcomer:
Judi Dench, *Four in the Morning*
Robert Flaherty Award (Best Feature-Length Documentary):
Tokyo Olympiad
Best Short Film:
Rig Move
Best Animated Film:
Be Careful Boys
Best Specialized Film:
I Do—And I Understand

Best Screenplay (British Film):
Frederic Raphael, *Darling*
Best Cinematography (British Film):
  Black and White:
  Oswald Morris, *The Hill*
  Color:
  Otto Heller, *Ipcress File*
Best Art Direction (British Film):
  Black and White:
  Ray Simm, *Darling*
  Color:
  Ken Adam, *The Ipcress File*
Best Costume Design (British Film):
  Black and White:
  No award this year
  Color:
  Osbert Lancaster, Dinah Greet, *Those Magnificent Men in Their Flying Machines*

1966

Best Film:
Who's Afraid of Virginia Woolf?
Best British Film:
The Spy Who Came In From the Cold
United Nations Award:
The War Game
Best British Actress:
Elizabeth Taylor, *Who's Afraid of Virginia Woolf?*
Best British Actor:
Richard Burton, *The Spy Who Came In From the Cold; Who's Afraid of Virginia Woolf?*
Best Foreign Actress:
Jeanne Moreau, *Viva Maria*
Best Foreign Actor:
Rod Steiger, *The Pawnbroker*
Best Promising Newcomer:
Vivien Merchant, *Alfie*
Robert Flaherty Award (Best Feature-Length Documentary):
Goal! The World Cup
Best Short Film:
The War Game
Best Specialized Film:
Exploring Chemistry

Best Screenplay (British Film):
David Mercer, *Morgan—A Suitable Case for Treatment*
Best Cinematography (British Film):
  Black and White:
  Oswald Morris, *The Spy Who Came In From the Cold*
  Color:
  Christopher Challis, *Arabesque*
Best Art Direction (British Film):
  Black and White:
  Tambi Larsen, *The Spy Who Came In From the Cold*
  Color:
  Wilfrid Shingleton, *The Blue Max*
Best Costume Design (British Film):
  Black and White:
  (No award given this year)
  Color:
  Julie Harris, *The Wrong Box*
Best Editing (British Film):
Tom Priestly, *Morgan—A Suitable Case for Treatment*

1967

Best Film:
A Man for All Seasons
Best British Film:
A Man for All Seasons
United Nations Award:
In the Heat of the Night
Best British Actress:
Edith Evans, *The Whisperers*
Best British Actor:
Paul Scofield, *A Man for All Seasons*
Best Foreign Actress:
Anouk Aimee, *A Man and a Woman*
Best Foreign Actor:
Rod Steiger, *In the Heat of the Night*
Most Promising Newcomer:
Faye Dunaway, *Bonnie and Clyde*

Robert Flaherty Award (Best Feature-Length Documentary):
To Die in Madrid
Best Short Film:
Indus Waters
Best Specialized Film:
Energy and Matter
Best Animated Film:
Notes on a Triangle
Best Screenplay (British Film):
Robert Bolt, *A Man for All Seasons*
Best Cinematography (British Film):
  Black and White:
  Gerry Turpin, *The Whisperers*
  Color:
  Ted Moore, *A Man for All Seasons*
Best Art Direction (British Film):
  Black and White:
  No award for this year
  Color:
  John Box, *A Man for All Seasons*
Best Costume Design (British Film):
  Black and White:
  Jocelyn Rickards, *Mademoiselle*

1968

Best Film:
The Graduate
United Nations Award:
Guess Who's Coming to Dinner?
Best Director:
Mike Nichols, *The Graduate*
Best Actress:
Katharine Hepburn, *Guess Who's Coming to Dinner?; The Lion in Winter*
Best Actor:
Spencer Tracy, *Guess Who's Coming to Dinner?*
Best Supporting Actress:
Billie Whitelaw, *The Twisted Nerve; Charlie Bubbles*
Best Supporting Actor:
Ian Holm, *The Bofors Gun*
Most Promising Newcomer:
Dustin Hoffman, *The Graduate*

Robert Flaherty Award (Best Feature-Length Documentary):
In Need of Special Care
Best Specialized Film:
The Threat in the Water
Best Animated Film:
Pas de Deux
Best Screenplay:
Calder Willingham, Buck Henry, *The Graduate*
Best Cinematography:
Geoffrey Unsworth, *2001: A Space Odyssey*
Best Art Direction:
Tony Masters, Harry Lange, Ernie Archer, *2001: A Space Odyssey*
Best Costume Design:
Danilo Donati, *Romeo and Juliet*
Best Sound Track:
Winston Ryder, *2001: A Space Odyssey*
Anthony Asquith Memorial Award (Original Film Music):
John Barry, *The Lion in Winter*
Best Film Editing:
Sam O'Steen, *The Graduate*

1969

Best Film:
Midnight Cowboy
United Nations Award:
Oh! What a Lovely War
Best Direction:
John Schlesinger, *Midnight Cowboy*
Best Actress:
Maggie Smith, *The Prime of Miss Jean Brodie*
Best Actor:
Dustin Hoffman, *Midnight Cowboy; John and Mary*
Best Supporting Actress:
Celia Johnson, *The Prime of Miss Jean Brodie*
Best Supporting Actor:
Laurence Olivier, *Oh! What a Lovely War*
Most Promising Newcomer:
Jon Voight, *Midnight Cowboy*
Robert Flaherty Award (Best Feature-Length Documentary):
Prologue

Best Specialized Film:
Let There Be Light
Best Short Film:
Picture to Post
Best Screenplay:
Waldo Salt, *Midnight Cowboy*
Best Cinematography:
Gerry Turpin, *Oh! What a Lovely War*
Best Costume Design:
Anthony Mendelson, *Oh! What a Lovely War*
Best Film Editing:
Hugh A. Robertson, *Midnight Cowboy*
Best Sound Track:
Don Challis, Simon Kaye, *Oh! What a Lovely War*
Best Art Direction:
Don Ashton, *Oh! What a Lovely War*
Anthony Asquith Memorial Award (Original Film Music):
Mikis Theodorakis, *Z*

1970

Best Film:
Butch Cassidy and the Sundance Kid
United Nations Award:
M*A*S*H
Best Direction:
George Roy Hill, *Butch Cassidy and the Sundance Kid*
Best Actress:
Katharine Ross, *Tell Them Willie Boy is Here; Butch Cassidy and the Sundance Kid*
Best Actor:
Robert Redford, *Tell Them Willie Boy is Here; Butch Cassidy and the Sundance Kid*
Best Supporting Actress:
Susannah York, *They Shoot Horses Don't They?*
Best Supporting Actor:
Colin Welland, *Kes*
Most Promising Newcomer:
David Bradley, *Kes*
Best Specialized Film:
The Rise and Fall of the Great Lakes
Best Short Film:
Shadow of Progress

Robert Flaherty Award (Best Feature-Length Documentary):
Sad Song of Yellow Skin
Best Screenplay:
William Goldman, *Butch Cassidy and the Sundance Kid*
Best Cinematography:
Conrad Hall, *Butch Cassidy and the Sundance Kid*
Best Art Direction:
Mario Garbuglia, *Waterloo*
Best Costume Design:
Maria de Metteis, *Waterloo*
Best Film Editing:
John C. Howard, Richard C. Meyer, *Butch Cassidy and the Sundance Kid*
Best Sound Track:
Don Hall, David Dockendorf, William Edmundson, *Butch Cassidy and the Sundance Kid*
Anthony Asquith Award (Original Film Music):
Burt Bacharach, *Butch Cassidy and the Sundance Kid*

1971

Best Film:
Sunday, Bloody Sunday
United Nations Award:
The Battle of Algiers
Best Direction:
John Schlesinger, *Sunday, Bloody Sunday*
Best Actress:
Glenda Jackson, *Sunday, Bloody Sunday*
Best Actor:
Peter Finch, *Sunday, Bloody Sunday*
Best Supporting Actress:
Margaret Leighton, *The Go-Between*
Best Supporting Actor:
Edward Fox, *The Go-Between*
Most Promising Newcomer:
Dominic Guard, *The Go-Between*
Best Specialized Film:
The Savage Voyage
Best Short Film:
Alaska—The Great Land

Robert Flaherty Award (Best Feature-Length Documentary):
The Hellstrom Chronicle
Best Screenplay:
Harold Pinter, *The Go-Between*
Best Cinematography:
Pasquale De Santis, *Death in Venice*
Best Art Direction:
Ferdinando Scarfiotti, *Death in Venice*
Best Costume Design:
Piero Tosi, *Death in Venice*
Best Film Editing:
Richard Marden, *Sunday, Bloody Sunday*
Best Soundtrack:
Giuseppe Muratori, *Death in Venice*
Anthony Asquith Award (Original Film Music):
Michel Legrand, *Summer of '42*

1972

Best Film:
Cabaret
United Nations Award:
The Garden of the Finzi-Continis
Best Direction:
Bob Fosse, *Cabaret*
Best Actress:
Liza Minnelli, *Cabaret*
Best Actor:
Gene Hackman, *The French Connection; The Poseidon Adventure*
Best Supporting Actress:
Cloris Leachman, *The Last Picture Show*
Best Supporting Actor:
Ben Johnson, *The Last Picture Show*
Most Promising Newcomer:
Joel Grey, *Cabaret*
Best Specialized Film:
Cutting Oils and Fluids
Best Short Film (John Grierson Award):
Memorial
Best Screenplay:
Paddy Chayefsky, *The Hospital*
Larry McMurtry, Peter

Bogdanovich, *The Last Picture Show*
Best Cinematography:
Geoffrey Unsworth, Cabaret; *Alice's Adventures in Wonderland*
Best Art Direction:
Rolf Zehetbauer, *Cabaret*
Best Costume Design:
Anthony Mendelson, *Young Winston; Macbeth; Alice's Adventures in Wonderland*
Best Film Editing:
Jerry Greenberg, *The French Connection*
Best Soundtrack:
David Hildyard, Robert Knudson, Arthur Piantadosi, *Cabaret*
Anthony Asquith Award (Original Film Music):
Nino Rota, *The Godfather*

1973

Best Film:
Day for Night
United Nations Award:
State of Siege
Best Direction:
Francois Truffaut, *Day for Night*
Best Actress:
Stephane Audran, *The Discreet Charm of the Bourgeoisie; Juste avant la nuit*
Best Actor:
Walter Matthau, *Pete'n' Tillie; Charley Varrick*
Best Supporting Actress:
Valentina Cortese, *Day for Night*
Best Supporting Actor:
Arthur Lowe, *O Lucky Man!*
Most Promising Newcomer:
Peter Egan, *The Hireling*
Best Specialized Film:
A Man's World
Best Short Film (John Grierson Award):
Caring for History
Best Feature-Length Documentary (Robert Flaherty Award):
Grierson
Best Animated Film:
Tchou-Tchou

Best Screenplay:
Luis Bunuel, Jean-Claude Carrière, *The Discreet Charm of the Bourgeoisie*
Best Cinematography:
Anthony Richmond, *Don't Look Now*
Best Art Direction:
Natasha Kroll, *The Hireling*
Best Costume Design:
Phyllis Dalton, *The Hireling*
Best Film Editing:
Ralph Kemplen, *The Day of the Jackal*
Best Soundtrack:
Les Wiggins, Gordon K. McCallum, Keith Grant, *Jesus Christ Superstar*
Anthony Squith Award (Original Film Music):
Alan Price, *O Lucky Man!*

1974

Best Film:
Lacombe, Lucien
United Nations Award:
Lacombe, Lucien
Best Direction:
Roman Polanski, *Chinatown*
Best Actress
Joanne Woodward, *Summer Wishes, Winter Dreams*
Best Actor:
Jack Nicholson, *Chinatown; The Last Detail*
Best Supporting Actress:
Ingrid Bergman, *Murder on the Orient Express*
Best Supporting Actor:
John Gielgud, *Murder on the Orient Express*
Most Promising Newcomer:
Georgina Hale, *Mahler*
Best Screenplay:
Robert Towne, *Chinatown; The Last Detail*
Best Cinematography:
Douglas Slocombe, *The Great Gatsby*
Best Art Direction:
John Box, *The Great Gatsby*
Best Costume Design:
Theoni V. Aldredge, *The Great Gatsby*
Best Editing:
Walter Murch, *Richard Chew, The Conversation*

Best Soundtrack:
Art Rochester, Nat Boxer,
Mike Evoe, Walter Murch,
The Conversation
**Anthony Asquith Award
(Original Film Music):**
Richard Rodney Bennett,
*Murder on the Orient
Express*

1975

Best Film:
*Alice Doesn't Live Here
Anymore*
United Nations Award:
Conrack
Best Direction:
Stanley Kubrick, *Barry Lyndon*
Best Actress:
Ellen Burstyn, *Alice Doesn't
Live Here Anymore*
Best Actor:
Al Pacino, *The Godfather II;
Dog Day Afternoon*
Best Supporting Actress:
Diane Ladd, *Alice Doesn't Live
Here Anymore*
Best Supporting Actor:
Fred Astaire, *The Towering
Inferno*
Most Promising Newcomer:
Valerie Perrine, *Lenny*
Best Specialized Film:
*The Curiosity That Kills the
Cat*
Best Animated Film:
Great
**Best Short Film (John
Grierson Award)**
Sea Area Forties
**Best Feature-Length
Documentary (Robert
Flaherty Award):**
The Early Americans
Best Screenplay
Robert Getchell, *Alice Doesn't
Live Here Anymore*
Best Cinematography:
John Alcott, *Barry Lyndon*
Best Art Direction:
John Box, *Rollerball*
Best Costume Design:
Ann Roth, *Day of the Locust*
Best Film Editing:
Dede Allen, *Dog Day
Afternoon*

Best Soundtrack:
William A. Sawyer, Jim Webb,
Chris McLaughlin, Richard
Portman, *Nashville*
**Anthony Asquith Award
(Original Film Music):**
John Williams, *Jaws; The
Towering Inferno*

1976

Best Film:
*One Flew Over the Cuckoo's
Nest*
Best Direction:
Milos Forman, *One Flew Over
the Cuckoo's Nest*
Best Actress:
Louise Fletcher, *One Flew
Over the Cuckoo's Nest*
Best Actor:
Jack Nicholson, *One Flew
Over the Cuckoo's Nest*
Best Supporting Actress:
Jodie Foster, *Bugsy Malone;
Taxi Driver*
Best Supporting Actor:
Brad Dourif, *One Flew Over
the Cuckoo's Nest*
Most Promising Newcomer:
Jodie Foster
Best Specialized Film:
Hydraulics
Best Short Factual Film:
The End of the Road
**Best Feature-Length
Documentary (Robert
Flaherty Award):**
Albert Kish, *Los Canadienses*
Best Screenplay:
Alan Parker, *Bugsy Malone*
Best Cinematography
Russell Boyd, *Picnic at
Hanging Rock*
Best Art Direction:
Geoffrey Kirkland, *Bugsy
Malone*
Best Costume Design:
Moidele Bickel, *The Marquise
of O*
Best Film Editing:
Richard Chew, Lynzee
Klingman, Sheldon Kahn,
*One Flew Over the
Cuckoo's Nest*
Best Soundtrack:
Les Wiggins, Clive Winter,
Ken Barker, *Bugsy Malone*

**Anthony Asquith Award
(Original Film Music):**
Bernard Herrmann, *Taxi Driver*

1977

Best Film:
Annie Hall
Best Direction:
Woody Allen, *Annie Hall*
Best Actress:
Diane Keaton, *Annie Hall*
Best Actor:
Peter Finch, *Network*
Best Supporting Actress:
Jenny Agutter, *Equus*
Best Supporting Actor:
Edward Fox, *A Bridge Too Far*
Most Promising Newcomer:
Isabelle Huppert, *La
Dentelliere*
Best Specialized Film:
Path of the Paddle
Best Short Factual Film:
The Living City
Best Short Fictional Film:
The Bead Game
Best Screenplay:
Woody Allen, Marshall
Brickman, *Annie Hall*
Best Cinematography:
Geoffrey Unsworth, *A Bridge
Too Far*
Best Art Direction:
Danilo Donati, *Fellini's
Casanova*
Best Costume Design:
Danilo Donati, *Fellini's
Casanova*
Best Editing:
Ralph Rosenblum, Wendy
Greene Bricmount, *Annie
Hall*
Best Soundtrack:
Peter Horrocks, Gerry
Humphrey, Simon Kaye,
Robin O'Donaoghue, Les
Wiggins, *A Bridge Too Far*
**Anthony Asquith Award
(Original Film Music):**
John Addison, *A Bridge Too
Far*
Fellowship Award:
Fred Zinnemann

1978

Best Film:
Julia
Best Direction:
Alan Parker, Midnight Express
Best Actress:
Jane Fonda, Julia
Best Actor:
Richard Dreyfuss, Goodbye
Girl
Best Supporting Actress:
Geraldine Page, Interiors
Best Supporting Actor:
John Hurt, Midnight Express
Most Promising Newcomer:
Christopher Reeve, Superman
Best Screenplay:
Alvin Sargent, Julia
Best Cinematography:
Douglas Slocombe, Julia
Best Art Direction:
Joe Alves, Close Encounters
of the Third Kind
Best Costume Design:
Anthony Powell, Death on the
Nile
Best Film Editing:
Gerry Hambling, Midnight
Express

Best Soundtrack:
Don MacDougall, Ray West,
Bob Minkler, Derek Ball,
Star Wars
**Anthony Asquith Award
(Original Film Music):**
John Williams, Star Wars
**Michael Balcon Award
(Outstanding British
Contribution to Cinema)**
Les Bowie, Colin Chilvers,
Denys Coops, Roy Field,
Derek Meddings, Zoran
Perisic, special effects for
Superman
Fellowship Award:
Lord Lew Grade

1979

Best Film:
Manhattan
Best Direction:
Francis Coppola, Apocalypse
Now
Best Actress:
Jane Fonda, China Syndrome

Best Actor:
Jack Lemmon, China
Syndrome
Best Supporting Actress:
Rachel Roberts, Yanks
Best Supporting Actor:
Robert Duvall, Apocalypse
Now
Most Promising Newcomer:
Dennis Christopher, Breaking
Away
Best Screenplay:
Woody Allen, Marshall
Brickman, Manhattan
Best Cinematography:
Vilmos Zsigmond, Deer Hunter
Hunter
Best Art Direction:
Michael Seymour, Alien
Best Costume Design:
Shirley Russell, Yanks
Best Film Editing:
Peter Zinner, Deer Hunter
Best Sound:
Derrick Leather, Jim Shields,
Bill Rowe, Alien
Robert Flaherty Award:
Tree of Wooden Clogs
**Anthony Asquith Award
(Original Film Music):**
Ennio Morricone, Days of
Heaven

7/THE LOS ANGELES FILM CRITICS ASSOCIATION

THE LOS ANGELES Film Critics Association, which includes more than 20 movie reviewers working in the Los Angeles area, presented its first awards in 1975, some 40 years after the New York Film Critics Circle established its prizes. The Los Angeles Association traditionally announces its winners during the third week of December, right after the "Christmas film flood." For the first three years, the presentations were made at informal receptions held in January, but the 1978 awards were presented on *The Merv Griffin Show*.

How do the L.A. prizes compare with their east coast counterparts? Between 1976 and 1978, the Los Angeles and the New York critics do not coincide once on their choices of Best Film, Best Director, Best Supporting Actor, or Best Supporting Actress. The two groups, however, have seen eye-to-eye during all three years on their selections for Best Script. And in 1979 the two organizations' prizes were almost identical.

The Los Angeles Film Critics Association also confers an annual Career Achievement Award during each summer. Winners include John Huston, Alan Dwan, King Vidor and Orson Welles.

1976

Best Picture:
  Network
  Rocky
Best Director:
  Sidney Lumet, *Network*
Best Actor:
  Robert De Niro, *Taxi Driver*
Best Actress:
  Liv Ullmann, *Face to Face*
Best Screenplay:
  Paddy Chayefsky, *Network*
Best Cinematography:
  Haskell Wexler, *Bound for Glory*
Best Musical Score:
  Bernard Herrmann, *Taxi Driver*
Best Foreign Film:
  Face to Face

Special Awards:
  Marcel Ophuls, *The Memory of Justice*
  Max Laemmle for his many years of innovative programming of specialized motion pictures in Los Angeles

1977

Best Picture:
  Star Wars
Best Director:
  Herbert Ross, *The Turning Point*
Best Actor:
  Richard Dreyfuss, *The Goodbye Girl*
Best Actress:
  Shelley Duvall, *Three Women*
Best Supporting Actor:
  Jason Robards, *Julia*

Best Supporting Actress
Vanessa Redgrave, *Julia*
Best Screenplay:
Woody Allen and Marshall Brickman, *Annie Hall*
Best Cinematography:
Douglas Slocombe, *Julia*
Best Foreign Language Film:
That Obscure Object of Desire
Best Musical Score:
John Williams, *Star Wars*
Special Award:
Gary Allison for initiative in writing and producing *Fraternity Row* and setting a pattern for film students to work on a profession level.

1978

Best Picture:
Coming Home
Best Director:
Michael Cimino, *The Deer Hunter*
Best Actor:
Jon Voight, *Coming Home*
Best Actress:
Jane Fonda, *Coming Home, Comes a Horseman*
Best Supporting Actor:
Robert Morley, *Who Is Killing The Great Chefs of Europe?*
Best Supporting Actress:
Maureen Stapleton, *Interiors*
Mona Washbourne, *Stevie*

Best Screenplay:
Paul Mazursky, *An Unmarried Woman*
Best Cinematography:
Nestor Almendros, *Days of Heaven*
Best Musical Score:
Giorgio Moroder, *Midnight Express*
Best Foreign Language Film:
Madame Rosa

1979

Best Picture:
Kramer v. Kramer
Best Director:
Robert Benton, *Kramer v. Kramer*
Best Actor:
Dustin Hoffman, *Kramer v. Kramer*
Best Actress:
Sally Field, *Norma Rae*
Best Supporting Actor:
Melvyn Douglas, *Being There; Seduction of Joe Tynan*
Best Supporting Actress:
Meryl Streep, *Manhattan; Seduction of Joe Tynan; Kramer v. Kramer*
Best Screenplay:
Robert Benton, *Kramer v. Kramer*
Best Cinematography:
Caleb Deschanel, *The Black Stallion*
Best Musical Score:
Carmine Coppola, *The Black Stallion*
Best Foreign Film:
Soldier of Orange

8/THE WRITERS GUILD OF AMERICA AWARDS

THE HOLLYWOOD WRITER has probably suffered more abuse and enjoyed less recognition than any other member of the filmmaking team. Accordinging to the Eastern literary establishment, the Hollywood writer betrays his talent and belittles his art if he stays in Hollywood too long. (Edmund Wilson, for example, once claimed that the failures of F. Scott Fitzgerald and Nathanael West to get the best out of their best years "may certainly be laid partly to Hollywood with its already appalling record of talent depraved and wasted.") According to the industry, the Hollywood writer is more of a commodity than an artist. (An efficiency expert at RKO during the 1930s once angrily announced, "I've been through the whole Writers Building, every office, 28 writers—and you know how many of them were writing? Three!") And according to the film scholar, the Hollywood writer hardly has anything to do with a film's success. (The influential *auteur* theory argues that it's the director and not the writer who is the author of a film.)

Recently the Hollywood writer's reputation has been rehabilitated, and he is at long last beginning to receive due recognition. Tom Dardis' *Some Time in the Sun,* for example, maintains that the famous novelists who went to Hollywood actually learned, not suffered from their Hollwood careers. Pauline Kael's *Raising Kane* claims that the importance of *Citizen Kane* is due

to as much to screenwriter Herman J. Mankiewicz as to director Orson Welles. And most important, Richard Corliss's *Talking Pictures: Screenwriters in the American Cinema* and his anthology. *The Hollywood Screenwriters,* radically revise our ideas about the screenwriter's importance.

D.W. Griffith, himself a director of overwhelming importance, once claimed that the director could only play "Paderewski to the screenwriter's Beethoven," that movies could not be a great art form without great screenwriters. Perhaps we are now approaching the day when Griffith's largely forgotten sentiments will be shared by the film community.

The Screen Writers Guild of America was founded in the 1920s and underwent extensive reorganization in 1933. In its attempt to protect the screenwriter's rights, the Guild met considerable opposition in the 1930s from the producers. in 1933, when the Guild prohibited its members from signing long-term contracts, Louis B. Mayer threatened to fire all Guild members who were under contract with his studio. Only after years of bitter conflict did the Guild win the right to be a collective-bargaining agent for writers.

Throughout the years, one of the principal activities of the Guild has been credit arbitration. Because Hollywood screenplays are so often written by a string of writers, it is frequently difficult to decide who rightfully deserves screen credit and the Guild has worked tirelessly in the field of credit jurisdiction. The Guild, then, is a divided creature; at once a labor union occupied with economics and an art guild concerned with the freedom of creativity.

In 1949 the guild presented its first awards for writing achievements and has continued to honor excellence in screenwriting down to the present day. The awards have filled an important gap, for although the Academy has honored screenwriting achievements since its first awards, film writing has been neglected by many other organizations. There are, for example, no Pulitzer Prizes for screenwriters, no Nobels. More than 20 years passed before the New York Film Critics included writing among their prizes, and the National Board of Review still does not confer annual awards for film scripts.

In 1954 the Screen Writers Guild merged with the Radio Writers Guild and the Television Writers Guild to form the Writers Guild of America, East and West. Motion-picture writers belong to the screen Branch of the Writers Guild of America, West. In addition to film awards, the Writers Guild also confers prizes in the fields of television and radio. These awards, however, are not listed here.

The following is a list of special film prizes conferred by the Guild:

The Robert Meltzer Award "given for the screenplay dealing most ably with problems of the American scene" (presented 1948-1951).

The Laurel Award for Achievement "given annually to that member of the Guild who, in the opinion of the current Executive Board of the Screen Branch, has advanced the literature of the motion picture through the years, and who has made outstanding contributions to the profession of the Screen Writer" (first presented 1953).

The Valentine Davies Award. "In memory of Valentine Davies, whose contribution to the motion picture community brought dignity and honor to writers everywhere" (first presented 1962).

Founders Award (first presented 1966).

The Morgan Cox Award "presented to that member or group of members whose vital ideas, continuing efforts and personal sacrifices best exemplify the ideal of service to the Guild which the life of Morgan Cox so fully represented" (first presented 1969).

Medallion Award (first presented 1971).

1948

Best-Written American Comedy:
F. Hugh Herbert, *Sitting Pretty*
Best-Written American Drama:
Frank Partos, Millen Brand, *The Snake Pit*
Best-Written American Western:
John Huston, *Treasure of Sierra Madre*
Best-Written American Musical:
Sidney Sheldon, Frances Goodrich, Albert Hackett (screenplay); Frances Goodrich, Albert Hackett (story), *Easter Parade*

Robert Meltzer Award:
Frank Partos, Millen Brand, *The Snake Pit*

1949

Best-Written American Comedy:
Joseph L. Mankiewicz, *A Letter to Three Wives*
Best-Written American Drama:
Robert Rossen, *All the King's Men*
Best-Written American Western:
Lamar Trotti (screenplay) W.R. Burnett (story), *Yellow Sky*

Best-Written American Musical:
Betty Comden, Adolph Green, *On the Town (based on an idea by Jerome Robbins)*
Robert Meltzer Award:
Robert Rossen, *All the King's Men*

1950

Best Written American Comedy:
Joseph L. Mankiewicz, *All About Eve* (also entered as Drama)
Best-Written American Drama:
Charles Brackett, Billy Wilder, D.M. Marshman, Jr., *Sunset Boulevard*

Best-Written American Western:
Michael Blankfort, *Broken Arrow*
Best-Written American Musical:
Sidney Sheldon, *Annie Get Your Gun*
Robert Meltzer Award:
Carl Foreman, *The Men*

1951

Best-Written American Comedy:
Frances Goodrich, Albert Hackett, *Father's Little Dividend*
Best-Written American Drama:
Michael Wilson, Harry Brown, *A Place in the Sun*
Best-Written American Low-Budget Film:
Samuel Fuller, *The Steel Helmet*
Best-Written American Musical:
Alan Jay Lerner, *An American in Paris*
Robert Meltzer Award:
Robert Buckner, *Bright Victory*

1952

Best-Written American Comedy:
Frank S. Nugent, *The Quiet Man*
Best-Written American Drama:
Carl Foreman, *High Noon*
Best-Written American Musical:
Betty Comden, Adolph Green, *Singin' in the Rain*
Laurel Award for Achievement:
Sonya Levien

1953

Best-Written American Comedy:
Ian McLellan Hunter, John Dighton (screenplay); Ian McLellan Hunter (story), *Roman Holiday*
Best-Written American Drama:
Daniel Taradash, *From Here to Eternity*
Best-Written American Musical:
Helen Deutsch, *Lili*
Laurel Award for Achievement:
Dudley Nichols

1954

Best-Written American Comedy:
Billy Wilder, Samuel Taylor, Ernest Lehman, *Sabrina*
Best-Written American Drama;
Budd Schulberg, *On the Waterfront*
Best-Written American Musical:
Albert Hackett, Frances Goodrich, Dorothy Kingsley *Seven Brides for Seven Brothers*
Laurel Award for Achievement:
Robert Riskin

1955

Best-Written American Comedy:
Frank Nugent, Joshua Logan, *Mr. Roberts*
Best-Written American Drama:
Paddy Chayefsky, *Marty*
Best-Written American Musical:
Daniel Fuchs, Isobel Lennart (screenplay); Daniel Fuchs (story), *Love Me or Leave Me*
Laurel Award for Achievement:
Frances Goodrich, Albert Hackett, Julius J. Epstein, and Philip G. Epstein

1956

Best-Written American Comedy:
James Poe, John Farrow, S.J. Perelman, *Around the world in 80 Days*
Best-Written American Drama:
Michael Wilson, *Friendly Persuasion*
Best American Musical:
Ernest Lehman, *The King and I*
Laurel Award for Achievement:
Charles Brackett and Billy Wilder

1957

Best-Written American Comedy:
Billy Wilder, I.A.L. Diamond, *Love in the Afternoon*
Best-Written American Drama:
Reginald Rose, *Twelve Angry Men*
Best-Written American Musical:
John Patrick (screenplay); Vera Casary (story), *Les Girls*
Laurel Award for Achievement:
John Lee Mahin

1958

Best-Written American Comedy:
S.N. Behrman, George Froeschel, *Me and the Colonel*

Best-Written American Drama:
Harold Jacob Smith, Nathan E. Douglas, *The Defiant Ones*
Best-Written American Musical:
Alan Jay Lerner, *Gigi*
Laurel Award for Achievement:
Nunnally Johnson

1959

Best-Written American Comedy:
Billy Wilder, I.A.L. Diamond, *Some Like It Hot*
Best-Written American Drama:
Frances Goodrich, Albert Hackett, *The Diary of Anne Frank*
Best-Written American Musical:
Melville Shavelson, Jack Rose (screenplay), Robert Smith (story), *Five Pennies*
Laurel Award for Achievement:
Norman Krasna

1960

Best-Written American Comedy:
Billy Wilder, I.A.L. Diamond, *The Apartment*
Best-Written American Drama:
Richard Brooks, *Elmer Gantry*
Best-Written American Musical:
Betty Comden, Adolph Green, *The Bells Are Ringing*
Laurel Award for Achievement:
George Seaton

1961

Best-Written American Comedy:
George Axelrod, *Breakfast at Tiffany's*
Best-Written American Drama:
Sidney Carroll, Robert Rossen, *The Hustler*
Best-Written American Musical:
Ernest Lehman, *West Side Story*
Laurel Award for Achievement:
Philip Dunne
Valentine Davies Award:
Mary C. McCall, Jr.

1962

Best-Written American Comedy:
Stanley Shapiro, Nate Monaster, *That Touch of Mink*
Best-Written American Drama:
Horton Foote, *To Kill a Mockingbird*
Best-Written American Musical:
Marion Hargrove, *The Music Man*
Laurel Award for Achievement:
Joseph L. Mankiewicz
Valentine Davies Award:
Allen Rivkin

1963

Best-Written American Comedy:
James Poe, *Lilies of the Field*
Best-Written American Drama:
Harriet Frank, Jr., Irving Ravetch, *Hud*
Best-Written American Musical:
(no award presented this year)

Laurel Award for Achievement:
John Huston
Valentine Davies Award:
Morgan Cox

1964

Best-Written American Comedy:
Stanley Kubrick, Peter George, Terry Southern (screenplay); Peter George (story), *Dr. Strangelove*
Best-Written American Drama:
Edward Anhalt, *Becket*
Best-Written American Musical:
Bill Walsh, Don Da Gradi, *Mary Poppins*
Laurel Award for Achievement:
Sidney Buchman
Valentine Davies Award:
James R. Webb

1965

Best-Written American Comedy:
Herb Gardner, *A Thousand Clowns*
Best-Written American Drama:
Morton Fine, David Friedkin, *The Pawnbroker*
Best-Written American Musical:
Ernest Lehman, *The Sound of Music (no other nominations this year in this category)*
Laurel Award for Achievement:
Isobel Lennart
Valentine Davies Award:
Leonard Spigelgass

1966

Best-Written American Comedy:
William Rose, *The Russians*

Are Coming, The Russians Are Coming
Best-Written American Drama:
Ernest Lehman, *Who's Afraid of Virginia Woolf?*
Best-Written American Musical:
(no award presented this year)
Laurel Award for Achievement:
Richard Brooks
Valentine Davies Award:
Edmund H. North
Founders Award:
Charles Brackett and Richard Breen

1967

Best-Written American Comedy:
Calder Willingham, Buck Henry, *The Graduate*
Best-Written American Drama:
David Newman, Robert Benton, *Bonnie and Clyde*
Best-Written American Musical:
Richard Morris, *Thoroughly Modern Millie*
Best-Written Original Screenplay:
David Newman, Robert Benton, *Bonnie and Clyde*
Laurel Award for Achievement:
Casey Robinson
Valentine Davies Award:
George Seaton

1968

Best-Written American Comedy:
Neil Simon, *The Odd Couple*
Best-Written American Drama:
James Goldman, *The Lion in Winter*
Best-Written American Musical:
Isobel Lennart, *Funny Girl*

Best-Written Original Screenplay:
Mel Brooks, *The Producers*
Laurel Award for Achievement:
Carl Foreman
Valentine Davies Award:
Dore Schary

1969

Best-Written American Comedy Written Directly for the Screen;
Paul Mazursky, Larry Tucker, *Bob & Carol & Ted & Alice*
Best-Written American Comedy Adapted from Another Medium:
Arnold Schulman, *Goodbye Columbus*
Best-Written American Drama Written Directly for the Screen:
William Goldman, *Butch Cassidy and the Sundance Kid*
Best-Written Drama Adapted from Another Medium:
Waldo Salt, *Midnight Cowboy*
Laurel Award for Achievement:
Dalton Trumbo
Valentine Davies Award;
Richard Murphy
Morgan Cox Award:
Barry Trivers

1970

Best-Written American Comedy Written Directly for the Screen:
Neil Simon, *The Out-of-Towners*
Best-Written American Comedy Adapted from Another Medium:
Ring Lardner, Jr., *M*A*S*H*
Best-Written American Drama Written Directly for the Screen:
Francis Ford Coppola, Edmund H. North, *Patton*

Best-Written Drama Adapted from Another Medium:
Robert Anderson, *I Never Sang for My father*
Laurel Award for Achievement:
James Poe
Morgan Cox Award:
Leonard Spigelgass
Founders Award:
Lamar Trotti
Valentine Davies Award:
Daniel Taradash

1971

Best-Written Comedy Written Directly for the Screen:
Paddy Chayefsky, *The Hospital*
Best-Written Comedy Adapted from Another Medium:
John Paxton, *Kotch*
Best-Written Drama Written Directly for the Screen:
Penelope Gilliatt, *Sunday Bloody Sunday*
Best-Written Drama Adapted from Another Medium:
Ernest Tidyman, *The French Connection*
Laurel Award for Achievement:
Ernest Lehman
Valentine Davies Award:
Michael Blankfort, Norman Corin
Morgan Cox Award:
Allen Rivkin
Medallion Award:
(first time presented)
Charles Chaplin

1972

Best-Written Comedy Written Directly for the Screen:
Buck Henry, David Newman, Robert Benton, *What's Up, Doc*

Best-Written Comedy Adapted from Another Medium:
Jay Presson Allen, *Cabaret*
Best-Written Drama Written Directly for the Screen:
Jeremy Larner, *The Candidate*
Best-Written Drama Adapted from Another Medium:
Mario Puzo, Francis Ford Coppola, *The Godfather*
Laurel Award for Achievement:
William Rose
Valentine Davies Award:
William Ludwig
Morgan Cox Award;
David Harmon

1973

Best-Written Comedy Written Directly for the Screen:
Melvin Frank, Jack Rose, *A Touch of Class*
Best-Written comedy Adapted from Another Medium:
Alvin Sargent, *Paper Moon*
Best-Written Drama Written Directly for the Screen:
Steve Shagan, *Save the Tiger*
Best-Written Drama Adapted from Another Medium:
Waldo Salt, Norman Wexler, *Serpico*
Laurel Award for Achievement:
Paddy Chayefsky
Valentine Davies Award:
Ray Bradbury, Philip Dunne
Morgan Cox Award:
James R. Webb

1974

Best-Written Comedy Written Directly for the Screen:
Mel Brooks, Norman Steinberg, Andrew Bergman, Richard Pryor, Alan Uger, *Blazing Saddles*

Best-Written Adapted Comedy;
Mordecai Richler, Lionel Chetwynd, *The Apprenticeship of Duddy Kravitz*
Best-Written Drama Written Directly for the Screen:
Robert Towne, *Chinatown*
Best-Written Drama Adapted from Another Medium:
Francis Ford Coppola, Mario Puzo, *The Godfather Part II*
Laurel Award for Achievement:
Preston Sturges (posthumously)
Valentine Davies Award;
Fay Kanin
Morgan Cox Award:
Edmund North

1975

Best-Written Comedy Written Directly for the Screen:
Robert Towne, Warren Beatty, *Shampoo*
Best-Written Comedy Adapted from Another Medium:
Neil Simon, *The Sunshine Boys*
Best-Written Drama Written Directly for the Screen:
Frank Pierson, *Dog Day Afternoon*
Best-Written Drama Adapted from Another Medium:
Laurence Hauben, Bo Goldman, *One Flew Over the Cuckoo's Nest*
Laurel Award for Achievement:
Michael Wilson
Valentine Davies Award:
Winston Miller
Morgan Cox Awards:
William Ludwig

1976

Best-Written Comedy Written Directly for the Screen:
Bill Lancaster, *The Bad News Bears*
Best-Written Comedy Adapted from Another Medium:
Frank Waldman, Blake Edwards, *The Pink Panther Strikes Again*
Best-Written Drama Written Directly for the Screen:
Paddy Chayefsky, *Network*
Best-Written Drama Adapted from Another Medium:
William Goldman, *All the President's Men*
Laurel Award for Achievement:
Samson Raphaelson
Valentine Davies Award:
Carl Foreman
Morgan Cox Award:
Herbert Baker
Medallion Award:
Cesare Zavattini

1977

Best-Written Comedy Written Directly for the Screen:
Woody Allen, Marshall Brickman, *Annie Hall*
Best-Written Comedy Adapted from Another Medium:
Larry Gelbart, *Oh, God*
Best-Written Drama Written Directly for the Screen:
Avery Corman, Arthur Laurents, *The Turning Point*
Best-Written Drama Adapted from Another Medium:
Alvin Sargent, *Julia*
Laurel Award for Achievement:
Edward Anhalt
Valentine Davies Award:
Norman Lear
Morgan Cox Award:
John Furia, Jr.

1978

Best-Written Comedy Written Directly for the Screen:
Larry Gelbart, Sheldon Keller, *Movie, Movie*
Best-Written Comedy Adapted from Another Medium:
Elaine May, Warren Beatty, *Heaven Can Wait*
Best-Written Drama Written Directly for the Screen:
Waldo Salt, Robert C. Jones, *Coming Home*, story by Nancy Dowd

Best-Written Drama Adapted from Another Medium:
Oliver Stone, *Midnight Express*
Laurel Award for Achievement:
Neil Simon
Valentine Davies Award:
Melville Shavelson
Morgan Cox Award:
George Seaton

1979

Best-Written Comedy Written Directly for the Screen:
Steve Tesich, *Breaking Away*

Best-Written Comedy Adapted from Another Medium:
Jerzy Kosinski, *Being There*
Best-Written Drama Written Directly for the Screen:
Mike Gray, T.S. Cook and James Bridges, *The China Syndrome*
Best-Written Drama Adapted from Another Medium:
Robert Benton, *Kramer vs. Kramer*
Laurel Award for Achievement:
Billy Wilder and I.A.L. Diamond
Morgan Cox Award:
Fay Kanin
Valentine Davies Award
David W. Rintels

9/THE DIRECTORS GUILD OF AMERICA AWARDS

THE FUNCTIONS AND status of the film director have changed considerably. During the earliest years of filmmaking, the director really did not have "much" to do. Because each scene in the first movies was filmed in one long take with no cutting and little or no camera movement, the director's influence was severely limited: he merely made sure that the story had continuity and that the actors' best performances were recorded by the camera.

When film technique advanced with the well-known discoveries of Edwin S. Porter and D.W. Griffith, the director's responsibility grew and his opportunities to infuse a film with his own personal style similarly expanded. The placement, angle and movement of the camera, as well as such important matters as casting, costumes, sets and acting, could all be influenced or determined by the director. Despite this influence, for most of cinema's history the director—particularly the Hollywood director—has been considered only one of many members in the filmmaking crew: he was thought to be subordinate to the producer; he often had no say whatsoever in editing the film; and his name was rarely known by the public, who selected films according to their stars. (There were, of course, obvious exceptions; D.W. Griffith, Cecil DeMille and Alfred Hitchcock were attractions in their own right.)

The director's status was greatly enhanced during the 1950s, when a group of French critics writing for *Cahiers du Cinéma* (among them Francois Truffaut, Jean-Luc Godard, Claude Chabrol, and Eric Rohmer) postulated that the director was in fact the *auteur,* or author, of a film, that he was in the most favorable position to infuse a film with artistic qualities. As a result of this influential theory, attention became focused on directors' themes and styles, and many earlier American directors were favorably reassessed.

Although the *auteur* theory has come under attack in recent years, no longer being considered a complete enough approach to the complex art of film, people still think and talk about a film largely in terms of its director. Movies are often advertised by their director's name, as in Robert Altman's *Nashville* or Martin Scorsese's *Taxi Driver.* (The Directors Guild and the Writers Guild had quite a battle in 1967 over that use of the possessive apostrophe.) And most international film festivals list their entries by title, director, and country, again suggesting that the director holds first place among the filmmaking team.

The Directors Guild of America was founded in 1936 by 15 of Hollywood's top directors who wished to insure creative freedom in their work. The founding members included Howard Hawks, Rouben Mamoulian, King Vidor, Gregory LaCava, William Wellman, John Cromwell, Leo

McCarey, Lewis Milestone, Wesley Ruggles, Rowland V. Lee, Frank Tuttle, Richard Wallace, Frank Borzage, William K. Howard, and Eddie Sutherland. King Vidor was the Guild's first president.

Like the Writers Guild, the Directors Guild is the official bargaining agent for its members. In 1939 the Guild won the right to establish minimal wages and working conditions for assistant directors, and in 1944 the agreement was extended to cover the directors' salaries as well. The Guild is now 5,300 members strong.

Since 1948 the Guild has honored one of its members as the best director of the year. During the first five years of the awards, quarterly awards were also presented. Seasonal years (1948/49, 1949/50, ect.) were used initially, but the calendar year became the basis for the awards in 1951, resulting in some overlapping prizes that year.

Because it announces its awards prior to the Academy Awards presentation, the Guild is often used to predict who will win the Academy's choice for Best Director. Over the past 29 years since it has given awards based on the calendar year, the Guild has only disagreed twice with the Academy for its choice of Best Director: in 1968, when the Guild selected Anthony Harvey *(The Lion in Winter)*, while the Academy chose Carol Reed *(Oliver!)*; and in 1972, when the Academy honored Bob Fosse *(Cabaret)*, while the Guild awarded Francis Ford Coppola *(The Godfather)*.

The Guild also confers prizes for best direction in the field of television. These awards have not been listed here.

In 1979 the Guild established the Frank Capra Achievement Award, to go to the assistant director or unit production manager "who has made an outstanding contribution for an extended period of years to both the Directors Guild of America and the industry."

1948/49

Quarterly Awards:
Fred Zinnemann, *The Search*
Howard Hawks, *Red River*
Anatole Litvak, *The Snake Pit*
Joseph L. Mankiewicz, *A Letter to Three Wives*
Annual Award:
Joseph L. Mankiewicz

1949/50

Quarterly Awards:
Mark Robson, *The Champion*
Alfred L. Werker, *Lost Boundaries*
Robert Rossen, *All the King's Men*
Carol Reed, *The Third Man*
Annual Award:
Robert Rossen

1950/51

Quarterly Awards:
Billy Wilder, *Sunset Boulevard*
John Huston, *The Asphalt Jungle*
Joseph L. Mankiewicz, *All About Eve*
Vincente Minnelli, *Father's Little Dividend*
Annual Award:
Joseph L. Mankiewicz, *All About Eve*

1951

Quarterly Awards:
Alfred Hitchcock, *Strangers on a Train*
George Stevens, *A Place in the Sun*
Vincente Minnelli, *An American in Paris*
Annual Award:
George Stevens, *A Place in the Sun*

1952

Quarterly Awards:
Charles Crichton, *The Lavender Hill Mob*
Joseph L. Mankiewicz, *Five Fingers*
Fred Zinnemann, *High Noon*
John Ford, *The Quiet Man*
Annual Award:
John Ford

1953

Most Outstanding Directorial Achievement:
Fred Zinnemann, *From Here to Eternity*
Outstanding Directorial Achievement:
Charles Walters, *Lili*
William Wyler, *Roman Holiday*
George Stevens, *Stalag 17*
Critic Award:
Bosley Crowther, *New York Times*

1954

Most Outstanding Directorial Achievement:
Elia Kazan, *On the Waterfront*
Outstanding Directorial Achievement:
George Seaton, *The Country Girl*
Alfred Hitchcock, *Rear Window*
Billy Wilder, *Sabrina*
William Wellman, *The High and the Mighty*
Critic Award:
Harold V. Cohen, Pittsburgh Post-Gazette

1955

Most Outstanding Directorial Achievement:
Delbert Mann, *Marty*
Outstanding Directorial Achievement:
John Sturges, *Bad Day at Black Rock*
John Ford and Mervyn LeRoy, *Mister Roberts*
Elia Kazan, *East of Eden*
Joshua Logan, *Picnic*
Critic Award:
John Rosenfield, Dallas Morning-Evening Star

1956

Most Outstanding Directorial Achievement:
George Stevens, *Giant*
Outstanding Directorial Achievement
Michael Anderson, *Around the World in 80 Days*
William Wyler, *Friendly Persuasion*
King Vidor, *War and Peace*
Walter Lang, *The King and I*
Critic Award:
Francis J. Carmody, Washington News

D.W. Griffith Award:
(for outstanding achievement throughout a career.)
King Vidor

1957

Most Outstanding Directorial Achievement:
David Lean, *The Bridge on the River Kwai*
Outstanding Directorial Achievement:
Joshua Logan, *Sayonara*
Sidney Lumet, *Twelve Angry Men*
Mark Robson, *Peyton Place*
Billy Wilder, *Witness for the Prosecution*
Critic Award:
Hollis Alpert and Arthur Knight, Saturday Review

1958

Grand Award for Direction:
Vincente Minnelli, *Gigi*
D.W. Griffith Award:
Frank Capra
Critic Award:
Philip K. Scheuer, Los Angeles Times
Special Award:
Louella Parsons
Best Directed Non-English Film:
René Clair, *Gates of Paris*

1959

Grand Award for Direction:
William Wyler, *Ben-Hur*
Critic Award:
John E. Fitzgerald, *Our Sunday Vistor*

1960

Grand Award for Direction:
Billy Wilder, *The Apartment*

Critic Award:
Paul Beckley, New York Herald Tribune
Special Award of Honorary Membership:
Y. Frank Freeman

1961

Director Award:
Robert Wise, Jerome Robbins, *West Side Story*
Critic Award:
John Beaufort, Christian Science Monitor

1962

Director Award:
David Lean, *Lawrence of Arabia*

1963

Director Award:
Tony Richardson, *Tom Jones*
Critic Award:
Paine Knickerbocker, San Francisco Chronicle

1964

Director Award:
George Cukor. *My Fair Lady*
Critic Award:
James Meade, San Diego Union

1965

Director Award:
Robert Wise, *The Sound of Music*
Critic Award:
Sam Lesner, Chicago Daily News

D.W. Griffith Award:
William Wyler

1966

Director Award:
Fred Zinnemann, *A Man for All Seasons*

1967

Director Award:
Mike Nichols, *The Graduate*

1968

Director Award:
Anthony Harvey, *The Lion in Winter*
D.W. Griffith Award:
Alfred Hitchcock

1969

Director Award:
John Schlesinger, *Midnight Cowboy*
D.W. Griffith Award:
Fred Zinnemann

1970

Director Award:
Franklin Schaffner, *Patton*

1971

Director Award:
William Friedkin, *The French Connection*

1972

Director Award:
Francis Ford Coppola, *The Godfather*

1973

Director Award:
George Roy Hill, *The Sting*

1974

Director Award:
Francis Ford Coppola, *The Godfather II*

1975

Director Award:
Milos Forman, *One Flew Over the Cuckoo's Nest*

1976

Director Award:
John G. Avildsen, *Rocky*

1977

Director Award:
Woody Allen, *Annie Hall*

1978

Director Award:
Michael Cimino, *The Deer Hunter*

1979

Best Director:
Robert Benton, *Kramer vs. Kramer*
Frank Capra Achievement Award:
Emmett Emerson

10/DIRECTORS OF THE YEAR AWARDS

THE *International Film Guide*, the annual compendium of world film information, each year honors five directors with a profile of each director's life, a critique of his work, and a thorough filmography. Although a director may be selected for his overall contribution to film rather than for any single work, each honored director must be both still living (so a great director like Sergei Eisenstein has never been cited) and must have produced *recent* major work (so great directors like Jean Renoir and Howard Hawks have been omitted). The awards are nonrecurrent: once a director is honored, he is ineligible for future selection.

Peter Cowie, editor of the *Guide*, realizes that authorship in cinema is not a clear issue, that screenwriters, producers, stars, cinematographers and editors can certainly exert a major influence over a movie. But despite these other contributors, it is the director who most clearly can impose his signature on the film, according to Cowie.

Years before the *auteur* theory ever originated in France, cinema, Cowie says, was almost exclusively appreciated in terms of directors. And he wishes to maintain that appreciation: the goal of the *International Film Guide*, Cowie says, is "to place an uncompromising emphasis on the role of the director."

In selecting the Directors of the Year, Cowie claims not to make any arbitrary distinctions between commercial Hollywood movies and the European "art" film; rather, his criterion is "quality within any given genre or style." A popular Hollywood movie can of course merit our attention, Cowie says, as much as an experimental film: what counts in the director's personal vision.

The Directors of the Year awards from the first ten volums of the *International Film Guide* have been collected in book form. Above quotations are taken from this collection, entitled *50 Major Film-Makers*.

1964	1965	1966	1967
Luchino Visconti	Federico Fellini	Akira Kurosawa	Georges Franju
Orson Welles	Satyajit Ray	Francesco Rosi	Joseph Losey
Francois Truffaut	Luis Buñuel	Jacques Demy	Roman Polanski
Andrzei Wajda	Louis Malle	Richard Brooks	John Frankenheimer
Alfred Hitchcock	Stanley Kubrick	Bert Haanstra	Leopoldo Torre Nilsson

1968

Bo Widerberg
Joris Ivens
Sidney Lumet
Jan Nemec
Michelangelo Antonioni

1969

Sergei Bondarchuk
Milos Forman
Miklos Jancso
Arthur Penn
Jacques Tati

1970

Lindsay Anderson
Claude Chabrol
Kon Ichikawa
Pier Paolo Pasolini
Jerzy Skolimowski

1971

Mark Donskoi
Elia Kazan
Jean-Pierre Melville
Nagisa Oshima
Ewald Schorm

1972

Bernardo Bertolucci
Jorn Donner
Grigori Kozintsev
Eric Rohmer
Jan Troell

1973

Ingmar Bergman
Robert Bresson
Dusan Makavejev
Alain Resnais
John Schlesinger

1974

John Boorman
Istvan Gaal
Jean-Luc Godard
John Huston
James Ivory

1975

Robert Altman
Marco Ferreri
Wojciech Has
Richard Lester
Vilgot Sjoman

1976

Michael Cacoyannis
John Cassavetes
Francis Coppola
Rainer Werner Fassbinder
Krzysztof Zannusi

1977

Woody Allen
George Cukor
Setsuo Kobayashi
Claude Sautet
Lina Wertmüller

1978

Claude Goretta
King Hu
Vincente Minnelli
Michael Ritchie
Carlos Saura

1979

Shyam Benegal
Werner Herzog
Marta Mészáros
Fons Rademakers
Martin Scorsese

1980

Hal Ashby
Henning Carlsen
Bertrand Tavernier
Peter Weir
Wim Wenders

11 / THE INDEPENDENT FILM AWARDS

EXPERIMENTAL ARTISTS HAVE often encountered problems in this country, but experimental filmmakers have a particularly difficult time here. Whereas an avant-garde poet or painter can at least practice his art (even if he can't always get published or exhibited), the expense of filmmaking severely limits the frequency with which an avant-garde filmmaker can even work in his medium. Despite the increasing availability of inexpensive 16mm stock and equipment, filmmaking is still much more costly than poetry or painting. Thus, experimental films look radically different from Hollywood productions not only by design but by necessity as well: without the financial resurces of a major studio, the independent filmmaker has had to rely on his own ingenuity to make films.

Experimental filmmakers have also suffered neglect by most of our major newspapers and magazines. Even today, many of our most highly respected film critics confine their attention largely to more "conventional" narrative movies. In order to rectify this situation, Jonas Mekas started to publish *Film Culture* in 1955, the first American journal to take the avant-garde cinema seriously. Calling for the "thorough revision of the prevalent attitude to the function of cinema," *Film Culture* has often been compared to the French journal *Cahiers du Cinéma,* which has also been a voice for innovative filmmakers.

The first issues of *Film Culture* focused on European films, although some attention—mostly negative—was given to the embryonic experimental cinema in America. Plagued by financial difficulties from its beginnings, in 1958 the magazine collapsed as a monthly and started publishing on an irregular basis. At that time, *Film Culture* reversed its position and began to give attention to the experimental cinema of which it had been so critical. The magazine also turned its eyes from European to American filmmakers, and Andrew Sarris—usually credited with introducing the *auteur* theory to America—began publishing his now famous series of essays on Hollywood directors in *Film Culture.*

With its 19th issue, in 1959, *Film Culture* established the Independent Film Award to "point out original and unique American contributors to the cinema." During the late 1950s and early 1960s, Mekas' concept of the independent film was broader than it has become under the policies of such editors of P. Adams Sitney. The first years the awards went to narrative films like *Shadows* and *Primary,* which many current experimental filmmakers would no longer consider quite so experimental now that conceptualism and minimalism are so strongly favored.

The American underground cinema is still a matter of controversy. When the Museum of Modern Art screened a seven-evening series of "The History of the American Avant-Garde Cinema" in the spring of 1976, it aroused numerous debates. Andrew Sarris wrote a long review in the *Village Voice,* claiming that experimental cinema simply wasn't as important, diverse, interesting or even as truly experimental as commercial cinema. And Amos Vogel published an article in *Film Comment* arguing that the seven programs did not represent the *real* American avant-garde cinema.

It is, of course, the nature of the avant-garde to be controversial. But whatever one thinks of American Independent Cinema, one can't deny its achievements and the necessity of diverse film forms.

The Independent Film Awards listed below are accompanied by texts written by *Film Culture's* editors. For Michael Snow's prize, however, no text was printed at the time of the award's announcement, since in the same issue as the prize, several pieces about and by Snow were published. The editors of *Film Culture* have asked that brief excerpts from those articles be included here to serve as an accompanying text.

FIRST INDEPENDENT FILM AWARD (for 1959) to:
John Cassavetes for *Shadows*

Since John Cassavetes's film *Shadows,* independently produced by Maurice McEndree and Seymour Cassel, more than any other recent American film, presents contemporary reality in a fresh and unconventional manner, it rightly deserves the first Independent Film Award.

Cassavetes in *Shadows* was able to break out of conventional molds and traps, and retain original freshness. The improvisation, spontaneity, and free inspiration that are almost entirely lost in most films from an excess of professionalism are fully used in this film. The situations and atmosphere of New York night life are vividly, cinematically, and truly caught in *Shadows.* It breathes an immediacy that the

cinema of today vitally needs if it is to be a living and contemporary art.

SECOND INDEPENDENT FILM AWARD (for 1960) to:
Robert Frank and Alfred Leslie's *Pull My Daisy*

Looking back through our last year's film production, we have found a sad and infested landscape, with our official cinema still perpetuating long-dead styles and long-dead subjects. Our official cinema is completely out of tune with the times. We however believe that no art in modern times has any value if it is not modern. Only modern art can be creative, and only modern can be moral, since it does not place obstacles of clichés of life and art between man and the immediacy of life.

Pull My Daisy has all these qualities. Its modernity and its honesty, its sincerity and its humility, its imagination and its humor, its youth, its freshness, and its truth is without comparison in our last year's pompous cinematic production. In its camera work, it effectively breaks with the accepted and 1,000-years-old official rules of slick polished Alton Y Co. cinematographic schmaltz. It breathes an immediacy that the cinema of today vitally needs if it is to be a living and contemporary art.

THIRD INDEPENDENT FILM AWARD (for 1961) to:
Ricky Leacock, Don Pennebaker, Robert Drew, Al Maysles for the film *Primary*

Looking back through our last year's film production, we have found that *Primary,* more than any other film, reveals new cinematic techniques of recording life on film. Whereas the usual fiction film is drowned in heavy theatrics, and the usual theatrical and television documentary has become a pallid and dehumanized illustration of literary texts, in *Primary,* as well as in their film *Cuba Si, Yankee No,* Robert Leacock, Don Pennebaker, Robert Drew, and Al Maysles have caught scenes of real life with unprecedented authenticity, immediacy, and truth. They have done so by daringly and spontaneously renouncing old controlled techniques; by letting themselves be guided by the happening scene itself; by concentrating themselves only on man himself, without imposing on him any preconceived "form" or "idea" or "importance." We see *Primary* as a revolutionary step and a breaking point in the recording of reality in cinema. We further believe that the fiction film too, could intelligently profit from *Primary's* techniques.

Shadows and *Pull My Daisy* have indicated new cinematic approaches stylistically and formally. *Primary* goes one step further: By exploring new camera, sound, and lighting methods, it enables the film-maker to pierce deeper into the area of new content as well. The main handicap of cinema has been its expensiveness and its need for teamwork. Since most of human creation is a private personal action, the most sensitive artists have avoided cinema. The techniques of *Primary* indicate that we are entering a long-awaited era, when the budget of a sound film is the same as that of a book of poems, and by himself and unobtrusively, almost the same way as a poet observing a scene. Thus, heralded by *Primary*, we see another turning point in cinema.

There is a feeling in the air that cinema is only just beginning.

FOURTH INDEPENDENT FILM AWARD (for 1962) to:
Stan Brakhage for his films *The Dead* and *Prelude*

Looking back through last year's film production, we have found that Stan Brakhage's films, *The Dead* and *Prelude*, stand out as works of exquisite beauty; they point to the unexplored possibilities of the poetic cinema.

Singlemindedly and persistently, during the last ten years, Stan Brakhage has been pursuing his own personal vision. He has developed a style and a filmic language that is able to express with utmost subtlety the unpredictable movements of his inner eye. He has mastered silence as no other film-maker has done, he has made it an integral part of his films. He has eliminated from his work all literary elements, making it a unique and pure cinematic experience.

Whereas the bulk of the independent film-making in America and elsewhere follows the dramatic and the documentary film traditions, Brakhage has chosen poetry for his artistic self-expression. He has directed his eye inwards, into man's subconscious, wherefrom he draws snatches of the beauty and the meaning of man and the world. He has kept away from the obvious, the explainable, the banal, giving the cinema an intelligence and a subtlety that is usually the province of the older arts, and he has done this with fanatical consistency, upholding—and setting an example for others—the absolute independence of the film artist.

FIFTH INDEPENDENT FILM AWARD (for 1963) to:
Jack Smith for his film *Flaming Creatures*

In *Flaming Creatures*, Smith has graced the anarchic liberation of new American cinema with graphic and rhythmic power worthy of the best of formal cinema. He has attained for the first time in motion pictures a high level of art that is absolutely lacking in decorum; and a treatment of sex that makes us aware of the restraint of all previous film-makers.

He has shown more clearly than anyone before how the poet's license includes all things, not only of spirit, but also of flesh; not only of dreams and of symbol, but also of solid reality. In no other art but the movies could this have so fully been done, and their capacity was realized by Smith.

He has borne us a terrible beauty in *Flaming Creatures*, at a time when terror and beauty are growing more and more apart, indeed are more and more denied. He has shocked us with the sting of mortal beauty. He has struck us with not the mere pity or curiosity of the perverse, but the glory, the pageantry of Transylvania and the magic of Fairyland. He has lit up a part of life, although it is a part which most men scorn.

No higher single praise can be given an artist than this, that he has expressed a fresh vision of life. We cannot wish more for Jack Smith that this: that he continues to expand that vision, and make it visible to us in flickering light and shadow, and in flame.

SIXTH INDEPENDENT FILM AWARD (for 1964) to:
Andy Warhol for his films *Sleep, Haircut, Eat, Kiss* and *Empire*

Andy Warhol is taking cinema back to its origins, to the days of Lumière, for a rejuvenation and a cleansing. In his work, he has abandoned all the "cinematic" form and subject adornments that cinema had gathered around itself until now. He has focused his lens on the plainest images possible in the plainest manner possible. With his artist's intuition as his only guide, he records, almost obsessively, man's daily activites, the things he sees around him.

A strange thing occurs. The world becomes transposed, intensified, electrified. We see it sharper than before. Not in dramatic, rearranged contexts and meanings, not in the service of something else (even Cinéma Vérité did not escape this subjection of the objective reality to ideas) but as pure as it is in itself: eating as eating, sleeping as sleeping, haircut as haircut.

We watch a Warhol movie with no hurry. The first thing he does is that he stops us from running. His camera rarely moves. It stays fixed on the subject like there was nothing more meaningful and nothing more important than that subject. It stays there longer than we are used to. Long enough for us to begin to free ourselves from all that we thought about haircutting or eating or the Empire State Building; or, for that matter, about cinema. We begin to realize that we have never, really, seen those actions. The whole reality around become *differently* interesting, and we feel like we have to begin filming everything anew. A new way of looking at things and the screen is given through the personal vision of Andy Warhol; a new angle, a new insight—a shift necessitated, no doubt, by the inner changes that are taking place in man.

As a result of Andy Warhol's work, we are going to see soon these simple phenomena, like Eating, or Trees, or Sunrise filmed by a number of different artists, each time differently, each time a new Tree, a new Eating, a new Sunrise. Some of them will be bad, some good, some mediocre, like any other movie—and somebody will make a masterpiece. In any case, it will be a new adventure; the world seen through a consciousness that is not running after big dramatic events but is focused on more subtle changes and nuances. Andy Warhol's cinema is a mediation

on the objective world; in a sense, it is a cinema of happiness.

SEVENTH INDEPENDENT FILM AWARD (for 1965) to:
Harry Smith

Harry Smith's creative work reaches across two important fields of film:

His abstract works, both in color and black and white are among the most complex and rich, among the most beautiful, yet to come out of cinema. The modulations of color and form are so certain and subtle, delicate and bold, that these films rank among the very few where attempt is absolutely realized in attainment.

As an animator, Harry Smith is remarkable in perfection of technique, and in intensity of vision, unique. To the decorative wasteland of contemporary animation, he has brought fantastic opulent growth and orgiastic opiate undergrowth, the purest ritual, the most direct uncompromising magic—whether viewed as enchantment, beguilement, invocation; or as Boschian document of possibilities of Earth, Heaven, and Hell in our world and time.

For a generation, Harry Smith has been creating unquestionable masterworks. Now his films have come to light, and we are delighted to give them and their maker this recognition so long and well deserved.

EIGHTH INDEPENDENT FILM AWARD (for 1966) to:
Gregory Markopoulos

It is now almost twenty years that Gregory Markopoulos has been perfecting that quality so unlikely in the avant-garde, in the independent film —an imagistic elegance, a measured eloquence of editing, a delicate balance of all elements of plot, character, theme—a harmony as classic as the Greek myths of his major works.

At the same time, he has constantly been at the forefront among innovators, developing techniques of rapid cutting and subjective treatments of narrative time that were more than experimental, that were and remain truly new.

Such is the achievement of Gregory Markopoulos, from *Psyche* and *Swain* through *Twice a Man* and his latest completed work *Galaxie*, an achievement in which the traditions of classic and romantic are fused with the most modern art in the roundedness and lucidity of crystal.

NINTH INDEPENDENT FILM AWARD (for 1967) to:
Michael Snow for his film *Wavelength*

Wavelength is a "definitive statement of pure Film space and time, a balancing of 'illusion' and 'fact,' all about seeing." A continuous zoom which takes 45 minutes to go from its widest field to its smallest and final field, *Wavelength* is a work "whose PROCESS is so profoundly simple, tragic and inevitable, that it offers no human consolation, no compromise . . . In terms of the relationship of the viewer and the work, Michael Snow is pushing into new areas." And *Wavelength* is a summation of everything he has thought about, his nervous system, his religious inklings, his aesthetic ideas, everything.

TENTH INDEPENDENT FILM AWARD (for 1969) to:
Kenneth Anger

for his film *Invocation of My Demon Brother* specifically, and for his entire creative work in general; for his unique fusion of magick, symbolism, myth, mystery, and vision with the most modern sensibilities, techniques, and rhythms of being; for revealing it all in a refreshed light, persistently, constantly and with a growing complexity of means and content; at the same time, for doing it with an amzaing clarity, directness and sureness; for giving to our eye and our senses some of the most sensuous and mysterious images cinema has created; for being the Keeper of the Art of Cinema as well as the Keeper of the Eternal Magick Directions.

ELEVENTH INDEPENDENT FILM AWARD (for 1972) to:
Robert Breer

for his film work of the last twenty years. Since 1952 he has continued to produce a cinema of the highest quality, fusing the best of the earliest abstract cinema with the dynamics of the American Avantgarde Film. The liveliness of his films had restored the root meaning to "animation" at a time when most animated films invoked deadly tradition. For his unique contribution to the language of cinema in the exploration of the thresholds of rapid montage; for his pioneering work in the collage film; for his enrichment of the formal cinema with works that are visually, rhythmically, and intellectually exciting, enduring, new and clear, this award is presented.

TWELFTH INDEPENDENT FILM AWARD (for 1975) to:
James Broughton

We here celebrate this mystery that for thirty years James Broughton has sustained the vitality and freshness of vision that make him—one suddenly sees—the grand classic master of Independent Cinema. He is, as well, the old master of comedy among all directors anywhere now and—that most incongruous phenomenon—an avantgarde film-maker not merely with humor but dedicated to primal panic sacraments, the ancient sudden gusto, breath of absolute release, very spirit of the laugh.

This comic career now culminates in the autopsychographical *Testament*, surely Broughton's most moving picture; a ritual mask with sardonic bite which opens to giddy depths and let out the roar of good old animal spirits.

And over all these years, constant formal innovation too, an exaltation of essential image over the conveniences and conveyances of narrative; a concentration of time and purification of action which serve the revel, revelation of, not just absurdities or even enormities, but the largeness of life which necessarily naturally evokes that most manifestly gut reaction—laughter.

12/LIFE ACHIEVEMENT AWARDS

THE AMERICAN FILM Institute (AFI) established the Life Achievement Award in 1973 to honor the total career contributions of a filmmaker—regardless of place of birth —whose "talent has fundamentally advanced the art of American film or television, whose accomplishments have been acknowledged by scholars, critics, professional peers, and the general public, and whose work has withstood the test of time." The award, based on the collective judgment of AFI's Board of Trustees, is also accompanied by: a televised salute featuring film clips from the winner's career; scholarships in the winner's name to deserving students at the Institute's Center for Advanced Film Studies; a retrospective in the AFI Washington theater; an attempt to preserve all the films of the awards' recipient; and (since 1976) a special tribute in *American Film,* the official publication of AFI and now one of the most widely circulated film and television publications in the world.

The American Film Institute is an independent nonprofit organization established in 1967 by the National Endowment for the Arts to advance the art of film and television in the United States. The Institute preserves films, operates an advanced conservatory for filmmakers, gives assistance to new American filmmakers through grants and internships, provides guidance to film teachers and educators, publishes film books, periodicals and reference works, supports basic research and operates a national film repertory exhibition program. One of AFI's admirable archival efforts, for example, is cataloguing the entire output of American cinema since 1893. So far, two decades of the Institute Catalog of Feature Films have been published— 1921–30 and 1961–70—and work on the volume covering 1911–20 is under way. The Directing Workshop for Women assists women already involved in film to develop their skills as directors, another example of AFI's valuable activities. Each workshop student selects her own script and assembles, with the help of AFI, a volunteer crew and cast to shoot and edit her own project with complete artistic control. Past graduates of the workshop include such notable actresses as Lee Grant, Ellen Burstyn, Dyan Cannon, Joanne Woodward, and Cicely Tyson.

George Stevens, Jr. was the director of AFI from the inception of the Institute through 1979. Jean Firstenberg was appointed director in 1980. Its Board of Trustees (now chaired by Charlton Heston) includes the presidents of both the Motion Picture Association of America and the Academy of Motion Picture Arts and Sciences, as well as representatives from the fields of acting, writing, directing, producing and scholarly research. Although it is impossible to deny AFI's achievements—it has already preserved more than 14,000 films from the early years of American filmmaking—the Institute does have its critics. Some complain that *American Film,* despite its claim to cover film and television without fear or favor, is rather a safe and cautious magazine, decidedly middle-brow. Others have argued that AFI is more interested in its image than in its activities. Paul Schrader, the celebrated writer of *Taxi Driver* and one of the first of the 2,000 Fellows selected by AFI for its Center for Advanced Film Study at Greystone Mansion in Beverly Hills, has argued that AFI wastes its money on luxuries. The definitive mistake in AFI's history, Schrader says, is the lavish Greystone Mansion itself, which mistakenly equates filmmaking with wealth and which offers students the rewards of being successful without demanding the successful products.

The AFI Independent Filmmaker Program, which awards grants to finance projects ranging from experimental and animated films to documentary and narrative productions and which, funded by the National Endowment for the Arts, is the nation's major competition for independent filmmakers, has also come under attack. So far, $1.7 million has been funded to 230 filmmakers, but some say that too many well-known and established filmmakers have been among the recipients.

The history of the American Film Institute, in short, mirrors those of many other film organizations. Like the Academy of Motion Picture Arts and Sciences or like the National Board of Review, AFI began as an organization to advance the art of film, but in doing so has itself become the target of criticism. Hollywood, always being attacked, has protected itself with agencies, institutes and academies that themselves have increased rather than decreased the industry's supposed flaws. At times the history of Hollywood resembles a series of attacks that arouses defenses that arouse renewed attacks.

Few people, however, have criticized the Life Achievement Awards; the qualifications of its recipients are unquestionable. The only complaint heard is that at the rate of only one award a year, AFI cannot pay tribute to the dozens of people who also deserve its honors.

1973	1975	1977	1979
John Ford	Orson Welles	Bette Davis	Alfred Hitchcock
1974	**1976**	**1978**	**1980**
James Cagney	William Wyler	Henry Fonda	James Stewart

13/"MOVIE WORSTS" AWARDS

IN 1940 THE *Harvard Lampoon* announced its first "Movie Worsts" awards for those films released in 1939. The Academy Awards were then little more than a decade old, the New York Film Critics Awards had been presented for only five years, and the Golden Globes had not even been established yet. But already the *Lampoon* realized that film awards were a great subject for parody: film awards could be as inane as they were becoming numerous. "Every time you buy a bag of peanuts in this town," a character says in *Citizen Kane*, "they give you an award." The *Lampoon* could hardly agree more. So almost every year since 1940, the *Lampoon*—with cruelty, acerbity and great wit—has presented its "Movie Worsts."

In its preface to the 1963 awards, the *Lampoon*—in a rare moment of seriousness —said the "Movie Worsts" had four functions: (1) to express rage and disappointment over the failure of Hollywood either to entertain or to educate; (2) to rectify this failure through criticism; (3) to supply a tonic to cure the ballyhoo and inanity of the Academy Awards; and (4) to infuriate people over trivialities.

Although the target of the *Lampoon*'s criticism has varied over the years, the "Movie Worsts" have most frequently attacked Hollywood's sentimentality and pretentiousness. Religious epics, overdone literary adaptations and silly spectaculars have consistently been lambasted for their "extravagance and blundering ineffectiveness," to quote the citation from one of the *Lampoon*'s funniest prizes, "The Please- Don't- Put-Us-Through- DeMille-Again Award." And children and animals —over which Americans can be infinitely sentimental—have similarly aroused the *Lampoon*'s wrath.

The "Movie Worsts" awards have often been received with great hostility. Lawsuits have been threatened, and many fans have attacked the magazine for its awards. According to *The Harvard Lampoon Centennial Celebration*, more people were enraged about the choice of Dean Martin and Jerry Lewis in 1952 than about any other single award. But starting in the sixties, more and more people received the awards in the humor with which they were given. In 1961 one staff member of Walt Disney Productions even nominated Annette Funicello for Worst Actress even before the film she was then working on was finished. And in 1966 Natalie Wood surprised everyone by showing up to receive her Worst Actress award, and thereby started a tradition. (Instead of the Academy's gold-plated Oscar, Natalie Wood received a living 220-pound man dressed in gold lamé.) Since then, such people as Judith Crist and George Peppard have written the *Lampoon* letters thanking the magazine for awarding them "Movie Worsts" prizes, and even Elizabeth Taylor has appeared at Harvard to pick up her Worst Actress awards.

In recent years—ever since American academics granted film studies legitimacy —it has been popular to find the art beneath the surface of Hollywood films. Al-though it would be impossible to deny that in many of our films there is indeed gold where we once thought there was only dross, the *Lampoon*'s "Movie Worsts" re-mind us that in all too many movies the dross is indeed only dross.

1939

Ten Worst Pictures:
The Rains Came
Hollywood Cavalcade
Winter Carnival
St. Louis Blues
Five Little Peppers
Bad Little Angel
The Fighting 69th
Idiot's Delight
20,000 Men a Year
The Man in the Iron Mask
Worst Actor:
Tyrone Power, *The Rains Came*
Worst Actress:
Norma Shearer, *Idiot's Delight*
Most Consistently Bad Performances:
Dorothy Lamour
Don Ameche
Most Colossal Flop:
The Wizard of Oz

1940

Ten Worst Pictures:
The Howards of Virginia
Swanee River
The Great Victor Herbert
1,000,000 B.C.
I Take This Woman
My Son, My Son
Green Hell
Lillian Russell
Typhoon
Boom Town

1941

Ten Worst Pictures:
Hudson's Bay

Wild Geese Calling
Belle Starr
Navy Blues
Honky Tonk
You Belong to Me
This Woman Is Mine
Lady Be Good
Aloma of the South Seas
Smilin' Through
Worst Performer:
Betty Grable
Worst Script:
Feminine Touch
Worst Discovery:
Veronica Lake
Most Unattractive Actress:
Jeanette MacDonald
Fastest-on-the-Downward-Pass Award:
Alice Faye, Nelson Eddy
Greatest Disappointment:
Sundown

1942

(Awards not presented this year)

1943

(Awards not presented this year)

1944

Ten Worst Pictures:
Kismet

A Song to Remember
Frenchman's Creek
Tonight and Every Night
Mr. Skeffington
Hollywood Canteen
Follow the Boys
Till We Meet Again
Thousands Cheer
Winged Victory
Worst Discovery:
Maria Montez in anything
Frank Sinatra and/or Van Johnson
Worst Script:
A Song to Remember
Most in Need of Retirement:
Paul Muni
Worst Scene:
The ketchup on the keys in *A Song to Remember*
Fastest-on-the-Downward-Pass Award:
Don Ameche
Most Unattractive:
Andrews Sisters in anything but a total blackout

1945

Ten Worst Pictures:
Weekend at the Waldorf
Music for Millions
This Love of Ours
The Enchanted Cottage
Where Do We Go from Here
Spellbound
Anchors Aweigh
Guest Wife
She Wouldn't Say Yes
Uncle Harry

Worst Single Performance—Female:
June Allyson, *Her Highness and the Bellboy*
Worst Single Performance—Male:
Van Johnson, *Thrill of a Romance*
Most Consistently Bovine Performances:
Alexis Smith
Oldest Actress of the Year:
Joan Crawford (honorable mention to Joan Bennett)

1946

Ten Worst Pictures:
(12 listed)
Night and Day
I've Always Loved You
Leave Her to Heaven
Margie
Adventure
Make Mine Music
The Searching Wind
No Leave, No Love
Road to Utopia
Of Human Bondage
Scarlet Street
The Harvey Girls
Worst Single Performance—Female:
Alexis Smith, *Night and Day*
Worst Single Performance—Male:
Orson Welles, *The Stranger*
Worst Supporting Performance—Female:
Linda Darnell, *Anna and the King of Siam*
Worst Supporting Performance—Male:
Andy Devine, *Canyon Passage*
Most Miscast—Female:
Ginny Simms as Ethel Merman, *Night and Day*
Most Miscast—Male:
Paul Henreid as Somerset Maugham in *Of Human Bondage*
Most Outrageous Misrepresentation of Fact:
Cornel Wilde as a former *Lampoon* editor in *Leave Her to Heaven*
Worst Juvenile Performance:
Jane Powell, *Holiday in Mexico*

Actress With Most Toes in the Graves:
Joan Crawford
Most Welcome Retirements:
Errol Flynn, Faye Emerson
Least Talented New Finds:
Glenn Ford, Catherine MacLeod
Worst Movie Couple:
Merle Oberon, Turhan Bey, *Night in Paradise*
Worst Script:
Three Strangers
Most Confusing Plot:
The Big Sleep
Worst Dialogue:
Adventure
Biggest Disappointment:
Song of the South
Least Stimulating Scene:
Nose-rubbing scene in *Notorious*
Most Ludicrous Scene:
Mickey Rooney, dancing with a 6'6" chorus girl in *Love Laughs at Andy Hardy*
Series Most in Need of Discontinuation:
Claudia and Co.
Most Tiresome Movie Device:
Twin-sister routine as exemplified in *A Stolen Life* (Bette Davis's) and *The Dark Mirror* (Olivia de Havilland's)
Most Frankly Cribbed Plot:
Angel on My Shoulder

1947

(Awards not presented this year)

1948

Ten Worst Movies:
Winter Meeting
Homecoming
The Emperor Waltz
The Miracle of the Bells
Beyond Glory
On an Island with You
The Paradine Case
The Three Musketeers
Arch of Triumph

Sorry, Wrong Number
Worst Performances:
Lana Turner, *The Three Musketeers*
Burt Lancaster, *I Walk Alone*
Shirley Temple, *Fort Apache*
Worst Fraud:
Eleanor Parker as Margaret Sullavan as Sally Middleton, *The Voice of the Turtle*
Worst Scene:
Ida Lupino sticking out her tongue at Errol Flynn in *Escape Me Never*
Worst Duo:
Dennis Morgan and Jack Carson alone, together, or in any combination
Worst Deception:
Joan Fontaine as a sixteen-year-old girl in *Letter from an Unknown Woman*
Worst Reincarnation:
Jeannette MacDonald, *Three Daring Daughters*
Worst Title:
That Wonderful Urge
Due for a Pension:
Deanna Durbin
Career up in Smoke:
Robert Mitchum
Most Stonefaced:
Lizabeth Scott
Best of this Year (OR ANY YEAR):
Four Feathers
Actress Most Likely to Drag Down Her Husband's Dubious Rep. as an Actor:
Mrs. Agar
All-Time Worst Hoyden:
Mrs. Agar
Most Nauseating Screen Voice:
Mrs. Agar

1949

Ten Worst Pictures of the Year:
Special Award:
Worst Picture of the Century:
Joan of Arc
The Other Nine:
The Great Gatsby
The Night Has a Thousand Eyes

Flamingo Road
Look for the Silver Lining
Top o' the Morning
The Fountainhead
The Fan
That Midnight Kiss
A Connecticut Yankee in King Arthur's Court

Worst Moment:
Ginger Rogers, in *The Barkeleys of Broadway* singing the "Marseillaise" to the "bravos" and "encores" of the Académie Francaise, in French, thank God

Worst Performance—Female:
Shirley Temple, *Mr. Belvedere Goes to College*

Worst Performance—Male:
Gregory Peck, *The Great Sinner*

Runner-up:
Gregory Peck in practically anything

Most Implausible:
Paulette Goddard as Lucrezia Borgia, *Bride of Vengeance*

Most Sickening Combination:
Claude Jarman, Jr., and Lassie

Most Consistently Unamusing:
Abbott and Costello

Least Likely to Warm Cockles of Heart:
Barry Fitzgerald

Least Likely to Warm Anything:
Barry Fitzgerald

Least Deserving but Most Due for a Pension:
Barry Fitzgerald

Also Overdue for Retirement:
Margaret O'Brien

Most Ridiculous Import:
Louis Jourdan

Worst Deceit:
Larry Parks as *Al Jolson*

Most Expressionless:
Alan Ladd

Least Frightening:
Mighty Joe Young

Most Frightening:
Tom Drake singing "Words and Music"

Finest Example for Clean-Cut American Youth:
Mrs. Aly Khan

Runner-Up:
Shirley Temple

Best-known Wife of Race-Horse Owner:
Mrs. Aly Khan

Meatball:
Aly Khan

1950

Ten Worst Pictures:
Our Very Own
Sampson and Delilah
Three Came Home
The Next Voice You Hear
An American Guerilla in the Philippines
Cheaper by the Dozen
Stromboli
The Flame and the Arrow
The Conspirators
The Duchess of Idaho

Worst Performances of the Year:
Clifton Webb, *Cheaper by the Dozen*
Elizabeth Taylor, *The Conspirators*

Worst Supporting Performances:
Cornell Wilde, *Two Flags West*
Celeste Holm, *All About Eve*

Most Depressing Discovery:
Faith Domergue

Least Likely to Succeed:
Cecile Aubrey

Worst Duo:
Esther Williams and Van Johnson, alone, together, or in any combination

Most Objectionable Movie Children:
Dean Stockwell
Elizabeth Taylor

Most Objectionable Ingénue:
Elizabeth Taylor

Most Unnecessary Contribution to the American Way of Life:
Bing Crosby, in anything

Most Miscast:
Burt Lancaster, as a sturdy Lombard peasant in *The Flame and the Arrow*

Greatest Travesty of the Holy Year:
Samson an Delilah

Worst Comedy:
Fancy Pants

Dullest:
Never a Dull Moment

Happiest Event of the Year:
Shirley Temple's announced retirement

Arrested Development:
William "Hopalong" Boyd

Worst Scene:
Micheline Presle huskily singing an old French Christmas carol between clinches with Tyrone Power in *An American Guerilla in the Philippines*

Worst Insult to the American Fighting Man:
John Wayne

Worst Assistant Producer:
Robert Goelet, Jr., for *Rapture*

Worst Title:
Oh, You Beautiful Doll

The Roscoe Award:
Elizabeth Taylor for so gallantly persisting in her career despite a total inability to act

---

1951

Ten Worst:
Tales of Hoffman
Valentino
Alice in Wonderland
That's My Boy
Texas Carnival
Take Care of My Little Girl
The Flame of Araby
Here Comes the Groom
David and Bathsheba
I Want You

Worst Performances of the Year:
Robert Taylor, *Quo Vadis*
Corinne Calvet, *On the Riviera*

Worst Supporting Performances:
Peter Lawford, *Royal Wedding*
Ava Gardner, *Showboat*

Worst Musical:
Painting the Clouds with Sunshine

Worst Double-bill:
Hard, Fast, and Beautiful
Rich, Young, and Pretty

Biggest Argument for Stricter Immigration Laws:
Mario Lanza

Finest Example of Idyllic Young Love:
Ava Gardner, Frank Sinatra

Most Unexpected Revival:
The Ape-man of Kawaloa
starring Barbara Peyton
Most Miscast:
Franchot Tone as a Boston
 Brahmin in *Here Comes the
 Groom*
**Most Noteworthy Examples
of Physical Fitness:**
Franchot Tone kicking Miss
 Florabella Muir
Humphrey Bogart felling
 unidentified girl in *El
 Morocco*
Great Travesty of the Year:
Alice in Wonderland
Should Have Stayed Home:
Ezio Pinza, principal victim of
 Mr. Imperium and *Strictly
 Dishonorable*
**Most Unattractive
Connotations:**
*The Model and the Marriage
 Broker*
Worst Dialogue:
St. Peter interviewing God in
 Quo Vadis
Worst Comic Duo:
Dean Martin and Jerry Lewis

1952

Ten Worst Pictures:
Jumping Jacks
Snows of Kilimanjaro
Quo Vadis
Son of Paleface
Million Dollar Mermaid
Bloodhounds of Broadway
Niagara
Because You're Mine
Affair in Trinidad
The Merry Widow
Worst Male Performance:
Jerry Lewis, *Sailor Beware,
 Jumping Jacks,* etc.
**Worst Support Male
Performance:**
Dean Martin, *Sailor Beware,
 Jumping Jacks,* etc.
Worst Female Performance:
Marilyn Monroe, *Niagara*
**Strongest Indictment of
Academic Freedom:**
Bonzo Goes to College
Most Ill-advised Refilming:
The Merry Widow

Worst Foreign Importation:
Brandy for the Parson
**Most Unattractive
Connotations:**
*She's Working Her Way
 Through College*
**Most Inspiring Example of
American Virility:**
Jerry Lewis
**Most Embarrassing
Infatuation with One's Own
Folksiness:**
Barry Fitzgerald
Edmund Gwenn
Most Brutally Exploited:
Ernest Hemingway
Sir Walter Scott
Hans Christian Andersen
Most Miscast:
Entire personnel of *Plymouth
 Adventure* as New England
 Puritans
Worst Moment:
Mitzi Gaynor mouthing "In the
 Sweet By and By" over her
 grandpappy's grave in
 Bloodhounds of Broadway
**Most Noteworthy Pre-Pubic
Flop:**
Tab "Sigh-Guy" Hunter
Shrewdest Business Move:
MGM's suspension of Mario
 Lanza
**Strongest Argument for
Laxer Divorce Laws:**
Marge and Gower Champion in
 Everything I Have Is Yours
**Most Sophisticated
Dialogue:**
The Thief
The Roscoe Award:
Jerry Lewis, who, by dint of
 incessant struggle, has
 unquestionably established
 himself as The Worst
 Commedian of All Time

1953

Ten Worst Movies:
The Robe
Salome
Beneath the Twelve-Mile Reef
Hondo
Torch Song
Call Me Madam
How to Marry a Millionaire
Easy to Love

I, the Jury
Gentlemen Prefer Blondes
Worst Performances:
Terry Moore, *Beneath the
 Twelve-Mile Reef*
Victor Mature, *The Robe*
**Worst Supporting
Performances:**
Brandon De Wilde, *Shane*
Zsa Zsa Gabor, *Moulin Rouge*
**Greatest Setback to
Christianity Since Nero:**
The Robe
Most Depressing Dotage:
Charles Laughton slavering
 over Rita Hayworth's
 abdominal dancing in *Salome*
Unsung Hero:
Musician who blew the bugle
 for Montgomery Clift in
 From Here to Eternity
Most Miscast:
Louis Calhern as a doddering
 Caesar in *Julius Caesar*
Silvana Mangano as a nun in
 Anna
**Best Argument for a
Stronger Navy:**
Paratroopers
Greatest Travesty:
Tony Curtis' systematic
 destruction of a legend in
 Houdini
**Most Unattractive
Connotations:**
Call Me Madam
Girls in the Night
Most Degrading Moment:
Charles Laughton being hit
 over the head with a shovel
 by Lou Costello in *Abbott
 and Costello Meet Captain
 Kidd*
**Most Unconvincing
Dialogue:**
Biff Elliot mouthing "It was
 easy" to a fading blonde in
 I, the Jury
**Grossest Exploitation of Old
Material:**
Refilming *King Solomon's
 Mines* backwards to achieve
 Mogambo
The Roscoe Award:
Terry Moore, the worst ingénue
 of 1953

1954

Ten Worst Movies:
Haaji Baba
There's No Business Like Show Business
The Egyptian
The High and the Mighty
Magnificent Obsession
Beau Brummel
The Student Prince
Knights of the Round Table
Demetrius and the Gladiators
White Christmas

Not Worth the Price of Admission:
Three Coins in the Fountain

Most Unconvincing Death Scene in Recent Years:
Stewart Granger in *Beau Brummel*

Most Fortuitous Drownings:
James Mason in *A Star Is Born* and *20,000 Leagues under the Sea*

Most Freudian Title:
River of No Return

Best Reasons for Healthy Paganism:
Demetrius and the Gladiators
The Silver Chalice

The Greatest Detriment to Anglo-Arabian Relations:
Haaji Baba

Most Thoughtful Deed of 1954:
The director of *The Student Prince* refusing to allow Mario Lanza to sing before the cameras

Most Convincing Nominee for Brood Mare of 1954:
Barbara Stanwyck, *Cattle Queen of Montana*

Greatest Mayhem Committed on a Myth:
White Christmas

Best Excuse for Another Thugee Rebellion in India:
The Bengal Brigade

Most Ingenuous Statement of the Year:
Gina Lollobrigida (quote in *Look*): "I am an actress, not a body."

Great Waste of Gas:
The Long, Long Trailer

Best Argument Against N.R.O.T.C.:
The Caine Mutiny

Saddest Evidence of Rapid Aging:
Jimmy Stewart impassively receiving a massage in *Rear Window*

The Roscoe Award:
Tony Curtis, whose marcelled and Mobilgreased locks have titillated scores of bobby-soxers, and Grace Kelly, who easily earns the title "Ironclad Virgin of 1954"

1955

Ten Worst Movies:
Not as a Stranger
Ulysses
The Prodigal
Hit the Deck
The Tall Men
The Rains of Ranchipur
Battle Cry
The Last Time I Saw Paris
The Long Grey Line
Underwater

Worst Actor:
Kirk Douglas, *Ulysses; Indian Fighter*

Worst Actress:
Debbie Reynolds, *Hit the Deck; Susan Slept Here*

Worst Supporting Actor:
Vic Damone, *Kismet*

Worst Supporting Actress:
Gloria Grahame, *Not as a Stranger*

First Annual Award for Crude Symbolism:
The fireworks in mounting crescendo as a backdrop for Grace Kelly and Cary Grant in their big scene in *To Catch a Thief*

Title With Most Interesting Alternatives:
Love Me or Leave Me

Most Pathetic Remnant of a Vanishing Race:
Victor Mature as Chief Crazy Horse in the movie of the same title

Most Mature Nature Movie:
The Seven-Year Itch

Most Unpropitious Return:
To Hell and Back

Greatest Threat to the Church Since Luther:
Johnny Ray becoming a priest in *There's No Business Like Show Business*

Most Heartening Decease:
Elizabeth Taylor, with Van Johnson at her deathbed, in *The Last Time I Saw Paris*

Greatest Gift to the Animal World Since Noah:
Walt Disney

Title With the Most Unattractive Connotations:
You're Never Too Young

Most Cretinous Performance:
Robert Mitchum, *Not as a Stranger*

Best Reason for Closing the Open Door:
Love Is a Many-Splendored Thing

Title With the Most Futile Advice:
Bring Your Smile Along

Most Monolithic Sleuth:
Jack Webb, *Pete Kelly's Blues*

Most Embarrassing Interlude:
Jennifer Jones, in *Love is a Many-Splendored Thing*, standing disconsolately on the proverbial high and windy hill, waiting for the show to end, to the tune of a stirring chant from an archangel chorus: "When your fingers touched my silent heart and taught it how to sing"

Bosco:
(in recognition of the advances recently made in the science of geriatrics)
June Allyson, who with eternally girlish hominess, an aura of fresh-baked deep-dish apple pie like Mother used to make, and an endless supply of tears, bravely but vainly attempts to resist the onslaught of the advancing years

The Roscoe Award:
Sheree North *(This award was followed by a parody of a Sheree North questionnaire,*

which is too long to be reprinted here.)

1956

Ten Worst Movies:
The Ten Commandments
Alexander the Great
Trapeze
The Benny Goodman Story
Gaby
Serenade
Bwohani Junction
Miracle in the Rain
The Vagabond King
The Proud and the Profane
Worst Actor:
Gregory Peck, *Moby Dick*
Worst Actress:
Jennifer Jones, *The Man in the Grey Flannel Suit*
Worst Supporting Actor:
Elvis Presley, *Love Me Tender*
Worst Supporting Actress:
Anne Baxter, *The Ten Commandments*
Life-Begins-at-Fifty Award:
A passionate Joan Crawford in throes of senilescence culminating her *Autumn Leaves* love affair by tossing about in the waves with Cliff Robertson
Best Alternative to the Ten Commandments:
All That Heaven Allows; Somebody Up There Likes Me; You Can't Run Away from It
Most Imaginative Locale:
Between Heaven and Hell
Greatest Argument for Birth Control:
Bundle of Joy
Most Thoroughly Unsatisfying Ending:
Rock Hudson's recovery in *All That Heaven Allows*
Publicity Agent of the Year:
Cardinal Spellman
The Mario Lanza Award for Most Oily Demise:
Oreste
Most Degrading Bow to American Morality Cults:
Tea and Sympathy's closing rebuttal of its own themes

Title With Most Unappealing Implications:
The Lieutenant Wore Tights
Hypocrisy-of-the-Year Award (Big-as-Texas Variety):
The five million dollars spent on the theme of antimaterialism in *Giant*
The Roscoe Award:
Anita Ekberg, who has breasted the tide of criticism in regard to her triumphant inability to act by spreading herself, in film after film, over CinemaScope screen like a great fleshy smörgasbord, proving once and for all that delicacy can be as un-Swedish as it is un-American

1957

Ten Worst Movies:
Raintree County
The Pride and the Passion
Peyton Place
Island in the Sun
Jeanne Eagels
Funny Face
The Hunchback of Notre Dame
The Sun Also Rises
Pal Joey
April Love
Worst Actor:
Rock Hudson, *A Farewell to Arms*
Worst Actress:
Kim Novak, *Jeanne Eagels; Pal Joey*
Worst Supporting Actor:
MacGeorge Bundy, *To the Age That Is Waiting*
Worst Supporting Actress:
Joan Collins, *Island in the Sun*
The Janos Kadar Award:
Tyrone Power for his superlatively impotent performance in *The Sun Also Rises*
Better-Things-for-Better-Living-Through-Chemistry: A Commendation:
To the producers of *A Hatful of Rain* for giving the movie industry a long overdue shot in the arm

The Wayward Bus Award:
Jayne Mansfield for her outstanding
The "Any Connection?" Prize:
Rita Hayworth, *Fire Down Below;* Bing Crosby, *Man on Fire*
The Most Deceptive Title:
Something of Value
The Elsa Maxwell Kudo:
Given for the first time in thirty-seven years to *The Bachelor Party* as the most unattractive social event of the season
The Suzy Parker Award:
For the most inauspicious male debut: Pat Boone, *Bernadine*
The Pat Boone Award:
For the most inauspicious female debut: Suzy Parker, *Kiss Them for Me*
Most Outrageous Case of On-Screen Discrimination Toward a Minority:
Walt Disney's ruthless suppression of the Weasels and Martens in *Perri*
The Gloria Swanson Award for the Most Unexpected Comeback:
James Dean, *The James Dean Story*
What the Bachelor Party Needed Most:
Les Girls
Special Commendation:
Kay Kendall for rescuing *Les Girls* from the dismal mediocrity which only Gene Kelly can add to a picture
Most Telling Argument for Birth Control:
Full of Life
Most Appalling Example of the Inadequacy of Our Present Social Security Program:
Fred Astaire, forced once more out of retirement to don his high-heeled tap shoes and pursue Audrey Hepburn before an ill-focused camera lens in *Funny Face*
The Marquis De Sade Award:
Operation Madball
"Oh Yeah?" Department:
The Girl Can't Help It

The Emilio Boscoe Award:
Natalie Wood whose saccharine, whining caricatures of American girlhood have, in film after tedious film, raised her above the obstacles of talented competition, first-draft scripts, pubescent co-stars, and sleepy directors to the top of the Hollywood heap

The Roscoe Award:
Jean Seberg, who, having allowed her ambition to outstrip her inability, has risen from student to starlet in little over a year, and demonstrated that she can be both soporific as a saint and insipid as a sinner

The Worst-Film-of-the-Century Award:
This award, given once every hundred years, is presented for the century 1857-1957 to Otto Preminger's *Saint Joan*

1958

Worst Ten Movies:
South Pacific
The Vikings
Roots of Heaven
The Last Hurrah
Marjorie Morningstar
The Buccaneers
Big Country
The Old Man and the Sea
A Certain Smile
Windjammer

Worst Actor:
Kirk Douglas, *The Vikings* (the trophy will be retired, since Mr. Douglas has won it for the third time)

Worst Actress:
Rita Hayworth, *Separate Tables*

Worst Supporting Actor:
Errol Flynn, *Roots of Heaven*

Worst Supporting Actress:
Christine Carrere, *A Certain Smile*

The "Any Connection?" Prize:
The Reluctant Debutante, *Home Before Dark*

The Venus De Milo Award:
A Farewell to Arms

The To-Say-the-Least Award:
Ingrid Bergman, *Indiscreet*

The Wilde Oscar:
(presented to that actor who is willing to flaunt convention and reputation in the pursuit of artistic fulfillment)
Jerry Lewis, *The Geisha Boy*

Most Shocking Film of the Year:
Some Came Running

Most Unreasonable Request:
Susan Hayward, *I Wanna Live*

Special Award:
(to those actors and actresses who, despite the lack of entertaining scripts, still manage extemporaneously to entertain the nation)
Eddie Fisher; Debbie Reynolds; Liz Taylor

The Fauntleroy Behest:
(a stipend set up in the will of the late Lord Fauntleroy to send a young lad to acting school)
James *(A Light In the Forest)* MacArthur, with all dispatch

The Thank-God Award:
Marilyn Monroe, who in a sweeping public service has made no movies this year

The Roscoe Award:
Kim Novak, who, not satisfied with a performance in *Vertigo* that would have assured her of the Worst Actress of the Year Award, spurred herself to even greater heights in *Bell, Book and Candle*, immortalizing herself and her directors

1959

Ten Worst Movies:
The Best of Everything
The Miracle
Career
Never So Few
Solomon and Sheba
The Tempest
A Summer Place
They Came to Cordura
Say One for Me

Hercules
One Too Many

Worst Actor:
Sal Mineo, *Tonka*

Worst Actress:
Lana Turner, *Imitation of Life*

Worst Supporting Actress:
Sandra Dee, *A Summer Place*

Worst Supporting Actor:
Dick Nixon, *The Best of Benson*

The Bratwurst Award:
(to the worst child actor of the year, presented by the Delicatessen Owners' Assn.)
Eddie Hodges, *A Hole in the Head*

The Ghandi Grant:
(for the year's most attractive ribs)
May Britt, *The Blue Angel*

The Wish-It-Were-True Award:
Bing Crosby as a celibate priest in *Say One for Me*

The Miss Nomer Award:
The Best of Everything

The Not-Worth-It Award:
Five Pennies

The "Any Connection?" Prize:
(presented annually to those films which would best appear as double features)
The Girl with an Itch and *The Tingler*
Happy is the Bride and *Middle of the Night*
The Nun's Story and *Ask Any Girl*
Arson for Hire and *Some Like It Hot*
Libel and *Say One for Me*
Thirty-Foot Bride of Candy Rock and *Cast a Long Shadow*
Room 43 and *Grand Canyon Suite*

The "It Was Funny the First Time" Award:
The Man Who Died Twice

The Eva Marie Saint Award:
(to the movie title most conducive to uninhibited speech-making)
Say One for Me

The Varsi Vase:
(awarded to the most dramatic walkout in the field of entertainment)

Jack Parr
The Luce Laurel:
Shirley MacLaine for gracing, if not monopolizing, the pages of *Life* magazine

1960

Ten Worst Movies:
Butterfield 8
Strangers When We Meet
The Gazeo
Ice Palace
Exodus
It Started in Naples
Pepe
Pollyanna
Because They're Young
High Time
Worst Actor:
Frank Sinatra, *Can-Can*
Worst Actress:
Eva Marie Saint, *Exodus*
Worst Supporting Actor:
Eddie Fisher, *Butterfield 8* (with honorable mention to Cameron Mitchell for failing to meet his alimony payments)
Worst Supporting Actress:
Annette Funicello, *The Horse Masters*
The Uncrossed Heart:
(awarded to the least promising young actor of the year)
Fabian, *North to Alaska*
The Merino Award:
(to that motion picture personality who, in the opinion of the officers, editors, and staff of the Harvard Lampoon, has done the most to enhance the fame and glory of the merino)
Maureen O'Hara
The Bratwurst Award:
(to the most obnoxious child star of the year)
David Ladd, *Dog of Flanders*
The But-Not-For-Us-Either Award:
But Not for Me
The Mirror-On-The-Wall Oblation:
(to the movie whose title reflects the action of the audience rather than that of its characters)

The Angry Silence
The-Off-Color Investiture
The Green Carnation
The Bad-Taste Citation:
Broth of a Boy
The Wilde Oscar:
(presented to that actor who is willing to flaunt convention and reputation in the pursit of artistic fulfillment)
Jerry Lewis, *Cinderfella*
The The-World-in-the-Future-if-Karl-Marx's-Basic-Political-Precepts-Are-Proved-Correct-but-His-Hypothesis-That-the-People-Will-Not-Be-Disgruntled-Is-Sorely-in-Error Award:
The Angry Red Planet
The Along-the-Mohawk Grant:
(to that film with the most drummed-up publicity campaign)
The Alamo
The Roscoe Award:
Robert Mitchum

1961

Ten Worst Movies:
Kings of Kings; Parrish (tied)
By Love Possessed
The Devil at 4 O'Clock
The Last Sunset
The Young Doctors
Ada
Flower Drum Song
Babes in Toyland
Sergeants Three
The Kirk Douglas Award to the Worst Actor:
Richard Beymer, *West Side Story*
Worst Actress:
Susan Hayward, *Ada; Back Street*
Worst Supporting Actor:
Robert Ryan as John the Baptist, *Kings of Kings*
Worst Supporting Actress:
Sandra Dee, *Romanoff and Juliet; Come September*
The Uncrossed Heart:
(to the least promising young actor of the year)

Richard Beymer, *West Side Story*
The Worst All-Around Performance By a Cast in Toto:
King of Kings, with special mention to Jeffrey Hunter, Siobhan McKenna, Robert Ryan, and Frank Thring
The Last Sunset, with special mention to Kirk Douglas, Rock Hudson, Dorothy Malone, and Carol Lynley
The Best Argument for Vivisection:
Lad a Dog
The Worst Duos of the Year:
Troy Donahue; Connie Stevens
Natalie Wood and (1) Warren Beatty, (2) Richard Beymer, (3) Anyone
The Greatest Setback to Christianity Since *The Robe*:
King of Kings
The Hon. "W.W." Corrigan Memorial Palm:
(to the worst director)
Elia Kazan, *Splendor in the Grass*
The Tin Pan:
(to the most nauseating movie song of the year)
"Pocketful of Miracles"
The Merino Award:
Rita Moreno for saving *West Side Story* from Richard Beymer and Natalie Wood
The Once-Was-Enough Award:
The Second Time Around
The Wilde Oscar:
(to that actor willing to flout convention and reputation in the pursuit of artistic fulfillment)
Mickey Rooney as Mr. Yunioshi, *Breakfast at Tiffany's*
The Great Ceremonial Hot Dog:
(for the worst scenes of the cinema season)
Kirk Douglas fighting a mad dog. *The Last Sunset*
Salome's Dance in *King of Kings'*
Richard Beymer singing "Maria" in *West Side Story*

The Along-the-Mohawk Grant:
(for the most drummed-up publicity campaign of the year)
Jayne Mansfield, her husband, and her publicity agent for the heroism they displayed during and after their near-tragic boating accident

The Arrested-Development Oblation:
(to that adult actor who displays the lowest level of maturity)
Jerry Lewis, *Errand Boy*

The Cellophane Figleaf:
This trophy, awarded annually for false modesty, is this year given to Warren Beatty, most of whose publicity has been based on his constant statements that he wants no publicity from the fact that he is Shirley MacLaine's younger brother

The Vanity Fair Citation:
(to that actress who most tirelessly champions the cause of womanhood)
Sophia Loren for carrying to court her fight to be billed above Charlton Heston for her performance in *El Cid*

The Off-Color Investiture:
The Green Mare

The Ok-Doc-Break-the-Arm-Again Award:
This citation, awarded annually for the most flagrant example of miscasting, goes this year to the producers of *A Majority of One* for putting Alec Guinness in the role of a Japanese businessman and Rosalind Russell in the role of a Jewish housewife

The Luce Laurel:
Awarded in 1960 to Shirley MacLaine for gracing, if not monopolizing, the pages of *Life* magazine, this year goes to...
Shirley MacLaine, for gracing, if not monopolizing, the pages of *Life* magazine

The "Any Connection?" Prize:
(awarded annually to those films which would best appear as double features)

The Unstoppable Man and *The Explosive Generation*
Anatomy of a Psycho and *The Man Who Wagged His Tail*
Capture That Capsule and *You Have to Run Fast*
The Sergeant Was a Lady and *Marines, Let's Go*
Deadly Campions and *Snow White and the Three Stooges*

Thank You:
Victor Mature for not making a picture this year

The Roscoe Award:
Natalie Wood for so gallantly persisting in her career despite a total inability to act.

1962

Ten Worst Movies:
The Chapman Report
If a Man Answers
Adventures of a Young Man
Diamond Head
The Wonderful World of the Brothers Grimm
White Slave Ship
Mutiny on the Bounty
Taras Bulba
Barabbas
The Mongols; The Tartars; The Huns

Worst Actress:
Jane Fonda, *The Chapman Report*

The Kirk Douglas Award to the Worst Actor:
Charlton Heston, *Diamond Head; The Pigeon That Took Rome*

Worst Supporting Actress:
Pier Angeli, Sodom and Gomorrah

Worst Supporting Actor:
William Frawley, *Safe at Home*

The Uncrossed Heart:
(to the least promising young performer)
Ann-Margret

The Tin Pan:
(to the most obnoxious movie song)
"Lolita, Yah-Yah"

The Wilde Oscar:
(to the performer who has been willing to flout convention and risk worldly reputation in order to pursue artistic fulfillment)
Pier Angeli, for her part as the Pillar of Salt in *Sodom and Gomorrah*

The Merino Award:
In 1960 To Maureen O'Hara; in 1961 to Rita Moreno; this year to Maureen O'Sullivan

The Diamond-in-the-Rough Award:
Rosalind Russell for making *Gypsy* palatable despite Natalie Wood, Karl Malden, etc.

The Cellophane Figleaf:
(for false modesty)
Sue Lyon, who played the part of Lolita, and thereafter drummed up most of her publicity by insisting that she is not a Lolita in real life

The Bratwurst Award:
(for the most obnoxious child star)
A tie between Kevin Corcoran in *In Search of the Castaways* and the entire Vienna Boys Choir in *Almost Angels*

The Hon. "W.W." Corrigan Memorial Palm:
(for the worst direction of a film)
Otto Preminger for *Lolita*

The Timothy Cratchit Memorial Crutch:
To that Hollywood personality who offers the lamest justification for unsavory behavior: to Tony Curtis for calling a press conference to insist that there was nothing immoral about his living with Christine Kaufman, since she had her parents' permission

The Arrested-Development Oblation:
(to that adult actor who has displayed the lowest level of maturity)
Jerry Lewis, *It's Only Money*

The Worst All-Around Performance by a Cast in Toto:
The Longest Day

The Please-Don't-Put-Us-Through-DeMille-Again Award:
Presented to that religious movie of the past year which best embodies the pretentious extravagance and blundering ineffectiveness of the traditional Christian Screen Spectacular:
Awarded this year to two equally poor movies: *Barabbas* and *Sodom and Gomorrah*

The Great Ceremonial Hot Dog:
(for the worst scenes of the past cinema season)
The naming of the fairy tale characters in *The Wonderful World of the Brothers Grimm* and the Polish army hurtling over the cliff in *Taras Bulba*

The Roscoe Award:
To Natalie Wood, for her unquestionably atrocious performance in *Gypsy*, which she did her utmost to ruin

1963

Ten Worst Movies:
Cleopatra
The V.I.P.s
The Prize
It's a Mad, Mad, Mad, Mad, World
How the West Was Won
Heavens Above
55 Days at Peking
Act One
The Birds and *Bye-Bye Birdie* (tied)
Gidget Goes to Rome; Tammy and the Doctor (tied)

Worst Film of the Century:
For the century 1863-1963 to *Cleopatra*
(This award was last presented in 1958 for the century ending in that year)

The Kirk Douglas Award to the Worst Actor:
Burt Lancaster, *The Leopard; Seven Days in May*

The Worst Actress:
Debbie Reynolds, *How the West Was Won; Mary, Mary*

The Worst Supporting Actor:
Roy Cohn, *Point of Order*

The Worst Supporting Actress:
Carol Burnett, *Who's Been Sleeping in My Bed?*

The Timothy Cratchit Memorial Crutch:
(to that Hollywood personality who offers the lamest justification for unsavory behavior)
Elizabeth Taylor for divorcing Eddie Fisher on the grounds of abandonment

The Tin Pan:
(to the most obnoxious movie song)
"Love with a Proper Stranger"

The Great Ceremonial Hot Dog:
(for the worst scenes of the cinema season)
The five ax murders in *Straitjacket*
The four murders in *Charade*
The delivery of a baby in the back seat of a Rolls Royce (with Doris Day as midwife) in *The Thrill of It All!*
Cliff Richards twisting his way across Europe in an open-mesh T-shirt in *Summer*

The Wilde Oscar:
(to that performer who has been willing to flout convention and risk worldly reputation to pursue artistic fulfillment)
To the producers of *Becket* and *Night of the Iguana* for casting Richard Burton in clerical roles

The Ok-Doc-Break-the-Arm-Again Award:
(for the most flagrant example of miscasting)
To the producers of *Take Her, She's Mine* for placing Sandra Dee in the role of a Wellesley College student

The Drums-Along-the-Mohawk Grant:
(for the most drummed-up publicity campaign)
Frank Sinatra, Frank Sinatra, Jr., and the three kidnappers of the latter

The Bratwurst Award:
(to the most obnoxious child star of the year)
the entire cast of *The Lord of the Flies*

Worst Performance by a Cast in Toto:
It's A Mad, Mad, Mad, Mad World

The Hon. Wrong-Way Corrigan Memorial Palm:
(for the worst direction of a film)
Stanley Kramer, *It's a Mad, Mad, Mad, Mad World*

The Uncrossed Heart:
(for the least promising young performer)
Annette Funicello, *Beach Party; The Misadventures of Merlin Jones*

Thank You Again:
Victor Mature for not making a film this year

The-Please-Don't-Put-Us-Through-DeMille-Again Award:
(for that film which best embodies pretentious extravagance and blundering ineffectiveness of the traditional Screen Spectacular)
Cleopatra

The Arrested-Development Oblation:
(to that adult actor who has displayed the lowest level of maturity)
Always given to Jerry Lewis

The Aerosol Bomb:
The Lord of the Flies

The Gilded Cage:
The Birds and *A Gathering of Eagles* with mention of *The Cardinal*

The Merino Award:
In 1960 to Maureen O'Hara; in 1961 to Rita Moreno; in 1962 to Maureen O'Sullivan; this year to the Marine standing sentry duty outside the American Embassy in Paris in *Charade*

Best Argument for Stricter Immigration Laws:
America America

The Gold Star-on-the-Wayne Laurel:
To *Donovan's Reef* and *McClintock*

The That-Was-the-Week-that-Was Trophy:
Seven Days in May

We-Heard-You-The-First-Time Award:
It's Mad, Mad, Mad World; America America and *Twice Told Tales*

Best Argument for Vivisection:
Miracle of the White Stallions

The Marquis De Sade Memorial Whip:
A New Kind of Love

The Cellophane Figleaf:
(for false modesty)
Ann-Margret for insisting that she is not oversexed

The Vanity Fair Citation:
To Rex Harrison for carrying to court his fight to be portrayed on the *Cleopatra* poster

The Ayn Rand Award:
(to that writer whose bad books made worse movies)
Irving Wallace, author of *The Chapman Report* and *The Prize*

The Roscoe Award:
Doris Day, who has gotten way with it once too often

1964

Ten Worst Movies:
The Greatest Story Ever Told
The Carpetbaggers, Sylvia, Cheyenne Autumn, Station Six Sahara, Kiss Me Stupid, (tied)
The Outrage
The Fall of the Roman Empire
One Potato, Two Potato
Youngblood Hawke
Kisses for My President
Good-by Charlie
The Unsinkable Molly Brown
Muscle Beach Party

The Kirk Douglas Award to the Worst Actor:
James Franciscus, *Youngblood Hawke*

Worst Actress:
Carroll Baker in *The Greatest Story Ever Told; Sylvia; Cheyenne Autumn; The Carpetbaggers; Station Six Sahara*

Worst Supporting Actor:
Laurence Harvey, *The Outrage*

Worst Supporting Actress:
Honor Blackman as Pussy Galore in *Goldfinger*

The Merino Award:
In 1960 to Maureen O'Hara; in 1961 to Rita Moreno; in 1962 to Maureen O'Sullivan; in 1963 to the Marine standing sentry duty outside the American embassy in Paris in *Charade*; this year to marinophile Jacques Cousteau for his underwater documentary *World Without Sun*

The Uncrossed Heart:
(to the least promising young performer)
For the second year in a row: Annette Funicello

The Tin Pan:
(to the most obnoxious movie song)
"Sex and the Single Girl"

The Arrested-Development Oblation:
(to that adult actor who has displayed the lowest level of maturity)
Always given to Jerry Lewis

The Hon. Wrong-Way Corrigan Memorial Palm:
(to the worst direction)
Billy Wilder, *Kiss Me Stupid*

The Diamond-in-the-Rough Award:
Ann Southern, *Sylvia*

The Cellophane Figleaf:
(for false modesty)
Elke Sommer who, when accused of making nude movie scenes, said, "Those pictures were of me in flesh-tight leotards—and photographers had the nerve to retouch them!"

The Bratwurst Award:
(to the most obnoxious child star)
Hayley Mills, *The Chalk Garden*

Worst Performance By a Cast in Toto:
The entire population of Western Europe for its performance in *The Fall of the Roman Empire*

The Timothy Cratchit Memorial Crutch:
(to that Hollywood personality who offers the lamest justification for unsavory behavior)
Ann-Margret, for hitting her director in the head with an ashtray, inflicting a 19-stitch wound, and then excusing herself as having a passionate absorption in her craft

The Wilde Oscar:
(to that performer who has been willing to flout convention and risk wordly reputation in order to pursue artistic fulfillment)
Carroll Baker, for spending two weeks with a prostitute in Tijuana to help her adjust to her public image

The Please-Don't-Put-Us-Through-DeMille-Again Award:
(to that movie of the past year which best embodies the pretentions, extravagance and blundering ineffectiveness of the traditional Screen Spectacular)
The Greatest Story Ever Told

Best Argument for Stricter Immigration Laws:
Tosh-Togo for his performance as Odd-Job in *Goldfinger*

Thank You Again:
Victor Mature for not making a film this year

The Great Ceremonial Hot Dog:
(for the worst scenes)
The on-screen rape in *The New Interns*
The entire first reel of *The Silence*

The Ok-Doc-Break-the-Arm-Again Award:
(for the most flagrant example of miscasting)
Sex and the Single Girl, with Natalie Wood in the role of a psychiatrist, and to *None*

But the Brave, featuring Frank Sinatra as an Irish medic

The Geritol Award:
Anthony Quinn, *Zorba the Greek*

The Gold Star-on-the-Wayne Laurel:
To John Wayne, for "licking the Big C"

Best Argument for Vivisection:
Flipper's New Adventure and *Father Goose*

The Curse-of-the-Living-Corpse:
Bette Davis

The Marquis De Sade Memorial Whip:
Ann-Margret for her performance in *Kitten with a Whip* and the entire cast of *Advance to the Rear*

The Ayn Rand Award:
(to that author whose bad books made worse movies)
Matthew, Mark, Luke and John for *The Greatest Story Ever Told*

The Roscoe Award;
Carroll Baker, who was the first performer ever to win the Movie Worst Triple Crown

1965

Ten Worst Movies:
The Sandpiper
The Hallelujah Trail
Lord Jim
What's New, Pussycat?
The Agony and the Ecstasy
Shenandoah
Genghis Kahn
Thunderball
The Great Race
The Yellow Rolls Royce

1966

Ten Worst Movies:
Is Paris Burning?
Hurry Sundown
The Oscar
The Fortune Cookie

The Bible
A Countess from Hong Kong
The Blue Max
Fantastic Voyage
Torn Curtain
Penelope

Kirk Douglas Award to Worst Actor:
George Peppard, *The Blue Max*

Natalie Wood Award to Worst Actress:
Ursula Andress, *Casino Royale*

Worst Supporting Actor:
John Huston, *The Bible*

Worst Supporting Actress:
Leslie Caron, *Is Paris Burning?*

The Ok-Doc-Break-the-Arm-Again Award:
(to that most flagrant example of miscasting)
John Huston as the voice of God in *The Bible*

Der Otto:
Awarded annually to Otto Preminger for his yearly excursions in to the tawdry, the sordid and the silly. This year for his direction of *Hurry Sundown*

The Hon. Wrong-Way Corrigan Memorial Palm:
(for worst direction)
Charles Chaplin, *A Countess from Hong Kong*

The Cellophane Figleaf:
(for false modesty)
Jane Fonda for suing *Playboy* magazine for having printed nude snapshots of her on set with husband-director Roger Vadim. "Nasty voyeurs," she said

The Please-Don't-Put-Us-through-DeMille-Again Award:
(for the film which best embodies the pretentions, extravagance and blundering ineffectiveness of the traditional Screen Spectacular)
The Bible

The Piltdown Mandible:
Presented annually for the lamest explanation of scientifically improbable phenomena: this year to the producers of *Fantastic Voyage* for assuming that the molecules which made up the submarine would not

re-expand to normal size simply because said submarine had been devoured by a white corpuscle; and to the lone cow in *The Bible* who supplied an estimated nine hundred seventy-four gallons of milk to all the animals on the Ark for forty days and forty nights

The Uncrossed Heart:
(for the least promising young performer)
Andrea Dromm, *The Russians Are Coming*

The Bratwurst Award:
(for the most obnoxious child star)
John Mark as the demented child in *Hurry Sundown*

The Best Argument for Vivisection:
To *Born Free* and the entire Ark in *The Bible*

The Ayn Rand Award:
(to the writer whose bad books make worst movies)
Norman Mailer, *The American Dream*

Worst Performance By a Cast in Toto:
The Charles Chaplin family in *A Countess from Hong Kong*

The Arrested-Development Oblation:
(to that adult actor who has displayed the lowest level of maturity)
Always given to Jerry Lewis

The Elsa Maxwell Kudo:
(for the most unattractive social event)
Sodom goat seduction in *The Bible*

The Great Ceremonial Hot Dog:
(for the worst scenes of the cinema season)
The birth scene in *Hawaii* and Jane Fonda's mouthing of a saxophone in *Hurry Sundown*

The In Pan:
(for the most obnoxious movie song)
"Alfie" and "Born Free"

The Diamond-in-the-Rough Award:
(to that performer whose genuine talent has shown through the drivel and dross that is so characteristic of modern cinema)
Margaret Rutherford, *A Countess From Hong Kong*

The Timothy Crachit Memorial Crutch:
(to that Hollywood personality who offers the lamest justification for unsavory behavior)
Raquel Welch, for marrying her manager in order to be seen in her flesh-colored mini-wedding gown

Best Argument for Stricter Immigration Laws:
Milos Forman, *Loves of a Blond*

The Tower of Babel Citation:
(to that foreign-language film which has the worst subtitles)
A Man and a Woman

The Bennett:
(to the worst suffering movie)
The Endless Summer

The Merino Award:
In 1960 to Maureen O'Hara; in 1961 to Rita Moreno; in 1962 to Maureen O'Sullivan; in 1963 to the Marine standing sentry duty outside the American embassy in Paris in *Charade*; in 1964 to marinophile Jacques Cousteau for his underwater documentary *World Without Sun*; in 1965 to Merina Mercouli; this year to the two merinos on the Ark in *The Bible*

The Roscoe Award:
Stephen Boyd for his starring roles in *The Oscar* and *Fantastic Voyage*, and his brief but significant appearance as Nimrod in *The Bible*

1967

Ten Worst Movies:
Guess Who's Coming to Dinner
Valley of the Dolls
Up the Down Staircase
One Million years B.C.
The Comedians
Reflections in a Golden Eye
Thoroughly Modern Millie
Doctor Dolittle
The Fox
Carmen Baby

Kirk Douglas Award for Worst Actor:
Richard Burton for his disheartening performance in *Doctor Faustus; The Comedians*

Natalie Wood Award for Worst Actress:
Raquel Welch, *One Million Years B.C.; The Biggest Bundle of Them All; Bedazzled*

Worst Supporting Actor:
Whatsisname, *Valley of the Dolls*

Worst Supporting Actress:
Jean Shrimpton, *Privilege*

The Ok-Doc-Break-the-Arm-Again Award:
(to the most flagrant example of miscasting)
The Comedians for the waste of Peter Ustinov and Alec Guinness in roles as dull as they were uninteresting; and to Charlton Heston for portraying a human being in *Planet of the Apes*

The Hey-Jack-Which-Way-to-Mecca Award:
(for worst direction)
Claude Lelouche, *Live for Life*

The Please-Don't-Put-Us-Through-DeMille-Again Award:
(to that film which best embodies the pretentions, extravagances and blundering ineffectiveness of the traditional Screen Spectacular)
Camelot

The Piltdown Mandible:
(to the most obviously and unabashedly spurious scientific phenomena)
One Million Years B.C., for the contemporaneous existence of Raquel Welch and a passel of dinosaurs; an unscientific juxtaposition redounding entirely to the credit of the dinosaurs

The Uncrossed Heart:
(to the least promising young performer)
Karharine Hepburn's niece Katharine Houghton, *Guess Who's Coming to dinner*

The Mobius Strip:
(to the most boring and unnecessary undressing scene)
Barbara Parkins preparing to meet the Fate Worse Than Death in *Valley of the Dolls*

The Beast of Buchenwald Award:
To those actors who most thoroughly degrade themselves in order to pull in the paycheck, this handsomely tooled lampshade goes to the extras who played the apes in the beginning of *2001: A Space Odyssey*

The Ayn Rand Award:
(for that writer whose bad books made worse movies)
Graham Green, an otherwise fine author, for *The Comedians*

The Dance of the Seven Scott Tissues Award:
(to the most lewd and completely unwarranted dancing scene)
Raquel Welch, *Bedazzled*

Worst Performance by a Cast in Toto:
The Mills family, *The Family Way*

The Arrested-Development Oblation:
(for the adult actor who has displayed the lowest level of maturity)
Always given to Jerry Lewis

The Elsa Maxwell Kudo:
(to the most unattractive event)
To the "show" in *Titicut Follies*

The Great Ceremonial Hot Dog:
(for the worst scenes of the cinema season)
Paty Duke's withdrawal fit in *Valley of the Dolls*

The Tedium Is the Medium Citation:
(to the worst student film)
Tim Hunter's *Desire Is the Fire*

The Exhausted Udder:
Presented by the Dairy Farmers Assn. in recognition of the attempts to milk every penny possible from a marketable idea, such as film versions of obviously unfilmable sellers, etc.; this year, the handsome prize in withered polyurethane goes to the producers of *The Fox*

The Tin Pan:
(to the most obnoxious movie song)
Leslie Bricuss's "Let's Talk to the Animals" in *Doctor Dolittle*, for blood-curdling anthropomorphism

The Best Argument for Reactivating Ellis Island:
(to the worst foreign film)
Poor Cow

The Sentimental Mushmelon:
(to the film that best reminds us of that true Poignancy, that bitter Sweetness, which we know as Life)
Elvira Madigan

The Cheap-at-Half-the-Price Award:
For the worst bargain in a film from the last year, to *Half a Sixpence*

The Guess-Who's-Stepping-Out-to-Tommy's-Lunch Award:
Guess Who's Coming to Dinner

The Timothy Cratchit Memorial Crutch:
(to that Hollywood personality who offers the lamest justification for unsavory behavior)
Mia Farrow, who followed the Maharishi all the way to India just to be able to cream an Indian reporter with her handbag

The H. J. Heinz Laurel Wreath:
(to that film that makes most extensive use of the company's various vegetable derivatives)
Bonnie and Clyde

The Bratwurst Award:
(to the most obnoxious child star)
Lulu, as the warbling

adolescent in *To Sir, With Love*

The Best Argument for Vivisection:
Doctor Dolittle, the Jungle Book and *The Fox*, an unusual spate of bad sentimentalism and worse symbolism

The Bennett:
(to the worst surfing movie)
Surfari

The On-a-Clear-Day-You-Can-See-Fall-River Citation:
(for the most stereotyped New England Scenery)
Valley of the Dolls for the eternally snow-blanketed shots of "Lawrenceville, N.H." which was really Bedford, N.Y.

The Merino Award:
To the Pushme-Pullyou in *Doctor Dolittle*, who is, as we take it, a distant cousin to merinos, and at any rate leads just as tenous an existence

The Roscoe Award:
Sandy Dennis, *Up the Down Staircase, The Fox*

1968

Ten Worst Movies:
The Lion in Winter
Ice Station Zebra
Rosemary's Baby
Star!
The Boston Strangler
Candy
Barbarella
You Are What You Eat
The Seagull
Boom

Kirk Douglas Award for Worst Actor:
Sidney Poitier, *For Love of Ivy*

Natalie Wood Award for Worst Actress:
Barbra Streisand, *Funny Girl*

Worst Supporting Actress:
Ewa Aulin, *Candy*

Worst Supporting Actor:
Rod Steiger, *No Way to Treat a Lady*

The Roscoe Award:
(to that performer who dis-

plays a certain unskilled, clumsy quality)
Tony Curtis, *The Boston Strangler*

1969

Ten Worst Movies:
Easy Rider
Medium Cool
Putney Swope
Bob & Carol & Ted & Alice
Topaz
The Maltese Bippy
True Grit
John and Mary
Hello, Dolly!
Last Summer

Kirk Douglas Award for Worst Actor:
Peter Fonda, *Easy Rider*

Natalie Wood Award for Worst Actress:
Jane Fonda, *Spirits of the Dead*, and for marrying Roger Vadim

Worst Supporting Actor:
Dennis Hopper, *Easy Rider*

Worst Supporting Actress:
Mia Farrow, *Secret Ceremony*

The Ok-Doc-Break-the-Arm-Again Award:
(to the most flagrant example of miscasting)
Omar Sharif for his west-of-center title role in *Che!*

The Hey-Jack-Which-Way-to-Mecca Award:
(for the worst direction)
Jean-Luc Godard, *Sympathy for the Devil*

The Uncrossed Heart:
(to the least promising young performer)
Goldie Hawn, *Cactus Flower*

The Please-Don't-Put-Us-Through-DeMille-Again Award:
(to that movie which best embodies the pretentions, extravagances and blundering ineffectiveness of the traditional Screen Spectacular)
Hello, Dolly!

The Piltdown Mandible:
(to the most obviously and una-bashedly spurious scientific phenomena)
Krakatoa, East of Java, since Krakatoa, by all recent accounts, is a good two hundred miles west of Java

The Sentimental Mushmelon:
(to the film that most reminds us of that true Poignancy, that bitter Sweetness, which we know as Life)
The Reivers, a sledgehammer-on-a-marshmallow rendition of a squishy Faulkner novel

The Cheap-at-Half-the-Price Award:
Woody Allen's *Take the Money and Run*

The OhGodohGod, the Lights, the Shapes, the Colors Award:
(to that movie which makes us glad we have lungs to inhale with)
The revival of Walt Disney's *Fantasia*

The Timothy Cratchit Memorial Crutch:
(to that personality who offers the lamest justification for un-savory behavior)
President Richard Nixon, who screened the film *Marooned,* an epic of three spacemen lost in the great beyond, for apprehensive astronauts Armstrong, Collins and Young at a White House *Kultur-fest*

The Beast of Buchenwald Award:
(to those actors who most thoroughly degrade them-selves in order to pull in the paycheck, this handsomely tooled lampshade is awarded)
The entire cast of Visconti's horror show, *The Damned*

The Great Ceremonial Hot Dog:
(for the worst scene of the cinema season)
Peter Fonda's I-love-you-I-hate-you acid trip

in a New Orleans cemetery in *Easy Rider*

The Arrested-Development Oblation:
(to that adult actor who has displayed the lowest level of maturity)
Always given to Jerry Lewis, who, in spite of making no films this year, has managed to perpetuate the infantile tradition by his inimitable Cerebral Palsy telethons

The Ayn Rand Award:
(to that writer whose bad books make worse movies)
Petronius, who should have know better, for *Satyricon*

The Exhausted Udder:
(presented by the Diary Farm-ers Assn. in recognition of at-tempts to milk every penny possible from a marketable idea)
Anyone who had anything to do with what we hope is the last James Bond film ever, *On Her Majesty's Secret Service*

The Tin Pan:
(to the most obnoxious movie song)
Rod McKuen's "Jean" from *The Prime of Miss Jean Brodie*

The Marquis De Sade Memorial Whip:
Raquel Welch in *The Magic Christian,* for a leather-and-chains performance which rivals Attila the Hun

The Dance to the Seven Scott Tissues Award:
(to the most lewd and com-pletely unwarranted dancing scene)
To the fag ball in Andy Warhol's *Lonesome Cowboys*

The Most Unnecessary Contribution to the American Way of Life:
To the hippest people we know, the cool and groovy stars of *Bob & Carol & Ted & Alice*

The Guess-Who's-Stepping-Out-to-Tommy's-Lunch Award:
(presented to that scene in a movie which makes us guess we'll step out to Tommy's lunch)
The blow job in the movie balcony of *Midnight Cowboy*

The Do-You-Know-the-Way-to-San-Jose Award:
(to that film which took the wrong turn on the Los Angeles freeway while shooting on the studio lot and ended up in the least likely location)
Butch Cassidy and the Sundance Kid for its Bolivian sequences

The Strongest Argument for Laxer Divorce Laws:
Paul Newman and Joanne Woodward for *Winning,* a loser

The Dr. Christiaan Barnard Award:
(to that movie which shows the worst job of cutting)
Dan Rowan and Dick Martin's *The Maltese Bippy*

The Bratwurst Award:
(to the most obnoxious child star)
The entire cast of *Goodbye, Mr. Chips,* a movie which made us wish we were back at St. Paul's

The Elsa Maxwell Kudo:
(to the most unattractive social event)
To the singles bar scenes in *John and Mary*

The Best Argument for Reactivating Ellis Island:
To the entire country of Sweden, for bringing us such screaming turkeys as *Without a Stitch; Woman Is a Female Animal* and *I, a Man*

The Twenty-Cent Token:
(to that film which does the most fashionable injustice to a minority class)
Putney Swope

The Thanks-for-Nothing Award:
(given to that Hollywood per-former who has blessedly not

made a motion picture this year)

Doris Day, who has saved us from guessing once again how it is that she will remain a post-menopausal virgin

The Wilde Oscar:
(to that performer who has been willing to flout convention and risk worldly reputation in order to pursue artistic fulfillment)

Dustin Hoffman for playing a consumptive Italian hunchback in Midnight Cowboy

The H.J. Heinz Laurel Wreath:
(to that film that makes most extensive use of the company's various vegetable derivatives)

The Battle of Britain

The Wrong-Way Corrigan Memorial Flight Jacket:
(to the one line a film which does more to distort the course of history than Lyndon Johnson's interviews with Walter Cronkite)

Given, with apologies to the American Barbers Assn., to the Virgin Mary in Buñuel's The Milky Way for her line, "Jesus, don't cut off your beard; you look handsome with it."

The Harvard Independent Award:
(to that film noted for its ignominious failure as both art and politics)

Medium Cool

The Curse-of-the-Living-Corpse Award:
A fully-paid burial insurance policy presented by the American Morticians Assn. as inducement to a speedy interment, the award this year goes to Mae West, who is going to do it again in Myra Breckenridge

The It-Can't-Happen-Here Award:
(presented to that film that shot a sequence which is geographically closest to The Lampoon Castle)

Goodbye, Columbus for a scene in which Ali MacGraw, an unconvincing "Cliffie," ambles down the steps of romantic Widener Library

The Babar Boo-Boo:
(to those movies which do most for the cause of bestiality)

Futz! and The End of the Road, two movies which were especially illuminating on the possibilities of doing it with pigs and chickens

The Hey-Boswell-Did-You-Get-That-One-Down Award:
(to that film whose dialogue was, when not monosyllabic, subhuman)

Easy Rider, for doing its own thing in its own time

The Charles Manson Memorial Scalpel:
Awarded without comment to the gallant army doctors in M*A*S*H

The Bosley:
(to that film critic who has done most to perpetuate the cult of kitsch)

Judith Crist, whose taste buds died in 1952

The Black-and-White-and-Red-All-Over Award:
(to that movie which has done the most to eliminate shades of grey)

The entire cast of Z

The Best Argument for Stricter Immigration Laws:
Ingrid Bergman, who changed the course of her career by her prickly performance in Cactus Flower

The Brass Brassiere:
(given to that man who, in the tradition of Hugh Hefner and Harold Robbins, has done most to advance the cause of male chauvinism)

Allen Funt for his epic of women's lib, What Do You Say to a Naked Lady?

The Best Argument for Keeping R.O.T.C. on Campus:
Awarded with much apprehension to this year's

most courageous war movie, Patton

The Doctor-Down Award:
(to that movie which would most likely cause a bummer trip)

They Shoot Horses, Don't They?

The Best Argument for Vivisection:
The Wild Bunch, which was as graphic as it was unappetizing

The On-a-Clear-Day-You-Can-See-Fall-River Citation:
(for the most stereotyped New England scenery)

Alice's Restaurant, whose Stockbridge, Massachusetts, was just like Life magazine said it would be

The Merino Award:
In 1960 this one-quarter scale Corfam mounted sheep went to Maureen O'Hara; in 1961 to Rita Moreno; in 1962 to Maureen O'Sullivan; in 1963 to Italian director Dario Moreno; in 1964 to marino-phile Jacques-Yves Cousteau; in 1965 to Merina Mercouli; in 1966 to the two merinos on board the Ark in The Bible; in 1967 to the Pushme-Pullyou in Doctor Dolittle, a distant cousin to merinos; in 1968 to the cast of The Green Berets, which included only one black Marine; and in 1969, to the accompaniment of dull thuds produced by beating a dead sheep, the Merino Award goes to Andy Warhol's Blue Movie, which was filmed entirely in lurid aqua-merino

The Ros(s)coe Award:
Katharine Ross, for her forgettable performances in Tell Them Willie Boy Is Here and Butch Cassidy and the Sundance Kid

---

1970

Ten Worst Movies:
Love Story

Airport
Patton
Joe
Soldier Blue
Getting Straight
The Strawberry Statement
Little Fauss and Big Halsy
Julius Caesar
The Statue

Kirk Douglas Award for Worst Actor:
Elliott Gould, for *Getting Straight* and for dumping Barbra Streisand

Natalie Wood Award for Worst Actress:
Ali MacGraw, *Love Story*

Worst Supporting Actor:
Jon Voight, *Catch-22*

Worst Supporting Actress:
Ruth Gordon, *Where's Poppa?*

The Where-is-Erik-Erikson-Now-That-We're-All-Going-Bananas Award:
The *Lampoon* is proud to present a set of gold-plated thumbscrews and a spicy meatball to Jack Nicholson, who, in *Five Easy Pieces*, showed that it's never too late to have an identity crisis

The Tin Pan:
(to the most lethal movie song)
"Suicide Is Painless," from *M*A*S*H*, written by Michael Altman, the fifteen-year old son of the director, Robert Altman

The Marquis De Sade Memorial Whip:
Richard Harris, for being a brave brave in *A Man Called Horse*

The Hey-Boswell-Did-You-Get-That-One-Down Award:
(to that film whose dialogue was, when not monosyllabic, subhuman)
The Sidelong Glances of a Pigeon Kicker

The Senuous Eunuch:
(to that man and / or woman who has done the most to advance the cause of male chauvinism)
The Christine Jorgensen Story

The Ok-Doc-Break-the-Arm-Again Award:
(to the most flagrant example of miscasting)

Dean Martin, who soberly piloted a 707 to a belly-landing in *Airport*

The Guess-Who's-Stepping-Out-to-Tommy's-Lunch Award:
To the shooting-up scene in *Trash*

The Strongest Argument for Laxer Divorce Laws:
Bob Evans, president of Paramount Pictures, and Ali MacGraw, for obvious reasons

The Dr. Christiaan Barnard Award:
(to that movie which shows the worst job of cutting)
Claude Chabrol's *Le Boucher*

The Please-Don't-Put-Us-Through-DeMille-Again Award:
(to that movie which best embodies the pretensions, extravagances and blundering ineffectiveness of the traditional Screen Spectacular)
Woodstock

The Beast of Buchenwald Award:
(to those actors who most thoroughly degrade themselves in order to pull in the paycheck, a handsomely tooled lampshade)
The entire cast of *Fellini's Satyricon*

The What's-a-Nice-Boy-from-Shaker-Heights-Doing-etc. Award:
(given to the most unnecessary contribution to the American way of life)
Paul Newman, who proved that he is no Merle Haggard in *WUSA*

The Julia Child Cleft Palate:
Ryan O'Neil, for calling the Hasty Pudding Club "boring"

The Cheap-at-Half-the-Price Award:
(for the worst bargain in a film)
Stewardesses in 3D, which in addition to its $3.00 admission price charges 25¢ for a sliver of twisted plastic. The eyeshades transform the colorful two-dimensional

slurry into a steamy three-dimensional cesspool

The Timothy Cratchit Memorial Crutch:
(to that personality who offers the lamest justification for unsavory behavior)
For the second year in a row, to President Nixon, who gave *Patton* a careful screening the night before he announced the Cambodian invasion

The Bratwurst Award:
(to the most endearing child star)
The entire cast of *Groupies*

The Dance of the Seven Scott Tissues Award:
(to the most lewd and completely unwarranted dancing scene)
Mick Jagger, who trips the light psychedelic in *Performance*

The Bare-assed in the Park Award:
This award, along with the traditional cellophane figleaf, is presented to Joey Heatherton, for marrying Lance Rentzel, whose let-it-all-hang-out performance in a Dallas park was the year's best argument for sex education in the locker room

The Piltdown Mandible:
(to the most obviously and unabashedly spurious scientific phenomenon)
On a Clear Day You Can See Forever, in which Yves Montand hypnotizes Barbra Streisand from twentieth-century Brooklyn into nineteenth-century England

The Sentimental Mushmelon:
(to that film which most reminds us of that true Poignancy, that bitter Sweetness, which we know as Life)
The squishy rendition of Robert Anderson's seedy play, *I Never Sang for My Father*

The Great Ceremonial Hot Dog:
(for the worst scene of the cinema season)
To Holly Woodlawn, for making it with a beer bottle in *Trash*

The Exhausted Udder:
(presented by the Diary Farmers Assn. in recognition of attempts to milk every penny possible from a marketable idea)
Anyone who had anything to do with *Beyond the Valley of the Dolls* or *Beneath the Planet of the Apes*

The Hey-Jack-Which-Way-to-Mecca Award:
(for the worst direction)
Michelangelo Antonioni's *Zabriskie Point*

The Uncrossed Heart:
(to the least promising young performer)
Presented in a serious vain to *Trash*'s mainliner, Joe Dallesandro

The Within-You-But-Not-Without-Me Award:
Kama Sutra, for getting it together

Best Argument for Pay-TV:
Loving, in which George Segal and Eva Marie Saint make it in a playpen before a closed-circuit TV camera for the benefit of party guests next door

The Bosley:
(to that film critic whose writing consistently explores the farthest limits of bad taste)
This year uncontested: it goes with a hip flask of bile and a mortal dose of henbane, to John Simon, for his muddle-headed, obfuscatory, artless, splenetic and interminable...self

The Women-and-Children-First-Lt.-Calley Award:
A Fanner Fifty and a roll of Greenie Stickum Caps to John Wayne, for surprising us with two new westerns, *Chisum* and *Rio Lobo*

The Charles Manson Memorial Scalpel:
Awarded without comment to

the side-splitting scene in *Catch-22*

The It-Can't-Happen-Here Award:
(presented to the film that shot a sequence which is geographically closest to The Lampoon Castle)
Love Story for showing the American public that the nicest things about Harvard are Cambridge winters, low-rent housing, Winthrop House and leukemia

The Merino Award:
In 1960 this one-quarter scale neoprene mounted sheep went to Maureen O'Hara; in 1961 to Rita Moreno; in 1962 to Maureen O'Sullivan; in 1963 to Italian director Dario Moreno; in 1964 to marinophile Jacques-Yves Cousteau; in 1965 to Merina Mercouli; in 1966 to the two merinos on board the Ark in *The Bible*; in 1967 to the Pushme-Pullyou in *Doctor Dolittle*, a distant cousin to merinos, leading as tenuous an existence; in 1968 to the cast of *The Green Berets*, which icluded only one black Marine; in 1969 with a dull thud to Andy Warhol's *Blue Movie*, filmed entirely in lurid aqua-merino; and in 1970 to the frumpy housewife from a frumpy movie, *Airport*, Maureen O. Stapleton

The Wrong-Way Corrigan Memorial Flight Jacket:
(for the worst direction)
Ken Hughes, *Cromwell*

The Harvard Independent:
(to that film noted for its ignominious failure as both art and politics)
Strawberry Statement

The-Curse-of-the-Living-Corpse Award:
Helen Hayes, *Airport*

The Wilde Oscar:
(for that performer who has been willing to flout convention and risk worldly damnation in the pursuit of artistic fulfillment)

Liza Minnelli, *Tell Me You Love Me Junie Moon*

The H.J. Heinz Laurel Clot:
(to the film that makes most extensive use of the company's various vegetable derivatives)
Soldier Blue

The Roscoe Award:
(to that performer who has most memorably displayed that certain unskilled clumsy quality that has marked the products of Hollywood since the early days)
Katharine Ross, *Fools*

The Elsa Maxwell Kudo:
(to the most unattractive social event of the year)
The party in *Boys in the Band*

The Best Argument for Activating Ellis Island:
Sexual Freedom in Denmark

The Twenty-Cent Token:
(to that film which does the most fashionable injustice to a minority class)
Little Big Man

Thanks for Nothing:
(to that Hollywood performer who has blessedly not made a motion picture this year)
Jane Fonda, for immigrating to the Third World

The Martha Mitchell Mug:
Peter Boyle for *Joe*

Prease Get off Tojo Award:
Darryl Zanuck for *Tora! Tora! Tora!*

Mary Martin Light-and-Lively Award:
(for worst musical)
Gimme Shelter

If Only Films Were Biodegradable Award:
To those who recycled *My Fair Lady, Lawrence of Arabia, Dr. Zhivago,* and *Mutiny on the Bounty*

The Ayn Rand Award:
(to that writer whose bad books made worse movies)
Harold Robbins, *The Adventurers*

1971

Ten Worst Movies:
Clockwork Orange
Carnal Knowledge
Summer of '42
Fiddler on the Roof
The Last Movie
T.R. Baskin
Kotch
Willard
The Music Lovers
Dealing

Kirk Douglas Award for Worst Actor:
Jack Nicholson, *Carnal Knowledge*

Natalie Wood Award for Worst Actress:
Candice Bergen, *T.R. Baskin*

Worst Supporting Actor:
The real-life cop in *French Connection*

Worst Supporting Actress:
Lana Wood, *Diamonds Are Forever*

H.J. Heinz Laurel Clot:
(to the film that makes most extensive use of the company's various vegetable derivatives)
Dirty Harry

The Mary Martin Light-and-Lively Award:
(for worst musical)
200 Motels

The Twenty-Cent Token:
(to that film which does the most fashionable injustice to a minority class)
McCabe & Mrs. Miller for its gratuitous Negro espousals

The W-W Corrigan Memorial Flight Jacket:
(to the worst directed film)
Nicholas and Alexandra

The Best Argument for Reactivating Ellis Island:
The Godfather

The Elsa Maxwell Kudo:
To Buck Henry for losing the strip poker game in *Taking Off*

The Roscoe Award:
(to that performer who has most memorably displayed that certain unskilled clumsy quality)
Art Garfunkel, *Carnal Knowledge*

The Thanks-for-Nothing Award:
(to that Hollywood performer who has blessedly not made a motion picture this year)
Katharine Ross

The Harvard Independent:
(to that film noted for its ignominious failure as both art and politics)
Sacco and Vanzetti

The Hey-Which-Way-Is-Mecca? Award:
(for worst direction)
Dennis Hopper, *The Last Movie*

The Hey-Boswell-Did-You-Get-That-One-Down Award:
(to the film with the worst dialogue)
To Steve McQueen for his exhaust-laden sweet nothings in *LeMans*

The Where-Is-Erik-Erikson-Now-That-We're-All-Going-Bananas Award:
Woody Allen, *Bananas*

The Wilde Oscar:
(to that performer most willing to flout convention and risk worldly damnation in the pursuit of artistic fulfillment)
John Wayne for making two more saddle movies and standing behind our boys in Vietman

The Sensuous Eunuch Award:
Jack Nicholson

The Ok-Doc-Break-the-Arm-Again Award:
(to the most flagrant example of miscasting)
To Ingmar Bergman for letting Elliott Gould turn *The Touch* into a karate chop

The If-He-Gets-Through-This-One-We'll-Name-Him-Houdini Award:
The cretin pharmacist in *Summer of '42*

The Within-You-But-Not-Without-Me Award:
Ecstasy '72

The Bosley:
(to the film critic whose writing has most consistently explored the limits of bad taste)

The entire Society of New York Film Critics for naming *Clockwork Orange* best film of the year

The Exhausted Udder:
(in recognition of attempts to milk every penny possible from a marketable idea)
Diamonds Are Forever

The Uncrossed Heart:
(to the least promising young performer)
Twiggy, the girl friend in *The Boy Friend*

The Ceremonial Hot Dog:
(to the worst movie scene)
The morning-after scene in *Macbeth*

The Piltdown Mandible:
(to the most obviously and unabashedly spurious scientific phenomenon)
The Andromeda Strain

The Cheap-at-Half-the-Price Award:
(for the worst movie bargain)
Experience (the Harvard promotional flick)

The Women-and-Children-First-Lt.-Calley Award:
(to the film whose violence was above and beyond the call of duty)
John Wayne, *Big Jake*

Ayn Rand Award:
(to that writer whose bad books made even worse movies)
Michael Crichton, *Andromeda Strain*

The If-Only-Films-Were-Biodegradable Award:
The recycling of Charlie Chaplin films

The Dance of the Seven Scott Tissues Award:
(to the most lewd and completely unwarranted dancing scene)
Malcolm MacDowell, *Clockwork Orange*

The Charles Manson Memorial Scalpel:
(to that film with the clumsiest job of cutting)
The Go Between for its time jumps

The Please-Don't-Put-Us-Through-DeMille-Again Award:
(to that film which best embodies the pretensions, extravagances, and blundering ineffectiveness of the traditional Screen Spectacular)
Waterloo

The Strongest Argument for Laxer Divorce Laws:
Renee Taylor and Joseph Bologna for Made for Each Other

The Guess-Who's-Stepping-Out-to-Tommy's-Lunch Award:
To the nuns who blew their wafers in The Devils

The Tar Baby:
(in recognition of Hollywood's continued exploitation of the black market)
To MGM for giving us Shaft

The Bratwurst Award:
(to the worst child actor)
The entire cast of Bless the Beasts and Children

The Cellophane Figleaf:
(to the most outstanding display of anemic false modesty)
Cybill Shepherd, The Last Picture Show

The Beast of Buchenwald Award:
(to that performer who most thoroughly degrades himself in order to pull in the paycheck, a handsomely tooled lampshade)
Ernest Borgnine, Willard

The Merino Award:
(to that figure who has done the most to enhance the fame and glory of the merino)
Murino eye drops for making Malcolm MacDowell see the light in Clockwork Orange

1972

Ten Worst Movies:
Last Tango in Paris
The Candidate
The Getaway
Sounder

Deliverance
Play It As It Lays
The Emigrants
What's Up, Doc?
Man of La Mancha
The Man

Kirk Douglas Award for Worst Actor:
Robert Redford, The Candidate

Natalie Wood Award for Worst Actress:
Ali MacGraw, Getaway

Worst Supporting Actor:
Burgess Meredith, The Man

Worst Supporting Actress:
Shelley Winters, The Poseidon Adventure

The We-Heard-You-the-First-Time Award:
Georgia, Georgia

The Charles Manson Memorial Scalpel:
(to the clumsiest job of cutting)
Play It As It Lays

The Jerry Van Dyke Clip-on Medallion:
(to the most consistently innocuous personality)
Fred MacMurray

The Please-Don't-Put-Us-Through-DeMille Award:
(to that movie which best embodies the pretensions, extravagances, and blundering ineffectiveness of the Screen Spectacular)
Lost Horizon

The Elsa Maxwell Kudo:
(to the most unattractive social event of the year)
The New Year's Eve splash party in The Poseidon Adventure

The Kill-It-Before-It-Spreads Citation:
(designed to cripple the career of a fledgling actor or actress)
Jeannie Berlin, The Heartbreak Kid

The Sentimental Mushmelon:
(to the film that most reminds us of that true Poignancy, that Bitter Sweetness, which we know as Life)
Butterflies Are Free

The Wrong-Way Corrigan Memorial Fight Jacket:
(for the worst direction)

Sam Peckinpah, The Getaway; Junior Bonner

The Uncrossed Heart:
(to the least promising young performer)
Cybill Shepherd, who has now gone two major films without once opening her eyes

The Twenty-Cent Token:
(to that film which does the most fashionable injustice to a minority class)
Sounder

The Women-and-Children-First-Lt.-Calley Award:
(designed to honor acts above and beyond the call of duty)
Sam Peckinpah, The Getaway, Junior Bonner

The Best Argument for Vivisection:
Fritz the Cat

The Tar Baby:
(in recognition of Hollywood's continued exploitation of the black market)
Blacula

The Brass Brassiere:
(to those who have done the most to advance the cause of male chauvinism)
Gene Hackman and Lee Marvin, Prime Cut

The Great Ceremonial Hot Dog:
(to the worst scene)
Carol Burnett, for her stunning impersonation of Charlie the Horse doing Medea in the bereavement scene of Pete 'n' Tillie

The Handlin Oscar:
(to the film which has most distorted the course of history)
Young Winston

The Yawns-of-Death Citation:
(to the most unremittingly depressing film)
The King of Marvin Gardens

The Tin Pan:
(to the most thoroughly obnoxious movie song)
"Cabaret," Cabaret

The Hey-Boswell-Did-You-Get-That-One-Down Award;
(to that film whose dialogue

was, when not monosyllabic, subhuman)

Charles Bronson, *Da Valachi Papers*; *Da Mechanic*

The Dark Fedora:
(this citation names the villain you might have waited to discover with bated breath or stifled yawns at the end of a three-hour movie)

Sleuth, now that you know Michael Caine is inspector Doppler

The Best Argument for Reactivating Ellis Island:
The Emigrants, for showing us that even Swedes can act like Polacks

The Ok-Doc-Break-the-Arm-Again Award:
(to the most flagrant example of miscasting)

Sam Peckinpah for hiring Ali MacGraw to do a woman's job in *The Getaway*

The Caploe:
(to the actor or actress in a porno film)

Linda Lovelace, *Deep Throat*

The Worst Film of the Century Award:
The Poseidon Adventure

The Cheap-at-Half-the-Price Award:
(to the worst bargain in a film)

Deep Throat

The Timothy Cratchit Memorial Crutch:
(to that personality who offers the lamest excuse for unsavory behavior)

Ms. Sacheen Littlefeather, Marlon Brando's Oscar-night stand-in, who later parlayed her status as a representative of the American Indian cause into a three-page nude photo spread in *Playboy*

The Dance of the Seven Scott Tissues Award:
(to the most lewd and completely unwarranted dancing scene)

Marlon Brando, *Last Tango*

Worst Performance by a Cast in Toto:
The Poseidon Adventure

The Life-of-the-Party Award:
(to that actor who most thoroughly degrades himself in order to pull in the paycheck)

Richard Burton in *Bluebeard*, for methodically murdering six wives whose lips are out of sync

The Roscoe:
(to that performer who has displayed that certain unskilled clumsy quality)

Jon Voight, *Deliverance*

The Cellophane Figleaf:
(for the most outstanding display of anemic false modesty)

Valerie Perrine, *Slaughterhouse Five*

The Wilde Oscar:
(to that performer who has been willing to flout convention in the pursuit of artistic fulfillment)

Linda Lovelace

The Bosley:
(to that critic whose writing explores the farthest limits of bad taste)

Pauline Kael, whose hysterical encomium loosed Bertolucci's *Last Tango* upon an all-too-trusting world

The Guess-Who's-Stepping-Out-to-Tommy's-Lunch Award:
To the Mothers and Fathers of Italian Ancestry for a castration in *The Valachi Papers*, which finally proves that sopranos are made, not born

The Ayn Rand Award:
(to that writer whose bad books made worse movies)

John Knowles, *A Separate Peace*

The Strongest Argument for Laxer Divorce Laws:
Paul Newman, who should learn to control his wife, for *The Effects of Gamma Rays.*
. .

The Well-It-Sure-Is-Different Award:
(to the most chicly incomprehensible film)

Fellini, *Roma*

The Curse-of-the-Living-Corpse Award:
Ernest Borgnine

The Arrested-Development Oblation:
(presented to that adult actor who has displayed the lowest level of maturity)

Jerry Lewis as always

The-Black-Symbolizes-Death, See? Award:
(to the worst student film)

Jean Pigozzi, *Hamburger*

The Victor Mature Memorial Award:
(to the most embarrassing line of dialogue since Richard Burton was asked at the foot of the cross, in The Robe, "Is this your first crucifixion?")

Nicholas and Alexandra, for a young Trotsky's angry reproach to the Father of Modern Communism: "Lenin, you've been avoiding me!"

The Piltdown Mandible:
(to the most unabashedly spurious scientific phenomenon)

Deep Throat, for the tired, hackneyed misplaced-clitoris routine

The Marquis de Sade Memorial Whip:
Ken Russell, *Savage Messiah*

The Harvard Independent Award:
(to that film noted for its ignominious failure as both art and politics)

The Candidate

The Not-Tonight-I-Have-a-Headache Award:
(to that movie which gave us the best excuse to turn in early)

Marcel Ophuls, *The Sorrow and the Pity*

The Stanislavsky Avardsk:
(to that performer who has undergone the greatest physical torment in the furtherance of Art)

Raquel Welch, who learned to roller-skate in *Kansas City Bomber*

The Exhausted Udder:
(in recognition of attempts to

milk every penny from marketable idea)
Conquest of the Planet of the Apes

The H. J. Heinz Award:
(to that film which makes most extensive use of the company's various vegetable derivatives)
The Valachi Papers

The Bratwurst Award:
(to the most endearing child stars)
The entire cast of *A Separate Peace*

The Thanks-for-Nothing Award:
(to that performer who has blessedly not made a film this year)
Stephan Boyd, whose career seems to have gone steadily downhill since his disembowlment in *Ben-Hur*

The Merino Award:
In 1960 to Maureen O'Hara; in 1961 to Rita Moreno; in 1962 to Maureen O'Sullivan; in 1963 to Italian director Dario Moreno; in 1964 to marinophile Jacques-Yves Cousteau; in 1965 to Merino Mercouli; in 1966 to the two merinos on board the Ark in *The Bible*; in 1967 to the Pushme-Pullyou in *Doctor Dolittle*, a distant cousin to the merino; in 1968 to the cast of *The Green Berets*, which included only one black marine; in 1969 to Andy Warhol's *Blue Movie*, filmed entirely in liquid aquamerino; in 1970 to Maureen O. Stapleton; in 1971 to Murino eye drops, for making Malcolm MacDonald see the light in *A Clockwork Orange*; and for 1972 to Marino Schneider in *Last Tango*

1973

Ten-Worst Movies:
The Great Gatsby

Day of the Dolphin
Jonathan Livingston Seagull
The Seven-Ups
A Touch of Class
Blume in Love
The Way We Were
The Exorcist
Save the Tiger
American Graffiti

The Kirk Douglas Award for Worst Actor:
Jack Lemmon, *Save The Tiger*

The Natalie Wood Award for Worst Actress:
Barbra Streisand, *The Way We Were*

Worst Supporting Actor:
Dustin Hoffman, *Papillon*

Worst Supporting Actress:
Dyan Cannon, *Shamus*; *The Last of Sheila*

The Ok-Doc-Break-the-Arm-Again Award:
(to the most flagrant example of miscasting)
The Great Gatsby, which cast Mia Farrow as Daisy Buchanan

The Wrong-Way Corrigan Memorial Flight Jacket:
(for worst direction)
Mike Nichols, *Day of the Dolphin*

The Women-and-Children-First-Lt.-Calley Award:
(for acts of violence above and beyond the call of duty)
Philip D'Antoni for the chase scene in *The Seven Ups*

The Jerry Van Dyke Clip-On Medallion:
(for the most innocuous personality)
Fred MacMurray

The Please-Don't-Put-Us-Through-DeMille-Again Award:
(to the film which best embodies the pretensions, extravagances, and blundering ineffectiveness of the Screen Spectacular)
Papillon

The Handlin Oscar:
(to the film which most distorts history)
Hitler: The Last Ten Days

The Worst Performance by a Cast in Toto Award:
Bang the Drum Slowly, with Least Valuable Players citations going to Michael Moriarty and Robert DeNiro

The Great Ceremonial Hot Dog:
(to the worst scene)
Neil Young, *Journey through the Past*, for assault with a flimsy weapon

The We-Heard-You-the-First-Time Award:
Money, Money, Money

The H. J. Heinz Laurel Clot:
(to that film which makes most extensive use of the company's vegetable derivatives)
Magnum Force

The Marquis de Sade Memorial Whip:
Clint Eastwood, *Magnum Force*

The Remember-You-Saw-It-Here-First Award:
Roberta Flack, who should kill us softly with her songs the first time we see her in the upcoming film biography of Bessie Smith

The Curse-of-the-Living-Corpse Award:
Lucille Ball, *Mame*, in which her actual age was cleverly concealed by a paper towel taped over the camera lens; someone should saw this lady in half and count the rings

The Elsa Maxwell Kudo:
(to the most unattractive social event)
The Grande Bouffe, for dishing up Death as a dessert at a banquet

The Wilde Oscar:
(to the performer who has been wiling to flout convention in the pursuit of artistic fulfillment)
John Wayne, for giving up that plot on Boot Hill in exchange for a modest shrine in Forest Lawn

The Roscoe Award:
(to that performer who has most memorably displayed that certain unskilled clumsy quality)

Ann-Margret, who showed a distinct falling off in her Las Vegas act, if not deliberate slipshodness, in *The Train Robbers*

The Tin Pan:
(to the most obnoxious movie song)
Paul McCartney, *Live and Let Die*

The Best Argument for Reactivating Ellis Island:
The New Land

The Sentmental Mushmelon:
(to that film that most reminds us of that true poignancy, that bitter Sweetness, which we know as Life)
Bang the Drum Slowly

The Guess-Who's-Stepping-Out-to-Tommy's-Lunch Award:
The probing scene in *The Exorcist*

The Harvard Independent Award:
(to that film that most reminds us of that true poignancy, that bitter Sweetness, which we know as Life)
State of Siege, which escaped the criticism it so richly deserved because nobody criticized it for its failure as art (since it never occurred to anybody that is was art) and because nobody criticized it for its failure as journalism (since it never occurred to anybody that it was journalism)

The Cosmic Blender:
Black Caesar, who brought the mob to Harlem

The Twenty-Cent Token:
(to that film which does the most fashionable injustice to a minority class)
Cleopatra Jones

The Timothy Cratchit Memorial Crutch:
(to that personality who offers the lamest justification for unsavory behavior)
Colleen Dewhurst, who appeared in *McQ* because, she said, "I needed the money."

The Yawns-of-Death Citation:
(to the most unremittingly depressing film)
The Way We Were

The Ayn Rand Award:
(to that writer whose bad books made worse movies)
Hermann Hesse, who should have been old enough to know better than to write *Siddhartha*

The Stanislavsky Avardsk:
(to that performer who has undergone the greatest physical torment in the furtherance of Art)
Mercedes McCambridge, who well, sounded like hell in *The Exorcist*

The Bratwurst Ward:
(to the most endearing child star)
Johnny Whitaker, "either Buffy or Jody" *Tom Sawyer*

The Strongest Argument for Laxer Divorce Laws:
To Mrs. Ryan O'Neal, who should have fought harder for custody of daughter Tatum

The Charles Manson Memorial Scalpel:
(for the clumsiest job of cutting)
O Lucky Man, whose shooting script was first published as a deck of flash-cards by Educational Playthings

The Brass Brassiere:
(to that personality who has done the most to advance the cause of male chauvinism)
Henry Fonda, for whom Elizabeth Taylor had her face lifted in *Ash Wednesday*

The Nippon-in-the-Bud Award:
To the current rash of Hong Kong Flu films

The Dance of the Seven Scott Tissues Award:
(to the most lewd and completely unwarranted dancing scene)
Rudolph Nureyev for his unexceptional Royal Canadian Air Force exercises in *I Am a Dancer*

The Cheap-at-Half-Price Award:
(to the worst bargain in a film)
The Exorcist, in which the devil gets far more than his due

The Exhausted Udder:
(in recognition of attempts to milk every penny possible from a marketable idea)
Anthony Quinn, *Th Don is Dead*

The Hey-Boswell-Did-You-Get-That-One-Down Award:
(to that film whose dialogue was, when not monosyllabic subhuman)
Bluce Ree, *Enter the Dragon*

The Dark Fedora:
(this citation reveals the tricky conclusion)
The Sting, which you will enjoy even less now that you know that Robert Redford doesn't really double-cross Paul Newman, that they don't really shoot each other, and of course, that they do "get away with it"

The Piltdown Mandible:
(to the most obviously and unabashedly spurious scientific phenomenon)
Chariots of the Gods (Could this film possibly be the remnant of a civilization vastly inferior to our own?)

The Uncrossed Heart:
(to the least promising young performer)
Linda Blair, *The Exorcist*, who turned a few heads around

The Life-of-the-Party Award:
(to that performer who most thoroughly degrades himself in order to pull in the paycheck)
The entire cast of *The Grande Bouffe*, who proved that what goes down must come up

The Bosley:
(to that critic who consistently explores the farthest limits of bad taste)
Penelope Gilliatt, who might have at least flipped a coin to decide whether or not she liked *The Great Gatsby*, if she saw *The Great Gatsby*, before she wrote about it—if

she was writing about it—in *The New Yorker*

The Kill-It-Before-It-Spreads Citation:
(designed to cripple the career of a fledgling performer)
Keith Carradine and Shelley Duval, *Thieves Like Us*

The Thanks-for-Nothing Award:
(to that Hollywood performer who has blessedly not made a film this year)
To two-time worst Actress Ali McGraw, who was busy this year two-timing somewhere else

The Cellophane Figleaf:
(to the most outstanding display of anemic false modesty)
Julie Christie, *Don't Look Now*, who couldn't see to brazen her buff charms until this blockbuster came along

The Merino Award:
(to that figure who has done the most to enhance the fame and glory of the merino)
To that Merican actor and performer *ordinaire* Mario Moreno, who has announced plans to reappear as Cantinflas on same screen in the near future

Best Argument for Vivisection:
Jonathan Livingston Seagull

1974

Ten Worst Movies:
Lenny
*S*P*Y*S*
Harry and Tonto
Airport 1975
Blazing Saddles
The Night Porter
The Trial of Billy Jack
Murder on the Orient Express
Daisy Miller
The Front Page

Kirk Douglas Award for Worst Actor:
Burt Reynolds, *The Longest Yard*

Natalie Wood Award for Worst Actress:
Julie Andrews, *The Tamarind Seed*

Worst Supporting Actor:
Gene Wilder, *The Little Prince*

Worst Supporting Actress:
Carol Burnett, *The Front Page*

Worst Performance by a Cast in Toto:
Murder on the Orient Express

The Exhausted Udder Award:
(in recognition of attepts to milk every penny possible from a marketable idea)
To the producers of *Our Time; Macon County Line; The Lords of Flatbush;* and *Buster and Billie* for trying to eke piquancy from an era as colorless as the tag on a pair of overlaundered pedal pushers

H. J. Heinz Laurel Clot:
(to the film that makes most extensive use of the company's various vegetable derivatives)
Andy Warhol's Frankenstein

Merino Award:
(to that figure who has done the most to enhance the fame and glory of the merino)
Maureen O. McGovern, the curtailment of whose adipose warbling in *The Poseiden Adventure* and now *The Towering Inferno* excuses in part the effects of the disasters that follow

Best Argument for Vivisection:
Tonto of *Harry and Tonto*

The Victor Mature Award:
(in memory of Victor Mature, who was heard to ask Barabbas in The Robe *"Is this your first crucifixion?," this award is given to the most embarrassing line of dialogue)*
George Kennedy's astute remark in *Earthquake* "Earthquakes bring out the worst in people"

The Ok-Doc-Break-the-Arm-Again Award:
(for the most flagrant example of miscasting)

Dean Martin as an intelligent lawyer in *Mr. Ricco*

The Life-of-the-Party Award:
(to that performer who most thoroughly degrades himself in order to keep the wolf from the door)
Harvey Korman, who showed us in *Blazing Saddles* what seven lean years of being straight man to Carol Burnett can do to a guy

The Remember-You-Saw-It-Here-First Award:
Warren Beatty, that pudgy, self-preening angel of banality, whose—for lack of a better word—performance in an upcoming film biography of John Reed will be—for lack of a worse word—excrable

The Curse-of-the-Living-Corpse Award:
Gloria Swanson, an actress only slightly older than the mountains she is imperiled above in *Airport '75*

The Bosley:
(to that film critic whose work consistently explores the farthest limits of bad taste)
Pat Mitchell, whose television hysterics can fortunately be shut off at a flick of the dial

The Kill-It-Before-It-Spreads Citation:
(designed to cripple the career of a fledgling performer)
Lee Strasberg, who unfortunately has already infected with bad acting habits more than just his portion of the screen in *Godfather part II*

The Dark Fedora:
(this citation reveals the tricky conclusion of a film)
Chinatown, in which Faye Dunaway is shot after confessing that her father actually sired her illigitimate daughter

The Please-Don't-Put-Us-Through-DeMille Award:
That's Entertainment, which wasn't

1975

Ten Worst Movies:
Barry Lyndon
Tommy
At Long Last Love
The Other Side of the
   Mountain
The Hindenburg
Day of the Locust
Story of O
Mahogany
Shampoo
Once Is Not Enough
**Kirk Douglas Award for
Worst Actor:**
Ryan O'Neal, Barry Lyndon
**Natalie Wood Award for
Worst Actress:**
Diana Ross, Mahogany
Worst Supporting Actor:
Burgess Meredith, Day of the
   Locust
Worst Supporting Actress:
Madeline Kahn, Sherlock
   Holmes' Smarter Brother
   and At Long Last Love
**The We-Heard-You-the-First-
Time Award:**
Daughters, Daughters
**The Please-Don't-Put-Us-
Through-DeMille Award:**
(to the movie which best em-
bodies the pretensions, ex-
travagances and blundering
ineffectiveness of the Screen
Spectacular)
John Huston, The Man Who
   Would Be King
The Ayn Rand Award:
(to the writer whose bad books
made worse movies)
Jacqueline Susann, Once is Not
   Enough
The Tin Pan:
(to the most thoroughly obnox-
ious movie song)
"Do You Know Where You're
   Going?" Mahogany
**Worst Performance by a
Cast in Toto:**
Let's Do It Again
The Bratwurst Award:
(to that juvenile actor or ac-
tress who most convincingly
presents a strong argument for
compulsory education)

Jodie Foster, Taxi Driver
**The Best Argument for
Reactivating Ellis Island:**
Sweet Movie
**The Curse-of-the-Living-
Corpse Award:**
The limping digits of Arthur
   Rubinstein for their distinctly
   separate performances in
   Love of Life
The Bosley:
(to that film critic whose jour-
nalism most consistently chal-
lenges the American ideal of a
free press)
John Simon, whose
   continuance in the critical
   cult constitutes the most
   shocking misuse of trees for
   paper pulp since the death
   of Hedda Hopper
**The Strongest Argument for
Laxer Divorce Laws:**
Paul Newman and Joanne
   Woodward, who made
   heavy water of Drowning
   Pool
**The Thanks-for-Nothing
Award:**
(to that Hollywood personality
who has blessedly not made a
motion picture this year)
Mel Brooks
**The Wrong-Way Corrigan
Memorial Flight Jacket:**
(for the worst direction
Stephen Spielberg, Jaws, for
   turning Moby Dick into King
   Kong and attempting to pass
   this fish story off as great
   cinematic art
**Cheap-at-Half-the-Price
Award:**
(for the worst bargain in a film)
Roger Corman and anyone else
   responsible for Tidal Wave,
   for splicing fifteen minutes
   of Lorne Green into
   Japanese footage of model
   cities annihilated by
   whirl-pool baths
The Handlin Oscar:
(to the film that has most distorted the cause of history)
The Wind and the Lion, which
   was actually quite accurate
   if you can accept Sean
   Connery as a North African
   chieftain and Candice
   Bergen as having a mental

edge over a five-year-old
   sufficient to be a governess
**The
Hey-Boswell-Did-You-Get-
That-One-Down Award:**
(to the film with the worst dialogue)
Cooley High which made the
   illiterate rumblings in
   American Graffiti look like
   crackling repartee at the
   Algonquin table
**The Women-and-Children-
First-Lt.-Calley Award:**
(designed to honor violence
above and beyond the call of
duty)
Sam Peckinpah, Killer Elite
The Exhausted Udder:
(in recognition of attempts to
milk every penny possible from
a marketable idea)
Once Is Not Enough
**The Not-Tonight-I-Have-a-
Headache Award:**
(to that movie which gave us
the best excuse to turn in early)
Walt Disney Studios, One of
   Our Dinosaurs Is Missing
**The Charles Manson
Memorial Scalpel:**
(to the film which shows the
clumsiest job of cutting)
Shoot It Black, Shoot It Blue
**The Lukewarm-Bathos
Award:**
(to that scene in a movie
whose stilted sentimentality
succeeds in watering the eyes
only by irritating them)
Little Bryan's deathbed scene
   in Barry Lyndon
The Roscoe:
(to that performer who has
most unflaggingly exhibited a
complete lack of talent, perception, screen presence and
intelligence)
Karen Black, who crawls the
   gamut of human emotions in
   Day of the Locust and
   Nashville
**The Arrested-Development
Oblation:**
(to that adult actor who has
displayed the lowest level of
maturity on or off the screen)
Jerry Lewis, as always

Best Argument for Vivisection:
Benji

The Dark Fedora:
(This award serves to save the unsuspecting public from suffering through two hours of cinematic waste for the cheap thrill of uncovering the ingenious conclusion to a contrived and facile story line)
Farewell, My Lovely, which you will enjoy even less now that you know that the long-lost girl has been married to the crooked ganster all along, and gets shot at the end by the pathetic ex-boxer who loved her

The Ok-Doc-Break-the-Arm-Again Award:
(for the most flagrant example of miscasting)
Man Who Would Be King, for casting Sean Connery as anyone but *James Bond*

The Life-of-the-Party Award:
(for that screen performer who most thoroughly demeans himself in order to pull in the paycheck, a handsomely tooled lampshade goes to)
Julie Christie, that formerly elegant and sophisticated actress, whose understated sensitive appeal to Warren Beatty, "Oh, God, let me suck it," firmly ensconces her in the ranks of the cheap

The Tar Baby:
(in recognition of Hollywood's Second Reconstruction program of employing and exploiting former athletes and would-be welfare recipients)
The producers of *Mandingo*

The Piltdown Mandible:
(to the most obviously and unabashedly spurious scientific phenomenon)
The Land that Time Forgot for its Pleistocene backdrops and plasticene dinosaurs

The If Only Film Were Biodegradable Citation:
Richard Lester, for recycling the Three Stooges into *The Four Musketeers*

The Victor Mature Memorial Award:
(to the most embarassing line of dialogue)
Gable and Lombard, for the screen great's insouciant comment following the incendiary demise of his beloved in a plane crash, as he gazes fondly over the twisted wreckage: "She should have taken the train."

The Harvard Independent Award:
(for that film noted for its ignominious failure as both art and politics)
Swept Away

The Merino Award:
(to that figure who has done the most to enhance the fame and glory of the merino)
Marino Berenson, whose name doesn't even come close to sounding like merino, for her threadbare performance in *Barry Lyndon*

1976

Ten Worst Movies;
A Star Is Born
The Enforcer
Murder By Death
Slapshot
The Omen
Lipstick
Mickey and Nicky
The Missouri Breaks
Carwash
King Kong

Kirk Douglas Award for Worst Actor:
Clint Eastwood in his third go-round as *Dirty Harry Callahan*

Natalie Wood for Worst Actress:
Barbra Streisand, *A Star Is Born* (Her performances should delight those who can't tell the difference between Eydie Gormé and Patti Smith.)

The Burgess Meredith Award for Worst Supporting Actor:
Chris Saradon, *Lipstick*

The Ava Gardner Award for Worst Supporting Actress:
Jodie Foster, *Bugsy Malone*

The Radioactive-Velveeta Award:
(for the most tedious treatment of a tawdry topic)
Survive, the sleazy Mexican production of the story of a stranded soccer team that turns to cannibalism. It's too bad the scriptwriter wasn't around when the boys got hungry.

The Liquid-Paper-Correction-Fluid Award:
Diana Ross for her portrayal of a fashion model in *Sparkle*. We could have sworn the woman used to be white.

The Volvo Trophy:
Liv Ullman in *Face to Face* as the Swedish import that always breaks down

The Arrested Development Oblation:
(to that adult actor who has displayed the lowest level of maturity on or off the screen)
Jerry Lewis, as always

The Fertilized Tombstone:
Gable and Lombard and *W.C. Fields and Me* for making the wildflowers on their subjects' graves grow ever more quickly

The Roscoe Award:
(to that screen performer who has demonstrated a complete absence of qualities even resembling talent, intelligence and appeal)
Margaux Hemingway, *Lipstick*

The Out-to-Pasteur Award:
(to the worst science fiction movie)
Jonah, Who Will be 25 in the year 2000. With any luck, World War III will wipe out the brat before then

The Bonavena Oscar:
Rocky, for heavyweight box-officing

The Golden Glob:
(for the pornographic movie that limps along most lamely)

How Funny Can Sex Be?
The You're-Getting-Old-and-Fat-and-Generally-Unappetizing Award:
Elizabeth Taylor

The Merino Award:
(to that figure who has done the most to enhance the fame and glory of the merino)
Shearlings, a horror flick about radioactive sheep in the Mojave Desert

1977

Ten Worst Movies:
Looking for Mr. Goodbar
It's Alive
The Turning Point
A Nightful of Rain
New York, New York
Coming Home
Oh, God
Semi-Tough
The Goodbye Girl
The Gauntlet

Kirk Douglas Award for Worst Actor:
Kris Kristofferson, *Semi-Tough*

Natalie Wood Award for Worst Actress:
Marthe Keller, *Black Sunday*

Best Argument for Vivisection:
Summerdog

Strongest Argument for Laxer Divorce Laws:
To the parents of those baseballing brats in *The Bad New Bears In Breaking Training*. If we had gotten them 10-12 years ago, this stinker might have been averted.

The Exhausted Udder Award:
(presented by the Dairy Farmer's Association in recognition of attempts to milk every possible penny from a marketable idea)
Walking Tall, Final Chapter and *The Last Remake of Beau Geste*

The California Reich Award:
(Awarded to those Hollywood producers who use mass slaughter for mass profit, who express a tacit "thank you" to Mr. Hitler and company every time they subject the moviegoing public to yet another unnecessary and unwanted account of the people and places of World War II.)
MacArthur and *A Bridge Too Far*

The Rocky Award:
(dedicated to the proposition that all underdogs deserve to lose)
Robby Benson for *One on One*

The Harvard Independent Award:
(to that film noted for its ignominious failure as both art and politics)
The Battle of Chile

The Roscoe:
(to that screen actor or actress who has most unflaggingly exhibited a complete lack of talent, perception, screen presence and intelligence)
Rudolph Nureyev, *Valentino*

The Arrested Development Oblation:
(to that adult actor who has displayed the lowest level of maturity on or off the screen)
Jerry Lewis, as always

1978

Ten Worst Movies:
Sgt. Pepper's Lonely Hearts Club Band
Rabbit Test
Interiors
Superman
Foul Play
Up in Smoke
F.I.S.T.
Magic
Ice Castles
Same Time Next Year

Kirk Douglas Award for Worst Actor:
Warren Beatty, *Heaven Can Wait*

Natalie Wood Award for Worst Actress:
Jane Fonda, *Coming Home*; *Comes a Horesman*; *The China Syndrome*; and for staying married to Tom Hayden

The Not Even Nominated Award:
(for the most ungraceful transition from small screen to big)
Farrah Fawcett-Majors, *Somebody Killed Her Husband*

The Exhausted Udder Award:
(presented by the Dairy Farmer's Association in recognition of attempts to milk every penny possible from a marketable idea)
The Bad News Bears Go to Japan

The Arrested Development Oblation:
(to that adult actor who has displayed the lowest level of maturity on or off the screen)
Jerry Lewis, as always

14/COMPARISON OF MAJOR AWARDS 1967-79

THESE CHARTS PROVIDE convenient comparisons of the major annual film awards. Because the various associations listed below do not confer prizes in exactly the same categories, the following qualifications should be kept in mind. The Best Script Prize for the Academy Awards is divided into Best Adaptation and Best Original. The Best Film Category for the National Board of Review is divided into Best English-Language and Best Foreign-Language categories. The Best Film and Acting awards for the Golden Globes are divided into Dramatic and Musical/Comedy. Because a film may or may not be released in England and the United States during the same year, a movie may be eligible for an Academy Award one year and a British Award the next.

1967	Best Film	Best Director	Best Actor
Academy Awards	*In the Heat of the Night*	Mike Nichols, *The Graduate*	Rod Steiger, *In the Heat of the Night*
National Society of Film Critics	*Persona*	Ingmar Bergman, *Persona*	Rod Steiger, *In the Heat of the Night*
New York Film Critics	*In the Heat of the Night*	Mike Nichols, *The Graduate*	Rod Steiger, *In the Heat of the Night*
National Board of Review	*Far from the Madding Crowd; Elvira Madigan*	Richard Brooks, *In Cold Blood*	Peter Finch, *Far from the Madding Crowd*
Golden Globes	*In the Heat of the Night; The Graduate*	Mike Nichols, *The Graduate*	Rod Steiger, *In the Heat of the Night;* Richard Harris, *Camelot*
British Academy	*A Man for All Seasons*		British: Paul Scofield, *Man for All Seasons.* Foreign: Rod Steiger, *In the Heat of the Night*

Best Actress	Best Sup. Actor	Best Sup. Actress	Best Script
Katharine Hepburn, *Guess Who's Coming to Dinner*	George Kennedy, *Cool Hand Luke*	Estelle Parsons, *Bonnie and Clyde*	S. Silliphant, *In the Heat of the Night;* William Rose, *Guess Who's Coming to Dinner*
Bibi Andersson, *Persona*	Gene Hackman, *Bonnie and Clyde*	Marjorie Rhodes, *The Family Way*	David Newman, Robert Benton, *Bonnie and Clyde*
Edith Evans, *The Whisperers*	*(No award)*	*(No award)*	David Newman, Robert Benton, *Bonnie and Clyde*
Edith Evans, *The Whisperers*	Paul Ford, *The Comedians*	Marjorie Rhodes, *The Family Way*	*(No award in this category)*
Edith Evans, *The Whisperers;* Anne Bancroft, *The Graduate*	Richard Attenborough, *Doctor Dolittle*	Carol Channing, *Thoroughly Modern Millie*	Stirling Silliphant, *In the Heat of the Night*
British: Edith Evans, *The Whisperers* Foreign: Anouk Aimée, *A Man and A Woman*	*(No award)*	*(No award)*	British: Robert Bolt, *A Man for Seasons*

1968	Best Film	Best Director	Best Actor
Academy Awards	*Oliver!*	Carol Reed, *Oliver!*	Cliff Robertson, *Charly*
National Society of Film Critics	*Shame*	Ingmar Bergman, *Shame; Hour of the Wolf*	Per Oscarsson, *Hunger*
New York Film Critics	*The Lion in Winter*	Paul Newman, *Rachel, Rachel*	Alan Arkin *The Heart is a Lonely Hunter*
National Board of Review	*The Shoes of the Fisherman; War and Peace*	Franco Zeffirelli, *Romeo and Juliet* ✓	Cliff Robertson, *Charly*
Golden Globes	*The Lion in Winter; Oliver!*	Paul Newman, *Rachel, Rachel*	Peter O'Toole, *Lion in Winter;* Ron Moody, *Oliver!*
British Academy	*The Graduate*	Mike Nichols, *The Graduate*	Spencer Tracy, *Guess Who's Coming to Dinner*

Best Actress	Best Sup. Actor	Best Sup. Actress	Best Script
K. Hepburn, *The Lion in Winter;* B. Streisand, *Funny Girl*	Jack Albertson, *The Subject Was Roses*	Ruth Gordon, *Rosemary's Baby*	James Goldman, *Lion in Winter;* Mel Brooks, *The Producers*
Liv Ullmann, *Shame*	Seymour Cassel, *Faces*	Billie Whitelaw, *Charlie Bubbles*	John Cassavetes, *Faces*
Joanne Woodward, *Rachel, Rachel*	*(No award)*	*(No award)*	Lorenzo Semple, Jr., *Pretty Poison*
Liv Ullmann, *Hour of the Wolf*	Leo McKern, *The Shoes of the Fisherman*	Virginia Maskell, *Interlude*	*(No awards in this category)*
J. Woodward, *Rachel, Rachel;* B. Streisand, *Funny Girl*	Daniel Massey, *Star!*	Ruth Gordon, *Rosemary's Baby*	Stirling Silliphant, *Charly*
K. Hepburn, *Guess Who's ... and The Lion in Winter*	Ian Holm, *The Bofors Gun*	Billie Whitelaw, *Charlie Bubbles; Twisted Nerve*	Calder Willingham, Buck Henry, *The Graduate*

1969	Best Film	Best Director	Best Actor
Academy Awards	*Midnight Cowboy*	John Schlesinger, *Midnight Cowboy*	John Wayne, *True Grit*
National Society of Film Critics	*Z*	Francois Truffaut, *Stolen Kisses*	Jon Voight, *Midnight Cowboy*
New York Film Critics	*Z*	Costa-Gavras, *Z*	John Voight, *Midnight Cowboy*
National Board of Review	*They Shoot Horses, Don't They?* and *Shame*	Alfred Hitchcock, *Topaz*	Peter O'Toole, *Goodbye, Mr. Chips*
Golden Globes	*Anne of the 1000 Days; Oh, What a Lovely War!*	Charles Jarrott, *Anne of the 1000 Days*	John Wayne, *True Grit;* Peter O'Toole, *Goodbye, Mr. Chips*
British Academy	*Midnight Cowboy*	John Schlesinger, *Midnight Cowboy*	Dustin Hoffman, *Midnight Cowboy; John and Mary*

Best Actress	Best Sup. Actor	Best Sup. Actress	Best Script
Maggie Smith, *The Prime of Miss Jean Brodie*	Gig Young, *They Shoot Horses, Don't They?*	Goldie Hawn, *Cactus Flower*	Waldo Salt, *Midnight Cowboy;* William Goldman, *Butch Cassidy ...*
Vanessa Redgrave, *The Loves of Isadora*	Jack Nicholson, *Easy Rider*	Sian Phillips, *Goodbye, Mr. Chips*	Paul Mazursky, Larry Tucker, *Bob & Carol & Ted & Alice*
Jane Fonda, *They Shoot Horses, Don't They?*	Jack Nicholson, *Easy Rider*	Dyan Cannon, *Bob & Carol & Ted & Alice*	Paul Mazursky, Larry Tucker, *Bob & Carol & Ted & Alice*
Geraldine Page, *Trilogy*	Philippe Noiret, *Topaz*	Pamela Franklin, *The Prime of Miss Jean Brodie*	*(No awards in this category)*
Genevieve Bujold, *Anne of the 1000 Days;* Patty Duke, *Me Natalie*	Gig Young, *They Shoot Horses, Don't They?*	Goldie Hawn, *Cactus Flower*	Bridget Boland, John Hale, *Anne of the 1000 Days*
Maggie Smith, *The Prime of Miss Jean Brodie*	Laurence Olivier, *Oh, What a Lovely War!*	Celia Johnson, *The Prime of Miss Jean Brodie*	Waldo Salt, *Midnight Cowboy*

1970	Best Film	Best Director	Best Actor
Academy Awards	*Patton*	Franklin J. Schaffner, *Patton*	George C. Scott, *Patton*
National Society of Film Critics	*M*A*S*H*	Ingmar Bergman, *The Passion of Anna*	George C. Scott, *Patton*
New York Film Critics	*Five Easy Pieces*	Bob Rafelson, *Five Easy Pieces*	George C. Scott, *Patton*
National Board of Review	*Patton; The Wild Child*	Francois Truffaut, *The Wild Child*	George C. Scott, *Patton*
Golden Globes	*Love Story; M*A*S*H*	Arthur Hiller, *Love Story*	George C. Scott, *Patton;* Albert Finney, *Scrooge*
British Academy	*Butch Cassidy and the Sundance Kid*	George Roy Hill, *Butch Cassidy...*	Robert Redford, *Butch Cassidy; Downhill Racer; Tell Them Willie Boy Is Here*

Best Actress	Best Sup. Actor	Best Sup. Actress	Best Script
Glenda Jackson, *Women in Love*	John Mills, *Ryan's Daughter*	Helen Hayes, *Airport*	Ring Lardner, Jr., *M*A*S*H*; F.F. Coppola, Edmund H. North, *Patton*
Glenda Jackson, *Women in Love*	Chief Dan George, *Little Big Man*	Lois Smith, *Five Easy Pieces*	Eric Rohmer, *My Night at Maud's*
Glenda Jackson, *Women in Love*	Chief Dan George, *Little Big Man*	Karen Black, *Five Easy Pieces*	Eric Rohmer, *My Night at Maud's*
Glenda Jackson, *Women in Love*	Frank Langella, *Diary of a Mad Housewife;* and *12 Chairs*	Karen Black, *Five Easy Pieces*	*(No award in this category)*
Ali MacGraw, *Love Story;* Carrie Snodgrass, *Diary of a Mad Housewife*	John Mills, *Ryan's Daughter*	Karen Black, *Five Easy Pieces;* Maureen Stapleton, *Airport*	Erich Segal, *Love Story*
Katharine Ross, *Butch Cassidy; Tell Them Willie Boy...*	Colin Welland, *Kes*	Susannah York, *They Shoot Horses, Don't They?*	William Goldman, *Butch Cassidy*

1971	Best Film	Best Director	Best Actor
Academy Awards	*The French Connection*	William Friedkin, *The French Connection*	Gene Hackman, *The French Connection*
National Society of Film Critics	*Claire's Knee*	Bernardo Bertolucci, *The Conformist*	Peter Finch, *Sunday Bloody Sunday*
New York Film Critics	*A Clockwork Orange*	Stanley Kubrick, *A Clockwork Orange*	Gene Hackman, *The French Connection*
National Board of Review	*Macbeth; Claire's Knee*	Stanley Kubrick, *A Clockwork Orange*	Gene Hackman, *The French Connection*
Golden Globes	*The French Connection; Fiddler on the Roof*	William Friedkin, *The French Connection*	Gene Hackman, *The French Connection;* Topol, *Fiddler on the Roof*
British Academy	*Sunday Bloody Sunday*	John Schlesinger, *Sunday Bloody Sunday*	Peter Finch, *Sunday Bloody Sunday*

Best Actress	Best Sup. Actor	Best Sup. Actress	Best Script
Jane Fonda, *Klute*	Ben Johnson, *The Last Picture Show*	Cloris Leachman, *The Last Picture Show*	Ernest Tidyman, *The French Connection;* Paddy Chayefsky, *The Hospital*
Jane Fonda, *Klute*	Bruce Dern, *Drive, He Said*	Ellen Burstyn, *The Last Picture Show*	Penelope Gilliatt, *Sunday Bloody Sunday*
Jane Fonda, *Klute*	Ben Johnson, *The Last Picture Show*	Ellen Burstyn, *The Last Picture Show*	tie betw. Penelope Gilliatt, *Sunday Bloody Sunday;* L. McMurtry, *Last Picture Show*
Irene Papas, *The Trojan Women*	Ben Johnson, *The Last Picture Show*	Cloris Leachman, *The Last Picture Show*	*(No award in this category)*
Jane Fonda, *Klute;* Twiggy, *The Boy Friend*	Ben Johnson, *The Last Picture Show*	Ann-Margret, *Carnal Knowledge*	Paddy Chayefsky, *The Hospital*
Glenda Jackson, *Sunday Bloody Sunday*	Edward Fox, *The Go-Between*	Margaret Leighton, *The Go-Between*	Harold Pinter, *The Go-Between*

1972	Best Film	Best Director	Best Actor
Academy Awards	*The Godfather*	Bob Fosse, *Cabaret*	Marlon Brando, *The Godfather*
National Society of Film Critics	*The Discreet Charm of the Bourgeoisie*	Luis Buñuel, *The Discreet Charm of the Bourgeoisie*	Al Pacino, *The Godfather*
New York Film Critics	*Cries and Whispers*	Ingmar Bergman, *Cries and Whispers*	Laurence Olivier, *Sleuth*
National Board of Review	*Cabaret; The Sorrow and the Pity*	Bob Fosse, *Cabaret*	Peter O'Toole, *Ruling Class* and *Man of La Mancha*
Golden Globes	*The Godfather; Cabaret*	Francis Ford Coppola, *The Godfather*	Marlon Brando, *The Godfather;* Jack Lemmon, *Avanti!*
British Academy	*Cabaret*	Bob Fosse, *Cabaret*	Gene Hackman, *The French Connection*

Best Actress	Best Sup. Actor	Best Sup. Actress	Best Script
Liza Minelli, *Cabaret*	Joel Grey, *Cabaret*	Eileen Heckart, *Butterflies Are Free*	Mario Puzo, F.F. Coppola, *The God- father;* Jeremy Larner, *The Candidate*
Cicely Tyson, *Sounder*	Joel Grey, *Cabaret;* Eddie Albert, *Heartbreak Kid*	Jeannie Berlin, *Heart- break Kid*	Ingmar Bergman, *Cries and Whispers*
Liv Ullmann, *Cries and Whispers*	Robert Duvall, *The Godfather*	Jeannie Berlin, *Heart- break Kid*	Ingmar Bergman, *Cries and Whispers*
Cicely Tyson, *Sounder*	Joel Grey, *Cabaret;* Al Pacino, *The Godfather*	Marisa Berenson, *Cabaret*	*(No award in this category)*
Liv Ullman, *The Emi- grants;* Liza Minnelli, *Cabaret*	Joel Grey, *Cabaret*	Shelley Winters, *The Poseidon Adventure*	Mario Puzo, F.F. Coppola, *The Godfather*
Liza Minnelli, *Cabaret*	Ben Johnson, *The Last Picture Show*	Cloris Leach- man, *The Last Picture Show*	Tie between P. Bogdanovich, L. McMurtry, *The Last Picture Show;* P. Chayefsky, *The Hospital*

1973	**Best Film**	**Best Director**	**Best Actor**
Academy Awards	*The Sting*	George Roy Hill, *The Sting*	Jack Lemmon, *Save the Tiger*
National Society of Film Critics	*Day for Night*	Francois Truffaut, *Day for Night*	Marlon Brando, *Last Tango in Paris*
New York Film Critics	*Day for Night*	Francois Truffaut, *Day for Night*	Marlon Brando, *Last Tango in Paris*
National Board of Review	*The Sting; Cries and Whispers*	Ingmar Bergman, *Cries and Whispers*	Al Pacino, *Serpico;* Robert Ryan, *The Iceman Cometh*
Golden Globes	*The Exorcist; American Graffiti*	William Friedkin, *The Exorcist*	Al Pacino, *Serpico;* George Segal, *A Touch of Class*
British Academy	*Day for Night*	Francois Truffaut, *Day for Night*	Walter Matthau, *Pete 'n' Tillie,* and *Charley Varrick*

Best Actress	Best Sup. Actor	Best Sup. Actress	Best Script
Glenda Jackson, *A Touch of Class*	John Houseman, *The Paper Chase*	Tatum O'Neal, *Paper Moon*	William Blatty, *The Exorcist;* David S. Ward, *The Sting*
Liv Ullmann, *The New Land*	Robert De Niro, *Mean Streets*	Valentina Cortese, *Day for Night*	George Lucas, Gloria Katz, William Huyck, *American Graffiti*
Joanne Woodward, *Summer Wishes, Winter Dreams*	Robert De Niro, *Bang the Drum Slowly*	Valentina Cortese, *Day for Night*	George Lucas, Gloria Katz, William Huyck, *American Graffiti*
Liv Ullman, *The New Land*	John Houseman, *The Paper Chase*	Sylvia Sidney, *Summer Wishes, Winter Dreams*	*(No award in this category)*
Marsha Mason, *Cinderella Liberty;* Glenda Jackson, *A Touch of Class*	John Houseman, *The Paper Chase*	Linda Blair, *The Exorcist*	William Blatty, *The Exorcist*
Stephane Audran, *The Discreet Charm of the Bourgeoisie* and *Juste avant la nuit*	Arthur Lowe, *O Lucky Man!*	Valentina Cortese, *Day for Night*	Luis Buñuel, Jean-Claude Carrière, *The Discreet Charm of the Bourgeoisie*

1974	Best Film	Best Director	Best Actor
Academy Awards	*Godfather II*	Francis Ford Coppola, *Godfather II*	Art Carney, *Harry and Tonto*
National Society of Film Critics	*Scenes from a Marriage*	Francis Ford Coppola, *Godfather II*	Jack Nicholson, *Chinatown* and *The Last Detail*
New York Film Critics	*Amarcord*	Federico Fellini, *Amarcord*	Jack Nicholson, *Chinatown*
National Board of Review	*The Conversation; Amarcord*	Francis Ford Coppola, *The Conversation*	Gene Hackman, *The Conversation*
Golden Globes	*Chinatown; The Longest Yard*	Roman Polanski, *Chinatown*	Jack Nicholson, *Chinatown;* Art Carney, *Harry and Tonto*
British Academy	*Lacombe, Lucien*	Roman Polanski, *Chinatown*	Jack Nicholson, *Chinatown* and *The Last Detail*

Best Actress	Best Sup. Actor	Best Sup. Actress	Best Script
Ellen Burstyn, *Alice Doesn't Live Here Anymore*	Robert De Niro, *Godfather II*	Ingrid Bergman, *Murder on the Orient Express*	F.F. Coppola, Mario Puzo, *Godfather II;* Robert Towne, *Chinatown*
Liv Ullman, *Scenes from a Marriage*	Holger Löwenadler, *Lacombe, Lucien*	Bibi Andersson, *Scenes from a Marriage*	Ingmar Bergman, *Scenes from a Marriage*
Liv Ullmann, *Scenes from a Marriage*	Charles Boyer, *Stavisky*	Valerie Perrine, *Lenny*	Ingmar Bergman, *Scenes from a Marriage*
Gena Rowlands, *A Woman Under the Influence*	Holger Löwenadler, *Lacombe Lucien*	Valerie Perrine, *Lenny*	*(No awards in this category)*
G. Rowlands, *A Woman Under the Influence;* R. Welch, *The Three Musketeers*	Fred Astaire, *The Towering Inferno*	Karen Black, *The Great Gatsby*	Robert Towne *Chinatown*
Joanne Woodward, *Summer Wishes, Winter Dreams*	John Gielgud, *Murder on the Orient Express*	Ingrid Bergman, *Murder on the Orient Express*	Robert Towne, *Chinatown*

1975	Best Film	Best Director	Best Actor
Academy Awards	*One Flew Over The Cuckoo's Nest*	Milos Forman, *Cuckoo's Nest*	Jack Nicholson *Cuckoo's Nest*
National Society of Film Critics	*Nashville*	Robert Altman, *Nashville*	Jack Niholson, *Cuckoo's Nest*
New York Film Critics	*Nashville*	Robert Altman, *Nashville*	Jack Nicholson, *Cuckoo's Nest*
National Board of Review	*Nashville* and *Barry Lyndon; Story of Adele H.*	R. Altman, *Nashville;* S. Kubrick, *Barry Lyndon*	Jack Nicholson, *Cuckoo's Nest*
Golden Globes	*Cuckoo's Nest; The Sunshine Boys*	Milos Foreman, *Cuckoo's Nest*	J. Nicholson, *Cuckoo's Nest;* W. Matthau, *Sunshine Boys*
British Academy	*Alice Doesn't Live Here Anymore*	Stanley Kubrick, *Barry Lyndon*	Al Pacino, *Godfather II; Dog Day Afternoon*

Best Actress	Best Sup. Actor	Best Sup. Actress	Best Script
Louise Fletcher, *Cuckoo's Nest*	George Burns, *Sunshine Boys*	Lee Grant, *Shampoo*	L. Hauben, Bo Goldman *Cuckoo's Nest;* F. Pierson, *Dog Day Afternoon*
Isabelle Adjani, *Story of Adele H.*	Henry Gibson, *Nashville*	Lily Tomlin, *Nashville*	Robert Towne, Warren Beatty, *Shampoo*
Isabelle, Adjani, *Story of Adele H.*	Alan Arkin, *Hearts of the West*	Lily Tomlin, *Nashville*	Francois Truffaut, Jean Gruault, Suzanne Shiffman, *Story of Adele H.*
Isabelle Adjani, *Story of Adele H.*	Charles Durning, *Dog Day Afternoon*	Ronee Blakely, *Nashville*	*(No awards in this category)*
L. Fletcher, *Cuckoo's Nest;* Ann-Margret, *Tommy*	Richard Benjamin, *Sunshine Boys*	Brenda Vaccaro, *Once Is Not Enough*	Laurence Hauben, Bo Goldman, *Cuckoo's Nest*
Ellen Burstyn, *Alice Doesn't Live Here Anymore*	Fred Astaire, *Towering Inferno*	Diane Ladd, *Alice Doesn't Live Here Anymore*	Robert Getchell, *Alice Doesn't Live Here Anymore*

1976	Best Film	Best Director	Best Actor
Academy Awards	*Rocky*	John G. Avildsen, *Rocky*	Peter Finch, *Network*
National Society of Film Critics	*All the President's Men*	Martin Scorsese, *Taxi Driver*	Robert De Niro, *Taxi Driver*
New York Film Critics	*All the President's Men*	Allan Pakula, *All the President's Men*	Robert De Niro, *Taxi Driver*
National Board of Review	*All the President's Men; The Marquise of O*	Alan Pakula, *All the President's Men*	David Carradine, *Bound For Glory*
Golden Globes	*Rocky; A Star Is Born*	Sidney Lumet, *Network*	Peter Finch, *Network;* Kris Kristofferson, *A Star Is Born*
British Academy	*One Flew Over the Cuckoo's Nest*	Milos Forman, *Cuckoo's Nest*	Jack Nicholson, *Cuckoo's Nest*
L.A. Film Critics	*Network; Rocky*	Sidney Lumet, *Network*	Robert De Niro, *Taxi Driver*

Best Actress	Best Sup. Actor	Best Sup. Actress	Best Script
Faye Dunaway, *Network*	Jason Robards, *All the President's Men*	Beatrice Straight, *Network*	William Goldman, *All the President's Men;* Paddy Chayefsky, *Network*
Sissy Spacek, *Carrie*	Jason Robards, *All the President's Men*	Jodie Foster, *Taxi Driver*	Alain Tanner and John Berger, *Jonah, Who Will Be 25 in the Year 2000*
Liv Ullmann, *Face to Face*	Jason Robards, *All the President's Men*	Talia Shire, *Rocky*	Paddy Chayefsky, *Network*
Liv Ullman, *Face to Face*	Jason Robards, *All the President's Men*	Talia Shire, *Rocky*	*(No awards in this category)*
Faye Dunaway, *Network;* Barbra Streisand, *A Star Is Born*	Laurence Olivier, *Marathon Man*	Katharine Ross, *Voyage of the Damned*	Paddy Chayefsky, *Network*
Louise Fletcher, *Cuckoo's Nest*	Brad Dourif, *Cuckoo's Nest*	Jodie Foster, *Taxi Driver* and *Bugsy Malone*	Alan Parker, *Bugsy Malone*
Liv Ullmann, *Face to Face*	*(No award)*	*(No award)*	Paddy Chayefsky, *Network*

1977	Best Film	Best Director	Best Actor
Academy Awards	*Annie Hall*	Woody Allen, Annie Hall	Richard Dreyfuss, *The Goodbye Girl*
National Society of Film Critics	*Annie Hall*	Luis Bunuel, *That Obscure Object of Desire*	Art Carney, *The Late Show*
New York Film Critics	*Annie Hall*	Woody Allen, *Annie Hall*	John Gielgud, *Providence*
National Board of Review	*The Turning Point; That Obscure Object of Desire*	Luis Bunuel, *That Obscure Object of Desire*	John Travolta, *Saturday Night Fever*
Golden Globes	*The Turning Point; The Goodbye Girl*	Herbert Ross, *The Turning Point*	Richard Burton, *Equus;* Richard Dreyfuss, *The Goodbye Girl*
British Academy	*Annie Hall*	Woody Allen, *Annie Hall*	Peter Finch, *Network*
L.A. Film Critics	*Star Wars*	Herbert Ross, *The Turning Point*	Richard Dreyfuss, *The Goodbye Girl*

Best Actress	Best Sup. Actor	Best Sup. Actress	Best Script
Diane Keaton, *Annie Hall*	Jason Robards, *Julia*	Vanessa Redgrave, *Julia*	Alvin Sargent, *Julia;* Woody Allen, Marshall Brickman, *Annie Hall*
Diane Keaton, *Annie Hall*	Edward Fox, *A Bridge Too Far*	Anne Wedgeworth, *Handle With Care*	Woody Allen, Marshall Brickman, *Annie Hall*
Diane Keaton, *Annie Hall*	Maximilian Schell, *Julia*	Sissy Spacek, *Three Women*	Woody Allen, Marshall Brickman, *Annie Hall*
Anne Bancroft, *The Turning Point*	Tom Skerritt, *The Turning Point*	Diane Keaton, *Annie Hall*	*(No award in this category)*
Jane Fonda, *Julia;* Marsha Mason, *The Goodbye Girl*	Peter Firth, *Equus*	Vanessa Redgrave, *Julia*	Neil Simon, *The Goodbye Girl*
Diane Keaton, *Annie Hall*	Edward Fox, *A Bridge Too Far*	Jenny Agutter, *Equus*	Woody Allen, Marshall Brickman, *Annie Hall*
Shelley Duvall, *Three Women*	Jason Robards, *Julia*	Vanessa Redgrave, *Julia*	Woody Allen, Marshall Brickman, *Annie Hall*

1978	Best Film	Best Director	Best Actor
Academy Awards	*The Deer Hunter*	Michael Cimino, *The Deer Hunter*	Jon Voight, *Coming Home*
National Society of Film Critics	*Get Out Your Handkerchiefs*	Terence Malick, *Days of Heaven*	Gary Busey, *The Buddy Holly Story*
New York Film Critics	*The Deer Hunter*	Terence Malick, *Days of Heaven*	Jon Voight, *Coming Home*
National Board of Review	*Days of Heaven; Autumn Sonata*	Ingmar Bergman, *Autumn Sonata*	Laurence Olivier, *The Boys From Brazil;* Jon Voight, *Coming Home*
Golden Globes	*Midnight Express; Heaven Can Wait*	Michael Cimino, *The Deer Hunter*	Jon Voight, *Coming Home;* Warren Beatty, *Heaven Can Wait*
British Academy	*Julia*	Alan Parker, *Midnight Express*	Richard Dreyfuss, *The Goodbye Girl*
L.A. Film Critics	*Coming Home*	Michael Cimino, *The Deer Hunter*	Jon Voight, *Coming Home*

Best Actress	Best Sup. Actor	Best Sup. Actress	Best Script
Jane Fonda, *Coming Home*	Christopher Walken, *The Deer Hunter*	Maggie Smith, *California Suite*	Oliver Stone, *Midnight Express;* N. Dowd, W. Salt, R.C. Jones, *Coming Home*
Ingrid Bergman, *Autumn Sonata*	Richard Farnsworth, *Comes A Horseman;* Robert Morley, *Who's Killing Great Chefs...?*	Meryl Streep, *The Deer Hunter*	Paul Mazursky, *An Unmarried Woman*
Ingrid Bergman, *Autumn Sonata*	Christopher Walken, *The Deer Hunter*	Colleen Dewhurst, *Interiors*	Paul Mazursky, *An Unmarried Woman*
Ingrid Bergman, *Autumn Sonata*	Richard Farnsworth, *Comes A Horseman*	Angela Lansbury, *Death on the Nile*	*(No award in this category)*
Jane Fonda, *Coming Home;* Maggie Smith, *California Suite,* Ellen Burstyn, *Same Time Next Year*	John Hurt, *Midnight Express*	Dyan Cannon, *Heaven Can Wait*	Oliver Stone, *Midnight Express*
Jane Fonda, *Julia*	John Hurt, *Midnight Express*	Geraldine Page, *Interiors*	Alvin Sargent, *Julia*
Jane Fonda, *Coming Home*	Robert Morley, *Who Is Killing the Great Chefs of Europe?*	Maureen Stapleton, *Interiors;* Mona Washbourne, *Stevie*	Paul Mazursky, *An Unmarried Woman*

1979	Best Film	Best Director	Best Actor
Academy Awards	*Kramer vs. Kramer*	Robert Benton, *Kramer vs. Kramer*	Dustin Hoffman, *Kramer vs. Kramer*
National Society of Film Critics	*Breaking Away*	Robert Benton, *Kramer vs. Kramer;* Woody Allen, *Manhattan*	Dustin Hoffman, *Kramer vs. Kramer*
New York Film Critics	*Kramer vs. Kramer*	Woody Allen, *Manhattan*	Dustin Hoffman, *Kramer vs. Kramer*
National Board of Review	*Manhattan; La Cage aux Folles*	John Schlesinger, *Yanks*	Peter Sellers, *Being There*
Golden Globes	*Kramer vs. Kramer; Breaking Away*	Francis Coppola, *Apocalypse Now*	Dustin Hoffman, *Kramer vs. Kramer;* Peter Sellers, *Being There*
British Academy	*Manhattan*	Francis Coppola, *Apocalypse Now*	Jack Lemmon, *China Syndrome*
L.A. Film Critics	*Kramer vs. Kramer*	Robert Benton, *Kramer vs. Kramer*	Dustin Hoffman, *Kramer vs. Kramer*

Best Actress	Best Sup. Actor	Best Sup. Actress	Best Script
Sally Field, *Norma Rae*	Melvyn Douglas, *Being There*	Meryl Streep, *Kramer vs. Kramer*	Robert Benton, *Kramer vs. Kramer;* Steve Tesich, *Breaking Away*
Sally Field, *Norma Rae*	Frederic Forrest, *The Rose, Apocalypse Now*	Meryl Streep, *Kramer vs. Kramer; Manhattan; Seduction of Joe Tynan*	Steve Tesich, *Breaking Away*
Sally Field, *Norma Rae*	Melvyn Douglas, *Being There*	Meryl Streep, *Kramer vs. Kramer; Seduction of Joe Tynan*	Steve Tesich, *Breaking Away*
Sally Field, *Norma Rae*	Paul Dooley, *Breaking Away*	Meryl Streep, *Kramer vs. Kramer; Manhattan; Seduction of Joe Tynan*	(No awards in this category)
Sally Field, *Norma Rae;* Bette Midler, *The Rose*	Robert Duvall, *Apocalypse Now;* Melvyn Douglas, *Being There*	Meryl Streep, *Kramer vs. Kramer*	Robert Benton, *Kramer vs. Kramer*
Jane Fonda, *China Syndrome*	Robert Duvall, *Apocalypse Now*	Rachel Roberts, *Yanks*	Woody Allen, Marshall Brickman, *Manhattan*
Sally Field, *Norma Rae*	Melyvn Douglas *Being There, Seduction of Joe Tynan*	Meryl Streep, *Kramer vs. Kramer; Manhattan; Seduction of Joe Tynan*	Robert Benton, *Kramer vs. Kramer*

VII. THE CODES AND REGULATIONS

1/THE PRODUCTION CODE

THE PRODUCTION CODE was one of the film industry's several attempts to prevent federal censorship. In 1908, for example, key figures in the business had helped establish the National Board of Censorship in order to curb growing criticism over the immorality of movies. And in 1922, after continued public disapproval and the passage of numerous state censorship bills, film producers had created the Motion Picture Producers and Distributors of America (MPPDA) to self-regulate the industry in the hope of curtailing criticism and preventing federal intervention. Will H. Hays, the conservative Postmaster General of the Harding Administration, was the organization's first president, and he grew so powerful that the MPPDA has been generally known, in fact, as "the Hays Office."

Before adopting the Production Code in 1930, the Hays Office tired two other self-regulatory policies. The first of these was the 1924 *Formula*. Faced with the "mature" themes of the jazz era's novelists and playwrights, the MPPDA passed a resolution asking its member studios to submit a summary of each play or novel it proposed to film in order to receive the MPPDA's advice about possible objections. Although there were 125 rejections of submitted material between 1924 and 1930, the *Formula* had limited applicability: for one thing, the MPPDA could only suggest, not enforce its guidelines; and for another, the *Formula* applied only to adapted material and not to original screenplays.

The second code the MPPDA adopted to regulate the subject matter of movies was the 1927 *Don'ts and Be Carefuls*, which listed 11 subjects that should never appear in films and 26 themes that should be handled with great care and discretion. Like the *Formula*, the *Don'ts and Be Carefuls* could not be legally enforced and it, too, proved of limited value.

So faced with continued public criticism and repeated calls for federal censorship, the MPPDA adopted the Production Code in 1930. Martin Quigley (the publisher of the influential *Motion Picture Herald*) and Reverend Daniel A. Lord (a St. Louis clergyman who had acted as adviser on many films) collaborated on the new code, which was to become one of the most important social documents in American history. On June 6, 1930, two months after the Code was ratified, an Advertising Code was also adopted.

Despite its length and explicitness, the code was not initially successful. It was not until the Catholic Legion of Decency's overwhelmingly effective campaign against movie immorality in 1934 that the Production Code really took effect. In July 1934 the MPPDA, frightened by the Legion's threats, organized the Production Code Administration Office (PCA), with Joseph Breen as its head. For the first time, the MPPDA had the power to enforce its regulations: if any member studio released a film without the PCA's certificate of approval, that studio would be fined $25,000.

For several years the PCA and the Legion of Decency worked in an unofficial and at times uneasy alliance. Together they managed to control the content of all films shown in this country, both domestic and foreign. The PCA functioned at all stages of production—selecting stories, examining scripts, approving the final cut. The Office even offered its services to nonmember producers to make its powers more complete.

But in 1943 the PCA received its first great challenge: Howard Hughes exhibited *The Outlaw* (starring Jane Russell) without code approval. Although the film was soon withdrawn from distribution, it reappeared in 1946 with an advertising campaign that has since become legendary: "What are the Two Great Reasons for Jane Russell's Rise to Stardom?" ads would coyly ask. (One Baltimore judge claimed that Russell's breasts "hung over the picture like a thunderstorm spread out over a landscape.")

The crowds of people who attended *The Outlaw* demonstrated a change in American morals and hinted at the PCA's increasing obsolescence. In 1945 Warner Bros. even temporarily withdrew from the MPPDA. (In that year Will Hays finally retired as president of the organization. Eric Johnston was his successor and soon after Johnston took over, the MPPDA changed its name to the Motion Picture Association of America—MPAA.)

Although the PCA made slight revisions in the code in 1946 and 1951 to accommodate changes in American morals, the code still came under severe criticism and there were many calls for complete re-examination of the code's usefulness. Even when the Supreme Court, in the famous case over Rossellini's *The Miracle*, decided that movies were an art form (and not an item of commerce, as previously thought) under the protection of the First Amendment, the PCA was still slow to loosen its reigns.

So in 1953 the PCA was once again defied, this time by Otto Preminger when he released *The Moon Is Blue* without the PCA's seal. Like *The Outlaw, The Moon Is Blue* attracted large crowds of moviegoers (although in some small towns police actually took down the names of those people who saw the film), and demonstrated once more that the code was outmoded. When the code refused its seal to Preminger's *The Man with the Golden Arm* in late 1955, United Artists, the film's distributor, pulled out of the MPAA. (Geoffrey Sherlock replaced Joe Breen in 1954.)

In 1956 the code, under continued attack, was considererably revised so that now only two subjects were prohibited: venereal disease and sexual perversion. When the Legion of Decency revised its classification system in 1958, the PCA also began to change. Despite controversies over films like *Suddenly, Last Summer* (1959), the PCA finally altered its attitude toward "sexual perversion" in 1961 when such major studio movies as *The Children's Hour* (1961) and *Advise and Consent* (1962) dealt with the subject.

In 1966 the code was once again revised, this time drastically. Now the PCA merely divided approved films into two categories, those for general audiences and those suggested for mature audiences. These categories were only suggestions—no legal restrictions were involved.

It was becoming increasingly obvious that an entirely new code was necessary. And in 1968 the MPAA initiated the Code of Self-Regulation.

The Don'ts and Be Carefuls

Resolved, That those things which are included in the following list shall not appear in pictures produced by the members of this Association, irrespective of the manner in which they are treated:

1. Pointed profanity—by either title or lip—this includes the words "God," "Lord," "Jesus," "Christ" (unless they be used reverently in connection with proper religious ceremonies), "hell," "damn," "Gawd,"

and every other profane and vulgar expression however it may be spelled;

2. Any licentious or suggestive nudity—in fact or in silhouette; and any lecherous or licentious notice thereof by other characters in the picture;

3. The illegal traffic in drugs;

4. Any inference of sex perversion;

5. White slavery;

6. Miscegenation (sex relationships between the white and black races);

7. Sex hygiene and venereal diseases;

8. Scenes of actual childbirth—in fact or in silhouette;

9. Children's sex organs;

10. Ridicule of the clergy;

11. Willful offense to any nation, race or creed;

And be it further resolved, That special care be exercised in the manner in which the following subjects are treated, to the end that vulgarity and suggestiveness may be eliminated and that good taste may be emphasized:

1. The use of the flag;

2. International relations (avoiding picturizing in an unfavorable light another country's religion, history, institutions, prominent people, and citizenry);

3. Arson;

4. The use of firearms;

5. Theft, robbery, safe-cracking, and dynamiting of trains, mines, building etc. (having in mind the effect which a too-detailed description of these may have upon the moron);

6. Brutality and possible gruesomeness;

7. Technique of committing murder by whatever method;

8. Methods of smuggling;

9. Third-degree methods;

10. Actual hangings or electrocutions as legal punishment for crime;

11. Sympathy for criminals;

12. Attitude toward public characters and institutions;

13. Sedition;

14. Apparent cruelty to children and animals;

15. Branding of people or animals;

16. The sale of women, or of a woman selling her virtue;

17. Rape or attempted rape;

18. First-night scenes;

19. Man and woman in bed together;

20. Deliberate seduction of girls;

21. The institution of marriage;

22. Surgical operations;

23. The use of drugs;

24. Titles or scenes having to do with law enforcement of law-enforcing officers;

25. Excessive or lustful kissing, particularly when one character or the other is a "heavy."

The 1930 Production Code

Preamble

Motion picture producers recognize the high trust and confidence which have been placed in them by the people of the world and which have made motion pictures a universal form of entertainment.

They recognize their responsibility to the public because of this trust and because entertainment and art are important influences in the life of a nation.

Hence, though regarding motion pictures primarily as entertainment without any explicit purpose of teaching or propaganda, they know that the motion picture within its own field of entertainment may be directly responsible for spiritual or moral progress, for higher types of social life, and for much correct thinking.

During the rapid transition from silent to talking pictures they realized the necessity and the opportunity of subscribing to a Code to govern the production of talking pictures and of acknowledging this responsibility.

On their part, they ask from the public and from public leaders a sympathetic understanding of their purposes and problems and a spirit of cooperation that will allow them the freedom and opportunity necessary to bring the motion picture to a still higher level of wholesome entertainment for all the people.

General Principles

1. No picture shall be produced which will lower the moral standards of those who see it. Hence the sympathy of the audience shall never be thrown to the side of crime, wrong-doing, evil or sin.

2. Correct standards of life, subject only to the requirements of drama and entertainment, shall be presented.

3. Law, natural or human, shall not be ridiculed, nor shall sympathy be created for its violation.

I. Crimes Against the Law

These shall never be presented in such a way as to throw sympathy with the crime as against law and justice or to inspire others with a desire for imitation.

1. Murder
    (a) The technique of murder must be presented in a way that will not inspire imitation.
    (b) Brutal killings are not to be presented in detail.
    (c) Revenge in modern times shall not be justified.
2. Methods of crime should not be explicitly presented.
    (a) Theft, robbery, safe-cracking, and dynamiting of trains, mines, buildings, etc., should not be detailed in method.
    (b) Arson must be subject to the same safeguards.
    (c) The use of firearms should be restricted to essentials.
    (d) Methods of smuggling should not be presented.
3. The illegal drug traffic must not be portrayed in such a way as to stimulate curiosity concerning the use of, or traffic in, such drugs; nor shall scenes be approved which show the use of illegal drugs, or their effects, in detail (as amended September 11, 1946).
4. The use of liquor in American life, when not required by the plot or for proper characterization, will not be shown.

II. Sex
The sanctity of the institution of marriage and the home shall be upheld. Pictures shall not infer that low forms of sex relationship are the accepted or common thing.

1. Adultery and illicit sex, sometimes necessary plot material, must not be explicitly treated or justified, or presented attractively.
2. Scenes of passion
    (a) These should not be introduced except where they are definitely essential to the plot.
    (b) Excessive and lustful kissing, lustful embraces, suggestive postures and gestures are not to be shown.
    (c) In general, passion should be treated in such manner as not to stimulate the lower and baser emotions.
3. Seduction or rape
    (a) These should never be more than suggested, and then only when essential

for the plot. They must never be shown by explicit method.
    (b) They are never the proper subject for comedy.
4. Sex perversion or any inference to it is forbidden.[1]
5. White slavery shall not be treated.[2]
6. Miscegenation (sex relationship between the white and black races) is forbidden.
7. Sex hygiene and venereal diseases are not proper subjects for theatrical motion pictures.[3]
8. Scenes of actual childbirth, in fact or in silhouette, are never to be presented.
9. Children's sex organs are never to be exposed.

III. Vulgarity
The treatment of low, disgusting, unpleasant, though not necessarily evil, subjects should be guided always by the dictates of good taste and a proper regard for the sensibilities of the audience.

IV. Obscenity
Obscenity in word, gesture, reference, song, joke or by suggestion (even when likely to be understood only by part of the audience) is forbidden.

V. Profanity[4]
Pointed profanity and every other profane or vulgar expression, however used, is forbidden.

No approval by the Production Code Administration shall be given to the use of words and phrases in motion pictures including, but not limited to, the following:

Alley cat (applied to a woman); bat (applied to a woman); broad (applied to a woman); Bronx cheer (the sound); chippie; cocotte; God, Lord, Jesus, Christ (unless used reverently); cripes; fanny; fairy (in a vulgar sense); finger (the); fire, cries of; Gawd; goose (in a vulgar sense); "hold your hat" or "hats"; hot (applied to a woman); "in your hat"; louse; lousy; Madam (relating to prostitution); nance, nerts; nuts (except when meaning crazy); pansy; razzberry (the sound); slut (applied to a woman); S.O.B.; son-of-a; tart; toilet gags; tom cat (applied to a man); traveling salesman and farmer's daughter jokes; whore; damn; hell (excepting when the use of said last two words shall be essential and required for portrayal, in proper historical context, of any scene or dialogue based upon historical fact or folklore, or for the presentation in proper literary context of a Biblical, or other religious quotation, or a quotation from a literary work provided that no such use shall be permitted which is intrinsically objectionable or offends good taste).

In the administration of Section V of the Production Code, the Production Code Administration may take cognizance of the fact that the following words and phrases are obviously offensive to the patrons of motion pictures in the

United States and more particularly to the patrons of motion pictures in foreign countries:

Chink, Dago, Frog, Greaser, Hunkie, Kike, Nigger, Spic, Wop, Yid.

VI. Costume
1. Complete nudity is never permitted. This includes nudity in fact or in silhouette, or any licentious notice thereof by other characters in the pictures.
2. Undressing scenes should be avoided, and never used save where essential to the plot.
3. Indecent or undue exposure is forbidden.
4. Dancing costumes intended to permit undue exposure of indecent movements in the dance are forbidden.

VII. Dances
1. Dances suggesting or representing sexual actions or indecent passion are forbidden.
2. Dances which emphasize indecent movements are to be regarded as obscene.

VII. Religion
1. No film or episode may throw ridicule on any religious faith.
2. Ministers of religion in their character as ministers of religion should not be used as comic characters or as villains.
3. Ceremonies of any definite religion should be carefully and respectfully handled.

IX. Locations
The treatment of bedrooms must be governed by good taste and delicacy.

X. National Feelings
1. The use of the flag shall be consistently respectful.
2. The history, institutions, prominent people and citizenry of all nations shall be represented fairly.

XI. Titles[5]
Salacious, Indecent, or obscene titles shall not be used.

XII. Repellent Subjects
The following subjects must be treated within the careful limits of good taste.
1. Actual hangings or electrocutions as legal punishments for crime.
2. Third-degree methods.
3. Brutality and possible gruesomeness.
4. Branding of people or animals.
5. Apparent cruelty to children or animals.
6. The sale of women, or a woman selling her virtue.
7. Surgical operations.

Reasons Supporting Preamble of Code
1. Theatrical motion pictures, that is, pictures intended for the theatre as distinct from pictures intended for churches, schools, lecture halls, educational movements, social reform movements, etc., are primarily to be regarded as entertainment.

Mankind has always recognized the importance of entertainment and its value in rebuilding the bodies and souls of human beings.

But it has always recognized that entertainment can be of a character either HELPFUL or HARMFUL to the human race, and in consequence has clearly distinguished between:

(a) Entertainment which tends to improve the race, or at least to re-create and rebuild human beings exhausted with the realities of life; and

(b) Entertainment which tends to degrade human beings, or to lower their standards of life and living.

Hence the Moral importance of entertainment is something which has been universally recognized. It enters intimately into the lives of men and women and affects them closely; it occupies their minds and affections during leisure hours; and ultimately touches the whole of their lives. A man may be judged by his standard of entertainment as easily as by the standard of his work.

So correct entertainment raises the whole standard of a nation.

Wrong entertainment lowers the whole living conditions and moral ideals of a race.

Note, for example, the healthy reactions to healthful sports, like baseball, golf; the unhealthy reactions to sports like cockfighting, bullfighting, bear baiting, etc.

Note, too, the effect on ancient nations of gladiatorial combats, the obscene plays of Roman times, etc.

2. Motion pictures are very important as **art.**

Though a new art, possibly a combination art, it has the same object as the other arts, the presentation of human thought, emotion, and experience, in terms of an appeal to the soul through the senses.

Here, as in entertainment,

Art enters intimately into the lives of human beings.

Art can be morally good, lifting men to higher levels. This has been done through good music, great painting, authentic fiction, poetry, drama.

Art can be morally evil in its effects. This is the case clearly enough with unclean art, indecent books, suggestive drama. The effect on the lives of men and women is obvious.

Note: It has often been argued that art in itself is unmoral, neither good nor bad. This is perhaps true of the **thing product** of some person's mind, and the intention of that mind was either good or bad morally when it produced the thing.

Besides, the thing has its **effect** upon those who come into contact with it. In both these ways, this is, as a product of a mind and as the cause of definite effects, it has a deep moral significance and an unmistakable moral quality.

Hence: The motion pictues, which are the most popular arts for the masses, have their moral quality from the intention of the minds which produce them and from their effects on the moral lives and reactions of their audiences. This gives them a most important moral quality.

1. They reproduce the morality of the men who use the pictures as a medium for the expression of their idea and ideals.

2. They affect the moral standards of those who, through the screen, take in these ideas and ideals.

In the case of the motion pictures, this effect may be particularly emphasized because no art has so quick and so widespread an appeal to the masses. It has become in an incredibly short period the art of the multitudes.

3. The motion picture, because of its importance as entertainment and because of the trust placed in it by the peoples of the world, has special **moral obligations:**

A. Most arts appeal to the mature. This art appeals at once to every class, mature, immature, developed, underdeveloped, law abiding, criminal. Music has its grades for different classes; so has literature and drama. This art of the motion picture, combining as it does the two fundamental appeals of looking at a picture and listening to a story, at once reached every class of society.

B. By reason of the mobility of a film and the ease of picture distribution, and because of the possibility of duplicating positives in large quantities, this art reaches places unpenetrated by other forms of art.

C. Because of these two facts, it is difficult to produce films intended for only certain classes of people. The exhibitor's theatres are built for the masses, for the cultivated and the rude, the mature and the immature, the self-respecting and the criminal. Films, unlike books and music, can with difficulty be confined to certain selected groups.

D. The latitude given to film material cannot, in consequence, be as wide as the latitude given to book material. In addition:

(a) A book describes; a film vividly presents. One presents on a cold page; the other by apparently living people.

(b) A book reaches the mind through words merely; a film reaches the eyes and ears through the reproduction of actual events.

(c) The reaction of a reader to a book depends largely on the keenness of the reader's imagination; the reaction to a film depends on the vividness of presentation.

Hence many things which might be described or presented in a book could not possibly be presented in a film.

E. This is also true when comparing the film with the newspaper.

(a) Newspapers present by description, films by actual presentation.

(b) Newspapers are after the fact and present things as having taken place, the film gives the events in the process of enactment and with apparent reality of life.

F. Everything possible in a play is not possible in a film:

(a) Because of the large audience of the film, and its consequential mixed character. Psychologically, the larger the audience, the lower the moral mass resistance to suggestion.

(b) Because through light, enlargement of character, presentation, scenic emphasis, etc., the screen story is brought closer to the audience than the play.

(c) The enthusiasm for and interest in the film actors and actresses, developed beyond anything of the sort in history, makes the audience largely sympathetic toward the characters they portray and the stories in which they figure. Hence the audience is more ready to confuse actor and actress and the characters they portray, and it is more receptive of the emotions and ideals presented by their favorite stars.

G. Small communities, remote from sophistication and from the hardening process which often takes place in the ethical and moral standards of groups in large cities, are easily and readily reached by any sort of film.

H. The grandeur of mass settings, large action, spectacular features, etc., affect and arouses more intensely the emotional side of the audience.

In general, the mobility, popularity, accessibility, emotional appeal, vividness, straightforward presentation of fact in the film make for more intimate contact with a larger audience and for greater emotional appeal.

Hence the larger moral responsibilities of the motion pictures.

Reasons Underlying the General Principles

1. No picture shall be produced which will lower the moral standards of those who see it. Hence the sympathy of the audience

should never be thrown to the side of the crime, wrong-doing, evil or sin.

This is done:

(1) When evil is made to appear attractive or alluring, and good is made to appear unattractive.

(2) When the sympathy of the audience is thrown on the side of crime, wrong-doing, evil, sin. The same thing is true of a film that would throw sympathy against goodness, honor, innocence, purity, or honesty.

Note: Sympathy with a person who sins is not the same as sympathy with the sin or crime of which he is guilty. We may feel sorry for the plight of the murderer or even understand the circumstances which led him to his crime. We may not feel sympathy with the wrong which he has done. The presentation of evil is often essential for art or fiction or drama. This in itself is not wrong provided:

a. That evil is not presented alluringly. Even if later in the film the evil is condemned or punished, it must not be allowed to appear so attractive that the audience's emotions are drawn to desire or approve so strongly that later the condemnation is forgotten and only the apparent joy of the sin remembered.

b. That throughout, the audience feels sure that evil is wrong and good is right.

2. Correct standards of life shall, as far as possible, be presented.

A wide knowledge of life and of living is made possible through the film. When right standards are consistently presented, the motion picture exercises the most powerful influences. It builds character, develops right ideals, inculcates correct principles, and all this in attractive story form.

If motion pictures consistently hold up for admiration high types of characters and present stories that will affect lives for the better, they can become the most powerful natural force for the improvement of mankind.

3. Law, natural or human, shall not be ridiculed, nor shall sympathy be created for its violation.

By natural law is understood the law which is written in the hearts of all mankind, the great underlying principles of right and justice dictated by conscience.

By human law is understood the law written by civilized nations.

1. The presentation of crimes against the law is often necessary for the carrying out of the plot. But the presentation must not throw sympathy with the crime as against the law nor with the criminal as against those who punish him.

2. The courts of the land should not be presented as unjust. This does not mean that a single court may not be represented as unjust, much less

than a single court official must not be presented this way. But the court system of the country must not suffer as a result of this presentation.

Reasons Underlying Particular Applications

1. Sin and evil enter into the story of human beings and hence in themselves are valid dramatic material.

2. In the use of this material, it must be distinguished between sin which repels by its very nature, and sins which often attract.

a. In the first class come murder, most theft, many legal crimes, lying, hypocrisy, cruelty, etc.

b. In the second class come sex sins, sins and crimes of apparent heroism, such as banditry, daring thefts, leadership in evil, organized crime, revenge, etc.

The first class needs less care in treatment, as sins and crimes of this class are naturally unattractive. The audience instinctively condemns all such and is repelled.

Hence the important objective must be to avoid the hardening of the audience, especially of those who are young and impressionable, to the thought and fact of crime. People can become accustomed even to murder, cruelty, brutality, and repellent crimes, if these are too frequently repeated.

The second class needs great care in handling, as the response of human nature to their appeal is obvious. This is treated more fully below.

3. A careful distinction can be made between films intended for general distribution, and films intended for use in theatres restricted to a limited audience. Themes and plots quite appropriate for the latter would be altogether out of place and dangerous in the former.

Note: The practice of using a general theatre and limiting its patronage during the showing of a certain film to "Adults Only" is not completely satisfactory and is only partially effective.

However, maturer minds may easily understand and accept without harm subject matter in plots which do younger people positive harm.

Hence: If there should be created a special type of theatre, catering exclusively to an adult audience, for plays of this character (plays with problem themes, difficult discussions and maturer treatment) it would seem to afford an outlet, which does not now exist, for pictures unsuitable for general distribution but permissible for exhibitions to a restricted audience.

I. Crimes Against the Law

The treatment of crimes against the law must not:

1. Teach methods of crime.
2. Inspire potential criminals with a desire for imitation.
3. Make criminals seem heroic and justified.

Revenge in modern times shall not be justified. In lands and ages of less developed civilization and moral principles, revenge may sometimes be presented. This would be the case especially in places where no law exists to cover the crime because of which revenge is committed.

Note: When Section 1, 3 of The Production Code was amended by resolution of the Board of Directors (September 11, 1946), the following sentence became inapplicable:

Because of its evil consequences, the drug traffic should not be presented in any form.

The use of liquor should never be excessively presented. In scenes from American life, the necessities of plot and proper characterization alone justify its use. And in this case, it should be shown with moderation.

II. Sex

Out of regard for the sanctity of marriage and the home, the triangle, that is, the love of a third party for one already married, needs careful handling. The treatment should not throw sympathy against marriage as an institution.

Scenes of passion must be treated with an honest acknowledgement of human nature and its normal reactions. Many scenes cannot be presented without arousing dangerous emotions on the part of the immature, the young, or the criminal classes.

Even within the limits of pure love, certain facts have been universally regarded by lawmakers as outside the limits of safe presentation. In the case of impure love, the love which society has always regarded as wrong and which has been banned by divine law, the following are important:

1. Impure love must not be presented as attractive and beautiful.
2. It must not be the subject of comedy or farce, or treated as material for laughter.
3. It must not be presented in such a way as to arouse passion or morbid curiosity on the part of the audience.
4. It must be made to seem right and permissible.
5. In general, it must not be detailed in method and manner.

III. Vulgarity; IV. Obscenity; V. Profanity; hardly need further explanation than is contained in the Code.

VI. Costume

General principles:

1. The effect of nudity or semi-nudity upon the normal man or woman, and much more upon the young and upon immature persons, has been honestly recognized by all lawmakers and moralists.
2. Hence the fact that the nude or semi-nude body may be beautiful does not make its use in the films moral. For, in addition to its beauty, the effect of the nude or semi-nude body on the normal individual must be taken into consideration.
3. Nudity or semi-nudity used simply to put a "punch" into a picture comes under the head of immoral actions. It is immoral in its effect on the average audience.
4. Nudity can never be permitted as being necessary for the plot. Semi-nudity must not result in undue or indecent exposures.
5. Transparent or translucent materials and silhouette are frequently more suggestive than actual exposure.

VII. Dances

Dancing in general is recognized as an art and as a beautiful form of expressing human emotions.

But dances which suggest or represent sexual actions, whether performed solo or with two or more; dances intended to excite the emotional reaction of an audience; dances with movement of the breasts, excessive body movements while the feet are stationary, violate decency and are wrong.

VIII. Religion

The reason why ministers of religion may not be comic characters or villains is simply because the attitude taken toward them may easily become the attitude taken toward religion in general. Religion is lowered in the minds of the audience because of the lowering of the audience's respect for a minister.

IX. Locations

Certain places are so closely and thoroughly associated with sexual life or with sexual sin that their use must be carefully limited.

X. National Feelings

The just rights, history, and feelings of any nation are entitled to most careful consideration and respectful treatement.

XI. Titles

As the title of a picture is the brand on that particular type of goods, it must conform to the ethical practices of all such honest business.

XII. Repellent Subjects

Such subjects are occasionally necessary for the plot. Their treatment must never offend good taste nor injure the sensibilities of an audience.

Special Regulations on Crime in Motion Pictures[6]

Resolved, that the Board of Directors of the Motion Picture Association of America, Inc., hereby ratifies, approves, and confirms the interpretations of the Production Code, the practices thereunder, and the resolutions indicating and confirming such interpretations heretofore adopted by the Association of Motion Picture Producers, Inc., effectuating regulations relative to the treatment of crime in motion pictures, as follows:

1. Details of crime must never be shown and care should be exercised at all times in discussing such details.
2. Action suggestive of wholesale slaughter of human beings, either by criminals, in conflict with police, or as between warring fractions of criminals, or in public disorders of any kind, will not be allowed.
3. There must be no suggestion, at any time, of excessive brutality.
4. Because of the increase in the number of films in which murder is frequently committed, action showing the taking of human life, event in the mystery stories, is to be cut to the minimum. These frequent presentations of murder tend to lessen regard for the sacredness of life.
5. Suicide, as a solution of problems occurring in the development of screen drama, is to be discouraged as morally questionable and as bad theatre—unless absolutely necessary for the development of the plot.
6. There must be no display, at any time, of machine guns, sub-machine guns or other weapons generally classified as illegal weapons in the hands of gangsters, or other criminals, and there are to be no off-stage sounds of the repercussions of these guns.
7. There must be no new, unique or trick methods shown for concealing guns.
8. The flaunting of weapons by gangsters, or other criminals, will not be allowed.
9. All discussions and dialogue on the part of gangsters regarding guns should be cut to the minimum.
10. There must be no scenes, at any time, showing law-enforcement officers dying at the hands of criminals. This includes private detectives and guards for banks, motor trucks, etc.
11. With special reference to the crime of kidnapping—or illegal abduction—such stories are acceptable under the Code only when the kidnapping or abduction is (a) not the main theme of the story; (b) the person kidnapped is not a child; (c) there are no details of the crime of kidnapping; (d) no profit accrues to the abductors or kidnappers; and (e) where the kidnappers are punished.
    It is understood, and agreed, that the word kidnapping, as used in paragraph 11 of these Regulations, is intended to mean abduction, or illegal detention, in modern times, by criminals for ransom.
12. Pictures dealing with criminal activities, in which minors participate, or to which minors are related, shall not be approved if they incite demoralizing imitation on the part of youth.
13. No picture shall be approved dealing with the life of a notorious criminal of current or recent times which uses the name, nickname or alias of such notorious criminal in the film, nor shall a picture be approved if based upon the life of such a notorious criminal unless the character[7] shown in the film be punished for crimes shown in the film as committed by him.

Special Resolution on Costumes

On October 25, 1939 the Board of Directors of the Motion Picture Association of America, Inc., adopted the following resolution:

Resolved, That the provisions of Paragraphs 1, 3 and 4 of sub-division VI of the Production Code in their application to costumes, nudity, indecent or undue exposure and dancing costumes, shall not be interpreted to exclude authentically photographed scenes photographed in a foreign land, of natives of such foreign land, showing native life, if such scenes are a necessary and integral part of a motion picture depicting exclusively such land and native life, provided that no such scenes shall be intrinsically objectional nor made a part of any motion picture produced in any studio; and provided further that no emphasis shall be made in any scenes of the customs or garb of such natives or in the exploitation thereof.

Special Regulations on Cruelty to Animals

On December 27, 1940 the Board of Directors of the Motion Picture Association of America, Inc., approved a resolution adopted by the Association of Motion Picure Producers, Inc., reaffirming previous resolutions of the California Association concerning brutality and possible gruesomeness, branding of people and animals, and apparent cruelty to children and animals:

Resolved, by the Board of Directors of the Association of Motion Picture Producers, Inc., that

(1) Hereafter, In the production of motion pictures there shall be no use by the members of the Association of the contrivance or apparatus in connection with animals which is known as the "running W," nor shall any picture submitted to the Production Code Administration be approved if reasonable grounds exist for believing that use of any similar device by the producer of such picture resulted in apparent cruelty to animals; and

(2) Hereafter, In the production of motion pictures by the members of the Association such member shall, as to any picture involving the use of animals, invite on the lot during the shooting and consult with the authorized representative of the American Humane Association; and

(3) Steps shall be taken immediately by the members of the Association and by the Production Code Administration to require compliance with these resolutions which shall bear the same relationship to the sections of the Production Code quoted

herein as the Association's special regulations re: Crime in Motion Pictures bear to the sections of the Production Code dealing therewith; and it is **Further resolved,** That the resolutions of February 19, 1925 and all other resolutions of this Board establishing its policy to prevent all cruelty to animals in the production of motion pictures and reflecting its determination to prevent any such cruelty be and the same hereby are in all respects reaffirmed.

Resolutions for Uniform Interpretation

as amended June 13, 1934

1. When requested by production managers, the Motion Picture Association of America, Inc., shall secure any facts, information or suggestions concerning the probable reception of stories or the manner in which in its opinion they may best be treated.

2. That each production manager shall submit in confidence a copy of each or any script to the Production Code Administration of the Motion Picture Association of America, Inc. (and of the Association of Motion Picture Producers, Inc., (California). The Production Code Administration will give the production manager for his guidance such confidential advice and suggestions as experience, research, and information indicate, designating wherein in its judgment the script departs from the provisions of the Code, or wherein from experience or knowledge it is believed that exception will be taken to the story or treatment.

3. Each production manager of a company belonging to the Motion Picture Association of America, Inc., and any producer proposing to distribute and/or distributing his picture through the facilities of any member of the Motion Picture Association of America, Inc., shall submit to such Production Code Administration every picture he produces before the negative goes to the laboratory for printing. Said Production Code Administration, having seen the picture, shall inform the production manager in writing whether in its opinion the picture conforms or does not conform to the Code, stating specifically wherein either by theme, treatment, or incident, the picture violates the provisions of the Code. In such latter event, the picture shall not be released until th changes indicated by the Production Code Administration have been made; provided, however, that the production manager may appeal from such opinion of said Production Code Administration, so indicated in writing, to the Board of Directors of the Motion Picture Association of America, Inc., whose finding shall be final, and such production manager and company shall be governed accordingly.

Footnotes

[1] Amended in October 1961 to permit "Sex aberration" when treated with "care, discretion, and restraint."

[2] Later changed to read: "The methods and techniques of prostitution and white slavery shall never be presented in detail, nor shall the subjects be presented unless shown in contrast to right standards of behavior. Brothels in any clear identification as such may not be shown."

[3] Sex hygiene included abortion. In the amended Code of December 1956, the following was specified: "The subject of abortion shall be discouraged, shall never be more than suggested, and when referred to shall be condemned. It must never be treated lightly, or made the subject of comedy. Abortion shall never be shown explicitly or by inference, and a story must not indicate that an abortion has been performed, the word 'abortion' shall not be used."

[4] As amended by resolution of the Board of Directors November 1, 1939, and September 12, 1945.

[5] Amended by resolution of the Board of Directors on December 3, 1947, to include prohibition of (2) Titles which suggest or are currently associated in the public mind with material, characters, or occupations unsuitable for the screen. (3) Titles which are otherwise objectionable.

[6] As adopted by the Board of Directors on December 20, 1938.

[7] As amended by resolution of the Board of Directors, December 3, 1947.

2/THE CODE OF SELF-REGULATION; THE CLASSIFICATION AND RATING ADMINISTRATION

THROUGHOUT THE 1950s, and early 1960s, it was obvious that the Production Code was becoming increasingly outmoded. Under the severe restrictions of the Code, American movies could not compete with European films like *La Dolce Vita, Two Women* and *Hiroshima Mon Amour* which were being distributed with greater frequency and popularity at this time. It was also argued that the very premise of the Production Code—that movies had to be carefully regulated because they were the nation's broadest based entertainment—was no longer valid, now that television had usurped much of film's mass audience. And so it was maintained that film, now subject to not one but many audiences, should be granted the freedoms long since conferred to novels and plays, which also had splintered audiences.

Throughout this time there were calls for a classification system that would recognize moviegoers' various tastes and that would thus allow for enhanced sophistication in American films. Many film scholars maintain that the pros and cons of such a system would have been debated even longer had it not been for two Supreme Court decisions

handed down on the same day, April 22, 1968. The first decision, *Ginsberg v. New York,* ruled that material which was not obscene for adults might be declared obscene for children. The second decision, *Interstate Circuit* v. *Dallas,* indicated that a classification system for movies could be declared constitutional were the guidelines for the system clearly defined.

Together, these two decisions would allow every city or state to devise its own classification code to protect its children should it desire to do so. Frightened by the chaos of a multitude of contradictory standards, the MPAA was quick to act: on Oct. 7, 1968, just six months after the two Court decisions, the MPAA announced its new self-regulatory code. The new code went into effect Nov. 1. (Jack Valenti had succeeded Eric Johnston as president of the MPAA in 1966.

According to the new classification system, any film regardless of its theme or treatment could be made, but it would be subject to one of four ratings: G (all ages admitted; general audiences); M (suggested for mature audiences—adults and mature young children); R (restricted; children under sixteen required an accompanying parent or adult); or X (no one under sixteen admitted). These ratings—which the MPAA said did not indicate a film's quality but only its suitability for children—were later modified. In March 1970 the R and X categories raised their age limits to 17, and the M category was now labeled GP (all ages admitted; parental guidance suggested), since many people had taken M to mean for mature audiences only. When the GP label also proved confusing—many thought it meant General Public—it was changed in 1972 to PG, to emphasize the parental guidance.

But the new rating system did not do away with the old Production Code entirely: a "Standards for Production" was retained, and many critics have said that this new list was merely a re-wording of the old Code.

Under the new system, the Production Code Administration was replaced by the Code and Rating Administration (CARA). Seven permanent members comprise this board, and they, like their predecessors on the PCA, still examine both scripts and final cuts of films, giving all G, PG and R movies their seal of approval. X-rated films are denied a seal but are still permitted to be shown. Any nonmember company of the MPAA may still use CARA's services.

Although it did ease many obviously anachronistic restrictions, the new classification system was heavily criticized by conservatives (who found the ratings not sufficient) and liberals (who found the ratings not accurate) alike. In 1971, for example, both the National Catholic Office for Motion Pictures and the National Council of Churches' Broadcasting and Film Commission, disturbed by the "clearly unrealistic ratings handed out," refused to support the MPAA any longer. Liberals, on the other hand, argued that the rating system was still a form of censorship and be-

moaned the fact that one short scene or phrase could change a movie's overall rating. The fact that sex still seemed to be restricted, while violence was treated much more leniently, was another cause of criticism. And when it was learned that studios were re-editing films to change a film's rating, film critics and scholars were quick to point out the destructive effects the new code could have on a director's artistry.

But the greatest blow to the new code's efficiency came in 1973 when the Supreme Court decided that the question of offensiveness could be judged against "local, not national, community standards," a decision that meant a local community could disregard the MPAA's rating and apply its own standard. The film industry, understandably disturbed, claimed that had the new code been more effective in the first place, the Supreme Court decision would never have been made. The new code, through its R and X ratings, made it easy for self-appointed guardians of public morality to know which films might contain "objectionable" material. And as a result, newspapers could refuse to advertise X-rated films and theaters could decline to show them. A 1969 survey, for example, revealed that 50% of theaters in this country would not shown an X-rated film. And newspapers representing approximately 11% of the national circulation have restrictions or bans on ads for X-rated films, including the *New York Times.*

Many believe that X-rated films should be divided into categories that distinguish run-of-the-mill porno flicks from exceptional erotic films like *In the Realm of the Senses* and *Salo,* but such a distinction would of course be arbitrary at times. Other critics of the code have lamented the disadvantages accrued to G-rated movies: many moviegoers stay away from G films, in the belief that such films would be boring and bland. In fact, *Variety* has reported that while 41% of films in 1968 were given G ratings, only 13% of the movies in 1977 were so rated. And independent producers have further charged that the code process favors the major studios.

Jack Valenti, however, maintains that the ratings still work, pointing to the annual surveys conducted by the Opinion Research Corp. of Princeton. According to the 1976 survey, 95% of the moviegoing public are aware of the ratings. Approximately 25% find the ratings "very useful" and about 40% believe the rating "fairly useful." Only 30% said they thought the ratings "not very useful."

After months of examination and debate, the MPAA revised its voluntary rating system on Aug. 1, 1977. Most of the changes were minor and did not take into account many of the system's alleged limitations.

Under the new system, the code concept has been eliminated and the administration —once called the Code and Rating Administration—is now known as the Classification and Rating Administration.

The PG category has also been altered. Whereas the explanation attached to the symbol formerly read "some material may not be suitable for pre-teenagers," it now reads "some material may not be suitable for children." The MPAA thought the redefinition of the PG tag "strengthens the PG rating by indicating that parents should exercise guidance concerning PG films for their children, not just pre-teenagers."

During the first 11 years of its work (November 1968 to November 1979), the Classification and Rating Administration assigned ratings to some 4,953 feature films. The films were rated as follows:

MPAA FILM RATINGS: 1968-78

	G	PG	R	X	Total
First Year: 11/68 - 10/69					
Majors-Minors*	120 (32%)	154 (42%)	81 (22%)	16 (4%)	371 (84%)
Independents	21 (30%)	18 (26%)	22 (31%)	9 (13%)	70 (16%)
Total	141 (32%)	172 (39%)	103 (23%)	25 (6%)	441 (100%)
Second Year: 11/69 - 10/70					
Majors-Minors*	59 (22%)	109 (40%)	91 (34%)	12 (4%)	271 (61%)
Independents	31(18%)	46 (27%)	73 (42%)	22 (13%)	172 (39%)
Total	90 (20%)	155 (35%)	164 (37%)	34 (8%)	443 (100%)
Third Year: 11/70 - 10/71					
Majors-Minors*	60 (25%)	105 (44%)	70 (30%)	3 (1%)	238 (46%)
Independents	41 (15%)	91 (33%)	100 (36%)	45 (16%)	277 (54%)
Total	101 (20%)	196 (38%)	170 (33%)	48 (9%)	515 (100%)
Fourth Year: 11/71 - 10/72					
Majors-Minors*	74 (29%)	127 (50%)	51 (20%)	1 (1%)	253 (50%)
Independents	20 (8%)	104 (40%)	127 (50%)	5 (2%)	256 (50%)
Total	94 (19%)	231 (45%)	178 (35%)	6 (1%)	509 (100%)
Fifth Year: 11/72 - 10/73					
Majors-Minors*	43 (18%)	112 (47%)	79 (33%)	3 (1%)	237 (43%)
Independents	42 (13%)	72 (23%)	182 (58%)	17 (5%)	313 (57%)
Total	85 (16%)	184 (33%)	261 (47%)	20 (4%)	550 (100%)
Sixth Year: 11/72 - 10/74					
Majors-Minors*	36 (20%)	88 (50%)	55 (31%)	(2) # (1%)	177 (35%)
Independents	36 (11%)	97 (30%)	477 (54%)	17 (5%)	327 (65%)
Total	72 (14%)	185 (37%)	232 (46%)	15 (3%)	504 (100%)
Seventh Year: 11/74 - 10/75					
Majors-Minors*	28 (18%)	68 (45%)	54 (35%)	3 (2%)	153 (36%)
Independents	28 (11%)	82 (30%)	148 (54%)	14 (5%)	272 (64%)
Total	56 (13%)	150 (35%)	202 (48%)	17 (4%)	425 (100%)
Eighth Year: 11/75 - 10/76					
Majors-Minors*	24 (16%)	75 (51%)	45 (30%)	4 (3%)	148 (30%)
Independents	40 (12%)	85 (24%)	179 (51%)	45 (13%)	349 (70%)
Total	64 (13%)	160 (32%)	224 (45%)	49 (10%)	497 (100%)

	G	PG	R	X	Total
Ninth Year: 11/76 - 10/77					
Majors-Minors*........	16 (14%)	71 (60%)	31 (26%)	0 (0%)	118 (30%)
Independents	35 (13%)	81 (30%)	127 (46%)	30 (11%)	273 (70%)
Total	51 (13%)	152 (39%)	158 (40%)	30 (8%)	391 (100%)
Tenth Year: 11/77 - 10/78					
Majors-Minors*........	14 (12%)	66 (55%)	41 (34%)	(1) # (1%)	120 (38%)
Independents	25 (13%)	70 (36%)	85 (43%)	15 (8%)	195 (62%)
Total	39 (12%)	136 (43%)	126 (40%)	14 (4%)	315 (100%)
Eleventh-Year: 11/78 - 10/79					
Majors-Minors*........	9 (6%)	89 (61%)	49 (34%)	(2) # (1%)	145 (40%)
Independents	15 (7%)	63 (29%)	114 (52%)	26 (12%)	218 (60%)
Total	24 (7%)	152 (42%)	163 (45%)	24 (6%)	363 (100%)
11-Year Cumulative: 11/68 - 10/79					
Majors-Minors*........	483 (22%)	1064 (48%)	647 (29%)	37 (1%)	2231 (45%)
Independents	334 (12%)	809 (30%)	1334 (49%)	245 (9%)	2722 (55%)
Total	817 (16%)	1873 (38%)	1981 (40%)	282 (6%)	4953 (100%)

* Includes AA, AIP, AvEmb, Buena Vista, Cinerama, Col, MGM, NGP, Par, 20th-Fox, UA, Universal, WB and all affiliated tradenames.

Denotes the rerating and removal of previous X films shifted to another category.

NOTE: Percentage figures after the number of films under each rating symbol denote the percentage of all films from that source (i.e., Majors-Minors, Independents or Total) in the yearly period indicated. The percentages add vertically to 100% only in the right hand "Total" column for each time period; they add horizontally by ratings categories.

This chart reveals how strongly the major/minor companies avoid the "X" rating: only 1% of those films distributed by the major/minor studios over the past 11 years have been assigned the dreaded "X."

Over the years fewer and fewer movies have been classified "G": whereas 32% of those films rated in 1968/69 were given the "G" label, only 12% of the movies rated in 1977/78 were assigned "G" ratings.

This chart also suggests what a toll the unavailability of tax shelter-financing took on independent production in 1977. Whereas 273 independent films were rated during the CARA's ninth year (1976/77) of work, only 195 independent pictures were assigned ratings during CARA's tenth year (1977/78), when tax shelters for films were no longer legal.

How do the MPAA ratings break down with regards to studio?

As you can see, United Artists leads in "X" ratings, followed by Paramount and Avco Embassy. Warner Brothers and Buena Vista (Disney) are the only studios whichhave never released an "X" film. But not surprisingly, Buena Vista leads in "G" ratings, followed by MGM and Paramount.

The three principal systems used by the MPAA during its history—the Production Code, the Code of Self-Regulation, and the Classification and Rating System—comprise one of the most important chapters of American social history. The Production Code especially, with its detailed prohibitions and very specific beliefs about film aesthetics, is a fascinating document.

Distributor	G	PG	R	X	Total
(between November 1968-December 1979)					
A.A.	6	21	21	5	55
AIP	14	109	83	1	207
AvEmb	10	49	53	6	118
BV (Disney)	105	1	0	0	106
Columbia	38	137	77	2	254
MGM	77	67	40	2	186
Paramount	57	106	76	7	246
20th C-F	28	117	51	2	198
United Artists	39	165	66	8	278
Universal	43	107	54	2	206
Warner Brothers	33	110	85	0	228

2A/THE CODE OF SELF-REGULATION

The Code of Self-Regulation of the Motion Picture Association of America shall apply to production, to advertising, and to titles of motion pictures.

The Code shall be administered by the Code and Rating Administration, headed by an Administrator.

There shall also be a Director of the Code for Advertising, and a Director of the Code for Titles.

Nonmembers are invited to submit pictures to the Code Administrator on the same basis as members of the Association.

Declaration of Principles of the Code of Self-Regulation of the Motion Picture Association

This Code is designed to keep in close harmony with the mores, the culture, the moral sense and change in our society.

The objectives of the Code are:

(1) To encourage artistic expression by expanding creative freedom; and

(2) To assure that the freedom which encourages the artist remains responsible and sensitive to the standards of the larger society.

Censorship is an odious enterprise. We oppose censorship and classification by governments because they are alien to the American tradition of freedom.

Much of this nation's strength and purpose is drawn from the premise that the humblest of citizens has the freedom of his own choice. Censorship destroys this freedom of choice.

It is within this framework that the Motion Picture Association continues to recognize its obligations to the society of which it is an integral part.

In our society parents are the arbitors of family conduct. Parents have the primary responsibility to guide their children in the kind of lives they lead, the character they build, the books they read, and the movies and other entertainment to which they are exposed.

The creators of motion pictures undertake a responsibility to make available pertinent information about their pictures which will assist parents to fulfill their responsibilities.

But this alone is not enough. In further recognition of our obligation to the public, and most especially to parents, we have extended the Code operation to include a nationwide voluntary film rating program which has as its prime objective a sensitive concern for children. Motion pictures will be reviewed by a Code and Rating Administration which, when it reviews a motion picture as to its conformity with the standards of the Code, will issue ratings. It is our intent that all motion picture exhibited in the United States will carry a rating.

These ratings are:

G **All ages admitted. General audiences.**
This category includes motion pictures that in the opinion of the Code and Rating Administration would be acceptable for all audiences, without consideration of age.

PG **All ages admitted. Parental Guidance suggested. Some material may not be suitable for pre-teenagers.**
This category includes motion pictures that in the opinion of the Code and Rating Administration would be acceptable to all audiences, without consideration of age, as to which because of their theme, content and treatment, parents may wish to obtain more information for their guidance.

R **Restricted. Under 17 requires accompanying parent or adult guardian.**

This category includes motion pictures that in the opinion of the Code and Rating Administration, because of their theme, content or treatment, should not be presented to persons under 17 unless accompaniedy by a parent or adult guardian.

X No one under 17 admitted. (Age limit may vary in certain areas.)

This category includes motion pictures submitted to the Code and Rating Administration which in the opinion of the Code and Rating Administration are rated X because of the treatment of sex, violence, crime, or profanity. Pictures rated X do not qualiffy for a Code Seal. Pictures rated X should not be presented to persons under 17.

The program contemplates that any distributors outside the membership of the Association who choose not to submit their motion pictures to the Code and Rating Administration will self-apply the X rating.

The ratings and their meanings will be conveyed by advertising; by displays at the theaters; and in other ways. Thus, audiences, especially parents, will be alerted to the theme, content, and treatment of movies. Therefore, parents can determine whether a particular picture is one which children should see at the discretion of the parent; or only when accompanied by a parent; or should not see.

We believe self-restraint, self-regulation, to be in the American tradition. The results of self-discipline are always imperfect because that is the nature of all things mortal. But this Code, and its administration, will make clear that freedom of expression does not mean toleration of license.

All members of the Motion Picture Association, as well as the National Association of Theater Owners, the International Film Importers and Distributors of America, and other independent producer-distributors are co-operating in this endeavor. Most motion pictures exhibited in the United States will be submitted for Code approval and rating, or for rating only, to the Code and Rating Administration. The presence of the Seal indicates to the public that a picture has received Code approval.

We believe in and pledge our support to these deep and fundamental values in a democratic society:

Freedom of choice . . .

The right of creative man to achieve artistic excellence . . .

The importance of the role of the parent as the guide to the family's conduct . . .

Standards for Production

In furtherance of the objectives of the Code to accord with the mores, the culture, and the moral sense of our society, the principles stated above and the following standards shall govern the Administrator in his consideration of motion pictures submitted for Code approval.

The basic dignity and value of human life shall be respected and upheld. Restraint shall be exercised in portraying the taking of life.

Evil, sin, crime and wrong-doing shall not be justified.

Special restraing shall be exercised in portraying criminal or anti-social activities in which minors participate or are involved.

Detailed and protacted acts of brutality, cruelty, physical violence, torture and abuse shall not be presented.

Indecent or undue exposure of the human body shall not be presented.

Illicit sex relationships shall not be justified. Intimate sex scenes violating common standards of decency shall not be portrayed.

Restraint and care shall be exercised in presentations dealing with sex aberrations.

Obscene speech, gestures or movements shall not be presented. Undue profanity shall not be permitted.

Religion shall not be demeaned.

Words or symbols contemptuous of racial, religious, or national groups, shall not be used so as to incite bigotry or hatred.

Excessive cruelty to animals shall not be portrayed and animals shall not be treated inhumanely.

Standards for Advertising

The principles of the Code cover advertising and publicity as well as production. There are times when their specific application to advertising may be different. A motion picture is viewed as a whole and may be judged that way. It is the nature of advertising, however, that it must select and emphasize only isolated portions and aspects of a film. It thus follows that what may be appropriate in a motion picture may not be equally appropriate in advertising. Furthermore, on application to advertising, the principles and standards of the Code are supplemented by the following standards for advertising:

Illustrations and text shall not misrepresent the character of a motion picture.

Illustrations shall not depict any indecent or undue exposure of the human body.

Advertising demeaning religion, race, or national origin shall not be used.

Cumulative overemphasis on sex, crime, violence, and brutality shall not be permitted.

Salacious postures and embraces shall not be shown.

Censorship disputes shall not be exploited or capitalized upon.

Standards for Titles

A salacious, obscene, or profane title shall not be used on motion pictures.

Regulations Governing the Operation of the Motion Picture Code and Rating Administration

1. The Motion Picture Code and Rating Administration (hereinafter referred to as the Administration) is established to be composed of an Administrator and staff members, one of whom shall be experienced in the exhibition of motion pictures to the public.

2 a. All motion pictures produced or distributed by members of the Association and their subsidiaries will be submitted to the Administration for Code and Rating.

b. Non-members of the Association may submit their motion pictures to the Administration for Code approval and rating in the same manner and under the same conditions as members of the Association or may submit their motion pictures to the Administration for rating only.

3. Members and non-members who submit their motion pictures to the Administration should, prior to the commencement of the production of the motion picture, submit a script or other treatment. The administration will inform the producer in confidence whether a motion picture based upon the submitted script appears to conform to the Standards of the Code and indicate its probable rating. The final judgment of the Administration shall be made only upon the reviewing of the completed picture.

4 a. When a completed motion picture is submitted to the Administration and is approved as conforming to the Standards of the Code, it will be rated by the Administration either as G (all ages admitted—general audiences) GP (all ages admitted—parental guidance suggested), or R (restricted), according to the categories described in the **Declaration of Principles.**

b. Completed motion pictures submitted by non-members for rating only will be rated according to the categories described in the **Declaration of Principles** as G, PG, R or X.

5. Motion pictures of member companies or their subsidiaries which are approved under the Code and rated: G, PG, or R, shall upon public release bear upon an introductory frame of every print distributed in the United States the official seal of the Association with the word "Approved" and the words "Certificate Number," followed by the number of the Certificate of Approval. Each print shall also bear a symbol of the rating assigned to it by the Administration. So far as possible the Seal of the Association and the rating shall be displayed in uniform type, size, and prominence. All prints of an approved motion picture bearing the Code seal shall be identical.

6. Motion pictures of non-member companies submitted for Code approval and rating or for rating only which receive a G, PG, or R rating shall bear such rating upon every print distributed in the United States, in uniform type, size, and prominence. Prints of such pictures may also display the official Seal of the Association if application is made to the Association for the issuance of a Code Certificate number.

7. If the Administration determines that a motion picture submitted for approval and rating or rating only should be rated X in accordance with the description of that category in the **Declaration of Principles,** the symbol X must appear on all prints of the motion picture distributed in the United States in uniform type, size, and prominence and in all advertising for the picture. Rating or a Rating Certificate shall condition such issuance upon the agreement by the producer or distributor that all advertising and publicity to be used for the picture shall be submitted to and approved by the Director of the Code for Advertising.

9. The producer or distributor applying for a Certificate of Approval for a picture or a Rating Certificate for those pictures receiving a rating only shall advance to the Administration at the time of application a fee in accordance with the uniform schedule of fees approved by the Board of Directors of the Association.

10. The Standards for Titles for motion pictures shall be applied by the Administration in consultation with the Director of the Code for Titles to all motion pictures submitted for approval and rating only and no motion picture for which a Certificate of Approval or Rating Certificate has been issued shall change its title

without the prior approval of the Administration.

Advertising Code Regulations

1. These regulations are applicable to all members of the Motion Picture Association of America, to all producers and distributors of motion pictures with respect to each picture for which the Association has granted its Certificate of Approval or Rating Certificate; and to all other producers and distributors who self-apply the X rating to their motion pictures and voluntary submit their advertising.

2. The term "advertising" as used herein includes all forms of motion picture advertising and exploitation and ideas therefore, including newspaper, magazine and trade paper advertising; publicity copy and art intended for use in pressbooks or other intended for general distribution in printed form or for theatre use; trailers; posters, lobby displays and other outdoor displays; including rear-projection trailers; advertising accessories, including the following: pressbooks, still photographs, heralds and throw-aways; novelties; copy for exploitation tieups; and all radio and television copy and spots.

3. All advertising for motion pictures which have been submitted to the Code and Rating Administration for approval and rating, or for rating only, shall be submitted to the Director of the Code for Advertising for approval before use, and shall not be used in any way until so submitted and approved. All print advertising shall be submitted in duplicate.

4. The Director of the Code for Advertising shall proceed promptly to approve or disapprove the advertising submitted.

The director of the Code for Advertising shall stamp "Approved" on one copy of all advertising approved by him and return the stamped copy to the company which submitted it. If the Director of the Code of Advertising disapproves any advertising, the Director shall stamp the word "Disapproved" on one copy and return it to the company which submitted it, together with the reasons for such disapproval; or, if the Director so desires, he may return the copy with suggestions for such changes or corrections as will cause it to be approved.

The Director of the Code for Advertising shall send a white form of approval for teaser and theater trailers. If the Director approves a trailer, a pink form is sent stating the reasons for disapproval. After the revisions have been made by the company, the trailers are rescreened and a white form of approval is sent.

After TV and radio spots are submitted, the Director shall send a form letter of approval. In cases where material is questionable, he advises the company and suggests changes.

5. The Director of the Code for Advertising shall require all approved advertising for pictures submitted to the Code and Rating Administration by members of the Motion Picture Association of America and their subsidiaries to carry the official Code Seal and a designation of the rating assigned to the picture by the Code and Rating Administration. Uniform standards as to type, size, and prominence of the display of the seal and rating as approved by The Advertising Advisory Council are set forth by the Advertising Code Administrator as follows:

A. Display Advertising and Posters

1. All display advertising and posters, including trade paper advertising shall carry the official Code seal, when authorized, and the rating letter, assigned to the picture.

2. The official Code seal is authorized for pictures rated G, PG, or R. For pictures rated X, the seal may not be used.

3. In all advertisements of 150 lines or more the definition of each rating shall be carried in conjunction with the letter symbol, both in the uniform type face as distributed by the Association.

4. The lettering size of the symbol should approximate 25 percent of the letter height of the main title.

5. In advertisements less than 150 lines, the rating letter and Code seal should appear next to the main title.

6. In the larger advertisements, the rating and definition shall be given reasonable emphasis in placement and every attempt should be made to avoid burying it in the billings credits. The Director of the Code for Advertising shall have the authority to object to faulty placements.

7. Teaser ads must be submitted for review, but are exempt from the above requirements.

B. Television Spots

60–30–20–10 second spots

Visual—

Show the MPAA Seal

Show the Rating Symbol Letter (G, PG, R or X)

Show the Full Definition of the Symbol.

Full Definition:

G—ALL AGES ADMITTED (General Audiences). PG—ALL AGES ADMITTED

(Parental Guidance Suggested. Some Material May Not Be Suitable for Pre-Teenagers.)

R—RESTRICTED (Under 17 Requires Accompanying Parent or Adult Guardian.) X—NO ONE UNDER 17 ADMITTED (Age limit may vary in certain areas.)

Audible—

State the Rating Symbol Letter: "Rated G," "Rated PG," "Rated R," "Rated X"

Note: The visual Code information (MPAA seal, Rating Symbol and Full Definition) should be included when the title of the film comes on the screen and remain for four seconds.

C. Radio Spots

60–30–20 second spots

State the Rating Symbol (G, PG or X)

State the Abbreviated Definition:

"Rated G—General Audiences"

"Rated PG—All Ages, Parental Guidance"

"Rated R—Under 17, Not Admitted Without Parent"

"Rated X—Under 17 Not Admitted"

10 second spots

"Rated G"

"Rated PG"

"Rated R"

"Rated X"

D. Theater Trailers

1. The complete rating definition and Code seal, as set forth in the attached trailer card Exhibits I, II, and III, for the appropriate rating, shall conform to the approved new format, screen right with key line of definition in reverse for pictures rated G, PG, or R.

2. For pictures rated X by the Code and Rating Administration, Exhibit IV shall appear as above except the seal may not be used.

3. Trailers are reviewed for two distinct audiences—GENERAL (G, PG) and RESTRICTED (R, X). Trailers for R and X pictures will not be shown during the exhibition of G and PG pictures.

The following exceptions will be applied to the above policy:

(a) The Director of the Code for Advertising will certify that a trailer for an R or X picture is acceptable (as revised) for use with G and PG pictures, if, in his judgment, the contents of the trailer meet the G and PG levels of approval.

or

(b) In lieu of the regular R or X trailer, the distributor will offer exhibitors a special alternate trailer or telop (showing only titles and credits) that has been approved for **Unrestricted** audiences.

(c) In May 1971 the following line was approved for use in trailers approved under (a) and (b) above: "This **Preview** has been approved by the Motion Picture Association of America for General Audiences." This statement should appear on the rating tag for the trailer.

E. Multiple Features

When more than one picture is being exhibited on the same bill, the more restrictive rating will apply to admissions. Advertising shall be governed accordingly.

6. Approved advertising for pictures submitted to the Code and Rating Administration by companies other than members of the Motion Picture Association of America, and their subsidiaries, for Code approval and rating, or for rating only, may bear the official seal at the distributor's option, but all such advertising shall bear the assigned rating.

7. Approved advertising for pictures rated X by the Code and Rating Administration shall bear the X rating but may not bear the official seal.

8. All pressbooks approved by the Director of the Code for Advertising, except for X-rated pictures, shall bear in a prominent place the official seal of the Motion Picture Association of America and a designation of the rating and the full definition assigned to the picture by the Code and Rating Administration. Pressbooks shall also carry the following notice:

Approved
(seal)
All advertising in this pressbook, as well as all other advertising and publicity materials referred to herein, has been approved under the Standards for Advertising of the Code of Self-Regulation of the Motion Picture Association of America. All inquiries on this procedure may be addressed to:
Director of Code Advertising
Motion Picture Association of America
522 Fifth Avenue/New York, New York 10036

9. Appeals. Any Company whose advertising has been disapproved may appear from the decision of the Director of the Code for Advertising, as follows:

It shall serve notice of such appeal on the director of the Code for Advertising and on the President of the Association. The President, or in his absence a Vice-President designated by him, shall thereupon promptly and within a week hold a hearing to pass upon the appeal. Oral and written evidence may be introduced by the Company and by the Director of the Code for Advertising, or their representatives. The appeal shall be decided as expeditiously as possible and the decision shall be final.

On appeals by companies other than members of the Motion Picture Association of America and their subsidiaries, the President shall, if requested, decide the appeal in consultation with a representative of International Film Importers and Distributors of America, as designated by its Governing Board.

10. Any company which has been granted a Certificate of Approval and which uses advertising without securing the prior approval of the Director of the Code for Advertising or if such advertising does not include the assigned rating may be brought up on charges before the Board of Directors by the President of the Association. Within a reasonable time, the Board may hold a hearing, at which time the company and the Director of the Code for Advertising or their representatives, may present oral or written statements. The Board, by a majority vote of those present, shall decide the matter as expeditiously as possible.

If the Board of Directors finds that the company has used advertising for a Code approved and rated picture without securing approval of the Director of the Code for Advertising, or without including the assigned rating, the Board may direct the Code and Rating Administration to void and revoke the Certificate of Approval granted for the picture and require the removal of the Association's seal from all prints of the picture.

11. Each company shall be responsible for compliance by its employees and agents with these regulations.

Code and Rating Appeals Board

1. A Code and Rating Appeals Board is established to be composed as follows:

(a) The President of the Motion Picture Association of America and 12 members designated by the President from the Board of Directors of the Association and executive officers of its member companies;

(b) Eight exhibitors designated by the National Association of Theater Owners from its Board of Directors;

(c) Four distributors designated by the International Film Importers and Distributors of America.

2. A pro tempore member for any particular hearing to act as a substitute for a member unable to attend may be designated in the same manner as the absent member.

3. The President of the Motion Picture Association shall be Chairman of the Appeals Board, and the Association shall provide its secretariat.

4. The presence of 13 members is necessary to constitute a quorum of the Appeals Board for a hearing of any appeal.

5. The Board will hear and determine appeals from:

(a) A decision of the Code and Rating Administration withholding Code approval from a picture submitted for approval and rating and which consequently received an X rating.

(b) A decision by the Code and Rating Administration applying an X rating to a picture submitted for rating only.

On such appeals a vote of two-thirds of the members present shall be required to sustain the decision of the Administration. If the decision of the Administration is not sustained, the Board shall proceed to rate the picture appropriately by majority vote.

6. The Board will also hear and determine appeals from the decision of the Code and Rating Administration applying any rating other than X to a motion picture.

Such appeals shall be decided by majority vote. If the decision of the Administration is not sustained the Board shall proceed to rate the picture appropriately.

7. (a) An Appeal from a decision of the Administration shall be instituted by the filing of a notice of appeal addressed to the Chairman of the Appeal Board by the party which submitted the picture to the Administration.

(b) Provision shall be made for the screening by the members of the Appeals Board at the Hearing or prior thereto of a print of the motion picture identical to the one reviewed and passed upon by the Administration.

(c) The party taking the appeal and the Administration may present oral or written statements to the Board at the hearing.

(d) No member of the Appeals Board shall participate on an appeal involving a picture in which the member or any company with which he is associated has a financial interest.

(e) The appeal shall be heard and decided as expeditiously as possible and the decision shall be final.

(f) The hearing of an appeal shall commence

with the screening of the motion picture involved.

(g) If either the party taking the appeal or the Code and Rating Administration desire to present oral or written statements to the Board pursuant to subparagraph (c) of Paragraph 7, any such written statement should be furnished to the Secretary at least two days before the date fixed for the hearing. The Secretary will reproduce such statements and circulate them to the members of the Appeals Board in advance or at the hearing of the appeal. Submission of written statements shall not diminish or alter the right also to present oral statements or arguments on behalf of the party taking the appeal.

(h) The Board will hear oral statements or argument on behalf of the party taking the appeal by not more than two persons, except by special permission. Oral statements or argument on behalf of the Code and Rating Administration shall be made only by the Administrator or his designated representative.

(i) Normally no more than a half hour will be allowed for oral argument to the party taking the appeal, and a like time to the Code and Rating Administration. If a party taking an appeal is of the opinion that statements or more than two persons or that additional time is necessary for the adequate presentation of the appeal, he may make such request by letter addressed to the Secretary stating the reasons why oral statements or more than two persons or more than a half hour is required for the adequate presentation of the appeal.

When such request is made by a party who is a member of the International Film Importers and Distributors of America, Inc., the Secretary shall consult with the Executive Directors or a member of the Governing Committee of that organization in determining whether and to what extent the request may be granted.

(j) In no circumstances shall the time allowed to any party for the hearing of an appeal extend beyond one hour.

A request for the participation of additional persons or for the allowance of additional time, to the extent that it is not granted, may be renewed to the Appeals Board at the commencement of the hearing of the appeal for disposition by the Appeals Board.

8. The board will also act as an advisory body on Code matters and, upon the call of the Chairman, will discuss the progress of the operation of the Code and Rating Program and review the manner of adherence to the Advertising Code.

2B/RULES AND REGULATIONS OF THE CLASSIFICATION AND RATING ADMINISTRATION

ARTICLE I POLICY REVIEW COMMITTEE
Section I. Organization

A. A Policy Review Committee is established to be comprised of representatives of the National Association of Theatre Owners ("NATO"), International Film Importers and Distributors of America ("IFIDA") and Motion Picture Association of America, Inc. ("MPAA").

B. Each organization shall have four representatives on the Policy Review Committee.

(1) The chairman of CARA shall participate in all meetings as an *ex officio* member of the Policy Review Committee.

(2) Each organization shall have the right to have an additional person attend for secretarial purposes.

C. Attendance by eight members, exclusive of *ex officio* members, shall constitute a quorum, provided that at least two members are present from each organization.

D. The Chairmanship of the Policy Review Committee shall rotate among the President of NATO, a member of the Board of Governors of IFIDA and the President of MPAA.

E. The Policy Review Committee shall meet at least twice a year at times scheduled through consultation among the President of NATO, a member of the Board of Governors of IFIDA and the President of MPAA. Special meetings may be called as circumstances require through the same procedure.

F. Minutes shall be kept and distributed to the members of the Policy Review Committee. Such minutes shall in all respects be confidential.

G. MPAA counsel, in cooperation with the Executive Director of NATO, shall serve as Secretary to the Policy Review Committee and shall be responsible for circulating minutes of the meetings and such other materials as the Policy Review Committee determines should be circulated.

Section II. Duties

A. The Policy Review Committee shall determine the policies, rules and procedures to be followed by the Classification and Rating Administration in the conduct of its duties.

B. The Policy Review Committee shall determine the policies, rules and procedures to be followed by the Classification and Rating Appeals Board and its subcommittees in the conduct of Appeals and other proceedings.

C. The Policy Review Committee shall have the authority to make changes in the Rating System and the policies, rules and/

or procedures necessary for implementation. Such changes may be made on the Policy Review Committee's own initiative or on the basis of proposals from members of the Appeals Board, the Chairman of CARA or other appropriate sources.

ARTICLE II CLASSIFICATION AND RATING ADMINISTRATION

Section I. Organization

A. A Classification and Rating Administration (CARA) is established.

B. It shall be comprised of a Chairman and staff members, one of whom, shall be designated Administrative Director.

Section II. CARA's Duties

A. All motion pictures produced or distributed by members of the MPAA and their subsidiaries shall be submitted to CARA for rating.

B. All motion pictures produced or distributed by non-members of the MPAA may be submitted to CARA in the same manner and under the same conditions as members of MPAA.

C. The actual rating of a motion picture shall be made only upon the viewing by CARA of the completed motion picture. Solely at the request of the producer or the distributor of a motion picture, CARA may consult with them on rating criteria at any time before completion of the motion picture.

Section III. Rating and Re-rating by CARA

A. CARA will rate or re-rate any motion picture at any time before it is exhibited in any theatre in the United States.

B. CARA will rate of re-rate any motion picture if that motion picture has not been exhibited in more than four theatres for a period not exceeding thirty days. The thirty-day period shall commence with first day of exhibition in any one theatre and run continuously therefrom.

C. CARA will re-rate any motion picture that has been exhibited and does not qualify under subsection B above, only if any and all versions of the motion picture are per-

manently withdrawn from exhibition and all such versions are not exhibited or advertised anywhere in the United States for a period of 90 days prior to the date the re-rated version is re-released in exhibition. The 90-day time period may be changed in exceptional cases by the Waiver Committee as prescribed in Section III-H below.

D. CARA will rate a motion picture released without previously being submitted to CARA at any time after release, provided it is submitted for a rating in exactly the same form in which it is in release. If the producer or distributor seeking the rating chooses to edit or otherwise revise the picture, CARA will rate the picture in accordance to Section III-C above.

E. CARA will rate any motion picture previously released with a self-applied X rating (or without a self-applied X rating, but under similar admissions policy) under the rules set out in Sections III B-C, except that if upon review CARA issues the motion picture an X rating, the producer or distributor submitting need not remove the motion picture nor certify that it has been removed from exhibition for the time period specified in Section III-C above.

F. CARA shall issue the Rating Certificate containing the rating or re-rating only after the producer or distributor who submitted the motion picture certifies that:

(1) All prints conform identically to the version rated or re-rated by CARA and only such conforming prints shall be exhibited in the United States; and

(2) The time period for which the motion picture must be withdrawn, if any, has been completed.

G. Motion picture submitted for rating or re-rating shall be subject to the advertising approval procedures provided in the rules for the Advertising Code.

H. A Waiver committee is established to be comprised of three members each from NATO, IFIDA and the MPAA. Upon the initiative of CARA or the producer or distributor of the motion picture, the Committee shall have the authority to hold a hearng and to decide either to lengthen or shorten the 90-day time period prescribed in Section III-C above.

(1) Five members shall constitute a quorum, provided that at least one member is present from each organization. Each member shall have one vote and a majority vote of those voting shall govern.

(2) The Waiver Committee shall have the final authority to set a time period of 90 days or less. If the Waiver Committee imposes a time period in excess of 90 days, the producer or distributor may appeal the decision to the Appeals Board.

(3) The Appeals Board has the authority to reduce the tme period set by the Waiver Committee down to 90 days exactly, affirm the time period set by the Waiver Committee or modify the decision of the Waiver Commitee to a time period of greater than 90 days but less than that imposed by the Waiver Committee. The procedures for such appeals are prescribed in Article III, Sections II and III.

I. For the purposes of determining the applicability of Section III A-F hereof, CARA or the Waiver Committee may require applicants to supply, in writing, all necessary and pertinent information.

Section IV. Rating Procedures

A. When the producer or distributor of a completed motion picture elects to release the motion picture with a CARA rating, it shall be submitted to CARA and rated either:

(1) G—General Audiences. All ages admitted.

(2) PG—Parental Guidance Suggested. Some material may not be suitable for children.

(3) R—Restricted. Under 17 requires accompanying parent or adult guardian. (Age may vary in some jurisdictions.)

(4) X—No one under 17 admitted. (Age may vary in some jurisdictions.)

B. The G, PG and R ratings set out above are Certification Marks registered by the MPAA with the United States Patent and Trademark Office.

(1) The G, PG, or R ratings may not be self-applied.

(2) The X rating may be self-applied by producers and distributors who are non-members of the MPAA.

C. In issuing the ratings provided in Section IV-A above, CARA shall consider as criteria among others as deemed appropriate the treatment of the theme, language, violence, nudity and sex.

D. A producer or distributor shall pay CARA a fee in accordance with the uniform schedule of fees.

Section V. Use of the Ratings

A. A rating is issued by CARA on the condition that all prints of a picture to be distributed for exhibition in the United States shall be identical to the print rated by CARA. The agents, assignees and other persons acting under the actual or apparent authority of the applicant are bound by this requirement.

B. A rating is issued by CARA on the condition that all the terms and conditions stated in the Rating Certificate are binding on the producer or distributor who submits the motion picture, as well as his agents, assignees and other persons acting under his actual or apparent authority.

C. Motion pictures of MPAA members companies rated G, PG, or R by CARA shall bear upon a prominent frame of every print distributed in the United States the number of Rating Certificate and the official Seal of the Association with the words "Certificate Number," followed by the number of the Rating Certificate and the symbol of the rating assigned to it. So far as possible, the Seal of the Association, the rating and number shall be displayed in uniform type, size and prominence.

D. Motion pictures of non-MPAA member companies rated G, PG, or R by CARA may bear upon a prominent frame of every print distributed in the United States the words "Certificate Number," followed by the number of the Rating Certificate and shall bear the symbol of the rating assigned to it. Prints of such pictures may also display the official Seal of the Association. So far as possible, the Seal of the Association and the number, if displayed and the rating shall be displayed in uniform type, size and prominence.

E. Motion pictures submitted for rating which are rated X, shall display the symbol X on all prints of the motion picture distributed in the United States in uniform type, size and prominence. The Seal of the Association shall not be displayed on a motion picture rated X.

Section VI. Unauthorized Use and Revocation

A. The use of CARA ratings without a duly issued CARA Rating Certificate is not permitted. In addition to the remedies provided in these rules, legal action may be instituted to prevent unauthorized use of the ratings.

B. Any producer or distributor issued a Rating Certificate who distributes the motion picture in violation of the terms and conditions specified in these rules or the Rating Certificate may have the rating revoked.

C. An action for revocation other than for a violation of the Advertising Code shall be commenced by CARA.

(1) CARA shall file a letter with the President of the MPAA stating the relevant facts on which the revocation is sought.

(2) A copy of the letter shall be sent to the producer or distributor and, where possible, be accompanied by telephone notice.

(3) In consultation with the President of the MPAA and the Chairman of CARA, a date and a time for a hearing shall be set to provide the producer or distributor an opportunity to be heard.

D. Hearings on revocation shall be heard by a representative designated by the President of the MPAA, a representative designated by the Board of Governors of IFIDA, and a representative designated by NATO, if, by majority vote, the three representatives of MPAA, IFIDA and NATO determine that the violation did occur, they may order the rating revoked and the Rating Certificate voided.

a) Only one request for a re-hearing shall be entertained and that must be filed within fifteen busness days after the date of the original appeal.

b) The producer or distributor may submit new information in support of the request for a re-hearing.

c) A majority vote of the members shall be required for a re-hearing to be granted and the decision shall be final. In the event of a tie vote, the Chairman of the Appeals Board shall decide whether to grant the re-hearing.

d) The re-hearing of an appeal shall be conducted under the same procedures as prescribed for appeals generally.

E. (1) After a motion picture has been initially rated or re-rated by CARA and such rating or re-rating sustained by the Appeals Board in the appeal provided for in Section II-A above, the producer or distributor may resubmit the motion picture to CARA for a subsequent re-rating one or more times, subject only to the fee schedule and rule requirements procided in Article II, Section III.

(2) The Appeals Board shall hear and determine appeals from decisions by

CARA issuing a subsequent re-rating in accordance with the same rules and procedures provided in this article for appeals generally, except that

a) The producer or distributor shall be granted only one appeal on a subsequent re-rating as a matter of right. This appeal of right may be taken after the first or after any subsequent re-submission to CARA at the option of the producer or distributor.

b) The producer or distributor shall be granted additional appeals, after the appeal of right provided for in subsection (a) above, only in exceptional cases and only with the express consent of the Chairman of the appeals Board. The approval of the Chairman shall be granted only where the producer or distributor demonstrates that there is a substantial change in the motion picture giving the reasons why such changes were not made prior to the last appeal of right.

ARTICLE III CLASSIFICATION AND RATING APPEALS BOARD
Section I. Organization

A. A Classification and Rating Appeals Board is established, to be composed as follows:

(1) The President of the MPAA and nine representatives designated one each by the member companies of the MPAA.

(2) Eight exhibitors designated by NATO.

(3) Four distributors designated by IFIDA.

B. A substitute member for any appeal, to replace a regular member unable to attend, may be designated in accordance with the same procedures for selecting regular members.

C. The President of the MPAA shall be Chairman of the Appeals Board, and the MPAA shall provide its Secretariat.

D. The presence of eleven members is necessary to constitute a quorum of the Appeals Board for the hearing of the appeal, provided that at least four members each, designated by MPAA and NATO, respectively, and one member designated by IFIDA are present. Upon the unanimous concurrence of the Chairman of the Appeals Board, the representative of CARA and the representative of the producer or distributor taking the appeal, the quorum requirements may be waived.

Section II. Duties

A. (1) The Appeals Board shall hear and determine appeals taken by producers or distributors from an initial decision by CARA. The Appeals Board may affirm the decision of CARA or apply a different rating as it deems appropriate.

(2) Upon the request of the producer or distributor whose appeal received a majority vote, but less than a two-thirds vote and therefore did not overturn CARA's rating, the Chairman of the Appeals Board shall poll the members of the Appeals Board who voted on the appeal on whether a re-hearing of the appeal should be granted.

c) When an appeal is sought pursuant to subsection (b) above, by a non-member of MPAA, the chairman shall, at the request of the producer or distributor, consult with a member of the Governing Board of IFIDA in determining whether to grant the appeal.

(3) If a producer or distributor seeking an appeal pursuant to Section II-B-2 (b and c) is denied the right to take an appeal, such producer or distributor may have that decision reviewed by the President of NATO, the Chairman of the Board of Governors of IFIDA and the President of MPAA. A majority vote shall decide whether an appeal shall be granted and such decision shall be final.

(4) In determining the appeal rights of a producer or distributor under Section

II-B, the grant or denial of a re-hearing of any prior appeal, as provided for in section II-A-2, shall be of no effect.

C. The Appeals Board shall hear and determine appeals from a waiting time period in excess of 90 days imposed by the Waiver Committee pursuant to Article II Section III-C.

D. The Appeals Board or any member may offer proposals to the Policy Review Committee regarding the policies, rules or procedures of the Appeals Board, CARA, the Waive Committee, or any other matter involving the Rating System. The final decision to adopt such proposals shall be made by the Policy Review Committee.

E. (1) No member of the Appeals Board shall participate in an appeal involving a motion picture in which the member or any company with which he or she is associated has a financial interest.

(2) Except as allowed in these rules, it shall be grounds for dismissal of the appeal or other appropriate sanction for the producer or distributor taking an appeal to discuss the subject of the appeal with one or more members of the Appeals Board, other than the Chairman of the Appeals Board, prior to the hearing of the Appeal. It shall be the duty of the member or members contacted to inform the Chairman who shall rule on the sanction to be imposed.

Section III. Appeals—Time for Filing

A. An appeal from a decision of the Waiver Committee on the time-period requirement provided for in Article II Section III-C may be made to the Appeals Board at any time during the time period originally established by the Waiver Committee.

B. An appeal from a decision by CARA may be filed at any time until the motion picture in question has opened at any theatre in the United States.

C. When the appeal from a decision by CARA involves a motion picture in exhibi-

tion, an appeal may be filed only with approval of the Waiver Committee. The producer or distributor seeking the appeal shall submit a letter, stating the reasons why the appeal was filed after the date of exhibition with a rating and providing the information required in Subsection D below. The decision of the Waiver Committee shall be final.

D. The Waiver Committee's consideration shall in part be based on:

(1) The date upon which the motion pictue was rated by CARA:

(2) The date upon which the motion picture was first exhibited;

(3) The number of theatres in which the motion picture has been exhibited, is being exhibited and is booked to be exhibited as of the dates upon which the appeal is filed and is to be heard, and

(4) The nature of the advertising and extent to which the motion picture has been advertised.

Section IV. Conduct of Appeals

A. An appeal from a decision by CARA or the Waiver Committee shall be instituted by the filing of a notice of appeal.

(1) The notice shall state the intention to appeal, the running time of the motion picture and certify that the print to be shown at the appeal conforms identically to the version rated by CARA.

(2) The information required in Article III, Section III-D.

(3) A check in the amount of $100 made out to the MPAA.

(4) The letter should be sent to the Chairman of the Appeals Board as follows: President Motion Picture Association of America, Inc, 1600 Eye Street Washington, D.C. 20006

B. With the filing of an appeal, the producer or distributor taking the appeal shall be required to pay a uniform fee in the amount of $100, said amount to be used exclusively towards the cost involved in scheduling and hearing of the appeals.

C. Appeals shall be scheduled no less than seven days after the filing of the notice of the appeal. In exceptional cases the executives of NATO, IFIDA and MPAA may modify this rule.

D. Provision shall be made for the screening by the members of the Appeals Board at the hearing or prior thereto of a print of the motion picture identical to the one rated by CARA.

(1) The hearing of an appeal from a rating by CARA shall commence with the screening of the motion picture involved.

(2) The hearing of an appeal from a time period decision by the Waiver Committee shall commence with the screening of the motion picture involved at the discretion of the Chairman of the Appeals Board.

E. The producer or distributor taking the appeal, CARA or the Waiver Committee may present written statements to the Appeals Board.

(1) If either the producer or distributor taking the appeal, CARA or the Waiver Committee deires to present such written statements to the Appeals Board, any such written statement should be furnished to the Secretary at least seven days before the date fixed for the hearing of the appeal. The Secretary will distribute such statements to the Executive Secretaries of IFIDA, NATO and MPAA for circulation to their respective members of the Appeals Board. If prior submission is not possible, the written statement shall be distributed at the hearing of the appeal.

(2) Submission of written statements shall not diminish or alter the right to present oral statements or arguments on behalf of the producer or distributor taking the appeal and CARA or the Waiver Committee.

F. The producer or distributor taking the appeal, CARA or the Waiver Committee may present oral statements to the Appeals Board at the hearing.

(1) The Appeals Board will hear oral statements on behalf of the producer or distributor by not more than two persons, except by special permission. Oral statements or arguments on behalf of CARA shall be made only by the Chairman of CARA or his designated representative and on behalf of the Waiver Committee by a member or a designated representative.

(2) On appeals of decisions by the Waiver Committee, the producer or distributor taking the appeal and the representative of the Waiver Committee may offer the oral testimony of two witnesses. Such witnesses shall be subject to questioning by the Appeals Board.

(3) The producer or distributor taking the appeal, the representative of CARA or the Waiver Committee shall be afforded the opportunity for rebuttal.

(4) Normally no more than a half hour will be allowed for oral arguments to the party taking the appeal, and a like time to CARA or the Waiver Committee. If a producer or distributor taking an appeal, CARA or the Waiver Committee is of the opinion that additional statements or additional time are necessary fo the adequate presentation of the appeal, the producer or distributor, CARA or the Waiver Committee may make such request by letter and addressed to the Secretary stating the reasons why such statements or time is required for the adequate presentation of the appeal.

(5) When such request is made by a non-member of MPAA, the Secretary shall consult with a member of the Governing Board of IFIDA in determining

whether and to what extent the request may be granted.

(6) A request for the participation of additional persons or for the allowance of additional time, to the extent that it is not granted, may be renewed to the Appeals Board at the commencement of the hearing of the appeal for disposition by the Appeals Board.

(7) In no circumstances shall the time allowed to any producer or distributor, the Waiver Committee or CARA, for the hearing of an appeal, extend beyond one hour.

G. The members of the Appeals Board shall have the opportunity to question the producer or distributor taking the appeal and/or the representative of CARA or the Waiver Committee.

(1) The time for questioning shall not run against the prescribed time allocations.

(2) At the conclusion of the questioning the producer or distributor taking the appeal and the representative of CARA or the Waiver Committee shall leave the room in which the hearing is being conducted.

H. After a reasonable time for discussion, the designated members of the Appeals Board shall vote to either sustain or to overrule the decision of CARA or the Waiver Committee.

(1) No decision of CARA shall be overruled upon appeal unless two-thirds of those present and voting shall vote to overrule. Upon an overruling of its decision, CARA shall rate the picture involved in conformity with the decision of the Appeals Board.

(2) No decision of the Waiver Committee shall be overruled unless a majority of those present and voting shall vote to overrule. Upon the overruling of its decision, the Waiver Committee shall implement the time requirement set by the Appeals Board in accordance with the provisions in Article II, Section III.

Advertising Code Regulations

The MPAA Code *for Advertising is administered through the California Office of the MPAA. All advertisements for films that are rated by the Classification and Rating Administration (CARA) must meet the following requirements of the MPAA Code for Advertising. They must be submitted for approval in advance of their public use.*

The MPAA Code for Advertising is designed to ensure that all advertisements for films rated by CARA carry the correct rating designation and to ensure that these advertisements are not offensive. Every advertisement must be suitable for all audiences except theatrical trailers, which are rated either G (suitable for all audiences) or R (suitable only for audiences viewing R or X rated features).

I. ADVERTISING CODE REGULATIONS

1. These regulations are applicable to all members of the Motion Picture Association of America, to all other producers and distributors of motion pictures with respect to each picture for which a Classification and Rating Administration rating is sought and to all other producers and distributors who self-apply the X rating to their motion pictures and voluntarily submit their advertising.

2. The term "advertising" as used herein shall be deemed to mean all forms of motion picture advertising and exploitation including but not limited to the following: pressbooks; still photographs; newspaper, magazine and trade paper advertising; publicity copy and art intended for use in pressbooks or otherwise intended for general distribution in printed form or for theatre use; trailers; posters, lobby displays and other outdoor displays; advertising accessories, including heralds and throwaways; novelties; copy for exploitation tieups; and all radio and television copy and spots.

3. All advertising for motion pictures which have been submitted to the Classification and Rating Administration for rating shall be submitted to the Director of Advertising for approval and shall not be used in any way until so submitted and approved. All print advertising with the exception of stills shall be submitted in duplicate, particularly pressbooks.

4. In reviewing advertising submitted to the Advertising Code office, the Director shall consider:

(1) Whether the advertising material misrepresents the character of the motion picture.

(2) Whether the advertising material depicts graphic displays of nudity or sexual activity.

(3) Whether the advertising material depicts graphic displays of violence or brutality.

(4) Whether the advertising material exploits or capitalizes upon censorship disputes or the designated rating.

(5) Whether the advertising material demeans religions, race or national origin.

5. Acting as promptly as feasible, the Director of Advertising shall stamp "Approved" on one copy of all advertising approved and return the stamped copy to the producer or distributor who submitted it. If the Director disapproves any advertising, the Director shall stamp the word "Disapproved" on one copy and return it to the producer or distributor who submitted it, together with the reasons for such disapproval.

6. The Director of the Code for Advertising shall require all approved advertising for pictures submitted to the Classification and Rating Administration by members of the Motion Picture Association of America and their subsidiaries to carry the official Association seal and a designation of the rating assigned to the picture by the Clas-

sification and Rating Administration. Uniform standards as to type, size and prominence of the display of the seal and rating will be set forth by the Advertising Code Administrator.

7. Approved advertising for pictures submitted for rating to the Classification and Rating Administration by companies other than members of the Motion Picture Association of America and their subsidiaries may bear the official Association seal at the distributor's option, but all such advertising shall bear the assigned rating.

8. Approved advertising for motion pictures rated X by the Classification and Rating Administration shall bear the X rating but may not bear the official Association seal.

9. All pressbooks approved by the Director of the Code for Advertising shall bear in a prominent place the rating and its definition assigned to the picture by the Classification and Rating Administration. Pressbooks shall also carry the following notice:

All advertising in this pressbook, as well as all other advertising and publicity materials referred to herein, have been approved under the standards for Advertising of the Motion Picture Association of America. All inquiries on this procedure may be addressed to:

Director of the Code for Advertising
Motion Picture Association of America
8480 Beverly Boulevard
Los Angeles, CA 90048

10. The Director of Advertising shall have the authority to promulgate supplementary regulations for the purpose of implementing the objectives of the Advertising Code.

11. Appeals. Any producer or distributor whose advertising has been disapproved may appeal the decision of the Director of the Code for Advertising as follows:

A producer or distributor shall serve notice of such appeal on the Director of the Code for Advertising and on the President of the Association. The President, or in his absence a Vice President designated by him, shall within a week hold a hearing to pass upon the appeal. Oral and written evidence may be introduced by the producer or distributor and by the Director of the Code for Advertising or their representatives. The appeal shall be decided as expeditiously as possible and the decision shall be final.

On appeals by companies other than members of the Motion Picture Association of America and their subsidiaries, the President shall, if requested, decide the appeal in consultation with a represntative of Int'l Film Importers and Distributors of America, as designated by its Governing Board.

12. Any producer or distributor issued a Rating Certificate by the Classification and Rating Administration must use approved advertising in accordance with the rules and supplemental regulations of the Advertising Code. Noncompliance shall be a violation of the terms and conditions upon which the rating was issued and shall constitute grounds for revocation of the rating.

An action for revocation shall be commenced by the Director of Advertising.

(1) The Director shall file a letter with the President of the Motion Picture Association of America stating the relevant facts on which the revocation is sought.

(2) A copy of the latter shall be sent to the producer or distributor and where possible be accompanied by telephone notice.

(3) In consultation with the President of the Motion Picture Association and the Director of Advertising a date and time for a hearing shall be set to provide the producer or distributor an opportunity to be heard.

Hearings on revocation shall be heard by the President of the Motion Picture Association or, in his absence, a designated Vice President of the Association. If the President determines that the violation did occur, he may order the Rating Certificate revoked and voided.

On hearings by producers or distributors other than members of the Motion Picture Association or America and their subsidiaries, the President shall, if requested, make the determination of whether a violation did occur in consultation with a representative of the Int'l Film Importers and Distributors of America, Inc., as designated by its Governing Board.

13. Each company shall be responsible for compliance by its employees and agents with these regulations.

HOW TO WORK MOST EFFECTIVELY WITH THE CODE FOR ADVERTISING

The main function of the Advertising Code is to make certain that all advertising with the exception of restricted trailers is suitable for general audiences and that such advertising contains nothing that most parents would find offensive for their children to see or hear. Experience has shown that advertising approved by the Advertising Code office is more readily accepted by the various media—newspapers, radio and TV —and oftentimes without such approval is totally rejected by the media. Therefore, it is in your best interest to submit your advertising in its earliest stages to prevent costly changes later on.

The following paragraphs are a few guidelines that will be beneficial to you concerning the submission of advertising material.

THE MPAA RATING MUST BE USED IN ALL ADVERTISING
II. PRINT ADVERTISING

This includes everything but theatre trailers and radio and TV spots.

A. STILLS. Any and all stills being contemplated for use as print advertising or exhibition of any kind—and this includes the trade papers and magazines—must be submitted for approval.

B. NEWSPAPER ADS. All newspaper ads must carry the designated rating and those ads 150 lines and over must carry the definition of the rating. Such rating definitions must be large enough to be legible in print and must be placed in a prominent position in the ad—preferably at the bottom but not buried in the credits.

C. TEASER ADS. No mention of the rating need be in a teaser ad UNLESS the theatre where the film will be playing is mentioned. If the theatre is noted in the ad, it must show a rating. However, all teaser ads as well as other advertising must be approved by the Advertising Code prior to release.

D. POSTERS AND BILLBOARDS. Submit art work and layouts for posters and billboards well in advance, even before the final rating of the picture. You can always add the correct rating symbol later. Use of rating symbol and full definition is required on all posters and billboards.

E. MAGAZINE AND TRADE ADS. Ads to appear in magazines or in the trades must be approved prior to their use.

F. PRESSBOOKS. Never go to fnal pressbook print unless all of the advertising elements and publicity stills used have been given earlier Advertising Code approval. Once everything in your pressbook is submitted and approved, please add the following notice for all films rated either "G", "PG" or "R" (not "X") in a prominent place: **APPROVED**—All advertising in this pressbook, as well as all other advertising and publicity materials referred to herein, have been approved under the standards for Advertising of the Motion Picture Association of America. All inquiries on this procedure may be addressed to: Director of the Code for Advertising, Motion Picture Association of America. All inquiries on this procedure may be ad-

dressed to: Director of the Code for Advertising, Motion Picture Association of America, 8480 Beverly Blvd., Los Angeles, CA 90048.

This picture was rated:

III. THEATRICAL TRAILERS

The theatrical trailer is the key element in every motion picture distribution campaign. We are aware of the importance of the theatrical trailer to every distributor and exhibitor. We also know—all too well—that it is one of the most sensitive areas in the industry's film rating program. Use of the official MPAA rating tags are required to be shown on all trailers for rated films. There are no audio requirements for theatrical trailers.

We examine trailers and approve them for TWO audiences only—"G" Unrestricted or General Audiences—and "R" Restricted (Under 17 must be accompanied by parent or adult guardian). Trailers for "PG" films should be suitable for "G" audiences, regardless of the content of the "PG" film. Remember, a patron selects a "PG" film after having been warned concerning the content. This *does not* mean that all of the material in the film can play to a "G" General Audience. Please note that in general, scenes approved for a "PG", "R" or "X" feature when spread out over a 90 minute film have a much stronger impact when reduced to a two minute trailer. It is important to keep this fact in mind when preparing trailers—and this applies particularly to those who may be working on their first feature release.

G—General Audience

A family audience viewing a "G-rated" film may object to a trailer they feel is unsuitable for their children who may be with them. Parents can be very protective about what they didn't select, and resent material that may be thrust upon them because they happen to be in the audience.

A trailer for General Audiences and television spots have the same standards. Oftentimes the 60-second television spot is used as a "teaser" or "crossplug" trailer for General Audiences Because a G trailer must be suitable for all audiences and must not contain any scenes which most parents would find objectionable to their young children, the following are some of the guidelines to be mindful of when preparing a G trailer:

No blood
No victim/weapon in the same frame
No exposed breasts or nudity of any kind
No bed scenes with any action
No use of blasphemous language (allowing only "hell" and "damn")

R—Restricted Audience

It should be clearly understood that Restricted trailers cannot carry the same scenes of sex, violence and language that may be approved in the R rated feature. The advertising must necessarily eliminate all strong sex or excessive violence in theatre trailers. Again, the impact of those scenes is heightened when compacted in a short trailer. Some of the scenes unacceptable in R trailers are:

Excessive sex or violence
Dismemberment
Genitals
Pubic hair
Use of sexually connotative words
Humping, lesbianism, fondling or masturbation

We suggest you use the following procedure; let us look at your rough cut before going to a composite. And even before we see it, you should eliminate excessive violence—close-up shootings, stabbings, hacking with axes, etc. Show the weapon, not the meeting against the flesh. Eliminate all blood in general audience trailers and as much as possible in R trailers. If guns are fired in a G trailer, do not use close-up shots where the bullet hits body, but cut to body on the ground or just before body hits the ground.

Where making a "G" audience trailer is not possible with an "R"-rated feature, we suggest accepting a restricted audience trailer and using a one-minute TV spot for the "G" rated general audience trailer. Many companies do this successfully.

IV. TEASER TRAILERS

Since a regular trailer cannot be released before the feature has been rated, many companies use a shorter teaser trailer. Any teaser trailer for a film not yet rated must be suitable for general audiences and must carry the front tag once it has been approved by the Director of the Code for Advertising. A teaser need not carry the end tag *unless* the feature has been rated.

V. TRAILER TAGS

There are two head tags which indicate for which audience the trailer is intended— either "All Audiences" or "Restricted Audiences."

ALL TAGS ARE TO REMAIN ON THE SCREEN FOR FIVE (5) SECONDS.

Trailer negatives have been supplied to most of the major labs in New York, Los Angeles and Miami. Contact the Code for Advertising office if you have trouble locating the trailer tag you need.

All trailers must carry the proper MPAA tags. Failure to attach the proper tag is cause for disapproval. Also, unless the trailer carries the tags, many exhibitors will refuse to run it.

VI. TELEVISION SPOTS

All television trailers should be made with a general audience in mind. TV spots containing sexual references, violence, blood or profanity are not acceptable. It is suggested that when possible, several spots be made of varying degree as stronger spots may be acceptable for late night viewing. TV standards are different for prime time viewing as opposed to late night viewing.

The MPAA Advertising Regulations which follow give specific information on the use of the rating symbols in TV spots both *visually* and *verbally* in 60–30–20 and 10-second spots. This arrangement was worked out in cooperation with the National Association of Broadcasters and must be carefully adhered to.

TV spots should carry rating and definition large enough to be legible on a home viewer's screen and can appear in the same frame with the film title and credits, but must remain on the screen for four (4) seconds.

> NOTE: IN PAST EXPERIENCES WHEN THE STATIONS FELT THAT THE RATING AND DEFINITION WERE NOT LARGE ENOUGH, THEY WOULD FLASH ON AN ADDITIONAL COPY OF THE RATING AND DEFINITION, USUALLY IN LARGE WHITE LETTERS, OVER SCENES IN THE SPOT.

VII. RADIO SPOTS

There is little difference in acceptable content between TV and radio spots. Most radio spots are acceptable provided there is no profanity, use of the Lord's name or sexually-oriented language. Many stations in the middle west will not accept vulgar references to racial or national groups. These should be avoided. In general, advertisers should be guided by good taste and use language in radio spots that is acceptable to family audiences.

MPAA REGULATIONS FOR TELEVISION AND RADIO SPOTS
(Worked out in cooperation with the National Association of Broadcasters)
I. Television Spots
  60–30–20–10 second spots
A. *Visual*
   Show the MPAA Seal (except when rating is X)
   Show the Rating Symbol Letter (G, PG, R or X)
   Show the *Full Definition* of the Symbol
   (See page 9 for samples.)
Full Definition

   G—GENERAL AUDIENCES
     All Ages Admitted
   PG—PARENTAL GUIDANCE SUGGESTED
     Some Material May Not Be Suitable for Children
   R—RESTRICTED
     Under 17 Requires Accompanying Parent or Adult Guardian
   X—NO ONE UNDER 17 ADMITTED
     (Age Limit may vary in certain areas)

B. *Audible—State the Rating Symbol Letter*
   "RATED G"
   "RATED PG"
   "RATED R"
   "RATED X"

Note: The visual code information (MPAA Seal, Rating Symbol and Full Definition) should be included when the title of the film comes on the screen and remain for *four* seconds.

II. Radio Spots
  60–30–20 second spots
A. *State the Rating Symbol* (G, PG, R or X) and also state the *Abbreviated Definition*

   "RATED G—GENERAL AUDIENCES"
   "RATED PG—PARENTAL GUIDANCE SUGGESTED"
   "RATED R—UNDER 17 NOT ADMITTED WITHOUT PARENT"
   "RATED X—UNDER 17 NOT ADMITTED"

   10 seconds spots

   "RATED G"   "RATED R"
   "RATED PG"   "RATED X"

VIII. GENERAL INFORMATION ON RATED FILMS
A. Sneak Previews:

When a film is sneaked, for everyone's protection, the rating must be in the ads. All advertising for a sneak preview must carry the rating.

B. Re-issues:

ALL ADVERTISING FOR A RE-ISSUE MUST BE RE-SUBMITTED

If a film is a re-issue, it is suggested that it be mentioned directly or inferred in the advertising to avoid confusion, i.e., "now you can see again," "brought back by popular demand," "a (company name) re-release."

C. Title Changes:

ALL ADVERTISING FOR A TITLE CHANGE MUST BE RE-SUBMITTED

It is suggested that the former title be mentioned in all advertising, such as "formerly released as . . . "

D. Kiddie Shows:

The only trailers that should be shown during a kiddie matinee are trailers for *future kiddie matinee* features.

E. Double Bills:

On a double bill where each feature has a different rating, *only the more restricted of the two ratings can be used in the advertising.* The more restricted rating governs box office admittance.

F. Foreign Language Films:

In the state of New York, if a foreign language film is released with sub titles, it must so state in *ALL ADVERTISING*, i.e., (French film-English sub-titles).

If a foreign language film is released in two versions, English and foreign, it must differentiate in the advertising which version is playing.

G. Rating Chages:

If your film has been *re-rated* by the Classification and Rating Administration, all advertising must reflect the change in rating.

In is advised that words such as "original," "uncut," not be used in the ad campaign. The change in rating cannot be exploited.

H. Distributor Changes:

If you have recently acquired a film carrying an MPAA rating, please notify us so that we can adjust our records accordingly.

Also, if you change your name, address or telephone number, we would appreciate your advising us for future correspondence.

I. Posting ("wild" etc.):

Posters seen in public places other than theatres are subjected to great criticism. Therefore, it is most important that these posters are approved before use and are inoffensive (see "AREAS IN ADVERTISING MOST SENSITIVE TO CRITICISM")

J. "G"-rated films:

Phrases such as, "for the whole family" or "family entertainment" cannot be used in any advertising unless the film has received a "G" rating.

K. New Campaigns:

If an ad campaign that has already been approved is revised or changed or a second campaign substituted, any new advertising must be submitted.

IX. AREAS IN ADVERTISING MOST SENSITIVE TO CRITICISM:

(1) SEX
(2) VIOLENCE, WEAPONS (i.e. gunsites)
(3) LANGUAGE AND GESTURES
(4) NUDITY
(5) DRUGS AND PARAPHERNALIA (i.e. needles)
(6) DEFAMATION
(7) ETHNIC OR MINORITY GROUPS
(8) SACRILEGE
(9) CHILD ABUSE
(10) CRUELTY TO ANIMALS
(11) BODY FUNCTIONS
(12) ASSASSINATION
(13) VENEREAL DISEASES
(14) MUTATIONS
(15) PHYSICAL HANDICAPS (i.e. amputations)
(16) CADAVERS (i.e. eyes opened, abuse)
(17) RAPE AND MOLESTATIONS
(18) LAVATORY OR LAVATORY JOKES

3/THE CATHOLIC LEGION OF DECENCY

IN OCTOBER 1933 Monsignor Amleto Giovanni Cicognani spoke to a Catholic Charities Convention in New York. "What a massacre of innocence of youth is taking place hour by hour!" he exclaimed. "How shall the crimes that have their direct source in immoral motion pictures be measured? Catholics are called by God, the Pope, the Bishops, and the priests to a united and vigorous campaign for the purification of the cinema, which has become a deadly menace to morals."

Thus was the Legion of Decency—the most powerful pressure group in the history of film—started.

At the annual American Bishops Convention held the month after Monsignor Cicognani's rousing speech, the bishops heeded the monsignor's advice by appointing an Episcopal Committee on Motion Pictures. After six months of work, the committee in April 1934 announced its plans for a crusade against the immorality and irresponsibility of movies: priests were instructed to preach on the "moral ills" of the movies; the clergy was advised to put pressure on local exhibitors; and millions of Catholics were asked to sign the Legion of Decency Pledge to do all they could to arouse public opinion against the immorality of films. (See Table 1.)

In Philadelphia, Catholics actually boycotted all motion picture theaters, an action that gave national attention to the Legion.

Even non-Catholic groups joined the Legion in its attempt to clean up the movies: representatives of the Knights of Columbus, B'nai B'rith, Elks, Masons and Odd Fellows all gave the Legion their support.

The Legion's effort proved so successful, in fact, that three months after it was formed the film industry agreed to establish the Production Code Administration Office to regulate movies. In November 1934 the Legion of Decency was made a permanent institution.

The Legion's main function was to publish lists of films which its staff had morally rated according to prescribed classifications. (See Table 2.) In deciding the ratings, the Legion ruled that no consideration should be given to artistic, technical or dramatic values. Only moral content was weighed.

The Legion did not consider its activities to be a form of censorship, but rather argued that its aim was to guide public opinion. Many people, however, have claimed that the Legion, in speaking for the movie morality of Catholics, has dictated the tastes of the entire nation.

The Legion continued its fight against immorality in movies even after public morals changed following World War II. In 1956, for example Francis Cardinal Spellman warned Catholics to stay away from *Baby Doll* on "penalty of sin," and bishops even placed a six-month boycott on theaters showing the film. The next year a similar controversy surrounded the Legion's diatribes against *And God Created Woman*, starring Brigitte Bardot.

But in December 1957 the Legion revised its classification system to take into account differences in adolescent and adult sensibilities. (See Table 2.) Even the pledge was revised to reflect the Legion's more lenient attitude toward movies. (See Table 1.) Although in 1966 the Legion created another furor over *The Pawnbroker*, it has in the main eased its standards, giving special classifications to such films as *La Dolce Vita, Lolita* and *Suddenly, Last Summer*.

In 1966 the Legion of Decency became the National Catholic Office for Motion Pictures. In 1972 the National Catholic Office for Motion Pictures and the National Catholic Office for Radio and Television were reorganized to form the Office for Film and Broadcasting (OFB). In addition to sponsoring workshops and seminars, the OFB publishes *SHARE*, a twice-monthly packet of film and broadcasting information, and *Film and Broadcasting Review* (formerly the *Catholic Film Newsletter*), which twice a month reviews and classifies current 35mm films. Reviews include artistic as well as moral examinations.

Table 1: The Legion of Decency Pledges

Original Pledge (1934)

"I wish to join the Legion of Decency, which condemns vile and unwholesome moving pictures. I unite with all who protest against them as a grave menace to youth, to home life, to country and to religion.

I condemn absolutely those salacious motion pictures, which, with other degrading agencies, are corrupting public morals and promoting a sex mania in our land.

I shall do all that I can to arose public opinion against the portrayal of vice as a normal condition of affairs, and against depicting criminals of any class as heroes and heroines, presenting their filthy philosophy of life as something acceptable to decent men and women.

I unite with all who condemn the display of suggestive advertisements on billboards, at theatre entrances, and the favorable notices given to immoral motion pictures.

Considering these evils, I hereby promise to remain away from all motion pictures except those which do not offend decency and Christian morality. I promise further to secure as many members as possible for the Legion of Decency.

I make this protest in a spirit of self-respect and with the conviction that the American public does not demand filthy pictures, but clean entertainment and educational features."

Revised Pledge (1934)

"I condemn indecent and immoral motion pictures, and those which glorify crime or criminals.

I promise to do all that I can to strengthen public opinion against the production of indecent and immoral films, and to unite with all who protest against them.

I acknowledge my obligation to my moral life. As a member of the Legion of Decency, I pledge myself to remain away from them. I promise, further, to stay away altogether from places of amusement which show them as a matter of policy."

Revised Pledge (1965)

"I promise to promote by word and deed what is morally and artistically good in motion picture entertainment. I promise to discourage by my good example and always in a responsible and civic-minded manner."

TABLE 2: THE LEGION OF DECENCY RATINGS

Original Classification (1936)
A-1:Morally Unobjectionable for General Patronage
The films are considered to contain no material which would be morally dangerous to the average motion picture audience, adults and children alike.
A-2:Morally Unobjectionable for Adults
These are films which in themselves are morally harmless but which, because of subject matter or treatment, require maturity and experience if one is to witness them without danger or moral harm. While no definite age limit can be established for this group, the judgment of parents, pastors and teachers

would be helpful in determining the decision in individual cases.

B:Morally Objectionable in Part for All
Films in this category are considered to contain elements dangerous to Christian morals or moral standards.

C:Condemned
Condemned films are considered to be those which, because of theme or treatment, have been described by the Holy Father as "positively bad."

Separate Classification
This is given to certain films which, while not morally offensive, require some analysis and explanation as a protection to the uninformed against wrong interpretations and false conclusions.

Revised Classification (1957)

A-1:Morally Unobjectionable for General Patronage

A-2:Morally Unobjectionable for Adults and Adolescents

A-3:Morally Unobjectionable for Adults

B:Morally Objectionable in Part for All

C:Condemned

Reasons for New Classification

(a) The Legion recognizes that in connection with motion picture attendance the average adolescent of our day will not infrequently consider himself more than a child and hence will seek pictures with more adult content and orientation. In keeping with the sound principles of modern Catholic educational psychology, it seems desirable that the Legion aid the adolescent in this quest for more mature movie-subjects and thereby contribute to his intellectual and emotional maturation. To this end the new A-s classification has been adopted; it is

hoped that this classification, while providing the necessary reasonable moral controls upon the adolescent, will at the same time aid him in his "growing up."

(b) The A-3 classification is an attempt on the part of the Legion to provide for truly adult subject matter in entertainment motion pictures, provided that the themes in question and their treatment be consonant with the moral law and with traditionally accepted moral standards.

(c) Although the B and C classifications remain unchanged, it is to be recognized that the new triple A classification is intended also to strengthen the meaning of the B category. Henceforth, there will be no doubt that a B film is one adjudged to contain material which in itself or in its offensive treatment is contrary to traditional morality and constitutes a threat not only to the personal spiritual life of even an adult viewer, but also to the moral behavior-patterns which condition public morality. Catholic people are urged to refrain from attendance at all B pictures, not only for the sake of their own consciences, but also in the interest of promoting the common good.

Current Classification

A-1:Morally Unobjectionable for General Patronage

A-2:Morally Unobjectionable for Adults and Adolescents

A-3:Morally Unobjectionable for Adults

A-4:For adults with reservations

B:Morally Objectionable in Part for All

C:Condemned

INDEX

M

MASON, James—224, 240, 278, 289
MASON, Marsha—65, 248, 253, 256, 296, 297
MASON, Sarah Y.—199
MASSEY, Daniel—242, 294
MASSEY, Raymond—206
MASSIE, Paul—301
MASSINA, Guilietta—103
MASTERS, Tony—304
MASTROIANNI, Marcello—104, 235, 253, 292, 293, 302
MATA Hari—18
MATE, Rudolph—206, 208, 209, 211, 212
MATEOS, Antonio—245
MATERNALE—166
MATHESON, Tim—65
MATHOT, Jacques—219
MATING Game, The—35
MATING Season, The—108, 220
MATTEI Affair, The—105, 159
MATTES, Eva—106
MATTHAU, Walter—60, 146, 147, 150–152, 154, 155, 239, 246, 251, 296, 305
MAUCH, Thomas—264
MAUMONT, Jacques—235
MAXSTED, Jack—246
MAX's Words—111
MAXWELL, Lois—287
MAXWELL, Marilyn—62
MAY, Elaine—255, 316
MAYBE I'll Come Home In the Spring—33
MAYER, Louis B.—220
MAYERLING—266, 274
MAYES, Wendell—231, 268
MAYNIEL, Juliette—109
MAYTIME—18
MAZURSKY, Paul—116, 155, 159, 244, 250, 255, 262, 264, 271, 309, 314
McBAIN, Diane—64
McBROOM, Amanda—298
McCABE and Mrs. Miller—157, 161, 163, 164, 166, 246
McCALL Jr., Mary C.—313
McCALLISTER, Lon—62
McCALLUM, Gordon K.—246, 305
McCAMBRIDGE, Mercedes—218, 227, 287
McCAREY, Leo—201, 205, 206, 211–213, 222, 260, 267
McCARTHY, Charlie—203
McCARTHY, Kevin—220, 288
McCAUGHEY, William—255
McCLEARY, Urie—208, 245
McCLOY, Terence—247
McCORD, Ted—217, 235, 239
McCORMACK, Patty—227
McCUNE, Grant—254
McDANIEL, Hattie—205, 276
McDONELL, Gordon—210
McDOWALL, Roddy—62, 275
McDOWELL, Malcolm—65
McGILL, Barney—198
McGUIRE, Dorothy—215, 279

McGUIRE, William Anthony—201
McKENNA, Virginia—300
McKERN, Leo—282
McKUEN, Rod—295
McLAGLEN, Victor—200
McLAUGHLIN, Chris—306
McLEAN, Barbara—212
McLINTOCK!—33, 35
McMURTRY, Larry—246, 269, 305
McNAMARA, Maggie—63, 223
McNUTT, William Slavens—199, 200
McQUEEN, Steve—60, 61, 68, 239, 294, 295
MEADE, James—319
MEAHL, E. Michael—243
ME and the Colonel—177, 279, 290, 312
MEAN Streets—117, 157, 160–163, 165, 167, 174, 178, 263
MEATBALLS—28
MEDAL for Benny, A—213
MEDDINGS, Derek—255, 307
MEDFORD, Kay—242
MEDIOLI, Enrico—244
MEDIUM Cool—149, 165
MEEHAN, John—198, 204, 218, 219, 225
MEET John Doe—19, 207, 275
MEET Marlon Brando—115
MEET Me in St. Louis—20, 132, 171, 183, 212, 276
MEKAS, Adolfas—114, 116
MEKAS, Jonas—114, 116
MELLOR, William C.—221, 229, 231, 239
MELODY Time—96
MELVILLE, Jean-Pierre—114, 117, 322
MELVIN, Murray—103
MELVIN Purvis, G-Man—33
MEMBER of the Wedding—176, 222, 288
MEMORANDUM—115
MEMORIAL—305
MEMORIES of Underdevelopment—116, 156, 160, 162–164, 166, 174, 263
MEMORY of Justice—117, 166, 175, 308
MEMPHIS Belle, The—276
MEN, The—67, 172, 176, 219, 277, 312
MEN Against the Arctic—226
ME, Natalie—294
MENDELSON, Anthony—304, 305
MENDY—97
MENJOU, Adolphe—198
MEN of Bronze—118
MEN Without Women—273
MENZEL, Jiri—115
MENZIES, William Cameron—197, 205
MERCER, David—303
MERCER, Johnny—214, 221, 234, 235, 295

MERCHANT, Vivien—240, 281, 303
MERCHANT of Four Seasons, The—116, 157, 162, 163, 166
MERCOURI, Melina—103, 232
MERCURE, Monique—105
MEREDITH, Burgess—251, 252, 280
MEREDYTH, Bess—197
MERKEL, Una—233
MERMAN, Ethel—288
MERRILL, Kieth—249
MERRILY We Live—204
MERRY Widow, The—116, 170, 200
MERRY Wives of Windsor Overture, The—223
MERTON of the Movies—170
MESCALL, John—209
MESENKOP, Louis—208, 210
MESHES of the Afternoon—140
MÉSZÁROS, Márta—118, 322
METCALFE, Melvin—250
METELO—104
METRO-Goldwyn Mayer Inc. (MGM)—200, 201, 203–214, 216, 217, 221–223, 225, 228, 231–233, 237, 239–242, 244, 250, 257, 260
METTY, Russell—232, 234
METZLER, Fred L.—234
MEYER, Dr. Herbert—243
MEYER, Nicholas—252
MEYER, Richard C.—304
MEYERS, Sidney—97, 218
MICHELSON, Manfred G.—248, 253
MICKEY Mouse—199
MICKEY One—114
MICKEY'S Polo Team—95
MIDDLEMAN, The—117
MIDDLE of the Night—177, 280
MIDDLE of the World—117, 141, 159
MIDLER, Bette—256, 298
MIDNIGHT Cowboy—6, 14, 25, 68, 144–146, 149, 150, 154, 155, 157, 159, 161, 163, 164, 174, 187, 243, 262, 269, 282, 294, 304, 314, 320
MIDNIGHT Express—254, 255, 284, 297, 307, 309, 316
MIDNIGHT Lace—24
MIDSUMMER Night's Dream, A—18, 178, 200
MIDWAY—6, 13, 28, 89
MIELZINER, Joe—226
MIFUNE, Toshiro—99
MIGHTY Joe Young—218
MIKABERITZE, Kote—118
MIKADO, The—95
MIKEY and Nicky—164
MILDRED Pierce—20, 213, 276
MILES, Bernard—276
MILES, Bill—118
MILES, Sarah—245
MILES, Sylvia—243, 251
MILESTONE, Lewis—197, 198
MILESTONES—117, 160

X

Y

Z